HANS WEHR

A DICTIONARY OF MODERN WRITTEN ARABIC

(Arabic - English)

Edited by

J MILTON COWAN

Fourth Edition

Considerably enlarged and amended by the author

This dictionary is an enlarged and includes a collection of new additional material (about 13,000 entries) by the same author.

Published by Snowball Publishing

Cover Design: Joe Petru

www.snowballpublishing.com

info@snowballpublishing.com

Preface to the Student Edition

This edition is intended to meet the demand of students & scholars for a compact, well-bound, economically priced version of A DICTIONARY OF MODERN WRITTEN ARABIC. It contains all of the entries of the larger, hard-bound, 4th edition.

Ithaca NY J MILTON COWAN
December 1993

Preface to the Fourth Edition

This edition of the Dictionary, published eighteen years after its first appearance, is an enlarged and improved version of the original corpus. During the past two decades, the Dictionary has achieved widespread acceptance and use. In the interim, modern written Arabic has continued to exhibit vigorous lexical growth. Therefore, feeling the need to fill in many gaps and update the corpus, the author again undertook systematic collection of material. In addition to many neologisms of recent origin, the author has incorporated much older material attested in present-day contexts, which had not yet appeared in the Dictionary, as well as numerous improvements and corrections. The result is that this revised edition has nearly 200 new pages.

All new entries have been derived from primary sources, i.e. from running contexts. The source texts, predominantly from the last ten years, cover a broad spectrum of content, style and origin, thereby providing a representative cross section of modern usage encountered in various fields such as technology, economics, sports, medicine, the oil industry and the natural sciences, as well as creative literature. Particular use was made of texts from Egypt, Syria, Lebanon and Saudi Arabia which were drawn from newspapers, periodicals, textbooks, official and private documents and belles-lettres; some use was also made of the press of the northwest African countries. —The number of new entries, including lemmata as well as compounds, idiomatic phrases and new definitions of head words, runs to approximately 13.000. Moreover, in ca. 3.000 instances, smaller additions (new transcriptions, plural forms, prepositional government of verbs, cross-references, etc.) have been inserted, errors corrected, obsolete entries eliminated. Some lemmata have been completely reworked.

The revised edition suffers from a technical limitation. For economic reasons, it was done by cutting and pasting-in of the new material rather than by new typesetting of the entire book. In order to keep the number of places requiring change within reason, no attempt was made to follow through consistently with all possible changes in presentation and arrangement. Insertions into longer lemmata and changes of order which would have required extensive new composition were avoided where they were not absolutely necessary. The user is asked to overlook certain inconsistencies in the ordering of sequences after the bold-faced colons. The mark (') indicating the glottal stop in the transcription should appear before initial vowels, wherever *hamzat al-qaṭʿ* would be written in voweled Arabic script or where *madda* occurs; thus one should read, for example: *'amr, 'umm, 'īrād, 'ādāb* instead of *amr, umm, īrād, ādāb,* since the glottal stop is a separate phoneme, also in initial position.—The "Introduction" remains essentially unchanged. The user is urged to become familiar with the principles on which the presentation of the contents is based and to study the explanations for use of the Dictionary at the end of the "Introduction" (pp. XII—XV) before attempting to use it.

My special thanks are due to the Editor, J Milton Cowan, who converted the new material from German into English. I am greatly indebted to Dr. Lorenz Kropfitsch, who worked a year with me in Münster and helped me prepare printer's copy. He also contributed some 600 entries, mainly from the newspapers of the Maghreb, and undertook the time-consuming revision of the cut-and-pasted page proof. I should like to express my gratitude to Dr. Karl Stowasser, who read galley proofs of the new composition and provided excellent contributions to the English translation as well as numerous valuable notes and suggestions. Some hundreds of additions came from the late Dr. Fahmi Abul-Fadl, whose premature death I deeply regret. Also, I am grateful for contributions of entries from Mr. Alex Sheffy of Jerusalem and from Dr. Mokhtar Ahmed, who came from Egypt and was my main informant. Furthermore, Dr. Omar Al Sasi of Saudi Arabia and students at our University from several Arab countries served as informants from time to time. Several colleagues submitted smaller numbers of entries and supplied information. To all those who contributed to the revision, and, last but not least, to the publisher who supported the work in various ways, I express my heartfelt thanks.

Münster
July 1979

HANS WEHR

Preface to the First Edition

Shortly after the publication of Professor Hans Wehr's *Arabisches Wörterbuch für die Schriftsprache der Gegenwart* in 1952, the Committee on Language Programs of the American Council of Learned Societies recognized its excellence and began to explore means of providing an up-to-date English edition. Professor Wehr and I readily reached agreement on a plan to translate, edit, and enlarge the dictionary. This task was considerably lightened and hastened by generous financial support from the American Council of Learned Societies, the Arabian American Oil Company, and Cornell University.

This dictionary will be welcome not only to English and American users, but to orientalists throughout the world who are more at home with English than with German. It is more accurate and much more comprehensive than the original version, which was produced under extremely unfavorable conditions in Germany during the late war years and the early postwar period.

Ithaca, New York
November 1960

J MILTON COWAN

Introduction

This dictionary presents the vocabulary and phraseology of modern written Arabic. It is based on the form of the language which, throughout the Arab world from Iraq to Morocco, is found in the prose of books, newspapers, periodicals, and letters. This form is also employed in formal public address, over radio and television, and in religious ceremonial. The dictionary will be most useful to those working with writings that have appeared since the turn of the century.

The morphology and syntax of written Arabic are essentially the same in all Arab countries. Vocabulary differences are limited mainly to the domain of specialized vocabulary. Thus the written language continues, as it has done throughout centuries of the past, to ensure the linguistic unity of the Arab world. It provides a medium of communication over the vast geographical area whose numerous and widely diverse local dialects it transcends. Indeed, it gives the Arab people of many countries a sense of identity and an awareness of their common cultural heritage.

Two powerful and conflicting forces have affected the development of the modern Arabic lexicon. A reform movement originating toward the end of the last century in Syria and Lebanon has reawakened and popularized the old conviction of educated Arabs that the ancient *ʿarabīya* of pre-Islamic times, which became the classical form of the language in the early centuries of Islam, is better and more correct than any later form. Proponents of this puristic doctrine have held that new vocabulary must be derived exclusively in accordance with ancient models or by semantic extension of older forms. They have insisted on the replacement of all foreign loanwords with purely Arabic forms and expressions. The purists have had considerable influence on the development of modern literary Arabic although there has been widespread protest against their extreme point of view. At the same time and under the increasing influence of Western civilization, Arab writers and journalists have had to deal with a host of new concepts and ideas previously alien to the Arab way of life. As actual usage demonstrates, the purists have been unable to cope with the sheer bulk of new linguistic material which has had to be incorporated into the language to make it current with advances in world knowledge. The result is seen in the tendency of many writers, especially in the fields of science and technology, simply to adopt foreign words from the European languages. Many common, everyday expressions from the various colloquial dialects have also found their way into written expression.

From its inception, this dictionary has been compiled on scientific descriptive principles. It contains only words and expressions which were found in context during the course of wide reading in literature of every kind or which, on the basis of other evidence, can be shown to be unquestionably a part of the present-day vocabulary. It is a faithful record of the language as attested by usage rather than a normative presentation of what theoretically ought to occur. Consequently, it not only lists classical words and phrases of elegant rhetorical style side by side with new coinages that conform to the demands of the purists, but it also contains neologisms, loan translations, foreign loans, and colloquialisms which may not be to the linguistic taste of many educated Arabs. But since they occur in the corpus of materials on which the dictionary is based, they are included here.

A number of special problems confront the lexicographer dealing with present-day Arabic. Since for many fields of knowledge, especially those which have developed outside the Arab world, no generally accepted terminology has yet emerged, it is evident that a practical dictionary can only approximate the degree of completeness found in comparable dictionaries of Western languages. Local terminology, especially for many public institutions, offices, titles, and administrative affairs, has developed in the several Arab countries. Although the dictionary is based mainly on usage in the countries bordering on the eastern Mediterranean, local official and administrative terms have been included for all Arab countries, but not with equal thoroughness. Colloquialisms and dialect expressions that have gained currency in written form also vary from country to country. Certainly no attempt at completeness can be made here, and the user working with materials having a marked regional flavor will be well advised to refer to an appropriate dialect dictionary or glossary. As a rule, items derived from local dialects or limited to local use have been so designated with appropriate abbreviations.

A normalized journalistic style has evolved for factual reporting of news or discussion of matters of political and topical interest over the radio and in the press. This style, which often betrays Western influences, is remarkably uniform throughout the Arab world. It reaches large sections of the population daily and constitutes to them almost the only stylistic norm. Its vocabulary is relatively small and fairly standardized, hence easily covered in a dictionary.

The vocabulary of scientific and technological writings, on the other hand, is by no means standardized. The impact of Western civilization has confronted the Arab world with the serious linguistic problem of expressing a vast and ever-increasing number of new concepts for which no words in Arabic exist. The creation of a scientific and technological terminology is still a major intellectual challenge. Reluctance to borrow wholesale from European languages has spurred efforts to coin terms according to productive Arabic patterns. In recent decades innumerable such words have been suggested in various periodicals and in special publications. Relatively few of these have gained acceptance in common usage. Specialists in all fields keep coining new terms that are either not understood by other specialists in the same field or are rejected in favor of other, equally short-lived, private fabrications.

The Academy of the Arabic Language in Cairo especially, the Damascus Academy, and, to a lesser extent, the Iraqi Academy have produced and continue to publish vast numbers of technical terms for almost all fields of knowledge. The academies have, however, greatly underestimated the difficulties of artificial regulation of a language. The problem lies not so much in inventing terms as it does in assuring that they gain acceptance. In some instances neologisms have quickly become part of the stock of the language; among these, fortunately, are a large number of the terms proposed by academies or by professional specialists. However, in many fields, such as modern linguistics, existential philosophy, or nuclear physics, it is still not possible for professional people from the different Arab states to discuss details of their discipline in Arabic. The situation is further complicated by the fact that the purists and the academies demand the translation into Arabic even of those Greek and Latin technical terms which make possible international understanding among specialists. Thus while considerable progress has been made in recent decades toward the standardization of Arabic terminology, several technical terms which all fit one definition may still be current, or a given scientific term may have different meanings for different experts.

Those technical terms which appear with considerable frequency in published works, or which are familiar to specialists in various fields and are considered by them to be standardized terminology, presented no particular problem. Nevertheless it has not always been possible to ascertain the terms in general acceptance with the experts of merely one country, let alone those of all. Doubtful cases are entered and marked with a special symbol. A descriptive dictionary such as this has no room for the innumerable academic coinages which experience has shown are by no means assured of adoption. Only those that are attested in the literature have been included.

Classicisms are a further special problem. Arab authors, steeped in classical tradition, can and do frequently draw upon words which were already archaic in the Middle Ages. The use of classical patterns is by no means limited to belles-lettres. Archaisms may crop up in the middle of a spirited newspaper article. Wherever an aesthetic or rhetorical effect is intended, wherever the language aims more at expressiveness than at imparting information, authors tend to weave in ancient Arabic and classical idioms. They are artistic and stylistic devices of the first order. They awaken in the reader images from memorized passages of ancient literature and contribute to his aesthetic enjoyment. Quotations from the Koran or from classical literature, whose origins and connotations may well elude the Western reader, are readily recognized by Arabs who have had a traditional education and who have memorized a wealth of ancient sources. In former years many writers strove to display their erudition by citing lexical rarities culled from ancient dictionaries and collections of synonyms. As often as not the author had to explain such *nawādir* in footnotes, since nobody else would understand them. This pedantic mannerism is going out of fashion and there is a trend in more recent literature toward smoothness and readability in style. Nevertheless it is clear from the foregoing that it is not possible to make a sharp distinction between living and obsolete usage. All archaic words found in the source material have, therefore, been included in this dictionary, even though it is sometimes evident that they no longer form a part of the living lexicon and are used only by a small group of well-read literary connoisseurs. Such included forms are but a small sample of what the user is likely to encounter in the writings of a few modern authors; the impossibility of including the entire ancient vocabulary is obvious. The user who encounters an old Arabic word which he does not understand will have to consult a lexicon of the *ʿarabīya*. Finally, some modern authors will occasionally take great liberties with older words, so that even highly educated Arabs are unable to understand the sense of certain passages. Items of this kind have not been entered. They would contribute nothing to a dictionary whose scope did not permit inclusion of source references.

The vocabulary of modern Arabic, then, is by no means standardized, its scope at times difficult to delimit. These results emerge from the very character of modern Arabic — a written language, powerfully influenced by traditional norms, which nevertheless is required to express a multitude of new foreign concepts, not for one country only, but for many distributed over a vast geographical area. Arabic phonology, morphology, and syntax have remained relatively unchanged from earliest times, as has much of the vocabulary. Here traditional adherence to ancient linguistic norms and to the models of classical literature, especially the Koran, has had the effect of preserving the language intact over the centuries. But as vocabulary and phraseology must adapt to the new and ever-changing requirements of external circumstances, these are more prone to change. Strictly speaking, every epoch of Arab history has had its own peculiar vocabulary, which should be set forth in a separate dictionary. But as we have seen, the vocabulary of modern Arabic confronts the lexicographer who aims at completeness with more than a fair share of problems and difficulties.

In the presentation of the entries in the dictionary, homonymous roots are given separately in only a few especially clear instances. The arrangement of word entries under a given root does not necessarily imply etymological relationship. Consistent separation of such roots was dispensed with because the user of a practical dictionary of modern Arabic will not generally be concerned with Semitic etymology. In conformity with the practice customary in bilingual dictionaries of modern European languages, where the material is treated in purely synchronic fashion, the origin of older loanwords and foreign terms is not indicated. For recent loans, however, the source and the foreign word are usually given. Personal names are generally omitted, but large numbers of geographical names are included; the *nisba* adjectives of these can be formed at will, hence are not entered unless some peculiarity such as a broken plural is involved. In transliteration, while the ending of *nisba* adjectives regularly appears as *-ī* (e.g., *janūbī, dirāsī, makkī*), the same ending is shown as *-īy* for nominal forms of roots with a weak third radical, i.e., where the third radical is contained in the ending (e.g., *qaṣīy, ṣabīy, maḥmīy, mabnīy*). This distinction, not present in Arabic script, may prove valuable to the user of the dictionary. Because of a distinction which retains importance in quantitative metrics, the third person singular masculine suffix is transcribed with a long vowel (*-hū, -hī*) following short syllables and with a short vowel (*-hu, -hi*) after long syllables. In any bilingual dictionary, the listing of isolated words with one or more isolated translations is, strictly speaking, an inadmissible abstraction. In order to provide the syntactical information to be expected in a dictionary of this size, a liberal selection of idiomatic phrases and sentences illustrating usage has been added. Symbols showing the accusative and prepositional government of verbs are also supplied. Synonyms and translations have been included in large numbers in order to delineate as accurately as possible the semantic ranges within which a given entry can be used.

The material for the dictionary was gathered in several stages. The major portion was collected between 1940 and 1944 with the co-operation of several German orientalists. The entire work was set in type, but only one set of galleys survived the war. The author resumed the collection of material in the years 1946 through 1948 and added a considerable number of entries. The German edition of the dictionary, *Arabisches Wörterbuch für die Schriftsprache der Gegenwart*, which appeared in 1952, was based on a corpus of approximately 45,000 slips containing citations from Arabic sources. The primary source materials consisted of selected works by Ṭāhā Ḥusain, Muḥammad Ḥusain Haikal, Taufīq al-Ḥakīm, Maḥmūd Taimūr, al-Manfalūṭī, Jibrān Ḵalīl Jibrān, and Amīn ar-Raiḥānī. Further, numerous Egyptian newspapers and periodicals, the Egyptian state almanac, *taqwīm miṣr*, for 1935 and its Iraqi counterpart, *dalīl al-ʿirāq*, for 1937, as well as a number of specialized Egyptian handbooks were thoroughly sifted. The secondary sources used in preparation of the German edition were the first edition of Léon Bercher's *Lexique arabe-français* (1938), which provides material from the Tunisian press in the form of a supplement to J. B. Belot's *Vocabulaire arabe-français*, G. S. Colin's *Pour lire la presse arabe* (1937), the third edition of E. A. Elias' comprehensive *Modern Dictionary Arabic-English* (1929), and the glossary of the modern Arabic chrestomathy by C. V. Odé-Vassilieva (1929). Items in the secondary sources for which there were attestations in the primary sources were, of course, included. All other items in the secondary sources were carefully worked over, in part with the help of Dr. Tahir Khemiri. Words known to him, or already included in older dictionaries, were incorporated. Apart from the primary and secondary sources, the author had, of course, to consult a number of reference works in European languages, encyclopedias, lexicons, glossaries, technical dictionaries, and specialized literature on the most diverse subjects in order to ascertain the correct translation of many technical terms. For older Arabic forms, the available indices and collections of Arabic terminology in the fields of religion (both Islam and Eastern Church), jurisprudence, philosophy, Arabic grammar, botany, and others were very helpful. These collections were, however, not simply accepted and incorporated en bloc into the dictionary, but used only to sharpen the definition of terms in the modern meanings actually attested in the primary source materials.

After publication of the German edition the author continued collecting and presented new material, together with corrections of the main work, in *Supplement zum arabischen Wörterbuch für die Schriftsprache der Gegenwart*, which appeared in 1959. The *Supplement* contains the results of extensive collection from the writings of ʿAbdassalām al-ʿUjailī, Mīkā'īl Nuʿaima, and Karam Malḥam Karam, from newspapers and periodicals of all Arab countries, as well as from Syrian and Lebanese textbooks and specialized literature. In the postwar years several lexicographical works dealing with modern Arabic became available to the author: the second edition of Bercher (1944), the fourth edition of Elias (1947), D. Neustadt and P. Schusser's Arabic-Hebrew dictionary, *Millōn ʿArabī-ʿIbrī* (1947), Charles Pellat's *L'arabe vivant* (1952), and C. K. Baranov's comprehensive Arabic-Russian dictionary, *Arabsko-Russkiy Slovar* (1957). In preparing the *Supplement*, the author compared these with his own work but was reluctant to incorporate items which he could not find attested in context, and which would merely increase the number of entries derived from secondary sources.

The author is indebted to Dr. Andreas Jacobi and Mr. Heinrich Becker who, until they were called up for military service in 1943, rendered valuable assistance in collecting and collating the vast materials of the German edition and in preparing the manuscript. A considerable amount of material was contributed by a number of Arabists. The author wishes to express his gratitude for such contributions to Prof. Werner Caskel, Dr. Hans Kindermann, Dr. Hedwig Klein, Dr. Kurt Munzel, Prof. Annemarie Schimmel, Dr. Richard Schmidt, and especially to Prof. Wolfram von Soden, who contributed a large amount of excellent material. I am deeply grateful to Dr. Munzel, who contributed many entries from newspapers of the postwar period and likewise to his colleague Dr. Muḥammad Safṭī. I appreciate having been able to discuss many difficult items with them. The assistance of Dr. Tahir Khemiri was especially useful. He contributed 1,500 very valuable items and, until 1944, his advice to the author during the collection and sifting of material shed light upon many dubious cases. Prof. Anton Spitaler likewise provided valuable observations and greatly appreciated advice. Contributions to the *Supplement* were supplied by Dr. Eberhard Kuhnt, Dr. Götz Schregle, and Mr. Karl Stowasser. Moreover, in the course of two visits to a number of Arab countries, many Arab contributors, students, scholars, writers, and professional people too numerous to mention generously provided useful information and counsel. Here, as in the prefaces to the German edition of the dictionary and the *Supplement*, the author wishes to express his sincere thanks to all those who have contributed to the success of this undertaking.

This English edition includes all the material contained in the German edition of the dictionary and in the *Supplement*, as well as a number of additions and corrections the need for which became obvious only after the publication of the *Supplement*. Additions have been inserted in the proof almost up to the present time. It was therefore possible to include a number of contributions made by Dr. Walter Jesser in Alexandria. The number of cross-references has been considerably increased. A new type font was introduced for the Arabic. The second edition of Webster's New International Dictionary was used as a standard reference for spelling and for certain definitions. On the suggestion of the editor, three changes were made in the system of transliteration used in the German edition, namely, *j* for ج, *ḵ* for خ, and *ḡ* for غ. Also, following his preference, proper names were transliterated without capital letters, since there is no capitalization in Arabic script. The author followed a suggestion made by Prof. Charles A. Ferguson in his review of the dictionary (Language 30: 174, 1954) to transcribe feminine endings of roots having a weak third radical (اة-) with the pausal form *-āh* instead of *-āt*. Also following Dr. Ferguson's advice, the author has transcribed many more foreign words than in the German edition. The letters *e*, *ē*, *ə*, *o*, *ō*, *č*, *ž*, *g*, *v*, and *p*, which have no counterpart in classical Arabic, have been added. The system of transcription for Arabic words throughout the dictionary is simply a transliteration of the Arabic script. For foreign words and Arabic dialect words, however, the usual transliteration of the Arabic is inadequate to indicate the pronunciation. In order to avoid discrepancy between spelling and pronunciation, the author, in his German edition, would often refrain from giving any transcription at all, but merely enter the foreign word as a rough guide to pronunciation. In the present edition practically all foreign words have been transcribed (e.g., *diblōmāsī*, *helikoptar*, *vīzā*, *vētō*) with the help of the added letters. Arab students at the University of Münster were consulted for the approximately correct pronunciation. Nevertheless, in many instances the foreign source word is also entered because pronunciation varies considerably from speaker to speaker, depending on the dialect and the degree of assimilation. One other deviation from a strict transliteration of the Arabic was made for certain foreign words in order to provide a closer approximation to the usual pronunciation. In writing European words with Arabic letters, ا, و, ى are, contrary to regular practice in Arabic, frequently used to indicate short vowels. Where this is the case, we have transcribed accordingly (e.g., اوتوماتيكى *otomātīkī*, الدانمارك *ad-danmark*).

Finally, the author wishes to express his sincere gratitude to the editor, Prof. J Milton Cowan, thanks to whose initiative and energy this English edition can now be presented to the public. His generous expenditure of time and effort on this project has been greatly appreciated by all involved. To Theodora Ronayne, who performed the exacting task of preparing a meticulously accurate typescript, thereby considerably lightening our labors, we are indeed grateful. Professor Cowan joins me in recording our special thanks to Mr. Karl Stowasser, whose quite remarkable command of the three languages involved and whose unusual abilities as a lexicographer proved indispensable. He has devoted his untiring efforts to this enterprise for the past four years, co-ordinating the work of editor and author across the Atlantic. The bulk of the translation was completed in 1957–1958, while he was in Ithaca. During the past two years in Münster he has completed the incorporation of the *Supplement* into the body of the dictionary and assisted the author in seeing the work through the press.

* * *

The following paragraphs describe the arrangement of entries and explain the use of symbols and abbreviations:

Arabic words are arranged according to Arabic roots. Foreign words are listed in straight alphabetical order by the letters of the word (cf. باريس *bārīs* Paris, كادر *kādir* cadre). Arabicized loanwords, if they clearly fit under the roots, are entered both ways, often with the root entry giving a reference to the alphabetical listing (cf. قانون *qānūn* law, نيزك *naizak* spear).

Two or more homonymous roots may be entered as separate items, including foreign words treated as Arabic forms (e.g., كريم *karīm* under the Arabic root [1]كرم and [2]كريم, the French word *crème*; cf. also the consonant combination *k-r-k*). In order to indicate to the reader that the same order of letters occurs more than once and that he should not confine his search to the first listing, each entry is preceded by a small raised numeral (cf. برد, مر).

Under a given root the sequence of entries is as follows. The verb in the perfect of the base stem, if it exists, comes first with the transliteration indicating the voweling. It is followed by the vowel of the imperfect and, in parentheses, the verbal nouns or *maṣādir*. Then come the derived stems, indicated by boldface Roman numerals II through X. For Arab users unaccustomed to this designation generally used by Western orientalists, the corresponding stem forms are: II فعل *fa''ala*, III فاعل *fā'ala*, IV افعل *af'ala*, V تفعل *tafa''ala*, VI تفاعل *tafā'ala*, VII انفعل *infa'ala*, VIII افتعل *ifta'ala*, IX افعل *if'alla*, X استفعل *istaf'ala*. Wherever there is any irregularity, for the rare stems XI through XV, and for the derived stems of quadriliteral verbs the Arabic form is entered and transliterated (cf. محو VII, وحد VIII, حدب XII, سلطح III). Then come nominal forms arranged according to their length. Verbal nouns of the stems II through X and all active and passive participles follow at the end. The latter are listed as separate items only when their meaning is not immediately obvious from the verb, particularly where a substantival or adjectival translation is possible (cf. حاجب *ḥājib* under حجب, ساحل *sāḥil* under سحل). The sequence under a given root is not determined by historical considerations. Thus, a verb derived from a foreign word is placed at the head of the entire section (cf. اقلم *aqlama*, [2]ترك II).

Essentially synonymous definitions are separated by commas. A semicolon marks the beginning of a definition in a different semantic range.

The syntactic markings accompanying the definitions of a verb are ه for the accusative of a person, ه for the accusative of a thing, ها for the feminine of animate beings, هم for a group of persons. It should be noted that the Arabic included in parentheses is to be read from right to left even if separated by the word "or" (cf. فهم X). Verb objects in English are expressed by s.o. (someone) and s.th. (something), the reflexive by o.s. (oneself).

A dash occurring within a section indicates that the following form of a plural or of a verbal noun, or in some instances the introduction of a new voweling of the main entry, holds for all following meanings in the section even if these are not synonymous and are separated by semicolons. This dash invalidates all previously given verbal nouns, imperfect vowels, plurals, and other data qualifying the main entry. It indicates that all following definitions apply only to this latest sub-entry (cf. خفق *ḵafaqa*, سبيل *sabīl*).

In the transcription, which indicates the voweling of the unpointed Arabic, nouns are given in pausal form without *tanwīn*. Only nouns derived from verbs with a weak third radical are transcribed with nunnation (e.g., قاض *qāḍin*, مقتضى *muqtaḍan*, مأتى *ma'tan* in contrast with بشرى *bušrā*).

A raised [2] following the transcription of a noun indicates that it is a diptote. This indication is often omitted from Western geographical terms and other recent non-Arabic proper names because the inflected ending is practically never pronounced and the marking would have only theoretical value (cf. استوكهولم *istokholm*, ابريل *abrīl*).

The symbol ○ precedes newly coined technical terms, chiefly in the fields of technology, which were repeatedly found in context but whose general acceptance among specialists could not be established with certainty (cf. تلفاز *tilfāz* television set, حدس *ḥads* intuition, محر *miḥarr* heating installation).

The symbol □ precedes those dialect words for which the Arabic spelling suggests a colloquial pronunciation (cf. حداف *ḥaddāf*, ²حدق II).

Dialect words are marked with abbreviations in lower-case letters (e.g., *syr.*, *leb.*, *saud.-ar.*, etc.). These are also used to indicate words which were found only in the sources of a particular area. This does not necessarily mean that a word or meaning is confined to that area (cf. جارور *jārūr*, طربيزة *ṭarabēza*).

The same abbreviations, but with capital letters, mark entries as the generally accepted technical terms or the official designations for public offices, institutions, administrative departments, and the like, of the country in question (cf. اطروحة *uṭrūḥa*, دائرة *dā'ira*, عميد *'amīd*).

The abbreviation *Isl. Law* marks the traditional terminology of Islamic *fiqh* (cf. حدث *ḥadaṯ*, لعان *li'ān*, متعة *mut'a*), as distinguished from the technical terms of modern jurisprudence which are characterized by the abbreviation *jur.* (cf. عمدى *'amdī*, تلبس *talabbus*). For other abbreviated labels see List of Abbreviations below.

Elatives of the form *af'alu* are translated throughout with the English comparative because this most often fits the meaning. The reader should bear in mind, however, that in certain contexts they will best be rendered either with the positive or the superlative.

The heavy vertical stroke | terminates the definitions under an entry. It is followed by phrases, idioms, and sentences which illustrate the phraseological and syntactic use of that entry. These did not have to be transcribed in full because it has been necessary to assume an elementary knowledge of Arabic morphology and syntax on the part of the user, without which it is not possible to use a dictionary arranged according to roots. Consequently, no transcription is given after the vertical stroke for:

1 the entry itself, but it is abbreviated wherever it is part of a genitive compound (e.g., *ṣ. al-ma'ālī* under *ṣāḥib*, *ḥusn al-u.* under *uḥdūṯa*);

2 nouns whose Arabic spelling is relatively unambiguous (e.g., فائدة, ساعة, آثار, دار);

3 words known from elementary grammar, such as pronouns, negations, and prepositions the third person perfect of the verb type *fa'ala*, occasionally also the definite article;

4 frequent nominal types, such as:

a) the verbal nouns (*maṣādir*) of the derived stems II and VII—X:
تفعيل *taf'īl*, انفعال *infi'āl*, افتعال *ifti'āl*, افعلال *if'ilāl*, استفعال *istif'āl*;

b) the active and passive participles of the basic verb stem:
فاعل *fā'il*, فاعلة *fā'ila*, and مفعول *maf'ūl*, مفعولة *maf'ūla*;

c) the nominal types فعيل *fa'īl*, فعيلة *fa'īla*, فعال *fi'āl*, and فعول *fu'ūl* (also as a plural); فعالة *fi'āla* and فعولة *fu'ūla* as well as افعل *af'al*;

d) the plural forms افعال *af'āl*, افعلاء *af'ilā'*, فعالل *fa'ālil*, افاعل *afā'il*, مفاعل *mafā'il*, فعائل *fa'ā'il*, فعاعل *fa'ā'il*, فعاليل *fa'ālīl*, افاعيل *afā'īl*, تفاعيل *tafā'īl*, مفاعيل *mafā'īl*, فعاللة *fa'ālila*.

All other possible vowelings are transcribed (e.g., *if'āl*, *fa''āl*, *fu'ail*, *fa'ūl*, *af'ul*, *fā'al*). Words with weak radicals belonging in the form types listed above are also transcribed wherever any uncertainty about the form might arise (cf. راغ *rāğin* under رغو, زيت الخروع under زيت *zait*, المسجد الاقصى under مسجد *masjid*).

In transcription, two nouns forming a genitive compound are treated as a unit. They are transcribed as noun — definite article — noun, with the entry word abbreviated (cf. under صاحب *ṣāḥib*, شبه *šibh*). In a noun compound where the second noun is in apposition or attributive, it alone is transcribed (cf. under جلد *jild*, حكم *ḥukm*). In this manner the difference between the two constructions is brought out clearly without resorting to transliteration of the *iʿrāb* endings. A feminine noun ending in *-a*, as first member of a genitive compound, is also abbreviated, and the construct ending *-t* is to be read even though it is not expressed in the transcription.

In view of the great variety and intricacy of the material presented, it is inevitable that inconsistencies will appear and that similar examples will be treated here and there in a different manner. For such incongruities and for certain redundancies, we must ask the user's indulgence.

Münster HANS WEHR

November 1960

* * *

List of Abbreviations

abstr.	abstract
acc.	accusative
A.D.	anno Domini
adj.	adjective
adm.	administration
adv.	adverb
A.H.	year of the Hegira
Alg.	Algeria
alg.	Algerian
a.m.	ante meridiem
anat.	anatomy
apoc.	apocopate form
approx.	approximately
arch.	architecture
archeol.	archeology
arith.	arithmetic
astron.	astronomy
athlet.	athletics
attrib.	attribute, attributively
biol.	biology
bot.	botany
Brit.	British
ca.	circa, about
caus.	causative
cf.	compare
chem.	chemistry
Chr.	Christian
coll.	collective
colloq.	colloquial
com.	commerce
conj.	conjunction
constr.-eng.	construction engineering
Copt.	Coptic
cosm.	cosmetics
dam.	Damascene
def.	definite
dem.	demonstrative
dial.	dialectal
dimin.	diminutive
dipl.	diplomacy
do.	ditto
du.	dual
E	east, eastern
econ.	economy

Eg.	Egypt	lit.	literally
eg.	Egyptian	m.	masculine
e.g.	for example	*magn.*	magnetism
el.	electricity	*Maǧr.*	Maghrib
ellipt.	elliptical	*maǧr.*	Maghribi
Engl.	English	masc.	masculine
esp.	especially	*math.*	mathematics
ethnol.	ethnology	*med.*	medicine
f.	feminine	*meteor.*	meteorology
fem.	feminine	*mil.*	military
fig.	figuratively	*min.*	mineralogy
fin.	finance	*Mor.*	Morocco
foll.	following	*mor.*	Moroccan
Fr.	French	*mus.*	music
G.	German	*myst.*	mysticism
G.B.	Great Britain	N	north, northern
genit.	genitive	n.	noun, nomen
geogr.	geography	*N.Afr.*	North Africa
geol.	geology	NE	northeast, northeastern
geom.	geometry	*naut.*	nautics
Gr.	Greek	neg.	negation
gram.	grammar	nom.	nominative
Hebr.	Hebrew	n. un.	nomen unitatis
ḥij.	Hejazi	n. vic.	nomen vicis
hort.	horticulture	NW	northwest, northwestern
i.e.	that is	obl.	obliquus
imp.	imperative	obs.	obsolete
imperf.	imperfect	*opt.*	optics
indef.	indefinite	o.s.	oneself
interj.	interjection	Ott.	Ottoman
Intern. Law	International Law	*Pal.*	Palestine
intr.	intransitive	*pal.*	Palestinian
invar.	invariable, invariant	*parl.*	parliamentary language
Ir.	Iraq	part.	particle
ir.	Iraqi	pass.	passive
Isl.	Islam, Islamic	*path.*	pathology
It.	Italian	perf.	perfect
Jord.	Jordan Kingdom	Pers.	Persian
journ.	journalism	pers.	person, personal
Jud.	Judaism	*pharm.*	pharmacy
jur.	jurisprudence	*philos.*	philosophy
Leb.	Lebanon	*phon.*	phonetics
leb.	Lebanese	*phot.*	photography
lex.	lexicography	*phys.*	physics
Lib.	Libya	*physiol.*	physiology
lib.	Libyan	pl.	plural

pl. comm.	pluralis communis
p.m.	post meridiem
poet.	poetry
pol.	politics
prep.	preposition
pron.	pronoun
pronun.	pronunciation
psych.	psychology
q.v.	which see
refl.	reflexive
rel.	relative
relig.	religion
rhet.	rhetoric
S	south, southern
Saudi Ar.	Saudi Arabia
saud.-ar.	Saudi-Arabian
SE	southeast, southeastern
sing.	singular
s.o.	someone
Span.	Spanish
specif.	specifically
s.th.	something
styl.	stylistics
subj.	subjunctive
subst.	substantive
surg.	surgery
SW	southwest, southwestern
Syr.	Syria
syr.	Syrian
techn.	technology
tel.	telephone
temp.	temporal
theat.	theatrical art
theol.	theology
trans.	transitive
Tun.	Tunisia
tun.	Tunisian
Turk.	Turkish
TV	television
typ.	typography
uninfl.	uninflected
verb.	verbal
W	west, western
Yem.	Yemen
yem.	Yemenite usage
zool.	zoology

ا *a* particle introducing direct and indirect questions; ا — ام *a — am* (also ا — ام ان *a — am anna*) whether — or (alternative questions); سواء ا — ام *sawā'un a — am* no matter whether — or; او *a-wa* particle indicating or implying doubt: or? perhaps? اوتشك فى ذلك (*tašukku*) you wouldn't doubt it, would you? do you perhaps doubt it? or do you doubt it? الا *a-lā* and اما *a-mā* intensifying interjections introducing sentences: verily, truly, indeed, oh yes, etc., الا فانظروا (*fa-nẓurū*) oh, do look! why, look! اما انه (*innahū*) why, he is ...!

1آب *āb*[2] August (month; *Syr., Leb., Jord., Ir.*)

2الآب *al-āb* (*Chr.*) the Father (God)

3اب see ابو

4اب *abba u* to long, yearn (الى وطنه *ilā waṭanihī* for one's homeland)

5ابيب look up alphabetically

اباجور *abāžūr*, اباجورة (Fr.) pl. *-āt* lampshade

ابتاه and يا ابت see ابو

ابجد *abjad* alphabet

ابجدى *abjadī* alphabetic(al); ابجديات elementary facts, simple truths | الحروف الابجدية the letters of the alphabet, the alphabet

ابد *abada i* (ابود *ubūd*) to stay (ب at), abide (ب in a place); to last, persist; — *i u* to be wild, untamed, be shy, shy away, run away (animal, game) **II** to make lasting or permanent, perpetuate, eternize (ه s.th.) **V** to be perpetuated, become lasting or permanent, be eternized; to return to a state of wildness

ابد *abad* pl. آباد *ābād* endless, eternal duration, eternity; ابدا *abadan* always, forever; ever, (with neg.) never (in the future), not at all, on no account; (alone, without negation) never! not at all! by no means! | الى الابد, على الابد and ابد الدهر *abada d-dahri* forever; ابد الابد *abada l-a.*, ابد الآبدين *a. l-ābidīn*, ابد الابدية *a. l-abadīya*, ابد الابدين *abada l-abadīn* and الى ابد الابدين *ilā abadi l-a.* forever and ever

ابدى *abadī* everlasting, eternal, endless

ابدية *abadīya* infinite duration, endless time, eternity

آبد *ābid* resident, nonmigratory (bird); wild, untamed

آبدة *ābida* pl. اوابد *awābid*[2] unusual thing, prodigious event; resident bird; wild animal; monster | اوابد الدنيا *a. ad-dunyā* the Wonders of the World

مؤبد *mu'abbad* eternal, endless, everlasting; lifelong, lifetime (e.g., sentence) | سجن مؤبد (*sijn*) life imprisonment

1ابر *abara i u* (*abr*) to prick, sting **II** to pollinate (ه a palm tree)

ابرة *ibra* pl. ابر *ibar* needle, pin; indicator (of an instrument); pointer (of a balance or scales); shot, injection (*med.*); sting, prick | ابرة الحياكة *i. al-ḥiyāka* knitting needle; ابرة الخياطة *i. al-ḵiyāṭa* sewing needle; ابرة الكروشيه *i. al-krūšēh* crochet needle; حقنه ابرة *ḥaqanahū ibratan* to give s.o. an injection; ابرة الراعى *i. ar-rā'ī* geranium (*bot.*); ابرة مغناطيسية (*maǧnāṭīsīya*) magnetic needle; شغل الابرة *šuǧl al-i.* needlework

مئبر *mi'bar* pl. مآبر *ma'ābir*[2] large packing needle; needlecase; ○ anther (*bot.*)

²آبار *ābār* see بئر

ابراهيم *ibrāhīm*² Abraham

ابرشية *abrašiya* and *abaršiya* pl. *-āt* (Gr. ἐπαρχία) eparchy, diocese, bishopric (*Chr.*); parish (*Chr.*)

ابرميس *abramīs,* ابراميس bream (*zool.*)

ابراهيم = ابرهيم

ابريز *ibrīz* pure gold

ابريزى *ibrīzī* golden, of pure gold

ابريسم *ibrīsam, ibrīsim* silk

ابريق *ibrīq* pl. اباريق *abārīq*², (*tun.*) ابارقة *abāriqa* pitcher; jug

ابريل *abrīl* April

ابزن *abzan* pl. ابازن *abāzin*² washbowl

ابزيم *ibzīm* pl. ابازيم *abāzīm*² buckle, clasp

ابستيمولوجيا *ebistēmolōjiyā* epistemology

ابض *ubḍ* pl. آباض *ābāḍ* and مأبض *ma'biḍ* pl. مآبض *ma'ābiḍ*² hollow of the knee, popliteal space

الاباضية *al-ibāḍīya* (usually *al-abāḍīya*) the Ibāḍites, a Moslem sect (in Oman, E Africa, Tripolitania and Algeria)

ابط V to take or carry under one's arm (ه s.th.); to put one's arm (ه, ه around s.o., around s.th.), hold in one's arm (ه, ه s.o., s.th.)

ابط *ibṭ* pl. آباط *ābāṭ* m. and f. armpit | تحت ابطه ready at hand, pat (e.g., answer), at one's finger tips (e.g., knowledge)

اباطرة see امبراطور

ابق *abaqa i* (اباق *ibāq*) to escape, run away (a slave from his master)

ابق *abaq* a kind of hemp

آبق *ābiq* pl. اباق *ubbāq* runaway, escaped; a fugitive

¹ابل *ibil* (coll.) camels

²ابالة *ibāla, ibbāla* bundle, bale

³ابلة *abla* (*eg.*) aunt, auntie (children's form of address); ابلة فلانة aunt So-and-so

ابليز *iblīz* alluvial deposits (of the Nile)

ابليس *iblīs*² pl. ابالسة *abālisa* devil, Satan

ابليسى *iblīsī* devilish, satanic, diabolic

¹ابن II to celebrate, praise, eulogize (ه a deceased person), deliver a funeral oration (ه in praise of s.o.)

ابنة *ubna* passive pederasty

ابان *ibbān* time; ابان *ibbāna* during, فى ابان at the time of, during

تأبين *ta'bīn* commemoration (of a deceased person) | حفلة التأبين *ḥaflat at-t.* commemorative celebration (in honor of a deceased person)

تأبينى *ta'bīnī*: كلمة تأبينية (*kalima*) eulogy for a deceased person, obituary speech

مأبون *ma'būn* catamite; weakling, mollycoddle, sissy; scoundrel

²ابن and ابنة see ¹بن

ابنوس *abnūs, abanūs,* آبنوس *ābinūs* ebony

ابه *abaha* and *abiha a* (*abh*) to pay attention (ل, also ب to), heed (ل, also ب s.th.), take notice (ل, also ب of) | امر لا يؤبه له (*yu'bahu*) an insignificant, unimportant matter V to display proud, haughty manners; to turn away, keep one's distance, remain aloof (عن from), look down (عن upon), think o.s. far above (عن s.o or s.th.)

ابهة *ubbaha* splendor, pomp, ostentation, pageantry; pride

اب (ابو) *ab* pl. آباء *ābā'* father (also *eccl.*); ancestor, forefather; يا ابت *yā abati,* ابتاه *abatāh,* يا ابتاه O my father! الابوان *al-abawān* the parents, father and mother; pl. الآباء fathers and mothers; ابونا *abūnā* reverend father, form of address and title of a priest (*Chr.*); (with genit.) possessor of, provided with, having . . ., e.g., ابو شوارب mustached, sporting a mustache | ابا عن جد *aban ʿan jaddin* handed down from father to son, as s.th. inherited from forefathers; ابو جعران *abū jiʿrān* scarabaeus; dung beetle; ابو زريق *abū zuraiq* jay (*zool.*); ابو سعن *abū suʿn* marabou; ابو ظبي *abū ẓaby* Abu Dhabi, name of an emirate on the Persian Gulf; ابو قير *abū qīr* Aboukir (Egyptian seaside resort on the Mediterranean); ابو النوم *abū n-naum* poppy; ابو الهول *abū l-haul* the Sphinx; ابو اليقظان *abū l-yaqẓān* rooster, cock; in compounds also look up the second word

ابوة *ubūwa* fatherhood, paternity

ابوى *abawī* paternal, fatherly; patriarchal, patriarchical

ابوية *abawīya* patriarchate, patriarchy

ابوا *abwā* (Fr. *hautbois*) oboe (*mus.*)

ابونيت ebonite

ابونيه (Fr. *abonné*) *abūnēh* pl. *-āt* subscription; subscription card (e.g., for public conveyances, a concert season, etc.)

ابى *abā a* (اباء *ibā'*, اباءة *ibā'a*) to refuse, decline; to turn down, reject, scorn, disdain (ه s.th.); to deny (على ه s.o. s.th.) | ابى الا ان يفعله (*illā an yafʿalahū*) he insisted on doing it; ابى الله الا ان God willed that . . . V to refuse, decline; to behave in a proud manner, be proud

اباء *ibā'*, اباءة *ibā'a* rejection; dislike, distaste, aversion, disdain; pride

ابى *abīy* disdainful, scornful; proud, lofty, lofty-minded

آب *ābin* pl. اباة *ubāh* reserved, standoffish; unwilling, reluctant, grudging

ابيب *abīb* the eleventh month of the Coptic calendar

ابيقور *abīqūr*[2] Epicurus

ابيقورى *abīqūrī* Epicurean

ابيقورية *abīqūrīya* Epicureanism

اترج *utrujj*, اترنج *utrunj* (n. un. ة) citron (Citrus medica; *bot.*)

آتشجى (Turk. *ateşçi*) *ātešgī* fireman, stoker

مأتم *ma'tam* pl. مآتم *ma'ātim*[2] obsequies, funeral ceremony; (female) mourners (at a funeral; treated as f. pl.)

[1]اتان *atān* pl. آتن *ātun*, اتن *utun*, *utn* female donkey, she-ass

[2]اتون *atūn*, *attūn* pl. اتن *utun*, اتاتين *atātīn*[2] kiln, furnace, oven

اتنولوجيا *etnolōjiyā*, *etnolōgiyā* ethnology

اتنولوجى *etnolōjī*, *etnolōgī* ethnological

اتاوة *itāwa* pl. *-āt*, اتاوى *atāwā* duty, tax, due, toll; extorted payment; tribute

اتوبيس (Fr.) *otobīs* pl. *-āt* autobus, bus

اتوماتيكى (Fr.) *otomātīkī* automatic

اتومبيل and اتوموبيل (Fr.) *otomobīl* pl. *-āt* automobile

اتى *atā i* (اتيان *ityān*, اتى *aty*, مأتاة *ma'tāh* to come (ه or الى to; على over s.o.), arrive (ه or الى at); اتى ب to bring, bring forward, produce, advance, accomplish or achieve s.th.; اتى ه ب to bring, give or offer s.o. s.th.; to do, perform (ه a deed), carry out, execute (ه e.g., movements); to commit, perpetrate (ه a sin, a crime); to mention (على s.th.); to finish off (على s.th., also s.o.); to finish, complete, carry through, dispose, settle, wind up, conclude, terminate, bring to a close (على s.th.); to destroy, annihilate, eradicate, wipe out (على s.th.); to eliminate, carry away, sweep away (على s.th.), do away (على with); to use up, exhaust (also a subject), present exhaustively, in great detail (على s.th.), elaborate (على on s.th.) | كما يأتى as follows; اتى بجديد to come out with s.th. new; اتى به الى to bring or lead s.o. to a place, to s.o., into a situation; اتى على آخره (*āḵirihī*) to complete, finish s.th.; to spend or use up the last of s.th.;

اتى على الاخضر واليابس to destroy everything, wreak havoc; اتى البيوت من ابوابها (*buyūta*) to tackle s.th. in the right way, knock on the right door; يؤتى من قبل *yu'tā min qibali* is undermined, weakened, ruined by **III** to offer, furnish, give, afford (ه ب to s.o. s.th.), provide, supply (ه ب s.o. with); to be propitious, be favorable (ه for s.o.), favor (ه s.o.); to turn out well (ه for s.o.), be in favor (ه of); to suit, befit, become (ه s.o.), be appropriate (ه for s.o.); to agree (ه with s.o.; food) | آتاه كل شىء (*kullu šai'in*) everything was in his favor, turned out well for him, came his way **IV** to bring (ه ه s.o. s.th.); to give (ه ه s.o. s.th.); to grant (ه ه to s.o. s.th.), bestow (ه ه upon s.o. s.th.) | آتى الزكاة (*zakāta*) to give alms; لم تؤت الثمرة اكلها (*ṯamaratu ukulahā*) it was a failure, nothing came of it **V** to originate, stem, derive, spring, arise, result (عن and من from); to end (عن with), result (عن in); to get (الى to), arrive (الى at); to be easy to do, be feasible without difficulty, be possible or attainable, go well, progress; to come off; to go about s.th. (فى) gently, cautiously **X** to ask to come, induce to come (ه s.o.)

اتيان *ityān* performance (ب of s.th.)

مأتى *ma'tan* pl. مآت *ma'ātin* place where s.th. comes from; place at which one arrives; access; pl. مآت place of origin; origin, source, provenance; place where one has been or to which one has come; place where s.th. starts, where s.th. ends

آت *ātin* coming, next; following | الاسبوع الآتى (*usbū'*) the coming week, next week; كالآتى as follows

موات *mu'ātin, muwātin* favorable, propitious, opportune, convenient, suitable

اث *aṯṯa u i a* (اثاثة *aṯāṯa*) to be luxuriant, grow profusely (hair, plants) **II** to fix up, prepare (ه s.th.); to furnish (ه an apartment) **V** to be or become rich, wealthy, to prosper; to be furnished

اث *aṯṯ*, اثيث *aṯīṯ* abundant, luxuriant, profusely growing (hair, plants)

اثاث *aṯāṯ* pl. *-āt* furniture, furnishings (of an apartment, of a room); equipment; pl. اثاثات furnishings, pieces of furniture

تأثيث *ta'ṯīṯ* furnishing

مؤثث *mu'aṯṯaṯ* furnished

[1]اثر *aṯara u i* (*aṯr*, اثارة *aṯāra*) to transmit, pass along, report, relate (ه s.th., عن from, or based on the authority of, s.o.) **II** to affect, influence (فى or على s.o., s.th.), act (فى or على upon), produce an effect, make an impression, have influence (فى or على on); to induce (*phys.*) **IV** to prefer (ه على s.th. to), like (ه s.th.) more (على than); to have a predilection, a liking (ه for), like (ه s.th.), be fond (ه of); to choose, deem wise or advisable (ان to do s.th.); to honour, hold in high esteem (ه, ه s.o., s.th.) | آثر نفسه ب (*nafsahū*) to take exclusive possession of, appropriate s.th., hold a monopoly over s.th.; آثر نفسه بالخير (*nafsahū bi-l-ḵair*) to think only of one's own welfare, demand good only for oneself, be egotistical **V** to be impressed, be influenced; to let o.s. be impressed, be impressible; to be moved, be touched (ب or ل by, also من); to be excited, be stimulated; to be affected (ب by, said of materials, e.g., iron by acid); to be induced (*phys.*); to follow in s.o.'s (ه) tracks, follow s.o.'s example, emulate (ه s.o.); to pursue, follow up (ه a question, a problem); to perceive, feel (ه s.th.) **X** to claim a monopoly; to possess alone, with the exclusion of others, monopolize (ب s.th.); to appropriate (ب s.th.), take exclusive possession (ب of); to preoccupy (ه s.th.), engross (ه the attention); to lay claim on, demand (ب e.g., s.o.'s interest) | استأثر الله به the Lord has taken him unto Himself

اثر *aṯar* pl. آثار *āṯār* track, trace, vestige; sign, mark (from the past); clue; slight touch (of s.th.); relic or remnant (preserved from the past); ancient monument; work of art, literary work (of former times); tradition, brief report (from early Islam); impression, effect, influence (ف or على on); — pl. آثار antiquities; (religious) relics; works, writings (esp. of deceased or ancient authors) | اثر قدم *a. qadam* footprint, trace, vestige; اثر سينمائى (*sīnamā'ī*) cinema classic, (art) film; علم الآثار *'ilm al-ā.* archeology; علم الآثار المصرية (*miṣrīya*) Egyptology; دار الآثار museum of antiquities; لا اثر له (*aṯara*) ineffective, ineffectual; بأثر رجعى (*raj'ī*) with retroactive force (*jur.*); اصبح اثرا بعد عين *aṣbaḥa aṯaran ba'da 'ainin* to be destroyed, be wiped out, leave nothing but memory behind; اعاده اثرا بعد عين (*a'ādahū*) to destroy or wipe s.th. out, leaving only a trace or memory; فى اثره , على اثره (also *fī iṯrihī*) on his (its) track, at his heels, after him; immediately afterwards, presently, thereupon; على الاثر immediately afterwards, presently; من اثر (with genit.) as a consequence or result of ...

اثر *iṯra* (prep.) immediately after, right after

اثرى *aṯarī* archeologic(al); (pl. *-ūn*) archeologist (also آثارى *āṯārī*); old, ancient, antique; antiquarian | عالم اثرى archeologist; لغة اثرية (*luġa*) dead language; صرح اثرى (*ṣarḥ*) historic castle

اثر *aṯir* egoistic, selfish

اثرة *aṯara* selfishness, egoism

اثير *aṯīr* favored, preferred (عند by s.o.), in favor (عند with s.o.); favorite (in compounds); select, exquisite, noble; see also alphabetically

اثارة *aṯāra* remainder, remnant; faint trace, vestige

مأثرة *ma'ṯara, ma'ṯura* pl. مآثر *ma'āṯir*[2] exploit, feat, glorious deed; pl. مآثر memorable events, achievements (handed down from the past)

تأثير *ta'ṯīr* pl. *-āt* action, effect, influence, impression (ف, على on); effectiveness, efficacy; induction (*phys.*)

تأثيرى *ta'ṯīrī* efficacious, highly effective; produced by induction, inductive, inductional, induced (*phys.*)

ايثار *īṯār* preference; altruism; predilection; love, affection

ايثارية *īṯārīya* altruism

تأثر *ta'aṯṯur* being influenced; agitation, emotion, feeling; excitability, sensitivity; induction (*phys.*); (pl. *-āt*) feeling, sensation, perception | سريع التأثر easily impressed, impressible, sensitive; تأثر مغناطيسى (*maġnāṭīsī*) magnetic induction (*phys.*)

تأثرى *ta'aṯṯurī*: المذهب التأثرى (*maḏhab*) the impressionistic movement

تأثرية *ta'aṯṯurīya* impressionism

استئثار *isti'ṯār* arrogation of a monopoly; monopolization; complete absorption, demand, claim; ○ captivation (*psych.*); presumption, presumptuousness; exclusive power

مأثور *ma'ṯūr* transmitted, handed down | قول مأثور (*qaul*) and كلمة مأثورة (*kalima*) proverb; مأثورات شعبية (*ša'bīya*) folklore

مؤثر *mu'aṯṯir* affecting, acting upon; effective; impressive; moving, touching, pathetic; (pl. *-āt*) influencing factor, influence; effect | مؤثرات صوتية (*ṣautīya*) sound effects

متأثر *muta'aṯṯir* under the influence (ب of); (following) as a result or effect (ب of)

اثير[2] look up alphabetically

اثفية *uṯfīya* pl. اثاف *aṯāfin* trivet, tripod (in ancient times: any one of the three stones supporting a cooking pot near the fire) | ثالثة الاثافى that which rounds out a number, caps s.th., puts the lid on s.th., the crowning touch

اثل *aṯala i* to consolidate, strengthen **II** to become rich **V** to be consolidated, be strengthened; to become rich

اثل *atl* pl. اثول *utūl* (coll.; n. un. ة, pl. *atalāt*) tamarisk (*bot.*)

اثيل *atīl* and مؤثل *mu'attal* deep-rooted; of noble origin, highborn

اثم *atima a* (*itm, atam,* مأثم *ma'tam*) to sin, err, slip **II** to sin, transgress; to accuse (ه s.o.) of sin, iniquity **V** to eschew sin, shun evil; to restrain o.s., hold back

اثم *itm* pl. آثام *ātām* sin, offense, misdeed, crime

مأثم *ma'tam* pl. مآثم *ma'ātim*[2] sin, offense, misdeed, crime

تأثيم *ta'tīm* sin, offense, misdeed, crime

آثم *ātim* pl. اثمة *atama* and اثيم *atīm* pl. اثماء *utamā'*[2] sinful, criminal, wicked, evil; sinner

اثمد *itmid* antimony

اثنوجرافيا *etnogrāfiyā* (Eg. spelling) and اثنوغرافيا ethnography

اثنولوجيا *etnolōjiyā, etnolōgiyā* ethnology

اثنولوجى *etnolōjī, etnolōgī* ethnological

اثير *atīr* ether

اثيرى *atīrī* ethereal

اثيلين *atīlīn* ethylene (*chem.*)

اثينا *atīnā* Athens

اثيوبيا *atyūbiyā* Ethiopia

اثيوبى *atyūbī* Ethiopian; (pl. *-ūn*) an Ethiopian | البلاد الاثيوبية Ethiopia

اج *ajja u i* (اجيج *ajīj*) to burn, blaze, flame (fire) **II** to light, kindle, start (ه a fire) **V** = **I**

ماء اجاج *mā' ujāj* bitter, salty water

اجاج *ajjāj* burning, blazing, hot

متأجج *muta'ajjij* burning, blazing, flaming

اجبية *ajabīya* horologium (*Copt.-Chr.*)

[1]اجر *ajara u* (*ajr*) to reward, recompense, remunerate (ه s.o.) **II** to let for rent, let out, hire out, rent, lease (ه s.th.); (with *nafsahū*) to hire o.s. out **IV** to let for rent, let out, hire out, rent, lease (ه s.th.); to rent, hire, lease, hold under a lease (ه s.th.), take a lease (ه on); to hire, engage, take on (ه s.o.), engage the services (ه of s.o.) **V** to hire o.s. out (also with بنفسه) **X** to rent, hire, lease, hold under a lease (ه s.th.), take a lease (ه on); to charter (ه a vessel); to hire, engage, take on (ه s.o.), engage the services (ه of s.o.)

اجر *ajr* pl. اجور *ujūr* wages, pay, honorarium, recompense, emolument, remuneration; price, rate, fee | اجور الدراسة (student) tuition, fees; اجور السفر *u. as-safar* fares

اجرة *ujra* hire, rent, rental; price, rate, fee; fixed rate, (official) charge; postage | اجرة البريد postage; اجرة النقل *u. an-naql* transport charges, freight(age), carriage, cartage; سيارة اجرة *sayyārat u.* taxi

اجير *ajīr* pl. اجراء *ujarā'*[2] hireling; workman, laborer, day laborer; employee

اجيرة *ajīra* working woman, factory girl, female laborer; woman employee | اجيرة للتنظيف cleaning woman, charwoman

تأجير *ta'jīr* letting, leasing, hiring out, letting on lease; lease | مشروع التأجير والاعارة (*i'āra*) Lend-Lease Act

ايجار *ījār* pl. *-āt* rent; letting, leasing, hiring out, letting on lease | للايجار for rent, to let

اجارة *ijāra* pl. *-āt* rent; letting, leasing, hiring out, letting on lease

استئجار *isti'jār* rent, lease, tenure

مأجور *ma'jūr* paid, salaried, on the payroll, gainfully employed; employee; mercenary, venal, hired, bribed; (pl. *-ūn*) a bribable, venal, corruptible person

مأجورى *ma'jūrī* pl. *-ūn* a bribable, venal, corruptible person

مؤجر *mu'ajjir* pl. *-ūn* landlord, lessor

مستأجر *musta'jir* leaseholder, lessee, tenant; employer

آجر[2] *ājurr* (n. un. ة) baked bricks

ماجور[3] see مجر[1]

اجزاجى see جزء

اجزاخانة see جزء

اجاص *ijjāṣ* (n. un. ة) pear; (*syr.*) a variety of plum

اجل *ajila a* (*ajal*) to hesitate, tarry, linger II to delay, postpone, put off, defer, adjourn (ه الى s.th. till) V to be postponed, be deferred, be adjourned (الى till, to) X to request postponement (ه of s.th.); to seek to delay (ه s.th.)

اجل *ajal* yes, indeed! certainly! by all means!

لأجل *li-ajli* or من اجل *min ajli* because of, on account of, for the sake of; for | لاجل ان in order that, that, so that; من اجل هذا therefore, for that reason, on this account

اجل *ajal* pl. آجال *ājāl* appointed time, date, deadline; instant of death; respite, delay | بالاجل on credit (*com.*); لاجل قريب for a short time; بعيد الاجل long-term; long-lasting; of unforeseeable duration; اقرب الاجلين the earlier of the two dates or deadlines, i.e., death or divorce (as due-date for deferred dowry payment; *Isl. Law*); قصير الاجل short-term, short-time; short-lived; الى اجل غير مسمى (*ġairi musamman*) for an indefinite period, sine die, until further notice

تأجيل *ta'jīl* delay, postponement, adjournment, deferment, respite; appointment of a time or date | تأجيل الدفع *t. ad-daf'* extension of payment, moratorium

آجل *ājil* delayed, protracted; deferred; later, future (as opposed to عاجل) | عاجلا او آجلا *'ājilan au ājilan*, فى عاجله او آجله sooner or later, now or later on; فى العاجل والآجل now and in the future

الآجلة *al-ājila* the life to come, the hereafter

مؤجل *mu'ajjal* delayed, late, postponed, deferred; due for later payment (portion of a dowry); fixed in time, deadlined

اجمة *ajama*, coll. اجم *ajam* pl. *-āt*, اجم *ujum*, آجام *ājām* thicket, jungle; canebrake, reedy place; swampy ground, fen

اجمية *ajamīya* malaria | بعوضة الاجمية *ba'ūḍat al-a.* anopheles

آجن *ājin* brackish (water)

اجندة *ajanda* notebook

اح *aḥḥa u* (*aḥḥ*) to cough

احد II to make into one, unite, unify (ه s.th.) VIII اتحد *ittaḥada* see وحد

احد *aḥad*, f. احدى *iḥdā* one; somebody, someone, anybody, anyone (esp. in negative sentences and questions); الاحد the One (God); (pl. آحاد) Sunday | احدهم *aḥaduhum* every one of them; يوم الاحد *yaum al-a.*, pl. ايام الآحاد *ayyām al-ā.* Sunday; احد السعف *a. as-sa'af* Palm Sunday; احد العنصرة *a. al-'anṣara* Whitsunday; احد النسبة *a. an-nisba* Sunday before Christmas; آحاد الالوف *āḥād al-ulūf* a few thousand (2—9000; as distinguished from عشرات الالوف and مئات الالوف)

احدى *aḥadī* dominical, Sunday (adj.)

احدية *aḥadīya* unity, oneness

احادى *uḥādī* single; mono-, uni- (in compounds) | احادى البعد *u. al-bu'd* one-dimensional; احادى اللغة *u. al-luġa* monoglot; احادى المرحلة *u. al-marḥala* single-phase, single-stage (attrib.; *techn.*)

آحاد *āḥād* (pl.) traditions attested only once (in Hadith and philology); الآحاد the units (*math.*)

آحادى *āḥādī* of unique occurrence, dubious, unauthentic (tradition)

[1]احن *aḥina a* (*aḥan*) to hate (على s.o.)

احنة *iḥna* pl. احن *iḥan* old feud, deep-rooted hatred

[2]آحين see اوح

اخ see اخو

اخت see اخو

اخذ *akada u* (*akd*) to take (ه من s.th. from or out of); to take (ه s.th.) along; to get, receive, obtain (ه من s.th. from); to take up, seize (ه s.th.); to grab (ب s.o., s.th.), take hold of (ب); to perceive, notice (ه s.o., said of the eye); to gather, understand, infer, deduce (ه من s.th. from), read (ه s.th.) between the lines (من of); to grip, captivate, thrill, spellbind (ب s.o.); to take up, acquire, make one's own (ب s.th., e.g., a method); to keep, adhere (ب to), observe, take over, adopt, embrace, follow, copy, imitate (ب s.th.); to accept (ب s.th.); to take, lead (ب الى s.o. to); to admonish, urge, drive (ه ب s.o. to do s.th.); to enjoin, impose (ه ب on s.o. s.th.); to take away (ه على from s.o. s.th.), strip, deprive (ه على s.o. of), cut off, bar (ه على s.o. from); to reproach, blame (ه على s.o. for); to hold against s.o. (على) that ... (ان), fix the blame (على on s.o., ان for the fact that); to obligate (ب على s.o. to); to gather (ه عن s.th. from a source); to take over, borrow (عن from others, ه e.g., literary subjects, etc.); to learn (على or عن from s.o., ه s.th.), acquire knowledge (على or عن from s.o.), اخذ العلم عنه (*'ilm*) to study under s.o.; to begin, start (فى or ب with s.th. or s.th., with foll. imperf.: to do s.th.), prepare, set out, be about (فى or ب to do s.th.) | اخذ اهبته (*uhbatahū*) to make preparations, prepare o.s., get ready; اخذ مأخذ فلان (*ma'kada f.*) to adopt the same course as s.o. else, follow s.o.'s example; اخذ منه مأخذا to seize s.o., take possession of s.o. (a sensation, or the like); اخذ منه كل مأخذ (*kulla ma'kadin*) to completely overcome, overpower, seize s.o. (also, e.g., of fatigue, emotion, sensation); اخذ الشىء مأخذ الجد (*ma'kada l-jidd*) to take s.th. seriously; اخذ الباخرة to go by boat; اخذ بالأبصار to catch everyone's eye; اخذ الثار and اخذ بالثار to take revenge (من on s.o.); اخذ مجراه (*majrāhu*) to take its course; اخذ مجلسه (*majlisahū*) to take one's seat, sit down; اخذ حذره (*ḥidrahū, ḥadarahū*) and اخذ حيطته (*ḥīṭatahū*) to be on one's guard, take precautions; اخذه بالحسنى (*ḥusnā*) to be friendly, be nice to s.o.; اخذ حقه (*ḥaqqahū*) to come into one's own, receive one's due, get what one deserves; اخذ بخاطره (*bi-kāṭirihī*) to show o.s. complaisant toward s.o., try to please s.o.; اخذته الدهشة (*dahša*), اخذه العجب (*'ajab*) he was overcome with astonishment; اخذه بذنبه (*bi-danbihī*) to punish s.o. for his offense; اخذ رأيه (*ra'yahū*) to ask s.o.'s opinion, consult s.o.; اخذ برأيه (*bi-ra'yihī*) take on s.o.'s opinion, agree with s.o.; اخذ الرأى عليه (*ukida r-ra'yu*) the matter was put to a vote; اخذ باسباب (*bi-asbābi*) to embrace, adopt s.th., e.g., اخذ باسباب الحضارة الاوربية (*ḥadāra*) to adopt European culture; اخذه بالشدة (*šidda*) to deal with s.o. severely, give s.o. a rough time; اخذ صورة (*ṣūratan*) to take a picture, make a photograph; اخذ عليه طريقه to obstruct s.o.'s way, hinder s.o. from moving on; اخذه على عاتقه to shoulder s.th., take s.th. upon o.s.; اخذ العدة ل (*'udda*) to prepare, set out, get ready to do s.th.; اخذ عليه عهدا (*'ahdan*) to put s.o. under an obligation, impose a commitment on s.o.; اخذت عينى كتابا (*akadat 'ainī*) I caught sight of a book; اخذ بعين الاعتبار (*bi-'aini l-i'tibār*) to consider seriously, bear in mind, take into consideration, weigh (ان that, ه s.th.); اخذ على غرة (حين) *ukida 'alā (ḥīni) ġirratin* to be taken by surprise, be caught unawares; اخذ بالمقابلة (*muqābala*) to repay like for like; شيء ياخذ القلوب s.th. which captivates the heart, a fascinating, thrilling thing; اخذنا المطر (*maṭaru*) we got caught in the rain; اخذ بناصره (*bi-nāṣirihī*) to help s.o., stand by s.o., take care of s.o., look after s.o.; اخذ نفسه (*nafasahū*) to draw breath; اخذ عليه انفاسه to take s.o.'s breath away; اخذه النوم (*naum*) sleep overwhelmed him; اخذ بيده (*bi-yadihī*) to help s.o., stand by s.o.; خذ على يمينك turn to the right! اخذ واعطى (*wa-aʿṭā*) to do business, deal with; to maintain relations (مع with) **II** to lay under a spell, enchant, bewitch (ه s.o.) **III** to censure, blame (ه على, ب s.o. for s.th.); to punish (ه على, ب s.o. for); to hold s.th. (على) against s.o. (ه), resent (على s.th. ه in s.o.) | لا تؤاخذنى! *lā tuʾāk̲id̲nī* pardon me! forgive me! no offense, I hope! **VIII** اتخذ *ittak̲ad̲a* to take (ه s.th.); to take on, assume (ه s.th.); to take up, occupy (ه s.th.); to pass, adopt (ه e.g., a resolution); to take, single out, have in mind (هه, ەه s.o. or s.th. as); to make use (ه of s.th.), use (ه s.th., ه من s.th. as); to imitate, affect (ه e.g., s.o.'s manner of speaking); to make (ه من s.th. out of, ه ه s.o. s.th.) | اتخذ شكلا (*šaklan*) to take on a form or shape; اتخذ موقفا (*mauqifan*) to take an attitude, assume a position; اتخذ التدابير اللازمة to take the necessary measures; اتخذ المناسب (*munāsib*) to act in a suitable or appropriate manner; اتخذ قرارا (*qarāran*) to pass or adopt a resolution; اتخذ المواقع الجديدة to take up new positions (troops)

اخذ *ak̲d̲* acceptance, reception; seizure; taking out, taking away, removal, etc. | اخذ الرأى *a. ar-raʾy* voting, vote; اخذ ورد (*wa-radd*) discussion, debate, dispute, argument; شيء لا يقبل اخذا ولا ردا (*yaqbalu*) an indisputable matter; اخذ وعطاء (*wa-ʿaṭāʾ*) give-and-take; traffic, trade; dealings, relations (esp. business, commercial); discussion, debate; fight, battle; ○ الاخذ عن كل شيء بطرف (*ṭaraf*) eclecticism

اخذة *uk̲d̲a* spell, charm

اخيذ *akīd̲* prisoner of war

اخيذة *akīd̲a* booty, spoils

اخاذ *akkād̲* captivating, fascinating, thrilling

مأخذ *maʾk̲ad̲* pl. مآخذ *maʾāk̲id̲*[2] place from which one takes s.th., source; wall socket, outlet (*el.*); adoption, borrowing, loan; manner of acting, mode of procedure, approach; fault, defect, shortcoming, reprehensible trait, reprehension; pl. مآخذ source references, bibliography (in books) | المأخذ الاقرب the simplest, easiest approach; قريب المأخذ easy to handle or to use; لا مأخذ فيه (*maʾk̲ad̲a*) flawless, faultless, irreproachable; see also *ak̲ad̲a* (middle of paragraph)

مؤاخذة *muʾāk̲ad̲a* objection, exception; censure, blame | لا مؤاخذة! (*muʾāk̲ad̲ata*) pardon me! no offense, I hope!

مأخوذ *maʾk̲ūd̲* taken, seized; taken by surprise, caught, trapped; surprised; taken (ب with), fascinated (ب by); مأخوذ به in force, valid

مأخوذات *maʾk̲ūd̲āt* receipts, takings, returns (*com.*)

مؤاخذ *muʾāk̲ad̲* responsible, held to account, accountable

اخر **II** to delay, put off, defer, postpone, adjourn (ه s.th.); to hinder, impede, obstruct, hold up (ه s.o., ه s.th.), slow down, retard (ه s.th.); to draw out, delay (ه عن s.th. beyond its appointed time); to put back (ه, ه s.o., s.th.), shelve (ه s.th.); to set back (ه a watch, a clock); to suspend, discharge, dismiss, remove (ه s.o. from an office) **V** to be late; to stay late, remain overtime; to keep waiting (على s.o.); to be delayed, fall or lag behind

(عن), tarry, linger, hesitate; to default (عن on), be behindhand, be in arrears (عن with), be behind (عن in); to hesitate (عن with); to be suspended (from service), be discharged, be dismissed | لم يتأخر بعد ذلك من ان after that, he did not hesitate long before he ..., presently, he ...; تأخر عن الموعد (mau'id) to be late (i.e., arrive after the agreed time), miss a deadline

اخرة akaratan and بأخرة at a later time, ultimately, finally, in the end

آخر ākir pl. -ūn, -āt, اواخر awākir[2] last, ultimate, utmost, extreme; end, close, conclusion; foot, bottom (of a paper); الآخر and الآخرة the hereafter; اواخر awākira and فى اواخر (with genit.) toward the end, at the end of | الدار الآخرة the abode in the hereafter, the everlasting abode; الى آخره ilā ākirihī and so forth, et cetera; آخر الامر ākira l-amri eventually, finally, in the end, after all; آخر الدهر ākira d-dahri forever; آخر الزمان ā. az-zamān time at which the Day of Judgment is to be expected, the end of the world; عن آخره to the last, down to the grass roots, entirely, completely, e.g., دمر عن آخره (dummira) to be completely destroyed, be wiped off the map; من آخره from behind, from the rear; ما له آخر endless, infinite; فى آخر الآخر after all, last of all; لآخر درجة li-ā. daraja exceedingly, in the highest degree; فى آخر المطاف (ā. al-maṭāf) in the long run, finally; فى اواخر العشرينات ('išrīnāt) at the end of the twenties; اواخر الشهر a. aš-šahr the end of the month, the last ten days of the month; اخيرا وليس آخرا last but not least

الآخرة al-ākira the hereafter

آخر ākar[2], f. اخرى ukrā, pl. comm. اخر ukar[2] (and آخرون ākarūn or اخريات ukrayāt respectively) another, one more, الآخر the other | مرة اخرى (marratan) once more; هو الآخر, هى الاخرى he also, she also, he in turn, she in turn, انا الآخر I also, هم الآخرون they also, they in turn; بعد ساعة اخرى after still another hour; ان كانت الاخرى (in kānat) otherwise; من آن الى آخر from time to time; من سنة الى اخرى (sana) from year to year; بين فترة واخرى (fatra) once in a while, from time to time; آونة — اخرى (āwinatan) sometimes — sometimes, at times — at times

الاخرى al-ukrā the hereafter

اخروى ukrawī of or relating to the life to come or the hereafter

اخير akīr last; latest; rearmost; the second of two; اخيرا eventually, finally, in the end, after all, at last; recently, lately, the other day; الاخير the latter | الاول — الاخير the former — the latter; اخيرا وليس آخرا last but not least

متخار mi'kār palm which retains its fruit into the winter

تأخير ta'kīr pl. -āt delay, deferment, postponement; obstruction, retardation; putting back, temporary shelving | دون تأخير without delay

تأخر ta'akkur delay, lag, retardation; hesitation, tarrying, lingering; slowness, tardiness; backwardness, underdevelopment (of a country)

مؤخر mu'akkar rear part, tail, end; stern (of a ship); remainder, balance (of a sum, to be paid later); مؤخرا mu'akkaran recently, lately, the other day; at last, finally, eventually

مؤخرة mu'akkara hind, rear part (of s.th.); background (also, e.g., of a picture); rear, rear guard (of an army); rear positions or lines (mil.); stern (of a ship)

متأخر muta'akkir delayed, belated, late; occurring later (عن than); behind, behindhand, in arrears; backward, underdeveloped; lagging, staying behind; defaulter; late, advanced (hour, age); المتأخرون the later, or modern, authors, writers, or the like (as opposed to المتقدمون); المتأخرات

arrears, balance of a sum remaining due after previous payment | البلدان المتأخرة (*buldān*) the underdeveloped countries

اخطبوط *uḵṭubūṭ* octopus

اخو III to fraternize, associate as brothers (ه with s.o.) V to act or show o.s. as a brother or friend VI to fraternize, associate as brothers

اخ *aḵ* pl. اخوة *iḵwa*, اخوان *iḵwān* brother; fellow man, neighbor; friend; pl. اخوان specif., brethren or members of an order; الاخوان religious brotherhood of the Wahabi sect, militant in character, established by Ibn Saʿūd in 1910 | يا اخى my dear friend! اخو ثقة *aḵū ṯiqa* trustworthy, reliable; اخ شقيق brother through both father and mother, brother-german; اخوانه العرب (*ʿarab*) his Arab brothers

اخت *uḵt* pl. اخوات *aḵawāt* sister; (*gram.*) cognate; counterpart | اختها the other (of two), its mate, its counterpart (after a fem. noun)

خوى *ḵuwaiy* little brother

اخوى *aḵawī* brotherly, fraternal

اخوية *aḵawīya* brotherhood (as a religious association)

اخاء *iḵāʾ*, اخوة *uḵūwa* brotherhood, brotherliness, fraternity

اخاوة *iḵāwa* fraternization, fraternity, brotherliness

تآخ *taʾāḵin* fraternization; fraternity, brotherliness

اخور *aḵūr* barn, stable

اد *adda u i* to befall, afflict (ه s.o.)

امر اد *amr idd* a terrible, evil, horrible thing

ادب *aduba u* (*adab*) to be well-bred, well-mannered, cultured, urbane, have refined tastes; — *adaba i* (*adb*) to invite (to a party or banquet, ه s.o.), entertain (ه s.o.) | ادب مأدبة (*maʾduba*) to arrange a banquet, give a formal dinner II to refine, educate (ه s.o.); to discipline, punish, chastise (ه s.o.) IV to invite as a guest (ه s.o.) V to receive a fine education; to be well-bred, well-educated, cultured, have refined tastes; to show o.s. polite, courteous, civil, urbane; to behave properly or decently, maintain good manners; to educate o.s., refine one's tastes (ب by, through); to let o.s. be guided (ب by) | تأدب بأدبه (*bi-adabihī*) to follow s.o.'s moral example

ادب *adab* pl. آداب *ādāb* culture, refinement; good breeding, good manners, social graces, decorum, decency, propriety, seemliness; humanity, humaneness; literature; — pl. آداب morals, decency; rules, rules of conduct; morale; the humanities; belles-lettres; literature (also on a subject) | فى ادب politely; بيت الادب toilet, water closet; قليل الادب and عديم الادب ill-mannered, ill-bred, impolite, uncivil; ادب الخواطر aphoristic literature; الادب الشعبى (*šaʿbī*) folk literature; الادب العامى (*ʿāmmī*) popular literature; رجال الادب literati, men of letters; كلية الآداب *kullīyat al-ā.* (= faculté des lettres) college of arts; آداب السلوك rules of decorum, etiquette; آداب المعاشرة *ā. al-muʿāšara* social etiquette; آداب المائدة table manners, etiquette; آداب الاسلام morality, ethics of Islam; آداب العمل *ā. al-ʿamal* work morale

ادبى *adabī* moral, ethic(al); literary | شجاعة ادبية (*šajāʿa*) moral courage; واجب ادبى moral obligation; ادبيا وماديا *adabīyan wa-māddīyan* morally and physically; الفلسفة الادبية (*falsafa*) ethics, moral science; القسم الادبى (*qism*) humanities division (higher education)

ادبيات *adabīyāt* literature, belles-lettres; the humanities

ادبخانة *adabḵāna* pl. *-āt* toilet, water closet

اديب *adīb* pl. ادباء *udabā'*[2] cultured, refined, educated; well-bred, well-mannered, civil, urbane; a man of culture and refined tastes; man of letters, writer, author

اديبة *adība* authoress, writer

مأدبة *ma'duba* pl. مآدب *ma'ādib*[2] banquet, formal dinner

تأديب *ta'dīb* education; discipline; punishment, chastisement; disciplinary punishment | مجلس التأديب *majlis at-t.* disciplinary board

تأديبي *ta'dībī* disciplinary; punitive, retaliatory | قضية تأديبية (*qaḍīya*) disciplinary action

تأدب *ta'addub* good breeding, good manners, civility, politeness, courteousness, tact

آدب *ādib* host

مؤدب *mu'addib* pl. *-ūn* educator; teacher in a Koranic school (*Tun.*); — *mu'addab* well-bred, well-mannered, civil, urbane

متأدب *muta'addib* polite, well-bred; المتأدبون educated people

ادرة *udra* scrotal hernia (*med.*); — *adra* hydrocele (*med.*)

ادرنة *adirna*[2] Edirne, Adrianople (city in NW Turkey)

الادرياتيك (Fr. *adriatique*) *al-adriyatīk* and بحر الادرياتيك *baḥr al-a.* the Adriatic Sea

ادريسى *idrīsī* belonging to the Idrisid dynasty; pl. الادارسة *al-adārisa* the Idrisids

[1]ادم *adama i* (*adm*) to take some additional food (ه with the bread), enrich (ه the bread) with some extra food or condiment

ادام *idām* anything eaten with bread; shortening, fatty ingredient

[2]ادم, ادمة *adam, adama* skin

اديم *adīm* pl. ادم *udum* skin; hide; tanned skin, leather; dyed piece of leather (made of goatskin; *Yem.*); surface | اديم الارض *a. al-arḍ* the surface of the earth; اديم الحقل *a. al-ḥaql* arable land, surface soil; اديم الغبراء *a. al-ġabrā'* lithosphere, earth's crust

ادام *addām* tanner

[3]آدم *ādam*[2] Adam | ابن آدم human being

آدمى *ādamī* human; humane; poor, inferior, meager; (pl. *-ūn*, اوادم *awādim*[2]) human being

آدمية *ādamīya* humaneness, humanity; humanism

اداة (ادو) *adāh* pl. ادوات *adawāt* tool; instrument; utensil, implement, device, appliance; apparatus; (*gram.*) particle | اداة الحكم *a. al-ḥukm* machinery of government; ○ اداة التصدير prefix (*gram.*); ○ اداة الانتهاء *a. al-intihā'* suffix (*gram.*); اداة النقل *a. an-naql* means of transport; اداة التعريف definite article (*gram.*); اداة التنكير and اداة النكرة *a. an-nakira* indefinite article (*gram.*); اداة تنفيذية (*tanfīḏīya*) executive agency; pl. ادوات materials, equipment, gear, ادوات حربية (*ḥarbīya*) war material; ادوات احتياطية (*iḥtiyāṭīya*) stand-by equipment (*techn.*); ادوات الزينة *a. az-zīna* toiletries, cosmetics; ادوات العمل *a. al-ʿamal* tools, implements; ادوات القراءة *a. al-qirā'a* reading matter; ادوات الكتابة *a. al-kitāba* writing materials; ادوات مكتبية (*maktabīya*) office requirements or supplies; ادوات منزلية (*manzilīya*) household utensils, household effects; ادوات المائدة knife, fork and spoon; ادوات النظافة *a. an-naẓāfa* cleaning apparatus

الادون *al-adōn* (Hebr.) Mr. . . . (*Isr.*)

ادى II to convey, take, bring, lead, steer, channel (ه, ه or ب s.o., s.th., الى to), see that s.o. or s.th. (ه, ه or ب) gets to (الى); to bring about, cause, effect, produce

(الى s.th.); to lead, contribute, be conducive (الى to a result); to amount, come practically (الى to); to tend (الى to), aim (الى at); to carry out, execute, discharge (ه s.th.); to perform (ه a ritual, etc.); to do (واجبه wājibahū one's duty); to fulfill (وظيفة a function, رسالة a mission); to accomplish (مأمورية a task); to take (يمينا an oath; امتحانا an examination); to render (خدمة kidmatan a service, ل or الى to s.o.; ه e.g., a meaning, a musical composition, etc.) | ادى السلام (salām) to greet, salute; ادى الشهادة (šahāda) to testify, give evidence V to lead, be conducive, contribute (الى to results); to be carried out, be performed, be accomplished; to arrive (الى at), be lead (الى to) X to demand, claim (ه ه from s.o. s.th.)

اداء adā' pl. -āt (as verbal noun of II) rendering (of a service); pursuit, performance, execution, discharge (of a duty), realization, effectuation, accomplishment (of a task); rendition, reading (e.g., of a musical composition); execution (of a song, a piece of music); acting (of a player); performance, conduct (of a ceremony, ritual); fulfillment (of a function); power, performance (e.g., of a car, motor); rendering (of a meaning); payment | حسن الاداء ḥusn al-a. good rendition (of a work of art, of a musical composition)

ادائى adā'ī functional

تأدية ta'diya rendering (of a service); pursuit, performance, execution, discharge (of a duty), realization, effectuation; accomplishment (of a task); fulfillment; payment

مؤدى mu'addan assignment, task, function; purport, significance, signification, import, underlying idea

اذ id 1. (introducing a verbal clause) (and) then; اذ ذاك id dāka (also written اذاك) then, at that time, at the same time, in doing so; 2. (conj.; temp. and caus.) as, when; since, as, the more so as, because; اذ ان id inna, id anna for; since, as, in view of the fact that

1اذا idā 1. (introducing a nominal clause the subject of which may be expressed by ب with foll. genit.) and then, and all of a sudden; (with noun in nominative case or with ب) there was ..., and all of a sudden there was ...; 2. (conj.) when; if, whenever; whether, if (introducing indirect questions); اذا ما when, whenever; الا اذا (illā) unless, if not; except when; ما اذا whether, if; see ما

2اذا and اذن idan then, therefore, in that case, hence, consequently

آذار ādār[2] March (month; Syr., Leb., Jord., Ir.)

1اذن adina a to listen (الى to s.o.); to allow, permit (فى ل s.o. s.th.); to hear, learn (ب of s.th.), be informed (ب about) II to call (ب to), esp. to call to prayer (بالصلاة); to crow (rooster) IV to announce, make known (ب s.th., ب ه to s.o. s.th.), inform, notify (ه s.o.); to call to prayer; to call upon s.o. (ه), urge, admonish, exhort (ه s.o.) to do s.th. (ب); to herald (ب or ه s.th.); to foreshadow (ب s.th.); to be on the verge (ان of doing s.th.) | آذن بالسقوط (بالزوال) (zawāl) to show signs of the imminent downfall (end); آذنت الشمس بالمغيب (magīb) the sun was about to set; آذن الليل بانتصاف (lailu bi-ntiṣāf) it was close to midnight V to herald, announce (ب s.th.) X to ask for permission (من s.o., فى to do s.th., rarely ب); to ask permission to enter (على s.o.'s house), have o.s. announced (على to s.o.); to take leave (من of s.o.), say good-by (من to)

اذن idn permission, authorization; leave; license; warrant; باذن الله if God choose, God willing; (pl. اذون udūn, اذونات udūnāt) (postal) order; bond (fin.) | عن باذنك or

اذنك with your permission; طالب الاذن بالكلام to ask the Chair for permission to speak, ask for the floor; اذن الاستيراد import license; اذن البريد pl. اذونات البريد postal money order; اذن البوسته do.; اذن على الخزينة treasury bond (*fin.*); اذن الصرف *i. aṣ-ṣarf* order to pay; اذن غياب عن العمل (*i. ġiyāb, ʿamal*) leave of absence, furlough

اذنى *iḏnī*: سند اذنى (*sanad*) promissory note, bill payable to order of s.o.

اذن *uḏun, uḏn* f., pl. آذان *āḏān* ear; handle (of a cup) | التهاب الاذن الوسطى (*wusṭā*) middle-ear infection, otitis media (*med.*)

اذان *aḏān* call to prayer

اذين *uḏain* auricle (*anat.*)

اذينة *uḏaina* little ear; ear lobe

مأذنة *ma'ḏana*, مئذنة *mi'ḏana* pl. مآذن *ma'āḏin*[2] minaret

ايذان *īḏān* declaration, proclamation, announcement (ب of s.th.); advance notice; imminence, threat, menace (ب of an event) | ايذانا بانتهاء الحديث as a sign that the conversation is (was) ended

آذن *āḏin* door-keeper, porter

مأذون *ma'ḏūn* authorized; licensed, legally allowed or recognized; holder of a diploma; slave with limited legal rights (*Isl. Law*); = مأذون شرعى (*šarʿī*) official authorized by the cadi to perform civil marriages (*Isl. Law*)

مأذونية *ma'ḏūnīya* leave, furlough (*mil. Syr.*); license, franchise (*Syr.*)

مؤذن *mu'aḏḏin* pl. *-ūn* muezzin, announcer of the hour of prayer

اذن[2] *iḏan* see اذا[2]

اذى *aḏiya a* to suffer damage, be harmed **IV** to harm, hurt, wrong (ه s.o.); to molest, annoy, irritate, trouble (ه s.o.); to cause pain (ه to s.o.), torture (ه s.o.) | لا يؤذى *lā yu'ḏī* innocuous, harmless, inoffensive **V** to suffer damage, be wronged; to feel offended, be hurt

اذى *aḏan*, اذاة *aḏāh*, اذية *aḏīya* damage, harm; pain, suffering; injury; trouble, annoyance, grievance, wrong, offense, insult

اذاية *iḏāya* damage, harm, harmfulness, noxiousness

ايذاء *īḏā'* harm, damage, prejudice; offense, hurt; grievance, nuisance

مؤذ *mu'ḏin* hurtful, harmful, injurious, detrimental, prejudicial; annoying, irksome, troublesome; painful, hurting, offensive, insulting

آر[1] *ār* are (land measure)

آرى[2] *ārī* pl. *-ūn* Aryan

آرية *ārīya* Aryanism

اراتيقى *arātīqī* and اراتيكى pl. اراتقة *arātiqa* a heretic (*Chr.*)

□اراجوز *aragōz* (*eg.*, < Turk.; popular spelling of قره جوز) Karagöz, chief character of the shadow play; Punch; buffoon, funny man

آرامى *ārāmī* Aramaean; Aramaic

ارب *ariba a* (*arab*) to be skillful, proficient (ب in s.th.); — *araba i* to tighten (ه a knot) **III** to try to outwit (ه s. o.)

ارب *arab* pl. آراب *ārāb* wish (فى for), desire, need (فى of s.th.); purpose, aim, goal, end

ارب *irb* pl. آراب *ārāb* limb | مزقه اربا اربا (*mazzaqahū*) to tear s.th. to pieces or to shreds

اربة *irba* skill, resourcefulness, cleverness, smartness

اربة *urba* pl. ارب *urab* knot, bow

اريب *arīb* skillful, resourceful, clever, intelligent

مأرب *ma'rab* pl. مآرب *ma'ārib*² wish, desire; object of desire, purpose, aim, goal, end

اربيل *arbīl*² Erbil (the ancient Arbela, city in N Iraq)

ارتوازى *artuwāzī* artesian (well)

ارث¹ II to sow dissension (بين between, among)

ارث² *irṯ* inheritance, heritage; estate (of inheritance)

الارثوذكس *al-urṯūḏuks* the adherents of the Orthodox Church | الروم الارثوذكس (*rūm*) the Greek Orthodox Church

ارثوذكسى *urṯūḏuksī* orthodox; الارثوذكسية the Orthodox Church

ارج¹ *arija a* (*araj*, اريج *arīj*) to be fragrant V do.

ارج *araj* fragrance, sweet smell

ارج *arij* fragrant, sweet-smelling

اريج *arīj* fragrance, sweet smell

ارج² *arg* pl. *-āt* (*eg.*) erg (unit of energy or work; *phys.*)

ارجح II *ta'arjaḥa* to rock, swing

تأرجح *ta'arjuḥ* oscillation (between two poles or states)

متأرجح *muta'arjiḥ* fluctuating

الارجنتين *al-arjantīn* Argentina

ارجنتينى *arjantīnī* Argentinian

ارجوان *urjuwān* purple

ارجوانى *urjuwānī* purple(-colored)

ارجوز *aragōz* see اراجوز

ارجيلة *argīla* (Eg. spelling) pl. اراجيل *arāgīl*² narghile, hookah

ارخ II to date (ه a letter, and the like, ب with a date); to write the history of s.th. (ه or ل)

تاريخ *ta'rīḵ* dating (of a letter, etc.); historiography; *tārīḵ* pl. تواريخ *tawārīḵ*² date; time; history; chronicle, annals; story, tale | تاريخ الحياة *t. al-ḥayāh* biography; curriculum vitae; تاريخ عام (*'āmm*) world history; تاريخ قديم an old story; علماء التاريخ the historians; ما قبل التاريخ pre-historic time

تاريخى *tārīḵī* historic(al)

مؤرخ *mu'arriḵ* pl. *-ūn* historiographer, historian, chronicler, annalist; — *mu'arraḵ* dated

ارخبيل *arḵabīl* archipelago

ارخميد *arḵamīd*² Archimedes

ارخن (ἄρχων) pl. اراخنة *arāḵina* archon, pl. notables (*Chr.-Copt.*)

اردب *irdabb* (now usually pronounced *ardabb*) pl. ارادب *arādib*² ardeb, a dry measure (*Eg.*; = 198 l)

اردبة *irdabba* cesspool

الاردن *al-urdunn* (m. and f.) Jordan (country); the Jordan river

اردنى *urdunnī* Jordanian | المملكة الاردنية الهاشمية *al-mamlaka al-u. al-hāšimīya* the Hashemite Kingdom of Jordan

اردواز (Fr. *ardoise*) *arduwāz* slate

ارز¹ *arz* (n. un. ة) cedar (Cedrus libani; *bot.*)

ارز² *aruzz* rice

ارزدرخت *arzdaraḵt* China tree, paradise tree (Melia azedarach; *bot.*)

ارس *arasa i* (*ars*) to till the land

اريس *irrīs* and *arīs* peasant, farmer

ارستوقراطى, ارستقراطى *aristuqrāṭī* aristocratic; aristocrat

ارستوقراطية, ارستقراطية *aristuqrāṭīya* aristocracy

ارسطو *arisṭū* and ارسطاطليس *arisṭāṭalīs*² Aristotle

ارش *arš* indemnity, amercement, fine, penalty; blood money (for the shedding of blood; *Isl. Law*)

ارشى ابسقوبس (Gr. ἀρχιεπίσκοπος) archbishop

ارشيدوق (Fr. *archiduc*) archduke, ارشيدوقة archduchess

ارشيف (Fr.) *aršīv, aršīf* archive

ارض II to ground, (Brit.) earth (ه antenna)

ارض *arḍ* f., pl. اراض *arāḍin*, ارضون *araḍūn* land, country, region; area; terrain, ground, soil; lot, parcel of land, estate, real estate (also قطعة ارض *qiṭʿat a.*); الارض earth (as opposed to heaven or as a planet); globe, world | الارض السفلى (*suflā*) the nether world; الارض المقدسة (*muqaddasa*) the Holy Land, Palestine; الاراضى المنخفضة (*munkafiḍa*) The Netherlands; تحت الارض underground

ارضى *arḍī* terrestrial, of the earth; soil-, land- (in compounds); situated on or near the ground, on the ground floor; ground (adj.); earthly; underground, subterranean | دور ارضى (*daur*), طابق ارضى (*ṭābaq*) ground floor; محطة ارضية (*mahaṭṭa*) ground station; مضيفة ارضية (*muḍīfa*) ground hostess; كرة ارضية (*kura*) ground shot (soccer)

ارضى شوكى *arḍī šaukī* artichoke

ارض *araḍ* (coll.; n. un. ة) termite; woodworm

ارضية *arḍīya* pl. *-āt* floor; ground (also, e.g., of a printed fabric); background (of a painting and fig.); flooring, floor covering; ground floor, first floor (*tun.*); storage, warehouse charges; groundwork, foundation, basis | ارضية باركيه *a. barkēh* parquet, parqueted floor

ارضروم *arḍurūm*[2] Erzurum (city in NE Turkey)

ارطة (also اورطة) *urṭa* pl. ارط *uraṭ* (اورط) battalion (formerly, *Eg.*; *mil.*)

ارطقة *arṭaqa* pl. *-āt* heresy (*Chr.*)

تاريع see ريع

ارغن *urğun* pl. اراغن *arāğin*[2] organ (mus. instr.)

ارغول *urğūl, arğūl* a wind instrument (related to the clarinet, consisting of two pipes of unequal length)

ارق *ariqa a* to find no sleep II to make sleepless (ه s.o.), prevent s.o. (ه) from sleeping

ارق *araq* sleeplessness, insomnia

اريكة *arīka* pl. ارائك *arāʾik*[2] couch, sofa; throne

اركيلة *argīla* pl. اراكيل *arāgīl*[2] (*syr.*) water pipe, narghile

ارلندا *irlandā*, ارلندة and ارلانده *irlanda* Ireland

ارلندى *irlandī* Irish

[1]ارم *arama i* to bite

ارم *urram* molar teeth | حرق الارم (*ḥaraqa*) to gnash one's teeth (in anger)

ارومة *arūma, urūma* root, origin; stump of a tree

مئرم *miʾram* root (of a tooth)

[2]آرام *ārām* (= ارآم pl. of رئم *riʾm*) white antelopes

الارمن *al-arman* the Armenians

ارمنى *armanī* Armenian (adj. and n.)

ارميا *irmiyā* Jeremiah (biblical prophet)

ارمينيا *armēniyā* Armenia

الارناوط *al-arnāwuṭ* the Albanians

ارناوطى *arnāwuṭī* Albanian

ارنب *arnab* pl. ارانب *arānib*[2] hare; rabbit | ارنب هندى (*hindī*) guinea pig

ارنبة *arnaba* female hare, doe | ارنبة الانف *a. al-anf* tip of the nose; nose, muzzle (of an animal)

ارنيك (Turk. *örnek*) *urnīk* pl. ارانيك *arānīk*[2] pattern, model; form, blank

اروبا *urubbā* Europe

اروبى *urubbī* European (adj. and n.)

ارى[1] *ary* honey

آرى[2] and آرية see under آر

اريحا *arīḥā* Jericho

اريل (Engl. *aerial*) *iriyal* antenna

از *azza u i* (*azz*, ازيز *azīz*) to drone, hum (e.g., plane, motor); to buzz (insect); to make a hissing sound or wheezing noise; to fizz (effervescent liquid); to whizz (bullet, arrow); to whistle (wind); to rattle, clatter

ازيز *azīz* drone, humming noise; buzz; whizz; rattling (see also the verb)

ازادرخت *azādarakt* see ارزدرخت

ازب[1] *azaba i* (*azb*) to flow, run (water)

مئزاب *mi'zāb* pl. مآزيب *ma'āzīb*[2] and ميزاب *mīzāb* pl. ميازيب *mayāzīb*[2] drain; gutter, eaves trough

ازب[2] *izb* dumpy, pudgy, stocky; small man

الازبك *al-uzbak* the Uzbeks

ازدرخت *azdarakt* see ارزدرخت

ازر *azara i* (*azr*) to surround (ه s.th.) **II** to clothe (ه s.o. with an ازار *izār* q.v.); to cover, wrap up (ه s.o., ه s.th.); to strengthen, brace (ه s.o., ه s.th.) **III** to help (ه s.o.); to support, back up, strengthen (ه s.o.) **V** and **VIII** to put on an *izār* (see below), wrap o.s. in an *izār* **VI** to help each other; to rally, unite, join forces

ازر *azr* strength | شد ازره *šadda azrahū* or شد من ازره (*min azrihī*) to help, support, encourage s.o., back s.o. up; *šadda azruhū* to be energetic, vigorous, lusty, courageous

ازار *izār* m. and f., pl. ازر *uzur* loincloth; wrap, shawl; wrapper, covering, cover

مئزر *mi'zar* pl. مآزر *ma'āzir*[2] apron; wrapper, covering, cover

مؤازرة *mu'āzara* support, aid, assistance, backing

تآزر *ta'āzur* mutual assistance; cooperation, coordination

متآزر *muta'āzir* cooperating, coordinated

ازف *azifa a* (*azaf*, ازوف *uzūf*) to come, approach, draw near (a time)

ازق *azaqa i* (*azq*) to be narrow **V** do.

مأزق *ma'ziq* pl. مآزق *ma'āziq*[2] narrow passageway, narrow pass, strait, bottleneck; predicament, fix, dilemma, critical situation, also مأزق حرج (*ḥarij*)

ازل *azal* pl. آزال *āzāl* eternity (without beginning), sempiternity

ازلى *azalī* eternal, sempiternal

ازلية *azalīya* sempiternity, eternity

ازم **V** to be or become critical, come to a head (situation, relations)

ازمة *azma* pl. *azamāt* emergency; crisis; attack, seizure (*med.*) | ازمة النقد الدولية *a. an-naqd ad-duwalīya* international monetary crisis; ازمة وزارية (*wizārīya*) cabinet crisis; ازمة قلبية (*qalbīya*) coronary or heart attack

تأزم *ta'azzum*: تأزم الحالة *t. al-ḥāla* critical development, aggravation of the situation

مأزوم *ma'zūm* victim of a crisis

متأزم *muta'azzim* critical (situation)

ازمير *izmīr*[2] Izmir (formerly Smyrna, seaport in W Turkey)

ازميل *izmīl* pl. ازاميل *azāmīl*[2] chisel

ازوت (Engl.) *azōt* azote, nitrogen

ازوتى *azōtī* nitrogenous

ازى III to be opposite s.th. (ه), face (ه s.o., ه s.th.)

ازاء *izā'a* (prep.) opposite, face to face with, facing; in front of; in the face of (e.g., of a situation); as compared with; بازاء *bi-izā'i* opposite, face to face with, facing; in front of; على ازاء *'alā izā'i* in the face of (e.g., of a situation)

[1]آس *ās* myrtle

[2]آس pl. *-āt* ace (playing card)

[3]اسّ II to found, establish, set up (ه s.th.), lay the foundation (ه for) V to be founded, be established, be set up

اس *uss* foundation, basis; exponent of a power (*math.*)

اساس *asās* pl. *-āt*, اسس *usus* foundation (also, of a building), fundament, groundwork, ground, basis; keynote, tonic (*mus.*); base (*math.*); اساسا *asāsan* primarily, basically | على اساس (with foll. genit.) on the basis of, on the strength of, on account of, according to; لا اساس له من الصحة (*asāsa, ṣiḥḥa*) completely unfounded (news, rumor); فى الاساس principally, mainly, chiefly; من اساسه in its essentials, completely, fundamentally, basically

اساسى *asāsī* fundamental, basic; elementary; essential; principal, chief, main | حجر اساسى (*ḥajar*) cornerstone, foundation stone

اساسيات *asāsīyāt* fundamentals, principles, basic problems

تأسيس *ta'sīs* founding, foundation, establishment, setting up, institution; grounding, laying of the substructure (*arch.*); pl. *-āt* facilities, utilities; institutions

تأسيسى *ta'sīsī* founding; foundational, fundamental | مجلس تأسيسى (*majlis*) constituent assembly

مؤسس *mu'assis* founder

مؤسسة *mu'assasa* pl. *-āt* foundation, establishment; firm (*com.*); industrial plant; (governmental) agency; institution; organization | مؤسسة انتاجية (*intājīya*) production plant or factory; مؤسسة تجارية (*tijārīya*) commercial firm, business house; مؤسسة الثقافة الشعبية *m. aṯ-ṯaqāfa aš-ša'bīya* school for adult education; مؤسسة شعبية (*ša'bīya*) state-owned enterprise; مؤسسة عامة (خاصة) state (private) institution

اسبارطة *isbarṭa* Sparta

الاسبان *al-asbān, al-isbān* the Spaniards

اسبانى *asbānī, isbānī* Spanish; (pl. *-ūn*) Spaniard

اسبانخ *isbānaḵ* spinach

اسبانيا *asbāniyā, isbāniyā* Spain

اسبداج *isbidāj* and اسبيداج *isbīdāj* white lead, ceruse

اسبرتو (It. *spirito*) *isbirto* alcohol

اسبليطة *isbalīṭa* epaulet

اسبور (Fr. *sport*) *isbōr* (*eg.*) sport, sporting, sportsmanlike | سيارة اسبور *sayyārat i.* sports car; قميص اسبور *qamīṣ i.* sport shirt

است see [1]ست

استاتيكا *istatīkā* statics

استاتيكى *istatīkī* static (*el.*)

استاد (Fr. *stade*) *istād* stadium (sports)

استاذ *ustāḏ* pl. اساتذة *asātiḏa* master; high school teacher; (*Ir.*) full professor; professor (academic title); form of address to intellectuals (lawyers, journalists, officials, writers and poets); ledger (*com.*) | الاستاذ الاعظم (*a'ẓam*) Grand Master (of a lodge); الاستاذ الاكبر title of the Rector of Al Azhar University; استاذ علوم and استاذ فنون (*Eg.*) renditions of Master of Science and Master of Arts; استاذ كرسى

(*kursī*; *Eg.*) and استاذ بكرسى (*Syr.*) full professor; استاذ بلا كرسى (*Syr.*) associate professor; استاذ غير متفرغ (*mutafarriḡ*; *Eg.*) part-time professor (holding an office outside the university); استاذ مساعد (*musāʿid*) assistant professor; استاذ زائر visiting professor; استاذ مشارك (*mušārik*) associate professor (*Ir.*); هم اساتذة فى الجدل (*jadal*) they are masters of disputation

استاذة *ustāḏa* professor (fem.)

استاذية *ustāḏīya* mastership; professorship, professorate; office of a professor or high school teacher

استانبول *istanbūl*² Istanbul, Constantinople

استانبولى *istanbūlī* of Istanbul

الآستانة *al-āsitāna*, الاستانة *al-astāna*, *al-istāna* Constantinople, Istanbul

استبرق *istabraq* brocade

استراتيجى *istrātījī* strategic

استراتيجية *istrātījīya* pl. *-āt* strategy

استرالى *usturālī* Australian

استراليا *usturāliyā* Australia

استرلينى *istarlīnī* sterling | جنيه استرلينى pound sterling; منطقة الاسترلينى *minṭaqat al-i.* sterling area

راقصة استريبتيز *rāqiṣat istribtīz* strip-tease dancer, stripper

استك (Fr. *élastique*) *astik* (*eg.*) elastic, rubber-insulated thread

استمارة see امر

استوبة (It. *stoppa*) tow, oakum; cotton waste

استوديو (It.-Engl. *studio*) *istūdiyō* pl. استوديوهات *istūdiyōhāt* studio; atelier

استوكهولم *istokholm* Stockholm

استونيا (Engl.) *istōniyā* Estonia

استياتيت *istiyātīt* steatite, soapstone (*min.*)

استيك (Fr. *élastique*) *astīk* pl. *-āt* (*eg.*) erasor; *ustēk* pl. اساتيك *asātīk*² (*eg.*) wrist watch band or strap; استيكة *astīka* pl. *-āt* (*eg.*) = *astīk*

اسوج look up alphabetically

اسد X to display the courage of a lion (على against); take possession, seize control (على of s.th.)

اسد *asad* pl. اسد *usud*, *usd*, اسود *usūd*, آساد *āsād* lion; الاسد Leo (sign of the zodiac; *astron.*); the fifth month of the solar year (*Saudi Ar.*, cf. حمل *ḥamal*) | اسد البحر *a. al-baḥr* sea lion; داء الاسد leontiasis (*med.*)

¹اسر *asara i* (*asr*) to bind, fetter, shackle, chain (ه s.o.); to capture, take prisoner (ه s.o.); to captivate, fascinate, hold spellbound (ه s.o.), absorb, arrest (ه the attention) X to surrender, give o.s. up as prisoner

اسر *asr* (leather) strap, thong; capture; captivity | شدة الاسر *šiddat al-a.* vigor, energy

اسرة *usra* pl. اسر *usar*, *-āt* family; dynasty; clan, kinsfolk, relatives; — *asirra* see سرير | الاسرة الاقتصادية الاوروبية the European Economic Community (*colloq.* Common Market)

اسرى *usrī* family (in compounds); dynastic

بأسره *bi-asrihī* entirely, completely, altogether, جاءوا بأسرهم all of them came, they came one and all

اسار *isār* (leather) strap, thong; captivity; captivation, enthrallment | وقع فى اساره to be subjected to s.th., fall into the clutches of s.th.

اسير *asīr* pl. اسراء *usarāʾ*², اسرى *asrā*, اسارى *asārā* prisoner, captive, prisoner of war

اسيرة *asīra* pl. *-āt* female prisoner, slave girl

اسف *asifa a* (*asaf*) to regret (على or ل s.th.), feel sorry (على for), be sad (على about) V do.

اسف *asaf* grief, sorrow, chagrin, regret | وا اسفاه! *wā asafāh!* oh, what a pity! it's too bad! ويا للاسف *wa-yā lal-asafi* (or only للاسف) unfortunately; مع الاسف and بكل اسف *bi-kulli asafin* do.

اسف *asif* and اسيف *asīf* regretful, sorry, sad, grieved, distressed

تأسف *ta'assuf* regret

آسف *āsif* regretful, sorry, sad | تركته غير آسف (*ġaira āsifin*) I left him without regret, I was only too glad to leave him

مأسوف عليه *ma'sūf 'alaihi* mourned (esp. of a dead person, = the late lamented)

مؤسف *mu'sif* distressing, sad, regrettable

متأسف *muta'assif* sad, sorry, regretful; متأسف! sorry!

اسفاناخ *isfānāḵ* and اسفانخ *isfānaḵ* spinach | اسفاناخ رومى (*rūmī*) garden orach (Atriplex hortensis, *bot.*)

اسفلت *asfalt* asphalt

اسفلتى *asfaltī* asphalt (in compounds)

اسفنج *isfanj*, *isfunj*, (Eg. pronun.) *isfing* sponge

اسفنجى *isfanjī* spongy; porous

اسفندان *isfindān* maple (*bot.*)

اسفيداج *isfīdāj* white lead, ceruse

اسفين *isfīn* pl. اسافين *asāfīn*[2] wedge

اسفينى *isfīnī*: الخط الاسفينى (*ḵaṭṭ*) cuneiform writing

اسقربوطى *isqarbūṭī*: مرض اسقربوطى (*maraḍ*) scurvy (*med.*)

اسقف *usquf* pl. اساقفة *asāqifa*, اساقف *asāqif*[2] bishop | رئيس الاساقفة archbishop

اسقفى *usqufī* episcopal

اسقفية *usqufīya* episcopate, bishopric

آسر *āsir* winning, captivating, fascinating; captor

مأسور *ma'sūr* captivated, fascinated, enthralled (ب by)

[2]اسرة *asirra* see سرير

[3]ماسورة look up alphabetically

اسرائيل *isrā'īl*[2] Israel | بنو اسرائيل *banū i.* the Israelites; دولة اسرائيل *daulat i.* the State of Israel

اسرائيلى *isrā'īlī* Israelitish; Israeli (adj.); — (pl. *-ūn*) Israelite; Israeli; اسرائيليات Judaica

اسرافيل *isrāfīl*[2] Israfil, the angel who will sound the trumpet on the Day of Resurrection

اسرب *usrub* lead (metal)

اسطانبول *isṭanbūl*[2] Istanbul, Constantinople

اسطبل *isṭabl* pl. *-āt* stable, barn

اسطبة (It. *stoppa*) *usṭubba* tow, oakum

اسطرلاب *asṭurlāb* astrolabe

اسطقس *isṭaqis* pl. *-āt* element

اسطوانة *usṭuwāna* pl. *-āt*, اساطين *asāṭīn*[2] column (*arch.*); cylinder (*math.*; of an engine); (pl. *-āt*) phonograph record; — pl. اساطين high-ranking, prominent personalities; stars, celebrities, authorities, masters (e.g., of art: اساطين الفن *a. al-fann*)

اسطوانى *usṭuwānī* cylindric(al)

اسطورة *usṭūra* pl. اساطير *asāṭīr*[2] legend, fable, tale, myth, saga

اسطورى *usṭūrī* fabulous, mythical, legendary

اسطول *usṭūl* pl. اساطيل *asāṭīl*[2] fleet; squadron

□ اسطى *usṭā* (colloq. for استاذ) pl. اسطوات *usṭawāt* master; foreman, overseer; also form of address to those in lower callings, e.g., to a cab driver, coachman, etc.

اسقمرى *usqumrī, isqumrī* mackerel (*zool.*)

اسقيل *isqīl* an Oriental variety of sea onion (Scilla)

اسكتش (Engl.) *isketš* pl. *-āt* sketch

اسكتلندا *iskotlandā, iskutlandā* Scotland

اسكتلندى *iskotlandī, iskutlandī* Scottish, Scotch; (pl. *-ūn*) Scotchman

اسكفة *uskuffa* see سكف

اسكلة *iskila* pl. اساكل *asākil*[2] seaport, commercial center (in the East)

اسكملة *iskamla* stool, footstool

اسكندرونة *iskandarūna*[2] Iskenderon (formerly Alexandretta, seaport in S Turkey)

الاسكندرية *al-iskandarīya* Alexandria (city in N Egypt)

اسكندينافيا, اسكندنافيا *iskandināfiyā* Scandinavia

اسكندنافى *iskandināfī* Scandinavian

اسل II to sharpen, point, taper (ه s.th.)

اسل *asal* (coll.) rush (*bot.*)

اسلة *asala* pl. *-āt* thorn, spike, prong; point (also, e.g., of a pen = nib); tip of the tongue

الحروف الاسلية *al-ḥurūf al-asalīya* the letters ز, س and ص

اسيل *asīl* smooth | خد اسيل (*ḵadd*) smooth cheek

اسالة *asāla* eliptic, oval form

مؤسل *mu'assal* pointed, tapered

اسلامبولى (variant of استانبولى) *islāmbūlī* of Istanbul

اسلاندا *islandā* and اسلانده *islanda* Iceland

اسم see سم[1]

اسماعيل *ismāʿīl*[2] Ishmael (legendary ancestor of the Arabs and son of Abraham)

الاسماعيلية *al-ismāʿīlīya* Ismailia (town in Egypt on the Suez Canal); Ismailism (a major branch of the Shiah in medieval Islam with numerous subdivisions)

اسمانجونى *asmānjūnī* sky-blue, azure, cerulean

اسمره *asmara* Asmara (city in Ethiopia)

اسمنت *asmant* cement

اسمنتى *asmantī* cement (adj.)

اسن *asana i u* and *asina a* to become brackish (water); to rot, decay, putrify, decompose

آسن *āsin* brackish; rotten, putrid

اسو and اسى) اسا *asā u* (*asw*, اسا *asan*) to nurse, treat (ه a wound); to make peace (بين between, among); — اسى *asiya a* (اسى, اسا *asan*) to be sad, grieved, distressed II to console, comfort (ه s.o.); to nurse (ه a patient) III to share (one's wordly possessions, ه with s.o.), be charitable (ه to s.o.); to assist, support (ه s.o.); to console, comfort (ه s.o.); to treat, cure (ه s.th., medically) V to be consoled, find solace; to take as one's model (ب s.o.), emulate, follow (ب s.o., an example) VI to share the worldly possessions; to assist one another, give mutual assistance; to give solace to one another, console each other

اسى *asan* grief, sorrow, distress

اسوة *uswa, iswa* example, model, pattern | اسوة ب *uswatan bi* following the model or pattern of, along the lines of; in the same manner as, just as, like

مأساة *ma'sāh* pl. مآس *ma'āsin* tragedy, drama

مأسوى *ma'sawī* and مأساوى *ma'sāwī* tragic

تأسية *ta'siya* consolation, comfort

مواساة *muwāsāh* (for *mu'āsāh*) consolation; charity, beneficence

اسوار *iswār, uswār* pl. اساور *asāwir*², اساورة *asāwira* bracelet, bangle

اسوان *aswān*² Aswan (city in S Egypt)

اسوج *asūj* Sweden

اسوجى *asūjī* Swedish; (pl. *-ūn*) Swede

اسو see اسى

آسيا *āsiyā* Asia | آسيا الصغرى (*ṣuḡrā*) Asia Minor

آسيوى *āsiyawī* Asiatic, Asian (adj. and n.)

اسيوط *asyūṭ*² Asyût (city in central Egypt)

ا. ش. ا. abbreviation of انباء الشرق الاوسط Middle East News (news agency), MENA

اشب V to be mixed, heterogeneous, motley (a crowd)

اشابة *ušāba* pl. اشائب *ašā'ib*² mixed, motley crowd

اشبيلية *išbīliya*² Seville (city in SW Spain)

اشبين *išbīn* pl. اشابين see شبن

اشر *ašara u* (*ašr*) to saw (ه s.th.); — *i* to file, sharpen with a file (ه s.th.) II to mark, indicate, state, enter, record (ه s.th.); to write a note or remark (ب s.th., على on an application, petition, of an official); to grant a visa; to provide with a visa (على s.th.)

اشر *ašar* liveliness, high spirits, exuberance; wildness; insolence, impertinence

اشر *ašir* lively, sprightly, in high spirits, exuberant; wild; insolent, impertinent, arrogant

منشار *mi'šār* pl. مواشير *mawāšīr*² saw

تأشير *ta'šīr* issuance of an official endorsement; entering a remark; official endorsement; visa

تأشيرة *ta'šīra* pl. *-āt* visa | تأشيرة دخول entry visa; تأشيرة خروج exit visa; تأشيرة مرور *t. murūr* or تأشيرة اجتياز transit visa

مؤشر *mu'aššir* pl. *-āt* pointer (of a scale; *techn.*), indicator, needle (of a measuring instrument); gauge, measuring apparatus; indicium, indication (على and عن of a state of affairs, a process, development); index, index number (statistics) | مؤشر الاسعار price index

مؤشر *mu'aššar* jagged, serrated; marked, designated (ب by, with)

اشعياء *iša'yā'*², اشعيا *aša'yā* Isaiah (biblical prophet)

اشفى *išfā* pl. اشاف *ašāfin* awl, punch

اشنان *ušnān* potash; saltwort (Salsola kali; *bot.*)

اشنة *ušna* moss

اشور *ašūr* Assyria

اشورى *ašūrī* Assyrian (adj. and n.); الاشوريون the Assyrians | علم الاشوريات *'ilm al-a.* Assyriology

اصيص *aṣīṣ* pl. اصص *uṣuṣ* flowerpot

اصد II to close, shut (a door, etc.)

اصر *iṣr* pl. آصار *āṣār* covenant, compact, contract; load, encumbrance, burden; sin; pl. آصار bonds, ties

آصرة *āṣira* pl. اواصر *awāṣir*² bond, tie (fig., e.g., اواصر الولاء *a. al-walā'* bonds of friendship); obligation, commitment

اصطبل *iṣṭabl* pl. *-āt* stable, barn

اصفهان *iṣfahān*² Isfahan (city in W central Iran)

اصل *aṣula u* (اصالة *aṣāla*) to be or become firmly rooted; to be firmly established; to be of noble origin II to found (ه s.th.), give s.th. (ه) a firm foundation, establish the foundation or origin of (ه) V to be

keeping; حسب الاصول (*ḥasaba*) properly, in conformity with regulations

اصلى *aṣlī* original, primary, primal, initial; genuine, authentic, pure; basic, fundamental, principal, chief, main; regular; real, true, actual | الثمن الاصلى (*ṯaman*) cost price; الجهات الاصلية (*jihāt*) the cardinal points (of the compass); عدد اصلى (*ʿadad*) cardinal number; عضو اصلى (*ʿuḍw*) regular member; تعليم اصلى fundamental education; الفاعل الاصلى the actual (or real) culprit; لغة اصلية (*luġa*) mother tongue

اصلة *aṣala* boa (*zool.*)

اصولى *uṣūlī* in accordance with the rules, conforming to prevailing principles; proper, regular; traditional, usual; legist

اصيل *aṣīl* pl. اصلاء *uṣalā'*[2] of pure, noble origin; original, authentic, genuine; pure; proper, actual; firm, solid; sound, reasonable, sensible; of strong, unswerving character, steadfast; deep-rooted; native, indigenous | الاصل الاصيل the actual reason; اصيل الرأى of sound, unerring judgment

اصيل *aṣīl* pl. آصال *āṣāl*, اصائل *aṣā'il*[2] time before sunset, late afternoon

اصالة *aṣāla* firmness, steadfastness, strength of character; nobility of descent, purity of origin; *aṣālatan* immediately, directly, personally | اصالة الرأى *a. ar-ra'y* clarity and firmness of judgment; judiciousness; بالاصالة عن نفسه spontaneously, of one's own accord, in one's own name, personally, privately (as opposed to بالنيابة عن غيره); اصالة ونيابة *aṣālatan wa-niyābatan* directly and indirectly

تأصيلة *ta'ṣīla* pedigree, genealogy

تأصل *ta'aṣṣul* deep-rootedness

استئصال *isti'ṣāl* extirpation, extermination, (radical) elimination; removal by surgery

or become firmly rooted, deep-rooted, ingrained; to take root, be or become firmly established; to derive one's origin (من from) X to uproot, root out, extirpate, exterminate, annihilate (ه s.th.); to remove (ه an organ by a surgical operation) | استأصل شأفته (*ša'fatahū*) to eradicate s.th., eliminate s.th. radically

اصل *aṣl* pl. اصول *uṣūl* root; trunk (of a tree); origin, source; inception; cause, reason; descent, lineage, stock (esp., one of a noble character); foundation, fundament, basis; the original (e.g., of a book, of a work of art); original version; original document; autograph; original script; theoretical basis, general foundation (as opposed to فرع *farʿ* practical application); — pl. اصول *uṣūl* principles, fundamentals, rudiments, elements (e.g., of a science); rules; basic rules, principles, axioms; code of conduct; guidelines; ancestors, progenitors, forefathers; real estate, landed property; assets (*fin.*); — اصلا *aṣlan* originally, primarily; (with neg.) by no means, not at all, not in the least | فى الاصل and فى اصل الامر originally, at first; really, actually; اصل تجارى (*tijārī*) fund (*com.*); commercial firm (*Maġr.*); اصل محرر (*muḥarrar*) original script, اصل مكرر (*mukarrar*) duplicate; اصل الدماغ *a. ad-dimāġ* brain stem (*anat.*); لا اصل له ولا فصل (*aṣla, faṣla*) of lowly origin (person); without basis or foundation; false, artificial (speech); اصله من دمشق (*dimašq*) he is from Damascus; اصول الفقه *u. al-fiqh* the 4 foundations of Islamic jurisprudence, i.e., Koran, Sunna, *qiyās* (analogy) and *ijmāʿ* (consensus); اصول ثابتة fixed assets (*fin.*); اصول وخصوم assets and liabilities; اصول رأسمالية capital assets (*fin.*); اصول عقارية (*ʿaqārīya*) real assets; اصول القوانين jurisprudence; اصول مباشرون immediate ancestors; اصول المحاكمات الجزائية (*jazā'īya*) code of criminal procedure (*jur.*); اصول مضاعفة (*muḍāʿafa*) double-entry book-

متأصل *muta'aṣṣil* deep-rooted, deep-seated; chronic (illness)

متآصل *muta'āṣil* of common origin (said of several things)

اطيط *aṭīṭ* the moaning bray of a camel

اطر[1] *aṭara i u* (*aṭr*) and II to bend, curve (ه s.th.)

اطار *iṭār* pl. *-āt*, اطر *uṭur* frame (also of a door, of eyeglasses); tire (of a wheel); hoop (of a barrel, etc.); skeleton, outline (of an action); (*Tun.*, *Alg.*, *Mor.*, as a loan translation from Fr. *cadre*) skeleton organization, cadre, permanent staff, (pl. اطارات) functionary, leading official or employee | فى اطار (with foll. genit.) within the compass of, within the scope of (e.g., an event, an activity); القانون الاطار (*Magr.*) skeleton law

اطارة *iṭāra* rim, felly (of a wheel)

اطارى *iṭārī* framelike, hoop-shaped

اطرية[2] see طرى

اطرغلة *uṭruğulla*, *aṭruğulla* turtledove

اطرون *aṭrūn* = نطرون

الاطلنطيق, الاطلانتيك *al-aṭlantīk*, *al-aṭlanṭīq* the Atlantic

اطلانطى *aṭlanṭīqī* and اطلانطق *aṭlanṭī* Atlantic

اطلس *aṭlas*[2] satin; (pl. اطالس *aṭālis*[2]) atlas, volume of geographical maps; الاطلس, جبال الاطلس Atlas Mountains

اطلسى *aṭlasī* Atlantic; الاطلسى the Atlantic | حلف الاطلسى and الحلف الاطلسى (*ḥilf*) the North Atlantic Treaty, the Atlantic Pact

اطلنطى *aṭlanṭī* Atlantic | حلف الاطلنطى and الحلف الاطلنطى (*ḥilf*) the North Atlantic Treaty, the Atlantic Pact

اطوم *aṭūm* sea turtle

اغا *ağā*, آغا *āğā* pl. اغوات *ağawāt* aga, lord, master, sir; eunuch, harem chamberlain

اغادير *ağādīr*[2] Agadir (city in Morocco)

اغبانى *ağabānī* (*syr.*) a kind of native muslin embroidered with silk

الاغريق *al-iğrīq*, الاغارقة *al-ağāriqa* the ancient Greeks

اغريقى *iğrīqī* classical Greek (adj.); a Greek (of antiquity)

اغسطس *ağusṭus* August (month)

اف V to grumble, mutter in complaint (من about)

اف *uff* dirt (in the ears or under the nails), earwax, cerumen

اف *uff* interj. expressing anger or displeasure

افف *afaf* displeasure; grumbling, grumble

تأفف *ta'affuf* displeasure; grumbling, grumble

افرقة *afraqa* Africanization

الافرنج *al-ifranj* the Franks, the Europeans | بلاد الافرنج Europe

افرنجى *ifranjī* European

افرنسى *ifransī* French; الافرنسية the French language; الافرنسيون the French

افروآسيوى *afro-āsiyawī* Afro-Asiatic

افريز *ifrīz* pl. افاريز *afārīz*[2] frieze; edge; curb; sidewalk | افريز المحطة *i. al-maḥaṭṭa* platform (of a railroad station); افريز الحائط molding (*arch.*)

افريقيا *afrīqiyā* (also *ifrīqiyā*) and افريقا *afrīqā* Africa | افريقيا الجنوبية (*janūbīya*), جنوب افريقيا and جنوبى افريقيا South Africa; افريقيا الشمالية (*šamālīya*) and شمالى افريقيا North Africa

افريقية *ifrīqiya*[2] Ifriqiya, medieval name for central N Africa (comprising approx.

present-day Tripolitania, Tunisia and E Algeria)

افريقى *ifrīqī*, now usually pronounced *afrīqī* African; (pl. *-ūn*, افارقة *afāriqa*) an African

افريل (Fr. *avril*) *afrīl* (*Alg., Tun.*) April

آفرين *āfirīn* bravo! well done!

افسنتين *afsintīn, ifsantīn* wormwood, absinthe (Artemisia absinthium; *bot.*)

افسيت (Engl.) *afsēt* offset (*typ.*)

افشين *ifšīn* pl. افاشين *afāšīn*[2] litany (*Chr.*)

الافغان *al-afġān* the Afghans; Afghanistan

افغانستان *afġānistān*[2] Afghanistan

افغانى *afġānī* Afghan (adj. and n.)

افق *ufq, ufuq* pl. آفاق *āfāq* horizon; range of vision, field of vision; — آفاق distant lands, faraway countries, remote regions; provinces, interior of the country (as distinguished from the capital) | آفاق الارض *ā. al-arḍ* the remotest parts of the earth; آفاق البلاد *ā. al-bilād* the outlying portions of the country; آفاق جديدة new horizons; اجتازت شهرته الآفاق (*šuhratuhū*) his fame spread throughout the world; شذاذ الآفاق *šuḏḏāḏ al-ā.* foreigners, travelers

افقى *ufqī* horizontal

آفاقى *āfāqī* coming from a distant country or region

افاق *affāq* wandering, roving, roaming; (pl. *-ūn*) tramp, vagabond; hoodlum

افك *afaka i* (*afk*) and *afika a* (*ifk, afk, afak,* افوك *ufūk*) to lie, tell a lie

افك *ifk* and افيكة *afīka* pl. افائك *afā'ik*[2] lie, untruth, falsehood

افاك *affāk* liar, lying

افل *afala u i* (افول *ufūl*) to go down, set (stars)

افول *ufūl* setting (of stars)

آفل *āfil* transitory, passing

افلاطون *aflāṭūn*[2] Plato

افلاطونى *aflāṭūnī* Platonic; (pl. *-ūn*) a Platonist

افلاطونية *aflāṭūnīya* Platonism | الافلاطونية المحدثة (الحديثة) (*muḥdaṯa, ḥadīṯa*) neo-Platonism

افلوطين *aflūṭīn*[2] Plotinus

افن *afan* stupidity

افين *afīn* and مأفون *ma'fūn* stupid, foolish, fatuous; fool

افندى *afandī* pl. *-īya* gentleman (when referring to non-Europeans wearing Western clothes and the tarboosh, formerly, after the name, also as a polite title, = Mr. So-and-so); (*eg.*) افندم *afandim!* Sir! (*eg.*) *afandim?* (I beg your) pardon? What did you say?

افوكاتو (It. *avvocato*) *avokātō* advocate, lawyer, attorney | الافوكاتو العمومى representative of the attorney general (= Fr. *avocat général*)

افيش (Fr. *affiche*) *afīš* pl. *-āt* placard, bill, poster

افيون *afyūn* opium | روح الافيون *rūḥ al-a.* laudanum

اقة *uqqa* pl. *-āt* oka, a weight, in Eg. = 1.248 kg, in Syr. = 1.282 kg

مؤقت *mu'aqqat* effective for a certain time, for a time only, temporary, transitory, provisional | مؤقتا temporarily; بصورة مؤقتة (*bi-ṣūra*) do.; حكومة مؤقتة provisional government; see also موقت *muwaqqat*

اقحوان *uqḥuwān* see under قحو

اقرباذين *aqrabāḏīn* composite medicament | علم الاقرباذين *'ilm al-a.* pharmaceutics, pharmacology

اقرباذينى *aqrabāḏīnī* pharmaceutic(al)

اقط *aqiṭ* cottage cheese

اقليد *iqlīd* look up alphabetically

اقلم *aqlama* to acclimate, acclimatize, adapt, adjust **II** *ta'aqlama* to acclimatize (o.s.)

اقليم *iqlīm* pl. اقاليم *aqālīm*[2] climate; geographical zone; area, region; province, district; administrative district; الاقاليم the country, countryside, provinces (as opposed to the capital)

اقليمى *iqlīmī* climatic; regional, local; territorial | المياه الاقليمية (*miyāh*) territorial waters

اقليمية *iqlīmīya* regionalism

اقليد *iqlīd* pl. اقاليد *aqālīd*[2] key

اقليدس *iqlīdis*[2] Euclid

اقليدى *iqlīdī* Euclidean

اقنوم *uqnūm* pl. اقانيم *aqānīm*[2] hypostasis, divine person within the Trinity (*Chr.*); constitutive element

اقونة (Gr. εἰκών) *iqūna* icon (*Chr.*)

اقيانوسية *uqyānūsīya* Oceania

اكادى *akkādī* Akkadian

اكادير (Mor. spelling) *agādīr*[2] Agadir (city in Morocco)

اكاديمى *akādīmī* academic

اكاديمية *akādīmīya* pl. *-āt* academy

اكتوبر *oktōbir* October

اكد **II** to assure (ه ل s.o. of, ان that); to give assurance (ه ل to s.o. of); to confirm (ه s.th., a view, a report, a fact, etc.); to corroborate (على or ه s.th.); to emphasize, stress, underscore (على s.th., ان that), place special emphasis (على on) **V** to be or become convinced, convince o.s.; to become certain (من of s.th.); to ascertain (من s.th.); to be confirmed (view, report, fact, etc.); to prove to be true (ل to s.o.), become clear; to be certain or sure; to be undeniable, be urgent (need)

تأكيد *ta'kīd* pl. *-āt* assurance; confirmation; emphasis; stylistic intensification of a meaning (*gram.*) | بالتأكيد most certainly! of course ! تأكيد الذات self-assertion; لام التأكيد the affirmative particle *la-* (*gram.*)

تأكد *ta'akkud* assurance, reassurance

اكيد *akīd* certain, sure; firm (resolve); definite (desire); urgent, imperative (need); اكيدا *akīdan* certainly! surely!

مؤكد *mu'akkad* certain, definite, sure; confirmed

متأكد *muta'akkid* convinced (من of)

[1]اكر *akara* *i* (*akr*) to plow, till, cultivate (ه the land)

اكار *akkār* pl. *-ūn*, اكرة *akara* plowman

[2]اكرة *ukra* pl. اكر *ukar* ball (for playing) | اكرة الباب round door knob

اكزيما *ekzēmā* eczema (*med.*)

اشعة اكس *aši''at iks* X-rays

اكسبريس (Engl.) *iksibrēs* (Eg. pronun.) express

اكسترا extra

اكسجين *oksižēn* oxygen

اكسد *aksada* (derived from اكسيد, see below) to oxidize, cause to rust **II** *ta'aksada* to oxidize, rust, become rusty

اكسدة *aksada* oxidation

مؤكسد *mu'aksid* oxidizing agent

مؤكسد *mu'aksad* oxidized

اكسسوار (Fr. *accessoire*) *akseswār* pl. *-āt* accessories, extras, fittings (automobile); ladies' accessories; props, sets (*theat.*)

اكسفورد *oksfōrd* Oxford

اكسيجين *oksižēn* oxygen

اكسيد *uksīd*, اوكسيد pl. اكاسيد *akāsīd*² oxide (*chem.*) | اوّل اكسيد *awwal u.* monoxide, ثانى اكسيد dioxide; اكسيد الكربون *u. al-karbōn* carbon oxide; اكسيد الكربون (ثانى) اول carbon monoxide (dioxide); اكسيد الحديد ferrous oxide

اكسير *iksīr* elixir

اكسيولوجيا *aksiyolōjiyā* axiology, theory of values

اكف *akuff* see كف

اكل *akala u* (*akl*, مأكل *ma'kal*) to eat (ه s.th.); to eat up, consume, swallow, devour, destroy (ه s.th.); to eat, gnaw (ه at), eat away, corrode, erode (ه s.th.); to spend unlawfully (ه s.th.), enrich o.s., feather one's nest (ه with) | اكل عليه الدهر وشرب (*dahru, šariba*) to be old and worn out, be timeworn; اكل الربا (*ribā*) to take usurious interest; يعلم من اين تؤكل الكتف *ya'lamu min aina tu'kalu l-katif* he knows how to tackle the matter properly; اكله جلده (*jilduhū*) his skin itched; اكل فى صحن (*ṣaḥn*) to eat off a plate; اكل حقه (*ḥaqqahū*) to encroach upon s.o.'s rights **II** and **IV** to give s.o. (ه) s.th. (ه) to eat, feed (ه ه s.o. s.th.) **III** to eat, dine (ه with s.o.) **V** to be devoured, be consumed; to be eaten away, corrode, undergo corrosion; to become old, worn, timeworn, full of cracks; to be destroyed by corrosion **VI** = **V**

اكل *akl* food; meal, repast; fodder, feed | غرفة الاكل *ġurfat al-a.* dining room; (*eg.*) اكل البحر *a. al-baḥr* land washed away by the sea or the Nile (as opposed to طرح البحر); اكل لحوم البشر *a. luḥūm al-bašar* cannibalism, anthropophagy

اكل *ukul, ukl* food; fruit | آتى اكله to bear fruit

اكلة *akla* pl. *akalāt* meal, repast; — *ukla* bite, morsel

اكال *ukāl* ○ prurigo, itch eruption (*med.*)

اكّال *akkāl*, اكيل *akīl*, اكول *akūl* voracious, gluttonous; hearty eater, gourmand, glutton

مأكل *ma'kal* pl. مآكل *ma'ākil*² food, eats

تأكّل *ta'akkul* wear; corrosion; erosion (*geol.*)

تآكل *ta'ākul* wear; corrosion; erosion (*geol.*)

ائتكال *i'tikāl* erosion (*geol.*)

آكل *ākil* eater | آكل لحوم البشر *ā. luḥūm al-bašar* cannibal

آكلة *ākila* gangrenous sore

مأكول *ma'kūl* eatable, edible; food, nourishment; pl. مأكولات food, foodstuffs, eatables, edibles

مؤاكل *mu'ākil* table companion

متأكّل *muta'akkil* and متآكل *muta'ākil* corroded; eroded; worn, timeworn; full of cracks; rusty, rust-eaten

اكلشيه *aklašēh* pl. *-āt* (*eg.*) cliché

اكليركى *iklīrikī* cleric(al)

اكليروس *iklīrūs* clergy (*Chr.*)

اكليروسية *iklīrūsīya* clericalism

اكليريكى *iklīrīkī* cleric(al)

اكلينيكى *iklīnīkī* clinical

اكمة *akama* pl. *-āt*, اكام *ikām*, اكم *ukum*, آكام *ākām* (coll. اكم *akam*) hill; reef; heap, pile | وراء الاكمة ما وراءها (*warā'a*) something's fishy! there is more to it than meets the eye

اكورديون *akōrdyun, akordiyon* accordion (*mus.*)

ال *ill* pact, covenant; blood relationship, consanguinity

الا[1] *a-lā* and اما *a-mā* see ا *a*

الا[2] *alā* see الو[1]

[3]الا *allā* (= ان لا *an lā*) lest, that ... not, in order that ... not, so as not to

[4]الا *illā* (= ان لا *in lā*) unless, if not; except, save; (with a preceding negation:) لا — الا, ما — الا, لم — الا, etc., only, nothing but, just; not till, not before | الساعة الثانية الا ربعا (*illā rubʿan*) it is a quarter to two; الا ان *illā anna* except that ...; (introducing the final clause of concessive sentences with "although, even if, despite the fact that") still, yet; (introducing main clauses) yet, however, but, nevertheless; الا اذا *illā iḏā* unless, if not; except when; والا *wa-illā* (and if not =) otherwise, or else; الا وهو *illā wa-huwa* (with a preceding negation) unless he ..., except that he ...; وما هى الا ان *wa-mā hiya illā an* (with following verb in perf.) it was not long until ...; presently, forthwith; وما هى الا ان ... حتّى *wa-mā hiya illā an ... ḥattā* no sooner had he ... than ..., e.g., فا هى الا ان هم حتّى فعل (*hamma*) he had no sooner made his plan than he carried it out, see also ما 4.; لا اظن الا انه (*aẓunnu*) I am quite sure that he ...

الاسكا *alaskā* Alaska

الاى *alāy* and آلاى *ālāy* (Turk.) pl. *-āt* (formerly, *mil.*) regiment

[1]الب *alaba u i* (*alb*) to gather, join forces, rally **II** to incite (ه على s.o. against) **V** to rally, band together, plot, conspire (على against)

الب *ilb* a crowd (of people) which rallies and sticks together | هم عليه الب واحد they are united against him, they are sworn to oppose him

[2]جبال الالب *jibāl al-alb* the Alps

البى *albī* Alpine | تزلج البى (*tazalluj*) Alpine skiing

الالبان *al-albān* the Albanians

البانيا *albāniyā* Albania

البوم *album* album

الخ abbreviation of الى آخره *ilā āḵirihī* and so on, etc.

الذى *allaḏī*, f. التى *allatī*, pl. m. الذين *allaḏīna* f. اللاتى *allātī*, اللواتى *allawātī*, اللائى *allāʾī* (relative pronoun) he who, that which; who, which, that | بعد اللتيا والتى *baʿda l-lutayyā wa-llatī* after lengthy discussions, after much ado

الزاس (Fr. *Alsace*) *alzās*[2] Alsace (region of NE France)

السن **II** to belittle, disparage (على s.o.)

الطو (It.) *alṭō* alto (voice register)

[1]الف *alf* pl. الوف *ulūf*, آلاف *ālāf* thousand; millennium | الوف مؤلفة (*muʾallafa*) or آلاف مؤلفة thousands and thousands; عشرات الالوف *ʿašarāt al-u.* tens of thousands; مئات الالوف *miʾāt al-u.* hundreds of thousands; وصلوا بالالوف they arrived by the thousands

الفى *alfī*: عيد الفى (*ʿīd*) millennial celebration, millenary

[2]الف *alif* name of the letter ا | من الفه الى يائه from beginning to end, from A to Z; يعرف الفه وياءه (*wa-yāʾahū*) he knows it from A to Z; الف باء ABC; الف بائى alphabetic

[3]الف *alifa a* (*alf*) to be acquainted, familiar, conversant (ه with s.th.); to be on intimate terms (ه with s.o.); to be or get accustomed, used, habituated (ه to); to like (ه s.th.), be fond of (ه); to become tame **II** to accustom, habituate (ه ه s.o. to s.th.); to tame, domesticate (ه an animal); to form (ه e.g., a committee, a government); to unite, join, combine, put together (بين different things); to compile, compose, write (ه a book) | الف بين قلوبهم to bring people back to harmony, reconcile people with each other **V** to be composed, be made up, consist (من

of); to be united, be combined **VI** to be attuned to each other, be in tune, be in harmony; to harmonize (مع with) **VIII** to be united, be linked, be connected; to be on familiar, intimate terms (ب with); to form a coalition (*pol.*); to fit, suit (مع s.th.), go well, agree, harmonize (مع with); to be well-ordered, neat, tidy **X** to seek the intimacy, court the friendship (ه of s.o.)

الف *ilf* pl. الاف *ullāf* intimate; close friend, intimate, confidant; lover

الفة *ulfa* familiarity, intimacy; friendship, love, affection; union, concord, harmony, congeniality

اليف *alīf* familiar, intimate; tame, domesticated (animal); friendly, amicable, genial; (pl. الائف *alā'if*[2]) intimate, close friend, associate, companion

الوف *alūf* familiar, intimate; tame, domesticated (animal); attached, devoted, faithful

مألف *ma'laf* object of familiarity

تأليف *ta'līf* formation (e.g., of a government); union, junction, combination (بين of separate things); composition, synthesis, formation (with genit.) of various components into a whole; literary work; composition, compilation, writing (of a book, of an article); (pl. تآليف *ta'ālīf*[2], تواليف) work, book, publication | تأليف الارقام dialing a number (by telephone)

تآلف *ta'āluf* harmony; familiarity, intimacy, mutual affection; comradeship, camaraderie; solidarity

ائتلاف *i'tilāf* concord, harmony; agreement (مع with); union; coalition, entente (*pol.*)

ائتلافى *i'tilāfī* coalition- (in compounds) | وزارة ائتلافية coalition cabinet

مألوف *ma'lūf* familiar, accustomed; usual, customary; custom, usage

مؤلف *mu'allif* pl. *-ūn* author, writer; — *mu'allaf* composed, consisting, made up (من of); written, compiled; (pl. *-āt*) book, publication; see also [1]الف *alf*

متآلف *muta'ālif* harmonious

[4]الفا اشعة الفا *aši''at alfā* alpha rays (*phys.*)

الق *alaqa* *i* (*alq*) to shine, radiate, flash, glitter, glisten; to sparkle **V** do. | تألق سعادة (*sa'ādatan*) to radiate with joy **VIII** = *alaqa*

الق *alaq* brightness, brilliance

الاق *allāq* bright, shining, brilliant, radiant; glittering, flashing, sparkling

تألق *ta'alluq* glow, radiance, effulgence

متألق *muta'alliq* bright, shining, brilliant, radiant

الكترود *elektrōd, iliktrōd* pl. *-āt* electrode

الكترون *elektrōn, iliktrōn* pl. *-āt* electron

الكترونى *elektrōnī, iliktrōnī* electronic | آلة الكترونية electronic apparatus; حاسب الكترونى electronic computer; عقل الكترونى (*'aql*) electronic computer; مخ الكترونى (*mukk*) electronic brain

الكترونيات *elektrōnīyāt, iliktrōnīyāt* electronics

الكلة *alkala* alkylation (oil refining; from الكيلات, Engl. *alkylate*)

[1]الم *alima* *a* (*alam*) to be in pain, feel pain; to suffer (ب from s.th.) **II** and **IV** to cause pain or suffering (ه to s.o.), pain, ache, hurt (ه s.o.) **V** = **I**; to complain

الم *alam* pl. آلام *ālām* pain, ache, suffering, agony | آلام نفسانية (*nafsānīya*) mental agony; اسبوع الآلام *usbū' al-ā.* Passion Week (*Chr.*); زهرة الآلام *zahrat al-ā.* passionflower; طريق الآلام Via Dolorosa; path of suffering

اليم *alīm* aching, sore; sad, grievous, painful, excruciating; hurting

آلم *ālam*[2] more painful (على for s.o.)

تألم *ta'allum* sensation of pain, pain, ache

مؤلم *mu'lim* aching, painful; sad, grievous, distressing

متألم *muta'allim* aching, painful; in pain, suffering, deeply afflicted; tormented

[2]الام *ilā-ma* see الى

الماس *almās* (*al* sometimes interpreted as definite article) diamond

الالمان *al-almān* the Germans

المانى *almānī* German (adj. and n.); الالمانية German, the German language | الجمهورية الديموقراطية الالمانية (*dīmūqrāṭīya*) German Democratic Republic

المانيا *almāniyā* Germany | جمهورية المانيا الاتحادية (*ittiḥādīya*) and جمهورية المانيا الفيدرالية (*fidrālīya*) Federal Republic of Germany, (inofficial designation: الجمهورية الفيدرالية الالمانية German Federal Republic)

المانية *almānīya* German character or characteristics, Germanity

المن II *ta'almana* to be Germanized; to become a German or like a German; to behave like the Germans, take on or imitate German characteristics or traits

المنيوم *alamonyum* (Eg. pronun.) aluminum

اله II to deify (ه s.o.), make a god of s.o. (ه) V to become a deity, a godhead; to deify o.s.

اله, الاه *ilāh* pl. آلهة *āliha* god, deity, godhead

الاهة *ilāha* pl. *-āt* goddess

الهى, الاهى *ilāhī* divine, of God; theological; الالاهيات *al-ilāhīyāt* theological, spiritual concerns | علم الالاهيات *'ilm al-i.* theology

الله *aḷḷāh* Allah, God (as the One and Only) | والله *wa-ḷḷāhi* by God! بالله *bi-llāhi* and بالله عليك for God's sake, I implore you, I beg of you; لله درك *li-llāhi darruka* exclamation of admiration and praise, see در; الله من هذا الشتاء (*šitā'*) oh God, what a winter! (*leb.*)

اللهم *aḷḷāhumma* O God! | اللهم الا (*illā*) unless, were it not that, except that, or at best (after a negative statement); اللهم اذا (*iḏā*) at least if or when; if only; اللهم نعم (*na'am*) by God, yes! most certainly!

الوهية *ulūhīya* divine power, divinity

تأليه *ta'līh* deification, apotheosis; theism

آله *ālih* (pagan) god

آلهة *āliha* pl. *-āt* goddess

آلهى *ālihī* divine

متأله *muta'allih* divine, heavenly

اللاهوت etc., see لاهوت

[1]الا (الو) *alā u* to neglect or fail to do, not to do (فى s.th.), desist, refrain (فى from s.th.) | لا يألو to stop at nothing, be eagerly or uninterruptedly active, be tireless (ه, ه in a matter or for s.o.; ه, also من, in doing s.th.); لا يألوها اسعادا (*is'ādan*) he is constantly striving to make her happy; لا يألوه نصحا وإرشادا (*nuṣḥan*) he never lets up giving him advice and guidance; لا يألو جهدا فى (*jahdan*) he will go to any length, he spares no effort, goes out of his way for IV to swear | آلى على نفسه ان he promised himself that he ...

ايلاء *īlā'* oath

[2]آلو (Fr. *hallo*) hello!

الومنيا *alūminyā* and الومنيوم *alūminyom* aluminum

[1]الى *ilā* (prep.) to, toward; up to, as far as; till, until; الى ان (conj.) until | الى آخره (*āḵirihī*) and so forth, et cetera; الى ذلك besides, moreover, furthermore, in addition to that; الى غد till tomorrow! الى اللقاء (*liqā'*) good-by! الام *ilāma*

(= الى ما) up to where? how far? الى متى till when? how long? اليك عنى (*'annī*) get away from me! away with you! الى جانب ذلك (*jānibi d.*) besides, moreover, in addition to that; هذا الى جانب (with genit.) add to this that ...; هذا الى ان moreover, furthermore; الى غير ذلك (*gairi d.*) and the like; وما اليه and the like, et cetera; ومن اليه (اليهم) (*wa-man*) and other people like that; اليك (addressing the reader) now here you have...; here is (are)...; following is (are) ..., e.g., والى القارئ ما in the following, the reader will find what...; اسلوب عبرانى الى العربية (*uslūb 'ibrānī*) a style of Hebrew approximating Arabic; لا الى هذا ولا الى ذاك neither this way nor that way, belonging to neither group; الامر اليك it's up to you, the decision is yours; الى يمينه at his right-hand side; الى اقصى اليمين (*aqṣā l-y.*) on the extreme right; يقع الى الجنوب من (*yaqa'u, janūb*) it is situated south of ...; رياح خفيفة الى معتدلة (*mu'tadila*) light to moderate winds

²آلاء *ālā'* (pl. of الى *ilan*) benefits, blessings

³الية *alya* pl. *alayāt* fat tail (of a sheep); — *ilya* buttock

الياذة *iliyāda* Iliad

¹ام *am* or? (introducing the second member of an alternative question, also ام ان *am anna*)

²امة *ama* pl. اماء *imā'*, اموات *amawāt* bondmaid, slave girl

³ام *amma u* (*amm*) to go, betake o.s., repair (ه to a place), go to see (ه s.o.); — (امامة *imāma*) to lead the way, lead by one's example (ه s.o.); to lead (ه s.o.) in prayer; — (امومة *umūma*) to be or become a mother **II** to nationalize (ه s.th.); to dispossess (ه private property, in a socialist economic system) **V** to go, betake o.s., repair (ه to a place), go to see (ه s.o.) **VIII** to follow the example (ب of s.o.)

ام *umm* pl. امهات *ummahāt* mother; source, origin; basis, foundation; original, original version (of a book); the gist, essence of s.th.; (as attribute) original, primary, basic, parent; pl. امهات matrix (*typ.*) | ام اويق *u. uwaiq* screech owl (*zool.*); ام جعران *u. ji'rān* Egyptian vulture (*zool.*); الام الجافية (*jāfiya*) dura mater (*anat.*); ام الحبر *u. al-ḥibr* cuttlefish, squid (*zool.*); ام الحسن *u. al-ḥasan* (*magr.*) nightingale; الام الحنون (*ḥanūn*) pia mater (*anat.*); ام الخلول *u. al-kulūl* river mussel (*zool.*); ام درمان *u. durmān* Omdurman (city in central Sudan, opposite Khartoum); ام الدماغ *u. ad-dimāg* meninges (*anat.*); ام الرأس *u. ar-ra's* skull, brain; cerebral membrane, meninges (*anat.*); ام اربع واربعين *u. arba' wa-arba'īn* centipede (*zool.*); ام شملة *u. šamla(ta)* this world, the worldly pleasures; بام العين *bi-u. al-'ain* or بام عينه with one's own eyes; شاهدوه بام اعينهم (*bi-u. a'yunihim*) they saw it with their own eyes; ام القرآن and ام الكتاب the first sura of the Koran; ام قرن *u. qarn* rhinoceros (*zool.*); ام القرى *u. al-qurā* Mecca; ام القيوين *u. al-qaiwain* Umm al Qaiwain, name of an emirate on the Persian Gulf; ام الكتاب also: the original text of the Book from which Koranic revelation derives; the uncontested portions of the Koran; ام النجوم the Milky Way; ام الوطن *u. al-waṭan* capital, metropolis; الشركة الام (*širka*) parent company (*com.*); الصخر الام pl. الصخور الام (*ṣakr, ṣukūr*) primitive rock, parent rock; اللغة الام (*luga*) mother tongue; امهات الحوادث the most important events; امهات الحروف matrix (*typ.*); امهات المسائل the main problems; امهات الصحف *u. aṣ-ṣuḥuf* the leading, most highly-respected newspapers; امهات الفضائل the principal virtues; امهات الكتب *u. al-kutub* handbooks, basic books, essential works; امهات المؤمنين *u. al-mu'minīn* Mohammed's wives

امة *umma* pl. امم *umam* nation, people; community | امة محمد Mohammed's community, the Mohammedans; الامم المتحدة (*muttaḥida*) the United Nations; الامة العربية the Arab nation, the sum total of all Arabs

امى *ummī* maternal, motherly; illiterate uneducated; (pl. *-ūn*) an illiterate

امية *ummīya* illiteracy; see also under اموى[2]

امى *umamī* international; UNO (in compounds) | الهيئة الامية (*hai'a*), المنظمة الامية (*munaẓẓama*) the United Nations Organization

امية *umamīya* Internationale (as federation of socialist parties)

امومة *umūma* motherhood; motherliness, maternity

امام *amāma* (prep.) in front of; in the presence of; facing, in the face of, opposite to | الى الامام (*amāmi*) to the front, forward, onward, ahead; للأمام forward march! (command; *mil.*); للامام انظر (*unẓur*) eyes front! (command; *mil.*); لم يكن امامه الا ان (*illā an*) he had no other alternative but to ...; مضى الى الامام and مضى امامه to stride ahead, go straight ahead, continue straight forward; فاز امام to win a match from . . ., خسر امام and انهزم امام or هزم امام (*huzima*) to lose against or to (a team or opponent, esp. in sports), be defeated by . . .; اقامة سد امام (*iqāmatu saddin*) erection of a bulwark against . . .; ازالة المعوقات امام (*izālatu l-mu'awwiqāt*) removal of obstacles or hindrances standing in the way of . . .; وقف امامه (*waqafa*) to oppose, resist, stop, check s.th.

امامى *amāmī* front, fore-, anterior, forward, foremost | نقطة امامية (*nuqṭa*) outpost

امام *imām* pl. أئمة *a'imma*, ايمة *ayimma* imam, prayer leader; leader; master; plumb line; standard, criterion | أئمة الاسلام *a'immat al-i.* the old teaching authorities or spiritual leaders of Islam; فضيلة الامام الاكبر (*akbar*) title of high-ranking religious dignitaries (esp. of the Rector of Azhar University)

امامة *imāma* imamah, function or office of the prayer leader; imamate; leading position; precedence

اماميات *imāmīyāt* standards

تأميم *ta'mīm* pl. *-āt* nationalization

[1]اما *a-mā* see ا *a*

[2]اما *ammā* (with foll. ف *fa*) as to, as for, as far as ... is concerned; but; yet, however, on the other hand | اما بعد (*ba'du*) (a formular phrase linking introduction and actual subject of a book or letter, approx.:) now then ..., now to our topic: ...; اما عن as to, as for, اما عنى فلا (*'annī, fa-lā*) as far as I'm concerned, no!

[3]اما *immā* if; اما — واما be it — or, either — or (also اما — او)

امبابة *imbāba*[2] Embabeh (a section of Giza)

امباشى *ombāšī* see اونباشى (alphabetically)

امبراطور *imbarāṭūr*, *imbaraṭōr* pl. *-āt*, اباطرة *abāṭira* emperor

امبراطورى *imbarāṭūrī*, *imbaraṭōrī* imperialist(ic)

امبراطورية *imbarāṭūrīya*, *imbaraṭōrīya* pl. *-āt* empire, imperium; imperialism | امبراطورية استعمارية colonial empire

امبريالى *imbiriyālī* imperialistic; (pl. *-ūn*) imperialist

امبريالية *imbiriyālīya* imperialism

امبير *ambīr*, *ambēr* pl. امابير *amābīr*[2] ampere (*el.*)

امبيق *imbīq* = انبيق

امت *amt* crookedness, curvedness, curvation, curvature; weakness

امر amr 1. pl. اوامر awāmir² order, command, instruction (ب to do s.th.); ordinance, decree; warrant (jur.); writ (jur.); power, authority; (gram.) imperative | امر عال (ʿālin) royal decree (formerly, Eg.); امر على (ʿalīy) decree, edict of the Bey (formerly, Tun.); امر قانونى ordinance having the force of law (Tun.); الامر والنهى (wa-n-nahy) pl. الاوامر والنواهى (lit.: command and interdiction, i.e.) sovereign power; full powers, supreme authority; امر جلب a. jalb writ of habeas corpus (jur.); امر حضور writ of summons (jur.); امر صرف a. ṣarf disbursement order, cash note, order for payment (econ.); الامر المطلق (muṭlaq) categorical imperative (philos.); امر اعتقال warrant of arrest (jur.); امر تفتيش search warrant (jur.); امر توريد (delivery) order (com.); امر يومى (yaumī) order of the day (mil.); تحت امرك at your disposal, at your service. — 2. pl. امور umūr matter, affair, concern, business | امر واقع (accomplished) fact; امر معروف common knowledge; فى اول الامر at first, in the beginning; لامر ما (amrin) for some reason or other; اليس الامر كذلك isn't it so? اما والامر كذلك (ammā wa-l-amru) things being as they are, there will, no doubt, . . .; مهما يكن من امر (min amrin) whatever may happen; however things may be; هو بين امرين he has two possibilities (or alternatives); الامر الذى which (introducing a relative clause the antecedent of which is another clause); قضى امره quḍiya amruhū it's all over with him; in the latter and similar phrases, امره is a frequent paraphrase of "he"; كل امره everything that concerns him; غلب على امره (ğuliba) he was totally overcome, he suffered a complete defeat; هزم على امره (huzima) do.

امر immar simple-minded, stupid

امرة imra power, influence, authority, command | تحت امرته under his command

امارة amāra pl. -āt, امائر amāʾir² sign, token, indication, symptom, mark, characteristic

امارة imāra position or rank of an emir; princely bearing or manners; principality; (pl. -āt) emirate; authority, power | امارة البحر i. al-baḥr office or jurisdiction of an admiral, admiralty; امارات الخليج the Persian Gulf emirates, (official designation:) الامارات العربية المتحدة (mutaḥida) United Arab Emirates, also دولة اتحاد الامارات العربية (daulat ittiḥād), short form: دولة الامارات; امارات ساحل عمان i. s. ʿumān = الامارات المتصالحة (mutaṣāliḥa) formerly: Trucial Oman

امير amīr pl. امراء umarāʾ² commander; prince, emir; title of princes of a ruling house; tribal chief | امير البحر a. al-baḥr admiral; (formerly, Eg.) rear admiral; (obs. military titles:) امير الاى a. alāy brigadier general (Eg., Sudan), امير البحار vice-admiral (Eg.), امير لواء a. liwāʾ major

امد amad pl. آماد āmād final point, goal, end, limit; (limited) time, stretch of time; (utmost) extent, scope | امد بعيد far distance; منذ امد بعيد since an early date, for a long time (past); امد الحياة a. al-ḥayāh life span, life expectancy; قصير الامد short-lived, of short duration, brief; short-term

امر amara u (amr) to order, command, bid, instruct (ه s.o. ب to do s.th.), commission, charge, entrust (ه s.o. ب with s.th. or to do s.th.); — amara, amura u (امارة imāra) to become an emir II to invest with authority, make an emir (ه s.o., على over) III to ask s.o.'s (ه) advice, consult (ه s.o.) V to come to power; to set o.s. up as lord and master; to behave like an emir; to assume an imperious attitude; to be imperious, domineering VI to take counsel, deliberate together, confer, consult with each other; to plot, conspire (على against) VIII to deliberate, take counsel (ب about); to conspire, plot, hatch a plot (ب against s.o.) | ائتمر بامره to carry out s.o.'s orders

general (*Ir., Jord.*), امير لواء العسة *a. l. al-ʿassa* commandant of the Bey's palace guard (formerly, *Tun.*); امير المؤمنين *a. al-mu'minīn* Commander of the Faithful, Caliph; امير الشعر *a. aš-šiʿr* and امير الشعراء *a. aš-šuʿarā'* prince of poets

اميرة *amīra* pl. *-āt* princess

اميرى *amīrī* (and □ ميرى *mīrī*) government(al), state-owned, state, public | ارض اميرى (*arḍ*) government land (*Syr.*); المطبعة الاميرية government press

امار *ammār* constantly urging, always demanding (ب to do s.th.); inciting, instigating | النفس الامارة بالسوء (*nafs, sū'*) the baser self (of man) that incites to evil

تأمور *ta'mūr* soul, mind, spirit; pericardium (*anat.*) | التهاب التأمور pericarditis (*med.*)

مؤامرة *mu'āmara* pl. *-āt* deliberation, counsel, conference; plot, conspiracy

تأمر *ta'ammur* imperiousness, domineeringness; imperious deportment, overbearing manners

تآمر *ta'āmur* joint consultation, counsel, deliberation, conference; plot, conspiracy

ائتمار *i'timār* deliberation, counsel, conference; plot, conspiracy

استئمارة *isti'māra* (frequently written استمارة) form, blank | استمارة بحث *i. baḥṯ* questionnaire

آمر *āmir* commander; commanding officer, commandant (*mil.*); lord, master; orderer, purchaser, customer, client | الآمر الناهى absolute master, vested with unlimited authority; الآمر بالسحب (*saḥb*) drawer of a bill or cheque (*fin.*)

مأمور *ma'mūr* commissioned, charged; commissioner; civil officer, official, esp., one in executive capacity; the head of a *markaz* and *qism* (*Eg.*) | مأمور البوليس superintendent of police; مأمور للتفليسة (*taflīsa*) receiver (in bankruptcy; *jur.*); مأمور الحركة *m. al-ḥaraka* traffic manager (railroad); مأمور التسوية *m. at-taswiya* land settlement officer; مأمور السجن *m. as-sijn* warden of a prison; مأمور التصفية *m. at-taṣfiya* receiver (in equity, in bankruptcy; *jur.*); مأمور التقدير (التخمين), مأمور الضرائب assessing officer, official who determines the amount of taxes

مأمورية *ma'mūrīya* pl. *-āt* order, instruction; errand; task, assignment, mission; commission; commissioner's office, administrative branch of a government agency, e.g., مأمورية قضائية (*qaḍā'īya*) judicial commission charged with jurisdiction in outlying communities (*Eg.*)

متآمرون *muta'āmirūn* conspirators, plotters

مؤتمرون *mu'tamirūn* conspirators, plotters; members of a congress, convention, or conference, conferees

مؤتمر *mu'tamar* pl. *-āt* conference; convention, congress | مؤتمر الامن *m. al-amn* security conference; مؤتمر الذروة *m. aḏ-ḏurwa* and مؤتمر القمة *m. al-qimma* summit meeting or conference; مؤتمر صحفى (*ṣuḥufī*) press conference; مؤتمر الصلح *m. aṣ-ṣulḥ* peace conference

امرك II *ta'amraka* to become Americanized, adopt the American way of life, imitate the Americans

تأمرك *ta'amruk* Americanization

امرلس *amarillis* amaryllis (*bot.*)

امريكا *amrīkā* (formerly, also امريقا) America | امريكا الجنوبية (*janūbīya*) South America; امريكا الشمالية (*šamālīya*) North America; امريكا اللاتينية Latin America; امريكا الوسطى (*wusṭā*) Central America

امريكى *amrīkī* American; (pl. *-ūn*) an American

الامريكان *al-amrīkān* the Americans

امريكانى *amrīkānī* American; (pl. *-ūn*) an American

تأمل *ta'ammul* pl. *-āt* consideration; contemplation; pl. تأملات meditations | تأمل باطني (*bāṭinī*) introspection (*psych.*)

تأملي *ta'ammulī* contemplative, meditative

آمل *āmil* hopeful

مأمول *ma'mūl* hoped for, expected

مؤمل *mu'ammil* hopeful

متأمل *muta'ammil* contemplative, meditative, reflective; pensive, wistful, musing

امن[1] *amuna u* (امانة *amāna*) to be faithful, reliable, trustworthy; — *amina a* (*amn*, امان *amān*) to be safe, feel safe (من or ه from) II to reassure (ه s.o.), set s.o.'s (ه) mind at rest; to assure, ensure, safeguard, guarantee, warrant, bear out, confirm, corroborate (على, ه s.th.); to secure (ه s.th.); to provide (ه s.th.); to insure (على s.o., s.th., ضد against, e.g., ضد الحريق against fire); to cover by insurance, underwrite (ه risk); to entrust (ه to s.o., على s.th.); to say "amen" (على to s.th.) IV to believe (ب in) VIII to trust (ه s.o.), have confidence, have faith (ه in); to entrust (على ه s.o. with, to s.o. s.th.) X = VIII; to ask for protection, for a promise of security, for indemnity (ه s.o.)

امن *amn* safety; peace, security, protection | الامن العام (*'āmm*) public safety; امن الدولة *a. ad-daula* state security; رجال الامن the police; مجلس الامن *majlis al-a.* Security Council; قوات الامن *quwwāt al-a.* police forces

امان *amān* security, safety; peace; shelter, protection; clemency, quarter (*mil.*); safeguarding, assurance of protection; indemnity, immunity from punishment | في امان الله (a valedictory phrase) in God's protection! امان المرور *a. al-murūr* safe-conduct; بكل امان without danger or risk; حزام امان *ḥizām a.* safety belt; زجاج امان *zujāj a.* safety glass; قفل امان *qufl a.*

امس *amsu* (acc. امسا *amsan*), الامس *al-a.* the day past, yesterday; the immediate past, recent time; — *amsi* (adv.) yesterday; recently, lately, not long ago | بالامس *bi-l-amsi* yesterday; not long ago; ليلة امس *lailata amsi* yesterday evening, last night; امس الاول *amsi l-awwal* and اول امس *awwala amsi* two days ago, the day before yesterday; امس القريب and بالامس القريب very recently; مسابقات الامس *musābaqāt al-a.* yesterday's competitions

امسية *umsīya* pl. *-āt*, اماسي *amāsīy* evening; الامسية *al-umsīyata* tonight, this evening; امسيات *umsīyātin* whole evenings, evening after evening | امسية شعرية (*ši'rīya*) poetry evening; امسية غنائية (*ġinā'īya*) soirée of song recital

امستردام *amstirdām* Amsterdam

امشير *amšīr* the sixth month of the Coptic calendar

امع *imma'* and امعة *imma'a* characterless person; opportunist, timeserver; yes-man

امعية *imma'īya* opportunism; timeserving

آماق see مؤق *mu'q*

امل *amala u* (*amal*) to hope (ه or ب for), entertain hopes (ه or ب of) II to hope; to expect (من ه s.th. of s.o.); to raise hopes (ه in s.o.), hold out hopes (ه for s.o.), give (ه s.o.) reason to hope or expect | امله خيرا (*kairan*) to let s.o. hope for the best V to look attentively (ه, ه at s.o. or s.th.), regard, contemplate (ه, في s.th.); to meditate; to consider, think over, ponder (ه, في s.th.), reflect (ه, في on)

امل *amal* pl. آمال *āmāl* hope, expectation (في of s.th., also ب) | امل كاذب fallacious hope; كلنا امل بأن (*kullunā amalun*) we are all full of hope that . . .; على امل ان in the hope that . . .

مأمل *ma'mal* pl. مآمل *ma'āmil*[2] hope

safety lock; كبريت امان *kibrīt a.* safety matches

امين *amīn* pl. امناء *umanā'*[2] reliable, trustworthy, loyal; upright, honest; faithful, true (description, report, etc.); safe, secure; innocuous, harmless (remedy, means, drug); authorized representative or agent; trustee; guarantor (على of); (also امين السر *a. as-sirr*) secretary; chief, head; superintendent, curator, custodian, guardian, keeper; chamberlain; master of a guild (*Tun.*); quartermaster sergeant (formerly, *Eg.*; *mil.*) | الامين الاول (*awwal*) Lord Chamberlain (formerly, at the Eg. Court); كبير الامناء approx.: Chief Master of Ceremonies (ibid.); امين ارشيف *a. aršīf* archivist; امين المحفوظات do.; امين بلوك *a. bulūk* staff sergeant, first sergeant (formerly, *Eg.*, *Sudan*; *mil.*); امين المخزن *a. al-makzan* warehouse superintendent; stock clerk; امين سر الدولة *a. sirr ad-daula* and امين السر *a. as-sirr* permanent secretary of state (*Syr.*); امين الصندوق *a. aṣ-ṣundūq* and امين المال treasurer; cashier; امين العاصمة mayor of the capital city; امين عام (*'āmm*) secretary general; امين متحف *a. mutḥaf* museum director; امين مكتبة *a. maktaba* librarian, library director; امين السجل المدنى *a. as-sijill al-madanī* registrar of vital statistics; صورة امينة (*ṣūra*) a true image, a faithful copy

امينة *amīna*: امينة عامة (*'āmma*) secretary general (fem.)

آمين *āmīn* amen!

امانة *amāna* reliability, trustworthiness; loyalty, faithfulness, fidelity, fealty; integrity, honesty; confidence, trust, good faith; deposition in trust; trusteeship; confidentiality, secrecy (of s.th.); (pl. *-āt*) s.th. deposited in trust, a deposit, trust, charge; secretariat; office of mayor in a capital city; municipal council of a capital city | امانة الصندوق *a. aṣ-ṣundūq* treasury department; امانة عامة (*'āmma*) secretariat general; مخزن الامانات *makzan al-a.* baggage checkroom

مأمن *ma'man* place of safety, safe place; shelter

تأمين *ta'mīn* securing, protection; assurance; safeguarding; reassurance; ensuring, providing, procurement, provision;—(pl. *-āt*) guaranty, warranty; security, surety; insurance; resigned mood (in which one says yea and amen; على to s.th.) | تأمين اجتماعى (*ijtimā'ī*) social security; تأمين شامل full-coverage insurance; تأمين ضد الحريق (*ḍidda*) fire insurance; تأمين على الحياة (*ḥayāh*) life insurance; تأمين على السيارات motor vehicle insurance

ايمان *īmān* faith, belief (ب in)

ائتمان *i'timān* trust, confidence; credit (also *fin.*) | ائتمان زراعى (*zirā'ī*) agricultural credit; سوء الائتمان breach of trust or confidence

ائتمانى *i'timānī* fiduciary (in compounds); credit (in compounds) | تسهيلات ائتمانية credit facilitations; اسواق ائتمانية credit markets

استئمان *isti'mān* trust, confidence

آمن *āmin* peaceful; safe, secure

مأمون *ma'mūn* reliable, trustworthy; mild, innocuous, harmless

مؤمن *mu'amman* pl. *-ūn* insured person, policy holder | مؤمن اجتماعى person covered by social security, social security pensioner; مؤمن عليه insured

مؤمن *mu'min* believing, faithful; believer

مؤتمن *mu'taman* entrusted (على with); trustworthy; confidant; sequestrator (*jur.*); fiduciary, trusted agent; custodian, trustee

امينى[2] look up alphabetically

امنيبوس *omnibus* omnibus, bus

امهات see ام *umm*

امهرى *amharī* Amharic

آمورى *āmūrī* pl. *-ūn* Amorite

[1]اموى *amawī* of or like a bondmaid or handmaid

[2]اموى *umawī* Umayyad (adj.); الامويون and بنو امية *banū umayya* the Umayyads

اميبا *amībā* amoebae

اميرال *amīrāl* admiral

اميرالية *amīrālīya* admiralty

اميركا, اميركه *amērikā, amērika* America (*Leb., Syr.*)

اميركى *amērikī* American

امينى : حمض امينى (*ḥamḍ*) pl. احماض امينية amino acid (*chem.*)

[1]ان *an* (conj.) that (with verb in the subj. indicating an action not yet realized, an expected or possible event; with verb in the perf. indicating that which has happened); — *in* 1. (conj.) if, in case; whether; وان *wa-in* although, even though, even if; وان — ان be it — or (be it); الا *illā* (= ان لا) look up alphabetically 2. (neg.) not, esp. in the phrase ان هو الا *in huwa illā* (f. ان هى الا) it is nothing but, it is no more than, ان هى الا لحظة حتى (*laḥẓa-tun*) it takes only a moment until . . .

[2]ان *anna* (conj.) that (with foll. subject in the acc. or as a suffix and with nominal or copulative clause); بما انه *bi-mā annahū* since he (it), because he (it); على انه *ʿalā annahū* while he (it), whereas he (it); introducing a main clause: however, yet; وذلك انه that is to say, namely, to wit; — *inna* (part. introducing a main clause, with foll. subject in the acc. or as a suffix) behold, verily, truly (in most cases not translated in English)

انما *innamā* nothing but, only; rather, much more, on the contrary

[3]ان *anna i* (انين *anīn*, تأنان *taʾnān*) to groan, moan (من at)

انة *anna* pl. *-āt* moan, groan | انات وآهات wails and laments

انين *anīn* plaintive sound, wail; groan, moan(ing)

انان *annān* moaning, lamenting

انا *anā* I | الانا the ego, الانا الاعلى (*aʿlā*) the superego (*psych.*)

O الانية *al-anīya* the ego (*psych.*)

انانى *anānī* egotistic; egoistic(al), selfish

انانية *anānīya* egoism, selfishness

الاناضول *al-anāḍūl, al-anaḍōl* Anatolia

اناضولى *anāḍūlī, anaḍōlī* Anatolian

اناناس *anānās* pineapple

انب II to blame, censure, reprehend, upbraid (ه s.o.); to scold, chide (ه s.o.)

تأنيب *taʾnīb* blame, censure, rebuke | تأنيب الضمير remorse

انبا (pronounced *ambā*) Abba, a high ecclesiastic title of the Coptic Church, preceding the names of metropolitans, bishops, patriarchs, and saints (< *Ἀββᾶ*)

انبار *anbār* pl. انابر *anābir*[2], انابير *anābīr*[2] warehouse, storehouse, storeroom

انباشى see اونباشى (alphabetically)

انبوب, انبوبة see نب

انبيق *imbīq, ambīq* pl. انابيق *anābīq*[2] alembic, retort

انت *anta*, f. *anti* thou, you (2nd pers. sing.); pl. m. انتم *antum*, f. انتن *antunna* you (2nd pers. pl. and polite form of address); dual انتما *antumā* both of you

انتذا *anta-ḏā* you there; it's you!

انتيكخانة *antīkkāna* museum

انتيكة *antīka* pl. *-āt* antique, object of ancient art; pl. انتيكات antiquities

انتيمون *antīmūn* antimony

انث *anuṯa u* (انوثة *unūṯa*) to be or become feminine, womanly, womanish, effeminate II to make feminine; to effeminate, make effeminate; to put into the feminine form (*gram.*) V to become feminine (also *gram.*)

انثى *unṯā* pl. اناث *ināṯ*, اناثى *anāṯā* feminine; female; a female (of animals); الانثيان *al-unṯayān* the testicles

انثوى *unṯawī* womanly, female, women's (in compounds); effeminate, womanish

انوثة *unūṯa* femininity, womanliness

تأنيث *ta'nīṯ* the feminine, feminine form (*gram.*)

مؤنث *mu'annaṯ* (*gram.*) feminine (adj.)

انثروبولوجيا *anṯrobolōjiyā* anthropology

انثروبولوجى *anṯrobolōjī* anthropological

انجاص *injāṣ* (< اجاص *ijjāṣ*; coll.; n. un. ة) pear (*syr.*)

انجل II *ta'angala* (Eg. spelling) to become English or anglicized; to take on English manners, imitate the English

انجلة *angala* anglicization

انجلترا (It. *Inghilterra*; Eg. spelling) *ingilterā* England

الانجلوسكسون (Eg. spelling) *al-anglosaksōn* the Anglo-Saxons

انجلوسكسونى *anglosaksōnī* Anglo-Saxon

الانجليز (Eg. spelling) *al-inglīz* the English

انجليزى *inglīzī* English; Englishman

انجولا (Eg. spelling) *angōlā* Angola

انجيل *injīl* pl. اناجيل *anājīl*[2] gospel

انجيلى *injīlī* evangelical; evangelist

انجيلية *injīlīya* evangelical creed

الاندلس *al-andalus* Andalusia; name of Arabicized Spain in the Middle Ages

اندلسى *andalusī* Andalusian

اندونيسيا *indūnīsiyā* Indonesia

اندونيسى *indūnīsī* Indonesian

انزيم *anzīm* pl. *-āt* enzyme (*chem.*)

انس *anisa a* and *anusa u* (*uns*) to be companionable, sociable, nice, friendly, genial; انس به to like s.o.'s company, like to be together with s.o.; to have confidence (الى in s.o.), take a liking (الى to s.o.); to be or get on intimate terms (ب or الى with s.o.); to be used, accustomed, habituated (الى to); to perceive, notice, find (ه a quality, فى, من in s.o.); to sense, feel, make out, recognize (ه s.th., فى in, at) | انس لحديثه (*li-ḥadīṯihī*) to like to listen to s.o. II to put at ease; to tame III to be friendly, nice (ه to s.o.); to entertain, amuse (ه s.o.) IV to keep s.o. (ه) company; to entertain, delight, amuse (ه s.o.); to perceive, discern, make out (with the eyes; ه s.th.); to sense (ه s.th.); to find, see, notice, observe, e.g., آنس فيه الكفاية he saw that he was duly qualified, that he was a capable man V to become incarnate (Son of God) X to be sociable, companionable; to get on familiar terms, become intimate; to become tame; to be friendly, nice, kind (ه to s.o.); to accommodate o.s., accustom o.s., settle down; to be familiar, familiarize o.s., acquaint o.s. (ب or الى with); to inform o.s., gather information (ب about); to take into consideration, take into account, bring into play (ب s.th.), draw upon s.th. (ب); to listen (ل to s.th.), heed (ب an opinion)

انس *uns* sociability; intimacy, familiarity, friendly atmosphere

انسى *unsī*: كعب انسى (*kaʿb*) talus, inner anklebone (*anat.*)

انس *ins* intimate friend; man, mankind, human race

انسى *insī* human; human being

اناس *unās* and ناس *nās* men, people, folks

اناسى *anāsīy* (pl.) people, human beings, humans

انيس *anīs* close, intimate; close friend; friendly, kind, affable, civil; sociable, companionable; tame

انسان *insān* man, human being; الانسان someone, somebody, one, a person, people | انسان العين *i. al-ʿain* pupil (of the eye)

انسانة *insāna* woman

انسانى *insānī* human; humane; humanitarian, philanthropist; الانسانيات the humanities

انسانية *insānīya* humanity, humaneness; politeness, civility; mankind, the human race

مؤانسة *mu'ānasa* intimacy, familiarity, friendliness, geniality, cordiality; sociability; conviviality

ايناس *īnās* exhilaration; friendliness, geniality; familiarity, intimacy, cordiality; sociability

تأنس *ta'annus* incarnation (*Chr.*)

ائتناس *i'tinās* social life, sociability

آنسة *ānisa* pl. *-āt*, اوانس *awānis*[2] young lady, miss

مأنوس *ma'nūs* familiar, accustomed

مستأنس *musta'nis* tame

انش (Engl.) *inš* pl. *-āt* inch

انشوجة (It. *acciuga*) *anšūga* (*eg.*) anchovy

انطاكية *anṭākiya*[2] Antioch (ancient city in Syria; now Antakya, in S Turkey)

انطولوجى *onṭōlōjī* ontologic(al) (*philos.*)

انغولا *angōlā* Angola

انف *anifa a* (*anaf*) to disdain, scorn (من s.th., ان to do s.th.); to reject haughtily (ه s.th.) X to begin (ه s.th.); to resume, renew, recommence (ه s.th.); (*jur.*) to appeal (ه a sentence)

انف *anf* pl. آناف *ānāf*, انوف *unūf* nose; spur (of a mountain); pride | رغم انفه *raḡma anfihī* in defiance of him, to spite him; على الرغم من انفه (*raḡmi*) and رغما عن انفه (*raḡman*) do.; كسر انفه (*anfahū*) to humiliate s.o., put s.o.'s nose out of joint; شامخ الانف haughty, proud, supercilious, arrogant

انفى *anfī* nasal

انفة *anafa* pride; rejection; disdain (من of s.th.)

انوف *anūf* proud, haughty, stuck-up, supercilious, disdainful

استئناف *isti'nāf* fresh start, recommencement, renewal, resumption, reopening (also, of a legal case); appeal (*jur.*) | قدم استئنافا (*qaddama*) to appeal, make an appeal (*jur.*)

استئنافى *isti'nāfī* of appeal, appellate; استئنافيا *isti'nāfīyan* by appeal

آنف *ānif* preceding, above | آنف الذكر (*ḏikr*) preceding, above, above-mentioned; آنفا *ānifan* previously, above, in the foregoing

مؤتنف *mu'tanaf* primordial, virginal state; beginning

مستأنف *musta'naf*: المستأنف عليه appellee, respondent in an appellate procedure (*jur.*)

انفرس (Fr. *Anvers*) *anvers* Antwerp (city in N Belgium)

انفلونزا *influwanzā* influenza, grippe

انق *aniqa a* to be neat, trim, smart, spruce, comely, pretty; to be happy (ب about), be delighted (ب by) **IV** to please (ه s.o.) | يؤنقه الشيء (*šai'u*) he likes the thing **V** to apply o.s. eagerly and meticulously (فى to); to be meticulous, fastidious, finical; to be chic, elegant

اناقة *anāqa* elegance

انيق *anīq* neat, trim, spruce, comely, pretty; elegant, chic

انوق *anūq* Egyptian vulture (Neophron percnopterus) | اعز من بيض الانوق *a'azz*[2] *min baiḍi l-a.* (lit.: rarer than the eggs of a vulture, i.e.) approx.: scarcer than hens' teeth (proverbially for s.th. rare)

تأنق *ta'annuq* elegance

مؤنق *mu'niq*, مونق *mūniq* pretty, comely, winsome, nice, pleasing

متأنق *muta'anniq* chic, elegant

انقره *anqara* Ankara

انقلترا (Tun. spelling) = انكلترا, انجلترا

الانقليز (Tun. spelling) = الانكليز, الانجليز

انقليس *anqalīs* (*syr.*) eel

آنك *ānuk* lead (metal)

انكشارى *inkišārī* pl. *-īya* Janizary

انكلترا, انكلترة (It. *Inghilterra*) *ingilterā*, *ingiltera* England

الانكلوسكسون *al-anglosaksūn* the Anglo-Saxons

الانكلوسكسونية *al-anglosaksūnīya* Anglo-Saxondom

الانكليز *al-inglīz* the English

انكليزى *inglīzī* English; Englishman

انكليس *ankalīs* (*syr.*) eel

انكليكانى *anglikānī* Anglican

انكولا *angōlā* Angola

[1]الانام *al-anām* and الآنام (coll.) mankind, the human race

[2]انما *innamā* see [2]ان *inna*

انموذج *unmūḏaj* model, pattern; type, example; sample, specimen

انمون *anamūn* anemone (*bot.*)

انود *anōd* pl. *-āt* anode (*el.*)

[1]انى *anā* *i* to mature, become ripe; to draw near, approach, come (esp. time) | انى له ان it is (high) time that he; esp. in negative statements: الم يأن *a-lam ya'ni?* isn't it about time ...? **V** to act slowly, proceed unhurriedly, bide one's time, be patient **X** to take one's time, hesitate (فى in, with); to wait

انى *anan* pl. آناء *ānā'* (span of) time, period | فى آناء الليل (*laili*) all night long; آناء الليل واطراف النهار *ānā'a l-laili wa-aṭrāfa n-nahār* by day and by night

اناة *anāh* deliberateness; perseverance, patience; equanimity, balanced judgment | طول الاناة *ṭūl al-a.* long-suffering, great patience; طويل الاناة long-suffering (adj.)

اناء *inā'* pl. آنية *āniya*, اوان *awānin* vessel, container, receptacle; plate; dish; الاوانى kitchenware, pots and pans | اناء الطبخ *i. aṭ-ṭabḵ* cooking pot; آنية الطعام *ā. aṭ-ṭa'ām* plates and dishes, tableware

تأن *ta'annin* slowness, deliberateness

متأن *muta'annin* slow, unhurried, deliberate

[2]انى *annā* (interrog. part.) where ... from? why is it that ...? why? where? (place and direction); how? wherever; however | ... وانى له الا (*allā*) and why shouldn't he ...?

انيسون *anīsūn*, آنيسون aniseed

انيميا *anīmiyā* anemia | ○ انيميا خبيثة pernicious anemia (*med.*)

آه *āhi!* آها *āhan!* (interj.) oh!

اهب **II** to prepare, make ready, equip (ل ه, ه s.o., s.th. for) **V** to be ready, be prepared; to prepare o.s., get ready; to equip o.s., be equipped (ل for)

اهبة *uhba* pl. اهب *uhab* preparation, preparedness, readiness, alertness; equipment, outfit, gear | اهبة الحرب *u. al-ḥarb* military equipment; على اهبة الرحيل ready to set out; على اهبة الاستعداد fully prepared; on the alert (*mil.*); اخذ اهبته to make one's preparations, get ready

اهاب *ihāb* skin, hide

تأهب *ta'ahhub* preparedness, readiness; (pl. *-āt*) preparation; (also حالة التأهب) stand-by (*mil.*), alert, state of alarm

متأهب *muta'ahhib* ready, prepared

اهل *ahala u i* (اهول *uhūl*) to take a wife, get married; — *ahila a* to be on familiar terms (ب with); — pass. *uhila* to be inhabited, be populated (region, place) **II** to make fit or suited, to fit; to qualify (ل ه, ه s.o., s.th. for, e.g., for a goal, a task, a job); to make possible (ه ل for s.o. s.th.), enable (ه ل s.o. to do s.th.), make accessible (ه ل to s.o. s.th.); to welcome (ب s.o.) **V** to be or become fit, suited, qualified (ل for s.th.); to qualify (ل for, e.g., for the next round in sport); to take a wife; to marry, get married **X** to deserve, merit (ه s.th.), be worthy (ه of)

اهل *ahl* relatives, folks, family; kin, kinfolk; wife; (with foll. genit.) people, members, followers, adherents, possessors, etc.; inhabitants; deserving, worthy (ل of s.th.); fit, suited, qualified (ل for); eligible, competent (ل for s.th.); — pl. اهلون members of the family, relatives; (with foll. genit.) adherents, followers, members (of a movement, religion, etc.); — pl. اهال *ahālin* population, inhabitants (of a city, a country); الاهالى the natives; the native population | اهل البيت *a. al-bait* members (of the house, i.e.) of the family; the Prophet's family; اهل الدار the people living in the house; اهل الحرفة *a. al-ḥirfa* people of the trade; اهل الحلف *a. al-ḥilf* people pledged by oath, members of a sworn confederacy; اهل الخبرة *a. al-ḵibra* people of experience, experts; اهل السفسطة *a. as-safsaṭa* Sophists; اهل السنة *a. as-sunna* the adherents of the Sunna, the Sunnis; اهل العلم *a. al-'ilm* learned people; اهل الكتاب *a. al-kitāb* people with a holy writ, monotheists (Christians, Jews); اهل المدر والوبر *a. al-madar wa-l-wabar* the resident population and the nomads; اهل الوجاهة *a. al-wajāha* people of rank and high social standing; اهلا وسهلا *ahlan wa-sahlan* welcome! اهلا بك *ahlan bika* welcome to you! له فى دارنا اهل وسهل he is a welcome guest in our house; اهل بأهل as members of one family, without formality and unceremoniously, informally; انت اهلها you are the right person for it; ما هو اهل للوزارة he is not fit for the office of minister

اهلى *ahlī* domestic, family (adj.); native, resident; indigenous; home, national; tame (animal) | بنك اهلى national bank (*Eg.*); حرب اهلية (*ḥarb*) civil war; محكمة اهلية (*maḥkama*) indigenous court, القضاء الاهلى (*qaḍā'*) jurisdiction of indigenous courts (formerly, *Eg.*; limited to Eg. nationals); فريق اهلى national team (sport); الانتاج الاهلى (*intāj*) domestic production; وقف اهلى (*waqf*) family wakf

اهلية *ahlīya* aptitude, fitness, suitableness, competence; capacity (e.g., for learning); eligibility (for an office, for membership); qualification | اهلية عقلية (*'aqlīya*) mental capacity; الاهلية القانونية legal capacity; اهلية الالتزام capacity for engagement, commitment; ذو اهلية suited, able, fit; capable; qualified; رد الاهلية *radd al-a.* rehabilitation; كامل الاهلية legally competent; عديم الاهلية legally incompetent, under tutelage; فاقد الاهلية unsuited; legally disqualified; نقص الاهلية *naqṣ al-a.* legal incapacity

تأهيل *ta'hīl* qualification; training, education (e.g., for a craft or profession) | تأهيل اكاديمى (*akādīmī*) academic education, qualification for a vocation by virtue of a college diploma; تأهيل مهنى (*mihnī*) vocational training

آهل *āhil* and مأهول *ma'hūl* inhabited, populated (region, place); مأهول (*saud.-ar.*) manned (space craft), provided with a crew | آهل بالسكان (*sukkān*) densely populated (city)

مؤهل *mu'ahhil* pl. *-āt* qualification, certificate of qualification; graduation certificate, diploma (for a course of training) | مؤهل دراسى (*dirāsī*) record of graduation from a school or other educational institution, diploma; مؤهل عال (*'ālin*) qualification by virtue of higher education, university diploma; مؤهل متوسط (*mutawassiṭ*) record of secondary education, secondary school certificate; مؤهلات شخصية (*šaḵṣīya*) personal aptitudes, abilities, qualifications

مؤهل *mu'ahhal* able, capable; qualified (esp. by an education)

متأهل *muta'ahhil* married

مستأهل *musta'hil* worthy, deserving, meriting; entitled

اهليلج *ihlīlaj* myrobalan, emblic (fruit of Phyllanthus emblica L.; *bot.*); ellipse (*geom.*)

اهليلجى *ihlīlajī* elliptic(al)

او *au* or; (with foll. subj.) unless, except that; او ان (*anna*) or it may be that ...

¹(اوب) آب *āba u* (*aub*, اوبة *auba*, اياب *iyāb*) to return; آب ب to catch, contract, suffer, incur s.th., be in for s.th., be left with, get one's share of

من كل اوب *min kulli aubin* from all sides or directions; من كل اوب وصوب (*wa-ṣaubin*) do.

اوبة *auba* return | ذهاب وأوبة (*ḏahāb*) comings and goings (of people)

اياب *iyāb* return | ذهابا وايابا *ḏahāban wa-iyāban* there and back; back and forth, up and down; مقابلة اياب *muqābalat i.* return match (as opposed to مقابلة ذهاب *m. ḏahāb*; sports; *Tun.*)

مآب *ma'āb* place to which one returns; (used as verbal noun:) return | ذهوب ومآب coming and going

آيب *āyib*: هو ذاهب آيب he goes up and down, back and forth

²آب look up alphabetically

اوبرا (It.) *ōbrā* f., pl. اوبرات *ōbirāt* (*eg.*) and اوپرا *ōprā*, *opirā* pl. *-āt* opera; opera house

اوبرج (Fr. *auberge*) *ōberj* restaurant, inn, tavern

اوبريت (Fr.) *ōprēt*, *oberet* (*eg.*) pl. *-āt* operetta

اوبك *ōbek*, اوبيك *ōbēk* OPEC (acronym for Organization of Petroleum Exporting Countries)

اوت (Fr. *août*) *ūt* August (month; *Alg.*, *Tun.*)

اوتوبيس (Fr.) *otobīs* pl. *-āt* autobus, bus

اوتوجراف (Fr.) *otogrāf* pl. *-āt* autograph

اوتوقراطى *otūqrāṭī* autocratic

اوتوماتيكى (Fr.) *otomātīkī* automatic

اوتوموبيل (Fr.) *otōmōbīl* pl. *-āt* automobile

اوتيل (Fr.) *ōtēl* pl. *-āt* hotel

اوج *auj* highest point, acme, pinnacle; culmination, climax; apogee (*astron.*); peak (fig.; of power, of fame)

آح *āḥ* albumen, eggwhite

آحين *āḥīn* albumin ○

اواخى *awāḵīy* (pl. of classical آخية) ties, bonds (e.g., of friendship) | صداقة متينة الاواخى an intimate, firm friendship

(اود) آد *āda* u (*aud*) to bend, flex, curve, crook (ه s.th.); to burden, oppress, weigh down (ه s.o.); — اود *awida* a (*awad*) to bend; to be bent V to bend; to bow

اودة *auda* burden, load

اود *awad:* قام بأوده to provide for s.o.'s needs, provide s.o. with barest subsistence, keep s.o. barely alive; اقام الأود and اقام اوده (*awadahū*) do.

عقدة اوديب *'uqdat udīb* Oedipus complex (*psych.*)

الاوديسة *al-udissa* the Odyssey

اوار *uwār* heat, blaze; thirst

اوراسيا *urāsiyā* Eurasia

اورانوس *uranōs* Uranus (planet)

اوربا *urubbā* Europe

اوربى *urubbī* European

لغة الاوردو *luğat al-urdū* the Urdu language

اوردى *urdī*: الاوردية or اللغة الاوردية the Urdu language

اورشليم *ūrušalīm*[2] Jerusalem

اورطة (= ارطة) *urṭa* pl. ارط *uraṭ* battalion (formerly, *Eg.*; *mil.*)

اورغواى *uruğuwāy* Uruguay

اوركسترا (It.) *orkestrā* m. and f. orchestra | اوركسترا سيمفونية (*simfūnī*), اوركسترا سيمفونى symphony orchestra

اورنيك (Turk. *örnek*) *urnīk* pl. ارانيك *arānīk*[2] sample, specimen; model, pattern; form, blank

اوروبا *urubbā*, اوروپا Europe

اوروبى *urubbī* European

اوروجواى *ūrūguwāy* (Eg. spelling), اوروغواى *ūrūğuwāy* Uruguay

اوز II (*eg.*) to ridicule (على s.o.), make fun of s.o. (على)

اوز *iwazz* (coll.; n. un.) goose, geese

اوزيريس *ūzirīs*[2] Osiris

آس *ās* myrtle; see also alphabetically

اوستراليا *usturāliyā* Australia

اوستريا (It.) *austriyā* Austria

اوسلو Oslo

اوسطى *usṭā* see اسطى

اوشية *ūšīya* pl. اواش *awāšin* prayer, oration (*Copt.-Chr.*)

اوضة (Turk. *oda*) *ōḍa* (*eg.*), *ūḍa* (*syr.*) pl. اوض *uwaḍ* room

اوغندا *uğandā*, اوغندة Uganda (country in E Africa)

آفة *āfa* pl. *-āt* harm, hurt, damage, ruin, bane, evil; epidemic, plague; plant epidemic

مؤوف *ma'ūf* stricken by an epidemic

اوفرول (Engl.) *ovirōl* overalls

اوفسيت *ofsēt* offset (*typ.*)

[1](اوق) آق *āqa* u to bring s.o. (على) bad luck, cause discomfort or hardship (على to) II to burden (ه s.o.) with s.th. unpleasant, troublesome or difficult

[2]اوقة see اقة

[3]اويقات *uwaiqāt* (dimin. of اوقات) short times; good times

[4]مآق see ماق

اوقيانوس, اوقيانس *oqiyānus*, *oqiyānūs* ocean

اوقية *ūqīya* pl. *-āt* ounce, a weight of varying magnitude (Eg.: 37.44 g; Aleppo 320 g; Jerusalem 240 g; Beirut 213.3 g)

اوكازيون (Fr. *occasion*) *okazyōn* clearing sale, special sale

اوكرانيا *ukrāniyā* Ukraine

اوكسجين (Fr.) *oksižēn,* (*eg.*) *uksojīn* oxygen

اوكسيد *uksīd* see اكسيد

(اول) آل *āla u* (*aul,* مآل *ma'āl*) to return, revert (الى to); to go back, be attributed, be attributable (الى to), spring, derive (الى from); to lead, conduce, tend (الى to), result eventually (الى in); to become (الى s.th.), turn, be converted (الى into), be reduced (الى to); to come or go eventually (الى to s.o.), pass into the hands of (الى); to attain (الى or ل to s.th.); to descend, fall (الى to an heir); to devolve (الى upon s.o.), accrue (الى to s.o.); to fall to the lot (الى of s.o.); to vest (الى in s.o.) | آل الامر الى the long and the short of it was that . . .; آل به المطاف الى (*maṭāfu*) he eventually got to the point where . . . **II** to interpret, explain (ه s.th.)

آل *āl* family, relatives, kinsfolk, clan; companions, partisans, people; mirage, fata morgana

آلة *āla* pl. *-āt* instrument, utensil; tool; apparatus; device, implement, appliance; machine | كالآلة mechanically; آلات الحس *ā. al-ḥiss* sensory organs; آلات الانتاج *ā. al-intāj* means of production; آلة بخارية (*bukārīya*) steam engine; آلة الجر *ā. al-jarr* tractor; آلة جهنمية (*jahannamīya*) infernal machine; آلة حربية (*ḥarbīya*) instrument of war; آلة التحريك motor, engine; آلة حاسبة calculating machine; آلة الكترونية (*elektrōnīya*) electronic apparatus; آلة حاسبة الكترونية electronic computer; آلة الحياكة *ā. al-ḥiyāka* power loom; آلة الخياطة sewing machine; آلة راديو radio; آلة رافعة hoisting machine, crane; derrick; pump; آلة راقنة (*alg.*) typewriter; آلة التسخين and آلة مسخنة (*musakkina*) heater; آلة التصوير (photographic) camera; آلة الطباعة printing press; آلة الغسل *ā. al-gasl* washing machine; آلة التفريخ incubator; آلة الاستقبال receiver, receiving set (radio); آلة مقطرة (*muqaṭṭira*) distilling apparatus, still; آلة قهوة *ā. qahwa* coffee maker; آلة الكتابة and آلة كاتبة typewriter; آلة لعب القمار *ā. la'b al-qimār* automatic gambling device; آلة موسيقية (*mūsīqīya*) musical instrument; آلة التنبيه alarm; siren; horn (of an automobile); آلة صماء (*ṣammā'*) (fig.) tool, creature, puppet

آلى *ālī* mechanic(al); mechanized; motorized; instrumental; self-acting (apparatus); automatic; automated (e.g., telephone connections with direct dialing); organic; pl. آليات motorized units | انسان آلى (*insān*) robot, automaton; قارب آلى motorboat; محراث آلى (*miḥrāṯ*) motor plow; القوات الآلية (*quwwāt*) motorized troops; حركة آلية (*ḥaraka*) a mechanical movement

آلية *ālīya* mechanics; automatism; mechanism

آلاتى *ālātī* pl. آلاتية *ālātīya* (*eg.*) musician; singer

اول *awwal*², f. اولى *ūlā*, pl. m. *-ūn*, اوائل *awā'il*², f. اوليات *ūlayāt*, pl. m. and f. اول *uwal*² first; foremost, most important, principal, chief, main; first part, beginning; (with def. article also) earlier, previous, former; see also under ولى | الانسان الاول (*insān*) primitive man; طبيب اول physician-in-chief; اول اكسيد *a. uksīd* monoxide (*chem.*); الاول *al-uwal* (attrib.) the most prominent, the most outstanding (of people); الاولون, الاوائل the forebears, forefathers, ancestors; the ancients (authors, religious authorities, etc., in classical times); الاولون والآخرون (*ākirūn*) the ancients and the moderns; اوائل الشىء the beginnings, the origins of s.th.; اوائل الطلبة *a. aṭ-ṭalaba* the most distinguished or the best of students; المسلمون الاوائل the ancient Muslims, Muslims of the earliest

ايالة *iyāla* pl. *-āt* province; regency

ايلولة *ailūla* see alphabetically

O اويل *uwayyil* pl. *-āt* proton (*phys.*)

مآل *ma'āl* end; outcome, final issue, upshot; result, consequence | فى الحال وفى المآل at present and in the future

تأويل *ta'wīl* pl. *-āt*, تآويل *ta'āwīl*² interpretation, explanation

آيل *āyil*: آيل للسقوط ripe for a fall, about to collapse, ramshackle (house)

اولاء *ulā'i*, اولئك, اولائك *ulā'ika* these; those, pl. of the demonstr. pron. ذا and ذلك

اولمبى *olimbī, ōlimbī*, also اوليمبى Olympic | الالعاب الاولمبية the Olympic games; دورة اوليمبية (*daura*) Olympiad

اولمبياد *olimbiyād* Olympiad

اولو *ulū* (pl. of ذو) owners, possessors, people (with foll.genit.: of) | اولو الأمر *u. l-amr* rulers, powerful leaders; اولو الحل والعقد *u. l-ḥall wa-l-'aqd* (lit.: masters of solving and binding) do.; اولو التحقيق precise, critical people; critical editors; اولو الشأن *u. š-ša'n* the responsible people; see also ذو

¹اوام *uwām* thirst

²اوم ohm (*el.*)

اومباشى *ombāšī* see اونباشى

اومنيبوس *omnībūs* omnibus, bus

¹آن *ān* time; الآن *al-āna* now | فى آن and فى آن واحد at the same time, simultaneously; من آن الى آخر (*ākara*) from time to time; ما بين آن وآخر (*wa-ākara*) and آنا بعد آن sometimes, at times, now and then, once in a while; آنا فآنا gradually, by and by, little by little; آنا — وآونة (*āwinatan*) sometimes — sometimes, at times — at times; قبل الآن *qabla l-āna* before, previously, formerly; للآن *li-l-āna*

times; اوائل *awā'ila* and فى اوائل at the very outset, at the beginning of, in the earliest stages of, e.g., فى اوائل الخمسينات at the beginning of the fifties; اوائل الشهر *a. aš-šahr* the first ten days of a month, beginning of a month; امس الاول *amsi l-awwala*, اول امس *awwala amsi*, اول البارحة day before yesterday; لاول مرة *li-awwali marratin* or للمرة الاولى for the first time; من اوله, من اوائله since its beginnings, from the very beginning; من اوله الى آخره (*ākirihī*) from beginning to end, from A to Z; اول الامر *awwala l-amri* at first, in the beginning; من اول امره (*a. amrihī*) from the very beginning; فى اول النهار at break of day, in the earliest morning; منذ الزمن الاول (*zaman*) since earliest time; الاول فالاول each time the first available; اول ما (*awwala*) the moment when, just when; at the very outset of; اكثر من الاول (*akṯara*) more than before

اولا *awwalan* first, firstly, in the first place; at first, in the beginning | اولا بأول and اولا فأولا by and by, gradually, one after the other, one by one; اولا واخيرا and اولا وآخرا (*ākiran*) first and last, altogether, simply and solely, merely

اولى *awwalī* prime, primary, primordial, original, initial, first; elemental, fundamental, basic, principal, chief, main; elementary; primitive, pristine, primeval; a priori (in compounds) | مدرسة اولية (*madrasa*) elementary school of the old type; مواد اولية (*mawādd*) raw materials; صخور اولية mother rock (*geol.*); مصادر اولية primary sources; عدد اولى (*'adad*) prime number; فاتورة اولية (*fātūra*) pro forma invoice

اولية *awwalīya* pl. *-āt* fundamental truth, axiom; primary constituent, essential component, element; original (of a typewritten letter); precedence; priority

ايل *ayyil, iyyal, uyyal* pl. ايائل *ayā'il*² stag

and حتى الآن *ḥattā l-āna* until now, hitherto, so far; بعد الآن *baʿda l-āna* from now on, henceforth, in the future; من الآن فصاعدا *min al-āna fa-ṣāʿidan* do.

آنى *ānī* timely, present, actual

آنئذ *āna'iḏin* that day, at that time, then

آنذاك *ānaḏāka* that day, at that time, then

اون *aun* calmness, serenity, gentleness

اوان *awān* pl. آونة *āwina* time | قبل اوانه prematurely; فى اوانه at the right time, timely, seasonably, فى غير اوانه at the wrong time, untimely, unseasonably; بين الآونة from time to time; بين الآونة والآخرى (*uḵrā*) and آونة بعد اخرى (*āwinatan, uḵrā*) at times, sometimes; آونة — واخرى sometimes — sometimes, at times — at times; فى الآونة الاخيرة in recent times; فات الاوان (*fāta*) it is too late; آن الاوان (*āna*) the time has come, it is time (ل for, to do s.th.)

ايوان[2] look up alphabetically

اونباشى (Turk. *onbaşı*) *ombāšī* pl. *-īya* corporal (formerly, *Eg.*, *Sudan*; *mil.*)

اونسكو *ūneskō* UNESCO

اونسة *unsa* and اونصة *unṣa* ounce

اونطة (Turk.) *awanṭa* (*eg.*, *syr.*) deceit, swindle

اونطجى *awanṭagī* (*eg.*), *awanṭaži* (*syr.*) pl. *-īya* cheat, swindler, impostor

(اوه) آه *āha u* and **II** to moan, sigh **V** to moan, sigh; to sigh with admiration (ل over), exclaim "ah!"

آه *āh*, آها *āhā*, اوه *awwah*, اواه *uwwāh* (interj.) ah! oh! alas!

آهة *āha* pl. *-āt* sigh, moan; pl. آهات sighs of admiration; rapturous exclamations

تأوه *ta'awwuh* pl. *-āt* moaning, sighing; admiring exclamation; plaintive sound, wail

اوى *awā i* to seek refuge, seek shelter (الى at a place); to go (الى to bed); to betake o.s., repair (الى to a place); to shelter, house, put up, lodge, accommodate, receive as a guest (ـه, ه s.o., s.th.) **II** to shelter, lodge, put up, accommodate, receive as a guest (ه s.o.) **IV** to seek shelter (الى at a place); to retire (الى to a place); to betake o.s., repair (الى to a place); to shelter, house, put up, lodge, accommodate (ه s.o.)

ايواء *īwā'* accommodation, lodging, housing, sheltering

مأوى *ma'wan* pl. مآو *ma'āwin* place of refuge, retreat, shelter; abode; resting place; dwelling, habitation | مأوى ليلى (*lailī*) shelter for the night; doss house; مأوى الأيتام orphanage

ابن آوى *ibn āwā* pl. بنات آوى *banāt ā.* jackal

آية[1] *āya*, coll. آى *āy*, pl. *-āt* sign, token, mark; miracle; wonder, marvel, prodigy; model, exemplar, paragon, masterpiece (فى of, e.g., of organization, etc.); Koranic verse, آى الذكر الحكيم (*āy aḏ-ḏikr*) the verses of the Koran; passage (in a book), utterance, saying, word; آيات (with foll. genit.) most solemn assurances (of love, of gratitude)

اى[2] *ay* that is (to say), i.e.; namely, to wit

اى[3] *ī* yes (with foll. والله yes, indeed! yes, by God!)

اى[4] *ayy*, f. اية *ayya* (with foll. genit. or suffix) which? what? what kind of? whoever, whosoever; any, every, no matter what...; (with neg.) no; ايما *ayyumā* whatever, whatsoever | ايا كان, اية كانت *ayyan kāna, ayyatan kānat* whoever he (or she) is, no matter who he (or she) is; اى من كان *ayyu man kāna* whoever it may be, whosoever; على اى حال (*ayyi ḥālin*) in any case, at any rate, at all events, by all means; اى واحد *ayyu wāḥidin* any one; ان له شأنا اى شأن *inna lahū ša'nan ayya ša'nin* it is of the greatest importance (lit.: it is of importance, and of what importance!); أعجب به ايما اعجاب *u'jiba bihī ayyamā i'jābin* how much he admired him! he admired him greatly; اقبل عليه ايما اقبال *aqbala 'alaihi ayyamā iqbālin* he showed the greatest interest in it

ايا *iyyā* with nominal suffix to express the accusative | اياك ان take care not to ..., be careful not to ...; اياك و, اياك من beware of...! واياك (dial. *wayyāk*), واياه (*wayyāh*) with you, with him

ايار see ²ار

ايبارشية *ībaršīya* pl. *-āt* = ابرشية *abrašīya*, see alphabetically

ايتها *ayyatuhā* see ايها

ايجار *ījār* see under اجر

بحر ايجه *baḥr ījih* the Aegean Sea

ايد II to back, support (ه s.o., ه a claim, an aspiration, etc.); to confirm, corroborate, endorse (ه news, a judgment, etc.) V = pass. of II

ايد *aid* strength

ايد *ayyid* strong

تأييد *ta'yīd* corroboration, confirmation, endorsement, backing, support; assent, sanction, approval (of a parliament, a party or meeting)

مؤيد *mu'ayyid* pl. *-ūn* supporter, helper; adherent, follower (of a politician or party), partisan

ايدروجين (Fr. *hydrogène*) *idrožēn* hydrogen

قنبلة ايدروجينية (*qunbula*) hydrogen bomb

ايديولوجيا *īdiyolōjiyā*, ايديولوجية *īdiyolōjīya* pl. *-āt* ideology

ايديولوجى *īdiyolōjī* ideological

¹ار *air* pl. ايور *uyūr* penis

²ايار *ayyār*² May (*Syr., Leb., Ir., Jord.*)

ايران *īrān*² Iran, Persia

ايرانى *īrānī* Iranian, Persian; (pl. *-ūn*) a Persian, an Iranian

ايرلندا *irlandā, ayirlandā* Ireland

ايرلندى *irlandī, ayirlandī* Irish; (pl. *-ūn*) Irishman

اريال (Engl.) *ēriyāl* aerial, antenna

ايزيس *īzīs* Isis

ايس *ayisa a* (اياس *iyās*) to despair (من of s.th.)

اياس *iyās* despair

ايسلانده *islanda, ayislanda* Iceland

ايشرب (Fr. *écharpe*) sash

(ايض) آض *āḍa i* (ايض *aiḍ*) to return, revert (الى to s.th.); to become (الى s.th.) II to metabolize (*physiol.*)

ايض *aiḍ* metabolism (*physiol.*) | ايض هدمى (*hadmī*) catabolism (*physiol.*)

ايضى *aiḍī* metabolic | امراض ايضية metabolic diseases

ايضا *aiḍan* also, too, as well, likewise, equally; again; in addition, besides, moreover

ايطاليا *īṭāliyā* Italy

ايطالى *īṭālī* Italian; (pl. *-ūn*) an Italian

ايقونة (Gr. εἰκών) *īqūna* and ايقونية *īqūniya* pl. *-āt* icon (*Chr.*)

ايك *aik* (coll.; n. un. ة) thicket, jungle

¹ايل, آيل and ايالة see under اول

ايلول[2] *ailūl*[2] September (*Syr., Leb., Ir., Jord.*)

ايلولة[3] *ailūla* takeover or transfer (of property, an inheritance, profits, power) in possession of another; (*Eg.*) title deed | رسم الايلولة estate tax, inheritance tax; ايلولة الميراث devolution of an inheritance

آم (ايم) *āma i*: آم من زوجته (*zaujatihī*) to lose one's wife, become or be a widower, آمت من زوجها (*zaujihā*) to lose one's husband, become or be a widow

ايمة *aima*, ايوم *uyūm* and تأيم *ta'ayyum* widowhood

ايم *ayyim* pl. ايائم *ayā'im*[2], ايامى *ayāmā* widower, widow

ايوم *aiwam*[2] see يوم

ايم الله and ايمن الله see يمين under يمن

ايام *ayyām* see يوم

ايما *ayyumā* see اى[4] *ayy*

ايماجسم *īmājism* (Engl.) imagism (liter. movement)

(اين)[1] آن *āna i* to come, approach, draw near (time) | آن الاوان (*awān*) the time has come; آن له ان it's time for him to ...

اون see آن

اين *aina* where? (= at or to what place?) | من اين *min aina* where ... from? الى اين where? (= to what place?) اين نحن من how far we still are from ..., worlds separate us from ... (fig.); اين هو منى what a difference there is between us! اين هذا من ذاك what is this compared with that!

الاين *al-ainu* the where; space (*philos.*)

اينما *ainamā* wherever

ايان *ayyāna* when? (conj.) when

اين[2] II to ionize (ه s.th.) V to be ionized (*el.*)

ايون *iyōn, iyūn* and *ayūn* pl. *-āt* ion (*el.*)

تأيين *ta'yīn* ionization

مؤين *mu'ayyan* ionized

متأين *muta'ayyin* ionized

ايه *īhi* (interj. of appeal or incitation) go ahead! come on! let's get going; — *ēh* (interj. of regret or pity) ah! alas!

ايها *ayyuhā*, f. ايتها *ayyatuhā* (vocative part., with article before the foll. noun) O...! يا ايها, f. يا ايتها do.

ايوب *ayyūb*[2] Job | ابو ايوب camel

الايوبيون *al-ayyūbīyūn* the Ayubites

ايوم *aiwam*[2] see يوم

ايون[1] see اين[2]

ايوان[2] *īwān* pl. *-āt* hall with columns, portico; hall or chamber on the ground floor opening through a high arched entrance onto a courtyard; dais opening onto the main room through an arcade (in traditional Arab houses)

ب

ب[1] abbreviation of باب chapter and بعد in ب م *ba'da l-mīlād* after Christ, A.D.

ب[2] *bi* (prep.) in, at, on (place and time); with (indicating connection, association, attendance); with, through, by means of (designating instrumentality or agency, also with pass. = by); for (= at the price of); by (= to the amount of); by (introducing an oath) | بالليل *bi-l-lail* at (by) night, بالنهار *bi-n-nahār* during the daytime, by day; شمالا بشرق *šamālan bi-šarqin* northeast; فبها ونعمت *fa-bihā wa-ni'mat* in that case it's all right; ليس بى ان it is not my intention to ...; هذا بذاك *hāḏā bi-ḏāka* now we are even, we are quits; هذا ب (with foll. price) that costs, amounts to ...; بأبى انت وأمى (*bi-abī, ummī*) you are as dear to me as my own father and mother (formula of veneration); العين بالعين (*'ain*) an eye for an eye; قبل مجيئه بساعة (*majī'ihī*) an hour before his arrival; ب "with" frequently gives causative meaning to a verb, e.g., نهض بشىء (lit.: to rise with s.th., i.e.) to boost, further, promote s.th.; بلغ به الى to cause s.o. to arrive at, lead s.o. to; for its use as copula after negations, etc., see grammar; بلا *bi-lā* without; بما ان *bi-mā anna* in view of the fact that; since, as, inasmuch as, because; بما فيه *bi-mā fīhi* including; فإذا به *fa-iḏā bi-hī* there he beheld before him, there stood before him ... (with foll. n.), see also [1]اذا; بالله *bi-llāhi* and بالله عليك for God's sake, I implore you, I beg of you

باء *bā'* name of the letter ب

بابا *bābā* pl. بابوات *bābawāt*, باباوات pope (also title of the pope and patriarch of the Coptic church); papa, father, daddy | بابا غنوج see under غنج

بابوى *bābawī*, باباوى papal

بابوية *bābawīya* papacy

[1]بأبأ *ba'ba'a* to say "papa" (child); to babble

[2]بؤبؤ *bu'bu'* root, source, origin; core, heart, inmost part; pupil of the eye, also بؤبؤ العين *b. al-'ain*

بابل *bābil*[2] Babel, Babylon

بابلى *bābilī* Babylonian

بابه *bābih* the second month of the Coptic calendar

بابوج *bābūj* pl. بوابيج *bawābīj*[2] slipper

بابور *bābūr* pl. *-āt*, بوابير *bawābīr*[2] (= وابور) locomotive, engine; steamship, steamer

بابونج *bābūnaj* camomile (*bot.*)

باتسته *bātista* batiste

باثولوجى *bāṯōlōjī* pathologic(al)

باثولوجيا *bāṯōlōjiyā* pathology

باذنجان *bāḏinjān* and بيذنجان *baiḏinjān* (coll.; n. un. ة) pl. *-āt* eggplant, aubergine; (*saud.-ar.*) tomatoes, باذنجان اسود (*aswad*) eggplant

[1]بار *bār* pl. *-āt* bar; taproom

[2]بأر *ba'ara a* to dig a well

بئر *bi'r* f., pl. آبار *ābār*, بئار *bi'ār* well, spring; water pit

بؤرة *bu'ra* pl. بؤر *bu'ar* center, seat (fig.); focus (*phys., opt.*); site; pit; abyss

بؤرى *bu'rī* focal (*phys., opt.*) | البعد البؤرى (*bu'd*) focal length (*opt.*)

باراشوت (Fr. *parachute*) *bārāšūt* parachute

باراغواى *bārāğuwāy* Paraguay

بارانويا *baranōyā* paranoia

باربونى see بربونى

بارفان (Fr. *parfum*) *barfān* (*eg.*) perfume

باركيه (Fr.) *barkēh* parquet, parquetry floor

بارناج see برناج

بارة *bāra* pl. *-āt* para (coin)

بارود *bārūd* saltpeter; gunpowder

بارودة *bārūda* pl. بوارىد *bawārīd*[2] rifle, carbine

بارون *bārōn*, *barūn* baron

باريس *bārīs*[2] Paris

باريسى *bārīsī* Parisian

باريوم *bāriyum* barium (*chem.*)

باز *bāz* pl. بيزان *bīzān* and بأز *ba'z* pl. بؤوز *bu'ūz*, بئزان *bi'zān* falcon

بازار *bāzār* pl. *-āt* bazaar

بازلت *bāzalt* basalt

بازوبند *bāzūband* bracelet

بؤس *ba'usa u* (بأس *ba's*) to be strong, brave, intrepid; — بئس *ba'isa a* (بؤس *bu's*) to be miserable, wretched **VI** to feign misery or distress **VIII** to be sad, worried, grieved

بئس الرجل *bi'sa r-rajulu* what an evil man!

بأس *ba's* strength, fortitude, courage, intrepidity (as verbal noun of بؤس *ba'usa*); power, might; harm, hurt, injury, impairment, detriment, wrong | شديد البأس and ذو بأس courageous, brave, intrepid; لا بأس به (*ba'sa*) there is no objection to it; unobjectionable; not bad, rather important, considerable, e.g., كيات لا بأس بها (*kammīyāt*) considerable quantities; لا بأس (*ba'sa*) never mind! it doesn't matter! it's all right! لا بأس ان it doesn't matter that ...; اى بأس؟ *ayyu ba'sin?* what does it matter? what of it? ليس عليه بأس من (*ba'sun*) he will be none the worse for ...; لا بأس عليك (*ba'sa*) it won't do you any harm! don't worry! don't be afraid! لم ير بأسا ب (*yara*) he saw nothing wrong in (doing it)

بنات بئس *banātu bi's* calamities, adversities, misfortunes

بؤس *bu's*, بأساء *ba'sā'*[2], بؤوس *bu'ūs* and بؤسى *bu'sā* pl. ابؤس *ab'us* misery, wretchedness, suffering, distress

بئيس *ba'īs* pl. *-ūn*, بؤساء *bu'asā'*[2] miserable, wretched

بائس *bā'is* miserable, wretched

باسبور (Fr.) *baspōr* pl. *-āt* passport

باستيل (Fr.) *bastēl* pastel

باسيل *bāsīl* bacilli

باش *bāš* senior, chief (in compounds)

باشجاويش *bāščāwīš*, باشجاويش and باش شاويش sergeant major (formerly, *Eg.*, *Sudan*; *mil.*)

باشحكيم *bāšḥakīm* physician-in-chief

باشكاتب *bāškātib* chief clerk

باشمفتى *bāšmuftī* chief mufti (*Tun.*)

باشمفتش *bāšmufattiš* chief inspector

باشمهندس *bāšmuhandis* chief engineer

باشا *bāšā* pl. باشوات *bāšawāt* (باشاوات) pasha

باشوية *bāšawīya* rank of a pasha

باشق *bāšaq*, *bāšiq* pl. بواشق *bawāšiq*[2] sparrow hawk

الباشقرد *al-bāšqird* the Bashkirs

باشكير see بشكير

[1]باص (Engl.) *bāṣ* pl. *-āt* bus, autobus

[2]باص (Fr.) *bāṣ* pl. *-āt* bass, double bass (mus. instrument)

باطون *bāṭūn* concrete, béton

باغة *bāga* celluloid; tortoise shell

باكتيريا see بكتيريا

الباكستان *al-bākistān* and باكستان *bākistān*[2] Pakistan

باكستانى *bākistānī* Pakistani (adj. and n.)

باكو *bākū* pl. باكوات *bākawāt* (*eg.*) packet, small package

[1]بال *bāl* whale (*zool.*)

[2]بالة *bāla* pl. *-āt* bundle, bale

بالرينا *balarīnā* and باللرينا *ballerīnā* ballerina

بالطو *balṭō* pl. بالطوات *balṭowāt,* بلاطى *balāṭī* overcoat; paletot

بالو (It. *ballo*) ball, dance

بالون *balōn* pl. *-āt* balloon

جزر البالیار *juzur al-bāliyār* the Balearic Islands

بالیه (Fr.) *bālēh* ballet

بامیا and بامية *bāmiya* gumbo, okra (Hibiscus esculentus L., *bot.*, a popular vegetable in Egypt)

بان see بون

بانتومیم *bantomīm* pantomime

بانداج (Fr.) *bandāž* bandage

بانطلون *banṭalōn* see بنطلون

بانما see بنما

شاشة بانوراميه *šāša banorāmīya* (= Fr. *écran panoramique*) cinemascope screen

بؤونة *ba'ūna* the tenth month of the Coptic calendar

بای *bāy*, f. باية *bāya* pl. *-āt* formerly, in Tunisia, a title after the names of the members of the Bey's family

دار البای *dār al-bāy* (formerly) the Tunisian government

ببر *babr* pl. ببور *bubūr* tiger

ببغاء *babġā'*[2] (and *babbaġā'*[2]) pl. ببغاوات *babġāwāt* parrot

بت *batta u i* (*batt*) to cut off, sever (ه s.th.); to complete, finish, achieve, accomplish, carry out (ه s.th.); to fix, settle, determine (ه s.th.), decide (ه s.th., فى on s.th.) **II** to adjudge, adjudicate, award (ه s.th.) **VII** to be cut off; to be finished, be done; to be decided | قد انبت الامر بينه وبينهم it's all over between him and them, they are through with each other

بت *batt* settlement, decision; بتا *battan* definitely, once and for all

بتة *batta* pl. *-āt* adjudication, award; final decision; a knocking down (at an auction), sale to the highest bidder (*Tun.*); البتة *al-battata* and بتة *battatan* definitely, positively, decidedly, esp. with negations: absolutely not, definitely not

بتى *battī* definite, definitive

بتية *battīya, bittīya* pl. بتاتى *batātīy* barrel; tub

بتاتا *batātan* decidedly, definitely, positively, categorically, unquestionably, absolutely; لا . . . بتاتا absolutely not, by no means

تبتیت *tabtīt* adjudication, award

بات *bātt* definite, definitive, categorical | منع بات (*man'*) categorical interdiction; رفض بات (*rafḍ*) firm refusal, categorical rejection

مبتوت *mabtūt*: مبتوت الصلة *m. aṣ-ṣila* having no connection (ب with), bearing no relation (ب to)

بتر[1] *batara u* (*batr*) to cut off, sever (ه s.th.); to amputate (ه s.th.); to mutilate, render fragmentarily (ه a text) **VII** to be cut off, be severed, be amputated

بتر *batr* cutting off, severance, separation; amputation

ابتر *abtar*[2] curtailed, docked, clipped, trimmed; imperfect, defective, incomplete; without offspring

بتار *battār* cutting, sharp

باتر *bātir* cutting, sharp

مبتور *mabtūr* broken, abrupt, unconnected; fragmentary, incomplete; mutilated, poorly and incompletely transmitted (text, tradition, account)

²بتراء bitrā'², batrā'² Petra (ancient city of Edomites and Nabataeans; ruins now in SW Jordan)

بترك batrak patriarch

بتروكيماوى bitrokīmāwī petrochemical

بترول bitrōl petroleum

بترولى bitrōlī petroleum- (in compounds) | حقل بترولى (ḥaql) oil field

بترون (Fr. patron) pl. -āt dress pattern (for women's clothing)

ابتع abta'² an assonant intensifier of اجمع ajma'² all, altogether, whole, entire

باتع bāti' strong; full, whole, entire

بتك II to cut off (ه s.th.)

¹بتل batala i u (batl) and II to cut off, sever (ه s.th.); to make final, close, settle, make conclusive, clinch (ه s.th.) V to retire from the world and devote one's life to God (الى الله); to be pious, chaste and self-denying; to live in chastity VII to be cut off, be curtailed, be docked

بتول batūl virgin; البتول the Virgin Mary

بتولى batūlī virginal

بتولية batūlīya virginity

متبتل mutabattil an ascetic, a recluse; a pious, godly man

²بتولا batūlā birch tree

بث baṯṯa u (baṯṯ) to spread, unroll, unfold (ه s.th., e.g., a rug); to scatter, disperse (ه s.th.); to disseminate, propagate, spread (ه s.th., e.g., a spirit, an ideology, a doctrine); to sprinkle (ه ه s.th. on); to let s.o. (ه, also ل) in on s.th. (ه, esp. on a secret); to give vent (to), express (ه feelings, desires); to radiate, send out (ه electr. waves); to transmit (ه s.th. by radio, TV broadcasts, برنامجا barnāmajan a program, pictures by satellite), broadcast (ه s.th., also by loudspeaker) | بث العيون to peer around; بث الالغام to plant, or lay, mines IV to let (ه s.o.) in on a secret (ه) VII to be spread; to be scattered

بث baṯṯ spreading, dissemination, propagation; announcement, expression; broadcast, radio transmission; radiation; grief, sorrow | بث مباشر (mubāšir) live broadcast; بث تلفزيونى (televizyōnī) TV broadcast; بث الأشواق expression of longing or desire; اجهزة البث ajhizat al-b. transmitting sets, transmitters (radio, TV)

بثر baṯara i (baṯira a) and V to break out with pimples or pustules (skin)

بثر baṯr pl. بثور buṯūr (n. un. بثرة baṯra pl. baṯarāt) pimples, pustules

بثر baṯir, بثير baṯīr pustulate, pimpled

بثق baṯaqa i u (baṯq) to open flood gates so that the river will overflow its banks (object: النهر an-nahra) VII to break forth, burst out, well out, pour out, gush out; to emanate, proceed, spring (من or عن from) | انبثق الفجر (fajr) dawn broke

انبثاق inbiṯāq outpouring, effusion, outpour, outburst; emanation

بجح bajiḥa a (bajaḥ) to rejoice (ب at) V to vaunt, flaunt (ب s.th.), boast, brag (ب of)

تبجح tabajjuḥ bragging, braggery

متبجح mutabajjiḥ braggart

بجدة bajda, bujda root, source, heart, essence, basis | بجدة الامر the heart of the matter, the actual state of affairs, the true facts; هو ابن بجدتها (ibn bujdatihā) he knows the job from the ground up, he is the right man for it

بجادى bijādī garnet (min.)

ابجر abjar² obese, corpulent

بجس bajasa u i (bajs) and II to open a passage (for the water), cause (the water)

to flow V and VII to flow freely, pour forth copiously, gush out

بجس *bajs*, بجيس *bajīs* flowing freely, streaming

بجع *baja'* (n. un. ة) pelican

بجل II to honor, revere, venerate, treat with deference (ه s.o.), show respect (ه to s.o.); to give precedence (ه على or ه to s.o. or s.th. over) V to be honored, be revered, be venerated

بجل *bajal* syphilis (*ir.*)

تبجيل *tabjīl* veneration, reverence; deference, respect

مبجل *mubajjal* revered, respected; venerable

بجم *bajama i* (*bajm*, بجوم *bujūm*) to be speechless, dumfounded

بجن II to clinch (ه a nail)

بح *baḥḥa a* (*baḥḥ*, بحح *baḥaḥ*, بحوح *buḥūḥ*, بحاح *baḥāḥ*, بحوحة *buḥūḥa*, بحاحة *baḥāḥa*) to be or become hoarse, be raucous, husky, harsh (voice) II and IV to make hoarse (ه s.o.)

بحة *buḥḥa* hoarseness

ابح *abaḥḥ*[2] hoarse

مبحوح *mabḥūḥ* hoarse

بحبح II *tabaḥbaḥa* to be prosperous, live in easy circumstances; to enjoy o.s., have a good time

بحبوح *baḥbūḥ* gay, merry

بحبوحة *buḥbūḥa* middle; (also بحبوحة العيش *b. al-'aiš*) life of ease and comfort, prosperity, affluence | في بحبوحة من amidst

مبحبح *mubaḥbaḥ* well-to-do, prosperous; enjoying an easy, comfortable life

بحت *baḥt* pure, unmixed, sheer; exclusive, also بحت الامر; بحتا *baḥtan* merely, solely, purely, exclusively, nothing but ...

بحتر *buḥtur* stocky, pudgy, thickset

بحترى *buḥturī* stocky, pudgy, thickset

بحث *baḥata a* (*baḥt*) to look, search (عن for s.th.), seek (عن s.th.); to inquire (ه into s.th.); to do research (في on, in a field); to investigate, examine, study, explore (ه or عن s.th.), look into (ه or عن); to discuss (ه a subject, a question) III to discuss (ه with s.o., في a question) VI to have a discussion, discuss together; to confer, have a talk (مع with s.o., في about)

بحث *baḥt* pl. بحوث *buḥūt*, بحوثات, ابحاث *abḥāt* search (عن for), quest (عن of); examination, study; research; investigation (with genit.: of an incident, etc.), inquiry (into s.th.), examination (of s.th.); exploration; discussion; treatise; (pl. ابحاث) study, scientific report (في on)

بحاث *baḥḥāt* pl. *-ūn* scholar, research worker

بحاثة *baḥḥāta* eminent scholar

مبحث *mabḥat* pl. مباحث *mabāḥit*[2] subject, theme, field of investigation or discussion, object of research; research, study, examination; investigation | المباحث العامة (*'āmma*) national inspection and controls (e.g., of drug traffic); secret police (*Eg.*)

مباحثة *mubāḥata* pl. *-āt* negotiation, parley, conference, talk, discussion

باحث *bāḥit* pl. *-ūn* and بحاث *buḥḥāt* scholar, research worker; examiner, investigator

بحثر *baḥtara* to disperse, scatter (ه s.th.); to waste, squander, dissipate (ه s.th.) II *tabaḥtara* pass. of I

بحترة *baḥtara* waste, dissipation

مبحثر *mubaḥtir* squanderer, wastrel, spendthrift

¹بحر *baḥira a* to be startled, be bewildered (with fright)

²بحر II to travel by sea, make a voyage IV do.; to embark, go on board; to put to sea, set sail, sail, depart (ship); to go downstream, be sea-bound (ship on the Nile) V to penetrate deeply, delve (في into); to study thoroughly (في a subject) X = V

بحر *baḥr* pl. بحار *biḥār*, بحور *buḥūr*, ابحار *abḥār*, ابحر *abḥur* sea; large river; a noble, or great, man (whose magnanimity or knowledge is comparable to the vastness of the sea); meter (*poet.*) | في بحر in the course of, during, في بحر سنتين (*sanatain*) in the course of two years, within two years; البحر الابيض المتوسط (*abyaḍ, mutawassiṭ*) the Mediterranean (sometimes shortened to البحر الابيض); بحر البلطيق *b. al-balṭīq* the Baltic Sea; بحر الجنوب *b. al-janūb* the South Seas; البحر الاحمر the Red Sea (also بحر القلزم *b. al-qulzum*); بحر الخزر *b. al-ḵazar* and بحر قزوين *b. qazwīn*² the Caspian Sea (also البحر الكسبياني); بحر الروم *b. ar-rūm* the Mediterranean; البحر الاسود (*aswad*) the Black Sea; بحر الظلمات *b. aẓ-ẓulumāt* the Atlantic; بحر لوط *b. lūṭ* and البحر الميت (*mayyit*) the Dead Sea; بحر النيل (*eg.*) the Nile; بحر الهند *b. al-hind* the Indian Ocean

البحرين *al-baḥrain* the Bahrein Islands; (State of) Bahrain

بحرانى *baḥrānī* of the Bahrein Islands; البحارنة *al-baḥārina* the inhabitants of the Bahrein Islands

بحرى *baḥrī* sea (adj.), marine; maritime; nautical; naval; navigational; (in Eg.) northern, *baḥrīya* (with foll. genit.) north of; (pl. *-ūn*, ة) sailor, seaman, mariner; (after a military rank) on active duty in the navy | بحرى ماهر approx.: seaman apprentice (*Eg.*); الصيد البحرى (*ṣaid*) deep-sea fishing; القوات البحرية (*quwwāt*) the naval forces; كابل بحرى (*kābil*) ocean cable; نباتات بحرية (*nabātāt*) marine flora, water plants; نقيب بحرى captain in the navy (*mil.*)

بحرية *baḥrīya* marine; navy | طالب بحرية naval cadet

بحرة *baḥra* pond, pool

بحار *baḥḥār* pl. *-ūn*, بحارة *baḥḥāra* seaman, mariner, sailor; pl. بحارة crew (of a ship, of an airplane)

بحيرة *buḥaira* pl. *-āt*, بحائر *baḥā'ir*² lake; (*tun.*) vegetable garden, truck garden

بحران *buḥrān* crisis (of an illness); climax, culmination (also, e.g., of ecstasy)

ابحار *ibḥār* navigation, seafaring

تبحر *tabaḥḥur* deep penetration, delving (في into a subject), thorough study (في of)

متبحر *mutabaḥḥir* thoroughly familiar (في with); profound, erudite, searching, penetrating

بحش *baḥaša a* (*syr.*) to dig

بحلق *baḥlaqa*: بحلق عينيه (*'ainaihi*) to stare, gaze (في at)

¹بخ بخ *baḵ baḵ* excellent! well done! bravo!

²بخ *baḵḵa u* (*baḵḵ*) to snore; to spout, spurt, squirt (ه s.th.); to sprinkle, splatter (ه ب s.th. with)

بخاخة *baḵḵāḵa* nozzle

بخيخة (*eg.*) *buḵḵēḵa* squirt, syringe

مبخة *mibaḵḵa* nozzle

بخت *baḵt* luck; a kind of lottery | قليل البخت unlucky; سوء البخت bad luck

بخيت *baḵīt* lucky, fortunate

مبخوت *mabḵūt* lucky, fortunate

بختر II *tabaḵtara* to strut, prance, swagger

تبختر *tabaḵtur* strutting gait

بخر II to vaporize, evaporate (ه s.th.); to fumigate (ه s.th.); to disinfect (ه s.th.); to perfume with incense, expose to aromatic smoke (ه s.th.) V to evaporate (water); to volatilize, turn into smoke or haze; to perfume o.s., or be perfumed, with incense

بخار *bukār* pl. *-āt*, ابخرة *abkira* vapor, fume; steam | بخار الماء water vapor

بخاری *bukārī* steam (adj.), steam-driven | حمام بخاری (*ḥammām*) steam bath; عجلة بخارية (*'ajala*) motorcycle

بخور *bakūr* incense; frankincense | بخور مريم *b. maryam* cyclamen (*bot.*)

ابخر *abkar*[2] suffering from halitosis

مبخرة *mibkara* pl. مباخر *mabākir*[2] (also *-āt*) censer; thurible; fumigator

تبخير *tabkīr* fumigation

تبخر *tabakkur* evaporation, vaporization

باخرة *bākira* pl. بواخر *bawākir*[2] steamer, steamship

بويخرة *buwaikira* small steamboat

بخس *bakasa a* (*baks*) to decrease, diminish, reduce (ه s.th.); to lessen (e.g., قيمته *qīmatahū* the value of s.th.); to disregard, neglect, fail to heed (ه s.th.)

بخس *baks* too little, too low; very low (price)

ابخس *abkas*[2] smaller; lower (price)

باخس *bākis* small, little, trifling, unimportant

بخشيش *bakšīš* pl. بخاشيش *bakāšīš*[2] tip, gratuity

بخع *baka'a a* (*bak'*) with نفسه: to kill o.s. (with grief, anger, rage)

ابخق *abkaq*[2], f. بخقاء *bakqā'*[2] one-eyed

بخل *bakila a* (*bakal*), *bakula u* (*bukl*) to be niggardly, be stingy (ب with s.th., عن or على with regard to s.o.), scrimp (عن, على s.o., ب for), stint (ب in, عن or على s.o.), withhold (عن, على from s.o., ب s.th.) VI to give reluctantly, grudgingly (عن, على to s.o., ب s.th.)

بخل *bukl* avarice, cupidity, greed

بخيل *bakīl* pl. بخلاء *bukalā'*[2] avaricious, greedy; miser, skinflint

مبخلة *mabkala* cause of avarice, that which arouses avarice or greed

بخنق *buknuq* pl. بخانق *bakāniq*[2] kerchief, veil (to cover the head)

بد *badda u* (*badd*) to distribute, spread, disperse II to divide, distribute, spread, scatter, disperse (ه s.th.); to remove, eliminate (ه s.th.); to waste, squander, fritter away, dissipate (ه s.th.) V pass. of II; X to be independent, proceed independently (ب in, e.g., in one's opinion, i.e., to be opinionated, obstinate, headstrong); to possess alone, monopolize (ب s.th.); to take possession (ب of s.o.), seize, grip, overwhelm, overcome (ب s.o.; said of a feeling, of an impulse); to dispose arbitrarily, highhandedly (ب of s.th.); to rule despotically, tyrannically, autocratically (ب over)

بد *budd* way out, escape | اذا لم يكن بد من ان (*buddun*) if it is inevitable that ...; لا بد (*budda*) definitely, certainly, inevitably, without fail; by all means; لا بد من it is necessary, inescapable, unavoidable, inevitable, لا بد له منه he simply must do it, he can't get around it; من كل بد *min kulli buddin* in any case, at any rate

اباديد *abādīd*[2] (pl.) scattered

تبديد *tabdīd* scattering, dispersal, dispersion; removal, elimination; waste, dissipation

استبداد *istibdād* arbitrariness, highhandedness; despotism; autocracy; absolutism

استبدادى *istibdādī* arbitrary, highhanded, autocratic, despotic; authoritarian; استبداديات *istibdādīyāt* arbitrary acts

استبدادية *istibdādīya* autocracy; authoritarianism

مبدد *mubaddid* scatterer, disperser; squanderer, wastrel, spendthrift

مستبد *mustabidd* arbitrary, highhanded, autocratic, tyrannical, despotic; autocrat, tyrant, despot | مستبد برأيه (*bi-ra'yihī*) opinionated, obstinate, headstrong; ملكية مستبدة (*malakīya*) absolute monarchy

بدأ **bada'a** *a* (بدء *bad'*) to begin, start (ب or فى with s.th., ه s.th.; ه with s.o.; with foll. imperf.: to do s.th. or doing s.th. respectively); to set in, begin, start, arise, spring up, crop up **II** to put (ه s.th., على before s.th. else), give precedence or priority (ه to s.th., على over s.th. else) **III** to begin, start (ب s.th., ه with regard to s.o.), make the first step, take the initiative or lead (ب in s.th., ه toward s.o.), e.g., باداه بالكلام (*kalām*) to accost s.o., speak first to s.o. **IV** to do or produce first (ه s.th.), bring out (ه s.th. new) | ما يبدئ وما يعيد *mā yubdi'u wa-mā yu'īdu* he can't think of a blessed thing to say; يبدئ ويعيد he says or does everything conceivable **VIII** to begin, start (ب with s.th.)

بدء *bad'* beginning, start | منذ البدء from the (very) beginning; فعله عودا وبدءا (*'audan wa-bad'an*) or عوده على بدئه (*'audahū 'alā bad'ihī*) or عودا الى بدء (*ilā bad'in*) he did it all over again, he began anew

بدأة *bad'a* and بديئة *badī'a* beginning, start

بداءة *badā'a* and □ بداية *bidāya* pl. *-āt* beginning, start; first step, first instance | بداءة بدء *badā'ata bad'in* right at the outset, at the very beginning; فى بداية الامر in the beginning, at first

بدائى *badā'ī* initial, original; (also *budā'ī*) primitive; البدائيون the primitives | مرحلة بدائية (*marḥala*) initial stage

بدائية *badā'īya, budā'īya* primitiveness

مبدأ *mabda'* pl. مبادئ *mabādi'*[2] beginning, start, starting point; basis, foundation; principle; invention; pl. principles, convictions (of a person); ideology; rudiments, fundamental concepts, elements | كتب المبادئ *kutub al-m.* elementary books

مبدئى *mabda'ī* original, initial; fundamental, basic; مبدئيا *mabda'īyan* originally; in principle

ابتداء *ibtidā'* beginning, start; novitiate (*Chr.*) | ابتداء من *ibtidā'an min* from, beginning ..., as of (with foll. date)

ابتدائى *ibtidā'ī* initial; preparatory, elementary, primary; of first instance (*jur.*); original, primitive | محكمة ابتدائية (*maḥkama*) court of first instance; التعليم الابتدائى elementary education; مدرسة ابتدائية (*madrasa*) primary school; شهادة ابتدائية (*šahāda*) certificate of elementary school completion

بادئ *bādi'* beginning, starting | بادئ الامر *bādi'a l-amr* and فى بادئ الامر in the beginning, at first; بادئ الرأى *bādi'a r-ra'yi* and فى بادئ الرأى beginning with the very first impression, right away, at once, (i.e., without closer consideration or reflection); بادئ ذى بدء *bādi'a ḏī bad'in* right at the outset, at the very beginning; at first, in the beginning; primarily; البادئ ذكره *al-bādi'u ḏikruhū* (the person or thing) mentioned at the outset, the first-mentioned

مبتدئ *mubtadi'* beginning; (pl. *-ūn*) beginner; novice (*Chr.*); neophyte

مبتدئة *mubtadi'a* pl. *-āt* beginner (fem.)

بدر[1] **badara** *u* (بدور *budūr*) to come suddenly (ه to, over s.o.), come unexpectedly, by surprise; to escape (من s.o.; e.g., words in excitement); to occur or be executed spontaneously (من by s.o., movement) **III** to come to s.o.'s (ه) mind, occur to s.o. (ه) all of a sudden, strike s.o. (idea, notion); to embark, enter (الى upon s.th.) or set out (الى to do s.th.) without delay; to rush, hurry (الى to s.o., to a place); to hurry up (ب with s.th.); بادر الى with foll. verbal noun: to do s.th. promptly, without delay, hasten to do s.th.; to fall upon s.o. (ه) with (ب), accost, assail, surprise (ه ب s.o. with s.th.; e.g., بادره بكلام غليظ to snap rudely at s.o.); to take advantage unhesitatingly (ه of chances); to react, respond (الى to s.th.) | بادر الى انجاز الوعد (*injāzi l-wa'd*) to set out to fulfill a promise **VI** تبادر الى الذهن (*dihn*) to suggest itself strongly, be obvious; to appear at first glance as if (أن); تبادر الى ذهنى أن (*dihnī*) it occurred to me all of a sudden that ...; تبادر الى الفهم (*fahm*) to be immediately understood **VIII** to hurry, rush, hasten (ه to); to get ahead of s.o. (ه), anticipate, forestall (ه s.o.) | ابتدرها قائلا before she could say a word he exclaimed ...

بدر *badr* pl. بدور *budūr* full moon

بدرة *badra* pl. *badarāt*, بدار *bidār* huge amount of money (formerly = 10,000 dirhams) | بدرات الاموال enormous sums of money

بدار *badāri* hurry! quick!

مبادرة *mubādara* pl. *-āt* spontaneous undertaking, unexpected action; sudden inspiration, impulse, idea; initiative

بادرة *bādira* pl. بوادر *bawādir*² herald, harbinger, first indication, sign; unforeseen act; stirring, impulse, fit (e.g., of rage); inconsiderate remark or act, slip, lapse; spontaneous idea | بادرة خير *b. kairin* a good, or generous, impulse

بيدر² *baidar* pl. بيادر *bayādir*² threshing floor

بدروم and بدرون (Turk. *bodrum*) *badrūm*, *badrūn* pl. *-āt* basement

بدع *bada'a a* (*bad'*) to introduce, originate, start, do for the first time (ه s.th.), be the first to do s.th. (ه); to devise, contrive, invent (ه s.th.) **II** to accuse of heresy (ه s.o.); to excel (فى in) **IV** = **I**; to create (ه s.th.); to achieve unique, excellent results (فى in); to be amazing, outstanding (فى in s.th.) **VIII** to invent, contrive, devise, think up (ه s.th.); to introduce s.th. new; to advocate innovations, newfangled, heretical doctrines (*relig.*) **X** to regard as novel, as unprecedented (ه s.th.)

بدع *bad'* innovation, novelty; creation | بدعا وعودا *bad'an wa-'audan* repeatedly

بدع *bid'* pl. ابداع *abdā'* innovator; new, original; unprecedented, novel | لا بدع *lā bid'a* no wonder! لا بدع ان *lā bid'a an* no wonder that ...; بدع من s.th. else than; unlike, different from

بدعة *bid'a* pl. بدع *bida'* innovation, novelty; heretical doctrine, heresy; pl. creations (of fashion, of art) | اهل البدع *ahl al-b.* heretics

بديع *badī'* pl. بدع *bud'* unprecedented, marvelous, wonderful, amazing, admirable, singular, unique; uncommon, original (style); — creator | علم البديع *'ilm al-b.* branch of Arabic rhetoric, dealing with figures of speech and (in general) the art of beautiful style

بديعة *badī'a* pl. بدائع *badā'i'*² an astonishing, amazing thing, a marvel, a wonder; original creation

بديعى *badī'ī* rhetorically excellent, of high stylistic value

ابدع *abda'*² more amazing, more exceptional; of even greater originality

ابداع *ibdā'* creation, fashioning, shaping; a marvelous, unique achievement; uniqueness, singularity, originality; creative ability

○ ابداعى *ibdā'ī* romantic

○ ابداعية *ibdā'īya* romanticism

ابتداع *ibtidā'* new creation, innovation; introduction of new, heretical doctrines

○ ابتداعية *ibtidā'īya* romanticism

مبدع *mubdi'* producing, creating; creative; creator; exceptional, unique, outstanding (in an achievement, esp. of an artist); pl. مبدعون creative personalities, great artists

مبتدع *mubtadi'* innovator; creator; heretic

بيدق look up alphabetically

بدل *badala u* (*badl*) to replace (ه ب s.th. by), exchange (ه ب s.th. for) **II** to change, alter (ه ه s.th. to), convert (ه ه s.th. into); to substitute (ه for s.th., ب or من s.th.), exchange, give in exchange (ه s.th., ب or من for); to change (ه e.g., one's clothes, one's occupation); to shift (ه gears of a car); to make a change, introduce a modification **III** to exchange (ه ه with s.o. s.th.) **IV** to replace (ه ب s.th. by), exchange (ه ب for s.th. s.th. else); to compensate (ه ب ه s.o. for s.th. with s.th. else), give s.o. (ه) s.th. (ه) in exchange for (ب) **V** to change; to be exchanged **VI** to exchange (ه s.th., also words, views, greetings); to alternate with each other, take turns (ه doing s.th.) **X** to exchange, receive in exchange, trade, barter (ه ب and ه ب s.th. for); to replace (ه ب and ه ب s.th. by), substitute (ه ب and ه ب for s.th. s.th. else)

بدل *badal* pl. *-āt*, ابدال *abdāl* substitute, alternate, replacement; equivalent, compensation, setoff; reimbursement, recompense, allowance; price, rate; (*gram.*) appositional substantive standing for another substantive | بدل الجراية *b. al-jirāya* allowance for food; بدل السفرية *b. as-safarīya* travel allowance; بدل سكن *b. sakan* extra allowance for housing; بدل الاشتراك subscription rate; بدل غربة *b. ġurba* separation pay (as an increment to salary); بدل التمثيل expense account, expense allowance

بدل *badala* (prep.) instead of, in place of, in lieu of

بدلا من *badalan min* in place of, instead of, in lieu of

بدلة *badla* pl. *badalāt*, بدل *bidal* suit (of clothes); costume | بدلة الحمام *b. al-ḥammām* bathing suit; بدلة تدريب training suit, sweat suit; بدلة رسمية (*rasmīya*) uniform; بدلة السهرة *b. as-sahra* dress suit, evening dress; بدلة تشريفاتية (*tašrīfātīya*) full-dress uniform; بدلة الفضاء *b. al-faḍā'* space suit; بدلة الورشة *b. al-warša* overalls, coveralls

بدلية *badalīya* compensation, smart money

بدال *badāla* (prep.) instead of, بدال ما (conj.) instead of (being, doing, etc.)

بديل *badīl* pl. بدلاء *budalā'*[2], بدائل *badā'il*[2] substitute, alternate (عن or من, also ل for); stand-in, double (*theat.*); (f. ة) serving as a replacement or substitute | مفرزة بديلة (*mafraza*) reserve detachment (*mil.*)

بدال *baddāl* grocer; money-changer; — (pl. *-āt*) pedal (auto, bicycle) | بدال السرعة *b. as-sur'a* gas pedal, accelerator (auto)

بدالة *baddāla* culvert; pipeline; telephone exchange, central

□ مبادل *mabādil*[2] see بذل

تبديل *tabdīl* change, alteration; replacement (of s.th., ب by s.th. else)

مبادلة *mubādala* pl. *-āt* exchange | مبادلات تجارية (*tijārīya*) commercial exchange, trade relations

ابدال *ibdāl* exchange, interchange, replacement (ب by), substitution (ب of); change; phonetic change

تبدل *tabaddul* change, shift, turn; transformation; transmutation, conversion

تبادل *tabādul* (mutual) exchange | تبادل الاسرى *t. al-asrā* exchange of prisoners; تبادل ثقافى وتجارى (*taqāfī, tijārī*) cultural and commercial exchange; تبادل اطلاق النيران *t. iṭlāq an-nīrān* exchange of shots; تبادل السلام *t. as-salām* exchange of greetings; تبادل الخبرات *t. al-ḵibarāt* exchange of experiences; تبادل الخواطر thought transference, telepathy

استبدال *istibdāl* exchange, replacement, substitution

مبدل *mubdil*: مبدل الاسطوانات *m. al-usṭuwānāt* automatic record changer

متبادل *mutabādal* mutual, reciprocal

مستبدل *mustabdal*: لاعب مستبدل reserve player (sports)

بدن *baduna u* and *badana u* (*budn*) to be fat, corpulent

بدن *badan* pl. ابدان *abdān*, ابدن *abdun* body, trunk, torso

بدنى *badanī* bodily, corporal, physical, somatic

بدانة *badāna* corpulence, obesity

بدين *badīn* pl. بدن *budun* stout, corpulent, fat, obese; pyknic (type)

بدونة *budūna* corpulence, obesity

بادن *bādin* pl. بدن *budn* stout, corpulent, fat, obese

بده *badaha a* to come, descend suddenly (ه upon s.o.), befall unexpectedly (ه s.o.); to surprise (ه s.o.) with s.th. (ب) III to appear suddenly, unexpectedly (ه ب before s.o. with s.th.) VIII to extemporize, improvise, do offhand, on the spur of the moment (ه s.th.)

بداهة *badāha* spontaneity, spontaneous occurrence, impulse; simple, natural way, naturalness, matter-of-factness; بداهة *badāhatan* and بالبداهة all by itself, spontaneously

بديهة *badīha* s.th. sudden or unexpected; improvisation; impulse, inspiration, spontaneous intuition; intuitive understanding or insight, empathy, instinctive grasp, perceptive faculty | على البديهة all by itself, spontaneously; offhand; حاضر البديهة quick-witted, quick at repartee; بديهة حاضرة presence of mind

بديهى *badīhī* and بدهى *badahī* intuitive; self-evident; a priori (adj.) | من البديهى ان and من البدهى ان it is immediately apparent, obvious, goes without saying that ...

بديهية *badīhīya* pl. *-āt* an axiom, a fundamental or self-evident truth; truism, commonplace, platitude

بدائه *badā'ih*[2] fundamental or self-evident truths

(بدو) بدا *badā u* to appear, show, become evident, clear, plain or manifest, come to light; to be obvious; to seem good, acceptable, proper (ل to s.o.) | بدا عليه انه one could see that he ... III to show, display, evince, manifest, reveal, declare openly | بادى بالعداوة (*'adāwa*) to show open hostility IV to disclose, reveal, manifest, show, display, evince (ه s th.); to demonstrate, bring out, bring to light, make visible (ه s.th.); to express, utter, voice (ه s.th.) | ابدى رأيه فى (*ra'yahū*) to express one's opinion about; ابدى رغبة (*raġbatan*) to express a wish or desire V = I; to live in the desert VI to pose as a Bedouin

بدو *badw* desert; nomads; Bedouins

بدوى *badawī* Bedouin, nomadic; rural (as distinguished from urban); a Bedouin

بدوية *badawīya* pl. *-āt* Bedouin woman, Bedouin girl

بداة *badāh* pl. بدوات *badawāt* whim, caprice; ill-humor

بداوة *badāwa* and *bidāwa* desert life, Bedouin life; Bedouinism, nomadism

بيداء *baidā'*[2] desert, steppe, wilderness, wild

ابداء *ibdā'* expression, manifestation, declaration

باد *bādin* apparent, evident, obvious, plain, visible; inhabiting the desert; pl. بداة *budāh* Bedouins

بادية *bādiya* desert, semidesert, steppe; peasantry; (pl. بواد *bawādin*) nomads, Bedouins

بداية *bidāya* = بداءة

بديكير (Fr. *pédicure*) *bedikēr* (*eg.*) pedicure

بذ *badda u* (*badd*) to get the better of (ه), beat, surpass (ه s.o.)

بذ *badd* and باذ *bādd* slovenly, untidy, shabby, filthy, squalid

بذاذة *badāda* slovenliness, untidiness, shabbiness, dirtiness, filth

بذأ *bada'a a* to revile, abuse (على s.o.), rail (على at s.o.); — بذئ *badi'a a*, بذؤ *badu'a u* to be obscene, bawdy

بذىء *badī'* disgusting, loathsome, nauseous, foul, dirty, obscene, bawdy, ribald

بذاء *badā'* and بذاءة *badā'a* obscenity, ribaldry, foulness (of language); disgust, loathing, aversion, contempt

بذخ *badaka a* to be haughty, proud

بذخ *badak* luxury, pomp, splendor; haughtiness, pride

باذخ *bādik* pl. بواذخ *bawādik*[2] high, lofty; proud, haughty

بذر *badara u* (*badr*) to sow, disseminate (ه s.th., seed, also fig. = to spread) **II** to waste, squander, dissipate (ه s.th.)

بذر *badr* spread, propagation (of a trend or ideology); — (pl. بذور *budūr*, بذار *bidār*) seeds, seed; seedling; pl. بذور pips, pits, stones (of fruit)

بذرة *badra* (n. un.) a seed, a grain; pip, pit, stone (of fruit); germ; (fig.) germ cell (of a development, and the like)

بذار *bidār* seedtime

تبذير *tabdīr* waste, squandering, dissipation

مبذر *mubaddir* pl. *-ūn* squanderer, wastrel, spendthrift

بيذق look up alphabetically

بذل *badala i u* (*badl*) to give or spend freely, generously (ه s.th.); to sacrifice (ه s.th.); to expend (ه s.th.); to offer, grant (ه s.th.) | بذل جهده (*jahdahū*) to take pains; بذل مجهودا do.; بذل كل مساعدة (*kulla musā'adatin*) to grant every assistance; بذل المساعى to make efforts; بذل الطاعة ل to obey s.o., defer to s.o.; بذل كل غال (*kulla ġālin*) and بذل الغالى والرخيص فى سبيل to spare no effort, go to any length, give everything, pay any price for or in order to; بذل ماء وجهه (*mā'a wajhihī*) to sacrifice one's honor; بذل نفسه دون فلان (or عن فلان) to sacrifice o.s. for s.o.; بذل وسعه (*wus'ahū*) to do one's utmost, do one's best **V** to fritter away one's fortune, be overgenerous; not to spare o.s.; to give o.s. over (e.g., to some low work or activity, to s.th. vulgar or common); to prostitute o.s. (woman); to display common, vulgar manners **VIII** to wear out in common service, make trite, vulgar, commonplace, to hackney (ه s.th.); to abuse (ه s.th.); to express o.s. in a vulgar manner, use vulgar language; ابتذل نفسه to degrade o.s., demean o.s., sacrifice one's dignity

بذل *badl* giving, spending; sacrifice, surrender, abandonment; expenditure; offering, granting; (also عملية بذل *'amalī-*

yat b.) puncture, tapping (*med.*) | بذل الذات self-sacrifice

بذلة *badla* suit (of clothes)

مبذل *mibdal* pl. مباذل *mabādil*² slipper; pl. مباذل casual clothing worn around home | فلان فى مباذله so-and-so in his private life

ابتذال *ibtidāl* triteness, commonness, commonplaceness; banality; debasement, degradation

باذل *bādil* spender

متبذل *mutabaddil* unstintingly involved; completely dedicated (to a job); vulgar, common

مبتذل *mubtadal* trite, hackneyed, banal, common, vulgar; everyday, commonplace (adj.)

¹بر *barra* (1st pers. perf. *barirtu, barartu*) *a i* (*birr*) to be reverent, dutiful, devoted; to be kind (ه or ب to s.o.); to be charitable, beneficent, do good (ب to s.o.); to give out of charity (ب ه to s.o. s.th.); to obey (ه s.o., esp. God); to treat with reverence, to honor (ب or ه the parents); to be honest, truthful; to be true, valid (sworn statement); to keep (ب a promise, an oath) **II** to warrant, justify, vindicate; to acquit, absolve, exonerate, exculpate, clear (ه, ه s.o., s.th.) | برر وجهه ب (*wajhahū*) to justify o.s. by; لا يبرر (*yubarraru*) unjustifiable **IV** to carry out, fulfill (ه s.th., a promise, an oath) **V** to justify o.s.; to be justified

بر *birr* reverence, piety; righteousness, probity; godliness, devoutness; kindness; charitable gift; charity | البر بالوالدين (*wālidain*) filial piety

بر *barr* and بار *bārr* pl. ابرار *abrār* and بررة *barara* reverent, dutiful (ب toward), devoted (ب to); pious, godly, upright, righteous; kind

مبرة *mabarra* pl. *-āt* and مبار *mabārr*² good deed, act of charity, benefaction; philanthropic organization; charitable institution, home or hospital set up with private funds

تبرير *tabrīr* pl. *-āt* justification, vindication; palliation, extenuation; pl. تبريرات pleas, excuses, pretexts (for vindication)

تبريرى *tabrīrī* justifying, vindicating; exonerating, extenuating

بار *bārr* reverent, faithful and devoted; see also under بر *barr* above

مبرور *mabrūr* (accepted into the grace of the Lord, i.e.) blessed (said of a deceased person)

مبرر *mubarrir* pl. *-āt* justification; excuse | لا مبرر له (*mubarrira*) unjustifiable

²بر *barr* land (as opposed to sea), terra firma, mainland; open country; برا *barran* out, outside | برا وبحرا *barran wa-baḥran* by land and sea

برى *barrī* pertaining to, or located on, the mainland; land (in compounds, as opposed to بحرى *baḥrī*); rural, belonging to open country; wild (of plants and animals) | سيارة برية مائية (*sayyāra, mā'īya*) amphibious vehicle; علامة برية (*'alāma*) landmark

برية *barrīya* pl. برارى *barārīy* open country; steppe, desert; see also ¹برأ

برانى *barrānī* outside, outer, exterior, external; foreign, alien

³بر *burr* wheat

¹برأ *bara'a a* (برء *bar'*) to create (ه s.th., said of God)

برء *bar'* creation

برية *barīya* pl. *-āt*, برايا *barāyā* creation (= that which is created); creature; see also ²بر

البارئ *al-bāri'* the Creator (God)

برئ **bari'a** *a* (براءة *barā'a*) to be or become free, be cleared (من from, esp. from guilt, blame, etc., الى toward s.o.); to recover (من from an illness) **II** to free, clear, acquit, absolve, exculpate (ه s.o., من from suspicion, blame, guilt) | برأ ساحة الرجل (*sāḥata r-rajul*) he acquitted the man **IV** to acquit, absolve, discharge, exculpate (ه s.o.); to cause to recover, cure, heal (ه s.o.) | ابرأ ذمته (*dimmatahū*) to clear s.o. or o.s. from guilt, exonerate s.o. or o.s.; to release s.o. from a charge **V** to clear o.s. (من from suspicion, from a charge), free o.s. (من from responsibility, etc.), rid o.s. (من of); to disclaim association (من with s.o.); to declare o.s. innocent, wash one's hands (من of); to be acquitted **X** to restore to health, cure, heal (ه s.o.); to free o.s. (من from), rid o.s. (من of)

برء *bur'* and بروء *burū'* convalescence, recovery

بريء *barī'* pl. ابرياء *abriyā'*[2], براء *burā'*, *birā'* free, exempt (من from), devoid (من of); guiltless, innocent; guileless; harmless, innocuous; recovered, restored to health; sound

براء *barā'* (also for f. and pl.) free, exempt (من from); innocent, guiltless (من of s.th.) | ذمته براء من (*dimmatuhū*) he is innocent of . . .

براءة *barā'a* being free; disavowal, withdrawal; innocence, guiltlessness; naiveté, guilelessness, artlessness; (pl. *-āt*) license, diploma, patent | براءة اختراع patent on an invention; براءة التنفيذ exequatur (a written authorization of a consular officer, issued by the government to which he is accredited); براءة الثقة *b. aṯ-ṯiqa* (*Tun.*) credentials (*dipl.*); براءة الذمة *b. ad-dimma* certification of clean slate; exoneration; exculpation; unspotted or cleared record; release from a legal obligation; على براءة harmless; without guilt, innocent

تبرئة *tabri'a* freeing, exemption; acquittal, absolution, discharge, exoneration

مباراة *mubāra'a* mubarat, divorce by mutual consent of husband and wife, either of them waiving all claims by way of compensation (*Isl. Law*)

ابراء *ibrā'* acquittal, absolution, release; release of a debtor from his liabilities, remission of debt (*Isl. Law*) | ابراء ذمته *i. dimmatihī* exoneration of s.o., discharge

استبراء *istibrā'*: استبراء الحمل *ist. al-ḥamal* the ceremony of selecting and purifying the Host before Mass (*Copt.-Chr.*)

براجواى (Eg. spelling) *baraguwāy* Paraguay

البرازيل *al-barāzīl* (m.) Brazil

برازيلى *barāzīlī* Brazilian (adj. and n.)

براسيرى (Fr. *brasserie*) *brāserī* beer parlor, taproom

براغ Prague

برافان (Fr. *paravent*) *baravān* folding screen

براهما *bərahmā, barahmā* Brahma

بربة *birba* and بربى *birbā* pl. برابى *barābī* ancient Egyptian temple, temple ruins dating back to ancient Egypt (*eg.*); labyrinth, maze

بربخ *barbak̠* pl. برابخ *barābik̠*[2] water pipe, drain, culvert, sewer pipe

بربر *barbara* to babble noisily (e.g., a large crowd), jabber, mutter, prattle

البربر *al-barbar* the Berbers

بربرى *barbarī* Berber (adj.); barbaric, uncivilized; — (pl. برابرة *barābira*) a Berber; a barbarian; البربرية the Berber language

بربرية *barbarīya* barbar(ian)ism, barbarity, savagery, cruelty

متبربر *mutabarbir* barbaric, uncivilized

بربيس look up alphabetically

[1]بربوش *barbūš* (*alg.*) coarse couscous

[2]بربيش *barbīš* (*syr.*) tube (of a narghile, of an enema, etc.)

بربط *barbaṭa* to splash, paddle, dabble (in water)

بربونى (It. *barbone*) *barbūnī*, also بربون red mullet (Mullus barbatus; *zool.*)

بربى see بربة

بربيس *barbīs* barbel (*zool.*)

البرتغال *al-burtuğāl* (m.) Portugal

برتغالى *burtuğālī* Portuguese (adj.); (pl. *-ūn*) a Portuguese

برتقال *burtuqāl*, برتقان *burtuqān* (coll.; n. un. ة) orange; oranges

برتقالى *burtuqālī*, برتقانى *burtuqānī* orange, orange-colored

برثن *burṯun* pl. براثن *barāṯin*[2] claw, talon

[1]برج V to display, show, play up her charms (woman); to adorn herself, make herself pretty (woman)

[2]برج *burj* pl. بروج *burūj*, ابراج *abrāj* tower; castle; constellation; (also برج الافلاك) sign of the zodiac | برج بابل *b. bābil* tower of Babel; confusion of tongues; برج حراسة *b. ḥirāsa* watch tower; برج حفر *b. ḥafr* drill rig, derrick (oil exploration); برج الحمام *b. al-ḥamām* pigeon house, dovecot; برج مراقبة *b. murāqaba* control tower (airport); برج عاجى ivory tower; برج المياه *b. al-miyāh* water tower

[3]بارجة *bārija* pl. بوارج *bawārij*[2] warship, battleship; barge

برجز II *tabarjaza* to become bourgeois or middle class

[1]لعب البرجاس *la'b al-birjās* a kind of equestrian contest, joust, tournament

[2]البرجيس *al-birjīs* Jupiter (*astron.*)

برجل *barjal* pl. براجل *barājil*[2] compass, (pair of) dividers

برجمة *burjuma* pl. براجم *barājim*[2] knuckle, finger joint

برجوازى etc. see بورجوازى

برح *bariḥa a* (براح *barāḥ*) to move or go away (from one's place); to leave (ه or من a place, الى for), depart (ه from, الى on one's way to); with neg.: to continue to be (= زال) | ما برح فى he is still in ...; ما برح غنيا (*ğanīyan*) he is still rich; برح الخفاء (*kafā'*) the matter has come out, has become generally known; غدا وبرح to come and go II to beset, harass, trouble, molest (ب s.o.) III to leave (ه a place, الى for), depart (ه from, الى on one's way to)

براح *barāḥ* departure; cessation, stop; a wide, empty tract of land, vast expanse, vastness; براحا *barāḥan* openly and plainly, patently

تباريح *tabārīḥ*[2] agonies, torments (e.g., of longing, of passion)

مبارحة *mubāraḥa* departure

بارح *bāriḥ* (showing the left side, i.e.) ill-boding, inauspicious, ominous (as opposed to سانح); البارح *al-bāriḥa* yesterday

البارحة *al-bāriḥata* yesterday | الليلة البارحة (*lailata*) last night; اول البارحة *awwala l-b.* the day before yesterday, two days ago

مبرح *mubarriḥ* violent, intense, excruciating, agonizing (esp., of pains)

مبرح به *mubarraḥ bihī* stricken, afflicted, tormented

[1]برد *barada* *u* to be or become cold; to cool, cool off (also fig.); to feel cold; to cool, chill (ه s.th.); to soothe, alleviate (ه pain); — *baruda* *u* to be or become cold **II** to make cold (ه s.th.); to refrigerate (ه s.th.); to cool, chill (ه s.th., also fig.); to soothe, alleviate (ه pain) **V** to refresh o.s., cool o.s. off; to be soothed, be alleviated **VIII** to become cold, cool off

برد *bard* coldness, chilliness, coolness; cooling; alleviation; cold, catarrh

برد *barad* hail, بردة *barada* (n. un.) hailstone

برود *barūd* collyrium

برود *burūd* coldness, coolness, chilliness; emotional coldness, frigidity

برودة *burūda* coldness, coolness, chilliness; emotional coldness, frigidity | برودة الدم *b. ad-dam* cold-bloodedness

بردية *bardīya* ague, feverish chill; see also below

برداء *buradā'*[2] ague, feverish chill

براد *barrād* (*leb.*) refrigeration plant; refrigerator, icebox; (*eg.*) teapot | براد شاى a pot of tea

برادة *barrāda* cold-storage plant; refrigerator, icebox

تبريد *tabrīd* cooling, chilling; cold storage, refrigeration; alleviation, mitigation | جهاز التبريد *jahāz at-t.* cold-storage plant, refrigerator; غرفة التبريد *ġurfat at-t.* cold-storage room

بارد *bārid* cold; cool, chilly; easy; weak; stupid, inane, silly, dull; dunce, blockhead | الحرب الباردة (*ḥarb*) the cold war; غنيمة باردة an easy prey; عيش بارد (*'aiš*) an easy life; حجة باردة (*ḥujja*) a weak argument; تبغ بارد (*tibġ*) light, mild tobacco

مبرد *mubarrid* cooling, refreshing; — (pl. *-āt*) radiator; cooling apparatus; pl. مبردات refreshments (beverages, etc.) | مبرد الهواء *m. al-hawā'* electric fan, ventilator

مبرد *mubarrad* cooled, chilled

[2]برد *barada* *u* to file (ه a piece of metal, etc.)

براد *barrād* pl. *-ūn* tool cutter

برادة *birāda* tool cutting, milling (as a trade in the metal industry)

برادة *burāda* iron filings

مبرد *mibrad* pl. مبارد *mabārid*[2] file, rasp; tool cutter, (milling) cutter (as a machine)

[3]برد *burd* pl. ابراد *abrād* garment

بردة *burda* Mohammed's outer garment

بردایة *burdāya* curtain, drape

[4]برد **IV** to send by mail, to mail (ه a letter)

بريد *barīd* post, mail | البريد الجوى (*jawwī*) air mail; البريد العادى (*'ādī*) surface mail

بريدى *barīdī* postal; messenger, courier; mailman

[5]بارود look up alphabetically

[6]بردى *bardī, burdī* papyrus (*bot.*)

بردية *bardīya* pl. *-āt* papyrus | علم البرديات *'ilm al-b.* papyrology

[7]بردى *baradā* Barada, name of a river in Syria

برداق *bardāq* pl. براديق *barādīq*[2] jug, pitcher

لعب البردج *la'b al-bridž* bridge (game)

بردخ *bardaḵa* to polish, burnish (ه s.th.)

□ بردعة = برذعة

بردقان = برتقان

بردقوش *bardaqūš* (= مردقوش) marjoram

بردورة (Fr. *bordure*) *bardūra* curbstone, curb

بردعة *barḏaʿa* pl. براذع *barāḏiʿ*[2] saddle, pack-saddle (for donkeys and camels)

براذعي *barāḏiʿī* maker of donkey saddles, saddler

برذون *birḏaun* pl. براذين *barāḏīn*[2] work horse, jade, nag

[1]برز *baraza u* (بروز *burūz*) to come out, show, appear, come into view, emerge; to step out (من e.g., of a building); to jut out, protrude, be prominent (also fig.); to stand out (امام against), contrast (with); to surpass, excel (على s.o.) **II** to cause to come out, bring out, expose, show, set off, accentuate (ه s.th.); to emboss, raise in relief from a surface (ه s.th.); to emphasize, highlight, give prominence to (ه a point, a theme); to excel, surpass (على ف s.o. in), stand out (ف for), distinguish o.s. (ف by) **III** to meet in combat or duel (ه s.o.); to compete in a contest (ه with s.o.) **IV** to cause to come out, bring out, expose, make manifest (ه s.th.); to emphasize, highlight, give prominence to (ه a point, a theme); to publish, bring out (ه a book, etc.); to present, show (ه e.g., an identity card) **V** to evacuate the bowels **VI** to vie, contend **VIII** to stand out, be conspicuous

بروز *burūz* prominence, projection, protrusion; protruding edge or corner

براز *birāz* excrement, feces; competition, contest, match (in sports); duel

بريزة *buraiza* (*birēza; eg.*) ten-piaster coin

ابرز *abraz*[2] more marked, more distinctive; more prominent | ابرز المظاهر *a. al-maẓāhir* the most outstanding or conspicuous phenomenon

مبارزة *mubāraza* competition, contest, match, esp. in sports; duel; fencing | المبارزة بالشيش (*šīš*) fencing with foils

ابراز *ibrāz* bringing out, displaying, setting off, accentuation; production; presentation

بارز *bāriz* protruding, projecting, salient; raised, embossed, in relief; marked, distinct, conspicuous; prominent (personality) | بارز الاسنان *b. al-asnān* buck-toothed

مبرز *mubarriz* surpassing (على s.o.), superior (على to s.o.); winner, victor (in contest)

مبرز *mubarraz* embossed, worked in relief

مبارز *mubāriz* competitor, contender; combatant, fighter; fencer

[2]بريز (Fr. *prise*) *brīz* pl. *-āt* (plug) socket, wall plug, outlet (*syr.*); بريزة *barīza* pl. برائز *barāʾiz*[2] do. (*eg.*)

[3]ابريز look up alphabetically

[4]برزان *barazān* trumpet

برزخ *barzaḵ* pl. برازخ *barāziḵ*[2] partition, barrier, bar; isthmus; straits; dividing space

برزوق *burzūq* sidewalk

[1]برسام *birsām* pleurisy

[2]ابريسم look up alphabetically

[3]برسيم *birsīm* clover, specif., berseem, Egyptian clover (Trifolium alexandrinum L.; *bot.*)

[1]برش *burš* pl. ابراش *abrāš* mat

ابرش *abraš*[2] spotted, speckled

[2]ابرشية look up alphabetically

برشت *birišt*: بيض برشت (*baiḍ*) soft-boiled eggs

برشلونه *baršilōna* Barcelona (seaport in NE Spain)

برشم *baršama* to stare, gaze (الى at s.th.); to rivet (ه s.th.)

برشمة *baršama* riveting

برشام *buršām* and برشان (n. un. ة) pl. *-āt* wafer; Host (*Chr.*)

برشامة *buršāma* rivet

برشامجى *buršāmjī* riveter

برشمجية *buršamjīya* riveting

برشومى *baršūmī* (*saud.-ar.*) prickly pear (*bot.*)

¹برص *bariṣa a* (*baraṣ*) to be a leper

برص *burṣ* wall gecko (Tarentola mauritanica, *zool.*)

برص *baraṣ* leprosy

ابرص *abraṣ*² leprous; leper | سام ابرص *sāmm a.* wall gecko

²برصة *burṣa* stock exchange

برض *baraḍa u* (بروض *burūḍ*) to germinate, sprout (plant)

برطوز *barṭūz*: برطوز البحرية *b. al-baḥrīya* forecastle, crew quarters (on a merchant vessel)

برطع *barṭaʿa* (برطعة *barṭaʿa*) to gallop

برطل *barṭala* (برطلة *barṭala*) to bribe (ه s.o.) II *tabarṭala* to take bribes, be venal

برطيل *birṭīl* pl. براطيل *barāṭīl*² bribe

¹برطم *barṭama* to rave, talk irrationally

برطوم *burṭūm*, *barṭūm* trunk of an elephant

²برطمان *barṭamān* pl. *-āt* (*eg.*) glass jar (for preserves, etc.), jelly jar

³برطمان (Fr. *appartement*) *barṭamān* pl. *-āt* (*tun.*) apartment

برع *baraʿa a* to surpass, excel (ه s.o.); (also *baruʿa u*) to distinguish o.s., be skillful, proficient V to contribute, give, donate (ب s.th.); to undertake (voluntarily, ب s.th.), volunteer (ب for), be prepared, willing (ب to do s.th.); to be ready, be on hand (ب with)

براعة *barāʿa* skill, proficiency; efficiency, capability, capacity

بروعة *burūʿa* superior skill, outstanding proficiency

ابرع *abraʿ*² more prominent or excellent; superior

تبرع *tabarruʿ* pl. *-āt* gift, donation; contribution

بارع *bāriʿ* skilled, skillful, proficient, capable, efficient; brilliant, outstanding (work of art)

متبرع *mutabarriʿ* donor, contributor

برعم *barʿama* to bud, burgeon, sprout II *tabarʿama* to bud, put forth buds; to reproduce by buds, be gemmiparous (*biol.*)

برعم *burʿum* pl. براعم *barāʿim*² and برعوم *burʿūm* pl. براعيم *barāʿīm*² bud, burgeon; blossom, flower

تبرعم *tabarʿum* formation of buds; gemmation (*biol.*)

برغوث *burġūṯ* pl. براغيث *barāġīṯ*² flea; pl. براغيث (*syr.*) small silver coins | برغوث البحر *b. al-baḥr* shrimp (*zool.*)

برغش *barġaš* (coll.; n. un. ة) gnat(s), midge(s)

برغل *burġul* bulgur, cracked wheat kernels, used in cooking and served together with other food

برغى (Turk. بورغى *burġu*) *burġī* pl. براغى *barāġī* screw

برفير *birfīr* pl. برافير *barāfīr*² purple

بروفة look up alphabetically

¹برق *baraqa u* to shine, glitter, sparkle, flash | برقت السماء (*samāʾu*) there was lightning IV = I; to emit bolts of lightning (cloud); to flash up, light up; to brighten (face); to cable, wire, telegraph (الى to)

برق *barq* pl. بروق *burūq* lightning; flash of lightning; telegraph | برق خلب *barqun ḵullabun* and *b. ḵullabin* lightning without a downpour; a disappointing, disillusioning matter; an unkept promise

برقى *barqī* telegraphic, telegraph- (in compounds)

برقية *barqīya* pl. *-āt* telegram, wire, cable

بريق *barīq* pl. برائق *barā'iq*[2] glitter, shine, gloss, luster | ذو بريق معدنى (*ma'dinī*) lustered, coated with metallic luster

براق *burāq* Alborak, name of the creature on which Mohammed made his ascension to the seven heavens (معراج)

براق *barrāq* shining, lustrous, sparkling, flashing, glittering, twinkling

مبرق *mabraq* glitter, flash | فى مبرق الصبح *fi m. iṣ-ṣubḥ* with the first rays of the morning sun

بارق *bāriq*: بارق الامل *b. al-amal* glimpse of hope

بارقة *bāriqa* pl. بوارق *bawāriq*[2] gleam, twinkle

مبرق *mubriq*: مبرق كاتب teletype; آلة مبرقة do.

[2]البرقة *al-barqa* Cyrenaica (region of E Libya)

[3]ابريق *ibrīq* pl. اباريق *abārīq*[2], (*tun.*) اباريقة *abāriqa* pitcher; jug

بريق *barīq* = ابريق

[4]استبرق look up alphabetically

برقش *barqaša* (برقشة *barqaša*) to variegate, paint or daub with many colors (ه s.th.); to embellish (ه s.th.; قوله one's speech) **II** *tabarqaša* reflex. and pass. of **I**

برقش *birqiš* and ابو براقش *abū barāqiš* bishop bird (*zool.*)

برقشة *barqaša* colorful medley, variety, variegation

مبرقش *mubarqaš* colorful, variegated, many-colored

برقع *barqa'a* to veil, drape (ه, ه s.o., s.th.) **II** *tabarqa'a* to put on a veil, veil o.s.

برقع *burqu'* pl. براقع *barāqi'*[2] veil (worn by women; long, leaving the eyes exposed)

برقوق *barqūq* (coll.; n.un. ة) plum (*eg.*) | برقوق برى (*barrī*) sloe plum

[1]برك *baraka u* to kneel down **II** and **IV** to make (ه the camel) kneel down **II** to invoke a blessing (على or فى on s.th., ل on s.o.) **III** to bless (فى or ه s.o., also ل or على), invoke a blessing on; to give one's blessing (ه to s.th.), sanction (ه s.th.) | بارك الله فيك God bless you! **V** to be blessed (ب by); to enjoy (ب s.th.), find pleasure, delight (ب in); to ask s.o.'s (ب) blessing; to seek a blessing (ب from a saint) **VI** to be blessed, be praised; ... تبارك *tabāraka* ... God bless ...!; الله تبارك وتعالى (*tabāraka wa-ta'ālā*) God the Blessed and Sublime **X** to be blessed

بركة *birka* pl. برك *birak* pond, small lake; puddle, pool | بركة السباحة *b. as-sibāḥa* swimming pool

بركة *baraka* pl. *-āt* blessing, benediction | قلة البركة *qillat al-b.* misfortune, bad luck

ابرك *abrak*[2] more blessed

تبريك *tabrīk* pl. *-āt* good wish; blessing, benediction

مبارك *mubārak* blessed; fortunate, lucky | مبارك يا عزيزى congratulations, my friend!

[2]براريك *barārīk*[2] (*mor.*) barracks

بركار *birkār* compass, (pair of) dividers

بركان *burkān* pl. براكين *barākīn*[2] volcano

بركانى *burkānī* volcanic

برلمان *barlamān* pl. *-āt* parliament

برلمانى *barlamānī* parliamentary

برلمانية *barlamānīya* parliamentarianism

برلنتى (It. *brillante*) *brillantī* brilliant, diamond

برلين *barlīn* Berlin

[1]برم *barima a* (*baram*) to be or become weary, tired (ب of), be fed up, be bored (ب with), find annoying, wearisome (ب s.th.) **V** to feel annoyed (ب by), be displeased (ب with); to be fed up (ب with), be sick and tired (ب of, also من); to be impatient, discontented, dissatisfied; to grieve, be pained

برم *barim* weary, tired (ب of), disgusted (ب at, with); dissatisfied, discontented

تبرم *tabarrum* weariness, boredom, disgust; discontent, dissatisfaction; uneasiness, discomfort, annoyance

متبرم *mutabarrim* cross, peevish, vexed, annoyed

[2]برم *barama u* (*barm*) to twist, twine (ه a rope); to shape (ه s.th.) round and long; to roll up (ه the sleeves); to settle, establish, confirm (ه s.th.) **IV** to twist, twine (ه a rope); to settle, establish, confirm (ه s.th.); to conclude (ه a pact); to confirm (ه a judicial judgment); to ratify (ه a treaty, a bill) **VII** to be settled, be established, be confirmed; to be twisted, be twined

برامة *barrāma* pl. *-āt* drilling machine

بريم *barīm* rope; string, cord, twine

بريمة *barrīma* pl. *-āt* drill, borer, gimlet, auger, bit; corkscrew | مسمار بريمة (*mismār*) screw

○ بريمية *barrīmīya* spirochete

ابرام *ibrām* settlement, establishment; confirmation; conclusion (of a pact, etc.); ratification | محكمة النقض والابرام *maḥkamat an-naqḍ wa-l-i.* Court of Cassation (*Eg.*)

مبروم *mabrūm* bent, twisted, crooked | ○ سلك مبروم (*silk*) wire rope, cable

مبرم *mubram* firm, strong; irrevocable, definitely established; confirmed, ratified | قضاء مبرم (*qaḍā'*) inescapable fate; بصورة مبرمة irrevocably

[3]برمة *burma* pl. برم *buram*, برام *birām* earthenware pot

برما *burmā* Burma

برمائى *barmā'ī* amphibious | دبابة برمائية (*dabbāba*) amphibious tank (*mil.*)

○ برمائية *barmā'īya* amphibian

برماننت (Engl.) *barmānant* permanent wave | برماننت على البارد cold wave (in hair)

برمج *barmaja* to program (ه s.th.)

برمجة *barmaja* programing; program planning

مبرمج *mubarmaj* programed, scheduled | تعليم مبرمج programed instruction; مواد مبرمجة (*mawādd*) programed learning materials

برمق *barmaq* pl. برامق *barāmiq*[2] baluster; spike (of a wheel)

برمهات *baramhāt* the seventh month of the Coptic calendar

برمنكهام Birmingham

برموده *barmūda* the eighth month of the Coptic calendar

برميل *barmīl* pl. براميل *barāmīl*[2] barrel; keg, cask: tun

برنية *barnīya* pl. برانى *barānīy* clay vessel

برنامج *barnāmaj* pl. برامج *barāmij*[2] program, plan, schedule; roster, list, index; curriculum

برنجك *burunjuk* gauze, crepe

برنز *barnaza* to bronze (ه s.th.)

[1]برنس *burnus* pl. برانس *barānis*[2] (also برنوس *barnūs*, *burnūs* pl. برانيس *barānīs*[2]) burnoose, hooded cloak; casula, chasuble (of Coptic priests) | برنس الحمام *b. al-ḥammām* bathrobe

برانسى *barānisī* pl. *-īya* maker of burnooses

[2]جبال البرانس *jibāl al-barānis* the Pyrenees

[3]برنس *brins* prince

برنسيسة *brinsēsa* princess

برنط II *tabarnaṭa* to wear a hat

برنيطة *burnaiṭa* pl. *-āt*, برانيط *barānīṭ*[2] (European) hat (men's and women's); lamp shade

برهة *burha* pl. *burahāt*, بره *burah* a while, a time; short time; instant, moment; برهة *burhatan* a little while | بعد برهتين (after two moments =) in a short time

□ برهم *barham* (*syr.*) = مرهم *marham*

برهما *bərahmā*, *barahmā* Brahma

برهمة *barhama* Brahmanism

برهمى *barhamī*, *barahmī* Brahman (adj.)

برهمية *barhamīya*, *barahmīya* Brahmanism

برهمن *barahman* pl. براهمة *barāhima* Brahman

برهن *barhana* to prove, demonstrate (على or عن s.th.)

برهان *burhān* pl. براهين *barāhīn*[2] proof

برهنة *barhana* proving, demonstration

بروة *barwa* waste, scrap

البروتستانت *al-brotostant* the Protestants

بروتستانتى *brotostantī* Protestant; (pl. *-ūn*) a Protestant

بروتستانتية *brotostantīya* Protestantism

بروتستو (It. *protesto*) *brotostō* protest (of a bill of exchange)

بروتوكول *brotokōl* protocol

بروتون *brōtōn* pl. *-āt* proton

بروتين *brōtīn*, *prōtīn* protein

بروجرام *brogrām* program

بروجى *burūjī* pl. *-īya* trumpeter, bugler

بروز *barwaza* to frame

برواز *barwāz*, *birwāz* pl. براويز *barāwīz*[2] frame

بروسيا (It. *Prussia*) *burūsiyā* Prussia

بروسى *burūsī* Prussian

بروشيه (Fr. *broché*) *brošēh* pl. *-āt* brochure, prospectus

بروفة and بروڤة (It. *prova*) *brōva*, *brōfa* pl. *-āt* test, experiment; proof sheet; rehearsal

بروفسور and بروفيسور *brofesōr* Professor (European and American)

بروكسل *broksel*, (*eg.*) *biruksil* and (*tun.*) بروكسال Brussels

بروليتاريا (Fr.) *broletāriyā* proletariat

بروليتارى *broletārī* proletarian

برونز (Fr.) *bronz* bronze

برونزى *bronzī* bronze, bronzy | العصر البرونزى (*ʿaṣr*) the Bronze Age

[1]برى *barā i* (*bary*) to trim, shape (ه s.th.), nib (ه a pen), sharpen (ه a pencil); to scratch off, scrape off (ه s.th.); to exhaust, tire out, wear out, emaciate, enervate (ه s.o.), sap the strength of (ه) III to vie, com-

pete (ه with s.o.), try to outstrip (ه s.o.) **VI** to vie, compete, contend, be rivals; to meet in a contest, try each other's strength (esp. in games and sports); to play a match, play (مع against; sports) **VII** to be trimmed, be nibbed, be sharpened; to defy, oppose (ل s.o.); to undertake, take in hand (ل s.th.), set out to do s.th. (ل), enter, embark (ل upon); to break forth (من from); to get going; to break out, let fly, explode (with words, esp. in anger or excitement)

برى *baran* dust, earth

براية *barrāya,* براية الاقلام *b. al-aqlām* pencil sharpener

مبراة *mibrāh* pencil sharpener; pocketknife

مباراة *mubārāh* pl. مباريات *mubārayāt* contest, tournament, match (in games and sports); competition, rivalry | مباراة ودية (*wuddīya*) friendly match (sport); مباراة نهائية (*nihā'īya*) final match, final (sport)

اعط القوس باريها : بار *a'ṭi l-qausa bāriyahā* give the bow to him who knows how to shape it, i.e., always ask an expert

متبار *mutabārin* participant in a contest, contestant, contender; competitor, rival

[2]برية see [1]برأ and [2]بر

بريدج (Engl.) *brīdž, brēdž* (= بردج), لعب البريدج game of bridge

بريطانيا *biriṭāniyā* Britain | بريطانيا العظمى (*uẓmā*) Great Britain

بريطانى *biriṭānī* British; Britannic; (pl. *-ūn*) Briton

[1]بز *bazza u* (*bazz*) to take away, steal, wrest, snatch (ه ه from s.o. s.th.), rob, strip (ه ه s.o. of s.th.); to defeat, beat, outstrip, excel (ه s.o.), triumph, be victorious (ه over); to surpass (ه s.th., ب by means of) **VIII** to take away, steal, pilfer (ه s.th.); to take away, snatch (ه money, من from s.o.); to rob, fleece (ه s.o.) | ابتز اموال الناس to lift money out of people's pockets, relieve people of their money

ابتزاز *ibtizāz* theft, robbery; fleecing, robbing (of s.o.)

[2]بز *bazza u* to bud, burgeon

بز *buzz, bizz* pl. بزاز *bizāz,* ابزاز *abzāz* nipple, mammilla (of the female breast); teat, female breast

بزازة *bazzāza* pacifier, nipple (for babies to suck on); baby's bottle

[3]بز *bazz* pl. بزوز *buzūz* linen; cloth, dry goods

بزة *bizza* clothing, dress; suit; uniform | بزة رسمية (*rasmīya*) uniform

بزاز *bazzāz* draper, cloth merchant

بزازة *bizāza* cloth trade

بزبوز *bazbūz* pl. بزابيز *bazābīz*[2] nozzle; spout, lip (of a teapot or kettle)

بزر *bazara i* (*bazr*) to sow

بزر *bizr* pl. بزور *buzūr* seed(s); pl. ابزار *abzār* and ابازير *abāzīr*[2] spice

بزرة *bizra* (n. un.) seed; kernel, pip, pit, stone (of fruit); germ

بزار *bazzār* seedsman

بزيرة *buzaira* pl. *-āt* spore (*bot.*)

بزغ *bazaġa u* to break forth, come out; to dawn (day); to rise (sun)

بزوغ *buzūġ* appearance, emergence; rise (of the sun)

بزق *bazaqa u* (*bazq*) to spit

بزاق *buzāq* spit, spittle, saliva

بزاقة *bazzāqa* snail; cobra

مبزقة *mibzaqa* pl. مبازق *mabāziq*[2] spittoon, cuspidor

[1]بزل *bazala* u (*bazl*) to split (ه s.th.); to pierce (ه s.th.), make a hole (ه in); to tap, broach (ه s.th.; a cask); to puncture, tap (ه s.o.; *med.*); to clear, filter (ه a liquid)

بزل *bazl* puncture, tapping, paracentesis (*med.*)

بزال *buzāl* bung (of a cask)

مبزل *mibzal* pl. مبازل *mabāzil*[2] spile, spigot, tap; cock, faucet

[2]بزلة (It. *piselli*) *bizilla* and بزلا green peas

ابزيم *ibzīm* pl. ابازيم *abāzīm*[2] buckle, clasp

بزموت *bizmūt* bismuth

ابزن *abzan* look up alphabetically

بزنطى *bizanṭī* Byzantine

باز *bāzin* pl. بزاة *buzāh*, بواز *bawāzin*, بيزان *bīzān* falcon

[1]بس *bassa* u to crush, pulverize (ه s.th.)

[2]بس *bass* and بسة *bassa* pl. بساس *bisās* cat

بسأ *basa'a* a (بسء *bas'*) to treat amicably (ب s.o.); to be intimate, be on familiar terms (ب with)

بسارابيا *besārābiyā* Bessarabia

بسباس *basbās*, بسباسة *basbāsa* (*eg.*) mace (*bot.*); (*maḡr.*) fennel

بسبوسة *basbūsa* (*eg.*) pastry made of flour, melted butter, sugar and oil

بستر *bastara* to pasteurize (ه milk)

مبستر *mubastar* pasteurized (milk)

بستلة *bastilla* pl. -*āt* (*eg.*) tub

[1]بستان *bustān* pl. بساتين *basātīn*[2] garden

بستانى *bustānī* gardener; garden (adj.); horticultural

بستنة *bastana* gardening, horticulture

[2]بستون (Fr. *piston*) *bistōn* pl. -*āt*, بستن (Engl.) *bistan* pl. بساتن *basātin*[2] piston

[3]بستونى (It. *bastone*) *bastūnī* spades (suit of playing cards)

بستيلية (Fr.) *bastīliya* pastilles, lozenges

بسخة *baska* Easter; Passion Week (*Chr.*)

بسر *basara* u (بسور *busūr*) to scowl, frown; — *basara* u (*basr*) and VIII to begin too early (ه with), take premature action, be rash (ه in s.th.)

بسر *busr* (n. un. ة) pl. بسار *bisār* unripe dates

باسور *bāsūr* pl. بواسير *bawāsīr*[2] hemorrhoids

بسط *basaṭa* u (*basṭ*) to spread, spread out (ه s.th.); to level, flatten (ه s.th.); to enlarge, expand (ه s.th.); to stretch out, extend (ه s.th.); to unfold, unroll (ه s.th.); to grant, offer, present (ه s.th.); to submit, state, set forth, expound, explain (ه s.th., ل or على to s.o.); to flog (ه s.o.; *Nejd*); to please, delight (ه s.o.) | بسط ذراعيه (*ḏirā'aihi*) to spread one's arms; بسط له مهاد العذر (*mihāda l-'uḏr*) to hold out a helping hand to s.o., ease the way to vindication for s.o.; بسط يد المساعدة ل (*yada l-musā'ada*) to extend a helping hand to s.o.; بسط المائدة to lay the table; — *basuṭa* u (بساطة *basāṭa*) to be simple, openhearted, frank, candid II to spread, spread out, extend, expand (ه s.th.); to level, flatten (ه s.th.); to simplify, make simple (ه s.th.) III to set forth, state, expound, explain; to be sincere (ه ب with s.o. about or in s.th.), confess frankly (ه ب to s.o. s.th.); to speak openly (ه to s.o., فى about s.th.) V to be spread, be unrolled, be spread out, be extended; to speak at great length (في about), enlarge (في on), treat exhaustively, expound in detail (في a theme); to be friendly, communicative, sociable, behave unceremoniously, be completely at ease | تبسط في الحديث to talk freely, without formality **VII** to spread, extend, expand (intr.); to spread out flat, open up (the palm of the hand), be open; to broaden, become broader (content); to be merry, gay; to be glad, be delighted, be or become happy

بسط *basṭ* extension, spreading, unrolling, unfolding; presentation, statement, explanation, exposition; broad, detailed treatment (of content in books); cheering, delighting, delectation; amusement; numerator (of a fraction; *math.*) | بسط اليد *b. al-yad* greed, cupidity

بسطة *basṭa* extension, extent, expanse; size, magnitude; skill, capability, abilities; excess, abundance; (pl. *-āt*) statement, exposition, presentation; — (pl. بساط *bisāṭ*) landing (of a staircase); estrade, dais, platform (*eg.*)

بساط *bisāṭ* pl. *-āt*, ابسطة *absiṭa*, بسط *busuṭ* carpet, rug | بساط الرحمة *b. ar-raḥma* winding sheet, shroud; بساط المعمور the civilized world; طرح (or وضع) مسألة على بساط البحث (*mas'alatan, baḥṯ*) to raise a question, bring a question on the carpet, also على بساط المناقشة (*b. il-munāqaša*) for discussion; طوى بساطه (*ṭawā*) to be finished, be done, come to an end, finish; طوى البساط بما فيه to bring the matter to an end, settle it once and for all

بسيط *basīṭ* pl. بسطاء *busaṭā'*[2] simple; plain, uncomplicated; slight, little, modest, inconsiderable, trivial, trifling; البسيط name of a poetical meter; pl. بسطاء simple souls, ingenuous people | بسيط اليدين *b. al-yadain* (pl. بسط *busuṭ*) generous, openhanded; بسيطة! a simple matter! no problem!

البسيطة *al-basīṭa* the earth, the world

بسائط *basā'iṭ*[2] elements; simple remedies, medicinal plants; basic facts

بساطة *basāṭa* simplicity, plainness | ببساطة merely, only, simply, easily, without further ado

○ ابسوطة *ubsūṭa* pl. اباسيط *abāsīṭ*[2] rim, felly (of a wheel)

ابسط *absaṭ*[2] simpler; wider, more extensive

تبسيط *tabsīṭ* simplification

تبسط *tabassuṭ* candor, frankness, ease (للناس toward people)

انبساط *inbisāṭ* (n. vic. ة) extensity, extensiveness, extension; expansion, expanse; joy, delight, happiness, gaiety, cheerfulness; extroversion (*psych.*)

عضلة باسطة *'aḍala bāsiṭa* extensor (*anat.*)

مبسوط *mabsūṭ* extended, outstretched; spread out; flat, open (hand); extensive, large, sizeable; detailed, elaborate (book); broadly treated; cheerful, happy, gay; feeling well, in good health; (*tun.*) well-to-do

منبسط *munbasiṭ* extending, spreading; gay, happy, cheerful; being in a merry mood; extroverted (*psych.*)

منبسط *munbasaṭ* level or flat surface

بسطرمة (Turk.) *basṭurma* a kind of jerked, salted meat (*eg.*)

البسفور *al-busfūr* the Bosporus

بسق *basaqa* u (بسوق *busūq*) to be high, tall, lofty, towering; to excel, surpass (ه or على s.o.)

باسق *bāsiq* high, tall, lofty, towering

مبسق *mubsiq* high, tall, lofty, towering

بسكاى *biskāy* Biscay

بسكليت (Fr. *bicyclette*) *biskilēt*, *baskilēt* f., pl. *-āt* and (*eg.*) بسكليته *baskaletta* pl. *-āt* bicycle

بسكوت (It. *biscotto*) *baskūt* biscuit

بسكويت *baskawīt* biscuit

[1]بسل *basula u* (بسالة *basāla*) to be brave, fearless, intrepid **V** to scowl, glower **X** to be reckless, defy death

بسالة *basāla* courage, intrepidity

استبسال *istibsāl* death defiance

باسل *bāsil* pl. بسلاء *busalā'*[2], بواسل *bawāsil*[2] brave, fearless, intrepid

مستبسل *mustabsil* death-defying, heroic

[2]بسلة *bisilla* peas

بسم *basama i* (*basm*) and **V** to smile **VIII** do.; to give s.o. (ل) a friendly smile

بسمة *basma* pl. *basamāt* smile

بسام *bassām* smiling

مبسم *mabsim* pl. مباسم *mabāsim*[2] mouth; mouthpiece (of a wind instrument); holder (for cigars, cigarettes, etc.)

ابتسام *ibtisām* and (n. vic.) ابتسامة pl. *-āt* smile

بسمل *basmala* to utter the formula بسم الله الرحمن الرحيم "In the name of God, the Benificent, the Merciful"; (among Christians) to utter the formula بسم الآب والابن والروح القدس "in the name of the Father, the Son, and the Holy Ghost"

بسملة *basmala* utterance of the above formulae; the respective formula itself

بسينة *busaina* kitty

بسيكولوجيا *psikolōjiyā* psychology

بسيكولوجى *psikolōjī* psychologic(al)

بش *bašša a* (*bašš*, بشاشة *bašāša*) to display a friendly, cheerful, happy mien; to smile; to be friendly (ل to s.o.), give s.o. (ل) a smile

بشوش *bašūš*, بشاش *baššāš* smiling, friendly, cheerful

بشاشة *bašāša* smile; happy mien

باش *bāšš* smiling, happy; friendly, kind

بشت *bušt* (*Nejd, Baḥr., Ir.*) a kind of cloak, = عباءة *ʿabā'a*

بشتة *bišta* (*eg.*) woolen cloak worn by Egyptian peasants

[1]بشر *bašara i, bašira a* to rejoice, be delighted, be happy (ب at s.th.) **II** to announce (as good news; ب ه to s.o. s.th.); to bring news (ب ه to s.o. of s.th. good); to forecast (ب s.th. good), give good prospect (ب of); to spread, propagate, preach (ب s.th.; a religion, a doctrine) | بشر نفسه ب (*nafsahū*) to indulge in the happy hope that ... **IV** to rejoice (at good news) **X** to rejoice, be delighted, be happy (ب at s.th., esp. at good news), welcome (ب s.th.); to take as a good omen (ب s.th.) | استبشر به خيرا (*kairan*) to regard s.th. as auspicious

بشر *bišr* joy

بشر *bušr* glad tidings

بشرى *bušrā* pl. بشريات *bušrayāt* glad tidings, good news

بشير *bašīr* pl. بشراء *bušarā'*[2] bringer of glad tidings, messenger, herald, harbinger, forerunner, precursor; evangelist (*Chr.*)

بشارة *bišāra* pl. *-āt*, بشائر *bašā'ir*[2] good news, glad tidings; annunciation, prophecy; gospel; بشائر good omens, propitious signs | عيد البشارة *ʿīd al-b.* the Annunciation, the Day of Our Lady (*Chr.*)

بشارة *bušāra* gift to a bringer of glad tidings

تبشير *tabšīr* announcement (of glad tidings); preaching of the Gospel; evangelization, missionary activity

تبشيرى *tabšīrī* missionary

تباشير *tabāšīr*[2] foretokens, prognostics, omens, first signs or indications, heralds (fig.); beginnings, dawn | تباشير الفجر *t. al-fajr* the first shimmer of aurora, the first glimpse of dawn

مبشر *mubaššir* pl. *-ūn* announcer, messenger (of glad tidings); evangelist (*Chr.*); preacher; missionary (*Chr.*)

مستبشر *mustabšir* happy, cheerful

2بشر *bašara u* to peel (ه s.th.); to scrape off, shave off, scratch off (ه s.th.); to grate, shred (ه s.th.) **III** to touch (ه s.th.), be in direct contact (ه with s.th.); to have sexual intercourse (ه with s.o.); to attend, apply o.s. (ه or ب to s.th.), take up, take in hand, pursue, practice, carry out (ه s.th., a job, a task, etc.)

بشر *bašar* man, human being; men, mankind

بشرى *bašarī* human; human being; epidermal, skin (adj.) | طبيب بشرى dermatologist

بشرة *bašara* outer skin, epidermis, cuticle; skin; complexion

بشرية *bašarīya* mankind, human race

مبشرة *mibšara* pl. مباشر *mabāšir*[2] scraper, grater

مباشرة *mubāšara* pursuit, practice; direct, physical cause (*Isl. Law*); *mubāšaratan* immediately, directly

مبشور *mabšūr*: جبنة مبشورة (*jubna*) shredded cheese

مباشر *mubāšir* direct; immediate; — (pl. *-ūn*) practitioner, pursuer, operator; director; manager (*Eg.*); court usher (*Syr.*) | غير مباشر indirect; اصابات مباشرة (*iṣābāt*) direct hits; المباشران للعقد (*'aqd*) the two partners of an agreement or contract; اذاعة مباشرة (*iḏā'a*) live transmission (radio, TV)

بشروش *bašarūš* flamingo

بشع *baši'a a* (بشاعة *bašā'a*) to be ugly, loathsome **II** to make ugly, disfigure, distort (ه s.th.); to disparage, run down (ه s.th.) **X** to regard as ugly, find ugly or repugnant (ه s.th.)

بشع *baši'* ugly; offensive, disgusting, distasteful, repugnant; unpleasant

بشيع *bašī'* ugly; offensive, disgusting, distasteful, repugnant; unpleasant

بشاعة *bašā'a* ugliness

ابشع *abša'*[2] uglier; more repulsive

1باشق look up alphabetically

2بشقه (*eg.*; Turk. *başka*; invar.) different

بشك **VIII** to lie, prevaricate

بشاك *baššāk* liar

ابتشاك *ibtišāk* lie, deceit, trickery

1بشكور *baškūr* pl. بشاكير *bašākīr*[2] poker, fire iron

2بشكير *baškīr* pl. بشاكير *bašākīr*[2] towel

بشلة (It.) *bišilla* pl. *-āt* bacillus

بشم *bašima a* (*bašam*) to feel nauseated, be disgusted (من by s.th.), be fed up (من with) **IV** to nauseate, sicken, disgust (ه s.o.)

بشم *bašam* surfeit, satiety, loathing, disgust

بشمار *bašmār* (*tun.*) lacework, trimmings

بشامرى *bašāmirī* (*tun.*) laceworker, lacemaker

بشمق *bašmaq* slipper (worn by *fuqahā'* and women)

بشنة *bašna* (*maġr.*) sorghum, millet

بشنس *bašans* the ninth month of the Coptic calendar

بشنوقة *bašnūqa* pl. بشانيق *bašānīq*[2] kerchief tied under the chin (*pal.*)

بشنين *bašnīn* lotus

بص *baṣṣa* *i* (*baṣṣ*, بصيص *baṣīṣ*) to glow, sparkle, glitter, shine; — (*eg.*) *u* to look

بصة *baṣṣa* embers

بصيص *baṣīṣ* glow, shine; glimpse, ray (e.g., of hope); lustrous, shining

بصاص *baṣṣāṣ* lustrous, shining; (*eg.*) spy, detective

بصبص *baṣbaṣa* (بصبصة *baṣbaṣa*) to wag (بذنبه *bi-ḏanabihī* its tail); (*eg.*) to ogle, make sheep's eyes, cast amorous glances

بصخة *baṣka* see بسخة

[1]بصر *baṣura* *u*, *baṣira* *a* (*baṣar*) to look, see; to realize, understand, comprehend, grasp (ب s.th.) **II** to make (ه s.o.) see, understand or realize (ه or ب s.th.), make (ه s.o.) aware (ه or ب of s.th.); to enlighten (ه ه or ب ه s.o. on or as to s.th.); to tell, inform (ه ه or ب ه s.o. about) **IV** to see, catch sight of, behold, discern, perceive (ه, ه or ب s.o., s.th.); to notice, observe (ه, ه or ب s.o., s.th., به يفعله s.o. doing s.th.); to make out, recognize (ه, ب s.th.); to try to discern or perceive (ه, ب s.th.) **V** to envisage, regard (فى s.th.); to try to get an insight (فى into); to consider, ponder (فى s.th.), reflect (فى on); to gain or have a keen insight (فى into) **X** to have the faculty of visual perception, be able to see; to be endowed with reason, be rational, reasonable, intelligent; to reflect (فى on s.th.), ponder (فى s.th.)

بصر *baṣar* pl. ابصار *abṣār* vision, eyesight; glance, look; insight; sight, discernment, perception | قصير البصر short-sighted, myopic; لمح البصر *lamḥ al-b.* glance of the eye; فى لمح البصر ,كلمح البصر, فى اقل من لمح البصر, دون لمح البصر (*dūna*), (*aqalla*) in the twinkling of an eye, in a moment, in a flash, instantly; على مدى البصر (*madā*) within sight; له بصر ب he is knowledgeable in, he is familiar with; اولو الابصار *ulū l-a.* people of deep insight

بصرى *baṣarī* optic(al), visual, ocular

بصريات *baṣrīyāt* optics

بصارة *baṣāra* perception, discernment; perspicacity, acuteness of the mind, sharp-wittedness

بصير *baṣīr* pl. بصراء *buṣarā'*[2] endowed with eyesight; acutely aware (ب of), having insight (ب into); possessing knowledge or understanding (ب of), discerning, discriminating, versed, knowledgeable, proficient (ب in), acquainted (ب with s.th.)

بصيرة *baṣīra* pl. بصائر *baṣā'ir*[2] (keen) insight, penetration, discernment, understanding, (power of) mental perception, mental vision | عن بصيرة deliberately, knowingly; كان على بصيرة من to have insight into s.th., be informed about s.th.; نافذ البصيرة discerning, clear-sighted, perspicacious, sharp-witted; نفاذ البصيرة *nafāḏ al.-b.* sharp discernment, perspicacity

ابصر *abṣar*[2] more discerning

تبصرة *tabṣira* enlightenment; instruction, information

ابصار *ibṣār* vision, sight, visual perception | ○ ابصار مزدوج (*muzdawij*) diplopia (*med.*)

ابصارى *ibṣārī* optic(al)

تبصر *tabaṣṣur* reflection, consideration; penetration, clear-sightedness, perspicacity

استبصار *ist'ibṣār* insight (*psych.*)

باصرة *bāṣira* pl. بواصر *bawāṣir*[2] eye

[2]البصرة *al-baṣra* Basra (port in S Iraq)

[3]بصارة *biṣāra*, *buṣāra* (*eg.*) a kind of porridge made of green beans, boiled with onions, garlic, parsley, etc.

بصق **baṣaqa** *u* to spit (على on s.o.); to spit out (ه s.th.)

بصقة **baṣqa** (n. vic.) expectoration; (expectorated) spit, spittle, saliva

بصاق **buṣāq** spit, spittle, saliva

مبصقة **mibṣaqa** spittoon, cuspidor

بصل **baṣal** (coll.; n. un. ة) onion(s); bulb(s) | بصل الفار *b. al-fa'r* sea onion (Scilla verna)

بصلى **baṣalī** bulbous

بصيلة **buṣaila** pl. *-āt*, بصيلة الشعر *b. aš-ša'r* bulb of the hair (*anat.*)

بصم **baṣama** *u* (*baṣm*) to print, imprint (ه s.th.); to stamp (ه s.th.); to make, or leave, an imprint (ه on)

بصمة **baṣma** pl. *baṣamāt* imprint, impression | بصمة الختم *b. al-ḵatm* stamp imprint, stamp; بصمة الاصابع fingerprint

بصوة **baṣwa** embers

بض **baḍḍ** tender-skinned

بضع **baḍa'a** *a* (*baḍ'*) to cut, slash or slit open (ه s.th.); to cut up, carve up, dissect, anatomize (ه s.th.); to amputate (*surg.*) **II** to cut up, carve up, dissect, anatomize **III** to sleep (ها with a woman) **IV** to invest capital (ه) profitably in a commercial enterprise **V** pass. of **II**; to trade; to shop, make purchases **X** to trade

بضع **baḍ'** amputation

بضع **biḍ'** (commonly, with genit. pl. of f. nouns, بضعة with genit. pl. of m. nouns; in classical Arabic بضع with both genders) some, a few, several | بضعة عشر *biḍ'ata 'ašara* m., بضع عشرة *biḍ'a 'ašrata* f. (invar.) some and ten (= 11—19); طوال بضعة عشر قرنا (*ṭiwāla, qarnan*) during more than ten centuries

بضعة **biḍ'a** pl. بضع *biḍa'* piece (of meat); meat; see also *biḍ'* above

بضع **buḍ'** vulva

بضاعة **biḍā'a** pl. بضائع *baḍā'i'*[2] goods, merchandise, wares, commodities; that which s.o. has to offer, which he has to show, with which he is endowed (also attributes, qualities) | قطار البضاعة freight train; اخرج ما عنده من بضاعة he said what he had intended to say

مبضع **mibḍa'** pl. مباضع *mabāḍi'*[2] dissecting knife, scalpel

ابضاع **ibḍā'** mandate for the management of affairs (*Isl. Law*); partnership in a limited company, capital investment

مبضع **mubḍi'** pl. *-ūn* limited partner (*com.*)

مستبضع **mustabḍi'** manager, managing agent (*Isl. Law*)

بط **baṭṭ** (n. un. ة) duck; بطة *baṭṭa* leather flask | بطة الساق calf (of the leg)

مبط **mibaṭṭ** lancet, scalpel

بطؤ **baṭu'a** *u* (بطء *buṭ'*, بطاء *biṭā'*, بطاءة *baṭā'a*) to be slow; to be slowgoing, slow-footed, slow-paced; to tarry, linger, wait, hesitate **II** to retard, slow down, delay, hold up (على ب s.o. in s.th.) **IV** to slow down, decelerate, retard, delay, hold up (ه s.th.); to be slow, go or drive slowly, slow down; to be late (عن for s.th., in meeting s.o.), keep s.o. (عن) waiting **V** to be slow, tardy (في in) **VI** to be slow, leisurely, unhurried; to go, drive, act or proceed slowly, leisurely; to be slowgoing, slow-footed, slow-paced; to slow down **X** to find slow (ه, ه s.o., s.th.); to have to wait a long time (ه for s.o.), be kept waiting (ه by s.o.)

بطء **buṭ'** slowness, tardiness | ببطء slowly, leisurely, unhurriedly

بطىء **baṭī'** pl. بطاء *biṭā'* slow, unhurried; slowgoing, slow-footed, slow-paced; tardy, late; sluggish, lazy; slow, gradual, imperceptible | ○ بطىء التردد *b. at-taraddud* of low frequency (*el.*)

ابطأ *abṭa'*[2] slower | ابطأ من غراب نوح (*ġurābi nūḥ*) tardier than Noah's raven, i.e., slower than a ten years' itch (proverbially of s.o. who is very tardy)

ابطاء *ibṭā'* slowing down, retardation, deceleration, reduction of speed; tarrying, delay; slowness | دون ابطاء without delay

تباطؤ *tabāṭu'* slowness; slowing down, retardation | اضراب التباطؤ *iḍrāb at-t.* slow-down strike

بطارية *baṭṭārīya* pl. *-āt* battery (*el.* and *mil.*)

بطاطا *baṭāṭā*, بطاطة *baṭāṭa* sweet potato, yam

بطاطس *baṭāṭis* potatoes | بطاطس محمرة (*muḥammara*) fried potatoes

بطاقة see بطق

بطبط *baṭbaṭa* (بطبطة *baṭbaṭa*) to quack (duck)

بطح *baṭaḥa a* (*baṭḥ*) to prostrate, lay low, fell, throw to the ground, throw down (ه, ه s.o., s.th.) V and VII to be prostrated, be laid low; to lie prostrate, sprawl, stretch out; to extend, stretch; to lie

ابطح *abṭaḥ*[2] flat, level; (pl. اباطح *abāṭiḥ*[2]) basin-shaped valley, wide bed of a wadi

بطحاء *baṭḥā'*[2] pl. بطاح *biṭāḥ*, بطحاوات *baṭḥāwāt* basin-shaped valley; plain, level land, flatland, open country; (*tun.*) public square

بطيحة *baṭīḥa* pl. بطائح *baṭā'iḥ*[2] wide bed of a stream or wadi; a stagnant, shallow and broad body of water

منبطح *munbaṭiḥ* prostrate; flat, level; level land, plain

بطيخ *biṭṭīḵ*, *baṭṭīḵ* (n. un. ة) melon, watermelon; *baṭṭīḵ* hub (of a wheel; *syr.*)

مبطخة *mabṭaḵa* melon patch

[1]بطر *baṭira a* (*baṭar*) to be wild, wanton, reckless; to be proud, vain; to be discontented (ه with s.th.); to disregard (ه s.th.) IV to make reckless; to make (ه s.o.) proud, haughty, vain

بطر *baṭar* wantonness, cockiness, arrogance, hubris, pride, vanity

اباطرة *abāṭira* (pl.) bons vivants, playboys, epicures

[2]البطراء *al-baṭrā'* Petra (ancient city of Edomites and Nabataeans; ruins now in SW Jordan)

[3]بطارية look up alphabetically

بطرخ *baṭraḵ* pl. بطارخ *baṭāriḵ*[2] roe (of fish); caviar (esp. the Egyptian sort from the gray mullet)

بطرس *buṭrus* Peter

بطرشيل *baṭrašīl* and بطرشين *baṭrašīn* stole (*Chr.*)

بطريق *biṭrīq* pl. بطارقة *baṭāriqa*, بطاريق *baṭārīq*[2] patrician; Romaean general; penguin (*zool.*)

بطرك *baṭrak*, بطريك *baṭrīk*, بطريرك *baṭriyark* pl. بطاركة *baṭārika* Patriarch (as an ecclesiastic title, *Chr.*)

بطركية *baṭrakīya*, بطريركية *baṭriyarkīya* patriarchate (*Chr.*)

بطركخانة *baṭrakḵāna* seat of authority or administrative post of a patriarchate (*Chr.*)

بطش *baṭaša i u* (*baṭš*) to attack with violence; to bear down on, fall upon s.o. (ب or في); to knock out (ه s.o.); to hit, strike (ب s.th.), land with a thud (ب on)

بطش *baṭš* strength, power, force, violence, outrage; ruthless action; opression, tyranny | قوى البطش *quwā l-b.* squads of thugs, goon squads

بطشة *baṭša* impact

بطاقة *biṭāqa* pl. *-āt*, بطائق *baṭā'iq*[2] slip (of paper), tag; card, calling card; ticket; label | بطاقة الزيارة calling card; بطاقة شخصية (*šaḵṣīya*) and بطاقة التعريف identity card; بطاقة المواد الغذائية *b. al-mawādd al-ġiḏā'īya*, بطاقة التموين food ration card; بطاقة المعايدة *b. al-mu'āyada* greeting card; بطاقة ضريبية (*ḍarībīya*) tax card; بطاقة عائلية family identity card

[1]بطل *baṭala u* (*buṭl*, بطلان *buṭlān*) to be or become null, void, invalid, false, untenable, vain, futile, worthless; to be abolished, fall into disuse, become obsolete; to cease, stop, be discontinued; to be inactive, be out of work **II** to thwart, foil, frustrate, make ineffective, counteract, neutralize, nullify, invalidate (ه s.th.); to abolish, cancel, annul, suppress (ه s.th.) **IV** = **II**; to talk idly, prattle; to paralyze, immobilize, hold down, pin down (ه the opponent)

بطل *buṭl* nullity; uselessness, futility, vanity; falsity, falseness, untruth

بطالة *biṭāla* and *baṭāla* idleness, inactivity; free time, time off, holidays, vacations; unemployment

بطال *baṭṭāl* pl. *-ūn* idle, inactive; unemployed, out of work

بطلان *buṭlān* nullity; uselessness, futility, vanity; falsity, untruth; invalidity

ابطال *ibṭāl* thwarting, frustration, invalidation; ruin, destruction; abolition, cancellation

باطل *bāṭil* nugatory, vain, futile; false, untrue; absurd, groundless, baseless; worthless; invalid, null, void; deception, lie, falsehood; بالباطل and باطلا *bāṭilan* falsely; futilely, in vain; pl. اباطيل *abāṭīl*[2] vanities, trivialities, trifles, flimflam, idle talk, prattle | تهمة باطلة (*tuhma*) false accusation

مبطل *mubṭil* prattler, windbag; liar

مبطل *mubṭal* nugatory, futile, vain

متبطل *mutabaṭṭil* unemployed

[2]بطل *baṭula u* (بطالة *baṭāla*, بطولة *buṭūla*) to be brave, be heroic, be a hero

بطل *baṭal* pl. ابطال *abṭāl* brave, heroic; hero; champion, pioneer; hero, protagonist (of a narrative, etc.), lead, star (of a play); champion (*athlet.*); (in compounds) championship-, champion- (sport) | بطل العالم *b. al-'ālam* world champion; الاندية البطلة (*andiya*) championship clubs (sport)

بطلة *baṭala* heroine (of a narrative), female lead, star (of a play); woman champion (*athlet.*)

بطالة *baṭāla* bravery, valor, heroism

بطولة *buṭūla* bravery, heroism; — (pl. *-āt*) leading role, starring role (theater, film); championship (*athlet.*) | البطولة العالمية (*'ālamīya*) and بطولة العالم *b. al-'ālam* world championship (*athlet.*); دور البطولة the part or role of the hero, leading role

بطولى *buṭūlī* heroic

البطالسة *al-baṭālisa* the Ptolemies

بطليموس *baṭlaimūs*[2] (also بطلميوس *baṭlamiyūs*[2]) Ptolemy

بطليموسى *baṭlaimūsī* Ptolemaic

بطليوس *baṭalyaus*[2] Badajoz (city in Spain)

بطم *buṭm*, *buṭum* terebinth (*bot.*)

[1]بطن *baṭana u* (*baṭn*, بطون *buṭūn*) to be hidden, concealed, to hide; — *baṭuna u* (بطانة *baṭāna*) to be paunchy **II** to line (ه a garment, ب ه s.th. with); to cover the inside (ب ه of s.th. with), hang, face, fill (ب ه s.th. with) **IV** to hide, conceal, harbor (ه s.th.) **V** to be lined, have a lining (garment); to penetrate, delve (ه into), become absorbed, engrossed (ه in) **X** to penetrate, delve (ه into), become absorbed, engrossed (ه in); to

try to fathom (ه s.th.); to fathom (ه s.th.), get to the bottom of (ه); to have profound knowledge (ه of s.th.), know thoroughly, know inside out (ه s.th.)

بطن **baṭn** m. and f., pl. بطون *buṭūn*, ابطن *abṭun* belly, stomach, abdomen; womb; interior, inside, inner portion; depth | بطن القدم *b. al-qadam* sole of the foot; بطن الكف *b. al-kaff* palm of the hand; رقص البطن and رقص البطون *raqṣ al-b.* belly dance; فى بطن (*baṭni*) in, within, in the midst of; فى بطون inside, within, in; ولدت بطنا واحدا (*waladat* she gave birth only once; بطنا لظهر (*li-ẓahrin*) upside down

بطنى **baṭnī** ventral, abdominal, belly (in compounds) | تكلم بطنى (*takallum*) ventriloquism; هبوط بطنى belly landing

بطن **baṭin** paunchy

بطنة **biṭna** gluttony; overeating, indigestion

بطان **biṭān** pl. ابطنة *abṭina* girth (of a camel)

بطانة **biṭāna** pl. بطائن *baṭā'in*[2] inside, inner side; lining (of a garment); retinue, suite, entourage | فى بطانة among, amidst; within

بطين **baṭīn** pl. بطان *biṭān* and مبطان *mibṭān* paunchy, fat, corpulent, stout; gluttonous

بطين **buṭain** ventricle (of the heart; *anat.*)

بطانية **baṭṭānīya** pl. *-āt*, بطاطين *baṭāṭīn*[2] cover; blanket; quilt

○ تبطن **tabaṭṭun** subjectivation (*psych.*)

○ استبطان **istibṭān** introspection (*psych.*)

باطن **bāṭin** pl. بواطن *bawāṭin*[2] inner, interior, inward, inmost, intrinsic; hidden, secret; الباطنة coastal plain of E Oman; باطنا *bāṭinan* inwardly, secretly | باطن الكف *b. al-kaff* palm of the hand; باطن القدم *b. al-qadam* sole of the foot; فى باطن الامر at bottom, after all, really; بواطن الامر the factors, circumstances or reasons at the bottom of s.th.; بواطن الارض *b. al-arḍ* the secret depths of the earth; اجر من الباطن (*ajjara*) to sublet, sublease (ه a rented room, etc.)

باطنى **bāṭinī** internal; adherent of the *bāṭinīya*, see below | ○ تأمل باطنى (*ta'ammul*) introspection (*psych.*); مرض باطنى (*maraḍ*) internal disease; الطب الباطنى (*ṭibb*) internal medicine

الباطنية **al-bāṭinīya** name of a school of thought in Islam, characterized by divining a hidden, secret meaning in the revealed texts

مبطون **mabṭūn** affected with a gastric or intestinal ailment

مبطن **mubaṭṭan** lined; filled (ب with, e.g., with anger, bitterness, cynicism; of words, etc.)

بطن[2] **II** (*tun.*) to full (ه s.th.)

باطان (Span. *batán*) **bāṭān** fulling mill

باطية **bāṭiya** pl. بواط *bawāṭin* pitcher, jug

بظ **baẓẓa** *u* to spout, gush out, well out

بظر **baẓr** pl. بظور *buẓūr* clitoris (*anat.*)

بعبع **buʿbuʿ** pl. بعابع *baʿābiʿ*[2] bugaboo, bogey

بعث **baʿaṯa** *a* (*baʿṯ*) to send, send out, dispatch (ه ,ه or ب s.o. or s.th. to الى); to forward (ب or ه s.th. to الى); to delegate (ب or ه s.o. to الى); to emit (ب or ه s.th.); to evoke, arouse, call forth, awaken (ه s.th.); to stir up, provoke, bring on (ه s.th.); to revive, resuscitate (ه s.th.); to resurrect (ه s.o., من الموت from death); to incite, induce (على to s.th.), instigate (على s.th.); to cause (على s.th.; e.g., astonishment) | بعث اليه هزة الخوف (*hazzat al-ḵauf*) to fill s.o. with trembling fear: بعث روح الحياة فى (*rūḥa l-ḥayāh*) to breathe life into s.th. or s.o., revive s.th. **VII** to be sent out, be emitted, be dispatched, be delegated; to be triggered, be caused, be provoked; to be resurrected (من الموت from death); to rise (من from, out of), get up; to originate (من in), come (من from), be caused (من by); to emanate (fragrance); to escape (gas, من or عن from); to arise, spring, proceed, develop (من from), grow out of (من); to set out to do s.th. (with foll. imperf.) **VIII** to send, dispatch (ه s.o.)

بعث *ba'ṯ* sending out, emission, dispatching, delegation; resurrection; awakening, revival, arousal, evocation; pl. بعوث *bu'ūṯ* delegations, deputations | حزب البعث *ḥizb al-b.* the Baath party (*pol.*); بعث سوريا *b. sūriyā* the Syrian Baath party; يوم البعث Day of Resurrection (from the dead)

بعثى *ba'ṯī* belonging to the Baath party

بعثة *ba'ṯa* (also *bi'ṯa*) pl. *ba'aṯāt* delegation, deputation, mission; dispatched group; group of select students sent to foreign universities; expedition; revival, rebirth, renaissance, rise | بعثة شرف *b. šaraf* a dispatched escort of honor; بعثة عسكرية (*'askarīya*) military mission; بعثة دبلوماسية diplomatic mission; بعثة اثرية (*aṯarīya*) archaeological expedition; رئيس البعثة *ra'īs al-b.* chief of mission (*dipl.*)

باعوث *bā'ūṯ* Easter (*Chr.*)

مبعث *mab'aṯ* sending, forwarding, dispatch; emission; awakening, arousal; — (pl. مباعث *mabā'iṯ*[2]) cause; factor

باعث *bā'iṯ* pl. بواعث *bawā'iṯ*[2] incentive, inducement, motive, spur, reason, cause, occasion

مبعوث *mab'ūṯ* dispatched, delegated; envoy, delegate; representative, deputy (in the Ottoman Empire)

منبعث *munba'aṯ* source, point of origin

بعثر *ba'ṯara* (بعثرة *ba'ṯara*) to scatter, strew around, fling about (ه s.th.); to disarrange, throw into disorder (ه s.th.); to squander, waste, dissipate (ه s.th.) **II** *taba'ṯara* pass.

مبعثر *muba'ṯar* scattered, widespread; tousled (hair)

بعج *ba'aja a* (*ba'j*) to slit open (ه the belly); to groove, dent, notch (ه s.th.) **VII** to have indentations or notches; to be bruised, dented, bumpy; to get battered

منبعج *munba'ij* notched, indented

بعد *ba'uda u* (*bu'd*) to be distant, far away, far off; to be away (عن from, ب a distance); to keep away, keep one's distance (عن from); to go far beyond (عن), exceed by far (عن s.th.); to be remote, improbable, unlikely | بعد به عن he kept him away from; لا يبعد ان it is not unlikely that ... **II** to remove (ه s.o.); to banish, exile, expatriate (ه s.o.) **III** to cause a separation (بين between) | باعد بين فلان وبين الشىء to prevent s.o. from attaining s.th.; باعد بين اجفانه (*ajfānihī*) to stare wide-eyed **IV** to remove (ه s.th., also ه s.o., عن from, out of); to take away (ه s.th.), to elimininate (ه s.th.), do away with (ه); to send away, dismiss (ه s.o.); to expatriate, banish, exile (ه s.o.); to exclude, make unlikely, improbable, impossible (ه s.th.); to go or move far away; to go very far (فى in or with s.th.); to exaggerate, go too far **VI** to be separated, lie apart, lie at some distance from one another; to separate, part company, become estranged; to move away, go away, withdraw, depart (عن from); to keep away, keep one's distance (عن from); to quit, leave, avoid (عن s.th.); to follow in regular intervals **VIII** to move or go away; to keep away, withdraw (عن from); to quit, leave, avoid (عن s.th.); to leave out of consideration, disregard (عن s.th.) **X** to single out, set aside (ه s.th.); to discard, sort out, reject (ه s.th. useless, old or rotten); to exclude, remove (ه s.o., ه s.th.); to exempt (ه من s.o. from military service); to think remote, farfetched (ه s.th.); to regard as unlikely (ه s.th.); to disqualify (ه s.o.); pass. *ustubʿida* to be eliminated, drop out (in sport competition) | لا يستبعد (*yustabʿadu*) it is not inconceivable, not improbable

بعد *buʿd* remoteness, farness; — (pl. ابعاد *abʿād*) distance; dimension (also fig.); interval (*mus.*); pl. ابعاد dimensions, proportions (e.g., of a catastrophe or a disaster) | على بعد and على البعد in the distance, far off; على بعد مئة متر at a distance of 100 meters; عن بعد and من بعد from a distance, from afar; ذو ثلاثة ابعاد three-dimensional; قياس الابعاد *qiyās al-a.* linear measure; بعد الهمة *b. al-himma* high aspirations, loftiness of purpose; بعد الشقة *b. aš-šiqqa* wide interval, wide gap; بعد الصيت *b. aṣ-ṣīt* renown, fame, celebrity; بعد الصوت *b. aṣ-ṣaut* do.; بعد النظر *b. an-naẓar* farsightedness, foresight; بعدا ل *buʿdan li* away with . . .!

بعد *baʿdu* then, thereupon; afterwards, later, after that, in the following; still, yet | فيما بعد afterwards, later; اما بعد see [1]اما; هو بعد صغير he is only a small boy, he is still young; لم يأت بعد (*yaʾti*) he hasn't come yet

بعد *baʿda* (prep.) after; in addition to, beside; aside from | . . . بعد كونه (*kaunihī*) aside from the fact that he is . . .; بعد ذلك afterwards, after that, later (on); besides, moreover; بعد ذاك besides, moreover; بعد ان *baʿda an* (conj.) after; بعد اذ (*iḏ*), بعد ما and من بعد ما (*baʿdi*) do.; سفه ما بعده سفه (*safahun*) the height of stupidity; كفر ما بعده كفر (*kufr*) an unequaled blasphemy; ص . . . وما بعدها page . . . ff. (in citations)

بعدئذ *baʿdaʾiḏin* then, thereafter, thereupon, after that, afterwards

○ بعدى *baʿdī* a posteriori (as attrib.)

بعيد *baʿīd* pl. *-ūn*, بعداء *buʿadāʾ*[2], بعد *buʿud*, بعدان *buʿdān*, بعاد *biʿād* distant, far away, far (عن from); remote, outlying, out-of-the-way; distant in time, long past, remote, bygone; far-reaching, extensive; farfetched, improbable, unlikely; unusual, strange, odd, queer; incompatible, inconsistent (عن with) | من بعيد from afar, from a distance; منذ سنين بعيدة (*sinīna*) for many years; منذ عهد بعيد (*ʿahd*) a long time ago; بعيد الاثر *b. al-aṯar* of far-reaching consequence; بعيد الاجل *b. al-ajal* long-lasting, of incalculable length; بعيد التاريخ remote in time, going way back in history, ancient; بعيد الشأو *b. aš-šaʾw* high-minded, bold; بعيد الشقة *b. aš-šiqqa* far apart; بعيد الغور *b. al-ġaur* deep; profound, unfathomable; بعيد المدى *b. al-madā* long-distance, long-range; extensive, far-reaching; مواصلات بعيدة المدى (*muwāṣalāt*) telecommunications; بعيد النظر *b. an-naẓar* farsighted; farseeing; بعيد المنال *b. al-manāl* hardly attainable, hard to get at; ذهب بعيدا to go far away, go to distant lands; تطلع الى بعيد to look off into the distance

بعيد *buʿaida* (prep.) shortly after, soon after

ابعد *abʿad*[2] pl. اباعد *abāʿid*[2] farther, remoter, more distant; more extensive; less likely, more improbable; pl. اباعد *abāʿid*[2] very distant relatives | الشرق الابعد (*šarq*) the Far East; الابعد the absent one (used as a polite periphrasis for s.o. who is being criticized or blamed for s.th.; also when referring to the 1st and 2nd persons); الى ابعد الغايات to the nth degree

ابعادية *abʿādīya* pl. *-āt* country estate

تبعيد *tabʿīd* banishment

بعاد *biʿād* distance

مباعدة *mubāʿada* sowing of dissension, estrangement, alienation

ابعاد *ibʿād* removal, separation, isolation; elimination; expatriation, banishment, deportation

تباعد *tabāʿud* interdistance; mutual estrangement

استبعاد *istibʿād* exclusion, removal, keeping at a distance

مبعد *mubʿid*: عضلة مبعدة (*ʿaḍala*) abductor (*anat.*)

مبعد *mubʿad* deported; deportee

متباعد *mutabāʿid* separate | فى فترات متباعدة (*fatarāt*) in wide intervals; فى فترات متباعدة من الزمن (*zaman*) at infrequent intervals, from time to time

مستبعد *mustabʿad* improbable, unlikely

¹بعر *baʿr, baʿar* droppings, dung (of animals)

²بعير *baʿīr* pl. ابعرة *abʿira*, بعران *buʿrān*, اباعر *abāʿir*², بعارين *baʿārīn*² camel

بعزق *baʿzaqa* (بعزقة *baʿzaqa*) to scatter, dissipate, squander, waste (ه s.th.)

مبعزق *mubaʿziq* squanderer, spendthrift, wastrel

بعض II to divide into parts or portions (ه s.th.) V to be divided, be divisible

بعض *baʿḍ* part, portion; one; some, a few; a little of, some of; البعض several (of a number or of a crowd), some people | بعض العلماء *b. al-ʿulamāʾ* one (or some) of the scholars; رفعنا بعضهم فوق بعض (*rafaʿnā*) we have exalted some of them above the others; البعض — البعض الآخر some — some, a few — others; بعضهم بعضا one another, each other, mutually, reciprocally; بعضه فى بعض one in the other, within one another; بعض الشىء *baʿḍa š-šaiʾ* to some extent, somewhat, a little, rather; بعض القرش *b. al-qirš* less than a piaster, a few pennies; فى بعض الطريق on the way, after passing a certain stretch of the way; فى بعض النهار (*b. an-nahār*) at a certain time of day, sometime or other during the day; فى بعض الوقت (*b. al-waqt*) sometimes; ماثله بعض المماثلة (*baʿḍa l-m.*) he resembled him somewhat, to some extent; منذ قرن وبعض قرن (*qarn*) for the last hundred years and more; هو من بعض خدامه (*b. ḵuddāmihī*) he is one of his servants; هذا من بعض ما عندكم that is proof of your goodness, very kind of you

بعوض *baʿūḍ* (n. un. ة) gnats, mosquitoes

تبعيض *tabʿīḍ* division, partition, portioning

بعكوكة *buʿkūka* club, society

بعل *baʿl* the god Baal; land or plants thriving on natural water supply; — (pl. بعول *buʿūl*, بعولة *buʿūla*) lord; husband

بعلة *baʿla* wife

بعلى *baʿlī* unirrigated (land, plants)

بعلبك *baʿlabakk*² Baalbek (ancient Heliopolis, village in E Lebanon)

بغت *baġata a* (*baġt*, بغتة *baġta*) to surprise (ه s.o.); to come unexpectedly, descend unawares (ه upon s.o.) III do. VII to be taken by surprise; to be taken aback, be aghast, be nonplused

بغتة *baġta* surprising event, surprise; *baġtatan*, على بغتة *ʿalā baġtatin* all of a sudden, suddenly, surprisingly

مباغتة *mubāġata* sudden arrival, surprising incident or event, surprise; sudden attack, raid

باغت *bāġit* sudden, unexpected

بغاث *buġāṯ* pl. بغثان *biġṯān* small birds

بغادة see بوغادة

بغاز see بوغاز

بغدد II *tabaġdada* to swagger, throw one's weight around, be fresh (properly, to behave like one from Baghdad)

بغداد *baġdād*² Baghdad

بغدادى *baḡdādī* pl. *-ūn,* بغاددة *baḡādida* a native of Baghdad

[1]بغش *baḡaša a*: بغشت السماء (*samā'u*) there was a light shower

بغشة *baḡša* light rain shower

[2]بغشة *buḡša* = بقشة

[3]بغاشة (*eg.*) *buḡāša* stuffed pastry made of flour, eggs and butter

بغض *baḡiḍa a, baḡuḍa u* (*buḡḍ,* بغاضة *baḡāḍa*) to be hated, hateful, odious **II** to make (ه s.o.) hateful (الى to s.o.) **III** to loathe, detest, hate (ه s.o.) **IV** to loathe, detest, hate (ه s.o.) **VI** to hate each other

بغض *buḡḍ,* بغضة *biḡḍa* and بغضاء *baḡḍā'*[2] hatred, hate

بغيض *baḡīḍ* hateful, odious (الى to s.o.), loathsome, abominable

تباغض *tabāḡuḍ* mutual hatred

مبغوض *mabḡūḍ* detested, hateful, odious

مبغض *mubḡiḍ* pl. *-ūn* hater; — *mubḡaḍ* detested, hateful, odious

بغل *baḡl* pl. بغال *biḡāl,* ابغال *abḡāl* mule; بغلة *baḡla* pl. *baḡalāt* female mule | بغال القنطرة *b. al-qanṭara* the piers of the bridge

بغال *baḡḡāl* pl. *-ūn* mule driver, muleteer

بغى *baḡā i* (بغاء *buḡā'*) to seek, desire, covet, seek to attain (ه s.th.), wish for s.th. (ه); — (*baḡy*) to wrong, treat unjustly (على s.o.); to oppress (على s.o.), commit outrage (على upon); to whore, fornicate **VII** ينبغى it is desirable, necessary; it is proper, appropriate, seemly; it ought to be, should be; with له: it behooves him; it is incumbent upon him; with عليه: he must, he should, he ought to | ينبغى لى ان I must . . . **VIII** to seek, desire (ه s.th.), aspire (ه to s.th.), strive (ه for) | ابتغى من فضل الله to strive for God's grace

بغى *baḡy* infringement, outrage, injustice, wrong

بغى *baḡīy* pl. بغايا *baḡāyā* whore, prostitute

بغية *buḡya, biḡya* object of desire; wish, desire; *buḡyata* (prep.) with the aim of, for the purpose of

بغاء *biḡā'* prostitution

بغاء *buḡā'* wish(ing), desire, endeavor, effort

مبغى *mabḡan* pl. مباغ *mabāḡin* brothel

مباغ *mabāḡin* coveted things, desiderata, wishes, desires

ابتغاء *ibtiḡā'* desire, wish; *ibtiḡā'a* (prep.) for the purpose of

باغ *bāḡin* pl. بغاة *buḡāh* desiring, coveting, striving; committing outrages, oppressive, unjust; oppressor, tyrant

مبتغى *mubtaḡan* aspired goal; aspiration, desire, endeavor, effort

بفتة *bafta* calico, Indian cotton cloth

بفتيك *biftēk* beefsteak

[1]بق *baqq* (n. un. ة) bedbug, chinch | شجرة البق elm (*bot.*)

[2]بق *baqqa u* (*baqq*) to give off in abundance

بقاق *baqqāq* garrulous, loquacious; chatterbox, prattler

بقبق *baqbaqa* (بقبقة *baqbaqa*) to gurgle, bubble, splutter, purl (water); to chatter, prattle

بقباق *baqbāq* garrulous, loquacious; chatterbox, prattler

بقبوقة *baqbūqa* blister (of the skin)

بقجة *buqja* pl. بقج *buqaj* bundle, pack, package

بقدونس *baqdūnis, baqdūnas* parsley

بقر *baqara u* to split open, rip open, cut open (ه s.th.) **IV** do.

بقر *baqar* (coll.; n. un. ة) pl. ابقار *abqār*, بقور *buqūr* bovines, cattle, cows

بقرة *baqara* pl. *-āt* cow

بقرى *baqarī* bovine, cattle-, cow- (in compounds); (*eg.*) beef | لحم بقرى (*laḥm*) beef

بقار *baqqār* pl. ة cowhand, cowboy

بقراط *buqrāṭ*[2] Hippocrates

بقس *baqs* box, boxwood (*bot.*)

بقسمات *buqsumāt* rusk, zwieback; biscuit

بقشة *buqša* Yemenite copper coin

بقشيش *baqšīš* pl. بقاشيش *baqāšīš*[2] present of money; tip, gratuity, baksheesh

بقع **II** to spot, stain, smudge (ه s.th.) **V** to become stained, get smudged; to be spotted, stained

بقعة *buqʿa* pl. بقع *buqaʿ*, بقاع *biqāʿ* spot, blot, smudge, stain; place, spot, site; plot; spot or patch (of the earth)

البقاع *al-biqāʿ* the Bekaa (name of a region in Lebanon)

ابقع *abqaʿ*[2] spotted, speckled

باقعة *bāqiʿa* pl. بواقع *bawāqiʿ*[2] sly dog, shrewd fellow

بقل *baqala u* (*baql*) to sprout (plant)

بقل *baql* (coll.; n. un. ة) pl. بقول *buqūl*, ابقال *abqāl* herbs, potherbs, greens, herbaceous plants; specif., legumes | البقلة الباردة hyacinth bean (Dolichos lablab L.); البقلة الحمقاء (*ḥamqāʾ*) purslane (*bot.*); البقلة الذهبية (*dahabīya*) garden orach (*bot.*); بقلة الخطاطيف celandine (*bot.*); بقلة الملك *b. al-malik* common fumitory (*bot.*)

بقلى *baqlī*: الفصيلة البقلية the Leguminosae (*bot.*)

بقال *baqqāl* pl. *-ūn*, بقالة *baqqāla* greengrocer; grocer

بقالة *biqāla* the grocery business; grocery store, shop for foodstuffs

بقلاوة *baqlāwa*, بقلاوا a kind of Turkish delight, pastry made of puff paste with honey and almonds or pistachios

بقم *baqqam* brazilwood

بقى *baqiya a* (بقاء *baqāʾ*) to remain, stay, continue to be (على in a state or condition); to keep up, maintain (على a state or condition); to be left behind, be left over; to last, continue, go on; (with foll. imperf. or part.) to continue to do s.th., keep doing s.th.; to become | لم يبق طفلا (*yabqa ṭiflan*) he is no longer a child **II** to leave, leave over, leave behind (ه s.th.) **IV** to make (ه s.o.) stay; to retain, leave unchanged, leave as it is, preserve, maintain, keep up (ه s.th.); to leave, leave over, leave behind (ه s.th., ه s.o.); to leave untouched, save, spare (على s.o., s.th., e.g., s.o.'s life) **V** to remain, stay, continue to be (على in a state or condition); to be left, be left over **X** to make stay, ask to stay, hold back, detain (ه s.o.); to spare, save, protect (ه s.o., ه s.th.); to preserve (ه s.th.); to retain, keep (ه s.th.); to store, put away (ه s.th.)

بقية *baqīya* pl. بقايا *baqāyā* remainder, rest; remnant, residue; continuation and conclusion (of an article, etc.) | بقية الدول *b. ad-duwal* the remaining countries, the rest of the countries; البقية الباقية (*bāqiya*) the last remnant

بقاء *baqāʾ* remaining, staying, lingering, abiding; continuation, continuance, duration; survival, continuation of existence after life; immortality, eternal life; existence; permanence | دار البقاء the hereafter

ابقى *abqā* more lasting, more durable, more permanent; better preserving; conducive to longer wear, better protecting

ابقاء *ibqā'* continuation, retention; maintenance, conservation, preservation | ابقاء الحالة على ما كانت عليه maintenance of the status quo

استبقاء *istibqā'* continuation, retention; maintenance, conservation, preservation

باق *bāqin* staying; remaining; left; remainder (*arith.*); lasting, continuing, permanent, unending; surviving; living on; everlasting, eternal (God) | الباقيات الصالحات the good works

متبق *mutabaqqin* residue, remnant, remainder, rest

بك (Turk.) *bē* (*eg.*) pl. بكوات *bakawāt*, بهوات *bahawāt* bey; see also بيه

بكوية *bakawīya* rank of a bey

بكة *bakka*[2] (by-form of مكة in the Koran) Mecca

بكئ *bakī'* pl. بكاء *bikā'* having or giving little, sparing (e.g., of words)

بكاسين *bikāsīn* bécassine, snipe (*zool.*)

بكالوريا (Fr. *baccalauréat*) *bakālōriyā* baccalaureate, bachelor's degree; (*Maġr.*) secondary school diploma

بكالوريوس *bakālōriyūs* bachelor (academic degree) | بكالوريوس علوم Bachelor of Science; بكالوريوس فنون Bachelor of Arts

بكباشي (Turk. *binbaşı*) *bimbāšī*, *bikbāšī* pl. *-īya* lieutenant colonel (formerly, *Eg.*, *Sudan*; *mil.*)

بكت[1] II to censure, blame (ه s.o.)

تبكيت *tabkīt* blame, reproach | تبكيت الضمير remorse

بكتة[2] (It.) *baketta* pl. *-āt* pack(et)

بكتيري *baktērī* bacterial, caused by bacteria

بكتيريا *baktēriyā* bacteria

بكر *bakara u* (بكور *bukūr*) to set out early in the morning, get up early; to come early (الى to), be early (الى at) **II** do., بكر في and بكر ب with foll. verbal noun: to do s.th. early, prematurely, ahead of its time | بكر عن الموعد (*mau'id*) to come earlier than the appointed time **III** to be ahead of s.o. (ه), anticipate, forestall (ه s.o.) **IV** = **I**; **VIII** to be the first to take (ه s.th.), be the first to embark (ه on s.th.); to deflower (ها a girl); to invent (ه s.th.); to create, originate, start (ه s.th.); to think up, think out (ه e.g., a ruse, a story)

بكر *bakr* pl. ابكر *abkur*, بكران *bukrān* young camel

بكر *bikr* pl. ابكار *abkār* first-born, eldest; firstling; unprecedented, novel, new; virgin; virginal

بكري *bikrī* first-born, first

بكرية *bikrīya* primogeniture

بكرة *bakra* and *bakara* pl. بكر *bakar*, *-āt* reel; pulley (*mech.*); spool, coil; winch, windlass | خيط بكرة *ḵaiṭ b.* thread

بكرة *bakra*: على بكرة ابيهم *'alā bakrati abīhim*, عن بكرة ابيهم and عن بكرتهم all without exception, all of them, all together; خرجت الجماهير عن بكرتها the crowd went forth as one man

بكرة *bukra* pl. بكر *bukar* early morning; *bukratan* early in the morning; tomorrow; on the following day, next day

بكير *bakīr* coming early; early, premature; precocious

بكور *bakūr* and باكور *bākūr* coming early; early, premature; precocious

بكور *bukūr* earliness, prematureness, premature arrival; early morning, daybreak | بكوري في العود (*'aud*) my early return

بكارة *bakāra* virginity

بكارة *bakkāra* pulley (*mech.*) | بكارة مركبة (*murakkaba*) set of pulleys, block and tackle

بكورة *bukūra* and بكورية *bukūrīya* primogeniture

باكورة *bākūra* pl. بواكير *bawākīr*[2] firstlings; first results, first fruits; first work (of an author); beginning, rise, dawn; (with foll. genit.) initial, early, first; pl. بواكير first signs or indications; initial symptoms; heralds, harbingers (fig.) | باكورة الفواكه early fruit; كان باكورة اعماله the first thing he did was ...

ابكر *abkar*[2] rising earlier; earlier

مبكار *mibkār* precocious

ابتكار *ibtikār* pl. *-āt* novelty, innovation; creation; invention; origination, first production; initiative; (also قوة الابتكار *quwwat al-i.*) creativity, originality; pl. ابتكارات specif., creations of fashion, fashion designs

ابتكارى *ibtikārī* original

ابتكارية *ibtikārīya* originality

باكر *bākir* early; premature; باكرا *bākiran* in the morning; early (adv.) | فى الصباح الباكر (*ṣabāḥ*) early in the morning; الى باكر till tomorrow

باكرة *bākira* pl. بواكر *bawākir*[2] firstlings, first produce, early fruits, early vegetables; pl. first indications or symptoms, heralds, harbingers

مبكر *mubakkir* doing early; early; مبكرا *mubakkiran* early in the morning, early | فى ساعة مبكرة at an early hour

مبتكر *mubtakir* creator; creative; inventor; — *mubtakar* newly created, novel, new; original; (pl. *-āt*) creation, specif. fashion creation, invention | ثوب مبتكر (*ṯaub*) original design, model, dress creation

بكرج *bakraj* pl. بكارج *bakārij*[2] kettle, coffee pot

بقسمات see بكسماط, بكسماد

بكل II to buckle, buckle up, button up (ه s.th.); to fold, cross (ه the arms)

بكلة *bukla* pl. بكل *bukal*, *-āt* buckle

بكلاه (It. *baccalá*) *bakalāh* codfish

بكلوريا and بكلوريوس see بكالوريا and بكالوريوس

بكم *bakima* *a* to be dumb; — *bakuma* *u* to be silent, hold one's tongue IV to silence (ه s.o.) V to become silent; to become dumb

بكم *bakam* dumbness

ابكم *abkam*[2], f. بكماء *bakmā'*[2], pl. بكم *bukm* dumb

بكوات and بكوية see بك

بكى *bakā* *i* (بكاء *bukā'*, بكى *bukan*) to cry, weep (على over); to bemoan, lament, bewail (ه s.o.), mourn (ه for) II and IV to make (ه s.o.) cry X to move (ه s.o.) to tears, make (ه s.o.) cry

بكاء *bukā'* crying, weeping (n.)

بكاء *bakkā'* given to weeping frequently, tearful, lachrymose

حائط المبكى *ḥā'iṭ al-mabkā* the Wailing Wall (in Jerusalem)

باكية *bākiya* pl. *-āt* wailing-woman, hired mourner; — (pl. بواك *bawākin*; *eg.*) arch, arcade

باك *bākin* pl. بكاة *bukāh* weeping, crying; weeper, wailer, mourner

مبك *mubkin*, *mubakkin* causing tears, tearful; sad, lamentable, deplorable

بكين *bikīn*, *pikīn* Peking

[1]بل *bal* (also with foll. و *wa-*) nay, — rather...; (and) even; but, however, yet

[2]بل *balla u* (*ball*) to moisten, wet, make wet (ه s.th., ه s.o.); — *balla i* to recover (من مرض from an illness) II to moisten, wet, make wet (ه s.th., ه s.o.) IV to recover (من مرض from an illness) V and VIII to be moistened, be wetted; to become wet

بل *ball* moistening, wetting; moisture

بل *bill* recovery, convalescence, recuperation

بلة *billa* moisture, humidity | ما زاد الطين بلة *mā zāda ṭ-ṭīna billatan* what made things even worse ...

بلل *balal* moisture, humidity; moistness, dampness, wetness

بليل *balīl* a moist, cool wind

بليلة *balīla* (*eg.*) porridge made of wheat or maize with milk and sugar

ابلال *iblāl* recovery, convalescence, recuperation

تبلل *taballul* moistness, dampness, humidity

مبلول *mablūl*, مبلل *muballal*, مبتل *mubtall* moist, damp, wet; drenched (by rain)

[3]بلى *billī* (from Fr. *bille*): كرسى بلى (*kursī*) ball bearing

بلا *bi-lā* (prep.) without

بلاتوه (Fr.) *blatōh* pl. بلاتوهات plateau; stage, boards (*theat.*)

بلاتين, پلاتين *blātīn*, *plātīn* platinum

بلاج (Fr. *plage*) *blāž* pl. *-āt* beach

بلاجرا *balagrā* pellagra

بلارج *balāraj* stork

بلاستيك (Fr. *plastique*) *blāstīk*, *blastik* plastic

بلاش (*dial.*; < بلا شيء) *balāš* free, gratis

بلاط see بلط

بلاك (Engl.) *blāg* pl. *-āt* spark plug (*ir.*)

بلان, بلانة see بلن

بلبط *balbaṭa* to gurgle

[1]بلبل *balbala* to disquiet, make uneasy or restive, stir up, rouse, disturb, trouble, confuse (ه s.o., ه s.th.) II *tabalbala* to feel uneasy, be anxious; to be or become confused, get all mixed up

بلبلة *balbala* pl. بلابل *balābil*[2] anxiety, uneasiness, concern; confusion, muddle, jumble, chaos

بلبال *balbāl* anxiety, uneasiness, concern

بلابل *balābil*[2] anxieties, apprehensions

تبلبل *tabalbul* muddle, confusion | تبلبل الالسنة *t. al-alsina* confusion of tongues (at the tower of Babel)

[2]بلبل *bulbul* pl. بلابل *balābil*[2] nightingale

[1]بلج *balaja u* (بلوج *bulūj*) to shine; to dawn (morning, aurora); — *balija a* (*balaj*) to be happy, be glad (ب about), be delighted (ب at) IV to shine (sun) V and VII = *balaja*

ابلج *ablaj*[2] gay, serene, bright, clear, fair, nice, beautiful

انبلاج الفجر *inbilāj al-fajr* daybreak

[2]بلاج look up alphabetically

بلجيكا *beljīkā* Belgium

بلجيكى *beljīkī* Belgian (adj. and n.)

بلح *balaḥ* (coll.; n. un. ة) dates (*bot.*)

بلد *baluda u* (بلادة *balāda*) to be stupid, idiotic, dull-witted II to acclimatize, habituate (ه s.th., to a country or region) V pass. of II; to become stupid, besotted, lapse into a state of idiocy; to show o.s. from the stupid side VI to feign stupidity

بلد **balad** m. and f., pl. بلاد *bilād* country; town, city; place, community, village; pl. بلاد country; countries (forming a whole); pl. بلدان *buldān* countries | بلاد الحبش *b. al-ḥabaš* Ethiopia; بلاد الصين *b. aṣ-ṣīn* China; بلاد الهند *b. al-hind* India; البلاد العربية the Arab countries

بلدة *balda* town, city; place, community, village; rural community; township

بلدى *baladī* native, indigenous, home (as opposed to foreign, alien); (fellow) citizen, compatriot, countryman; a native; communal, municipal; popular, national, folk (in compounds) | مجلس بلدى (*majlis*) city council, local council; رقص بلدى (*raqṣ*) folk dance; زى بلدى (*ziyy*) national costume; طب بلدى (*ṭibb*) folk medicine; قهوة بلدى (*qahwa*) local coffee shop; (*eg.*); موسيقى بلدية (*mūsīqā*) folk music

بلدية *baladīya* pl. *-āt* township, community, rural community; ward, district (of a city); municipality, municipal council, local authority

بليد *balīd* and ابلد *ablad*[2] stupid, doltish, dull-witted, idiotic; obtuse, spiritless, apathetic (person)

بلادة *balāda* stupidity, silliness; apathy

تبلد *taballud* idiocy, dullness, obtuseness, apathy

متبلد *mutaballid* besotted, dull, stupid; spiritless, apathetic, dull (feeling)

بلور ,بلورة ,بلورى look up alphabetically

ابليز look up alphabetically

ابليس pl. ابالسة look up alphabetically

بلسان **balasān** balm; garden balm (Melissa officinalis; *bot.*); balm-tree; elder, elder tree (*bot.*)

بلسم **balsam** pl. بلاسم *balāsim*[2] balsam, balm

بلسمى *balsamī* balsamic, balmy

بلشف **balšafa** to Bolshevize II *tabalšafa* to be Bolshevized

بلشفة *balšafa* Bolshevization

بلشفى *bulšifī* pl. بلاشفة *balāšifa* Bolshevist(ic); Bolshevik, Bolshevist

بلشفية *bulšifīya* Bolshevism

بلشون **balašūn** heron (*zool.*)

[1]بلص **balaṣa** *u* (*balṣ*) and II to extort, wring forcibly (من ه from s.o. s.th.); to blackmail (ه s.o.)

بلص *balṣ* extortion, blackmail; forcible imposition of taxes

[2]بلاص **ballāṣ** pl. بلاليص *balālīṣ*[2] (*eg.*) earthenware jar

[1]بلط **II** to pave (ه s.th., with flagstones or tiles)

بلاط *balāṭ* pavement, tiled floor; floor tiles; palace; court (of a prince); pl. ابلطة *ablīṭa* floor tiles | البلاط الملكى (*malakī*) the royal court; حداد البلاط *ḥidād al-b.* court mourning

بلاطة *balāṭa* floor tile; flagstone, slabstone; paving stone

تبليط *tablīṭ* paving, tile-laying

مبلط *muballaṭ* paved, tiled

[2]بلوط **ballūṭ** oak; acorn

[3]بلطة **balṭa** pl. *-āt*, بلط *bulaṭ* ax

بلطجى *balṭajī* pl. *-īya* sapper, pioneer (*mil.*); — (*eg.*) *balṭagī* pl. *-īya* gangster; rowdy, bully, ruffian; bouncer; bruiser (in urban underworld)

[4]بلطة **balaṭa** balata gum

[5]بلطو (Fr. *paletot*) **balṭō** pl. *-āt*, بلاطى *balāṭī* paletot, overcoat

[6]بلطى **bulṭī** bolti (Tilapia nilotica), a food fish of the Nile

البلطيق *al-balṭīq* the Baltic countries | بحر البلطيق *baḥr al-b.* the Baltic Sea

بالوظة *bālūẓa* hand press; (*eg.*) a kind of cream made of cornstarch, lemon juice and honey, or the like

بلع *bala'a* and *bali'a a* (*bal'*) to swallow, swallow up (ه s.th.); to gulp down (ه s.th.); to put up (ه with s.th.), swallow, stomach, brook (ه s.th.) | بلع ريقه (*rīqahū*) lit.: to swallow one's saliva, i.e., to catch one's breath, take a little rest, have a break; to restrain o.s., hold back (said of one in a rage) **II** and **IV** to make (ه s.o.) swallow (ه s.th.) | بلعه ريقه (*rīqahā*) to grant s.o. a short rest **VII** to be swallowed; capable of being swallowed **VIII** = **I**

بلعة *bal'a* large bite, big gulp

بلاعة *ballā'a*, بلوعة *ballū'a* pl. *-āt*, بلاليع *balālī'*[2] sink, drain

بالوعة *bālū'a* pl. *-āt*, بواليع *bawālī'*[2] sewer, drain; sink (in a kitchen)

بلعم *bul'um* pl. بلاعم *balā'im*[2] and بلعوم *bul'ūm* pl. بلاعيم *balā'īm*[2] pharynx (*anat.*); بلعوم gullet, esophagus (*anat.*)

بلغ[1] *balaġa u* (بلوغ *bulūġ*) to reach (ه s.o., ه s.th.), get (ه, ه to), arrive (ه at); to come, amount (ه to), be worth (ه so and so much); to come to s.o.'s (ه) ears; to attain puberty (boy); to ripen, mature (fruit, or the like); to come of age; to exhaust, wear out (من s.o.); to act (من upon s.o.), have its effect (من on), affect (من s.o.); to go far (فى, من in s.th.), attain a high degree (فى, من of s.th.) | بلغ به الى to make s.o. or s.th. get to or arrive at, lead or take s.o. or s.th. to, get s.o. or s.th. to the point where; بلغ به الجحود ان (*juḥūdu*) his ingratitude went so far that he ...; بلغ به الترنح ان (*tarannuḥ*) he began to reel so violently that ...; بلغ اوجه (*aujahū*) to reach its peak, attain its climax; بلغ الامر مبلغ الجد (*mablaġa l-jidd*) the matter became serious; بلغ السيل الزبى *b. s-sailu z-zubā* the matter reached a climax, things came to a head; بلغ مبلغ الرجال (*mablaġa r-rijāl*) to be sexually mature, attain manhood, come of age; بلغ مبلغ الفتوة (*m. al-futūwa*) to attain the age of a young man; بلغ اشده (*ašuddahū*) to attain full maturity, come of age; to reach its climax; بلغ فى الشىء مبلغا (or من الشىء) (*mablaġan*) to attain a high degree of s.th.; حين بلغت بذكرياتى هذا المبلغ (*ḥīna, ḏikrayātī, mablaġa*) when I had come to this point in my reminiscences; بلغ منه كل مبلغ (*kulla mablaġin*) to work havoc on s.o.; بلغ منتهاه (*muntahāhu*) to reach its climax, come to a head; اللهم انى بلغت *allāhumma innī balaġtu* in any case, I have fulfilled my task, done or said everything I could **II** to make (ه s.o.) reach or attain (ه s.th.); to take, bring (ه الى s.th. to s.o.), see that s.th. (ه) gets (الى to); to convey, transmit, impart, communicate, report (ه ه to s.o. s.th.); to inform, notify (ه ه s.o. of s.th.), tell, let know (ه ه s.o. about); to report (عن about), give an account of (عن); to inform (عن against s.o.), report, denounce (عن s.o.) | بلغ رسالة to fulfill a mission; بلغه سلامى *balliġhu salāmī* give him my best regards! **III** to exaggerate (فى in s.th.); to overdo, do too long (فى s.th.); to go to greatest lengths, do one's utmost (فى in); to intensify (فى s.th.) **IV** to make (ه, ه s.o., s.th.) reach or attain (الى s.th.); to make (ه s.th.) amount (الى to), raise (ه an amount, a salary, الى to); to inform, notify (ب or عن ه s.o. of s.th.), tell, let know (ب or عن ه s.o. about); to announce, state, disclose (ه s.th.); to inform (عن against s.o.), report, denounce (عن s.o.) | ابلغ البوليس ب to report s.th. to the police; ابلغ نفسه عذرها (*nafsahū 'uḏrahā*) he did his utmost, but without success **V** to content o.s., be content (ب with); to eke out an existence; to still one's hunger (ب with), eat (ب s.th.);

to be delivered, be transmitted; to be informed (ه about s.th.)

سمعا لا بلغا *sam'an lā balğan!* may it be heard but not fulfilled, i.e., God forbid! (used at the mention of s.th. unpleasant)

بلغة *bulğa* and بلاغ *balāğ* sufficiency, competency, adequacy (see also ²بلغة below)

بلاغ *balāğ* pl. *-āt* communication, information, message, report; announcement, proclamation; communiqué; statement; notification (of the police), charge, complaint | بلاغ اخير ultimatum; بلاغ عسكرى (*'askarī*) armed forces' report, military communiqué

بليغ *balīğ* pl. بلغاء *bulağā'*[2] eloquent; intense, lasting, deep, profound (e.g., an impression); serious, grave (e.g., an injury)

بلوغ *bulūğ* reaching, attainment, arrival (at); maturity, legal majority

بلاغة *balāğa* eloquence; art of good style, art of composition; literature | علم البلاغة *'ilm al-b.* rhetoric, rhetorical art of the Arabs

ابلغ *ablağ*[2] more emphatic, farther reaching, deeper; more intense, stronger; more serious, graver; rhetorically superior, of higher stylistic value (expression; *rhet.*)

مبلغ *mablağ* pl. مبالغ *mabāliğ*[2] amount, sum of money; extent, scope, range; (see also examples under بلغ I) | مبلغ اسمى (*ismī*) nominal par; المبالغ المودعة (*mūda'a*) the deposits (at a bank); ليتبين مبلغ قولى من الجد (*li-yatabayyana, qaulī, jidd*) in order to find, out to what extent my words were meant seriously

تبليغ *tablīğ* pl. *-āt* conveyance, transmission, delivefy (الى to s.o.); conveyance or revelation of a message (by a prophet); information (عن about); report, notification (عن of); communication, announcement, notice | كتاب التبليغ credentials

مبالغة *mubālağa* pl. *-āt* exaggeration; intensification, strengthening (of an expression)

ابلاغ *iblāğ* conveyance, transmission

بالغ *bāliğ* extensive, far-reaching; considerable; serious (wound), deep, profound, violent, vehement (feelings), strong, intense; mature; of age, legally major

مبلغ *muballiğ* bearer (of news), messenger; informer, denouncer; detective

²بلغة *bulğa, balğa* pl. *-āt, bulağ* slipper of yellow leather

البلغار *al-bulğār* the Bulgarians

بلغارى *bulğārī* Bulgarian (adj. and n.)

بلغاريا *bulğāriyā* Bulgaria

بلغم *balğam* phlegm; (pl. بلاغم *balāğim*[2]) expectoration, sputum

بلغمى *balğamī* phlegmatic; phlegmy, mucous

بلف *balafa i* (*balf*) to bluff II do.

بلف *balf*, بلفة *balfa* bluff

ابلق *ablaq*[2] piebald

بلقيس *bilqīs*[2] Muslim name of the Queen of Sheba

البلقان *al-balqān* the Balkans

بلقانى *balqānī* Balkan

بلقع *balqa'* and بلقعة *balqa'a* pl. بلاقع *balāqi'*[2] wasteland

بلك see بلوك

بلكون *balkōn* and (*eg.*) بلكونة *balakōna* pl. *-āt* balcony

¹بلم *balam* anchovy

²بلم *balam* pl. ابلام *ablām* sailing barge (*ir.*)

بلم[3] IV to be silent, hold one's tongue

بلمر *balmara* to polymerize (ه s.th.; *chem.*) II *tabalmara* to be polymerized

بلمرة *balmara* polymerization | البلمرة الهيدروجينية (*hidrōjēnīya*) hydrocracking (process in oil refining)

بلان *ballān* bathhouse attendant; name of a plant growing near stagnant waters

بلانة *ballāna* female bathhouse attendant; lady's maid

بلنسية *balansiya*[2] Valencia (region and city in E Spain)

بلين pl. بلالين look up alphabetically

بله *baliha* *a* to be stupid, simple-minded VI to feign foolishness, pretend to be stupid X to deem (ه s.o.) stupid or simple-minded

بله *balah* and بلاهة *balāha* stupidity, foolishness, simple-mindedness; feeble-mindedness | بلاهة مبكرة (*mubakkira*) dementia praecox

بله *balha* (with foll. acc. or genit.) let alone, not to speak of, not to mention

ابله *ablah*[2], f. بلهاء *balhā'*[2], pl. بله *bulh* stupid, doltish, dull-witted; simple-minded; feeble-minded

بلهارسيا *bilharsiyā* bilharziasis, schistosomiasis (*med.*)

بلهنية *bulahniya* abundance, wealth, variety (of earthly possessions)

بلهوان[1] see بهلوان

□ بلهون[2] *bulhōn* pl. بلاهين *balāhīn*[2] (= ابو الهول; *eg.*) sphinx

(بلو and بلى) بلا *balā* *u* (*balw*, بلاء *balā'*) to test, try, put to the test (ه s.o., ه s.th.); to know from long experience (ه s.th.); to afflict (ه s.o.); — بلى *baliya* *a* (بلى *bilan*, بلاء *balā'*) to be or become old, worn, shabby (clothes); to dwindle away, vanish; to deteriorate, decline, become decrepit; to disintegrate (a corpse), decay, rot, spoil III to care, be concerned (ب or ه, ه about), be mindful (ب or ه, ه of s.o., of s.th.); to pay attention (ب or ه to), mind, heed, take into consideration, take into account (ب or ه s.th.); to take notice (ب of) | ما ابالى *mā ubālī*, لا ابالى I don't care! I don't mind! it's all right with me! لا يبالى (as a relat. clause) unconcerned, heedless, careless, reckless IV to try, test, put to the test (ه s.o.); to make experienced, harden, inure (ه s.o.; said of trials, experiences); to work havoc (ه on s.th.); to wear out (ه s.th.) | ابلى بلاء حسنا (*balā'an ḥasanan*) to stand the test; to prove o.s. brave (in war) VIII to try, tempt, put to the test (ه s.o.); to afflict (ب ه s.o. with), visit (ب ه on s.o. s.th.); pass. *ubtuliya* to become or be afflicted (ب with, by), suffer (ب from)

بلى *bilan* decline, deterioration; decay, putrefaction, decomposition; worn condition; wear; shabbiness

بلى *balīy* worn, old, shabby, threadbare; decrepit, dilapidated, decaying, decomposed, rotten

بلية *balīya* pl. بلايا *balāyā* trial, tribulation, visitation, affliction, distress, misfortune, calamity

بلاء *balā'* trial, tribulation, visitation, affliction, distress, misfortune; scourge, plague; creditable performance, bravery, gallantry, heroic action | بلاء حسن (*ḥasan*) favor, blessing, grace (of God); good performance

بلوى *balwā* trial; tribulation, visitation, affliction, distress, misfortune, calamity; necessity, need | عمت البلوى به (*'ammat*) it has become a general necessity

مبالاة *mubālāh* consideration, regard, heed, attention | لامبالاة *lā-mubālāh* indifference, unconcern, carelessness

ابتلاء *ibtilā'* trial, tribulation, affliction, visitation

بال *bālin* old, worn, worn out; shabby, threadbare, ragged, tattered; decrepit, dilapidated; decayed, rotten; obsolete, antiquated

مبال *mubālin* observant, heedful, mindful (ب of) | غير مبال ب heedless of

مبتلى *mubtalan* (less correctly مبتل *mubtalin*) afflicted (ب with, by), suffering (ب from)

بلوجينز (Engl.) *blūjīnz* and بنطلون بلوجين (*banṭalōn*) blue jeans

بلور *balwara* to crystallize out (ه s.th.); to visualize (ه future goals, objectives); to zero-in on (ه s.th., e.g., an idea) **II** *tabalwara* to crystallize; to be crystallized; to be covered with crystals; to crystallize out

بلور *billaur*, (*colloq.*) *ballōr* pl. *-āt* crystal; crystal glass, flint glass, glass | بلور صخرى (*ṣakrī*) rock crystal, transparent quartz

بلورة *billaura, ballōra* (n. un.) pl. *-āt* crystal; crystal glass, flint glass, glass; tube (radio); crystal, quartz plate (of a detector; radio); negative (*phot.*) | بلورة جليدية (*jalīdīya*) ice crystal

بلورى *billaurī, ballōrī* crystalline; crystal (adj.)

بلورية *billaurīya, ballōrīya* pl. *-āt* lense (*opt.*)

مبلور *mubalwar*: فواكه مبلورة candied fruits

متبلور *mutabalwir* crystalline

بلوز، بلوزة (Fr. *blouse*) *bəlūz, bəlūza* pl. *-āt* blouse

بلوطو *blūṭō* Pluto (planet)

بلوفر (Engl.) *blōver* pl. *blōvrāt* (*eg.*) pullover

بلوك (Turk. *bölük*) *bulūk* pl. *-āt* company (formerly, *Eg.*; *mil.*) | بلوك امين *b. amīn* quartermaster, paymaster (formerly, *Eg.*, *Sudan*; *mil.*)

بلون *balōn* pl. *-āt* balloon

بلى[1] *balā* (after a negation) oh yes! but of course! certainly!

بلى[2] *baliya* etc., see بلو

بلى[3] (Fr. *bille*) *bily* (*eg.*) marbles | لعبة البلى *laʿbat al-b.* game of marbles

بلياتشو (It. *pagliaccio*) *palyatšō* clown, buffoon

بلياردو (It. *bigliardo*) *bilyardō* billiards

بليزر (Engl.) *blēzer* pl. *blēzrāt* (*eg.*) blazer

بليسيه *bilīsēh* plissé, pleating

بلين[1] *ballīn* pl. بلالين *balālīn*[2] pallium, liturgical vestment of a bishop worn over the chasuble (*Chr.*); monk's robe (*Copt.-Chr.*)

بليون[2] *bilyōn* (*eg.*), *bilyūn* (*leb.-syr.*) pl. بلايين *balāyīn*[2] billion (U.S.: 1000 millions, G.B.: a million millions)

بم see ب

بم *bamm* lowest string of a musical instrument

بمباشى *bimbāšī* see بكباشى

بمباغ *bumbāḡ*, بمباغة *bumbāḡa* bow tie

بمباى *bombāy* Bombay

بامية look up alphabetically

بن[1] **V** تبنى *tabannā* to adopt as son (ه s.o.); to adopt, embrace (ه s.th.)

ابن *ibn* pl. ابناء *abnā'*, بنون *banūn* son (written بن after the personal name, before the father's name, e.g., زيد بن احمد); descendant, scion; offspring, son (of a nation or people); pl. ابناء (with genit.) inhabitants (of a place); pl. بنون boys; children (of a family, including girls) | ابن الأخ (الأخت) nephew; ابن آدم pl. بنو آدم (son of Adam) man, human being; ابن آوى *ibn āwā* jackal; ابن البلد *ibn al-balad* local inhabitant, native; ابناء البلاد natives, native population; ابن الحرب *ibn al-ḥarb* warrior, soldier; warlike, bellicose; ابناء الحى *a. al-ḥayy* the inhabitants of a city ward; ابن الزوج (الزوجة) *i. az-zauj* stepson; ابن السبيل wayfarer, wanderer; ابن خمسين سنة 50 years old; ابن ساعته *ibn sā'atihī* temporal, transient, passing; ابن صلبه *ibn ṣulbihī* his own son; ابن عرس *ibn 'irs* weasel; ابن العم *i. al-'amm* cousin on the father's side; periphrastically for husband; ابن اكابر person from a respected family, coming from a good family; بنو ماء السماء *banū mā' as-samā'* the Arabs; بنى سويف Beni Suef (city in Egypt, S of Cairo); السيد فلان الابن Mr. So-and-so, Jr.

ابنة *ibna* and بنت *bint* pl. بنات *banāt* daughter; بنت girl | ابنة الأخ (الأخت) niece; ابنة الزوج (الزوجة) *i. az-zauj* stepdaughter; ابنة العم *i. al-'amm* and بنت العم female cousin on the father's side; periphrastically for wife: ابنة عمك your wife; بنت الفكر *b. al-fikr* pl. بنات الافكار thought, idea; بنت اكابر fem. of ابن اكابر; بنت الهوى *b. al-hawā* a prostitute; بنات الارض *b. al-arḍ* insects and worms; بنات بئس *b. bi's* calamities, adversities, misfortunes; بنات الحياة *b. al-ḥayāh* and بنات الدهر *b. ad-dahr* afflictions, sufferings, sorrows bestowed by fate; بنات حواء *b. ḥawwā'* daughters of Eve, women; بنت الشفة *b. aš-šafa* word; بنات الصدر *b. aṣ-ṣadr* worries, fears, anxieties; بنات وردان *b. wardāna* earthworms, rainworms

بنى *bunaiya* my little son

بنية *bunaiya* little girl

بنوة *bunūwa* sonship, filiation

بنوى *banawī* filial

تبن *tabannin* adoption (also fig., e.g., of ideas, principles, etc.)

²بن *bunn* coffee beans, (unground) coffee | شجرة البن *šajarat al-b.* coffee tree, coffee shrub (*bot.*)

بنى *bunnī* coffee-colored, brown

³بنان *banān* finger tips | يشار عليه ببنان (*yušāru*) lit.: he is pointed at with fingers, i.e., he is a famous man; انا طوع بنانك *anā ṭau'a banānika* I am at your disposal, I am at your service

بنادورة *banādōra* (*syr.;* from It. *pomodoro*) tomato(es)

بنارس *banāris*² Banaras or Benares (the Holy City of the Hindus, in N India)

بنباشى see بكباشى

بنت see ¹بن

بنتو *bintū* napoleon, louis d'or (gold coin of 20 francs)

بنج II to dope, narcoticize (with *banj*; ه s.o.); to anesthetize (ه s.o.)

بنج *banj* henbane (Hyoscyamus niger; *bot.*); an anesthetic, a narcotic

البنجاب *al-banjāb* the Punjab (region, NW Indian subcontinent)

بنجر *banjar* beet, sugar beet; red beet (*eg.*)

بنجلاديش *bangladēš* (Eg. spelling) Bangladesh

بند *band* pl. بنود *bunūd* article, clause, paragraph (of a law, contract, etc.); point (of an explanation, presentation, etc.); banner; large body of troops | البنود الرئيسية the main points

¹بندر *bandar* pl. بنادر *banādir*² seaport; commercial center; district capital (*Eg.*); بنادر see also under بندرة below | بندر عباس *b. 'abbās* Bandar Abbas (seaport in S Iran)

²بندورة look up alphabetically

بندق *bunduq* (coll.; n. un. ة) pl. بنادق *banādiq*[2] hazelnut(s), filberts; hazel, hazel tree; بندقة hazelnut, filbert; bullet

بندقى *bunduqī* Venetian sequin

بندقية *bunduqīya* pl. بنادق *banādiq*[2] rifle, gun | بندقية رش *b. rašš* shotgun; بندقية هوائية (*hawā'īya*) air gun

البندقية *al-bunduqīya* Venice

بندقانى *bunduqānī* pl. *-ūn*, بنادقة *banādiqa* a Venitian

بندوق *bundūq* pl. بناديق *banādīq*[2] bastard

بندورة *banadōra* (*syr.*; from It. *pomodoro*) tomatoes

احمر بندورى *aḥmar*[2] *banadōrī* tomato-red

بندول (Fr. *pendule*) *bandūl* pendulum

بنديرة (Span. *bandera*) *bandēra* pl. بنادر *banādir*[2] pennon, flag, banner

بنور *bannūr* (= بلور *ballūr*) glass

بنزهير *banzahīr* bezoar, bezoar stone

بنزول *binzōl* benzol

بنزين *banzīn, benzīn* gasoline, benzine

بنس (Engl.) *bens* pl. *-āt* pence

بنسلين *benisilīn* penicillin

بنسيه (Fr. *pensée*) *bansēh* pansy (*bot.*)

بنسيون *bansiyōn* pl. *-āt* boardinghouse; boarding school

بنصر *binṣir* f., pl. بناصر *banāṣir*[2] ring finger

بنط *bunṭ* pl. بنوط *bunūṭ* point (stock market)

بنطة (It. *punta*) *bunṭa* pl. بنط *bunaṭ* (*eg.*) drill bit

بنطال *banṭāl* trousers, pants

بنطلون *banṭalōn* (It. *pantaloni*) pl. *-āt* trousers, pants

بنغازى *banġāzī* Bengasi (city in NE Libya)

البنغال *al-banġāl* Bengal (region, NE Indian subcontinent)

بنغلاديش *banġladēš* (Leb.-Syr. spelling) Bangladesh

بنفسج *banafsaj* (coll.; n. un. ة) violet (*bot.*)

بنفسجى *banafsajī* violetlike, violetish; violet (adj.) | فوق البنفسجى or وراء البنفسجى ultraviolet

بنفش *banfaš, banafš* amethyst (*min.*)

بنقة *binaqa* and بنيقة *banīqa* gore, gusset (of a shirt or garment)

[1]بنك *bunk* root, core, heart, best part | بنك العمر *b. al-'umr* the prime of life, the best years

[2]بنك *bank* pl. بنوك *bunūk* bank, banking house | بنك الترحيل transfer bank; بنك الاصدار *b. al-iṣdār* bank of issue; بنك التسليف credit bank; بنك التسليف العقارى (*'aqārī*) mortgage bank; بنك التوفير deposit bank; بنك الدم *b. ad-dam* blood bank; البنك الدولى (*daulī*) the World Bank; بنك القرض *b. al-qarḍ* (*Tun.*) loan bank

بنكى *bankī* bank (in compounds) | ضمان بنكى (*ḍamān*) bank guarantee

[3]مبنك *mubannak* stranded

[4]محنك مبنك *muḥannak mubannak* shrewd, sly, astute

بنكنوت (Engl.) *banknōt* banknote

بنما *banamā* Panama

بنها *banhā* Benha (town in N Egypt)

بنوة and بنوى see [1]بن

بنوار (Fr. *baignoire*) *banwār* baignoire, theater box of the lowest tier

[1]بنى *banā i* (بناء *binā'*, بنيان *bunyān*) and **VIII** to build, erect, construct, set up (ه s.th.);

to build, establish, rest (على ه s.th. on); to consummate the marriage (بها and عليها with a woman); pass. *buniya, ubtuniya* to be based, be built, rest (على on) | بنى العزم على (*'azma*) and بنى عزمه على (*'azmahū*) to determine or be firmly determined to do s.th.; بنى كلمة على (*kalimatan*) to give a word an indeclinable ending in (a certain vowel or a vowelless consonant; *gram.*) **V** see بن[1] **VII** to be built

بناء *binā'* building, construction, erection, setting up; structure (also, e.g., of an organism), setup, make-up; masonry; (pl. *-āt*) construction work; (pl. ابنية *abniya, alg.* also *-āt*) building, structure, edifice | عامل بناء construction worker; اعادة البناء *i'ādat al-b.* reconstruction; البناء الحر (*ḥurr*) Freemasonry; بناء على *binā'an 'alā* according to, in accordance with, on the basis of, by virtue of, on the strength of; بناء على هذا accordingly, thus

بنائى *binā'ī* constructional, building (used attributively); architectural; structural

بنية *binya, bunya* pl. بنى *binan, bunan* structure, setup, make-up; *binya* build, frame, physique, physical constitution | ضعيف البنية of delicate constitution; صحيح البنية and سليم البنية of sound constitution, healthy; قوى البنية *qawīy al-b.* husky, sturdy

بنيوى *binyawī, bunyawī* structural; structuralist

بنيوية *binyawīya, bunyawīya* structuralism

بنى *bunaiy* and بنية *bunaiya* see بن[1]

بناء *bannā'* pl. *-ūn* builder; mason, bricklayer; — constructive (e.g., action, plan) | بناء حر (*ḥurr*) Freemason

بناية *bināya* pl. *-āt* building, structure, edifice

بنيان *bunyān* building, construction, erection, setting up; building, structure, edifice; physique, stature

مبنى *mabnan* pl. مبان *mabānin* building, construction, erection, setting up; building, structure, edifice; form; foundation, fundament, basis | الرأى والمبنى (*ra'y*) content and form

تبن *tabannin* see بن[1]

بان *bānin* pl. بناة *bunāh* builder

مبنى *mabnīy* built, set up, erected; founded, based, resting (على on); fixed, established; indeclinable; ending indeclinably (على in; *gram.*)

[2]پنى (Engl.) penny

بنيو (It. *bagno*) *banyō* bath, bathtub

بهت *bahita a, bahuta u* and pass. *buhita* (*baht*) to be astonished, amazed, bewildered, startled, perplexed, flabbergasted, speechless; — *bahita* to be or become pale, fade (color); — *bahata a* to astonish, amaze, bewilder, startle, stagger, flabbergast (ه s.o.); (بهتان *buhtān*) to slander, defame (ه s.o.) **III** to come or descend unexpectedly (ه upon s.o.); to startle, stagger, flabbergast (ه s.o.) **IV** to surprise, astonis' amaze (ه s.o.) **VII** = **I**

بهت *buht* and بهتان *buhtān* sl..der, false accusation; lie, untruth

بهتة *bahta* perplexity, amazement, bewilderment, stupefaction

باهت *bāhit* pale, pallid, faded (color); wan, lusterless, mat; perplexed, aghast

مبهوت *mabhūt* perplexed, astonished, amazed, startled, flabbergasted, aghast

بهج *bahija a* to be glad, be happy (ب about), be delighted (ب at); — *bahuja u* to be beautiful, look wonderful **IV** to gladden, delight, make happy (ه s.o.) **VIII** to be glad, be happy (ب about), be delighted (ب at)

بهجة *bahja* splendor, magnificence, beauty, resplendence; joy, delight | بهجة الانظار delight of the eyes, welcome sight

بهج *bahij*, بهيج *bahīj* magnificent, splendid, beautiful; happy, joyous; delightful

مبهجة *mabhaja* a moment of happiness and joy

مباهج *mabāhij*² joys, delights; pleasures, amusements, diversions; splendid things; splendor, pomp, magnificence

ابتهاج *ibtihāj* joy, rejoicing, delight (ب at)

مبهج *mubhij* pleasant, charming, delightful

مبتهج *mubtahij* happy, glad, delighted

بهدل **bahdala** to insult (ه s.o.); to treat contemptuously, meanly (ه s.o.); to expose (ه s.o.) to ridicule, make a laughingstock (ه of s.o.); bring into disorder (ه s.th.) **II** *tabahdala* pass. of I

بهدلة *bahdala* insult, affront, abuse, outrage; meanness; triteness, insipidity

مبهدل *mubahdal* maltreated, oppressed, miserable; disorderly, neglected

بهر **bahara** *a* (*bahr*) and **IV** to glitter, shine; to dazzle, overwhelm (ه s.o., ه s.o.'s eyes) | شئ يبهر الابصار a dazzling, overwhelming thing; — pass. *buhira* to be out of breath, to pant **VII** to be dazzled, blinded; to be smitten with blindness; to be out of breath **VIII** to flaunt, parade, show off, present in a dazzling light (ب s.th.)

بهر *bahr* deception, dazzlement (ب by)

بهر *buhr* difficult respiration, labored breathing

بهرة *bahra* (n. vic.) being dazzled, dazzlement

بهرة *buhra* middle, center | في بهرة ... amidst

ابهر *abhar*² more brilliant, more magnificent

ابهر *abhar*² aorta (*anat.*)

بهار *bahār* pl. *-āt* spice

ابتهار *ibtihār* dazzling display, show (ب of s.th.)

باهر *bāhir* dazzling, brilliant, splendid

مبهور *mabhūr* breathless, out of breath, panting

بهرج **bahraja** (بهرجة *bahraja*) to adorn, deck out, dress up showily; to give a deceptive brightness (ه to); to glamorize (ه s.th.); to reject as false (ه a witness); to fake, counterfeit (ه s.th.) **II** *tabahraja* to adorn o.s., spruce o.s. up, dress up; to be fake

بهرج *bahraj* false, spurious, fake, sham, worthless, bad; counterfeit money; tinsel, frippery, cheap finery; trash, cheap stuff

بهرجة *bahraja* empty show, hollow pomp

بهرجان *bahrajān* tinsel, frippery

مبهرج *mubahraj* showy, tawdry, gaudy, ornate, ostentatious; trashy, rubbishy, cheap, inartistic

بهريز **bahrīz** (*eg.*) a soup

بهز **bahaza** *a* (*bahz*) to push or drive away (ه s.o.)

بهزة *bahza* (n. vic.) rejection, repulsion

بهظ **bahaẓa** *a* (*bahẓ*) to oppress, weigh down (ه s.o.; a load, work), weigh heavily (ه on s.o.) **IV** do.

باهظ *bāhiẓ* heavy, oppressive, trying; excessive, exorbitant, enormous; expensive, costly

بهق **bahaq** a kind of lichen (*bot.*); herpetic eruption, tetter; vitiligo alba, a mild form of leprosy (*med.*)

بهل bahala a (bahl) to curse (ه s.o.) V and VI to curse one another VIII to supplicate, pray humbly (to God); to implore, beseech (الى الله God)

ابهل abhal savin (Juniperus sabina; bot.)

ابتهال ibtihāl pl. -āt supplication, prayer

باهل bāhil pl. بهل buhl, buhhal free, independent

بهلول buhlūl, bahlūl pl. بهاليل bahālīl[2] buffoon, jester, clown, fool

بهلوان bahlawān pl. -āt, بهالين bahālīn[2] acrobat, tumbler, equilibrist, ropedancer, tightrope walker

بهلوانى bahlawānī acrobatic | حركات بهلوانية (ḥarakāt) acrobatics; antics, capers of a tumbler; طيران بهلوانى (ṭayarān) aerial acrobatics, stunt flying

بهم IV to make obscure, dubious, unintelligible (ه s.th.) V and X to be obscure, ambiguous, unintelligible (على to s.o.)

بهمة bahma lamb, sheep

بهيم bahīm pl. بهم buhum jet-black

بهيمة bahīma pl. بهائم bahā'im[2] beast, animal, quadruped; pl. livestock, cattle, (large) domestic animals

بهيمى bahīmī animal, bestial, brutish

بهيمية bahīmīya brutishness, bestiality, brutality

ابهام ibhām obscurity; vagueness, ambiguity

ابهام ibhām f., pl. اباهيم abāhīm[2] thumb; big toe

باهم bāhim big toe

مبهم mubham obscure, dark, cryptic, doubtful, vague, ambiguous; unintelligible | عدد مبهم ('adad) abstract number (math.); ○ العصب المبهم ('aṣab) the vagus (anat.); الاسم المبهم (ism) the demonstrative pronoun (gram.)

[1](بهو) بها bahā u, bahuwa u and بهى bahiya a (بهاء bahā') to be beautiful III to vie, compete (ه ب with s.o. in s.th.); to pride o.s. (ب on), be proud (ب of), boast (ب of, ه ب to s.o. of s.th.) VI to compete with one another; to be proud (ب of), pride o.s. (ب on)

بهو bahw pl. ابهاء abhā' hall; parlor, drawing room, reception hall

بهى bahīy beautiful, magnificent, splendid; brilliant, radiant, shining

بهاء bahā' beauty, magnificence, splendor; brilliancy

بهائى bahā'ī Bahai (adj.); (pl. -ūn) an adherent of the Bahai sect, a Bahai

البهائية al-bahā'īya the Bahai sect; Bahaism

ابهى abhā more splendid, more brilliant

مباهاة mubāhāh and تباه tabāhin pride, vainglory, boastfulness

متباه mutabāhin proud, boastful

[2]بهوات see بك

(بوء) باء bā'a u to come again, return; to come back (ب with s.th.), bring back, yield, bring in (ب s.th.) | باء بالخيبة or بالفشل (kaiba, fašal) to fail II to provide accommodations (ل and ه for s.o., ه at a place), put up (ل or ه s.o., ه at) | بوأ مكانا (makānan) to take a place, settle down, live or stay at a place; بوأه مكانا to put s.o. in a place, make s.o. take a position or place IV to provide accommodations (ه for s.o., ه at a place); to settle down, reside, live (ب at a place) V to settle down (ه at a place), occupy (مركزا markazan a place), hold (مقاما maqāman a position) | تبوأ مكانا (makānan) to gain ground, become generally accepted; تبوأ العرش

(*'arš*) to ascend the throne; تبوأ الحكم (*ḥukm*) to come to power, take over power; تبوأ منصبا (*manṣiban*) to take on a position, take over a post; to fill an office

بيئة *bī'a* pl. *-āt* milieu, surroundings; environment; situation (in which s.o. lives); place where s.o. feels at home; home, habitat

بيئى *bī'ī* conditioned by the milieu, environmental | عوامل بيئية environmental factors

مباءة *mabā'a* place to which s.th. comes; abode, dwelling, habitation

تبوء *tabawwu'*: تبوء العرش *t. al-'arš* accession to the throne

بواط (Fr. *boîte*) pl. *-āt* (*eg.*) tin, can, box

بوب II to divide into chapters or sections (ه s.th.); to arrange in groups, arrange systematically, class, classify (ه s.th.)

باب *bāb* pl. ابواب *abwāb*, بيبان *bībān* door; gate; opening, gateway; entrance; chapter, section, column, rubric; group, class, category; field, domain (fig.) | الباب العالى the Sublime Porte; باب المندب *b. al-mandab* Bab el Mandeb (strait between SW Arabia and Africa; *geogr.*); على الابواب near, imminent; فتح بابا جديدا to open up a new way, a new possibility; فتح باب *futiḥa bābu* ... was (were) begun, ... got under way; قفل باب الشىء (*qafala*) to put an end to s.th., terminate, close s.th.; من باب الفضل (*b. il-faḍl*) as a favor; من باب اولى (*aulā*) with all the more reason, the more so; فى هذا الباب about this matter, about this; من باب الضرورة ان (*b. iḍ-ḍarūra*) it is necessary that ...; ليس هذا من باب الصدفة (*b. iṣ-ṣudfa*) that's no coincidence; دخل فى باب or كان من باب (with foll. genit.) to belong to, fall under; فريد فى بابه unique of its kind; طلع على باب الله to pursue one's livelihood, earn one's bread

بابة *bāba* pl. *-āt* kind, sort, class, category

بواب *bawwāb* pl. *-ūn* doorman, gatekeeper

بوابة *biwāba* office of gatekeeper

بوابة *bawwāba* pl. *-āt* (large) gate, portal | بوابة القنطرة *b. al-qanṭara* lock gate

تبويب *tabwīb* division into chapters, sectioning, classification, systematic arrangement, grouping

مبوب *mubawwab* arranged in groups, classed, classified

بوبلين *boblīn* poplin

بوبينة (Fr. *bobine*) *bobīna* spool, reel

بويت *buwait* see بيت

بوتاجاز *būtāgāz* pl. *-āt* (*eg.*) gas stove

بوتاس، بوتاسا (It. *potassa*) *būtāsā*, *būtās* potash

بوتقة *būtaqa* (usually pronounced *bautaqa*) crucible, melting pot | فى بوتقة الزمان (*zamān*) in the melting pot of time

بوتيك (Fr.) *būtēk* pl. *-āt* (*eg.*) boutique

بوجيه (Fr. *bougie*) *bužīh* pl. *-āt* spark plug (*eg.*)

باح (بوح) *bāḥa u* (*bauḥ*) to become known, be revealed, be divulged, leak out (secret); to reveal, disclose, divulge (ه or ب s.th., a secret; الى and ل to s.o.) IV to disclose, reveal (ه or ب s.th., ل to s.o.); to release, abandon, make public property, declare ownerless (ه s.th.); to permit, allow, leave (ه s.th., ل to s.o.) X to reveal (ه s.th.); to regard as public property, as ownerless, as fair game; to deem permissible, lawful (ه s.th.); to hurt (حرمته *ḥurmatahū* s.o.'s honor); to take possession (ه of), appropriate, take as booty (ه s.th.); to seize, confiscate (ه s.th.); to give over (ه s.th., for pillage, appropriation, etc.); to plunder (ه s.th.) | استباح دمه (*damahū*) to proscribe, outlaw s.o.

بوح *bauḥ* divulgence, disclosure (of a secret); confession

بوح *būḥ* wide, open space; courtyard; hall

باحة *bāḥa* pl. *-āt* wide, open space; open place, square, plaza; courtyard; hall

اباحة *ibāḥa* divulgence, disclosure (of a secret); permission, authorization; licentiousness

اباحى *ibāḥī* licentious, unrestrained, uninhibited; anarchist; freethinker

اباحية *ibāḥīya* freethinking, libertinism; anarchism

استباحة *istibāḥa* appropriation, capture, seizure; spoliation, confiscation

مباح *mubāḥ* permitted, allowed, permissible; legal, lawful, licit, legitimate; open to everyone, permitted for all, free; ownerless (*Isl. Law*); indifferent (said of actions for which neither reward nor punishment is to be expected, but which are permissible, pl. مباحات indifferent, permissible actions, *Isl. Law*)

باخ (بوخ) *bāḵa* *u* to abate, subside, let up, decrease; to die, go out (fire); to fade, bleach; to spoil, rot (e.g., meat) **II** to spoil (ه s.th.)

بواخ *buwāḵ* evaporation, exhalation, vapor, steam

تبويخ *tabwīḵ*: تبويخ النكتة *t. an-nukta* the spoiling of the point of a story

□ بايخ *bāyiḵ* spoiled, bad; vapid, insipid, stale (also, e.g., of a joke)

بوخارست *būḵārest* Bucharest

بودرة (Fr. *poudre*) *būdra* powder

بودقة *būdaqa* pl. بوادق *bawādiq*[2] crucible, melting pot

بوذا *būḏā* Buddha

بوذى *būḏī* Buddhistic; Buddhist

بوذية *būḏīya* Buddhism

بار (بور) *bāra* *u* (*baur*, بوار *bawār*) to perish; to lie fallow, be uncultivated (land); to be futile, unsuccessful, unprofitable, lead to nothing (work); to be unsalable, be dead stock (merchandise) | بارت البنت (*bint*) the girl could not get a husband **II** to let lie fallow (ه land); to make unprofitable, useless (ه s.th.) **IV** to destroy

بور *būr* uncultivated, fallow | ارض بور (*arḍ*), pl. اراض بور (*arāḍin*) fallow land, wasteland

بورى and بوريه see below alphabetically

بوار *bawār* perdition, ruin | دار البوار hell

بائر *bā'ir* uncultivated, fallow (land)

بورانى *būrānī* (*eg.*) a vegetable stew

بور سعيد *būr sa'īd* Port Said (seaport in NE Egypt)

بور سودان *būr sūdān* Port Sudan (seaport in NE Sudan)

بور فؤاد *būr fu'ād* Port Fuad (seaport in NE Egypt, opposite Port Said)

بورتريه (Fr.) *bortrēh* pl. *-āt* portrait

بورتوريكو *burturīkū* Puerto Rico

بورتوغال *burtuġāl* = البرتغال Portugal

بورجوازى (Fr.) *burjuwāzī* bourgeois (adj.); (pl. *-ūn*) member of the bourgeoisie, bourgeois | المجتمع البورجوازى (*mujtama'*) middle-class society; بورجوازى صغير petit bourgeois

بورجوازية *burjuwāzīya* bourgeoisie, middle classes | البورجوازية الصغيرة petty bourgeoisie

بورصة *burṣa* pl. *-āt* stock exchange

بورق *bauraq, bōraq* borax

بورما *burmā* Burma

بورندى and بوروندى *burundī* Burundi (country in Africa)

[1]بورى (Turk. *boru*) *būrī* pl. *-āt* bugle; signal horn (esp. *mil.*)

بوروجى *būrūjī* pl. *-īya* bugler

[2]بورى *būrī* pl. □ بوارى *bawārī* gray mullet (*zool.*) | بورى احمر (*aḥmar*) red mullet (*zool.*)

[3]بوريه (Fr.) *būrēh* purée

[1]بوز II to pout, sulk, look glum, sullen

بوز *būz* pl. ابواز *abwāz* muzzle, snout

تبويزة *tabwīza* sullen mien

مبوز *mubawwiz* sullen, glum

[2]بوز *būz*, بوزة *būza* ice cream

[3]بوزة *būza* a beerlike beverage

[4]باز *bāz* pl. ابواز *abwāz*, بيزان *bīzān* falcon

[1]بوس *būs* bus

[2](بوس) باس *bāsa u* (*baus*) to kiss (ه s.o.)

بوسة *bausa, būsa* kiss

بوستر (Engl.) *bōstar* poster

بوستو (It. *busto*) *bustū* corset

بوسطة, بوستة (It. *posta*) *busṭa, busta* post, mail

بوسطجى *busṭagī* pl. *-īya* (*eg.*) mailman

البوسفور *al-busfūr* the Bosporus

(بوش) باش *bāša u* (*bauš*) to be boisterous, shout, roar (crowd) II do.

بوش *bauš* pl. اوباش *aubāš* (for ابواش) mob, rabble

[1]بوص *būṣ* (coll.; n. un. ة) reed

بوصة *būṣa* pl. *-āt* inch

[2]بوص *būṣ* pl. ابواص *abwāṣ* linen or silk fabric

بوصلة (It. *bussola*) *boṣla, bauṣala* pl. *-āt* compass

بويضة see under بيض

بواط see alphabetically

بوطة *būṭa* crucible, melting pot

بوظة *būẓa* a beerlike beverage; (*syr.*) ice cream

[1]بوع *būʿ* metatarsal bone (*anat.*) | لا يعرف الكوع من البوع he wouldn't know his knee from his elbow (proverbially, of a stupid person)

[2]باع *bāʿ* pl. ابواع *abwāʿ* the span of the outspread arms, fathom; in Eg. today = 4 *ḏirāʿ miʿmārīya* = 3 m | طول الباع *ṭūl al-b.* power, mastery; capability, ability; knowledge; generosity; طويل الباع mighty, powerful; capable, able; knowledgeable; generous, liberal, openhanded; قصير الباع powerless, helpless, impotent, weak, incapable; niggardly, stingy; قصور الباع impotence, weakness; incapability (عن of); بالباع والذراع with might and main

[1]بوغ II to surprise

[2]باغة *bāġa* celluloid; tortoise shell

بوغادة *būġāda* and بوغاضة *būġāḍa* potash, lye

بوغاز *būġāz* pl. بواغيز *bawāġīz*[2] strait(s); harbor | بوغاز الدردنيل the Dardanelles

بوفيه (Fr. *buffet*) *būfēh* buffet; bar; sideboard

بوق II to blow the trumpet

بوق *būq* pl. *-āt*, ابواق *abwāq* trumpet, bugle; fanfare; horn (of an automobile, of a gramophone); acoustic signaling device; megaphone; funnel (= funnel-shaped opening); mouthpiece, spokesman; duplicity, treachery, betrayal | بوق الصوت *b. aṣ-ṣaut* or بوق الراديو loudspeaker (*radio*); ○ بوق رحمى (*raḥimī*) oviduct,

grave; فراغ البال *farāġ al-b.* leisure; مشغول البال anxious, uneasy, concerned, worried; طويل البال long-suffering, patient; ... ما باله (with verb) why is it that he (it) ...? why ...? ما بالك how about you? what do you think? خلا باله *kalā băluhū* his mind is at rest, he has no worries; خطر بباله it occurred to him, it came to his mind; اعطى (القى, جعل) باله الى (ل) (*a'ṭā, alqā, ja'ala*) to turn one's mind to, give one's attention to, pay attention to, take into account, be mindful of, bear in mind, heed s.th.; لم يلق لقولى بالا *lam yulqi li-qaulī bālan* he didn't pay any attention to what I said; لا يقل عنه بالا (*yaqillu*) no less significant than this

³بول *būl* postage stamp

⁴بال *bāl* whale (*zool.*)

⁵بالة look up alphabetically

□ بولاد *būlād* (= فولاذ) steel

بولفار (Fr.) *bulvār* boulevard

بولاق *būlāq*² a district of Cairo

بولندا *bulandā, bōlandā* and بولندة Poland

بولندى *bulandī, bōlandī* Polish; (pl. *-ūn*) Pole

بولو *bōlō* polo

بولونيا (It. *Polonia*) *bōlōnyā* Poland

بولونى *bōlōnī* Polish; (pl. *-ūn*) Pole

¹بوليس (Fr. *police*) *būlīs* police | بوليس الآداب vice squad; البوليس الجنائى (*jinā'ī*) criminal police; البوليس الحربى (*ḥarbī*) military police; البوليس السرى (*sirrī*) secret police; بوليس المرور traffic police

رواية بوليسية *riwāya būlīsīya* detective story

²بوليسة and بوليصة (Fr. *police*) *būlīsa, būlīṣa* pl. بوالص *bawāliṣ*², بوالس *bawālis*² certificate of insurance, policy | بوليسة

Fallopian tube (*anat.*); على شكل بوق (*šakli b.*) funnel-shaped, infundibular

بواق *bawwāq* trumpeter, bugler

باقة *bāqa* bundle; bunch of flowers, nosegay, bouquet

بائقة *bā'iqa* pl. بوائق *bawā'iq*² misfortune, calamity

بوقال *būqāl*, بوقالة *būqāla* pl. بواقيل *bawāqīl*² vessel without handles, mug

بوكر (Engl.) *bōkar, bōker* poker

بوكس *boks* boxing

بوكسفورد *boksəford* patrol wagon, paddy wagon, Black Maria

بوكسكاف (Engl.) *boksəkāf* box calf

¹بال (بول) *bāla u* (*baul*) and V to make water, urinate IV to be diuretic X to cause to urinate

بول *baul* pl. ابوال *abwāl* urine | مرض البول السكرى *maraḍ al-b. as-sukkarī* diabetes

بولى *baulī* uric, urinary, urinous | المسالك البولية the urinary passages; الامراض البولية diseases of the kidney and urinary bladder; تسمم بولى (*tasammum*) uremia (*med.*)

بيلة *bīla*: ○ بيلة آحينية (*āḥīnīya*) albuminuria; ○ بيلة دموية (*damawīya*) hematuria (*med.*)

بوالة *bawwāla* public lavatory

مبولة *mabwala* pl. مباول *mabāwil*² urinal; a diuretic; — *mibwala* chamber pot; toilet, water closet

تبول *tabawwul*: تبول لاارادى (*lā-irādī*) enuresis, bed-wetting

استبوال *istibwāl*: ○ استبوال الدم *ist. ad-dam* uremia (*med.*)

²بال *bāl* mind; frame of mind; attention, regard, mindfulness | ذو بال significant, notable, considerable, important, serious,

الشحن *b. aš-šaḥn* bill of lading; بوليصة التأمين insurance policy

بوليفيا *būlīfiyā* Bolivia

بوليفى *būlīfī* Bolivian

○داء البولينا *dā' al-baulīnā* uremia

بوم *būm* (coll.; n. un. ة) pl. ابوام *abwām* owl

بون[1] *baun, būn* interval, distance; difference

بان[2] (coll.; n. un. ة) ben tree (Moringa; *bot.*); horse-radish tree (Moringa oleifera; *bot.*); Egyptian willow (Salix aegyptiaca L.; *bot.*)

بونى (Engl.) *bōnī* pl. بوانى *bawānī* pony

بونيق *būnīqī* Punic

باه *bāh* coitus; sexual potency

بوهيميا *bōhēmiyā, bōhīmiyā* Bohemia

بوهيمى *bōhēmī* Bohemian (adj. and n.)

بوهيمية *bōhēmīya* Bohemianism, Bohemian life

بؤونة *ba'ūna* the tenth month of the Coptic year

بوية (Turk. *boya*) *bōya* pl. *-āt* paint; shoe polish

بوياجى, بويجى *bōyajī,* (*eg.*) *boyagī* pl. *-īya* house painter, painter; shoeshine, bootblack

بوينس ايرس *buwēnos airis* Buenos Aires

بية *bayya* = باية look up alphabetically

بوء see بيئة

بيادة (Pers.) *biyāda* infantry (formerly, *Eg.*)

بيادى *biyādī* infantryman, foot soldier

بيانو *biyānō* pl. بيانوهات, also بيان *biyān* pl. *-āt* piano

بيب[1] (Fr.) *bīb* pipe, tube; feed pipe, spout (of a reservoir or tank)

بيبة[2] (It.) *bība* (Western) smoking pipe

(بيت) بات *bāta i* (مبيت *mabīt*) to pass or spend the night; to stay overnight; to become, come to be, have become; to get, have gotten (فى into a situation or state), be (فى in a situation, etc.); with foll. imperf.: to have now got to a point where . . ., have gotten so far that now . . .; to go on, keep on doing s.th. | بات من المقرر (*muqarrar*) it has become a sure thing, is now certain; بات فى حكم المؤكد (*fī ḥukmi l-mu'akkad*) it is now as good as certain **II** to brood (by night; ه about s.th.); to contrive, hatch (ه an evil plan, ل against s.o.), plot (ل against s.o.); to put up for the night (ه s.o.) | بيت فى الصف (*ṣaff*; *eg.*) to flunk, fail promotion (pupil) **IV** to put up for the night (ه s.o.)

بيت *bait* pl. بيوت *buyūt*, بيوتات *buyūtāt* house, building; tent (of nomads); room; apartment, flat; (garden) bed; family; case, box, covering, sheath; pl. بيوتات large, respectable houses; respectable families; (pl. ابيات *abyāt*) verse | بيت الابرة *b. al-ibra* (navigator's) compass; اهل البيت *ahl al-b.* family, specif., the family of the Prophet; اهل البيوتات people from good, respectable families; بيوتات تجارية (*tijārīya*) commercial houses; البيت الابيض (*abyaḍ*) the White House (in Washington); البيت الحرام (*ḥarām*) the Kaaba; بيت الخلاء *b. al-ḵalā'* and بيت الادب *b. al-adab* toilet, water closet; بيت الداء origin or seat of the disease; بيت ريفى (*rīfī*) country house; بيت الشباب *b. aš-šabāb* youth hostel; بيت المقدس *b. al-maqdis* Jerusalem; بيت القصيدة and بيت القصيد (the essential, principal verse of the kasida, i.e.) the quintessence; the gist, the essentials, the hit of s.th.; s.th. that stands out from the rest, the right thing; بيت لحم *bēt laḥm,* بيتلحم *baitalaḥm* Bethlehem; البيت المالك the ruling house; بيت المال treasure house; fisc, treasury, exchequer (*Isl. Law*); (*Tun.*) administration of vacant

Muslim estates; بيت الماء toilet, water closet

بيتى *baitī* domestic, private, home, of the house, house- (in compounds); domesticated (animals); homemade

بويت *buwait* pl. *-āt* small house; small tent

بيات *bayāt*: بيات شتوى (*šatawī*) hibernation (of animals)

بيات *bayyāt* pl. *-ūn* and بياتة *bayyāta* boarder (student); (pl. *-ūn*) pupil of a boarding school (*tun.*)

بيوت *bayyūt* stale, old

مبيت *mabīt* overnight stop, overnight stay; shelter for the night

بائت *bā'it* stale, old; (*eg.*) not promoted, فى الصف (*ṣaff*) in school

مبيت *mubayyit* plotter, schemer, intrigant

بيتا *bētā*: اشعة بيتا *aši''at b.* beta rays (*phys.*)

بيجاما *bījāmā* and بيجامة *bījāma* pl. *-āt* pajama

[1](بيد) باد *bāda i* to perish, die, pass away, become extinct IV to destroy, exterminate, extirpate (ه, ه s.o., s.th.)

بيد ان *baida anna* although, whereas; (esp., introducing a sentence:) yet, however, but, ... though

بيداء *baidā'*[2] pl. بيد *bīd*, بيداوات *baidāwāt* desert, steppe, wilderness

ابادة *ibāda* annihilation, extermination, eradication, extirpation

بائد *bā'id* passing, transitory, temporal; past, bygone | العرب البائدة the genuine Arabs of the past (who have become extinct)

مبيد *mubīd* destructive, annihilative; (pl. *-āt*) means of extermination | مبيدات حشرية (*ḥašarīya*) insecticides; مبيدات حيوية (*ḥayawīya*) antibiotics (*biol., med.*)

[2]بيادة look up alphabetically

بيداغوجى *bidaġōjī* (*tun., alg.*) pedagogical

بيدر *baidar* pl. بيادر *bayādir*[2] threshing floor

بيدق *baidaq* (and بيذق) pl. بيادق *bayādiq*[2] pawn (in chess)

بيذنجان see باذنجان alphabetically

[1]□ بيارة *bayyāra* pl. *-āt* (*pal.*) irrigation wheel; plantation

[2]بيرا, بيرة (It. *birra*) *bīrā, bīra* beer | مصنع البيرا *maṣna' al-b.* brewery

بيرق *bairaq* pl. بيارق *bayāriq*[2] flag, banner, standard

بيرقدار *bairaqdār* color-bearer, standard-bearer

جبال البيرنيه (Fr. *Pyrénées*) *jibāl al-bīrinēh* the Pyrenees

[1]بيرو *bērū* Peru

[2]بيرو (Fr. *bureau*) *bīrō* pl. *-āt* office, bureau

بيروت *bairūt*[2] Beirut (capital of Lebanon)

بيروتى *bairūtī* pl. بوارتة *bawārita*, بيارتة *bayārita* a native or inhabitant of Beirut

بيروقراطى *bīruqrāṭī* bureaucratic; (pl. *-ūn*) bureaucrat

بيروقراطية *bīruqrāṭīya* bureaucracy; red tape

بيزنطيا *bīzanṭiyā* Byzantium

بيزنطى *bīzanṭī* Byzantine

بيسون *bīsōn* bison

(بيض) باض *bāḍa i* to lay eggs (also ه); to stay, settle down, be or become resident (ب at a place) | باض بالمكان وفرخ (*wa-farraka*) to be born and grow up in a place; to establish itself and spread (plague) II to make white, paint white, whitewash, whiten (ه s.th.); to bleach, blanch (ه

s.th., textiles, laundry, rice, etc.); to tin, tinplate (ه s.th.); to make a fair copy (ه of s.th.) | بيض وجهه (*wajhahū*) to make s.o. appear blameless, in a favorable light, to whitewash, exculpate, vindicate, justify s.o., play s.o. up, make much of s.o.; to honor s.o., show honor to s.o.; بيض الله وجهه may God make him happy! لا يبيض من صحيفته this doesn't show him in a favorable light **V** pass. of **II**; **IX** to be or become white

بيض *baiḍ* pl. بيوض *buyūḍ* eggs | بيض مقلى (*maqlīy*) fried eggs; بيض مضروب scrambled eggs

بيضة *baiḍa* (n. un.) pl. *-āt* egg; testicle; helmet; main part, substance, essence | بيضة الديك *b. ad-dīk* (the egg of a rooster i.e.) an impossible or extraordinary thing; بيضة البلد *b. al-balad* a man held in high esteem in his community; فى بيضة النهار (*b. in-nahār*) in broad daylight; بيضة الصيف *b. aṣ-ṣaif* the hottest part of the summer; بيضة الاسلام the territory or pale of Islam; الدفاع عن بيضة الدين, عن بيضة الوطن (*b. id-dīn, b. il-waṭan*) defense of the faith, of the country; بيضة الخدر *b. al-ḵidr* a woman secluded from the outside world, a chaste, respectable woman

بيضى *baiḍī*, بيضوى *baiḍawī* and بيضاوى *baiḍāwī* egg-shaped, oviform, oval, ovate

بييضة *buyaiḍa* and بويضة *buwaiḍa* pl. *-āt* small egg, ovule; ovum (*biol.*)

بياض *bayāḍ* white, whiteness; whitewash; — (pl. *-āt*) barren, desolate, uncultivated land, wasteland; gap, blank space (in a manuscript); blank; leucoma (*med.*); linen, pl. بياضات white goods, linens; (*syr.*) milk, butter, and eggs | بياض البيض *b. al-baiḍ* white of egg, albumen; بياض العين *b. al-ʿain* the white of the eye; بياض النهار *b. an-nahār* daylight, (acc.) by day, during the daytime; بياض يومه وسواد ليله *bayāḍa yaumihī wa-sawāda lailihī* by day and by night; بياض الوجه *b. al-wajh* fine character, good reputation; سمك بياض *samak b.* a Nile fish (*eg.*); على بياض blank, free from writing, printing or marks, uninscribed; لبس (or ارتدى) البياض (*labisa, irtadā*) to dress in white

بيوض *bayūḍ* pl. بيض *buyuḍ, bīḍ* (egg-) laying

ابيض *abyaḍ*², f. بيضاء *baiḍā'*², pl. بيض *bīḍ* white; a white, a member of the white race; bright; clean, shiny, polished; blameless, noble, sincere (character); empty, blank (sheet of paper); pl. البيض and البيضان *al-bīḍān* the white race; الابيض white of egg, albumen | ارض بيضاء (*arḍ*) barren, uncultivated land, wasteland; ثورة بيضاء (*ṯaura*) peaceful, bloodless revolution; الخيط الابيض (*ḵaiṭ*) first light of dawn; الذهب الابيض (*ḏahab*) platinum; بالسلاح الابيض with cold steel; صحيفته بيضاء (*ṣaḥīfatuhū*) his reputation is good; he has noble deeds to his credit, he has a noble character; صحف بيضاء (*ṣuḥuf*) noble, glorious deeds; اكذوبة بيضاء (*ukḏūba*) white lie, fib; ليلة بيضاء (*laila*) a sleepless night, a night spent awake; الموت الابيض (*maut*) natural death; يد بيضاء (*yad*) beneficent hand, benefaction; يا خبر ابيض (*colloq.*, euphemistically instead of يا خبر اسود *yā ḵabar aswad*) oh what terrible news! what a misfortune! a fine thing!

البيضاء *al-baiḍā'* (short for الدار البيضاء) Casablanca

بيضاوى *baiḍāwī* (from الدار البيضاء) from Casablanca, a resident of Casablanca

مبيض *mabīḍ, mibyaḍ* ovary (*anat.*)

تبييضة *tabyīḍa* fair copy

○ ابيضاض *ibyiḍāḍ* leukemia (*med.*)

بائض *bā'iḍ* pl. بوائض *bawā'iḍ*² (egg-) laying

مبيض *mubayyiḍ* pl. *-ūn* whitewasher; bleacher; tinner; copyist, transcriber (of fair copy)

مبيضة *mubayyaḍa* fair copy

بيطر *baiṭara* to practice veterinary science; to shoe (ه a horse)

بيطار *baiṭār* pl. بياطرة *bayāṭira* veterinarian; farrier

بيطرى *baiṭarī* veterinary | الطب البيطرى (*ṭibb*) veterinary medicine; طبيب بيطرى veterinarian

بيطرة *baiṭara* veterinary science; farriery

1(بيع) باع *bāʿa i* (*baiʿ*, مبيع *mabīʿ*) to sell (ه s.th., ه or ل to s.o., ب for a price) **III** to make a contract (ه with s.o.); to pay homage (ه to s.o.); to acknowledge as sovereign or leader (ه s.o.), pledge allegiance (ه to) | بويع له بالخلافة (*būyiʿa*) he was acknowledged with homage as Caliph **IV** to offer for sale (ه s.th.) **VI** to agree on the terms of a sale, conclude a bargain **VII** to be sold, be for sale **VIII** to buy, purchase (ه من s.th. from s.o. and ه ه from s.o. s.th.) | لا ابتاع منه ولا ابيعه (*abtāʿu, abīʿuhū*) I don't trust him

بيع *baiʿ* pl. بيوع *buyūʿ*, بيوعات *buyūʿāt* sale | للبيع for sale; بيوع (or بيوعات) جبرية (*jabrīya*) forced sales, compulsory sale by auction; بيع بالجملة (*jumla*) wholesale sale; بيع بالخيار (*ḵiyār*) optional sale (*Isl. Law*); بيع لآخر راغب (*li-āḵiri rāġibin*) sale to the highest bidder; بيع العينة *b. al-ʿīna* credit operation (*Isl. Law*)

بيعة *baiʿa* conclusion of a bargain; business deal, commercial transaction, bargain; sale; homage, profession of loyalty, pledge of allegiance (to a ruler or head of state) | على البيعة into the bargain

بياع *bayyāʿ* salesman, merchant, dealer, commission agent, middleman

مبايعة *mubāyaʿa* pl. *-āt* conclusion of contract; homage, profession of loyalty, pledge of allegiance (to a ruler or head of state); transaction

ابتياع *ibtiyāʿ* purchase

بائع *bāʾiʿ* pl. *-ūn*, باعة *bāʿa* seller, vendor; dealer, merchant; salesman

بائعة *bāʾiʿa* saleswoman

مبيع *mabīʿ* and مباع *mubāʿ* sold; pl. مبيعات sales | المشتريات والمبيعات (*muštarayāt*) buying and selling (esp. stock market); ادارة المبيعات *idārat al-m.* sales management

مبتاع *mubtāʿ* buyer, purchaser

2بيعة *bīʿa* pl. *-āt*, بيع *biyaʿ* (*Chr.*) church; synagogue

بيفتيك *biftēk* beefsteak

بيك (Turk.) *bēg, bēk* pl. بيكوات *bēgawāt* (*syr.*), *bē* pl. *bēkawāt* (*eg.*) bey; see also بيه

بيكوية *bēkawīya* (*eg.*) rank of bey

بيك اب (Engl.) *bik-ab* pickup; record player, phonograph

بيكار *bīkār* compass, (pair of) dividers

بكباشى see بيكباشى

بيكه (Fr.) *bīkeh* piqué (fabric)

بيكين *bekīn, pekīn* Peking

1بيل (Fr. *bille*) *bīl* ball | كرسى بيل *kursī b.* ball bearing

2بيلة *bīla* see بول

بيلسان *bailasān* elder, elder tree (*bot.*)

بيلهارسيا *bilharsiyā* bilharziasis, schistosomiasis (*med.*)

بيليه (Fr. *bille*) *bīlya* pl. *-āt* little ball, marble

بيمارستان *bīmāristān* hospital; lunatic asylum

1(بين) بان *bāna i* (بيان *bayān*) to be or become plain, evident, come out, come to light; to be clear (ل to s.o.); (بين *bain*, بينونة *bainūna*) to part, be separated (من from) **II** to make clear, plain, visible, evident (ه s.th.); to announce (ه s.th.); to state (ه s.th.); to show, demonstrate (ه s.th.); to explain, expound, elucidate (ه s.th.), throw light (ه on); to separate, clearly differentiate, set apart (ه من s.th. from) **III** to part, go away (ه from), leave (ه s.o.); to differ, be different (ه, ه from), be unlike s.th. (ه); to contradict (ه s.th.), be contrary (ه to); to conflict, be at variance, be inconsistent (ه with s.th.) **IV** to explain, expound, elucidate (ه ل s.th. to s.o.); to separate, sift, distinguish (ه من s.th. from); to be clear, plain, evident; to speak clearly, understandably; to speak out, express distinctly (عن s.th.) **V** to be or become clear, intelligible (ل to s.o.); to turn out, prove in the end, appear, become evident; to follow (من from), be explained (من by); to be clearly distinguished (من from); to seek to ascertain (ه s.th.), try to get at the facts (ه of); to eye or examine critically, scrutinize (ه, ه s.o., s.th.); to look, peer (ه at); to see through s.th. (ه), see clearly, perceive, notice, discover, find out (ه s.th.); to distinguish (ه من s.th. from) **VI** to differ, be different, be opposed, be contrary; to vary greatly, differ widely; to vary, differ, fluctuate (بين between two amounts or limits) **X** to be or become clear, plain, evident, understandable; to make clear, clear up (ه s.th.); to see, know, perceive, notice (ه s.th.); pass. *ustubīna* to follow clearly, be clearly seen (من from) | استبان له ان it became clear to him that . . .

بين *bain* separation, division; interval; difference | ذات البين enmity, disunion, discord; فى البين in the meantime, meanwhile

بين *baina* (prep.) or ما بين, فيما بين *fī-mā b.* between; among, amidst | بين — و either — or, partly — partly, e.g., كان القوم بين صامت ومتكلم (*ṣāmitin wa-mutakallimin*) some of the group were silent and some were talking; بين يديه (*yadaihi*) in front of him, before him; in his presence; with him, on him, in his possession, e.g., لا سلاح بين يديه (*silāḥa*) he hasn't got a weapon on him, he is unarmed; فيما بين ذلك meanwhile, in the meantime; فيما بينى وبين نفسى in my heart, at heart, inwardly; بين ذراعيه in his arms; من بينهم *min bainihim* from among them, from their midst; بين بين something between, a cross, a mixture, a combination; neither good nor bad, medium, tolerable; شىء بين بين something between, a cross, a mixture, a combination; بين حين وحين (*ḥīnin*) and بين وقت وآخر (*waqtin wa-āḵara*), بين فترة واخرى (*fatra, uḵrā*) at times, from time to time; ما بين يوم وليلة (*yaumin wa-lailatin*) overnight, suddenly; ما بين يوم وآخر (*wa-āḵara*) from one day to the next, suddenly; ما بين الساعة ٩ والساعة ١٢ between 9 and 12 o'clock; ما بين النهرين (*nahrain*) Mesopotamia

مابين *mā-bain* look up alphabetically

بينا *bainā*, بينما *bainamā* (conj.) while; whereas

بين *bayyin* clear, plain, evident, obvious, patent; (pl. ابيناء *abyinā'*[2]) eloquent

بيان *bayān* pl. *-āt* clearness, plainness, patency, obviousness; statement, information (also, e.g., in a questionnaire, عن about); declaration, announcement; manifestation; explanation, elucidation, illustration; exposé; demonstration (of technical devices, equipments, etc.); (official) report, (official) statement; communiqué, official bulletin (of a government); enumeration, index, list; eloquence; البيان the Koran; pl. بيانات data | بيان الحقيقة correction (*journ.*); بيان مشترك (*muštarak*) joint communiqué; بيان صحفى (*ṣuḥufī*) press release; بيانات احصائية (*iḥṣā'īya*) statistical data; بيانات رقمية (*raqmīya*) numerical data; غنى عن البيان (*ġanīy*) self-explanatory, self-evident; علم البيان *'ilm al-b.* branch of Arab rhetoric, dealing with metaphorical language; (in general) rhetorical art of the Arabs; عطف البيان *'atf al-b.* explicative apposition (*gram.*)

بياني *bayānī* explanatory, illustrative; rhetorical | خطوط بيانية graphical representation (with lines, curves)

بينة *bayyina* pl. *-āt* clear proof, indisputable evidence; evidence (*Isl. Law*); a document serving as evidence | بينة ظرفية (*ẓarfīya*) circumstantial evidence; على بينة as has been proved; كان على بينة من to be fully aware of; to be well-informed, well-posted, up-to-date about

مبيان *mibyān* ○ device for measurement and graphical representation (esp. of physical events) | ○ مبيان نفسى (*nafsī*) psychograph

ابين *abyan*[2] clearer, more distinct, more obvious

تبيان *tibyān* exposition, demonstration, explanation, illustration

تبيين *tabyīn* and ابانة *ibāna* exposition, demonstration, explanation, illustration

تباين *tabāyun* difference, unlikeness, dissimilarity, disparity

تبايني *tabāyunī* different, differing, conflicting

استبانة *istibāna* clarification, explanation

استبيان *istibyān* poll, questioning or canvassing of persons; questionnaire

بائن *bā'in* clear, plain, evident, obvious, patent; final, irrevocable (divorce; *Isl. Law*); of great length | بائن الطول *b. aṭ-ṭūl* towering, of unusual height (person)

بائنة *bā'ina* bride's dowry

مبيونة *mabyūna* distance

مبين *mubayyin* pl. *-āt* indicator | مبين السرعة *m. as-sur'a* speed indicator (*techn.*)

مبين *mubīn* clear, plain, evident, obvious, patent | الكتاب المبين the Koran

متباين *mutabāyin* dissimilar, unlike, differential, differing, varying

بيان[2], بيانو look up alphabetically

بينباشى see بكباشى

بينتو see بنتو

بيه (Turk.; = بك and بيك) *bēh* bey; (honorific address and title of courtesy) يا بيه Sir! (after the name) فلان بيه Mr. So-and-so

بيوريه[1] (Engl.) *biyūrēh* purée

بيوريه[2] (Fr. *pyorrhée*) *biyōrēh* pyorrhea (*med.*)

بيولوجيا *biyolōjiyā* biology

بيولوجى *biyolōjī* biological

بيونس ايرس *byūnis airis* Buenos Aires

ت

ت[1] abbreviation of تلفون telephone and تشرين *tišrīn*[2] (name of a month), تشرين الاول = ت ١, تشرين الثانى = ت ٢

ت[2] *ta* (particle introducing oaths) by, تالله *ta-llāhi* by God!

تاء *tā'* name of the letter ت

تابلوه (Fr. *tableau*) *tablōh* pl. *-āt* painting; set (*theat.*); scene, number on a program

تابوت *tābūt* pl. توابيت *tawābīt*[2] box, case, chest, coffer; casket, coffin, sarcophagus | تابوت العهد *t. al-'ahd* ark of the covenant; تابوت رفع المياه *t. raf' al-miyāh* Archimedean screw; تابوت الساقية *t. as-sāqiya* scoop wheel, Persian wheel

تابيوكا *tābiyōkā* tapioca

تأتأ *ta'ta'a* to stammer (with fright)

تاج see توج

تؤدة see وأد

تأر[1] IV اتأر البصر (*baṣara*) to stare (ه or الى at s.o.)

تارة[2] see تور

تازة *tāza* (= طازة; invar. for gender) fresh, tender, new

تأق *ta'q* allergy (*med.*)

تاك *tāka* fem. of the demonstrative pronoun ذاك *dāka* (dual nom. تانك *tānika*, genit., acc. تينك *tainika*)

تاكسى *taksī* pl. *-āt*, (*saud.-ar.*) □ تكاسى *takāsī* taxi

تامبر *tambar* see تنبر

التاميز *at-tāmīz* the Thames

تانزانيا see تنزانيا

تاى *tāy* (*maḡr.*) tea | تاى احمر black tea

تايلند and تايلاند *tailand* Thailand

التايمز *at-taimz* the Thames

تايور *tāyōr* and تايير *tāyēr* (Fr. *tailleur*) pl. *-āt* ladies' tailored suit, tailleur

تب *tabba* *i* (*tabb*, تبب *tabab*, تباب *tabāb*) to perish, be destroyed **X** to stabilize, be stabilized, be or become stable; to be settled, established, well-ordered, regular, normal; to progress well | استتب له الامر everything went well with him

تبا له *tabban lahū!* may evil befall him! may he perish!

استتباب *istitbāb* normalcy, regularity, orderliness, order; stability; favorable course or development

التبت *at-tibit* Tibet

تبتى *tibitī* Tibetan

تبر *tabara* *i* (*tabr*) to destroy, annihilate (ه s.th.)

تبر *tibr* raw metal; gold dust, gold nuggets; ore

تبار *tabār* ruin, destruction

تبرية *tibrīya* dandruff

تبريز *tabrīz*[2] Tabriz (city in NW Iran, capital of Azerbaijan province)

تبع *tabi'a* *a* (*taba'*, تباعة *tabā'a*) to follow, succeed (ه s.o., ه s.th.), come after s.o. or s.th. (ه, ه); to trail, track (ه, ه s.o., s.th.), go after s.o. or s.th. (ه, ه); to walk behind s.o. (ه); to pursue (ه s.th.); to keep, adhere, stick (ه to s.th.), observe (ه s.th.); to follow, take (ه a road), enter upon (ه a road or course); to comply (ه with s.th.); to belong, pertain (ه to); to be subordinate, be attached (ه to s.o.), be under s.o.'s (ه) authority or command, be under s.o. (ه) | تبع الدروس (*durūsa*) to attend classes regularly **III** to follow (ه, ه s.o., s.th.; also = to keep one's mind or eyes on, e.g., on a development); to agree, concur (ه with s.o., على in s.th.), be in agreement or conformity (ه, على with); to pursue, chase, follow up (ه s.o., ه s.th.); to continue (ه s.th.; سيره *sairahū* on one's way), go on (ه with or in) **IV** to cause to succeed or follow (in time, rank, etc.); to place (ه s.o.) under s.o.'s (ه) authority or command, subordinate (ه ه to s.o. s.o., ه ه to s.th. s.th.) **V** to follow (ه s.th., esp. fig.: a topic, a development, the news, etc., = to watch, study); to pursue, trail, track (ه, ه s.o., s.th.); to trace (ه s.th.); to be subordinate (ه, ه to), be attached (ه to s.o.) **VI** to follow in succession, be successive or consecutive, come or happen successively; to form an uninterrupted sequence **VIII** to follow, succeed (ه s.o., ه s.th.), come after (ه, ه); to make (ه s.th.) be succeeded or followed (ب by s.th. else); to prosecute (ه s.o.), take legal action (ه against); to follow, obey, heed, observe, bear in mind (ه s.th.); to pursue (ه s.th.); to examine, investigate, study (ه s.th.); pass. *uttubi'a* to have or find followers, adherents (على for s.th., e.g., for an idea) | اتبع سياسة (*siyāsatan*) to pursue a policy; اتبع يمينه (*yamīnahū*) to keep (to the) right X to make (ه s.o.) follow, ask (ه s.o.) to follow; to seduce (ه s.o.); to have as its consequence, engender, entail (ه s.th.); to subordinate to o.s., make subservient to o.s. (ه s.th.)

تبع *taba'* succession; subordinateness, dependency; following, followers; subordinate, subservient (ل to s.th.); بالتبع successively, consecutively; تبعا ل *taba'an li* according to, in accordance with, pursuant to, in observance of; due to, in consequence of, as the result of; — (pl. اتباع *atbā'*) follower, companion, adherent, partisan; subject, national, citizen; appertaining, appurtenant, pertinent, incident

تبعى *taba'ī*: عقوبة تبعية (*'uqūba*) incidental punishment (*jur.*)

تبعة *tabi'a* pl. *-āt* consequence; responsibility, responsibleness | القى التبعة على (*alqā*) to make s.o. or s.th. responsible

تبيع *tabī'* pl. تباع *tibā'* following attached, attending, adjunct; — (pl. تبائع *tabā'i'*[2]) follower, adherent, partisan; aide, help, assistant, attendant, servant

تبعية *taba'īya* pl. *-āt* subordination, subjection; subordinateness, dependency; state of being subject, of pertaining or belonging to s.th. (e.g., a group, class, country), affiliation; citizenship, nationality; بالتبعية subsequently, afterwards; consequently, hence, therefore, accordingly

تباعا *tibā'an* in succession, successively, consecutively, one after the other, one by one

متابعة *mutāba'a* following, pursuing, pursuit, prosecution; tracking; continuation | متابعة التدريب continuation training; محطة متابعة *maḥaṭṭat m.* tracking station (for satellites)

اتباع *itbā'* (*gram.*) intensification by repeating a word with its initial consonant changed, such as *kaṯīr baṯīr*

تتبع *tatabbu'* following (esp. fig., of an argument, of a development, see V above); pursuit; prosecution; succession, course | التتبع التاريخى the course of history; تتبعات عدلية (*'adlīya*) legal action, prosecution

تتابع *tatābu'* succession; relay (*athlet.*); بالتتابع consecutively, successively, in succession; serially, in serialized form | مسابقة التتابع relay race (sport)

اتباع *ittibā'* following; pursuit (e.g., of a policy); adherence (to), compliance (with), observance (of); اتباعا ل *ittibā'an li* according to, in accordance or conformity with, pursuant to, in observance of

○ اتباعى *ittibā'ī* classical

○ اتباعية *ittibā'īya* classicism

تابع *tābi'* pl. تبعة *taba'a*, تباع *tubbā'* following, succeeding, subsequent; subsidiary, dependent; minor, secondary; subordinate (ل to s.o.), under s.o. (ل); belonging (ل to); subject to s.o.'s (ل) authority or competence; adherent (ل to), following (ل s.o. or s.th.); — (pl. اتباع *atbā'*) adherent, follower, partisan; subject, citizen, national; subordinate, servant; factotum; (pl. توابع) appositive (*gram.*); appendix, addendum, supplement; ○ function (*math.*) | الدول التابعة (*duwal*) the satellite countries

تابعة *tābi'a* pl. توابع *tawābi'*[2] female attendant, woman servant; a female demon who accompanies women; appurtenance, dependency; consequence, effect, result; responsibility; — pl. توابع dependencies, dependent territories; ○ satellites (*pol.*), = الدول التوابع (*duwal*) the satellite countries; things of minor importance belonging to s.th.; وتوابعه and everything else that belongs to it

تابعية *tābiʿīya* nationality, citizenship

متبوع *matbūʿ* followed, succeeded (ب by); one to whom service or obedience is rendered, a leader, a principal (as distinguished from تابع subordinate)

متتابع *mutatābiʿ* successive, consecutive; pl. متتابعات sequence of pieces (*mus.*)

متبع *muttabaʿ* observed, adhered to, complied with (e.g., regulation, custom); followed, traveled (road, course)

تبغ *tibḡ* pl. تبوغ *tubūḡ* tobacco

تبل *tabala i* to consume, waste, make sick (ه s.o.; said of love) **II, III** and توبل *taubala* to spice, season (ه s.th.)

تابل *tābal, tābil* pl. توابل *tawābil*[2] coriander (*bot.*); spice, condiment, seasoning

تبولة *tabbūla* (*syr., leb.*) a kind of salad made of bulgur, parsley, mint, onion, lemon juice, spices, and oil

متبول *matbūl* (love-)sick, weak, ravaged, consumed

متبل *mutabbal* spiced, seasoned, flavored; (*syr., leb.*) stuffed with a mixture of rice, chopped meat and various spices, e.g., باذنجان متبل (*bāḏinjān*) stuffed eggplant

تبلوه see تابلوه

تبن *tibn* chopped straw, chaff (for feed and building material)

تبنى *tibnī* straw-colored, flaxen

تبان *tabbān* straw vendor

درب التبانة *darb at-tabbāna* the Milky Way

متبن *matban* pl. متابن *matābin*[2] strawstack

تبيوكا *tabiyōkā* tapioca

التتر[1] *at-tatar* and التتار *at-tatār* the Tatars

تترى *tatarī* Tatarian; Tatar

تترى[2] *tatrā* (from وتر) one after the other, successively, in succession

تتك *titik* trigger

تتن *tutun* tobacco

تتنوس *tetanūs* tetanus (*med.*)

تجر *tajara u* to carry on commerce **III** to do business, trade (ه with s.o.) **VIII** to do business; to trade, deal (في or ب in s.th.)

تجارة *tijāra* commerce; traffic, trade; merchandise | تجارة خاسرة a losing business

تجارى *tijārī* commercial, mercantile, trade, trading, business (used attributively); commercialized; commercially profitable or productive; pl. تجاريون merchants, vendors, business people | بيت تجارى (*bait*) commercial house, business house; الحركة التجارية (*ḥaraka*) trade, traffic; شركة تجارية (*širka*) trading company; اتفاق تجارى (*ittifāq*) trade agreement

متجر *matjar* pl. متاجر *matājir*[2] business, transaction, dealing; merchandise; store, shop

متجرى *matjarī* commercial, trade, trading, business (used attributively)

متاجرة *mutājara* commerce

اتجار *ittijār* trade, business (في or ب in s.th.)

تاجر *tājir* pl. تجار *tujjār, tijār* merchant, trader, businessman, dealer, tradesman | تاجر الجملة *t. al-jumla* wholesale dealer; تاجر التجزئة *t. at-tajziʾa* and تاجر القطاعى *t. al-qiṭāʿī* retailer

بضاعة تاجرة *biḍāʿa tājira* salable, marketable merchandise

تجاه *tujāha* (prep.) in front of, opposite, face to face with, facing

تحت *taḥta* (prep.) under; below, beneath, underneath | تحت التجربة (*tajriba*) on probation; in an experimental state; تحت التحضير in preparation; تحت الحفظ (*ḥifẓ*) in custody, under guard; تحت السداد (*sadād*), تحت التسديد due, outstanding, unsettled, unpaid (*com.*); تحت السلاح under arms; تحت سمعهم (*sam'ihim*) in their hearing, for them to hear; تحت التسوية (*taswiya*) outstanding, unpaid, unsettled (*com.*); تحت اشراف (*išrāfi*) under the patronage or superintendence of; تحت الشعور subconscious; تحت تصرفه (*taṣarrufihī*) at his disposal; تحت الطبع (*ṭab'*) in press; تحت عنوان (*'unwāni*) under the title of; تحت اعيننا (*a'yuninā*) before our eyes; تحت التمرين in training; تحت اليد (*yad*) in hand, at hand, available, handy; تحت يده in his power; من تحت *min taḥti* from under, from beneath; under

تحت *taḥtu* (adv.) below, beneath, underneath

تحتى *taḥtī* under- (in compounds) | بناء تحتى infra-structure

تحتانى *taḥtānī* lower, under- (in compounds) | ملابس تحتانية underwear

تحتمس *tuḥutmis*[2] Thutmose (king of Egypt)

تحف IV to present (ه ب or ه ه s.o. with s.th.)

تحفة *tuḥfa* pl. تحف *tuḥaf* gift, present; gem (fig.), curiosity, rarity, article of virtu, objet d'art; work of art | تحفة فنية (*fannīya*) unique work of art

متحف *mutḥaf* (also pronounced *matḥaf*) pl. متاحف *matāḥif*[2] museum | متحف الشمع *m. aš-šam'* wax museum, waxworks

تخ *takka u* to become sour, ferment (dough)

تخت *takt* pl. تخوت *tukūt* bedstead, bedframe; wooden sofa, couchlike wooden bench; throne; dais, platform; (oriental) band, orchestra | تخت الثياب *t. aṯ-ṯiyāb* wardrobe; تخت الملك *t. al-mulk* throne; royal residence, capital; تخت المملكة *t. al-mamlaka* capital (of a country)

تختة *takta* pl. تخت *tukat* board; desk; blackboard

تختخ *taktaka* to rot, decay

تختروان *taktarawān* pl. *-āt* sedan chair, palanquin (litter for one person, borne on poles by two men or mules)

[1]تخم *takima a* to suffer from indigestion, feel sick from overeating IV to surfeit, satiate (ه s.o.); to give (ه s.o.) indigestion, make sick (ه s.o.); to overstuff, cloy (ه the stomach) VIII = I

تخمة *tukama, tukma* (also pronounced *takma*) pl. تخم *tukam, -āt* indigestion, dyspepsia; illness from overeating

متخوم *matkūm* suffering from indigestion, dyspeptic

[2]تخم *takama i* to fix the limits of (ه), delimit, limit, confine, bound (ه s.th.) III to border (ه on), be adjacent (ه to s.th.)

تخم *takm, tukm* pl. تخوم *tukūm* boundary, border, borderline, limit

متاخم *mutākim* neighboring, adjacent

تدرج *tadruj*[2], تدرجة *tadruja* pheasant

تدمر *tadmur*[2], usually pronounced *tudmur*[2] Palmyra (ancient city of Syria, now a small village)

تدمرى *tadmurī*, usually pronounced *tudmurī* anyone | لا تدمرى nobody, not a living soul

ترابيزة (*eg.*; *tarābēza*) pl. *-āt* table

تراجيديا *trajēdiyā*, (*eg.*) *tragēdiyā* pl. *-āt* tragedy

تراجيديان (Fr. *tragédien*) *tragedyān* (*eg.*) tragedian, tragic actor

تراخوما *trākōmā* trachoma (*med.*)

تراخومة *trākōma* = تراخوما

تراس (Fr. *terrasse*) *terās* terrace

ترام, ترامواى *trām, tramwāy* pl. *-āt* tramway

ترانزستر *tranzistar* and ترانزستور *tranzistor* pl. *-āt* transistor

ترانسفورم *transform* pl. *-āt* transformer (*el.*)

ترب *tariba a* to be or become dusty, covered with dust **II** and **IV** to cover with dust or earth (ه s.o., ه s.th.) **III** to be s.o.'s (ه) mate or comrade, be of the same age (ه as s.o.) **V** to be dusty, be covered with dust

ترب *tirb* pl. اتراب *atrāb* person of the same age, contemporary, mate, companion, comrade

ترب *tarib* dusty, dust-covered

تربة *turba* pl. ترب *turab* dust; earth, dirt; ground (also fig.); soil; arable soil; grave, tomb; graveyard, cemetery, burial ground

تربى *turabī* pl. *-īya* (*eg.*) gravedigger

تراب *turāb* pl. اتربة *atriba*, تربان *tirbān* dust, earth, dirt; ground, soil; (without pl.) home soil, territory (of a country)

ترابى *turābī* dusty; dustlike, powdery; earthlike, earthy; dust-colored, gray; territorial

ترابة *turāba* dust; ○ cement

تريبة *tarība* pl. ترائب *tarā'ib*[2] chest, thorax

متربة *matraba* poverty, misery, destitution; (pl. متارب *matārib*[2]) dirt quarry

مترب *mutrib* dusty, dust-covered

تربس *tarbasa* (= دربس) to bolt (ه a door)

ترباس *tirbās* pl. ترابيس *tarābīs*[2], ترابس *tarābis*[2] bolt, latch (of a door or window)

تربنتين *tarbantīn* turpentine

تربيزة (*eg.*) *tarabēza* table

تربين *turbīn* pl. *-āt* turbine

تراث see ورث

ترتر *tirtir* gold and silver spangles (*eg.*)

ترجم *tarjama* to translate (ه s.th. عن from one language الى to another); to interpret (ه s.th.); to treat (ه of s.th.) by way of explanation, expound (ه s.th.); to write a biography (ل of s.o., also ه)

ترجمة *tarjama* pl. تراجم *tarājim*[2] translation; interpretation; biography (also ترجمة الحياة); introduction, preface, foreword (of a book) | الترجمة السبعينية (*sab'īnīya*) the Septuagint; ترجمة ذاتية (*dātīya*) autobiography

ترجمان *turjumān* pl. تراجمة *tarājima*, تراجيم *tarājīm*[2] translator, interpreter

مترجم *mutarjim* translator, interpreter; biographer

مترجم *mutarjam* translated | مترجم على الفلم (*film*) synchronized (film)

ترجيديا etc. see تراجيديا

ترح *tariḥa a* (*taraḥ*) and **V** to grieve, be sad **II** and **IV** to grieve, distress (ه s.o.)

ترح *taraḥ* pl. اتراح *atrāḥ* grief, distress, sadness

تاريخ, تواريخ and تاريخى see under ارخ

ترزى *tarzī* pl. ترزية *tarzīya* (*eg.*) tailor

ترزية *tarzīya* tailoring

ترس[1] look up alphabetically

ترس[2] **II** to provide with a shield or armor

ترس *turs* pl. اتراس *atrās*, تروس *turūs* shield; disk of the sun; — *tirs* pl. *turūs* cogwheel, gear-wheel; pl. gear (*techn.*) | ذراع التروس gearshift lever; ناقل التروس gearshift; صندوق التروس *ṣundūq at-t.* gearbox, transmission; سمك الترس *samak at-turs* turbot (*zool.*)

مترس *matras, mitras* pl. متارس *matāris*[2] and متراس *mitrās* pl. متاريس *matārīs*[2] bolt, door latch; rampart, bulwark, barricade; esp. pl. متاريس barricades

ترسانة *tirsāna* and *tarsāna* (obs. ترسخانة *tarsḵāna*) pl. *-āt* arsenal; shipyard, dockyard

ترسكل (Fr. *tricycle*) tricycle

ترسو (It. *terzo*) *tersō* (*eg.*) 3rd class (in trains); cheapest seats in movies or theater

ترسينة (It. *terrazzino*) *tarasīna* balcony

ترع *tariʿa a* to be or become full (vessel) IV to fill (ه s.th., esp. a vessel)

ترعة *turʿa* pl. ترع *turaʿ*, *-āt* canal; artificial waterway | ترعة الايراد *t. al-īrād* feeder, irrigation canal; ترعة التصريف drainage canal (*Eg.*); الترعة الشريفة the Residence of the Sultan of Morocco

مترع *mutraʿ* filled (ب with), full (ب of)

ترغل, ترغلة *turğul, turğulla* turtledove

ترف *tarifa a* to live in opulence, in luxury IV to effeminate (ه s.o.); to provide with opulent means, surround with luxury (ه s.o.) V = I

ترف *taraf* and ترفة *turfa* luxury, opulence, affluence; effemination

ترف *tarif* opulent, sumptuous, luxurious

مترف *mutraf* living in ease and luxury; luxurious; luxuriously equipped (ب with); pl. المترفون the rich

ترفاس *tirfās* (*mağr.*) truffle (*bot.*)

ترفل *tarfala* to strut

ترقوة *tarquwa* pl. تراق *tarāqin* collarbone, clavicle (*anat.*)

ترك[1] *taraka u* (*tark*) to let be, leave, relinquish, renounce, give up, forswear (ه s.th.); to desist, refrain, abstain (ه from s.th.); to leave, quit (ه s.o., ه a place); to leave out, omit, drop, neglect, pass over, skip (ه s.th.); to leave (ل or الى ه s.th. to); to leave behind, leave, bequeath, make over (ه s.th., ل to s.o.; as a legacy) | تركه يفعل to let s.o. do s.th.; ترك مكانا الى to leave one place for (another); تركه فى ذمته (*fī ḏimmatihī*) to leave s.th. in s.o.'s care, leave s.th. to s.o.; تركه على حاله to leave s.th. or s.o. unchanged, leave s.th. or s.o. alone; تركه وشأنه (*wa-šaʾnahū*) to leave s.o. alone, leave s.o. to his own devices; ترك الحبل على الغارب (*ḥabla*) to give free rein, impose no restraints, let things take their course; ترك حبله على غاربه to give free rein to s.o. or s.th.; تركه جانبا to leave s.th. aside III to leave (ه s.o.); to leave alone (ه s.o.); to leave off hostilities (ه against s.o.)

ترك *tark* omission, neglect; relinquishment, abandonment; leaving, leaving behind

تركة *tarika* pl. *-āt* (also *tirka*) heritage, legacy, bequest

تريكة *tarīka* pl. ترائك *tarāʾik*[2] old maid, spinster

متاركة *mutāraka* truce

متروك *matrūk* pl. *-āt* heritage, legacy

ترك[2] II to Turkify, Turkicize (ه s.o.) X to become a Turk, become Turkified, adopt Turkish manners and customs

الترك *at-turk* and الاتراك *al-atrāk* the Turks

تركى *turkī* Turkish; Turk; التركية *at-turkīya* theTurkish language

تركيا *turkiyā* Turkey

تتريك *tatrīk* Turkification

تركتر *traktar* and تركتور *traktor* pl. *-āt* tractor

تركستان *turkistān*[2] Turkistan

التركمان *at-turkumān* the Turkmen

ترمبيط *turumbēṭ* (*syr.*) pl. *-āt* (Western) drum; ترمبيطة *turumbēṭa* (*eg.*) pl. *-āt* do.; specif., bass drum

ترمبطجی *turumbaṭgī* (*eg.*) drummer; bandsman (*mil.*)

ترمس *turmus*, ترموس *turmūs* lupine (*bot.*)

ترمومتر *termūmitr* thermometer

ترنج *turunj* see اترج, اترنج

تره *tariha a* to concern o.s. with trifles

ترهة *turraha* pl. *-āt* sham, mockery, farce; lie, humbug, hoax, fairy tale

ترواده (Fr. *Troade*) *tirwāda* Troy

تروب (Engl. *troop*) squad, platoon; squadron | تروب سوارى (*sawārī*) cavalry squadron (*Eg.*)

ترومبيتجى = ترمبطجى see under ترمبيط above

ترياق *tiryāq* theriaca; antidote

تريكو (Fr.) tricot

تسعة *tis'a* (f. تسع *tis'*) nine

تسعة عشر *tis'ata 'ašara*, f. تسع عشرة *tis'a 'ašrata* nineteen

تسع *tus'* pl. اتساع *atsā'* one ninth, the ninth part

تسعون *tis'ūn* ninety

التسعينات *at-tis'īnāt* the nineties (decade of a century)

التاسع *at-tāsi'* the ninth

تشاد *tšād* Chad (country in Africa)

تشرين الاول *tišrīn*[2] *al-awwal* October, تشرين الثانى *t. aṯ-ṯānī* November (*Syr.*, *Ir.*, *Leb.*, *Jord.*)

تشيكوسلوفاكيا *tšekoslovākiyā* Czechoslovakia

تشيكوسلوفاكى *tšekoslovākī* Czechoslovakian

تشيكى *tšīkī* Czech (adj.)

تشيلى *tšīlī* Chile; Chilean (adj.); (pl. *-ūn*) a Chilean

تطوان *tiṭwān*[2] Tetuán (city in N Morocco)

تع abbreviation of تعالى, see علو

تعب *ta'iba a* (*ta'ab*) to work hard, toil, slave, drudge, wear o.s. out; to be or become tired, weary (من of s.th.) **IV** to trouble, inconvenience (ه s.o.); to irk, bother, weary, tire, fatigue (ه s.o.)

تعب *ta'ab* pl. اتعاب *at'āb* trouble, exertion, labor, toil, drudgery; burden, nuisance, inconvenience, discomfort, difficulty, hardship; tiredness, weariness, fatigue; pl. اتعاب fees, honorarium

تعب *ta'ib* and تعبان *ta'bān* tired, weary, exhausted

متاعب *matā'ib*[2] troubles, pains, efforts; discomforts, inconveniences, difficulties, troubles; complaints, ailments, ills (attending disease); hardships, strains

متعب *mut'ib* troublesome, inconvenient, toilsome, laborious; burdensome, irksome, annoying; wearisome, tiresome, tiring; tedious, dull, boring

متعب *mut'ab* tired, weary

تعتع *ta'ta'a* to stammer; to shake (ه s.o.); اتعتع *itta'ta'a* to move, stir

تعز *ta'izz*[2] Taizz (city in S Yemen, seat of government)

تعس *ta'asa a*, *ta'isa a* to fall, perish; to become wretched, miserable; *ta'asa* and **IV** to make unhappy or miserable, ruin (ه s.o.)

تعس *ta's* and تعاسة *ta'āsa* wretchedness, misery

تعس *ta'is* and تعيس *ta'īs* pl. تعساء *tu'asā'*[2] wretched, miserable, unfortunate, unhappy

متعوس *mat'ūs* pl. متاعيس *matā'īs*[2] wretched, miserable, unfortunate, unhappy

تف *taffa* to spit **II** to say "phew"

تف *tuff* dirt under the fingernails;

تفا لك *tuffan laka* phew! fie on you!

○ تفافة *taffāfa* spittoon, cuspidor

تفتا *tafettā*, تفتاه taffeta

تفاح *tuffāḥ* (coll.; n. un. ة) pl. *-āt*, تفافيح *tafāfīḥ*[2] apple(s)

تفكة *tufka* pl. تفك *tufak* (*ir.*) gun, rifle

تفل *tafala u i* (*tafl*) to spit

تفل *tufl* and تفال *tufāl* spit, spittle, saliva

تفل *tafil* ill-smelling, malodorous

متفلة *mitfala* spittoon, cuspidor

تفه *tafiha a* (*tafah*, تفاهة *tafāha*, تفوه *tufūh*) to be little, paltry, insignificant; to be flat, tasteless, vapid, insipid

تفه *tafah* and تفوه *tufūh* paltriness, triviality, insignificance

تفاهة *tafāha* paltriness, triviality, insignificance; flatness, vapidity, insipidity, tastelessness; inanity, stupidity, silliness

تفه *tafih* and تافه *tāfih* little, paltry, trivial, trifling, insignificant; worthless; commonplace, common, mediocre; flat, tasteless, vapid, insipid; trite, banal

اتفه *atfah*[2] more trivial, insignificant; commoner; more tasteless

تافهة *tāfiha* pl. توافه *tawāfih*[2] worthless thing; triviality, trifle

تقاوى see قوى

تقلية see قلى

تقن IV to perfect, bring to perfection (ه s.th.); to master, know well (ه s.th., e.g., a language), be proficient, skillful, well-versed (ه in s.th.)

تقن *tiqn* skillful, adroit

تقنى *taqnī* technical; (pl. *-ūn*) engineer, technician

تقنية *taqnīya* pl. *-āt* technique (also artistic); perfection

تقانة *taqāna* firmness, solidity; perfection

اتقن *atqan*[2] more perfect, more thorough

اتقان *itqān* perfection; thoroughness, exactitude, precision; thorough skill, proficiency; mastery, command (e.g., of a special field, of a language) | فى غاية الاتقان to greatest perfection; of excellent workmanship

متقن *mutqan* perfect; exact, precise

تقى *taqā i* to fear (esp. God) VIII see وقى

تقى *taqīy* pl. اتقياء *atqiyā'*[2] God-fearing, godly, devout, pious

اتقى *atqā* more pious

تقى *tuqan* and تقوى *taqwā* godliness, devoutness, piety

[1]تك *takka u* to trample down, trample underfoot, crush (ه s.th.); to intoxicate (ه s.o.; wine)

[2]تكة *tikka* pl. تكك *tikak* waistband (in the upper seam of the trousers)

[3]تك *takka* to tick (clock)

تكة *tikka* pl. *-āt* ticking, ticktock (of a clock), ticking noise

[4]تكية look up alphabetically

تكوت *tukūt* pl. of Engl. *ticket*

[1]تكتك *taktaka* to trample down, trample underfoot (ه s.th.)

[2]تكتك *taktaka* to bubble, simmer (boiling mass)

[3]تكتك *taktaka* to tick (clock)

تكتكة *taktaka* ticking, ticktock (of a clock), ticking noise

[4]تكتيك *taktīk* tactics

تكتيكى *taktīkī* tactical

تكرز (Engl.) *tikarz* tickers, teletype (*techn.*)

تكلة see وكل

تكنوقراط *tiknoqrāṭ* technocrat

تكنولوجيا *tiknolōjiyā* and تكنولوجية *tiknolōjīya* technology

تكنولوجى *tiknolōjī* technological

تكنيك *taknīk* pl. -*āt* technique (also artistic); technical process

تكية *takīya* pl. تكايا *takāyā* monastery (of a Muslim order); hospice; home, asylum (for the invalided or needy)

تل[1] *tall* pl. تلال *tilāl*, اتلال *atlāl*, تلول *tulūl* hill, elevation | تل ابيب *t. abīb* Tel Aviv (city in W Israel)

تلة *talla* heap

تل[2] *tull* tulle

تلاتل *talātil*[2] hardships, troubles, adversities

تليد *talīd*, تالد *tālid*, تلاد *tilād* inherited, time-honored, old (possession, property)

تلسكوب *tiliskūb*, *teliskōb* pl. -*āt* telescope

تلسكوبى *tiliskūbī*, *teliskōbī* telescopic

تلع IV to stretch one's neck; to crane (ه the neck)

تلعة *tal'a* pl. تلاع *tilā'* hill, hillside, mountainside; (torrential) stream

تليع *talī'* long, outstretched, extended; high, tall

تلغراف *tiliġrāf*, *taliġrāf* pl. -*āt* telegraph; telegram, wire, cable | ارسل تلغرافا الى to send a wire to

تلغرافى *tiliġrāfī*, *taliġrāfī* telegraphic

تلف *talifa a* (*talaf*) to be annihilated, be destroyed; to be or become damaged or spoiled, be ruined, break, get broken, go to pieces II to ruin (ه s.th.); to wear out, "finish" (ه s.o.) IV to destroy, annihilate (ه s.th.); to ruin, damage, spoil, break (ه s.th.); to waste (ه s.th.)

تلف *talaf* ruin, destruction; ruination, damage, injury, harm; loss; waste

تلفان *talfān* spoiled; useless, worthless, good-for-nothing

متلف *matlaf*, متلفة *matlafa* pl. متالف *matālif*[2] desert

متلاف *mitlāf* wastrel; ruinous, harmful, injurious

اتلاف *itlāf* pl. -*āt* annihilation, destruction; damage, injury, harm

تالف *tālif* ruined, damaged, broken; out of order, kaput; spoiled

متلوف *matlūf* and متلف *mutlaf* ruined, damaged, broken; out of order, kaput; spoiled

متلف *mutlif* annihilator, destroyer; injurer; damaging, ruinous, harmful, injurious, noxious

تلفز *talfaza* to televise, transmit by television

تلفزة *talfaza* television

اذاعة تلفزية *iḏā'a talfazīya* television broadcast, telecast

○ تلفاز *tilfāz* television set

تلفزيون (Fr. *télévision*) *tilivizyōn*, *televizyōn*, *talavizyōn* television, telecast; (pl. -*āt*) television set, TV

تلفزيونى *tilivizyōnī* etc. TV- (in compounds) | اذاعة تلفزيونية (*iḏā'a*) television broadcast, telecast

تلفن *talfana* to telephone

تلفون *tilifūn*, *telefōn*, *talifōn* and تليفون pl. -*āt* telephone

تلفونى *tilifūnī*, *telefōnī* and تليفونى telephonic

تلقاء, تلقائى and تلقائية see under لقى

تلك *tilka* fem. of the demonstrative pronoun ذلك

تلكس and تليكس *teleks* telex

تلم *talam* pl. اتلام *atlām* (plow) furrow

تلمذ *talmaḏa* to take on as, or have for, a pupil or apprentice (ه s.o.); to be or become a pupil or apprentice (ل of s.o., also على), receive one's schooling or training (على, ل from) **II** *tatalmaḏa* to be or become a pupil or apprentice (ل or على يده of s.o.), work as an apprentice (ل or على يده under s.o.)

تلمذة *talmaḏa* school days, college years; apprenticeship; (time of) probation

تلماذ *tilmāḏ* learning, erudition

تلميذ *tilmīḏ* pl. تلاميذ *talāmīḏ*², تلامذة *talāmiḏa* pupil, student, apprentice; probationer; trainee; disciple; cadet (*Ir.*; *mil.*)

تلميذة *tilmīḏa* pl. *-āt* pupil (fem.)

تلمسان *tilimsān*² Tlemcen (city in NW Algeria)

تلمود *talmūd* Talmud

تله *taliha a* (*talah*) to be astonished, amazed, perplexed, at a loss

تاله *tālih* and متله *mutallah* at a loss, bewildered, perplexed | تاله العقل *t. al-ʿaql* absent-minded, distracted

(تلو) تلا *talā u* (تلو *tulūw*) to follow, succeed; to ensue; — (تلاوة *tilāwa*) to read, read out loud (ه s.th., على to s.o.); to recite (ه s.th.) **VI** to follow one another, be successive **X** to continue | استتلى يقول he went on saying, he continued with the words . . .

تلو *tilwa* (prep.) after, upon | ارسل كتابا تلو كتاب to send letter after letter

تلاوة *tilāwa* reading; public reading; recital, recitation (esp. of the Koran)

تال *tālin* following, succeeding, subsequent, next; بالتالى *bi-t-tālī* then, later, subsequently; consequently, hence, therefore, accordingly

متتال *mutatālin* successive, consecutive

تلى (Turk. *telli*) *tallī* (*eg.*, *tun.*) glittering fabric with interwoven gold or silver threads

تليباثى *tilībāṯī* telepathic

تليس *tallīs*, *tillīs* pl. تلاليس *talālīs*² sack

تليفريك (Fr. *téléférique*) cableway, funicular

تليفزيون and تليفزيونى see تلفزيون

تليفون and تليفونى see تلفون

تم *tamma i* to be or become complete, completed, finished, done; to be performed, be accomplished (ل by s.o.); to come to an end, be or become terminated; to come about, be brought about, be effected, be achieved, come to pass, come off, happen; to take place; to be or become a fact; to come into being, be concluded (contract); to persist (على in); to continue (على s.th. or to do s.th.) **II** and **IV** to complete, finish, wind up, conclude, terminate (ه s.th.); to make complete, supplement, round out, fill up (ه s.th.); to carry out, execute, perform, accomplish, achieve (ه s.th.) **X** to be complete, completed, finished

تمام *tamām* completeness, wholeness, entirety, perfection; full, whole, entire, complete, perfect; separate, independent; تماما *tamāman* completely, entirely, wholly, perfectly, fully, quite; precisely, exactly | بدر تمام (*badr*) and قمر تمام (*qamar*) full moon; فى تمام الساعة السادسة at 6 o'clock sharp; بتمام معنى الكلمة (*maʿnā l-kalima*) in the full sense of the word; بالتمام entirely, completely

تميمة *tamīma* pl. تمائم *tamāʾim*² amulet

اتم *atamm*² more complete, more perfect | على اتم استعداد perfectly prepared, totally ready

تتمة *tatimma* completion; supplementation; — (pl. *-āt*) supplement; final episode, continuation and end (e.g., of an article or a serial)

تتميم *tatmīm* completion; perfection; consummation, execution, fulfillment, realization, effectuation, accomplishment

اتمام *itmām* completion; perfection; termination, conclusion; consummation, execution, fulfillment, realization, effectuation, accomplishment

استتمام *istitmām* termination, conclusion

تام *tāmm* complete, perfect, entire; consummate; of full value; self-contained, needing no completion (*gram.*)

تمباك *tumbāk* Persian tobacco (esp. for the narghile)

تمبر *tambar* and متمبر *mutambar* see تنبر, متنبر

تمتم *tamtama* to stammer, mumble, mutter; to recite under one's breath (ب s.th.)

تمتمة *tamtama* murmuring, babble

تمر *tamr* (coll.; n. un. ة, pl. *tamarāt*, تمور *tumūr*) dates, esp. dried ones | تمر هندى (*hindī*) tamarind (*bot.*); tamarind juice (a refreshing drink)

تمرجى (*eg. tamargī*), تومرجى ,تيمارجى ,تمورجى pl. *-ya* male nurse, hospital attendant; تمرجية pl. *-āt* female nurse

تموز look up alphabetically

تمساح *timsāḥ* pl. تماسيح *tamāsīḥ*[2] crocodile

تمغة *tamḡa* stamp; stamp mark | ورق تمغة *waraq t.* stamped paper

تمن *tumman* rice

تموز *tammūz*[2] July (*Syr., Ir., Leb., Jord.*)

[1]تن *tunn* tuna (*zool.*)

[2]تنين *tinnīn* pl. تنانين *tanānīn*[2] dragon; Draco (*astron.*); waterspout (*meteor.*); see also alphabetically

تانئ *tāniʾ* pl. تناء *tunnāʾ* resident

تنوب *tannūb* (coll.; n. un. ة) fir (*bot.*)

تنباك *tunbāk* (pronounced *tumbāk*) and تنبك *tumbak* Persian tobacco (esp. for the narghile)

تنبال *tinbāl* pl. تنابيل *tanābīl*[2] short, of small stature

تنبر (Fr. *timbre*) *tambar* pl. تنابر *tanābir*[2] (*maḡr.*) stamp; duty stamp; postage stamp

متنبر *mutambar* (*maḡr.*) stamped, postmarked; postage paid (letter)

تنبل (Turk. *tembel*) *tambal* pl. تنابلة *tanābila* lazy; idler, lazy fellow

تنجستين (Fr. *tungstène*) *tongəstēn* tungsten

تندة (It. *tenda*) *tanda* awning; roofing, sun roof

تنور *tannūr* pl. تنانير *tanānīr*[2] a kind of baking oven, a pit, usually clay-lined, for baking bread

تنورة *tannūra* (*syr., leb.*) (lady's) skirt

تنزانيا *tanzāniyā* Tanzania (country in E Africa)

تنزانى *tanzānī* Tanzanian (adj. and n.)

تنس *tenis* tennis | تنس الطاولة *t. aṭ-ṭāwula* table tennis, ping pong

[1]تنك *tanak* tin plate; (*syr.-leb.*) jerry cans made of tin plate

تنكة *tanaka* pl. *-āt* tin container, can; tin pot; jerry can; (*syr.-leb.*) can made of tin plate; (*eg.*) (copper) coffee pot | تنكة غاز (*syr.-leb.*) gasoline can

تنكجى *tanakjī* pl. *-īya* tinsmith, whitesmith

[2]تانك *tānika* see تاك alphabetically

تنوة *tanwa* coffee dregs, grounds

تنيس tennis

تنين *tannīn* tannin, tannic acid

تهته *tahtaha* to stammer, stutter

تهمة[1] *tuhma* pl. تهم *tuham* accusation, charge; suspicion; insinuation

تهامة[2] *tihāma*[2] Tihama, coastal plain along the southwestern and southern shores of the Arabian Peninsula

توا *tawwan* right away, at once, immediately; just (now), this very minute | للتو *li-t-tawwi* at once, right away, also with pers. suffixes: لتوى *li-tawwī*, لتوها *li-tawwihā* (I have, she has) just ...; at once, presently, immediately; فى التو straight, directly

تواليت (Fr. *toilette*) *tuwālēt* toilette

توأم, تومم *tau'am*, f. ة, pl. توائم *tawā'im*[2] twin

توأمة *tau'ama* (*Maġr.*) formation of a partnership (e.g., between two cities)

متوأم *mutau'am* (*Maġr.*) joined in partnership

تاب (توب) *tāba u* (توب *taub*, توبة *tauba*, متاب *matāb*) to repent, be penitent, do penance; with عن: to turn from (sin), be converted from, renounce, forswear s.th.; (said of God) to restore to His grace, forgive (على s.o.) | تاب الى الله to turn to God in repentance II to induce to repentance or penitence, make repent (ه s.o.) X to call on s.o. (ه) to repent

توبة *tauba* repentance, penitence, contrition; penance

تواب *tawwāb* doing penance; repentant, penitent, contrite; forgiving, merciful (God)

تائب *tā'ib* repentant, penitent, contrite

توبل see تبل

توبوغرافيا *toboġrāfiyā* topography

توت[1] *tūt* mulberry tree; mulberry | توت ارضى (*arḍī*) and توت افرنجى (*ifranjī*) strawberry; توت شوكى (*šaukī*) and توت العليق *t. al-ʿullaiq* raspberry (*syr.*); توت شامى mulberry juice (a refreshing drink)

توت[2] *tūt* the first month of the Coptic calendar

توتيا *tūtiyā*, توتياء *tūtiyā'*, توتية *tūtiya* zinc

توج II to crown (ه s.o.; also fig. ب ه s.th. with) V to be crowned

تاج *tāj* pl. تيجان *tījān* crown; miter (of a bishop) | تاج العمود *t. al-ʿamūd* capital (of a column or pilaster); تاج الكرة *t. al-kura* calotte

تاجى *tājī* coronal | شريان تاجى للقلب (*širyān*) coronary artery (*anat.*)

تويج *tuwaij* pl. *-āt* little crown, coronet; corolla (*bot.*)

تتويج *tatwīj* crowning, coronation

توجو *tōgō* (Eg. spelling) Togo (country in W Africa)

توجولند *tōgōland* former designation of Togo

تيح see تاح (توح)

تارة *tāratan* once; sometimes, at times | تارة — اخرى, تارة — طورا (*ṭauran*), تارة — تارة (*uḵrā*) sometimes — sometimes, at times — at other times

توراة *taurāh* Torah, Pentateuch; Old Testament

توربيد, توربيد *turpīd*, *turbīd* torpedo (submarine missile)

توربين *turbīn* pl. *-āt* turbine

تورتة *torta* pl. *-āt* pie, tart

توغو *tōgō* = توجو

تاق (توق) *tāqa u* (*tauq*, توقان *tawaqān*) to long, yearn, wish (الى for), hanker (الى after), desire, crave, covet (الى s.th.), strive (الى for), aspire (الى to)

توق *tauq*, توقان *tawaqān* longing, yearning, craving, desire

تواق *tawwāq* longing, yearning, eager (الى for), craving (الى s.th.)

تائق *tā'iq* longing, yearning, eager (الى for), craving (الى s.th.)

توكة امامية (*tōka amāmīya; eg.*) belt buckle (*mil.*)

تول *tūl* tulle

تمرجى see تومرجى

تون *tūn* and تونة *tūna* tuna (*zool.*)

تونج (Turk. *tunç*) *tunj* bronze

تونس *taunasa* to make Tunisian, Tunisify (ه, ه s.o., s.th.)

تونس *tūnus*², *tūnis*² Tunis; Tunisia

تونسى *tūnusī*, *tūnisī* pl. -*ūn*, توانسة *tawānisa* Tunisian (adj. and n.) | الجمهورية التونسة (*jumhūrīya*) Republic of Tunisia

تونية *tūniya* pl. توانى *tawānī* alb of priests and deacons (*Chr.*)

(توه) تاه *tāha u* and II = (تيه) تاه *tāha i* and II

توهة *tūha* daughter

تياترو (It. *teatro*) *tiyātrō* theater

□ تيتل *taital* pl. تياتل see ثيتل

تيتانوس *tītānūs* tetanus (*med.*)

(تيح) تاح *tāḥa i* to be destined, be foreordained (by fate, by God; ل to s.o.); to be granted, be given (ل to s.o.) IV to destine, foreordain (ه ل to s.o. s.th.); to grant, afford, offer (ه ل s.o. s.th.); to vouchsafe, make possible (ل ه s.th. for s.o.); pass. *utīḥa* to be destined, be foreordained, be granted, be given (ل to s.o.) | اتيح له التوفيق (*utīḥa*) he met with success, he was successful; اتيح له الفرصة (*furṣa*) he was given the opportunity, he had the chance

متاح *mutāḥ* granted, given (ل to s.o.); bestowed by nature (e.g., mineral resources, energy sources); available (e.g., funds)

تيار *tayyār* pl. -*āt* flow, stream, course, current, flood; fall (of a stream); movement, tendency, trend; draft (of air); (*el.*) current | ○ تيار مباشر (*mubāšir*) and تيار مستمر (*mustamirr*) direct current; ○ تيار متناوب (*mutanāwib*) and ○ تيار متغير (*mutaǧayyir*) alternating current; ○ تيار متذبذب (*mutaḏabḏib*) oscillating current (*el.*); ○ تيار نابض (*nābiḍ*) pulsating current; ○ تيار سريع التردد (*sarī' at-taraddud*) high-frequency current; ○ تيار بطىء التردد (*baṭī' at-taraddud*) low-frequency current; ○ تيار عالى الجهد (*'ālī l-jahd*) high-tension current; ○ تيار واطىء الجهد (*wāṭi' al-jahd*) low-tension current; ○ تيار ذاتى (*ḏātī*) self-induced current

○ متار *matār* (*syr.*) dynamo, generator

تيزه (Turk. *teyze*) *tēza* maternal aunt

تيس *tais* pl. اتياس *atyās*, تيوس *tuyūs* billy goat

اتيس *atyas*² foolish, crazy

الحمى التيفودية *al-ḥummā t-tīfūdīya* typhoid fever

تيفوس *tīfūs* typhus

¹تيك *tīka* fem. of the demonstrative pronoun ذاك *ḏāka*

²تيك *tīk* teakwood

¹تيل II (from Turk. *tel*) to cable, wire, telegraph (*syr.*)

²تيل *tīl* (*eg.*) flax; linen

تيلة *tīla* (*eg.*) fiber, staple (esp. of cotton)

¹(تيم) تام *tāma i* (*taim*) to become enslaved, enthralled by love; to enslave, make blindly subservient (ه s.o.; through love) II to enslave, enthral (love; ه s.o.); to make blindly subservient, drive out of his mind, infatuate (ه s.o.; love)

متيم *mutayyam* enslaved, enthralled (by love), infatuated

²تيماء *taimā'*² Taima (oasis in NW Arabia)

تمرجى see تيمارجى

تين *tīn* (coll.; n. un. ة) fig | تين شوكى (*šaukī*) fruit of the Indian fig (Opuntia ficus indica Haw.)

تينك *tainika* see تاك alphabetically

(تيه) تاه *tāha i* to get lost, wander about, lose one's way, go astray; to stray, wander (thoughts); to waver, vacillate (بين between two feelings); to escape (من s.o.), slip (من s.o.'s memory); to perish, be lost; to be perplexed, startled, astonished; to be haughty; to swagger, boast, brag (على to s.o.) | تتيه على وجهه ابتسامة a smile flits over his face **II** to mislead, lead astray (ه s.o.); to distract, divert (ه s.o.); to confuse, confound, bewilder (ه s.o.) **IV** = **II**

تيه *tīh* desert, trackless wilderness; maze, labyrinth; haughtiness, pride

تياه *tayyāh* straying, stray, wandering; haughty

تيهان *taihān*[2] straying, stray, wandering; perplexed, at a loss, bewildered; proud, haughty

تيهاء *taihā'*[2] a trackless, desolate region

متاهة *matāha* pl. *-āt* maze, labyrinth; a trackless, desolate region

تائه *tā'ih* straying, stray, wandering, roving, errant; lost in thought, distracted, absent-minded; lost, forlorn; haughty | ○ العصب التائه (*'aṣab*) the vagus nerve (*anat.*)

تيوليب (Engl.) tulip

ث

ث abbreviation of ثانية second (time unit)

ثاء *ṯā'* name of the letter ث

ثئب *ṯa'iba a* (ثأب *ṯa'b*) and **VI** to yawn

ثؤباء *ṯu'abā'*[2] yawning, yawn; fatigue, weariness

ثأر *ṯa'ara a* (*ṯa'r*) to avenge the blood of (ه or ب), take blood revenge (ه or ب for s.o. killed), take vengeance, avenge o.s. (ب ه on s.o. for, also من or ل for) **IV** and **VIII** اثأر *iṯṯa'ara* to get one's revenge, be avenged

ثأر *ṯa'r* pl. *-āt*, اثآر *aṯ'ār*, آثار *āṯār* revenge, vengeance, blood revenge; retaliation, reprisal | اخذ بالثأر or اخذ ثأره to take revenge, avenge o.s.; مباراة الثأر *mubārāt aṯ-ṯ.* return match (sports)

ثائر *ṯā'ir* avenger

ثؤلول *ṯu'lūl* and ثؤلولة *ṯu'lūla* pl. ثآليل *ṯa'ālīl*[2] wart

ثأى *ṯa'ā* scars

ثبت *ṯabata u* (ثبات *ṯabāt*, ثبوت *ṯubūt*) to stand firm, be fixed, stationary, immovable, unshakable, firm, strong, stable; to hold out, hold one's ground (ل against s.o. or s.th.), be firm, remain firm (ل toward s.o. or s.th.), withstand, resist, defy (ل s.o. or s.th.); to be established, be proven (fact); to remain, stay (ب at a place); to maintain (على s.th.), keep, stick, adhere (على to s.th.), abide or stand by s.th. (على; e.g., by an agreement); to insist (على on) | ثبت فى وجهه (*fī wajhihī*) to hold one's own against s.o., assert o.s. against s.o.; ثبت وجوده (*wujūduhū*) to exist definitely, be certain, proven **II** to fasten, make fast, fix (ه s.th.); to consolidate, strengthen (ه s.th.); to stabilize (ه s.th.); to fix (ه a film or print; *phot.*); to confirm, corroborate, substantiate (ه s.th.); to appoint permanently (ه s.o.; to an office); to prove, establish (ه s.th.), demonstrate, show (بأن that); to prove guilty, convict (على a defendant); to confirm (*Chr.*) | ثبت بصره به (*baṣarahū*) to fix one's eyes on, gaze at; ثبت قدميه (*qadamaihi*) to gain a foothold **IV** to establish, determine (ه s.th.); to pinpoint (ه, e.g., a place); to assert as valid or authentic, affirm (ه s.th.); to confirm, corroborate, substantiate (ه s.th.); to prove (ه على s.th. to s.o.; ل to s.o., ان that); to demonstrate, show (ه s.th.); to furnish competent evidence (ه for); to bear witness, attest (ه to); to acknowledge (ه s.th., e.g., a qualification, a quality, ل in s.o.), concede (ه ل s.th. to s.o.); to prove guilty, convict (على a defendant); to enter, record, register, list (ه فى s.th. in a book, in a roster, etc.) | اثبته فى الورق (*waraq*) to put s.th. down in writing, get s.th. on paper; اثبت الشخص (*šaḵṣa*) to determine s.o.'s identity, identify s.o.; اثبت شخصيته (*šaḵṣīyatahū*) to identify o.s., prove one's identity; اثبت الكلام (*kalāma*) to fix the precise wording of a text **V** to ascertain, verify (فى s.th., هل if), make sure (فى of s.th., هل if); to consider carefully (فى s.th.), proceed with caution (فى in) **X** to show o.s. steadfast, persevering; to seek to verify (ه s.th.), try to make sure (ه of), seek confirmation of or reassurance with regard to (ه); to ascertain, verify (ه s.th.), make sure (ه of s.th.); to find right, proven or true, see confirmed (ه s.th.); to regard as authentic (ه s.th.)

ثبت *ṯabt* firm, fixed, established; steadfast, unflinching; brave

ثبت *ṯabat* reliable, trustworthy, credible

ثبت *ṯabat* pl. اثبات *aṯbāt* list, index, roster

ثبات *ṯabāt* firmness; steadiness, constancy, permanence, stability; certainty, sureness; reliability (of statements, reports); perseverance, persistence, endurance; continuance, maintenance, retention (على of s.th.), adherence (على to)

ثباتية *ṯabātīya* stability, static nature (of s.th.)

ثبوت *ṯubūt* constancy, immutability, steadiness; permanence, durability; certainty, sureness | ثبوت الشهر *ṯ. aš-šahr* the official determination of the beginning of a lunar month

ثبوتى *ṯubūtī* (*Syr.*): وثائق ثبوتية documents of proof, evidence

اثبت *aṯbat*[2] more reliable, firmer, steadier, etc.

تثبيت *taṯbīt* consolidation, strengthening; stabilization; confirmation; corroboration, substantiation | سر التثبيت *sirr at-t.* the Sacrament of Confirmation (*Chr.*)

اثبات *iṯbāt* establishment; assertion; confirmation; affirmation, attestation; demonstration; proof, evidence; registration, entering, listing, recording; documentation, authentication, verification | شاهد اثبات witness for the prosecution; عبء الاثبات *'ib' al-i.* burden of proof (*jur.*); اثبات التملك *i. at-tamalluk* official confirmation of property rights (by a religious tribunal)

اثباتى *iṯbātī* affirmative, confirmatory, corroborative, positive

تثبت *taṯabbut* ascertainment; verification, examination, check; careful, cautious procedure, circumspection; interment (of the remains of a saint; *Chr.*)

ثابت *ṯābit* firm, fixed, established; stationary, immovable; standing on firm ground, unshaken; steady, invariable, constant, stable; permanent, lasting, durable, enduring; confirmed, proven; a constant (*math., phys.*); constant factor | ثابت الجاش *ṯ. al-ja'š* undismayed, fearless, staunch, steadfast; ثابت العزم *ṯ. al-'azm* firmly resolved, determined; املاك ثابتة and اموال ثابتة immovable property, real estate, realty; ○ ثابت الاتجاه *ṯ. al-ittijāh* unidirectional, rectified (*el.*); فكرة ثابتة idée fixe; ثابت وجوده (*wujūduhū*) definitely existing, proven

ثابتة *ṯābita* pl. ثوابت *ṯawābit*[2] fixed star

مثبوت *maṯbūt* established, confirmed; certain, sure, positive, assured; proven

مثبت *muṯabbit* fixative, fixing fluid (*phot.*)

ثبر *ṯabara u* to destroy, ruin (ه s.o.); (ثبور *ṯubūr*) to perish III to apply o.s. with zeal and perseverance (على to s.th.), persevere, persist (على in)

ثبور *ṯubūr* ruin, destruction | نادى (دعا or) بالويل والثبور *nādā* (*da'ā*) *bi-l-wail wa-ṯ-ṯ.* to wail, burst into loud laments

مثابرة *muṯābara* persistence, perseverance, endurance; diligence, assiduity

ثبط *ṯabaṭa u* and II to hold back, keep, prevent (ه عن s.o. from doing s.th.); to hinder, handicap, impede, slow down, set back (ه, ه s.o., s.th.); to bring about the failure (ه of s.th.), frustrate (ه s.th.)

ثبنة *ṯubna* pl. ثبن *ṯuban* lap, fold of a garment (used as a receptacle)

ثبان *ṯibān* = ثبنة *ṯubna*

ثيتل look up alphabetically

ثج *ṯajja u* to flow copiously

ثجاج *ṯajjāj* copiously flowing, streaming

ثخن *ṯakuna u* to be or become thick, thicken; to be firm, solid, compact IV to wear out, exhaust, weaken (ه s.o.) | اثخنه ضربا (*ḍarban*) to wallop s.o., give s.o. a sound thrashing; اثخن فى العدو (*'adūw*) to massacre the enemy; اثخنه بالجراح to weaken s.o. by inflicting wounds

ثخن *ṯikan*, ثخانة *ṯakāna*, ثخونة *ṯukūna* thickness, density; consistency; compactness

ثخين *ṯakīn* pl. ثخناء *ṯukanā'*[2] thick; dense

ثدى *ṯady* and *ṯadan* m. and f., pl. اثداء *aṯdā'* female breast; breast (also of a man); udder; du. ثديان breasts (of a woman), bosom

ثدياء *ṯadyā'*[2] f. full-bosomed

ثديي *ṯadyī*: حيوانات ثديية (*ḥayawānāt*) mammals

ثر *ṯarr* abounding in water | ثرة من الدمع (*dam'*) tear-wet, tear-blurred (eye)

ثرب *ṯaraba i* (*ṯarb*) and II to blame, censure (ه and على s.o.)

يثرب see also alphabetically

تثريب *taṯrīb* blame, censure, reproof

ثرثر *ṯarṯara* (ثرثرة *ṯarṯara*) to chatter, prattle

ثرثار *ṯarṯār* pl. *-ūn* prattler, chatterbox; ثرثارة *ṯarṯāra* pl. *-āt* do. (fem.)

ثرثرة *ṯarṯara* chatter, prattle

ثرد *ṯarada u* to crumble and sop (ه bread)

ثريد *ṯarīd* a dish of sopped bread, meat and broth

مثرد *miṯrad* bowl

ثرم *ṯarama i* (*ṯarm*) to knock s.o.'s (ه) tooth out; — *ṯarima a* (*ṯaram*) to have a gap between two teeth

ثرى (ثرى and ثرو) *ṯariya a* to become wealthy IV to become or be rich, wealthy (ب or من through s.th.); to make rich (ه s.o.); to enrich (ه s.th., ب by means of)

ثرى *ṯaran* moist earth; ground, soil | اين الثرى من الثريا *aina ṯ-ṯ. min aṯ-ṯurayyā* (proverbially of things of disproportionate value) what has the ground to do with the Pleiades? طيب الله ثراه (*ṭayyaba*) approx.: may God rest him in peace! يبس الثرى بينهم (*yabisa*) they became enemies

ثرى *ṯarīy* pl. اثرياء *aṯriyā'*[2] wealthy, rich | ثرى الحرب *ṯ. al-ḥarb* war profiteer, nouveau riche

ثريات *ṯarīyāt* plantations

ثروة *ṯarwa* pl. *-āt* and ثراء *ṯarā'* fortune, wealth, riches | اهل الثروة *ahl aṯ-ṯ.* the rich, the wealthy; ثروة قومية (*qaumīya*) national wealth; ثروة مائية (*mā'īya*) abundance of water, abundant supply of water (of a region); ثروة سمكية (*samakīya*) abundance of fish; ثروة طبيعية natural resources (of a country); ثروات وطنية *ṯarawāt waṭanīya* national resources

ثريا *ṯurayyā* Pleiades; (also ثرية) pl. ثريات *ṯurayyāt* chandelier

مثر *muṯrin* wealthy, rich

ثعبان *ṯu'bān* pl. ثعابين *ṯa'ābīn*² snake | ثعبان الماء *ṯ. al-mā'* and سمك ثعبان *samak ṯ.* eel

ثعبانى *ṯu'bānī* snaky, snakelike, serpentine; eely

مثعب *maṯ'ab* pl. مثاعب *maṯā'ib*² drain

ثعالة *ṯu'āla* fox

ثعلب *ṯa'lab* pl. ثعالب *ṯa'ālib*² fox | داء الثعلب alopecia (*med.*), loss of hair

ثعلبي *ṯa'labī* foxy, foxlike

ثعلبة *ṯa'laba* vixen; ○ tetter (*med.*)

ثغر *ṯaġr* pl. ثغور *ṯuġūr* front tooth; mouth; port, harbor, inlet, bay; seaport

ثغرة *ṯuġra* pl. ثغر *ṯuġar*, *ṯuġarāt* breach, crevasse, crack, rift, crevice; opening, gap; cavity, hollow; narrow mountain trail

ثغام *ṯaġām* white, whiteness

ثاغم *ṯāġim* white (adj.)

ثغا (ثغو) *ṯaġā u* (ثغاء *ṯuġā'*) to bleat (sheep)

ثغاء *ṯuġā'* bleating, bleat

ثاغ *ṯāġin* bleating | ما له ثاغية ولا راغية (*rāġiya*) he has absolutely nothing, he is deprived of all resources, prop.: he has neither a bleating (sheep) nor a braying (camel)

ثفر *ṯafar* pl. اثفار *aṯfār* crupper (of the saddle)

ثفل *ṯufl* dregs, lees, sediment; residues

ثفن III to associate (ه with s.o.), frequent s.o.'s (ه) company; to pursue, practice (ه s.th.)

ثفنة *ṯafina* pl. *-āt*, ثفن *ṯifan* callus, callosity

اثفية look up alphabetically

ثقة see وثق

ثقب *ṯaqaba u* (*ṯaqb*) to bore, or drill, a hole (ه in s.th.), pierce, puncture, perforate (ه s.th.) II do. II and IV to light, kindle (ه s.th.) V and VII to be pierced, be punctured, be perforated

ثقب *ṯaqb* piercing, boring, puncture, perforation; (also *ṯuqb* pl. ثقوب *ṯuqūb*, اثقاب *aṯqāb*) hole, puncture, borehole, drill hole | ثقوب التفجير blasting holes; ○ الثقب بالابر (*ṯaqb, ibar*) acupuncture (*med.*)

ثقبة *ṯuqba* pl. ثقب *ṯuqab* hole

ثقاب and عود الثقاب *'ūd aṯ-ṯiqāb* matchstick; matches

ثقوب *ṯuqūb* keenness, acuteness (of the mind)

ثقابة *ṯaqqāba* pl. *-āt* drilling machine, drilling rig

مثقب *miṯqab* pl. مثاقب *maṯāqib*² borer, drill, gimlet, auger, brace and bit, wimble, perforator; drilling machine

مثقاب *miṯqāb* drilling machine, drilling rig

اثقاب *iṯqāb* kindling, lighting

ثاقب *ṯāqib* penetrating, piercing, sharp (mind, eyes) | ثاقب النظر *ṯ. an-naẓar* perspicacity; sharp-eyed; ثاقب الفكر *ṯ. al-fikr* sagacity, acumen, mental acuteness; shrewd, sagacious, sharp-witted

ثاقبات *ṯāqibāt* borers (*zool.*)

ثقف *ṯaqifa a* (*ṯaqf*) to find, meet (ه s.o.); —

taqifa a and *taqufa u* to be skillful, smart, clever **II** to make straight, straighten (ه s.th.); to correct, set right, straighten out (ه s.th.); to train, form, teach, educate (ه s.o.); to arrest (ه s.o.); to seize, confiscate (ه s.th.) **III** to fence (ه with s.o.) **V** to be trained, be educated

ثقافة *taqāfa* culture, refinement; education; (pl. *-āt*) culture, civilization

ثقافى *taqāfī* educational; intellectual; cultural | ملحق ثقافى (*mulḥaq*) cultural attaché

تثقيف *tatqīf* cultivation of the mind; training, education; instruction

مثاقفة *mutāqafa* fencing, art or sport of fencing, swordplay, swordsmanship

تثقف *tataqquf* culturedness, culture, refinement, education

مثقف *mutaqqaf* educated; trained; cultured; pl. المثقفون educated people, intellectuals, the intelligentsia, المثقفات educated ladies, women intellectuals

ثقل *taqula u* (*tiql*, ثقالة *taqāla*) to be heavy; with ب: to load or burden s.th., make s.th. heavy; to be hard to bear (على for s.o.), weigh heavily (على on), be burdensome, cumbersome, oppressive (على to s.o.); to be heavy-handed, sluggish, doltish, dull-witted; to be too dull, too sluggish (عن for s.th., to do s.th.), not to bother (عن about) **II** to make heavy, weight (ه s.th.); to burden, encumber (على s.o., ه with s.th.), overburden (على s.o.), overtax s.o.'s (على) strength, ask too much (على of s.o.); to trouble, inconvenience, bother (على s.o., ب with s.th.), pester, molest (على s.o.) | ثقل كاهله and اثقل كاهله (*kāhilahū*) to burden s.o. or s.th.; ثقل كاهل الميزان to burden the budget **IV** to burden (ه, ه s.o., s.th.); to oppress, distress (ه s.o.), weigh heavily (ه on); to be hard to bear (ه for s.o.) | اثقل كاهله (*kāhilahū*) see **II**; **VI** to become or be heavy; to be troublesome, burdensome (على to s.o.), trouble, oppress (على s.o.); to be sluggish, doltish, slow; to be in a bad mood, be sullen; to be bored; to find burdensome and turn away (عن from s.th.); not to bother (عن about); to be too dull, too sluggish (عن for s.th., to do s.th.) **X** to find heavy, hard, burdensome, troublesome (ه s.th.), find annoying (ه, ه s.o., s.th.) | استثقل ظله (*ẓillahū*) to find s.o. unbearable, dislike s.o.

ثقل *tiql* pl. اثقال *atqāl* weight; burden, load; gravity; heaviness | رفع الاثقال *raf' al-a.* weight lifting (*athlet.*); الثقل النوعى (*nau'ī*) specific gravity

ثقل *tiqal* heaviness; sluggishness, dullness

ثقل *taqal* pl. اثقال *atqāl* load, baggage

الثقلان *at-taqalān* the humans and the jinn

ثقلة *taqla* trouble, inconvenience, discomfort

ثقالة *taqāla* heaviness; sluggishness, doltishness; dullness

ثقيل *taqīl* pl. ثقلاء *tuqalā'*[2], ثقال *tiqāl* heavy; weighty, momentous, grave, serious, important; burdensome, troublesome, cumbersome, oppressive; unpleasant, disagreeable, distasteful (person) | ثقيل الدم *t. ad-dam* insufferable, unpleasant, disagreeable (person); ثقيل الروح *t. ar-rūḥ* doltish, dull (person); a bore; ثقيل الظل *t. aẓ-ẓill* disagreeable, insufferable (person); ثقيل الفهم *t. al-fahm* slow of understanding, slow-witted; ثقيل السمع *t. as-sam'* hard of hearing; صناعة ثقيلة (*ṣinā'a*) heavy industry; ماء ثقيل heavy water (*phys.*); ثقيل الاذن *t. al-udn* hard of hearing, deaf; هو ثقيل عليهم he is a burden to them

اثقل *atqal*[2] heavier; more oppressive

مثقال *mitqāl* pl. مثاقيل *matāqīl*[2] weight (also s.th. placed as an equipoise on the scales of a balance); miskal, a weight (in Egypt = 24 قيراط = 4.68 g) | مثقال ذرة *m. ḏarra* the weight of a dust speck, i.e., a tiny amount; a little bit; مثقال من a little of, a little bit of

تثقيل *taṯqīl* weighting, burdening; molestation

تثاقل *taṯāqul* sluggishness, dullness

مثقل *muṯaqqal* and *muṯqal* burdened, encumbered; overloaded; weighted (ب with s.th.); oppressed (ب by); heavy

متثاقل *mutaṯāqil* sluggish, dull; sullen, grumpy; bored

ثكل **ṯakila** *a* (*ṯakal*) to lose a child (ه) through death (esp. of a mother); to be bereaved of a loved one (ه) by death **IV** اثكل الام ولدها *aṯkala l-umma waladahā* to bereave a mother of her son

ثكل *ṯakal, ṯukl* bereavement (esp. of a woman, by the death of her child); state of one who has lost a friend or relative; mourning over the loss of a loved one

ثكلان *ṯaklān*(²) bereaved of a child or a loved one

ثكلى *ṯaklā* bereaved of a child (mother)

ثاكلة *ṯākila* pl. ثواكل *ṯawākil*² bereaved of a child (mother)

ثكنة **ṯukna** (now also pronounced *ṯakna*) pl. ثكن *ṯukan*, *-āt*, *ṯakanāt* barracks (*mil.*)

ثل **ṯalla** *u* (ثلل *ṯalal*) to tear down, destroy, overthrow, subvert (ه s.th., esp. عرشا *'aršan* to topple a throne) **VII** to be subverted, overthrown (throne)

ثلة *ṯulla* pl. ثلل *ṯulal* troop, band, party, group (of people); military detachment

ثلب **ṯalaba** *i* (*ṯalb*) to criticize, run down (ه s.o.); to slander, defame (ه s.o.)

ثلب *ṯalb* slander, defamation

مثلبة *maṯlaba* pl. مثالب *maṯālib*² shortcoming, defect, blemish, stain, disgrace

ثالب *ṯālib* slanderous, defamatory; slanderer

ثلث **II** to triple, make threefold (ه s.th.); to do three times (ه s.th.)

ثلث *ṯulṯ* pl. اثلاث *aṯlāṯ* one third; *ṯuluṯ* a sprawling, decorative calligraphic style | الساعة الثانية الا الثلث (*illā ṯ-ṯulṯa*) 20 minutes to 2 o'clock

ثلاثة *ṯalāṯa* (f. ثلاث *ṯalāṯ*) three; ثلاثا *ṯalāṯan* three times, thrice

ثلاثى *ṯalāṯī* tertiary; Tertiary (*geol.*) | ما قبل الثلاثى pre-Tertiary

ثلاثة عشر *ṯalāṯata 'ašara*, f. ثلاث عشرة *ṯalāṯa 'ašrata* thirteen

الثالث *aṯ-ṯāliṯ* the third; ثالثا *ṯāliṯan* thirdly; ثالثة ¹/₆₀ of a second

ثلاثون *ṯalāṯūn* thirty

الثلاثينات *aṯ-ṯalāṯīnāt* the thirties (decade of a century)

الثلاثاء *aṯ-ṯulāṯā'* and يوم الثلاثاء *yaum aṯ-ṯ.* Tuesday

ثلاث *ṯulāṯ*² and مثلث *maṯlaṯ*² three at a time

ثلاثى *ṯulāṯī* tripartite, consisting of three, (*gram.*) triliteral, consisting of three radicals; tri-; group of three, set of three people; trio (*mus.*) | ثلاثى الزوايا *ṯ. z-zawāyā* triangular; ثلاثى الورقات *ṯ. l-waraqāt* trifoliate; حلف ثلاثى (*ḥilf*) tripartite pact; مخطط ثلاثى (*mukaṭṭaṭ*) 3-year plan; وثبة ثلاثية (*waṯba*) hop-skip-and-jump (sport)

ثالوث *ṯālūṯ* Trinity (*Chr.*); trinity, triad; triplet | زهرة الثالوث *zahrat aṯ-ṯ.* pansy (*bot.*)

تثليث *taṯlīṯ* doctrine of the Trinity; Trinity (*Chr.*)

تثليثى *taṯlīṯī* trigonometric(al)

مثلث *muṯallaṯ* tripled, triple, threefold; having three diacritical dots (letter); triangular; (pl. *-āt*) triangle (*geom.*) |

الراية المثلثة الالوان (*rāya*), العلم المثلث (*'alam*) and المثلث the tricolor; المثلث الحاد (*ḥādd*) acute-angled triangle; مثلث الزوايا *m. az-zawāyā* triangular; المثلث المتساوى الساقين (*mutasāwī s-sāqain*) isosceles triangle; المثلث المتساوى الاضلاع equilateral triangle; المثلث القائم right-angled triangle

المثلثات *al-muṯallaṯāt* and حساب المثلثات *ḥisāb al-m.* trigonometry

ثلج **ṯalaja** *u:* ثلجت السماء (*samā'u*) it snowed, was snowing; — *ṯalija a* to be delighted, be gladdened (soul, heart; ب by) **II** to cool with ice (ه s.th.); to freeze, turn into ice (ه s.th.) **IV** اثلجت السماء it snowed, was snowing; to cool, moisten (ه s.th.) | اثلج صدره (*ṣadrahū*) to delight, please, gratify s.o. **V** to become icy, turn into ice, congeal; to freeze

ثلج *ṯalj* pl. ثلوج *ṯulūj* snow; ice; artificial ice | ثلج غذائى (*ġiḏā'ī*) ice cream; ندفة الثلج *nudfat aṯ-ṯ.* snowflake

ثلجى *ṯaljī* snowy, snow- (in compounds); icy, glacial, ice- (in compounds)

ثلج *ṯalij* icy

ثلاج *ṯallāj* pl. *-ūn* ice vendor

ثلاجة *ṯallāja* pl *-āt* iceberg, ice floe; refrigerator, icebox; cold-storage plant (for foodstuff)

مثلجة *maṯlaja* pl. مثالج *maṯālij*² icebox, refrigerator; cold-storage plant

تثليج *taṯlīj* deepfreezing

مثلوج *maṯlūj* snow-covered; iced, icy; مثلوجات frozen food; iced beverages

مثلج *muṯallaj* iced; icy, ice-cold; deep-frozen; — (pl. *-āt*) iced drink; ice cream | لحم مثلج (*laḥm*) frozen meat; قهوة مثلجة (*qahwa*) iced coffee

ثلم **ṯalama** *i* (*ṯalm*) to blunt, make jagged (ه s.th.), break the edge of (ه); to make a breach, gap or opening (ه in a wall); to defile, sully (ه reputation, honor); — *ṯalima a* to be or become jagged, dull, blunt **II** to blunt (ه s.th.) **V** to become blunt **VII** to be defiled, be discredited (reputation)

ثلم *ṯalm* nick, notch; breach, opening, gap; crack, fissure, rift | ثلم الصيت *ṯ. aṣ-ṣīt* defamation

ثلمة *ṯulma* pl. ثلم *ṯulam* = *ṯalm* | سد ثلمة *sadda ṯulmatan* to fill a gap; ثلمة لا تسد (*tusaddu*) a gap that cannot be closed, an irreparable loss

ثالم *ṯālim* dull, blunt

مثلوم *maṯlūm* defiled, sullied (reputation, honor)

متثلم *mutaṯallim* blunted, blunt; cracking (voice)

منثلم الصيت *munṯalim aṣ-ṣīt* of ill repute, of dubious reputation

ثم **ṯamma** there; there is | من ثم *min ṯamma* hence, therefore, for that reason

ثم *ṯumma* then, thereupon; furthermore, moreover; and again, and once more (emphatically in repetition) | كلا ثم كلا (*kallā*) no and a hundred times no! من ثم *min ṯumma* then, thereupon

ثمة *ṯammata* (ثمت) there; there is | ليس ثمة there isn't

ثمام *ṯumām* a grass | على طرف الثمام (*ṭarafi ṯ-ṯ.*) within easy reach, handy; جعله على طرف الثمام he made it readily understandable, he presented it plausibly for all

ثمامة *ṯumāma* blade of grass, a thin blade (of a plant) | الشيء كالثمامة it is a trifle, easy to accomplish

اثمد look up alphabetically

ثمر **ṯamara** *u* to bear fruit **IV** do.; to have as a result (عن s.th.), result (عن in) **X** to profit, benefit (ه from); to exploit, utilize (ه s.th.); to invest profitably (ه money)

ثمر *ṯamar* pl. ثمار *ṯimār*, اثمار *aṯmār* fruits, fruit (coll.); result, effect, fruit, fruitage; yield, profit, benefit, gain

ثمرة *ṯamara* (n. un. of *ṯamar*) pl. *-āt* fruit; result, effect; yield, profit, benefit, gain

استثمار *istiṯmār* exploitation (also *pol.-econ.*), utilization, profitable use; (pl. *-āt*) investment (of money, capital) | استثمار المدخرات *i. al-muddakarāt* investment of savings

مثمر *muṯmir* fruitful, productive, profitable, lucrative

مستثمر *mustaṯmir* pl. *-ūn* exploiter (*pol.-econ.*); beneficiary; investor

مستثمر *mustaṯmar* exploited (e.g., the masses); invested, profit earning (money, capital)

ثمل *ṯamila a* (*ṯamal*) to become drunk **IV** to make drunk, intoxicate (ه s.o.)

ثمل *ṯamal* intoxication, drunkenness

ثملة *ṯamala* drunken fit, drunkenness

ثمل *ṯamil* intoxicated, drunk(en)

ثمالة *ṯumāla* residue, remnant, dregs (of a liquid), heeltap (of wine); scum, foam, froth

[1]ثمن **II** to appraise, assess, estimate (ه s.th.), determine the price or value (ه of s.th.); to price (ه s.th.) | لا يثمن *lā yuṯammanu* invaluable, inestimable, priceless

ثمن *ṯaman* pl. اثمان *aṯmān*, اثمنة *aṯmina* price, cost; value | الثمن الاصلى (*aṣlī*) cost price; الثمن الاساسى (*asāsī*) par, nominal value

ثمين *ṯamīn* pl. ثمان *ṯimān* costly, precious, valuable

اثمن *aṯman*[2] costlier, more precious, more valuable

تثمين *taṯmīn* estimation, appraisal, assessment, valuation, rating (of the price or value)

مثمون *maṯmūn* object of value

مثمن *muṯammin* estimator, appraiser | خبير مثمن assessor

مثمن *muṯamman* prized, valued, valuable, precious

مثمن *muṯmin* costly, precious, valuable

مثمن *muṯman* object of value

[2]ثمانية *ṯamāniya* (f. ثمان *ṯamānin*) eight

ثمانية عشر *ṯamāniyata ʿašara*, f. ثمانى عشرة *ṯamāniya ʿašrata* eighteen

ثمن *ṯumn* pl. اثمان *aṯmān* one-eighth

ثمنة *ṯumna* pl. *-āt* a dry measure (*Eg.* = $^1/_8$ قدح = .258 l; *Pal.* = ca. 2.25 l)

ثمانون *ṯamānūn* eighty

الثمانينات *aṯ-ṯamānīnāt* the eighties (decade of a century)

الثامن *aṯ-ṯāmin* the eighth

مثمن *muṯamman* eightfold; octagonal

ثنة *ṯunna* pl. ثنن *ṯunan* fetlock

ثندوة *ṯundu'a*, *ṯunduwa* pl. ثناد *ṯanādin* breast (of the male)

ثنوى, ثنوية, ثانوى and ثانوية see under ثنى

ثنى *ṯanā i* (*ṯany*) to double, double up, fold, fold up, fold under (ه s.th.); to bend, flex (ه s.th.); to turn (الى ه s.th. to); to turn away, dissuade, keep, prevent, divert (ه s.o. from) عن | ثنى عنان فرسه (*ʿināna farasihī*) he galloped off; ثنى طرفه اليه (*ṭarfahū*) he turned his glance on him **II** to double, make double (ه s.th.); to do twice, repeat (ه s.th.); to pleat, plait (ه s.th.); to form the dual (ه of a word); to provide with two diacritical dots (ه a letter) **IV** to commend, praise, laud, extol (على s.th., s.o.), speak appreciatively (على of) | اثنى عليه عاطر الثناء (*ʿāṭira ṯ-ṯanāʾ*) to speak in the most laudatory terms of s.o. **V** to double, become double; to be doubled; to be repeated; to bend, fold; to be bent, be folded, be folded up or under; to walk with a swinging gait **VII** to bend, bend up, down or over, lean, incline, bow; to fold up, pull or bend together; to fold, be foldable, be folded back; to turn away (عن from), give up, renounce (عن s.th.); to turn, face (الى toward); to apply o.s., turn (الى to s.th.); (with foll. imperf.) to set out, prepare (to do s.th.) **X** to except, exclude (من ه or ه s.th. or s.o. from), make an exception (ه of s.th.)

ثنى *ṯany* bending; folding; turning away, dissuasion, keeping, prevention

ثنى *ṯiny* pl. اثناء *aṯnā'* fold, pleat, plait, crease (in cloth); bend, twist | ثنيا بعد ثنى *ṯinyan ba'da ṯinyin* from time to time

اثناء *aṯnā'a* (prep.) during; within; in; in the course of | فى اثناء *fī aṯnā'i* do.; فى اثناء ذلك, فى تلك الاثناء, فى هذه الاثناء in the meantime, during all this time, meanwhile

ثنية *ṯanya* pl. *-āt* fold, pleat, plait, crease (in cloth); turn-up, cuff (of trousers and sleeves), hem of a garment

ثنية *ṯanīya* pl. ثنايا *ṯanāyā* middle incisor, front tooth; fold, plait; crease (of trousers); narrow pass; mountain trail | فى ثنايا in, inside, among, between, frequently only a fuller, rhetorically more elegant expression for "in", e.g., فى ثنايا نفسه in his heart, inwardly, فى ثنايا الكتب in the books; بين ثنايا in, inside, among, between; طلاع الثنايا *ṭallā' aṯ-ṯ.* one with high-flung aspirations

ثنوى *ṯanawī* dualist

ثنوية *ṯanawīya* dualism

ثناء *ṯanā'* commendation, praise, eulogy; appreciation

ثنائى *ṯanā'ī* laudatory, eulogistic

ثناء *ṯunā'*[2] and مثنى *maṯnā* two at a time; *ṯunā'a* (adv.) as a pair or duo, two and two

ثنائى *ṯunā'ī* twofold, double, dual, binary, bi-; bilateral; biradical (*gram.*); — (pl. *-āt*) pair, a group of two; duet, duo (*mus.*); ثنائيا (adv.) as a pair or duo | محرك ثنائى المشوار *muḥarrik ṯ. l-mišwār* two-cycle engine; ثنائى البعد *ṯ. al-bu'd* two-dimensional; علاقات ثنائية (*'alāqāt*) bilateral relations; اتفاق ثنائى (*ittifāq*) bilateral agreement

ثنائية *ṯunā'īya* dualism; duet, duo (*mus.*)

اثنان *iṯnāni*, f. اثنتان *iṯnatāni* two

اثنا عشر *iṯnā 'ašara*, f. اثنتا عشرة *iṯnatā 'ašrata* twelve

يوم الاثنين *yaum al-iṯnain* and الاثنين Monday

الثانى *aṯ-ṯānī* the second; the next; (*colloq.*) the other (one), ثان, ثانية an other (one), a different one; ثانيا *ṯāniyan* and ثانية *ṯāniyatan* secondly; for the second time, once more, again | ثانى اثنين *ṯ. ṯnain* the second of a pair, pendant, companion piece, match; ثانى اكسيد *ṯ. uksīd* dioxide, O_2, ثانى اكسيد الكربون *ṯ. u. al-karbōn* carbon dioxide, CO_2 (*chem.*); ثانى اكبر (with foll. genit.) the second largest

ثانية *ṯāniya* pl. ثوان *ṯawānin* second (time unit)

ثانوى *ṯānawī* secondary; minor | امور ثانوية matters of secondary importance, minor matters; مدرسة ثانوية secondary school; تسويغ ثانوى subletting; شهادة ثانوية (*šahāda*) secondary school diploma

ثانوية *ṯānawīya* pl. *-āt* secondary school; — secondary importance

تثنية *taṯniya* repetition; plaiting, pleating; doubling, gemination; (*gram.*) dual; second sequel (e.g., of a collection of short stories); commendation, praise, eulogy | تثنية الاشتراع Deuteronomy

انثناء *inṯināʼ* bending, flection; flexibility, foldability | قابل للانثناء foldable, folding

انثناءة *inṯināʼa* pl. *-āt* (n. vic.) bend, flexure, curve

استثناء *istiṯnāʼ* pl. *-āt* exception, exclusion | باستثناء with the exception of, except; بدون استثناء without exception

استثنائى *istiṯnāʼī* exceptional; استثنائيا *istiṯnāʼīyan* as an exception | احوال استثنائية emergencies; جلسة استثنائية (*jalsa*) emergency session

مثنى *maṯnīy* folded; plaited, pleated; doubled

مثنى *muṯannan* double, twofold; in the dual (*gram.*); dual (*gram.*)

مستثنى *mustaṯnan* excepted, excluded (من from)

ثوة *ṯuwwa* see ثوى

[1](ثوب) ثاب *ṯāba* *u* to return, come back (also, e.g., a state or condition, الى or ل to s.o.); with ب: to return s.th. (الى to s.o.) | ثاب الى نفسه to regain consciousness, come to; ثاب اليه رشده (*rušduhū*) to recover one's senses II to reward (ه s.o.; said of God) IV to cause to return (ه, ه s.o., s.th., الى to); to repay, requite (ه ه s.th. with); to reward (ه على s.o. for) X to seek reward

ثوب *ṯaub* pl. ثياب *ṯiyāb*, اثواب *aṯwāb* garment, dress; cloth, material; (fig.) garb, outward appearance, guise, cloak, mask; pl. ثياب clothes, clothing, apparel | ثوب السهرة *ṯ. as-sahra* evening gown; ثياب السهرة *ṯ. as-sahra* formal dress, evening clothes; فى ثوب بسيط in plain, homely form; طاهر الثياب of flawless character, irreproachable; دنس الثياب *danis aṯ-ṯ.* of bad character

ثواب *ṯawāb* requital, recompense, reward (for good deeds); (*Isl. Law*) merit, credit (arising from a pious deed)

مثوبة *maṯwaba* requital, recompense, reward (bestowed by God for good deeds)

مثاب *maṯāb* place to which one returns; meeting place; rendezvous; resort, refuge

مثابة *maṯāba* (with foll. genit.) place or time at which s.th. appears or recurs; place or spot to which s.o. regularly returns; resort, refuge; manner, mode, fashion | بمثابة (with foll. genit.) like, as; tantamount to, equivalent to, having the same function as

[2]تثاوب = تثاءب (ثئب VI) to yawn

(ثور) ثار *ṯāra* *u* to stir, be stirred up, be aroused, be excited; to swirl up, rise (dust); to arise (question, problem; a difficulty, فى وجهه *fī wajhihī* before s.o.); to be triggered, be unleashed, break out; to revolt, rebel, rise (على against); to rage, storm | ثار ثائره (*ṯāʼiruhū*) to fly into a rage, become furious, flare up IV to agitate, excite (ه s.o., ه s.th.); to stimulate (ه s.o., ه s.th.); to irritate (ه s.o., ه s.th.); to arouse, stir up, kindle, excite (ه s.th., e.g., feelings), cause, provoke, awaken (ه s.th.); to raise, pose, bring up (مسألة *masʼalatan* a question, a problem) | اثار ثائرته (*ṯāʼiratahū*) to infuriate s.o., excite s.o.; اثار غبارا (*ḡubāran*) to stir up dust X to excite (ه s.o.), stir up, kindle (ه s.th., esp. passions); to rouse (ه s.th.); to arouse, awaken (ه s.th., esp. feelings); to elicit, evoke (ه wails, outcries, من from s.o.); to incite, set (ه على s.o. against) | استثار غضبه (*ḡaḍabahū*) to infuriate s.o., make s.o. angry

ثور *ṯaur* pl. ثيران *ṯīrān* bull, steer; ox; الثور Taurus (sign of the zodiac; *astron.*); the second month of the solar year (*Saudi Ar.*, cf. حمل *ḥamal*)

ثورة *ṯaura* excitement, agitation; outbreak, outburst, fit (of fury, of despair, etc.); eruption (of a volcano); (pl. *-āt*) upheaval, uprising, insurrection, riot, rebellion, revolt (على against); revolution | ثورة اهلية (*ahlīya*) popular revolt, civil war; ثورة ثقافية (*ṯaqāfīya*) cultural revolution; ثورة مضادة (*muḍādda*) counter-revolution

ثورى *ṯaurī* revolutionary (adj. and n.)

ثورية *ṯaurīya* revolutionary spirit

ثوروى *ṯaurawī* revolutionary (adj. and n.)

ثوران *ṯawarān* agitation, excitation, flare-up, eruption, outbreak, outburst; dust whirl

مثار *maṯār* incentive, stimulus, motive, spur, occasion, cause | مثار الجدل *m. al-jadal* and مثار النزاع object of controversy, point of contention

اثارة *iṯāra* excitation, stirring up, kindling; agitation, incitement; provocation, (a)rousing, awakening; irritation, stimulation

ثائر *ṯā'ir* excited, agitated, raving, furious, mad; rebellious; refractory, stubborn; fury, rage (in the idiomatic phrase ثار ثائره see above); (pl. *-ūn*, ثوار *ṯuwwār*) insurgent, rebel, revolutionary

ثائرة *ṯā'ira* pl. ثوائر *ṯawā'ir*[2] tumult; excitement, agitation; fury, rage

مثير *muṯīr* exciting; provocative; stimulative, irritative; excitant, irritant, stimulant; instigator; germ, agent; pl. مثيرات stimulants

ثوريوم *ṯōriyūm* thorium (*chem.*)

ثول VII to swarm, crowd, throng (على around s.o.); to come over s.o. (على)

ثول *ṯaul* and ثول النحل *ṯ. an-naḥl* swarm of bees

ثوم *ṯūm* (coll.; n. un. ة) garlic

ثوى *ṯawā* i (ثواء *ṯawā'*, ثوى *ṯuwīy*, مثوى *maṯwan*) to stay, live (ب at a place); to settle down (ب at a place); to lie, remain forever, slumber (also of objects; فى in one place); pass. *ṯuwiya* to be buried IV to stay, live; to lodge, put up as a guest (ه s.o.)

ثوى *ṯawīy* guestroom

ثوة *ṯuwwa* pl. ثوى *ṯuwan* signpost, road-sign

مثوى *maṯwan* pl. مثاو *maṯāwin* abode, habitation, dwelling; place of rest

ثيب *ṯayyib* pl. *-āt* a deflowered but unmarried woman, widow, divorcée

ثيتل *ṯaital* pl. ثياتل *ṯayātil*[2] a variety of wild goat (Capra jaela)

ج

ج abbreviation of جزء part (of books), جمهورية republic (e.g., الجمهورية العربية = ج ع س السورية Syrian Arab Republic), جنيه *ginēh*, *junaih* pound (ج م and ج . م . *g. miṣrī* = Eg. pound) and جواب answer

الجابون *al-gābūn* (Eg. spelling) Gabon (country in W Africa)

جاثليق *jāṯalīq* = جثليق

جؤجؤ *ju'ju'* pl. جآجئ *ja'āji'*[2] breast; prow, bow (of a ship)

جأر *ja'ara* a (*ja'r*, جؤار *ju'ār*) to low, moo; to supplicate, pray fervently (الى to God)

جأر *ja'r* and جؤار *ju'ār* lowing, mooing (of cattle)

[1]جاز *gāz* pl. *-āt* (Eg. spelling) gas; gasoline; kerosene

[2]جاز *jāz* jazz

جازون (Fr. *gazon*, Eg. spelling) *gāzōn* lawn

جأش *ja'aša* a (*ja'š*) to be agitated, be convulsed (with pain or fright)

جأش *ja'š* emotional agitation; heart, soul | ربط جأشه *rabaṭa ja'šahū* to remain calm, composed, self-possessed; رابط الجأش or ثابت الجأش calm, composed, cool, self-possessed, undismayed; بجأش رابط with unswerving courage, unflinchingly

جاكت *jaket,* جاكيت *jakēt* (Fr.) f., pl. *-āt* jacket, coat

جاكتة, جاكته *jaketta,* جاكيته *žakēta* (It.) pl. *-āt* jacket, coat

جالوت *jālūt*[2] Goliath

جالون *galōn* gallon

جالبرى (Eg. spelling) *galērī* gallery (*theat.*)

جام *jām* pl. *-āt* cup; drinking vessel; bowl

اشعة جاما *aši''at gāmā* (Eg. spelling) gamma rays (*phys.*)

جامبون (Fr. *jambon*) ham

جامكية *jāmakīya* pl. *-āt,* جوامك *jawāmik*[2] pay

جاموس *jāmūs* pl. جواميس *jawāmīs*[2] buffalo

جاموسة *jāmūsa* buffalo cow

جانرك (pronounced *žānəreg,* from Turk. *caneriği*; coll.; n. un. *žānərgēye*) a variety of small green plum with several stones (*syr.*)

جانفى *žānfī* (*Alg., Tun.*) January

جاه *jāh* rank, standing, dignity, honor, glory, fame

جاوه, جاوة *jāwa* and جاوا *jāwā* Java

جاوى *jāwī* Javanese; benzoin; (pl. *-ūn*) a Javanese

جاودار *jāwadār* rye

چاويش (Turk.) *čāwīš,* جاويش pl. *-īya* sergeant (formerly, *Eg., Sudan*; *mil.*), see also شاويش

جب[1] *jubb* pl. اجباب *ajbāb,* جباب *jibāb* well, cistern; pit

جبة[2] *jubba* pl. جبب *jubab,* جباب *jibāb,* جبائب *jabā'ib*[2] jubbah, a long outer garment, open in front, with wide sleeves

جبح *jabḥ* pl. اجبح *ajbuḥ,* جباح *jibāḥ,* اجباح *ajbāḥ* beehive

جبخانة *jabkāna, jabakāna* powder magazine; ammunition; artillery depot

جبر *jabara u* (*jabr,* جبور *jubūr*) to set (ه broken bones); to restore, bring back to normal (ه s.th.); to help back on his feet, help up (ه s.o.; e.g., one fallen into poverty); to force, compel (ه على s.o. to do s.th.) | جبر خاطره (*kāṭirahū*) to console, comfort, gratify, oblige s.o.; to treat (s.o.) in a conciliatory or kindly manner **II** to set (ه broken bones) **III** to treat with kindness, with friendliness (ه s.o.), be nice (ه to s.o.) **IV** to force, compel (ه على s.o. to do s.th.); to hold sway (على over) **V** to show o.s. proud, haughty; to act strong, throw one's weight around; to show o.s. strong or powerful, demonstrate one's strength or power; to tyrannize (على s.o.); to be set (broken bones) | تجبر الله بابنك (*bi-bnika*) God has demonstrated His power on your son, i.e., He has taken him unto Himself **VII** to be mended, repaired, restored

جبر *jabr* setting (of broken bones); force, compulsion; coercion, duress; power, might; (predestined, inescapable) decree of fate; determinism; جبرا *jabran* forcibly, by force | علم الجبر *'ilm al-j.* algebra; يوم جبر البحر *yaum j. al-baḥr* a local holiday of Cairo (the day on which, in former times, the water of the Nile was channeled into the now-abandoned *kalīj,* or City Canal, thus marking the beginning of the irrigation season)

جبرى *jabrī* algebraic; compulsory, forced; — *jabarī* an adherent of the doctrine of predestination and the inescapability of fate; fatalist

جبرية *jabarīya* an Islamic school of

thought teaching the inescapability of fate; fatalism

جبار *jabbār* pl. *-ūn*, جبابر *jabābir*², جبابرة *jabābira* giant; colossus; tyrant, oppressor; almighty, omnipotent (God); gigantic, giant, colossal, huge; mighty, powerful; الجبار Orion (*astron.*) | جبار الخطوة *j. al-kuṭwa* striding powerfully, taking huge strides; جبار العزمة *j. al-ʿazma* of strong determination or resoluteness; كف جبارة (*kaff*) a strong slap in the face

جبارة *jibāra* (art of) bonesetting

جبيرة *jabīra* pl. جبائر *jabā'ir*² splint (*surg.*)

جبروت *jabarūt* omnipotence; power, might; tyranny

جبرياء *jibriyā'*² pride, haughtiness

O تجبير *tajbīr*, تجبير العظام orthopedics

اجبار *ijbār* compulsion, coercion

اجبارى *ijbārī* forced, forcible, compulsory, obligatory | التجنيد الاجبارى compulsory recruitment; military conscription; تعليم اجبارى compulsory instruction

اجبارية *ijbārīya* compulsoriness, obligatory character (of s.th.)

جابر *jābir* and مجبر *mujabbir* bonesetter

مجبور *majbūr* and مجبر *mujbar* forced, compelled

متجبر *mutajabbir* tyrant

جبرئيل *jabra'īl*², جبرائيل *jabrā'īl*², *jibrā'īl*², جبريل *jibrīl*² Gabriel

¹جبس II to plaster, coat, patch, or fix with plaster (ه s.th.); to put in a cast, set in plaster (ه s.th.)

جبس *jibs* gypsum; plaster of Paris

جباسة *jabbāsa* gypsum quarry; plaster kiln

²جبس *jabas* (coll.; n. un. ة; *syr.*) watermelon(s)

¹جبل *jabala u i* (*jabl*) to mold, form, shape, fashion (ه s.th.); to knead (ه s.th.); to create (على ه s.o. with a natural disposition or propensity for); pass. جبل على (*jubila*) to be born for, be naturally disposed to, have a propensity for

جبلة *jibla*, *jibilla* pl. *-āt* natural disposition, nature, temper

²جبل *jabal* pl. جبال *jibāl*, اجبال *ajbāl* mountain; mountains, mountain range | جبال الالب *j. al-alb* the Alps; جبال الاوراس the Aurès Mountains (in E Algeria); جبل جليد iceberg; جبل سينا *j. sīnā* Mount Sinai; جبل طارق Gibraltar; جبل نار volcano; جبل الشيخ *j. aš-šaik* Mount Hermon

جبلى *jabalī* mountainous, hilly; mountain (adj.); montane; (pl. *-ūn*) highlander, mountaineer

جبلاوى *gabalāwī* (*eg.*) highlander, mountaineer

جبلاية *gabalāya* pl. *-āt* (*eg.*) grotto, cave

³جبيل *jubail*² small port in Lebanon, ancient Byblos

جبن *jabuna u* (*jubn*, جبانة *jabāna*) to be a coward, be fearful; to be too much of a coward (عن to do s.th.), shrink (عن from s.th.) II to cause to curdle (ه milk); to make into cheese (ه s.th.); to curdle; to accuse of cowardice, call a coward (ه s.o.) V to curdle (milk), turn into cheese

جبن *jubn* and جبانة *jabāna* cowardice

جبن *jubn* pl. جبون *jubūn* cheese

جبنة *jubna* cheese

جبان *jabān* pl. جبناء *jubanā'*² coward; cowardly

جبان *jabbān* cheese merchant

جبين *jabīn* pl. جبن *jubun*, اجبنة *ajbina*, اجبن *ajbun* forehead, brow; façade, front; face | من جبينى *min jabīnī* I alone; على جبين السماء in the sky

جبينى *jabīnī* frontal

اجبن *ajban*² more cowardly

جبانة *jabbāna* pl. *-āt* cemetery

مجبنة *majbana* cheese dairy, cheesery

تجبين *tajbīn* cheese making, processing into cheese

[1]جبه *jabaha* a to meet, face, confront (ه s.o.) **II** to present a front (ه against s.th.), oppose, defy, reject, refuse, repulse (ه s.th.) **III** to face, confront, oppose, defy (ه s.o., ه s.th.), show a bold front (ه to); to face (ه a problem, a difficulty)

جبهة *jabha* pl. جباه *jibāh*, جبهات *jabahāt* forehead, brow; front, face, façade; front-line, battle front | جبهة شعبية (*šaʿbīya*) people's front, popular front

تجبيه *tajbīh* opposition, resistance (ل to), rejection, repulsion (ل of ideologies, attacks, enemies)

مجابهة *mujābaha* facing, confrontation, opposition

[2]جبخانة see جبه خانة

جبى *jabā* i (جباية *jibāya*) to collect, raise, levy (ه taxes, duties) **II** to prostrate o.s. (in prayer) **VIII** to pick, choose, elect (ه s.th., ه s.o.)

جباية *jibāya* raising, levying (of taxes); (pl. *-āt*) tax, duty, impost

جبائى *jibā'ī* tax- (in compounds); fiscal

مجبى *majban* pl. مجاب *majābin* tax, impost

جاب *jābin* pl. جباة *jubāh* tax collector, revenue officer, collector; (bus, etc.) conductor (*ir.*)

جابية *jābiya* pl. جواب *jawābin* pool, basin

جتا *jatā* (abbreviation of جيب التمام) cosine (*math.*)

جتاية (*ir.*) *čtāya* head-scarf

جث *jaṯṯa* u (*jaṯṯ*) and **VIII** to tear out, uproot (ه a tree, also fig.)

جثة *juṯṯa* pl. جثث *juṯaṯ*, اجثاث *ajṯāṯ* body; corpse, cadaver; carcass

مجتث *mujtaṯṯ* uprooted (also fig.); المجتث name of a poetical meter

جثل *jaṯl* thick, dense (esp. hair)

جثليق *jiṯlīq* pl. جثالقة *jaṯāliqa* catholicos, primate of the Armenian Church

جثم *jaṯama* u i (*jaṯm*, جثوم *juṯūm*) to alight, sit, perch (bird); to crouch, cower; to fall or lie prone, lie face down; to lie, weigh heavily (على on s.o., s.th.); to beset, oppress (على s.th.) | جثم على صدره (*ṣadrihī*) to weigh heavily on s.o.'s soul (problem, difficulty)

جثمة *jaṯma* (n. vic.) motionless sitting or lying

جثام *juṯām* and جاثوم *jāṯūm* nightmare, incubus

جثمان *juṯmān* pl. *-āt* body, mortal frame

جثمانى *juṯmānī* bodily, physical, corporeal

جاثم *jāṯim* pl. جثم *juṯṯam* squatting, crouching; perching; prostrate, prone

جثا (جثو) *jaṯā* u (*juṯūw*) to kneel, rest on the knees; to bend the knee, genuflect; to fall on one's knees

جثو *juṯūw* kneeling position

جثوة *juṯwa* rock pile, mound; sepulchral mound, tumulus

مجثى *majṯan* hassock

جاث *jāṯin* kneeling; الجاثى Hercules (*astron.*)

جحد *jaḥada* a (*jaḥd*, جحود *juḥūd*) to negate (ه s.th.); to disclaim, disavow, disown, deny (ه s.th.); to refuse, reject, repudiate (ه s.th.); not to want to recognize (ه s.o.), not want to know anything (ه, ه about s.o., s.th.); to renounce, forswear, adjure (ه a belief); to deny (ه ه s.o. his right) | جحد جميله (*jamīlahū*) to be ungrateful to s.o.

جحد *jaḥd* denial; repudiation, disavowal, rejection, disclaimer; unbelief (*rel.*)

جحود *juḥūd* denial; evasion, dodging, shirking (of a moral obligation); ingratitude; repudiation, disavowal, rejection, disclaimer; unbelief (*rel.*)

جاحد *jāḥid* denier; infidel, unbeliever

جحر VII to hide in its hole or den (animal) VIII to seek refuge, take one's refuge (في in)

جحر *juḥr* pl. اجحار *ajḥār*, جحور *juḥūr* hole, den, lair, burrow (of animals)

جحش *jaḥš* pl. جحاش *jiḥāš*, جحشان *jiḥšān*, اجحاش *ajḥāš* young donkey; (pl. جحوش *juḥūš*) trestle, horse

جحشة *jaḥša* young female donkey

جحظ *jaḥaẓa a* (جحوظ *juḥūẓ*) to bulge, protrude (eyeball); to look at wide-eyed, stare

جحوظ العين *juḥūẓ al-ʿain* exophthalmic goiter, abnormal protrusion of the eyeball

جحف *jaḥafa a* (*jaḥf*) to peel off, scrape off (ه s.th.); to sweep away (ه s.th.); to have a bias (مع for), side (مع with s.o.) IV to harm, hurt, injure, prejudice (ب s.o., s.th.); to ruin, destroy (ب s.o., s.th.); to wrong (ب s.o.)

اجحاف *ijḥāf* injustice, wrong; bias, prejudice

مجحف *mujḥif* unjust, unfair; biased, prejudiced

جحفل *jaḥfal* pl. جحافل *jaḥāfil*[2] multitude, legion, host, large army; army corps (*Syr.*); eminent man

جحيم *jaḥīm* f. (also m.) fire, hellfire, hell

جحيمى *jaḥīmī* hellish, infernal

جخ *jakka* (*eg.*) to lord it, give o.s. airs; to boast, brag; (*syr.*) to dress up (slightly ironical)

جخاخ *jakkāk* boaster, braggart

جد[1] *jadd* pl. جدود *judūd*, اجداد *ajdād* grandfather; ancestor, forefather | الجد الاعلى (*aʿlā*) ancestor; جدى لأبى (*li-abī*) my paternal grandfather

جدة *jadda* pl. *-āt* grandmother

جد[2] *jadda i* to be new; to be a recent development, have happened lately, have recently become a fact; to be added, crop up or enter as a new factor (circumstances, costs); to appear for the first time (also, e.g., on the stage); to be or become serious, grave; to be weighty, significant, important; to take (في s.th.) seriously; to strive earnestly (في for), go out of one's way (في to do s.th.), make every effort (في in); to be serious, be in earnest (في about), mean business; to hurry (في one's step) | جد فى طريقه he strode quickly on his way, strained forward in a hurry; جد فى سيره (*sairihī*) do. II to renew (ه s.th.); to make anew, remake (ه s.th.); to modernize (ه s.th.); to restore, renovate, remodel, refit, recondition, refurbish (ه s.th.); to be an innovator, a reformer; to feature s.th. new or novel, produce s.th. new; to rejuvenate, regenerate, revive, freshen up (ه s.th.); to renew, extend (ه a permit); to begin anew, repeat (ه s.th.), make a new start (ه in s.th.); to try again (حظه *ḥaẓẓahū* one's luck) IV to strive, endeavor, take pains; to apply o.s. earnestly and assiduously (في to), be bent, be intent (في on s.th.); to hurry (في one's step); to renew, make new (ه s.th.) | جد فى سيره = اجد فى سيره V to become new, be renewed; to revive; to crop up anew (e.g., problems) X to be new, be added or enter as a new factor, come newly into existence; to make new, renew (ه s.th.)

جد *jadd* pl. جدود *judūd* good luck, good fortune

جد *jidd* seriousness, earnestness; diligence, assiduity, eagerness; جدا *jiddan* very, much | بجد and من جد earnestly, seriously; جد باهظ *jiddu bāhiẓin* very high (price); جد عظيم *j. ʿaẓīmin* very great; يختلفون جد الاختلاف (*jidda l-iktilāf*) they differ widely; وقف على ساق الجد ل (*sāqi l-j.*) to apply o.s. with diligence to, take pains in, make every effort to

جدى *jiddī* serious; earnest; جديا *jiddīyan* in earnest, earnestly, seriously

جدية *jiddīya* earnestness; seriousness, gravity (of a situation)

جدة *jidda* newness, recency, novelty; modernness, modernity; ○ rebirth, renaissance | بجدة وطرافة (*ṭarāfa*) in a new and unusual fashion

جدة *judda*[2], usually pronounced *jidda*, Jidda (seaport in W Saudi Arabia, on the Red Sea)

جديد *jadīd* pl. جدد *judud, judad* new, recent; renewed; modern; novel, unprecedented | الجديدان *al-jadīdān* day and night; من جديد anew, again; (*eg.*) جديد لنج *gadīd lang* brand-new هل من جديد ؟ anything new?

اجد *ajadd*[2] more serious, more intent; newer, more recent

تجديد *tajdīd* renewal (also, e.g., of a permit); creation of s.th. new, origination; new presentation, new production (*theat.*); innovation; reorganization, reform; modernization; renovation, restoration, remodeling, refitting, reconditioning, refurbishing; rejuvenation, regeneration; pl. *-āt* innovations; new achievements

تجدد *tajaddud* renewal, regeneration, revival

جاد *jādd* in earnest, earnest; serious

جادة *jādda* pl. *-āt*, جواد *jawādd*[2] main street; street

مجدود *majdūd* fortunate, lucky

مجدد *mujaddid* renewer; innovator; reformer

مجدد *mujaddad* renewed, extended; remodeled, reconditioned, renovated, restored; rejuvenated, regenerated; new, recent, young; مجددا *mujaddadan* anew

مجد *mujidd* painstaking, diligent, assiduous

مستجد *mustajidd* new, recent; — (pl. *-ūn*) incipient; recruit (*mil.*), also جندى مستجد (*jundī*) and عسكرى مستجد (*'askarī*)

جدب *jaduba u* (جدوبة *judūba*) and *jadaba u* (*jadb*) to be or become dry, arid (soil); to be barren, dried up, infertile, sterile **IV** to suffer from drought, poverty or dearth; to be barren, sterile; to come to nothing, go up in smoke, fall flat, fizzle out; (*syr.*) to explode in the barrel (shell; *mil.*)

جدب *jadb* drought, barrenness, sterility; sterile, barren

جديب *jadīb* and اجدب *ajdab*[2], f. جدباء *jadbā'*[2] barren, sterile

مجدب *mujdib* barren, sterile; desolate, arid; unproductive, unprofitable

جدث *jadaṯ* pl. اجداث *ajdāṯ* grave, tomb

جدجد *judjud* pl. جداجد *jadājid*[2] cricket (*zool.*)

[1]جدر *jadura u* (جدارة *jadāra*) to be fit, suitable, proper, appropriate (ب for s.o., for s.th.); to befit, behoove (ب s.o., s.th.); to be worthy (ب of), deserve (ب s.th.) | يجدر ذكره (*ḏikruhū*) and يجدر بالذكر it is worth mentioning

جدر *jadr* wall

جدير *jadīr* pl. *-ūn*, جدراء *judarā'*[2] worthy, deserving (ب of s.th.); becoming, befitting (ب s.th.); proper, suited, suitable, fit (ب for), appropriate (ب to) | جدير بالذكر (*ḏikr*) worth mentioning

اجدر *ajdar*[2] worthier; more appropriate; better suited, more suitable

جدارة *jadāra* worthiness; fitness, suitability, aptitude, qualification; appropriateness | شهادة الجدارة certificate of merit, citation (for bravery; *mil.*)

جدار *jidār* pl. جدر *judur*, جدران *judrān* wall

جدارى *jidārī* mural, wall (adj.)

[2]جدر *judira* (pass.) and **II** to have smallpox

جدرى *judarī, jadarī* smallpox

مجدور *majdūr* and مجدر *mujaddar* infected with smallpox; pock-marked

مجدرة *mujaddara* dish made of rice or (in Syr.) of bulgur with lentils, onions and oil (*eg., syr.*)

[1]جدع *jadaʿa a* (*jadʿ*) to cut off, amputate (ه s.th., esp. some part of the body)

بجدع الانف *bi-jadʿi l-anf* (prop., at the cost of having the nose cut off) at any price, regardless of the sacrifice involved

اجدع *ajdaʿ*[2] mutilated (by having the nose, or the like, cut off)

[2]□ جدع *gadaʿ* (= جذع *jadaʿ*) pl. جدعان *gidʿān* (*eg.*) young man, young fellow; he-man

[1]جدف **II** to curse, blaspheme (على s.o., esp. God)

تجديف *tajdīf* imprecation, blasphemy

مجدف *mujaddif* blasphemer

[2]جدف *jadafa i* and **II** to row (ه a boat)

مجداف *mijdāf* pl. مجاديف *majādīf*[2] oar

تجديف *tajdīf* rowing (sport)

[1]جدل *jadala u i* (*jadl*) to twist tight, tighten, stretch (ه a rope); to braid, plait (ه s.th., the hair, etc.) **II** to braid, plait, (ه s.th.) **III** to quarrel, wrangle, bicker (ه with s.o.); to argue, debate (ه with s.o.); to dispute, contest (فى s.th.) **VI** to quarrel, have an argument; to carry on a dispute

جدل *jadal* quarrel, argument; debate, dispute, discussion, controversy | فرض جدلا *farada jadalan* to assume for the sake of argument, propose as a basis for discussion, assume hypothetically (ان that)

جدلى *jadalī* controversial; disputatious; a disputant; dialectical | المادية الجدلية (*māddīya*) dialectical materialism (*philos.*)

جدلية *jadalīya* dialectics (*philos.*)

جدال *jaddāl* and مجدال *mijdāl* disputatious, argumentative; *mijdāl* see also below

جديلة *jadīla* pl. جدائل *jadāʾil*[2] braid, plait; tress

مجدال *mijdāl* pl. مجاديل *majādīl*[2] flagstone, ashlar; see also above under *jaddāl*

جدال *jidāl* and مجادلة *mujādala* pl. *-āt* quarrel, argument; dispute, discussion, debate | لا يقبل الجدال (*yaqbalu*) incontestable, indisputable; لا جدال *lā jidāla* and بلا جدال *bi-lā j.* incontestably, indisputably

مجدول *majdūl* tightly twisted; braided, plaited; interwoven, intertwined (tress of hair); slender and trim, shapely (e.g., leg)

مجادل *mujādil* disputant, opponent in dispute

[2]جدول *jadwal* pl. جداول *jadāwil*[2] creek, brook, little stream; column; list, roster; index; chart, table, schedule | جدول دراسى (*dirāsī*) curriculum; جدول البورصة stock list, خارج جدول البورصة (*kārija*) not quoted (stock exchange); جدول الاعمال agenda; working plan; جدول ارتباط correlation table (*math.*); جدول مواعيد القطارات (*qitārāt*) time table (for trains); railroad guide; جدول الضرب *j. ad-darb* multiplication table

جدا (جدو) *jadā u* to give a present (على to s.o.) **IV** to give as a present (على ب s.o. s.th.), present (على ب s.o. with); to be of use, be useful; to be appropriate, serve the purpose (means, device) | اجدى نفعا (*nafʿan*) to be useful; هذا لا يجديك that won't help you, that will be of no use (to you); ما يجدى عنك هذا do.; لا يجدى فتيلا

(*fatīlan*) = لا يجدى ;فتيل see ,لا يغنى فتيلا شروى نقير see شروى X to beg for alms; to implore, beg (ه ه s.o. for s.th.), plead (ه for s.th.)

جداء *jadā'* advantage, gain (عن for s.o.)

جدوى *jadwā* gift, present; advantage, benefit, gain | بلا جدوى (*bi-lā*) and على غير جدوى (*ğairi*) of no avail, useless, futile, in vain

اجدى *ajdā* more useful, more advantageous

استجداء *istijdā'* fervent plea, supplication

مجد *mujdin* useful, helpful; suitable, appropriate, serving the purpose | غير مجد useless

جدى *jady* pl. جداء *jidā'*, جديان *jidyān* kid, young billy goat; الجدى Capricorn (sign of the zodiac; *astron.*); the tenth month of the solar year (*Saudi Ar.*, cf. حمل *ḥamal*); the North Star

جذ *jaḏḏa u* (*jaḏḏ*) to cut off, clip (ه s.th.)

جذاذة *juḏāḏa* pl. *-āt* slip of paper; pl. جذاذات small pieces, shreds, scraps, clippings

جذب *jaḏaba i* (*jaḏb*) to pull, draw (ه s.th.); to attract (ه s.th.); to sniff (ه the air, a fragrance); to pull out, draw out, whip out (ه s.th.), draw (ه a weapon, or the like); to appeal, prove attractive (ه to s.o.), attract, captivate, charm, allure (ه s.o.), win (ه s.o.) over (اليه to one's side) **III** to contend (ه with s.o.) at pulling, tugging, etc. (ه s.th.) | جاذبه الحبل (*ḥabla*) to vie with s.o.; (to be able) to compete with s.o., measure up to s.o., be a match for s.o.; جاذبه الكلام or جاذبه اطراف الحديث or حديثا (*aṭrāfa l-ḥ.*) he engaged him in conversation, involved him in a discussion; جاذبه اطراف الحضارة (*aṭrāfa l-ḥaḍāra*) to vie with s.o. in culture **VI** to pull back and forth (ه s.o.); to contend; to contend with one another (ه, ه for); to attract each other | تجاذبوا اطراف الحديث (*aṭrāfa l-ḥ.*) they were deep in conversation, they were talking together **VII** to be attracted; to be drawn, gravitate (الى toward, to); to be carried away, be in ecstasy **VIII** to attract (ه s.o., ه s.th., اليه to o.s.; also *magn.*); to allure, entice (ه s.o.); to win (ه s.o.) over (اليه to one's side); to draw, inhale (ه puffs from a cigarette, etc.)

جذب *jaḏb* attraction; gravitation; appeal, lure, enticement, captivation; ○ ecstasy | اخذ جذبا to wrest away, take away by force; الجذب الجنسى (*jinsī*) sex appeal

جذاب *jaḏḏāb* attractive; magnetic (fig.); suction, suctorial; winning, fetching, engaging; charming, enticing, captivating, gripping

اجذب *ajḏab*[2] more attractive, more captivating

انجذاب *injiḏāb* attraction, inclination, proneness, tendency; ecstasy

اجتذاب *ijtiḏāb* attraction; enticement, lure

جاذب *jāḏib* attractive; magnetic (fig.); winning, fetching, engaging; charming, enticing, captivating, gripping

جاذبية *jāḏibīya* gravitation; attraction; attractiveness; charm, fascination; magnetism (fig.); lure, enticement | ○ جاذبية الثقل *j. aṯ-ṯiql* gravitational force; جاذبية مغنطيسية (*mağnaṭīsīya*) magnetism; جاذبية الجنس *j. al-jins* sex appeal

مجذوب *majḏūb* attracted; possessed, maniacal, insane; (pl. مجاذيب *majāḏīb*[2]) maniac, lunatic, madman, idiot | مستشفى المجاذيب *mustašfā l-m.* mental hospital

متجاذب *mutajāḏib* mutually attractive; belonging together, inseparable

منجذب *munjaḏib* attracted; inclined, tending (الى to)

جذر *jaḏara u* (*jaḏr*) to uproot, tear out by the

roots (ه s.th.) **II** do.; to extract the root (ه of a number; *math.*); to take root; to cause (ه s.o., ه s.th.) to become deeply rooted

جذر *jidr, jadr* pl. جذور *judūr* root (also *math.*); stem, base, lower end; (pl. اجذار *ajdār*) stub (of a receipt book, or the like) | جذر تربيعى (*tarbīʿī*) square root (*math.*)

جذرى *jidrī* radical, root (adj.); radical (= fundamental, extreme) | تحسينات جذرية radical improvements; حل جذرى (*ḥall*) a radical solution

تجذير *tajdīr* evolution, root extraction (*math.*)

جذع *jadaʿ* pl. جذعان *judʿān* young man, young fellow (cf. □ جدع *gadaʿ*); new, incipient | عادت الحرب جذعة (*ḥarbu, jadaʿatan*) the war broke out again, started all over again; اعاد الامر جذعا (*l-amra*) he reopened the whole affair, he reverted to the earlier status

جذع *jidʿ* pl. اجذاع *ajdāʿ*, جذوع *judūʿ* stem, trunk; stump, tree stump; torso

جذعى *jidʿī* truncal

جذف **II** to row (ه a boat)

مجذاف *mijdāf* pl. مجاذيف *majādīf*[2] oar

جذل *jadila a* (*jadal*) to be happy, gay, exuberant, rejoice **IV** to make happy, gladden, cheer (ه s.o.)

جذل *jidl* pl. اجذال *ajdāl*, جذول *judūl* stump (of a tree)

جذيل *judail* wooden post on which camels rub themselves

جذل *jadal* gaiety, hilarity, exuberance, happiness

جذل *jadil* pl. جذلان *judlān* gay, hilarious, cheerful, in high spirits, exuberant. happy

جذلان *jadlān*[2] gay, hilarious, cheerful, in high spirits, exuberant, happy

جذم *jadama i* (*jadm*) to cut off, chop off (ه s.th., esp. a part of the body); to remove, take out, excise (ه e.g., the tonsils, the appendix; *surg.*); pass. *judima* to be afflicted with leprosy

جذم *jidm* pl. جذوم *judūm*, اجذام *ajdām* root

جذام *judām* leprosy

جذامة *judāma* stubble

اجذم *ajdam*[2] pl. جذمى *jadmā* mutilated (from having an arm, a hand, etc., cut off); leprous; leper

مجذوم *majdūm* leprous; leper

جذمور *judmūr* stump

جذوة *jadwa, jidwa, judwa* pl. جذى *jidan, judan*, جذاء *jidāʾ* firebrand; burning log

جر *jarra u* (*jarr*) to draw, pull (ه s.th.); to drag, tug, haul (ه s.th.); to tow (ه s.th.); to trail (ه s.th.); to drag along (ه s.o., ه s.th.); to draw (ه على s.th. on s.o.), bring (ه s.th.) down (على upon s.o.); to lead (الى to), bring on, cause (الى s.th.); to entail (ه e.g., some evil, على for s.o.); (*gram.*) to pronounce the final consonant with *i*, put (a word) into the genitive | جر جريرة (*jarīratan*) to commit an outrage, a crime (على against s.o.); جر قيودا (*quyūdan*) to be in shackles, go shackled; جر النار الى قرصه (*qurṣihī*) to secure advantages for o.s., feather one's nest; لا يجر لسانه بكلمة (*lisānahū bi-kalima*) he won't let a word escape his lips; جر قدميه (*qadamaihī*) to drag one's feet, have a dragging gait **IV** to ruminate **VII** passive of **I**; to be driven; to be swept along, drift, float; to be derived, stem (عن from, out of; esp. rights, claims from a contract or a legal situation) | انجر الى الوراء (*warāʾi*) to withdraw, fall back, give way **VIII** to ruminate; to repeat constantly (ه the same words, ideas, etc.) | اجتر آلامه (*ālāmahū*) to mull over one's grief; اجتروا

احاديثهم they chewed the old cud over, kept saying the same things

جر *jarr* pull(ing), drawing, draft; traction; drag(ging), tugging, towage, hauling; bringing on, causing; genitive; pronunciation of the final consonant with *i* (*gram.*) | حرف الجر *ḥarf al-j.* (*gram.*) preposition; وهلم جرا *wa-halumma jarran* and so forth

جرة *jarra* pl. جرار *jirār* (earthenware) jar

جرة *jarra, jurra* trail, track; rut (left by a wagon) | بجرة قلم *bi-j. qalam* with one stroke of the pen

جرة *jirra* cud (of a ruminant)

من جرى *min jarrā* because of | من جراك because of you, on your account, for your sake

من جراء *min jarrā'i* because of, due to | من جراء أن because

جرار *jarrār* dragging along behind itself a great store of things; huge (army); producer and seller of clay jars (from جرة *jarra*); — (pl. *-āt*) tractor; tugboat, steam tug, towing launch | جرار مجنزر (*mujanzar*) tracklaying tractor; عربة جرارة (*'araba*) motor car (tram); tractor vehicle (truck)

جارور *jārūr* pl. جوارير *jawārīr*[2] (*syr.*) drawer (of a desk, etc.)

جارورة *jārūra* (*leb.*) rake (tool)

جريرة *jarīra* pl. جرائر *jarā'ir*[2] guilt; offense, outrage, crime | من جريرة *min jarīrati* because of, on account of

جرارة *jarrāra* pl. *-āt* a variety of scorpion; tractor

مجر *mijarr* trace, tug (of a harness)

مجرة *majarra* pl. *-āt* galaxy

مجرى *majarrī* galactic

انجرارية *ingirārīya* (*eg.*) towage charges for watercraft

جار *jārr* governing the genit. (of a preposition; *gram.*)

مجرور *majrūr* drawn, dragged, towed, etc.; word governed by a preposition, word in the genitive form; (pl. مجارير *magārīr*[2]) drain, sewer (*eg.*); مجارير sewers, sewage system (*eg.*)

مجتر *mujtarr* ruminant (adj. and n.)

جرؤ *jaru'a u* (جرأة *jur'a*, جراءة *jarā'a*) to dare, venture, risk, hazard (على s.th.), take the risk (على of, ان of doing s.th.), have the courage (على for s.th.) **II** to encourage (ه على s.o. to s.th.) **V** to dare, venture, risk, hazard (على s.th.) **VIII** to be venturesome, be daring; to become bold, make bold (على with s.o.); to venture (على s.th. or upon s.th.), have the audacity (على to do s.th.)

جرىء *jarī'* pl. اجرياء *ajriyā'*[2] bold, courageous (ب, على in s.th.); forward, immodest, insolent; daring, reckless, foolhardy

جرأة *jur'a* and جراءة *jarā'a* courage, boldness, daring; forwardness, insolence

مجترئ *mujtari'* bold, forward

جراج (Fr.; Eg. spelling) *garāž* pl. *-āt* garage

جرام (Eg. spelling) *grām* pl. *-āt* gram

جرانيت (Eg. spelling) *granīt* granite

جرانيتى *granītī* granitic

[1]جرب *jariba a* (*jarab*) to be mangy; (*eg.*) to fade (color) **II** to test (ه s.th.); to try, try out, essay (ه s.th.); to sample (ه s.th.); to rehearse, practice (ه s.th.); to attempt (ه s.th.); to put to the test, try, tempt (ه s.o.) | جرب نفسه فى to try one's hand at; جرب الايام (*ayyāma*) to gather experience

جرب *jarab* mange; itch, scabies

جرب *jarib* mangy; scabby

اجرب *ajrab*[2], f. جرباء *jarbā'*[2], pl. جرب *jurb* and جربان *jarbān*[2] mangy; scabby

جراب *jirāb* pl. اجربة *ajriba*, جرب *jurub* sack, bag, traveling bag; knapsack; scrotum; covering, case; sheath, scabbard (for the sword)

جراب *jurāb* pl. *-āt* stocking, sock

جريب *jarīb* a patch of arable land

تجربة *tajriba* pl. تجارب *tajārib*² trial, test; tryout; attempt; practice, rehearsal; scientific test, experiment; probation; trial, tribulation; temptation; experience, practice; proof sheet, galley proof, also تجربة مطبعية (*maṭbaʿīya*)

تجريب *tajrīb* trial, test(ing); trial, tribulation; temptation

تجريبي *tajrībī* trial, test (adj.); experimental; based on experience, empirical | علم النفس التجريبي (*ʿilm an-nafs*) experimental psychology; حفر تجريبي (*ḥaf.*) drilling of a test hole, exploration drilling; مدرسة تجريبية (*madrasa*) experimental school

تجريبية *tajrībīya* empiricism (*philos.*)

مجرب *mujarrib* experimental; tester; examiner; tempter

مجرب *mujarrab* tried, tested; proven or established by experience, time-tested, time-tried; experienced, practiced, seasoned; man of experience

جورب² look up alphabetically

جربذة *jarbaḏa* = جربزة

جربز *jurbuz* pl. جرابزة *jarābiza* impostor, confidence man, swindler

جربزة *jarbaza* (also جربذة) deception, swindle

جربوع *jarbūʿ* (= يربوع) pl. جرابيع *jarābīʿ*² jerboa (*zool.*)

جربندية *jarabandīya* (and جرابندية) knapsack; (*eg.*) *garabandīya* cartridge pouch; small leather pouch

جرثم II *tajarṯama* to take root, come into existence, germinate

جرثوم *jurṯūm*, جرثومة *jurṯūma* pl. جراثيم *jarāṯīm*² root; origin; germ; microbe, bacillus, bacterium | تحت الجرثوم *taḥt al-j.* inframicrobe; علم الجراثيم *ʿilm al-j.* bacteriology

جراج look up alphabetically

جرجر *jarjara* (جرجرة *jarjara*) to gargle; to jerk or pull back and forth; to trail, drag (ه s.th.); to tow away (ه s.th.) | جرجر خطاه (*kuṭāhu*) to drag one's feet, shuffle along **II** *tajarjara* pass. and refl. of I

جرجرة *jarjara* gargling; rumbling noise; rumble, clatter (of a wagon)

جرجر *jirjir* (large, thick) beans

جرجير *jirjīr* watercress (*bot.*)

جرح *jaraḥa a* (*jarḥ*) to wound (ه s.o.); to injure, hurt (ه s.o.; also fig., the feelings) **II** to invalidate (ه testimony), challenge, declare unreliable (ه a witness), take formal exception (ه, ه to) **VIII** to commit (ه an outrage, a crime); to bring about (ه wonders) | اجترح السيآت (*sayyiʾāt*) to do evil things

جرح *jurḥ* pl. جراح *jirāḥ*, جروح *jurūḥ*, جروحات *jurūḥāt*, اجراح *ajrāḥ* wound, injury, lesion

جراح *jarrāḥ* pl. *-ūn* surgeon | جراح الاسنان dental surgeon

جراحة *jirāḥa* surgery

جراحي *jirāḥī* surgical | عملية جراحية (*ʿamalīya*) surgical operation

جريح *jarīḥ* pl. جرحى *jarḥā* wounded, injured, hurt

تجريح *tajrīḥ* surgery; defamation, disparagement

جارح *jāriḥ* injuring; wounding, stinging, painful, hurting; rapacious (beast), predatory

جارحة *jāriḥa* pl. جوارح *jawāriḥ*² predatory animal or bird | جوارح الطير *j. aṭ-ṭair* predatory birds

جوارح *jawāriḥ*² limbs, extremities (of the body) | بكل جوارحه with might and main, with all his strength

مجروح *majrūḥ* pl. مجاريح *majārīḥ*² wounded, injured, hurt

جرد *jarada u* (*jard*) to peel, pare (ه s.th.); to remove the shell, peel, rind or husk (ه of s.th.); to denude, divest, strip, bare (ه s.th.); (*com.*) to take stock; to make an inventory (البضائع of goods on hand) **II** to peel, pare (ه s.th.); to remove the shell, peel, rind or husk (ه of s.th.); to denude, divest, strip, dispossess, deprive (ه من or ه s.o. or s.th. of); to withhold (ه من from s.o. s.th.); to draw, unsheathe (السيف the sword); to unleash (ه على s.th. against s.o.); to send, dispatch (ه a military detachment, troops, ضد or على against s.o.); to free (ه من or ه s.o. or s.th. from); to isolate (ه s.th.); to abstract (ه s.th.); to divest (ه من s.o. of his citizenship, of a rank, of a vested right, etc.) | جرده من السلاح to disarm s.o.; جرد نفسه من to free o.s. from, rid o.s. of, give up s.th.; جرده من ملابسه (*malābisihī*) to undress s.o. **V** pass. of **II**; to strip o.s., rid o.s., get rid (من or عن of), free o.s. (من or عن from); to be free (من or عن from, ل for a task); to devote o.s. exclusively (ل to s.th.); to give up, renounce (من or عن s.th.); to isolate o.s.; to be absolute

جرد *jard* bare, threadbare, shabby, worn; (*com.*) inventory; stocktaking

جرد *jarid* without vegetation, barren, bleak, stark (landscape)

اجرد *ajrad*[2], f. جرداء *jardā'*[2], pl. جرد *jurd* desolate, bleak, without vegetation; hairless, bald; threadbare, shabby, worn (garment); open, unprotected (border)

جراد *jarād* (coll.; n. un. ة) locust(s) | جراد رحال (*raḥḥāl*) migratory locust(s); جراد البحر *j. al-baḥr* langouste, sea crayfish; بجرادها *bi-jarādihā* in its entirety

جريد *jarīd* palm branches stripped of their leaves; jereed, a blunt javelin used in equestrian games

جريدة *jarīda* pl. جرائد *jarā'id*[2] (n. un. of جريد) palm-leaf stalk; list, register, roster, index; newspaper | جريدة يومية (*yaumīya*) daily newspaper; جرائد المساء *j. al-masā'* the evening papers; الجريدة الناطقة and الجريدة السينمائية the newsreel; جريدة رسمية (*rasmīya*) official gazette, government paper for publishing laws

اجرودى *ajrūdī* (*syr.*) beardless, hairless

مجرد *mijrad* pl. مجارد *majārid*[2] scraper

تجريد *tajrīd* peeling, paring; disrobement, stripping; denudation; deprivation; divestment; disarmament; dispatching (of troops); freeing; isolation; abstraction | تجريد من السلاح disarmament; تجريد الدين عن الاسطورية (*usṭūrīya*) demythologization of religion

تجريدة *tajrīda* pl. *-āt*, تجاريد *tajārīd*[2] military detachment, expeditionary force

تجريدى *tajrīdī* abstract | الفن التجريدى (*fann*) abstract art

تجريدية *tajrīdīya* abstract trend (in art)

تجرد *tajarrud* freedom (من or عن from); isolatedness, isolation; independence, impartiality; absoluteness; abstractness, abstraction

مجرد *mujarrad* denuded, bare, naked; freed, free (من or عن from); pure, mere, nothing more than; sole; very, absolute; abstract; selfless, disinterested; 1st stem of the verb (*gram.*); pl. مجردات abstract matters, abstracts | (with foll. noun in genitive = mere, sheer, nothing but:) مجرد لهو *mujarradu lahwin* mere play, just fun; بالعين المجردة with the naked eye; لمجرد ان *li-mujarradi an* for the simple reason that ...; بمجرد ما *bi-mujarradi mā* as soon as, at the very moment when; منطقة مجردة من السلاح (*minṭaqa*) demilitarized zone

متجرد *mutajarrid* impartial; selfless, free of selfish interest

جردل *jardal* pl. جرادل *jarādil*[2] bucket, pail

جرذ *jurad* pl. جرذان *jirdān*, *jurdān* large rat

جرذون *jirḏaun* pl. جراذين *jarāḏīn*² large rat

جرزة *jurza* pl. جرز *juraz* bundle (of hay, etc.); ponytail (hairdress)

¹جرس *jarasa i* (*jars*) to ring, toll, knell, (re)sound **II** to make experienced, inure by severe trials, sorely try (ه s.o.; time, events); to compromise, disgrace, discredit, expose, bring into disrepute (ب s.o.)

جرس *jars, jirs* sound, tone

جرس *jaras* pl. اجراس *ajrās* bell

جرسة *jursa* defamation, public exposure; scandal, disgrace

²جرساية *jirsāya*, جرسية *jirsīya* pl. *-āt* jersey, woolen sweater; جرسى jersey cloth

جرسون (Fr. *garçon*) *garsōn* pl. *-āt* (*eg.*) waiter

جرسونة *garsōna* pl. *-āt* (*eg.*) waitress

جرسونيره (Fr. *garçonnière*) *garsōnēra* (*eg.*) bachelor quarters; rented quarters where a man can meet with his paramour

جرش *jaraša u* (*jarš*) to crush (ه s.th.); to grate, bruise, grind (ه s.th.)

جرش *jarš* a grating, scraping noise

جريش *jarīš* crushed, bruised, coarsely ground; crushed grain; grits

جراشة *jarrāša* crusher (*techn.*)

جاروشة *jārūša* pl. جواريش *jawārīš*² quern, hand mill (for grinding grain)

جرض *jariḍa a* (*jaraḍ*): جرض بريقه (*bi-rīqihī*) he choked on his saliva, could not swallow his saliva (because of excitement, alarm, or grief), he was very upset, in a state of great agitation, deeply moved; — *jaraḍa u* (*jarḍ*) to choke, suffocate (ه s.o.) **IV** اجرضه بريقه (cf. I) to alarm s.o., fill s.o. with apprehension

جريض *jarīḍ*: حال الجريض دون القريض *ḥāla l-j. dūna l-qarīḍ* (proverb; lit.: choking prevented poetry, i.e.) in the face of death one does not think of rhyming (among other interpretations)

جرع *jaraʿa a* (*jarʿ*) and *jariʿa a* (*jaraʿ*) to swallow, gulp, devour (ه s.th.); to pour down, toss down (ه a drink) **II** to make (ه s.o.) swallow (ه s.th.); to gulp down **V** to drink (ه s.th.); to swallow (ه s.th., also suffering, woes) **VIII** to swallow, gulp down (ه s.th.)

جرعة *jurʿa, jarʿa* pl. جرع *juraʿ*, *-āt* gulp, mouthful, draught; dose, dosage (of a medicine or drug; *med., pharm.*); oral vaccination (*med.*, = جرعة الطعم *j. aṭ-ṭuʿm*)

جرف *jarafa u* (*jarf*) and **VIII** to sweep away (ه s.th.); to wash away (ه s.th.); to shovel away (ه s.th.); to remove (ه s.th.); to tear away, carry off (ه s.th.); to carry along (ه or ه s.o. or s.th.) **VII** to be swept away, be carried away

جرف *jarf* clearance, shoveling away | جرف الرمال *j. ar-rimāl* dredging

جرف *jurf, juruf* pl. جروف *jurūf*, اجراف *ajrāf* undercut bank or shore; cliff, steep slope, precipice; bluff (along a river or coast) | جرف جليدى (*jalīdī*) avalanche

جرافة *jarrāfa* pl. *-āt*, جراريف *jarārīf*² rake; harrow; ○ bulldozer | جرافة رمال dredger

مجرف *majraf* pl. مجارف *majārif*² torrent, strong current

مجرفة *mijrafa* shovel, scoop; (*syr.*) mattock; trowel

مجراف *mijrāf* pl. مجاريف *majārīf*² shovel, scoop

انجراف *injirāf* erosion (by water)

جارف *jārif* torrential (stream, mountain creek); stormy, violent (emotions, passions)

الجركس *al-jarkas* the Circassians

جركسى *jarkasī* pl. جراكسة *jarākisa* Circassian (adj. and n.)

جرم *jarama i* (*jarm*) to bone (اللحم *al-laḥma*

the meat); — to commit an offense, a crime, an outrage (على or الى against s.o.), sin (على or الى against s.o.), injure, harm, wrong (على or الى s.o.) **II** to incriminate, charge with a crime (ه s.o.; *syr.*); to make (ه s.th.) a criminal offense (*jur.*) **IV** to commit a crime, to sin (على or الى against s.o.), do wrong (على or الى to s.o.), harm, wrong (على or الى s.o.) **VIII** = **IV**

جرم *garm* pl. جروم *gurūm* (*eg.*) long, flat-bottomed barge, lighter (*naut.*)

جرم *jirm* pl. اجرام *ajrām*, جرم *jurum* body; mass, bulk, volume (of a body); (pl. اجرام) celestial body | الاجرام الفلكية (*falakīya*) and الاجرام السماوية (*samāwīya*) the celestial bodies

جرم *jurm* pl. اجرام *ajrām*, جروم *jurūm* offense, crime, sin

لا جرم *lā jarama* surely, certainly, of course

جريم *jarīm* hulking, bulky, huge, voluminous, of great size

جريمة *jarīma* pl. جرائم *jarā'im*² crime; offense; sin | جريمة كبرى (or عظمى) (*kubrā*, *'uẓmā*) capital offense; قانون الجرائم penal code

تجريم *tajrīm* incrimination; crimination

اجرام *ijrām* crime; culpability, delinquency; criminality | اجرام الاحداث *i. al-aḥdāṯ* juvenile criminality

اجرامى *ijrāmī* criminal

لحم مجروم *laḥm majrūm* fillet (meat)

سنة مجرمة *sana mujarrama* an entire year

مجرم *mujrim* criminal; (pl. *-ūn*) a criminal; evildoer, culprit, delinquent | مجرم عائد recidivous criminal; مجرم حرب *m. ḥarb* war criminal

جرامز *jarāmiz*² and جراميز *jarāmīz*² limbs, legs | ضم جراميزه (*ḍamma*) he beat it, he made off

الجرمان *al-jarmān* the Germanic tribes, the Teutons

جرمانى *jarmānī* Germanic, Teutonic

¹جرن *jurn* pl. اجران *ajrān* (stone) basin; mortar; (*eg.*) threshing floor, barn | جرن المعمودية *j. al-ma'mūdīya* baptismal font

²جران *jirān* the front part of a camel's neck | ضرب بجرانه to become established, take root; القى عليه جرانه (*alqā, jirānahū*) to apply o.s. to s.th. and adjust to it, accustom o.s. to s.th.

جرنال *žurnāl* (*eg.* also *gurnāl*) pl. جرانيل *žarānīl*² (*eg.*, *garānīl*²) journal, newspaper, periodical

جرانيت *granīt* granite

جرانيتى *granītī* granitic

جرو *jarw* (*jirw*, *jurw*) pl. اجر *ajrin*, جراء *jirā'*, اجراء *ajrā'*, اجرية *ajriya* puppy, whelp, cub (of a dog or beast of prey)

جروسة *grōsa* gross (= 12 dozen)

جرى *jarā i* (*jary*) to flow, stream (water); to run; to hurry, rush; to blow (wind); to take place, come to pass, happen, occur; to be under way, be in progress, be going on (work); to befall (ل s.o.), happen (ل to); to be in circulation, circulate, be current; to wend one's way (الى to), head (الى for); to proceed (على in accordance with); to conform (على to s.th.); to be guided, go (على by), take as a criterion (على s.th.); to follow (مع s.th.), yield, give way (مع to, e.g., to a desire); to entail (ب s.th.); (with وراء) to run or be after s.th., seek to get s.th. | جرى له حديث مع he had a talk with; جرى مجراه (*majrāhu*) to take the same course as, be analogous to, follow the same way as, proceed or act in the same manner as; to function the same as, be used in the same sense as (of a word); جرى على المذكر

(*mudakkar*) to be used in the masculine (*gram.*); جرى منه الشىء مجرى الدم (*minhu š-šai'u majrā d-dam*) it had become second nature to him; جرى على الالسن (*alsun*) to circulate, make the rounds (rumor); جرى على كل لسان to be on everyone's lips; جرى على قلمه (*qalamihī*) to come to s.o.'s pen (e.g., a poem); جرى على خطة (*kiṭṭa*) to follow a plan; يجرى على هذا السنن (*sanan*) he acts in accordance with this rule, follows this principle; ما يجرى عليه العمل (*'amalu*) the way things are handled, what is customary practice; جرى به العمل to be in force, be valid, be commonly observed (law, custom); جرت العادة ب to be customary, be common practice, be a common phenomenon, have gained vogue; جرى بالعادة على to do s.th. customarily, be in the habit of doing s.th.; جرت بذلك عادتهم that was their habit; جرى لسانه ب (*lisānuhū*) to articulate, pronounce, utter, express s.th.; ما جرت به الليلة what the night brought, what happened in the night **II** to cause to run | جرى ريقه (*rīqahū*) to make s.o.'s mouth water **III** to concur, agree, be in agreement (ه with s.o., فى in s.th.); to keep pace, keep up (ه with s.o.; also intellectually); to be able to follow (ه s.o.); to go (along) (ه with); to adapt o.s., adjust, conform (ه to), be guided (ه by) **IV** to cause to flow, make flow (ه s.th.); to cause to run, set running (ه, ه s.o., s.th.); to make (ه s.th.) take place or happen, bring about (ه s.th.); to carry out, execute, implement, put into effect, apply (ه s.th., e.g., rules, regulations); to carry out, perform (ه an action); to hold, conduct (ه talks, examinations); to set going, set in motion (ه a project), launch (ه an undertaking); to channel (ه ل or على s.th. to), bestow, settle (ه ل or على s.th. upon s.o.); to impose, inflict (ه على s.th., a penalty, on s.o.) | اجرى تجربة (*tajribatan*) to carry out an experiment; اجرى حديثا to conduct an interview; اجرى تحقيقا to conduct an investigation; اجرى له اعانة (*i'ānatan*) to grant s.o. a subsidy; اجراه مجرى (*majrā*, with foll. genitive) to treat s.th. in the same manner as, put s.th. on equal footing with; اجرى السنتهم ب (*alsinatahum*) he brought them to the expression of ..., caused them to voice or utter s.th.

جرى *jary* course | جريا على *jaryan 'alā* in accordance with, according to

من جراك *min jarāka* and من جرائك *min jarā'ika* because of you, on your account, for your sake

جراء *jarrā'* runner, racer

جراية *jirāya* pl. *-āt* daily (food) rations; pay, salary | عيش جراية *'ēš girāya* (*eg.*) coarse bread

جريان *jarayān* flow, flux; course; stream

مجرى *majran* pl. مجار *majārin* watercourse, stream, rivulet, gully; torrent or flood of water; pipeline; canal, channel; drain, sewer; pl. sewers, sewage system; power line (*el.*); current (*el.*); current (of a stream); track, path, course (of a ship, star); guide rail (*techn.*); course (of events), progress, passage; trend (in life, of events) | مجرى البول *m. l-baul* urethra (*anat.*); مجارى التنفس *m. t-tanaffus* respiratory tract (*anat.*); مجارى الكلام *m. l-kalām* the syntactic means, forms of continuous discourse (of a language); مجرى ملاحى (*milāḥī*) fairway, waterway (*naut.*); مجرى الهواء *m. l-hawā'* air stream, current of air, draft; اخذ مجراه to take its course; see also جرى I and IV

ماجريات *mājarayāt*, *mājariyāt* (pl. of ما جرى) (course of) events, happenings

مجاراة *mujārāh* keeping up (with foll. genitive: with); conformity (with foll. genitive: with) | مجاراة ل *mujārātan li* in conformity with, in accordance with, according to

اجراء *ijrā'* pl. *-āt* performance (of an action); execution; enforcement; holding (of talks, examinations, etc.); measure, step, proceeding; practical application, effectuation (of a plan, a recommendation, a rule); pl. اجراءات (*Tun.*, *Alg.*) decrees, orders, regulations (*jur.*) | اتخذ اجراءات (*ittakada*) to take measures; اجراءات قانونية (*qānūnīya*) legal steps, proceedings at law

اجرائى *ijrā'ī* operational

جار *jārin* flowing, streaming, running; circulating; current, present | الشهر الجارى (*šahr*) the current month

جارية *jāriya* pl. -*āt*, جوار *jawārin* girl; slave girl; maid, servant; ship, vessel

جز *jazza u* (*jazz*) and **VIII** to cut off, clip (ه s.th.); to shear, shear off (ه s.th.; esp. the wool of sheep)

جزة *jizza* (now also pronounced *jazza*) pl. جزز *jizaz*, جزائز *jazā'iz*² shorn wool, fleece, clip

جزازة *juzāza* pl. -*āt* slip of paper; label, tag

جزاز *jazzāz* pl. -*ūn* shearer, woolshearer

مجز *mijazz* woolshears

جزأ *jaza'a a* to be content, content o.s. (ب with) **II** to divide, part, separate, break up, cut up, partition (ه s.th.) **V** to divide, break up, be or become divided; to be separated, be detached, be partitioned off; to be divisible, separable (عن from) **VIII** = *jaza'a*; to divide up, do gradually, do a bit at a time (ه an action, activity)

جزء *juz'* pl. اجزاء *ajzā'* part, portion; constituent, component; fraction; division; section; the 30th part of the Koran (= 2 *ḥizb*) | اجزاء احتياطية spare parts, replacements (*techn.*)

جزئى *juz'ī* partial; minor, trivial, insignificant, unimportant; (*jur.*) minor, petty; جزئيا *juz'īyan* partly; جزئيات bagatelles; petty cases (*jur.*) | مواد جزئية (*mawādd*) petty cases (*jur.*); جنح جزئية (*junaḥ*) summary delicts (*jur.*); محكمة جزئية see under محكمة; نيابة جزئية see under نيابة; حادثة جزئية minor incident; تسوية جزئية (*taswiya*) part payment; ○ تشابه جزئى (*tašābuh*) partial assimilation (*phon.*)

جزئية *juz'īya* pl. -*āt* detail, particular; subordinate part; particle | جزئيات صخرية (*ṣakrīya*) rock fragments, mineral particles; الجزئيات والكليات (*kullīyāt*) the particular and general aspects, the minor and the major issues

جزىء *juzai'* pl. -*āt* molecule

جزيئى *juzai'ī* molecular

اجزائى *ajzā'ī* pl. -*ūn* pharmacist, druggist

اجزاجى *ajzājī* pl. -*īya* pharmacist, druggist

اجزائية *ajzā'īya* and اجزاخانة *ajzākāna* pl. -*āt* pharmacy, drugstore

تجزئة *tajzi'a* division; partition; separation; dissociation; breakdown (into classes, categories, etc.); fragmentation | قابل للتجزئة divisible; قابلية التجزئة divisibility; تاجر التجزئة retailer, retail merchant

جزأرة *jaz'ara* (from الجزائر, see جزيرة) Algerianization

جزدان *juzdān*, *jizdān* pl. -*āt* wallet; change purse

جزر¹ *jazara u* (*jazr*) to slaughter; to kill, butcher (ه an animal); — *i u* (*jazr*) to sink, fall, drop, ebb (water)

جزر *jazr* slaughter; butchering; ebb (of the sea)

جزرة *jazra* blood sacrifice

جزور *jazūr* pl. جزر *juzur* slaughter camel

جزارة *jizāra* butcher's trade, butchery

جزار *jazzār* pl. ة, -*ūn* butcher

جزيرة *jazīra* pl. جزر *juzur*, rarely جزائر *jazā'ir*² island | شبه جزيرة *šibhu j.* peninsula; الجزيرة Al Jazira, (Northwest)

Mesopotamia; الجزائر Algeria; Algiers (capital of Algeria); جزيرة العرب *j. al-ʿarab* Arabia, the Arabian Peninsula; الجزائر الخالدات (*kālidāt*) the Canary Islands; الجزيرة الخضراء (*kaḍrā'*) Algeciras (seaport in SW Spain); جزيرة الامان *j. al-amān* safety island

جزرى *jazarī* insular; (pl. *-ūn*) islander

جزائرى *jazā'irī* pl. *-ūn* Algerian (adj. and n.); islander | الجمهورية الجزائرية الديموقراطية الشعبية (*jumhūrīya, šaʿbīya*) Democratic and Popular Republic of Algeria

مجزر *majzir* pl. مجازر *majāzir*² slaughterhouse, abattoir; butchery

مجزرة *majzara* pl. مجازر *majāzir*² butchery; slaughterhouse (*Tun.*); massacre, carnage

²جزر *jazar* (coll.; n. un. ة) carrot(s)

جزع *jaziʿa a* (*jazaʿ*, جزوع *juzūʿ*) to be or become anxious, worried, concerned; to be sad, unhappy (من about); to feel regret (على for s.o.), pity (على s.o.); to mourn (على for s.o.) V to break apart, break, snap

جزع *jazʿ* onyx

جزع *juzʿ* axle; shaft (*techn.*)

جزع *jazaʿ* anxiety, uneasiness, apprehension, concern; anguish, fear; sadness

جزع *jaziʿ* restless, impatient; anxious, worried, uneasy, apprehensive

جزوع *jazūʿ* and جازع *jāziʿ* restless; impatient; anxious, worried, uneasy, apprehensive

مجزع *mujazzaʿ* marbled, veined; variegated, dappled

جزف III to act at random, blindly, indiscriminately, take a chance; to speculate (*fin.*); to speak vaguely, in general terms; to risk, stake (ب s.th.) | جازف بنفسه to risk one's life; جازف به في to plunge s.o. into (some adventure)

جزاف *juzāf* purchase of a certain amount of things (*Isl. Law*); جزافا *juzāfan* at random, haphazardly

مجازفة *mujāzafa* rashness, recklessness, foolhardiness; risk, hazard; adventure, venture

مجازف *mujāzif* rash, reckless, foolhardy; adventurous; venturesome

¹جزل *jazula u* to be considerable, abundant, plentiful IV اجزل له العطاء (*ʿaṭā'a*) to give generously, openhandedly, liberally to s.o.

جزل *jazl* and جزيل *jazīl* pl. جزال *jizāl* abundant, plentiful, ample, much; pure, lucid, eloquent (style) | جزل الرأى of sound, unerring judgment; شكره شكرا جزيلا *šakarahū šukran jazīlan* he thanked him profusely; شكرا جزيلا many thanks!

جزلة *jizla* piece, slice

جزالة *jazāla* profusion, abundance; (*rhet.*) purity (of style)

²جوزل look up alphabetically

³جزلان *juzlān* = جزدان

¹جزم *jazama i* (*jazm*) to cut off, cut short, clip (ه s.th.); to judge; to decide, settle (ه s.th.); to be positive (ب about), be absolutely certain (ب of s.th.); to assert authoritatively (ب s.th.); to make up one's mind, decide, resolve (على to do s.th.); to impose, make incumbent (ه على s.th. on s.o.); (*gram.*) to pronounce the final consonant (of a word) without a vowel; to put (ه a verb) into the apocopate form or the imperative

جزم *jazm* cutting off, clipping; decision; resolution, resolve; apodictic judgment; (*gram.*) apocopate form | علامة الجزم *ʿalāmat al-j.* = *jazma*

جزمة *jazma* diacritical mark (°) indicating vowellessness of a final consonant

جازم *jāzim* decisive; peremptory, definite, definitive, final; firmly convinced, absolutely certain (ب of s.th.); (pl. جوازم *jawāzim*[2]) governing the apocopate form (*gram.*)

مجزوم *majzūm* cut off, cut short, clipped; decided, settled; (*gram.*) vowelless (final consonant); in the apocopate form

منجزم *munjazim* (*gram.*) in the apocopate form

جزمة[2] *jazma* pl. *-āt*, جزم *jizam* (pair of) shoes, (pair of) boots | جزمة برباط (*bi-ribāṭ*) laced boots; جزمة لماعة (*lammāʿa*) patent-leather shoes

جزمجى *gazmagī* (*eg.*) and جزماتى *gizamātī* (*eg.*), *jazmātī* (*syr.*) pl. *-īya* shoemaker

جزى *jazā i* (جزاء *jazāʾ*) to requite, recompense (ه s.o., ب or على for), repay (ه to s.o., ب or على s.th.); to reward (ه s.o., ب or على for); to punish (ه s.o., ب or على for); to satisfy (ه s.o.), give satisfaction (ه to s.o.); to compensate, make up (ه ب for s.th. with or by); to compensate, offset (عن s.th.) | جزاك الله خيرا (*ḵairan*) may God bless you for it! جزاه جزاء سنمار (*jazāʾa sinimmāra*) he returned to him good for evil **III** to repay, requite (ه ب s.th. with, ه ب s.o. for), recompense (ه ب s.o. for); to reward (ه ب or على s.o. for); to punish (ه ب or على s.o. for) | جازاهم خيرا (*ḵairan*) he invoked God's reward upon them **IV** to suffice (ه s.o.), do for s.o. (ه); to take the place, serve instead (عن of), replace (عن s.th.)

جزاء *jazāʾ* requital, repayment; recompense, return; compensation, setoff; amends, reparation; punishment, penalty; final clause in a conditional sentence (*gram.*). = جزاء الشرط *j. aš-šarṭ* | جزاء نقدى (*naqdī*) fine; منطقة الجزاء *minṭaqat al-j.* penalty area (soccer)

جزائى *jazāʾī* penal

جزية *jizya* pl. جزى *jizan*, جزاء *jizāʾ* tax; tribute; head tax on free non-Muslims under Muslim rule

تجزية *tajziya* reward

مجازاة *mujāzāh* requital, repayment; punishment

جس *jassa u* (*jass*, مجسة *majassa*) to touch, feel, handle (ه s.th.); to palpate, examine by touch (ه s.th.); to test, sound, probe (ه s.th.); to try to gain information (ه about), try to find out (ه s.th.); to spy out (ه s.th.) | جس نبضه (*nabḍahū*) to feel s.o.'s pulse, (fig.) جس نبض الشىء to probe, sound out, try to find out s.th. **V** to try to gain information (ه about), try to find out (ه s.th.); to reconnoiter, scout, explore (ه s.th.); to be a spy, engage in espionage; to spy, pry, snoop (على on s.o.) | تجسس له اخبارا (*aḵbāran*) to gather information for s.o., spy for s.o. **VIII** to touch, feel, handle (ه s.th.); to spy out (ه s.th.)

جس *jass*: طرى الجس *ṭarīy al-j.* delicate to the touch, having a tender surface, fresh

جاسوس *jāsūs* pl. جواسيس *jawāsīs*[2] spy

جاسوسة *jāsūsa* woman spy

جاسوسى *jāsūsī* of espionage, spy- (in compounds)

جاسوسية *jāsūsīya* spying, espionage

جوسسة *jausasa* spying, espionage

مجس *majass* spot which one touches or feels; sense of touch | خشن المجس *ḵašin al-m.* coarse to the touch, having a rough surface

مجس *mijass* probe (*med.*)

تجسس *tajassus* spying, espionage

تجسسى *tajassusī* espionage (in compounds), contributing to or caused by spying

جاسئ *jāsiʾ* hard, rough, rugged

جسد **II** to make corporeal, invest with a

body, embody, incarnate (ه s.th.), give concrete form (ه to s.th.); to render or represent in corporeal form (ه s.th.); to concretize (ه s.th.); to represent (ه a role or character); to personify (ه s.th.) **V** to become corporeal, assume concrete form, materialize; to assume a visible shape (فى in); to be personified; to become incarnate (*Chr.*); to become three-dimensional

جسد *jasad* pl. اجساد *ajsād* body | عيد الجسد *ʿīd al-j.* and خميس الجسد Corpus Christi Day (*Chr.*); جسد الجريمة corpus delicti

جسدى *jasadī* bodily, fleshly, carnal

جسدانى *jusdānī* bodily

تجسد *tajassud* materialization; incarnation (*Chr.*)

مجسد *mujassad* embodied, corporified

متجسد *mutajassid* corporeal; incarnate (*Chr.*)

جسر *jasara* *u* to span, cross, traverse (ه s.th.); (جسارة *jasāra*, جسور *jusūr*) to venture, risk (على s.th.), have the courage (على to do s.th.) **II** to build a dam or dike; to embolden, encourage (ه s.o., على to do s.th.) **VI** to dare, venture, risk (على s.th.), have the audacity (على to do s.th.); to be bold, forward, insolent, impudent (على with s.o.) **VIII** to span, cross, traverse (ه s.th.)

جسر *jisr* pl. اجسر *ajsur*, جسور *jusūr* bridge; dam, dike, embankment, levee; — (pl. جسورة *jusūra*) beam, girder; axle, axletree | جسر متحرك (*mutaḥarrik*) movable bridge; جسر معلق (*muʿallaq*) suspension bridge; جسر عائم pontoon bridge, floating bridge; جسر قلاب (*qallāb*) bascule bridge, drawbridge; جسر جوى (*jawwī*) airlift

جسور *jasūr* bold, daring; forward, insolent, impudent

جسارة *jasāra* boldness, recklessness, intrepidity; forwardness, insolence

تجاسر *tajāsur* boldness, recklessness, intrepidity; forwardness, insolence

متجاسر *mutajāsir* bold, daring; forward, insolent, impudent

جصطن see جسطن

جسم *jasuma* *u* (جسامة *jasāma*) to be great, big, large, bulky, huge, immense **II** to make corporeal, invest with a body (ه s.th.), give (ه s.th.) shape or form; to materialize (ه s.th.); to cause to stand out, bring out (ه s.th.); to embody, cause to appear clearly and palpably, make obviously recognizable (ه a fact; *Tun.*); to enlarge, magnify (ه s.th.; e.g., microscope); to make big, bulky, huge (ه s.th.); to play up, exaggerate (ه s.th.) **V** to become corporeal, become embodied; to materialize; to assume a form, take shape, become tangible or concrete; to be materialized; to become big, large, huge, increase in volume, grow in size

جسم *jism* pl. اجسام *ajsām*, جسوم *jusūm* body (also ○ of an automobile); substance, matter; mass; form, shape

جسمى *jismī* bodily, physical; substantial, material

جسيم *jasīm* pl. جسام *jisām* great, big, large; voluminous, bulky, huge; vast, immense; stout, corpulent; weighty, most significant, momentous, prodigious; gross, grave (offense) | اهمال جسيم (*ihmāl*) gross negligence (*jur.*)

جسيم *jusaim* pl. *-āt* particle (*phys.*); corpuscle (*biol.*)

اجسم *ajsam*[2] more voluminous, larger; stouter, more corpulent

جسامة *jasāma* size, volume; stoutness, corpulence

جسمان *jusmān* body, mass

جسمانى *jusmānī* bodily, physical, corporal | التأديب الجسمانى corporal punishment

تجسيم *tajsīm* embodiment; relief; enlargement, magnification, magnifying power

مجسم *mujassam* bodily, corporeal; (*math.*) body; three-dimensional; tangible, material, concrete; raised, relieflike, standing out in relief (e.g., خريطة مجسمة relief map); relief; enlarged, magnified | فلم مجسم (*film*) three-dimensional (stereoscopic) film, 3-D motion picture; الهندسة المجسمة (*handasa*) stereometry

جسمانية *jasmānīya*² Gethsemane

(جسو) جسا *jasā u* to become hard, solid

جش *jašša u* (*jašš*) to grind, crush, bruise, grate (ه s.th.)

جشة *jušša* hoarseness, huskiness, raucity (of the voice)

جشيش *jašīš* ground, grated, crushed

اجش *ajašš*², f. جشاء *jaššā'*² hoarse, husky, raucous (voice)

جشأ II and V to belch, burp

جشاء *jušā'* and جشأة *juš'a* belch(ing), burp(ing)

جشار *jušār* livestock

جشطلتى (G.) *geštaltī*: علم النفس الجشطلتى Gestalt psychology

جشع *jašiʿa a* (*jašaʿ*) and V to be covetous, greedy

جشع *jašaʿ* greed, avidity, inordinate desire

جشع *jašiʿ* greedy, covetous

جشم *jašima a* (*jašm*, جشامة *jašāma*) to take upon o.s. (ه some hardship) II to make (ه s.o.) suffer or undergo (ه s.th.); to impose (ه ه on s.o. s.th. difficult), burden (ه ه s.o. with s.th.) V to take upon o.s., suffer, undergo (ه s.th., e.g., hardships)

جشنى (*eg.*, cf.ششنى *šišnī*) sample, specimen; sampling

جص II to plaster, whitewash (ه s.th.)

جص *jiṣṣ* gypsum; plaster of Paris

جصاص pl. *-ūn* plasterer

جصطن II *tajaṣṭana* to lounge, stretch lazily, loll

جعة *jiʿa* beer

جعب II to corrugate (ه s.th.)

جعبة *jaʿba* (now also pronounced *juʿba*) pl. جعاب *jiʿāb* quiver; tube, pipe; gun barrel; ○ cartridge pouch (*Syr.*) | جعبة اخبار *j. akbār* town gossip (person)

جعجع *jaʿjaʿa* (جعجعة *jaʿjaʿa*) to clap (mill); to gobble (turkey); to cause a rumbling noise; to bluster (in anger); to make a big fuss (about s.th.), make a noise; (*syr.*) to roar

جعجعة *jaʿjaʿa* clapping (of a mill); rumbling; rattle; bluster; noise

جعجاع *jaʿjāʿ* clamorous, boisterous, noisy; rumbling; blustering; (*syr.*) vociferous, clamorous; bawler, loud-mouthed person

جعد *jaʿuda u* (جعودة *juʿūda*, جعادة *jaʿāda*) and V to become curly, frizzed, kinky, curl (hair); to be wavy; to be creased; to be wrinkled II to curl, frizz (ه s.th.; the hair); to wave (ه s.th.; the hair); to crease, pleat, plait (ه cloth); to wrinkle (ه the skin)

جعد *jaʿd* (or جعد اليد *j. al-yad*, جعد الكف *j. al-kaff*) stingy, niggardly, tightfisted

جعدة *jaʿda* curl, lock, ringlet

جعدى *jaʿdī* and اجعد *ajʿad*² curly

جعيدى *gəʿēdī* (*eg.*) bum, loafer, good-for-nothing

تجاعيد *tajāʿīd*² wrinkles, lines (of the face)

تجعدات *tajaʿʿudāt* wrinkles

مجعد *mujaʿʿad* curled, frizzed; wavy; furrowed, creased; wrinkled

متجعد *mutajaʿʿid* curled, frizzed; wavy; furrowed, creased; wrinkled

جعدنة *jaʿdana* idle talk, gossip (*leb.*)

جعر *jaʿara a* (*jaʿr*) to drop its manure (animal)

ابو جعران *abū ji'rān*[2] scarabaeus; dung beetle; ام جعران *umm j.* Egyptian vulture (*zool.*)

ج ع س see ج

جعفر *ja'far* little river, creek

جعفرى *ja'farī*: المذهب الجعفرى the Shiah (*Ir.*)

ج ع ل abbreviation of الجمهورية العربية الليبية the Libyan Arab Republic

جعل *ja'ala a* (*ja'l*) to make (ه s.th.); to put, place, lay (ه s.th.); to create (ه s.th.); to effect, bring about (ه s.th.); to make (ه ه s.th. a rule, a principle, or the like, ه ه s.o., e.g., leader, king, etc.), appoint (ه ه s.o. to an office, rank, or the like); to fix, set (ه ه a sum, a price, at); to think, deem, believe (ه ب or ه ه s.o. to be ..., ه ه s.th. to be ...), take (ه ب or ه ه s.o. for, ه ه s.th. for); to represent (ه s.th., فى صورة as, or in the form of, s.th. else); to appoint, settle (ه ل s.th. for s.o., in s.o.'s favor); to give, grant, concede (ه ل s.th., an advantage, to s.o.), put s.o. (ل) in the way of s.th. (ه); to attribute (ه ل to s.o. s.th.), maintain that s.th. (ه) belongs to s.o. (ل); to entrust (ه الى s.th. to s.o.); to put, get (ه s.o., ه s.th., into a specific state or condition); (with foll. imperf.) to begin to, set out to| جعله يفعل to induce s.o. to do; to bring about that s.o. does s.th. or that s.th. happens; to make s.o. do s.th. (in a narrative); جعله بمنزلة (*bi-manzilati*) to place s.o. on equal footing with; جعله فى متناول يده (*fī mutanāwali yadihī*) to bring or put s.th. within s.o.'s reach III to seek to bribe, try to win (ه ب s.o. with s.th.)

جعل *ju'l* pl. اجعال *aj'āl* pay, wages; piece wages; reward, prize

جعلى *ju'lī*: اتفاق جعلى (*ittifāq*) piece-work contract

جعل *ju'al* pl. جعلان *ji'lān* dung beetle; scarabaeus

جعالة *ji'āla, ja'āla, ju'āla* pl. جعائل *ja'ā'il*[2] pay, wages; allowance; reward, prize; bribe

ج ع ى abbreviation of الجمهورية العربية اليمنية Yemen Arab Republic

جغرافيا *juġrāfiyā* and جغرافية *juġrāfīya* geography | جغرافية طبيعية (*ṭabī'īya*) physical geography; جغرافيا اقتصادية (*iqtiṣādīya*) economic geography

جغرافى *juġrāfī, jiġrāfī* geographical; geographer

جف *jaffa* (1st pers. perf. *jafaftu*) *i* (جفاف *jafāf*, جفوف *jufūf*) to dry, become dry; to dry out II to dry, make dry (ه s.th.)

جفاف *jafāf* dryness; desiccation; drying up; dullness | فى جفاف in a cold, unemotional tone, coldly

تجفاف *tijfāf* pl. تجافيف *tajāfīf*[2] protective armor

تجفيف *tajfīf* drying; desiccation; dehydration; drainage

جاف *jāff* dry | قلم حبرجاف (*qalam ḥibr*) ball-point pen

مجفف *mujaffif* dryer | مجفف الشعر *m. aš-ša'r* hair dryer

مجفف *mujaffaf* dried, desiccated, dehydrated; مجففات dehydrated foods

جفاء *jufā'* useless, vain, futile; a mere nothing, trifle | ذهب جفاء *ḏahaba jufā'an* to be in vain, be of no avail, pass uselessly; — see also جفو

جفت *jift* (*eg.*) forceps (esp. *med.*); tweezers, metal clamp (*med.*) | جفت شريان *j. širyān* arterial clamp

چفتشى (pronounced *šiftišī*; *eg.*) filigree

جفتلك *jiftlik* farm, country estate; government land (*Pal.*)

جفر *jafr*, علم الجفر *'ilm al-j.* divination, fortunetelling

جفرة *jufra* pl. جفر *jufar* pit, hole

جفل *jafala i u* (*jafl*, جفول *jufūl*) and **IV** to start, jump with fright; to shy (horse); to be startled **II** to start, rouse (ه s.th., ه s.o.); to scare away (ه s.o.)

جفل *jafl* and جفول *jufūl* fright, alarm; shying

چفلك (pronounced *šiflik*; *eg.*) = جفتلك

جفن *jafn* pl. جفون *jufūn*, اجفان *ajfān* eyelid

جفنة *jafna* pl. جفان *jifān*, جفنات *jafanāt* bowl; grapevine

(جفو) جفا *jafā u* (*jafw*, جفاء *jafā'*) to be rough, coarse; to treat (ه s.o.) roughly, harshly; to turn away (ه from), shun, avoid, flee (ه s.o.) **III** to treat (ه s.o.) roughly, rudely, harshly; to be cruel (ه to s.o.); to be cross (ه with s.o.); to shun, avoid (ه s.o.), keep aloof (ه from); to elude, flee (ه s.o.; slumber); to offend (ه against good taste, one's sense of honor, or the like) **VI** to withdraw (عن from), shun, avoid (ه s.o.); to loathe (عن s.o., s.th.), have an aversion (عن to); to display rude manners, act the ruffian

جفو *jafw* roughness, harshness

جفوة *jafwa* roughness; estrangement, alienation (between two people); disagreement, brusque or harsh attitude; tense or unfriendly relation (بين between); rupture

جفاء *jafā'* roughness, harshness; sternness; antipathy, aversion, distaste, loathing; estrangement, alienation; — see also جفأ

اجفى *ajfā* refraining even more (ل from), more averse (ل to s.th.)

جاف *jāfin* pl. جفاة *jufāh* harsh, rough, coarse; brutish, uncouth, rude

جاكت and جاكتة look up alphabetically

جكر **III** (*syr.*) to tease (ه s.o.)

جل[1] *jalla i* (جلال *jalāl*) to be great, lofty, exalted, illustrious, sublime; to be too great (عن for), be beyond s.th. (عن), be far above s.th. (عن) | جل عن الحصر (*'an il-ḥaṣr*) to be innumerable **II** to honor, dignify, exalt (ه s.o.); to cover (ه s.th., esp. the ground, as snow, plants, etc.); to envelop, wrap, drape, clothe; to border, edge (ه s.th., ب with) **IV** to honor, dignify, revere, venerate, esteem highly, exalt (ه s.o.); to deem too high, too exalted (عن for s.th.), consider far beyond s.th. (عن) **VI** to deem o.s. far above s.th. (عن) **X** to be great, exalted, sublime

جل *jall* great, outstanding; bulky

جل *jull* major portion, bulk, majority, main part | جله *julluhū* most of it; جل الامة *j. al-umma* the majority of the people; جل ما فيه its main contents; وجل ما يقال انه (*jullu*) that much, at least, can be said that ...

جلل *jalal* important, significant, momentous, weighty

جلى *jullā* pl. جلل *julal* matter of great importance, momentous undertaking, great feat, exploit

جلة *julla*, *jilla* droppings, dung (of animals); *julla* pl. جلل *julal* ball, bowl; marble; shot (= spherical weight); (cannon) ball; bomb | رمى الجلة *ramy al-j.* shot put(ting) (*athlet.*); — see also جليل

جليل *jalīl* pl. اجلاء *ajillā'*[2], اجلة *ajilla*, جلائل *jalā'il*[2], جلة *jilla* great, important, significant, weighty, momentous; lofty, exalted, sublime; revered, honorable, venerable; glorious, splendid

الجليل *al-jalīl* Galilee

جلال *jalāl* loftiness, sublimity, augustness; splendor, glory

جلالة *jalāla* loftiness, sublimity, augustness; majesty | صاحب (صاحبة) الجلالة His (Her) Majesty, جلالة الملك *j. al-malik* His Majesty, the King

اجل *ajall*[2] greater; more sublime; more splendid

مجلة *majalla* pl. *-āt* periodical; review, magazine | مجلة دورية (*daurīya*) periodical; مجلة اسبوعية (*usbūʿīya*) weekly magazine; مجلة شهرية (*šahrīya*) monthly publication; مجلة خاصة ب (*ḵāṣṣa*) professional journal for . . .; مجلة الاحكام lawbook, code; مجلة القوانين do.

تجلة *tajilla* and اجلال *ijlāl* honor, distinction; esteem, deference, respect; reverence

جل[2] *jull* rose

جلاب *julāb, jullāb* rose water; julep, refreshing drink made of mulberry and lemon juice

جلاتين (Fr. *gélatine*) *želātīn* jelly

جلاسيه (Fr. *glacé*) *glasēh* (*eg.*) kid leather

جلب[1] *jalaba i u* (*jalb*) to attract (ه s.th.); to bring along, bring to the spot (ه s.th.); to arraign (ه s.o.), present (ه the accused before the court); to fetch, get, bring (ه s.th., ل to s.o.); to import (ه goods); to bring about (ه a state, condition); to bring (ه harm, shame, etc., على upon s.o.); to gain, win, obtain (ه s.th.); to earn (ه s.th.) | جلبه معه to bring s.th. along, take s.th. along with o.s.; جلب النار لقرصه (*li-qurṣihī*) to secure advantages for o.s., feather one's nest; — (جلوب *julūb*) to scar over, heal (wound) **II** to shout, clamor; to be noisy, boisterous **IV** to earn, gain, acquire (ه s.th.); = **II**; **VII** pass. of **I** **VIII** to procure, bring, fetch, get (ه s.th.); to draw (ه on s.th.); to import (ه goods) **X** to import (ه goods); to fetch, summon, call in (ه s.o.); to attract, draw (ه, ه s.o., s.th.); to seek to attract or win (ه, ه s.o., s.th.); to get, procure (ه s.th.)

جلب *jalb* bringing, fetching; arraignment (of the accused before the court); procurement; acquisition; importation, import; causation, bringing on, bringing about

جلب *jalab* imported; foreign

جلب *jalab* and جلبة *jalaba* clamor; uproar, tumult, turmoil

جلبة *julba* scar

جليب *jalīb* imported, foreign; (pl. جلبى *jalbā*, جلباء *julabā'*[2]) foreign slave

جلاب *jallāb* attractive, captivating; importer, trader; see also alphabetically | جلاب العبيد slave trader

جلابية *gallābīya* (*eg.*) pl. *-āt*, جلاليب *galālīb*[2] galabia, a loose, shirtlike garment, the common dress of the male population in Egypt

جلباب see below under جلبب

اجلب *ajlab*[2] more attractive, more captivating

مجلبة *majlaba* pl. مجالب *majālib*[2] causative factor, motive, reason, cause, occasion

استجلاب *istijlāb* procurement, acquisition; importation, import; supply; attraction | استجلاب السائحين promotion of tourist traffic

جالب *jālib* causative factor, motive, reason, cause, occasion

مجلوب *majlūb* imported from a foreign country, exotic

جلاب[2] *julāb, jullāb* rose water; julep

جلبا[3] *jalabā* jalap (*bot.*)

جلبب **II** *tajalbaba* to clothe o.s. (ب with), be clothed, be clad (ب in a garment, also fig.)

جلباب *jilbāb* pl. جلابيب *jalābīb*[2] long, flowing outer garment, loose robe-like garment

جلبان *julubbān* chickling vetch, grass pea (Lathyrus sativus; *bot.*)

جلبوت (Engl. *jolly boat*) pl. جلابيت *jalābīt*[2] (*saud.-ar.*) flat fishing boat

جلتن II *tajaltana* to turn into gelatin

جلجل[1] *jaljala* to reverberate; to resound, ring out; to rattle; to shake (ه s.th.)

جلجل *juljul* pl. جلاجل *jalājil*[2] (little) bell, sleigh bell; cowbell; jingle

جلجلة *jaljala* sound of a bell; loud, shrill sound

مجلجل *mujaljil* shrill, piercing; ringing, resounding, reverberant

جلجلة[2] *juljula*, جبل الجلجلة *jabal al-j.* Golgotha

جلجلان[3] *juljulān*, *jiljilān* sesame

جلح *jaliḥa a* (*jalaḥ*) to be or become bald

اجلح *ajlaḥ*[2], f. جلحاء *jalḥā'*[2], pl. جلح *julḥ* bald-headed, bald

جلخ *jalaka a* and II to sharpen (ه s.th.); to whet, hone (ه a knife), strop (ه a razor); to stretch, extend, roll out (ه metal)

جلخ *jalk* grindstone, whetstone, hone

جلد *jalada i* (*jald*) to whip, flog, lash (ه s.o.); — *jalida a* to be frozen, freeze; — *jaluda u* to be tough, hardy, undismayed, steadfast, patient II to bind (ه a book); (to cause) to freeze (ه s.th.) III to fight (ه s.o.) IV to freeze; to be frozen, be covered with ice V to take heart; to show o.s. tough, hardy, robust; to resign o.s. to patience; to bear, suffer VI to engage in a sword fight

جلد *jald* flogging; — (pl. اجلاد *ajlād*) staunch, steadfast; strong, sturdy

جلد *jild* pl. جلود *julūd*, اجلاد *ajlād* skin, hide; leather | جلد سختيان (*suktiyān*) morocco; جلد لماع (*lammā'*) patent leather

جلدة *jilda* skin, hide; piece of leather; race | ابن جلدتنا *ibn jildatinā* our countryman, our fellow tribesman, pl. بنو جلدتنا *banū j.*; جلدة الرأس *j. ar-ra's* scalp; جلدة الساعة (*eg.*) leather wrist-watch strap

جلدى *jildī* dermal, cutaneous, skin (adj.) | امراض جلدية skin diseases

جليدة *julaida* pl. *-āt* membrane, pellicle; ○ film (*phot.*)

جلد *jalad* endurance; tolerance, indulgence; patience; firmament

جلدة *jalda* lash, stroke with a whip

جليد *jalīd* pl. جلداء *juladā'*[2] staunch, steadfast; strong, sturdy

جليد *jalīd* ice | جبل جليد *jabal j.* iceberg; قطعة من الجليد (*qiṭ'a*) ice floe

جليدى *jalīdī* icy, ice-covered, glacial, ice (adj.); snow-covered | العصر الجليدى (*'aṣr*) the Ice Age; بلورة جليدية (*ballōra*) ice crystal

جلود *jalūd* long-suffering, patient

جلاد *jallād* pl. *-ūn* leather merchant; executioner, hangman

جلادة *jalāda* and جلودة *julūda* endurance, patience

مجلدة *mijlada* whip, lash, scourge

تجليد *tajlīd* freezing; bookbinding

جلاد *jilād* fight, battle (against)

تجلد *tajallud* endurance, patience

مجلد *mujallid*: مجلد الكتب *m. al-kutub* bookbinder

مجلد *mujallad* frozen, icy, ice-covered; bound (book); (pl. *-āt*) volume (book)

مجالد *mujālid* pl. *-ūn* gladiator

متجلد *mutajallid* patient

جلوز *jillauz* (coll.; n. un. ة) hazelnut; hazel

جلس *jalasa i* (جلوس *julūs*) to sit down (الى with s.o., at a table, etc., على on a chair); to sit (الى with s.o., at a table, على on a chair) | جلس الى الرسام (*rassām*) to sit for a painter III to sit (ه with s.o., next to s.o., in s.o.'s company); to keep s.o. (ه) company IV to ask to sit down, make sit down, seat (ه s.o.)

جلسة *jalsa* (used as n. vic. of the verbal noun) sitting; (pl. *-āt*) seat (in an auditorium); session (of parliament, of a committee, of a court, etc); party, gathering, meeting | عقد جلسة *'aqada jalsatan* to convene a session; جلسة عامة (*'āmma*) open session; جلسة علنية (*'alanīya*) do.; جلسة عمل *j. 'amal* (pl. جلسات عمل) work session

جلسة *jilsa* manner of sitting

جليس *jalīs* pl. جلساء *julasā'*[2] participant in a social gathering; table companion; one with whom one sits together; جليسه the man who was at the party with him | جليس الاطفال babysitter

جليسة *jalīsa* lady companion; fem. of جليس

جلوس *julūs* sitting; sitting down; accession to the throne; pl. of جالس *jālis* sitting; sit down! (as command in school)

مجلس *majlis* pl. مجالس *majālis*[2] seat; session room, conference room; living room; party, gathering, meeting; social gathering; session, sitting; council meeting; council; concilium; collegium, college; board, committee, commission; administrative board; court, tribunal | في مجلسه in s.o.'s presence, in s.o.'s company; مجلس الآباء parents' council; مجلس التأديب and مجلس تأديبي disciplinary board; مجلس تأسيسي constituent assembly; مجلس آفاق regional court (*tribunal régional; Tun.*); مجلس الامة *m. al-umma* parliament; مجلس الامن *m. al-amn* the Security Council; مجلس البلدية *m. al-baladīya* and مجلس بلدى (*baladī*) local council, municipal council; مجلس الحرب *m. al-ḥarb* war council; مجلس حسبي (*ḥasbī*) probate court (for Muslims; *Eg.*); مجلس مختلط (*mukṭaliṭ*) mixed court (*eg.*); مجلس الدفاع defense council; مجلس الادارة *m. al-idāra* administrative board, committee of management, directorate; board of directors (of a corporation or bank); مجلس المديرية *m. al-mudīrīya* provincial council, provincial parliament (*Eg.*); مجلس الدولة *m. ad-daula* state council, council of state (*Eg.*); مجلس روحى (*rūḥī*) religious court, clerical court (of the Coptic Church); مجلس الشعب *m. aš-ša'b* people's chamber (name of the parliament in several Arab countries); مجلس شورى الدولة *m. šūrā d-daula* state council, council of state (formerly, *Eg.*); مجلس الشيوخ council of elders; senate (also of the U.S.A.); مجلس عدلى (*'adlī*) court, tribunal (*Syr.*); مجلس عرفى (or عسكرى) (*'urfī, 'askarī*) court-martial; مجلس عصبة الامم *m. 'uṣbat al-umam* Council of the League of Nations; مجلس العموم the House of Commons; مجلس الاعيان *m. al-a'yān* senate (*Jord.*); مجلس الاقتراع draft board, recruiting commission (*mil.*); مجلس قروى (*qarawī*) local council; مجلس اقتصادى (*iqtiṣādī*) economic council; مجلس قومى (*qaumī*) national assembly; مجلس قيادة الثورة *m. qiyādat aṯ-ṯaura* the Supreme Revolutionary Council; المجلس الكبير and المجلس الاكبر (*akbar*) the Grand Council (= *le Grand Conseil; Tun.*); مجلس اللوردات the House of Lords; مجلس النواب *m. an-nuwwāb* lower house, chamber of deputies; مجلس نيابي (*niyābī*) parliament; مجلس الجهة *m. al-jiha* approx.: provincial council (= *conseil de région; Tun.*); مجلس الوزراء *m. al-wuzarā'* cabinet, council of ministers

مجالسة *mujālasa* social intercourse

جالس *jālis* pl. جلوس *julūs*, جلاس *jullās* sitting; pl. جلاس participants in a social gathering

جالوص *jālūṣ* (*eg.*) large heap

جلط *jalaṭa* i (*jalṭ*) to chafe, gall, abrade (ه the skin); to shave (الرأس *ar-ra'sa* the head)

جلطة *julṭa* lump, clot | جلطة دموية (*damawīya*) blood clot, thrombus

جلف *jilf* pl. اجلاف *ajlāf* boorish, rude, uncivil; lout, uncivilized chap

جلفانومتر (Eg. spelling) *galvānomitr* galvanometer

جلفط *jalfaṭa* (جلفطة *jalfaṭa*) to calk (ه a ship)

جلفن *galfana* (*eg.*) to galvanize

جلفنة *galfana* galvanization

مجلفن *mugalfan* galvanized

جلاقة *julāqa*: جلاقة قروية (*qarawīya*) yokel, bumpkin

جلق *jilliq*² (and *jillaq*²) poetical designation for Damascus

جلم *jalama i* (*jalm*) to clip, shear off (ه s.th.)

جلم *jalam* pl. اجلام *ajlām* shears

ابو جلمبو *abū galambū* (*eg.*) a variety of crab

جلمد II *tajalmada* to be petrified

جلمد *jalmad* pl. جلامد *jalāmid*² and جلمود *julmūd* pl. جلاميد *jalāmīd*² rock, bolder

جلنار *jullanār* pomegranate blossom

(جلو and جلى) جلا *jalā u* to burnish, polish (ه s.th.); to clear (ه the view); to make clear, make plain, clarify, clear up (ه s.th.), throw light on (ه); to reveal, unveil, disclose (ه s.th.); to dislodge, oust, remove (ه عن or ه s.o. or s.th. from); to shine, be brilliant, distinguish o.s. (فى in s.th.); to be or become clear, evident, manifest; to pull out, move out (عن of a place), go away, depart (عن from a place), leave, quit, evacuate (عن a place); — جلى *jalā i* to polish, burnish (ه s.th.) **II** to elucidate, clear up, make clear (ه s.th.); to reveal, disclose, bring to light (عن or ه s.th.); to show, represent (ه s.o., ه s.th.); **IV** to remove, dislodge, oust, drive away (ه, ه s.o., s.th.); to evacuate (ه s.o., عن from); to move away, go away (عن from a place), leave (عن a place) **V** to become clear, evident, manifest; to reveal itself, be revealed; to appear, show, come to light, come out, manifest itself; to be manifested, be expressed, find expression **VII** to be clean or cleaned, be polished, be burnished; to be removed, be dislodged, be ousted; to move away (عن from a place), vacate, evacuate (عن a place); to be dispelled, vanish, go away, pass (crisis, difficulty, etc.); to disappear; to reveal itself, be revealed, be disclosed; to be unveiled (bride); to become manifest, manifest itself; to become clear or plain; to clear up and reveal (عن s.th.); to lead, come (عن to), end (عن in); to result (عن in) | ما ينجلى عنه الامر the outcome of the matter, what will come of it **VIII** to reveal, disclose (ه s.th.); to unveil (ها a bride); to regard, contemplate, observe (ه s.th.), look at (ه) **X** to seek to clarify (ه s.th.); to clarify, clear up (ه s.th.), throw light (ه on); to uncover, unearth, bring to light, find out, discover, detect (ه s.th.)

ابن جلا *ibn jalā* a famous, well-known man, a celebrity

جلى *jalīy* clear, plain, evident, patent, manifest, obvious, conspicuous; جليا *jalīyan* obviously, evidently

جلية *jalīya* pl. جلايا *jalāyā* sure thing, plain fact | جلية الامر *jalīyat al-amr* the true state of the affair

اجلى *ajlā* clearer, more obvious, more distinct

جلوة *jilwa* unveiling (of the bride) | ليلة الجلوة *lailat al-j.* wedding night; جلوة العريس preparation of the groom for a wedding (by men who bathe and clothe him, etc.)

جلاء *jalā'* clarification, elucidation; clarity, clearness, plainness, distinctness; departure, (e)migration (عن from); evacuation (عن of an area; *mil.*); withdrawal (of an army of occupation); بجلاء clearly, plainly, obviously, visibly

جليان *jalayān* vision, revelation, apocalypse (*Chr.*)

مجال *majālin* (pl. of مجلى *majlan*) manifestations

تجلية *tajliya* clarification; revelation (of a religion by a prophet) | تجلية الاهية (*ilāhīya*) divine revelation; theophany (*Chr.*)

اجلاء *ijlā'* evacuation, withdrawal (of troops, عن from) | اجلاء القواعد abandoning of bases (*mil.*)

تجل *tajallin* revelation, manifestation; Transfiguration (of Christ) | عيد التجلى *'īd at-t.* Transfiguration Day (*Chr.*)

اجتلاء *ijtilā'* revelation; unveiling; observation, contemplation

استجلاء *istijlā'* clarification, elucidation

جالية *jāliya* pl. *-āt*, جوال *jawālin* colony (of foreigners); colony of emigrants

المجلى *al-mujallī* the winner (in a race)

متجل *mutajallin* obvious, evident, manifest, patent

جلوكوز (Eg. spelling) *glukōz* glucose (*chem.*)

جلوكوما (Eg. spelling) *glūkōmā* glaucoma (*med.*)

جلون *galōn* pl. *-āt* gallon (*eg.*)

مجلون *mugalwan* galvanized (*eg.*)

جلى *jullā* see [1]جل

جليوتين *gilyotīn* guillotine (*eg.*)

[1]ج م abbreviation of جنيه مصرى Egyptian pound

[2]جم *jamma i u* (*jamm*) to gather; to collect one's thoughts, concentrate; to rest II and V to grow luxuriantly (plants) X to gather; to collect one's thoughts, concentrate; to rest, relax, seek recreation (من from); to be covered with luxuriant vegetation (ground) | استجم عافيته to recuperate

جم *jamm* abundant, plentiful; much, a great deal of; many, numerous; manifold, multiple; crowd, group of people | جم الاثر *j. al-aṯar* effective, efficacious; احبه حبا جما (*aḥabbahū ḥubban*) to be more than fond of; فوائد جمة numerous advantages, ample benefits; جم غفير large crowd, throng

جمام *jamām* rest, relaxation, recreation, gathering of new strength

مجم *majamm* place where s.th. gathers or flows together | مجم هذا الرأى ومستجمعه (*mustajma'uhū*) what this opinion amounts to

تجميم *tagmīm* (*eg.*) bobbed hairdo (of women)

استجمام *istijmām* collectedness; concentration; attentiveness, attentive reverence; rest, relaxation, recreation | استجمام العافية recuperation

الجمايك *al-jamāyik* Jamaica

جمبية *jambīya* see جنبية

جمباز, جمبازى see جنباز, جنبازى

جمبرى (from It. *gambero*) *gambarī*, جمرى *gammarī* (*eg.*) shrimps (*zool.*)

[1]جمجم *jamjama* (جمجمة *jamjama*), جمجم الكلام (*kalāma*) and II *tajamjama* to articulate indistinctly, stammer; to express o.s. poorly, speak incoherently; to mumble

[2]جمجمة *jumjuma* pl. جماجم *jamājim*[2] skull, cranium

جمجمى *jumjumī* cranial

جمح *jamaḥa a* (*jamḥ*, جماح *jimāḥ*, جموح *jumūḥ*) to bolt (horse); to be refractory, unruly, recalcitrant; to be defiant; to be capricious, whimsical; to run out on her husband, run away from home (wife), to soar (fantasy), run wild | جمح به خياله (*kayāluhū*) his imagination ran away with him

جماح *jimāḥ* recalcitrance, defiance; willfulness

جموح *jumūḥ* recalcitrance, defiance; willfulness

جموح *jamūḥ* headstrong, defiant, unruly, ungovernable

جامح *jāmiḥ* headstrong, defiant, unruly; indomitable, untamable

1جمد *jamada u*, *jamuda u* (*jamd*, جمود *jumūd*) to freeze; to congeal, harden, stiffen, be or become hard or solid, solidify; to coagulate, clot (blood); to be rigid; inflexible (in one's thinking); to stiffen, freeze, remain rigid (of a person; because of fear, surprise); to stagnate; to be apathetic, indolent, dull, indifferent | جمدت نفسه على to be indifferent toward, put up with, acquiesce in; جمدت يده (*yaduhū*) to be niggardly, tightfisted **II** to freeze, frost, congeal (ه s.th.); to solidify, coagulate, harden, stiffen (ه s.th.); to densify, make solid, compact (ه a soft or fluid mass or substance); to curdle (ه s.th.); to freeze (ه assets); to put on ice, postpone indefinitely (ه a suit, request) **V** to freeze, become frozen, turn into ice, freeze up, become icebound; to freeze to death; to congeal; to solidify; to be densified, compacted, become solid; to harden, set (e.g., cement); to coagulate, clot (blood) **VII** to freeze up, become icebound; to freeze, become frozen, turn to ice

جمد *jamd* freezing; congelation, solidification, coagulation | درجة الجمد *darajat al-j.* freezing point

جمد *jamad* ice

جماد *jamād* pl. *-āt* a solid; inorganic body; mineral; inanimate body, inanimate being; ○ neuter (*gram.*); — see also 2جمد

جمود *jumūd* frozen state; solid, compact state, compactness, solidity; rigor, rigidity, stiffness; inorganic state; hardening, induration; hardness, inflexibility; deadlock, standstill; inertia, inaction, inactivity; lethargy, apathy, passivity, indifference

جمودة *jumūda* solidity, hardness

تجميد *tajmīd* solidification, hardening; consolidation; reinforcement (of a foundation); freezing | تجميد الاسعار fixing of prices, freeze of prices (by a government); تجميد الاموال *t. al-amwāl* freezing of assets; تجميد الرئة *t. ar-ri'a* densification of pulmonary tissue, atelectasis (*med.*)

تجمد *tajammud* freezing; frost; congelation; solidification; coagulation

انجماد *injimād* freezing up or over, icing up; ice formation

جامد *jāmid* hard, solid; stiff; rigid; in a solid state (*phys.*); motionless; inanimate, inorganic; (*gram.*) defective; dry, dull (book, and the like); impervious to progress or innovation, ossified, ultraconservative; — pl. جوامد *jawāmid*[2] substances in a solid state (*phys.*); inanimate things, inorganic matter, minerals

متجمد *mutajammid* frozen, icy; stiff, congealed; coagulated

منجمد *munjamid* frozen, icy, ice (adj.); arctic | المحيط المنجمد (*muḥīṭ*) the Arctic Ocean

2جمادى *jumādā* name of the fifth and sixth months of the Muslim year (جمادى الاولى *j. l-ūlā* Jumada I and جمادى الآخرة *j. l-āḵira*, also جمادى الثانى *j. ṯ-ṯānī*, Jumada II); *colloq.* also جماد *jumād* (جماد الاول *j. al-awwal* and جماد الثانى; *lib.*)

1جمر **II** to roast (ه meat) **VIII** to burn incense

جمر *jamr* embers, live coal | كان على احر من الجمر (*aḥarra*) to be on tenterhooks; to be in greatest suspense, be dying with curiosity

جمرة *jamra* (n. un. of جمر) pl. *jamarāt* ember; live coal; smoldering embers; rankling resentment; carbuncle; anthrax (*med.*); pebble, small stone (in the stone-throwing ceremony at Minā near Mecca; also any one of the three piles of pebbles thus created)

جمار *jummār* palm pith, palm core (edible tuber growing at the upper end of the palm trunk)

مجمرة *mijmara* pl. مجامر *majāmir*² brazier; censer

جمرى² see جمبرى

جمرك *jumruk, gumruk* pl. جمارك *jamārik*², *gamārik*² customs; customhouse | رسم الجمرك *rasm al-g.* customs duty, tariff

جمركى *jumrukī, gumrukī* customs, tariff (used attributively); customs collector | اتحاد جمركى (*ittiḥād*) customs union; رسوم جمركية customs duties, tariffs

مجمرك *mujamrak, mugamrak* duty paid

جميز *jummaiz* (coll.; n. un. ة) sycamore (Ficus sycomorus; *bot.*)

جاموس look up alphabetically

جمش *jamaša i u* (*jamš*) to unhair (ه s.th.) II to make love, caress, pet

جمشت *jamašt* amethyst (*min.*)

ج م ع abbreviation of جمهورية مصر العربية Arab Republic of Egypt

جمع *jamaʿa a* (*jamʿ*) to gather (ه s.th.); to collect (ه e.g., money); to unite, combine, bring together (parts into a whole); to put together, join (ه things); to set, compose (ه type; *typ.*); to compile (ه a book); to summarize, sum up (ه s.th.); to rally, round up (هم people); to pile up, amass, accumulate (ه s.th.); to assemble (هم several persons); to convoke, convene, call (ه a meeting); to bring together (ب ه s.o. with others); to add (ه numbers), add up (ه a column); (*gram.*) to make plural, pluralize (ه a word); to unite, link, bring together (بين several things or persons); to combine (بين — و e.g., both strength and courage); to contain, hold, comprise (ه s.th.) | جمع اطراف الشىء (*aṭrāfa*) to summarize, sum up s.th.; to give a survey of s.th.; جمع البراعة من اطرافها (*barāʿata*) to be very efficient, do an excellent job, do superlatively good work; جمع شمل القطيع (*šamla l-q.*) to round up the herd; جمع القرآن to learn or know the entire Koran by heart; جمع كفه (*kaffahū*) to clench one's hand into a fist; يجمع الكتاب بين صفحاته (*ṣafaḥātihī*) the book contains, lists ...; يجمع بيت على بيوت (*yujmaʿu*) the plural of *bait* is *buyūt* II to pile up, amass, accumulate (ه s.th.); to rally, round up (ه s.th., هم s.o.); to pull together into unity (هم people); to assemble (ه the parts of a machine, an auto); to gather together, collect (ه e.g., information, reports, figures, from various sources); to compile (ه diverse materials in a book); to combine (ه a variety of things into a unit); to consolidate (also *econ.*, *fin.*), unite into a compact mass, combine into a single whole (ه several things) III to have sexual intercourse (ها with a woman) IV to agree (على on s.th., to do s.th.); to be agreed (على on); to decide unanimously (على on), resolve (على to do s.th.) | اجمعوا امرهم (*amrahum*) they came to terms, they made a joint decision V to gather; to assemble, congregate; to rally, band together, flock together (people); to pile up; to accumulate (also fig., e.g., signs, indications, mistakes); to unite, be combined (e.g., efforts); to gather into a mass, agglomerate; to cluster; to coagulate VIII to be close together; to come together, meet, join; to unite, combine (ب with); to assemble, meet, convene (an organization, a committee, etc.); to be or get together, have a meeting, interview or conference, hold talks (مع ,ب with s.o.), meet (مع ,ب s.o.); to concur (على in), agree, be agreed (على on s.th.) **X** to gather, collect (ه s.th.; also قواه *quwāhu* one's strength, افكاره *afkārahū* one's thoughts); to summarize, sum up (ه s.th.); to possess, combine (ه s.th.)

جمع *jam'* gathering; collection; combination; connection, coupling, joining; accumulation; (*arith.*) addition; union, merger, aggregation, integration (بين of); holding together (بين of divergent, separate things); — (pl. جموع *jumū'*) gathering, crowd, throng; assembly, meeting (of people); group; gang, troop; (*gram.*) plural | جمع الشمل *j. aš-šaml* union, integration; جمع التكسير the broken (= internal) plural, الجمع السالم the regular (= external) plural; اسم الجمع *ism al-j.* collective noun (*gram.*), see also اسم (under سم); جموع الشعب *j. aš-ša'b* masses of people, crowds

جمعى *jam'ī* collective, social, group (in compounds); common, joint, mutual | رقص جمعى (*raqṣ*) social dance, ball; الشعور الجمعى feeling of solidarity, sense of community, collective consciousness; العقل الجمعى (*'aql*) group mind; مقابلة جمعية group interview

جمع *jum'*, جمع الكف *j. al-kaff*, جمع اليد *j. al-yad* fist, clenched hand | بجمع يديه with clenched fists

جمعة *jum'a* pl. جمع *juma'*, -*āt* week; Friday | يوم الجمعة *yaum al-j.* Friday; جمعة الآلام Passion Week; الجمعة العظيمة and يوم الجمعة الحزينة Good Friday (*Chr.*)

جمعية *jam'īya* pl. -*āt* club, association, society; corporation, organization; assembly | جمعية الامم *j. al-umam* League of Nations; جمعية خيرية (*ḵairīya*) charitable organization; جمعية الاسعاف *j. al-is'āf* approx.: civil ambulance service; جمعية تشريعية (*tašrī'īya*) legislative assembly; جمعية عمومية (*'umūmīya*) and جمعية عامة (*'āmma*) general assembly; general meeting; plenum, plenary session; جمعية تعاونية (*ta'āwunīya*) cooperative; جمعية تجارية (*tijārīya*) business company or corporation

جميع *jamī'* (with foll. genitive) total; whole, entire; all; entirety; e.g., جميع الناس all men, all mankind; الجميع all people, everybody; the public at large; جميعا *jamī'an* in a body, altogether, one and all, all of them; entirely, wholly, totally

اجمع *ajma'*[2] pl. -*ūn*, f. جمعاء *jam'ā'*[2], pl. جمع *juma'*[2] entire, whole, all | العالم الاسلامى اجمع (*ajma'a*) the entire Islamic world; الدار جمعاء (*jam'ā'a*) the whole house; باجمعه *bi-ajma'ihī* in its entirety, to its full extent, completely, altogether; جاؤوا با جمعهم all of them came

جماع *jammā'* pl. -*ūn* typesetter | ○ جماع كهربائى (*kahrabā'ī*) storage battery

جماع *jummā'* aggregate; total, total amount

جماعة *jamā'a* pl. -*āt* group (of people); band, gang, party, troop; community; squad (*mil.*) | جماعات وافرادا *jamā'ātin wa-afrādan* in groups and individually

جماعى *jamā'ī* social, group (in compounds); common, joint, mutual; collective (as opposed to فردى *fardī* individual) | عمل جماعى (*'amal*) team work; علاج جماعى (*'ilāj*) group therapy; غناء جماعى (*ġinā'*) choral singing; لعب جماعى (*la'b*) party game

مجمع *majma'* pl. مجامع *majāmi'*[2] place where two or more things meet, place or point of union, junction; meeting, congregation, convention, assembly; (also مجمع علمى *m. 'ilmī*) academy (scientific); college (e.g., of ecclesiastical dignitaries); synod | مجمع بلدى (*baladī*) provincial synod (*Chr.*); مجمع اكليريكى (*iklīrīkī*) clerical synod (of the Coptic Church); المجمع المسكونى (*maskūnī*) the Ecumenical Council; اخذ بمجامع القلوب to win or captivate the hearts; بمجامع عينيه bi-m. ʻainaihi (to look at s.o.) with complete concentration, intently

مجمعى majmaʻī academy member, academician

تجميع tajmīʻ gathering, concentration, joining (of individuals); assembly, assemblage (of the parts of machinery); composition, bringing together; typesetting (*typ.*); compilation; combination; consolidation (*econ.*, *fin.*) | تجميع الارقام combination of numbers; dialing a number (telephone); تجميع السيارات *t. as-sayyārāt* automobile construction, assembly; تجميع الانتاج *t. al-intāj* combination, tie-in of different production branches (industry); آلة التجميع typesetting machine; خط التجميع *ḵaṭṭ at-t.* assembly line; assembly belt

جماع jimāʻ sexual intercourse; s.th. comprising or involving another thing or a number of things | الخمر جماع الاثم *al-ḵamr j. al-iṯm* wine involves sin, wine is the vessel of sin

اجماع ijmāʻ agreement, unanimity (also اجماع الرأى); unanimous resolution (على to do s.th.); (*Isl. Law*) consensus (of the authorities in a legal question; one of the four *uṣūl* of Islamic Law) | بالاجماع unanimously

اجماعى ijmāʻī based on general agreement, unanimous; collective, universal

تجمع tajammuʻ pl. -āt coming together, meeting; gathering; (*Alg.*) assembly; aggregation; aggregate; troop concentration; concourse, confluence of people, crowd; agglomeration; ○ agglutination (*chem.-med.*)

اجتماع ijtimāʻ pl. -āt meeting (ب with s.o.; of a corporate body; of parliament); get-together, gathering, assembly; reunion; rally; convention; conjunction, constellation (*astron.*); confluence (of rivers); life in a social group, community life, social life; الاجتماع human society | اجتماع الطرق *ijtimāʻ aṭ-ṭuruq* crossroads, intersection, junction; اجتماع عمل *i. ʻamal* work session; علم الاجتماع *ʻilm al-ijt.* sociology; علماء الاجتماع sociologists

اجتماعى ijtimāʻī community, group (used attributively); social; socialist(ic); sociological; (*Maḡr.*) concerning a corporation or business firm, corporate (in compounds); pl. اجتماعيات society news, society column (in newspapers) | وزارة الشئون الاجتماعية ministry for social affairs; الحالة الاجتماعية personal status; الخدمة الاجتماعية (*ḵidma*) social service, social work; المساواة الاجتماعية (*musāwāh*) social equality; الهيئة الاجتماعية (*hai'a*) human society; علم النفس الاجتماعى social psychology; رأس المال الاجتماعى corporate capital or assets

اجتماعية ijtimāʻīya socialism

جامع jāmiʻ comprehensive, extensive, broad, general, universal; — (pl. *-ūn*) collector; compiler (of a book); compositor, typesetter; (pl. جوامع *jawāmiʻ*[2]) mosque | جامع اعقاب cigaret-butt hoarder, butt rustler; مسجد جامع (*masjid*) great, central mosque where the public prayer is performed on Fridays; مصطلح جامع (*muṣṭalaḥ*) comprehensive term

جامعة jāmiʻa pl. -āt league, union, association; community; federation; religious community, communion; commonness, community of interests or purpose; university | ○ جامعة الكهرباء *j. al-kahrabā'* storage battery, accumulator; جامعة الامم *j. al-umam* League of Nations; الجامعة الاسلامية (*islāmīya*) Pan-Islamism; الجامعة العربية (*ʻarabīya*) and جامعة الدول العربية (*duwal*) the Arab League; جامعة شعبية (*šaʻbīya*) university extension, adult education courses, evening courses; جامعة رياضية (*riyāḍīya*) sport association

جامعى *jāmiʿī* academic, collegiate, university (adj.); university graduate | مدينة جامعية (*madīna*) student housing area

مجموع *majmūʿ* collected, gathered; totality, whole; total, sum (*arith.*) | الحروف المجموعة matter (*typ.*); مجموع أراضى القطر *m. arāḍī l-quṭr* the total area of the country; مجموع طوله *m. ṭūlihī* its total length; المجموع العصبى (*ʿaṣabī*) the nervous system

مجموعة *majmūʿa* pl. *-āt*, مجاميع *majāmīʿ*[2] collection (e.g., of works of art, of stamps, etc., also of stories); compilation, list; group (of persons belonging together, also, e.g., of trees, of islands, etc.); series (e.g. of articles in a newspaper); ○ battery (*el.*); alliance, league, bloc (e.g., of states); collective, collectivistic organization; aggregate (*techn.*); a self-contained unit, made up of several individual components; complex, block (of buildings); system; composition, matter (*typ.*) | مجموعة اجرامية (*ijrāmīya*) a group of criminals; مجموعة الدول الاوربية (*duwal*) the bloc of European countries; المجموعة الشمسية (*šamsīya*) the solar system; مجموعة صناعية (*ṣināʿīya*) syndicate; العمل فى مجموعة (*ʿamal*) group work; نظرية المجموعات *naẓarīyat al-m.* set theory (*math.*)

مجمع *mujammiʿ* collector (*techn.*); ○ storage battery, accumulator | مجمع ذرى (*ḏarrī*) atomic pile, nuclear reactor

مجمع *mujammaʿ* consolidated (*econ., fin.*); combined, etc.; (pl. *-āt*) collective combine, government controlled industrial enterprise in which several production branches are united (*Eg.*); government building housing offices of several agencies (*Eg.*); — وحدة مجمعة (*waḥda*) community center for social services (with a doctor, agricultural advisor, social worker, small workshops, etc., *Eg.*)

مجمع عليه *mujmaʿ ʿalaihi* (that which is) agreed upon, unanimous

مجتمع *mujtamiʿ*: pl. المجتمعون the assemblage, participants of a meeting

مجتمع *mujtamaʿ* pl. *-āt* gathering place, place of assembly; meeting place, rendezvous; assembly, gathering, meeting; society; human society; community, commune, collective | مجتمع طبقى (*ṭabaqī*) class society; مجتمع الاقطاع *m. al-iqṭāʿ* feudal society; مجتمع الاستهلاك consumer society

جمكية = جامكية look up alphabetically

[1]جمل *jamala u* (*jaml*) to sum up, summarize (ه s.th.); — *jamula u* (جمال *jamāl*) to be beautiful; to be handsome, pretty, comely, graceful; to be proper, suitable, appropriate (ب for s.o.), befit (ب s.o.) **II** to make beautiful, beautify, embellish, adorn (ه, ه s.o., s.th.) **III** to be polite, courteous, amiable (ه to s.o.) **IV** to sum, total, add (ه s.th.); to treat as a whole, mention collectively (ه s.th.); to sum up, summarize (ه s.th.); to act well, decently, be nice **V** to make o.s. pretty, adorn o.s. **VI** to be courteous, be friendly to one another

جملة *jumla* pl. جمل *jumal* totality, sum, whole; group, troop, body; crowd; wholesale; (*gram.*) sentence, clause; جملة *jumlatan* completely, wholly, on the whole, altogether, in general, at all | جملة واحدة *jumlatan wāḥidatan* all at once, at one swoop; جملة الكائنات everything in existence; كان من جملة اصحابه he was one of his companions, he belonged to his companions; قال فى جملة ما قاله (*jumlati*) among other things, he said ...; وجملة القول ان *wa-jumlatu l-qauli anna* or وجملة الامر ان in short ..., to sum up ..., briefly stated ...; جملة وتفصيلا (*jumlatan*) on the whole and in detail; على الجملة in short, in a word; seen as a whole; بالجملة wholly, on the whole, altogether, in general, at all; by wholesale (*com.*); جملة الاجرة المستحقة *j. al-ujra al-mustaḥiqqa* gross wages; تاجر الجملة wholesaler, wholesale dealer; سعر الجملة si'r al-j. wholesale price; جملة اسمية (ismīya) nominal clause; جملة فعلية (fi'līya) verbal clause; جملة اخبارية (ikbārīya) or جملة خبرية (kabarīya) declarative sentence (or clause); جملة انشائية (inšā'īya) exclamatory sentence; جملة حالية (ḥālīya) circumstantial clause; جملة شرطية (šarṭīya) conditional clause; جملة معترضة (mu'tariḍa) parenthetical clause

حساب الجمل ḥisāb al-jummal (or jumal) use of the letters of the alphabet according to their numerical value

جمال jamāl beauty | علم الجمال 'ilm al-j. and فلسفة الجمال falsafat al-j. aesthetics

جمالى jamālī aesthetic

جميل jamīl beautiful, graceful, lovely, comely, pretty, handsome; friendly act, favor, service, good turn; courtesy | معرفة الجميل, اعتراف بالجميل ma'rifat al-j. and عرفان بالجميل ('irfān) gratitude; نكران الجميل nukrān al-j. ingratitude; ناكر الجميل ungrateful; حفظ له جميلا (ḥafiẓa) to keep s.o. in fond remembrance, remember s.o. with gratitude

اجمل ajmal² more beautiful

تجميل tajmīl beautification, embellishment; cosmetics

تجميلى tajmīlī cosmetic

مجاملة mujāmala pl. -āt (act of) courtesy; civility, amiability; flattery; مجاملة mujāmalatan amicably, in a friendly way | زيارة مجاملة ziyārat m. courtesy call; قواعد المجاملات etiquette

اجمال ijmāl summation, summing up; summarization; اجمالا ijmālan on the whole, in general, generally speaking, as a general principle | اجمالا لذلك اقول to sum up, I (would) say ...; فى اجماله in its entirety, as a whole; بالاجمال and على الاجمال in general, on the whole, altogether; بوجه الاجمال bi-wajhi l-i. = اجمالا

اجمالى ijmālī comprehensive, summary, general, over-all, total, collective; the whole sum, total amount | تقرير اجمالى over-all report; غرامة اجمالية (ġarāma) collective penalty; نظرة اجمالية (naẓra) general view

مجمل mujmil pl. -ūn wholesaler, wholesale dealer

مجمل mujmal summary, résumé, synopsis, compendium; general concept; sum, total | بالمجمل by wholesale

²جمل jamal pl. جمال jimāl, اجمال ajmāl camel | جمل اليهود j. al-yahūd chameleon

جمال jammāl pl. -ūn camel driver

جملون jamalūn gable (arch.)

جمان jumān (coll.; n. un. ة) pearls

جمهر jamhara to gather, collect (ه, ه s.th., s.o.); to assemble (ه s.o.) II tajamhara to gather, flock together (crowd)

جمهرة jamhara and جمهرة الناس multitude, crowd, throng; the great mass, the populace; general public; a large number (من of people)

جمهور jumhūr pl. جماهير jamāhīr² multitude; crowd, throng; general public, public; الجماهير the masses, the people

جمهورى jumhūrī republican (adj. and n.); governmental, national (in a republic)

جمهورية jumhūrīya pl. -āt republic | الجمهورية العربية المتحدة (muttaḥida) the (former) United Arab Republic; جمهورية المانيا الاتحادية (ittiḥādīya) and جمهورية المانيا الفيدرالية (fidrālīya) the Federal Republic of Germany; الجمهورية الديموقراطية الالمانية (dīmūqrāṭīya) the German Democratic Republic; جمهورية شعبية (ša'bīya) people's republic; official names of Arab republics see under country names

جماهيرى jamāhīrī mass (in compounds); arising from or concerning the mass of the people

جماهيرية jamāhīrīya (Lib.) state representing the interests of the great masses, see ليبى lībī

تجمهر *tajamhur* gathering (of people); crowd, concourse; riotous assembly (*jur.*)

جن *janna u* (*jann*, جنون *junūn*) to cover, hide, conceal, veil (ه, على s.th.); to descend, fall, be or become dark (night); pass. *junna*: to be or become possessed, insane, mad, crazy | جن جنونه (*junūnuhū*) to get madly excited, become frantic **II** to craze, make crazy, drive insane, madden, enrage, infuriate (ه s.o.) **IV** to cover, veil, hide, conceal (ه s.th.); = **II**; **V** to go mad, become crazy **X** to be covered, veiled, concealed; to regard (ه s.o.) as crazy, think (ه s.o.) mad

جن *jinn* (coll.) jinn, demons (invisible beings, either harmful or helpful, that interfere with the lives of mortals)

جنى *jinnī* demonic; jinni, demon

جنية *jinnīya* female demon

جنة *janna* pl. *-āt*, جنان *jinān* garden; paradise | جنات النعيم paradise; ساكن الجنان inhabitant of paradise, deceased person, one of blessed memory; جنة عدن *j. ʿadn* the Garden of Eden

جنينة *junaina* pl. *-āt*, جنائن *janāʾin*² little garden; garden

جنائنى *janāʾinī* gardener

جنة *jinna* possession, obsession; mania, madness, insanity

جنة *junna* pl. جنن *junan* protection, shelter, shield

جنان *janān* pl. اجنان *ajnān* heart, soul

جنان *jannān* gardener

جنين *janīn* pl. اجنة *ajinna*, اجنن *ajnun* embryo, fetus; germ (in a seed, etc.)

جنون *junūn* possession, obsession; mania, madness, insanity, dementia; foolishness, folly; frenzy, rage, fury; ecstasy, rapture | الجنون فنون *al-j. funūn* madness has many varieties, manifests itself in many ways

جنونى *junūnī* crazy, insane, mad; frantic, frenzied

مجن *mijann* pl. مجان *majānn*² shield

مجنة *majanna* madness, insanity

جان *jānn* jinn, demons

مجنون *majnūn* pl. مجانين *majānīn*² possessed, obsessed; insane, mad; madman, maniac, lunatic; crazy, cracked; crackpot; foolish; fool

جنب *janaba u* to avert, ward off (ه ه from s.o. s.th.) **II** to keep away, avert, ward off (ه ه from s.o. s.th.), keep s.o. (ه) out of the way of (ه), spare (ه ه s.o. s.th.) **III** to be or walk by s.o.'s (ه) side; to run alongside of (ه), run parallel to (ه), skirt, flank (ه s.th.); to avoid (ه s.th.) **V** to avoid (ه s.th., ه s.o.); to keep away (ه, ه from), steer clear, get out of the way (ه, ه of) **VI** and **VIII** = **V**; **VIII** to be at the side of (ه), run side by side with (ه), run alongside of (ه), skirt, flank (ه s.th.)

جنب *janb* pl. جنوب *junūb*, اجناب *ajnāb* side; *janba* (prep.) beside, next to, near, at | جنبا الى جنب (also جنبا لجنب) side by side; بين جنبيه (*janbaihi*) inside (it), within; in his very soul, within his inner being; ما بين جنبيه (*baina janbaihi*) what it contains, comprises, its contents; على جنب aside, apart; ذات الجنب pleurisy, (also = ذات الرئة) pneumonia (*med.*)

جنبة *janba* pl. *janabāt* side; pl. جنبات fringe areas, remote parts (of a country or region), flanks | فى جنباته in it, within, inside; ضمه بين جنباته (*ḍammahū*) to comprise, hold, contain s.th.; جنبات الغرفة *j. al-ġurfa* the whole room; بين جنبات الغرفة in (the middle of) the room; زاخر الجنبات crammed, chock-full, brimful, filled to overflowing or bursting; فى جنبات البيت all over the house; فى جنبات المدينة throughout the whole town; اهتزت جنباته (*ihtazzat*) to be shaken in every joint or seam

جنبي *janbī* lateral, side (adj.)

جنبية and جمبية *jambīya* pl. *-āt*, جنابي *janābī* (*yem., saud.-ar.*) dagger

جنب *junub* in a state of major ritual impurity; not belonging to the tribe, not a kinsman | الجار الجنب the neighbor not belonging to the family

جناب *janāb* (title of respect) approx.: Right Honorable; جنابكم Your Honor; you (polite form)

جنابة *janāba* major ritual impurity (*Isl. Law*)

جناب *junāb* (= ذات الجنب) pleurisy

جنوب *janūb* south; (f.) south wind; جنوبا *janūban* southward, to the south | جنوب افريقيا *j. afrīqiyā* South Africa; جنوب شرق (*šarqī*) southeast; جنوب غربي (*ğarbī*) southwest

جنوبي *janūbī* southern; *janūbīya* (with foll. genit.) south of | جنوبي افريقيا South Africa

جانب *jānib* pl. جوانب *jawānib*[2] side; lateral portion; sidepiece; flank; wing; face (*geom.*); part, portion, partial amount; partial view, section (من of a scene, picture or panorama); quantity, amount; a certain number (من of), a few, some; pl. جوانب (with foll. genit.) the various aspects (of a problem or task, etc.) | من جانبه on his part; من جانب — من جانب آخر on the one hand — on the other hand; الى جانبه to him, to his address; at his (its) side, next to him (it); بجانبه beside him (it), next to him (it); الى جانب and بجانب side by side with; in addition to; apart from, aside from; وضعه جانبا to put s.th. aside; ودعه جانبا to leave s.th. aside, omit s.th.; فى جانب in comparison with, as compared with, as against; regarding, with regard to; ما بين جوانبهم their hearts; جانبا الفم *jānibā l-fam* the corners of the mouth; جانب من a considerable, or certain, degree of; a considerable amount of, a good deal of; جانب كبير من a great deal of, a large portion of; هو على جانب كبير من he is very ...; كان على جانب عظيم من الكرم (*karam*) to be very generous; على جانب عظيم من الاهمية (*ahammīya*) of great importance; على اعظم جانب من الخطورة *'alā a'ẓami jānibin min al-kuṭūra* of utmost importance, of greatest significance; فى كل جانب everywhere, on all sides; خفض له جانبه (*kafaḍa, jānibahū*) to show o.s. condescending, affable or gracious to s.o.; to meet s.o. on fair terms; امن جانبه *amina jānibahū* to be safe from s.o.; لم اعره جانب اهتمام (*u'irhu*) I paid not the least attention to him; خاف (رهب, هاب) جانبه (*jānibahū*) to fear s.o., be afraid of s.o.; ملك الجانب *milk al-j.* crown lands; جانب الميرى *j. al-mīrī* (*eg.*) fisc, treasury; لين الجانب *layyin al-j.* gentle; docile, tractable, compliant; لين الجانب *līn al-j.* gentleness; رحب الجوانب *raḥb al-j.* roomy; spacious, unconfined; رقيق الجانب friendly, amiable, gentle; مرهوب الجانب feared, dreaded; عزيز الجانب powerful, mighty, strong; عزة الجانب *'izzat al-j.* power; قوى الجانب *qawīy al-j.* mighty, influential; ملحوظ الجانب noticeable, conspicuous; مهيب الجانب *mahīb al-j.* dreaded, respected; فى جوانب الدار about the house, all over the house; often فى جوانبه = فيه; فى جوانب السوق in the midst of the market; جوانب من حياته fragments, episodes, single pages out of his life

جانبي *jānibī* lateral, side, by- (in compounds); marginal, happening on the margin, occurring as a side issue | نظرة جانبية (*naẓra*) side glance; تأثيرات جانبية side effects

اجنبي *ajnabī* foreign, alien; (pl. *-ūn*, اجانب *ajānib*[2]) foreigner, alien | البلاد الاجنبية the foreign countries, the outside world; فرقة الاجانب *firqat al-ajānib* the Foreign Legion

جنابية *gannābīya* pl. *-āt* (*eg.*) curb; embankment, levee; side channel, lateral (following a road or railroad tracks); bypass (of a lock or sluice)

تجنب *tajannub* avoidance

اجتناب *ijtināb* avoidance

مجنبة *mujanniba* flank, wing (of an army)

جمبرى see جنبرى

جنباز *jumbāz*, جمباز calisthenics; gymnastics

جنبازى *jumbāzī* (جمبازى) calisthenic(al), gymnastic | الالعاب الجمبازية gymnastic exercises, physical exercises

جنح *janaḥa* a (جنوح *junūḥ*) to incline, be inclined, tend (ل or الى to); to lean (ل or الى to or toward); to turn, go over (الى to), join (الى s.th.), associate o.s. (الى with); to strand (على or الى on a coast; ship); to diverge, deviate, depart (عن from); to turn away (عن from), break (عن with) **II** to provide (ه s.th.) with wings, lend wings (ه to s.th.) **IV** to incline, be inclined, tend (ل or الى to); to lean (ل or الى to or toward); to turn (ل or الى to s.th.); to strand (ship)

جنح *jinḥ* side

جنح *junḥ*, *jinḥ* darkness, gloom | فى جنح الليل (*j. il-lail*) in the dark of night, under cover of night; بين جنحى الكرى (*junḥay il-karā*) lit.: between the two halves of slumber, i.e., at night when everyone's asleep

جنحة *junḥa* pl. جنح *junaḥ* misdemeanor (*jur.*, less than a felony, جناية, and more than an infraction, مخالفة)

جناح *janāḥ* pl. اجنحة *ajniḥa*, اجنح *ajnuḥ* wing (of a bird, of an airplane, of a building, of an army); side; flank | انا فى جناحه I am under his protection; على جناح الاثير over the ether, by radio; على جناح السرعة (*j. as-sur'a*) with winged haste; جناح الهجوم wing forward (soccer); الجناح الايمن (*aiman*) outside right, الجناح الايسر (*aisar*) outward left (soccer)

جناح *junāḥ* misdemeanor (*jur.*); sin | لا جناح عليه ان (*junāḥa*) it won't be held against him if he ...; it won't do any harm if he ...

اجنح *ajnaḥ*[2] more inclined (الى to)

جنوح *janūḥ* inclined (الى to s.th.)

جنوح *junūḥ* inclination, leaning, bent, tendency (الى to)

جانح *jāniḥ* side, flank, wing

جانحة *jāniḥa* pl. جوانح *jawāniḥ*[2] rib; pl. also bosom, heart, soul | بين جوانحى in my bosom, at heart; طفرت جوانحها (*ṭafarat*) she became happily excited, she trembled with joy

مجنح *mujannaḥ* winged

جند **II** to draft, conscript, enlist, recruit (ه s.o.; *mil.*); to mobilize (ه an army, على against; also fig. = to induce to action, هم people) **V** to be drafted, be conscripted, be enlisted (for military service); to be mobilized, be set in action, be ready for action

جند *jund* m. and f., pl. جنود *junūd*, اجناد *ajnād* soldiers; army | جند الخلاص *j. al-kalāṣ* Salvation Army

جندى *jundī* pl. جنود *junūd* soldier; private (*Ir.*, *Leb.*, etc.; *mil.*) | جندى اول (*awwal*) private first class; lance corporal (*Jord.*, *Ir.*, *Leb.*, etc.; *mil.*); جندى ثان (*ṯānin*) private (*Jord.*; *mil.*); جندى مستجد (*mustajidd*) recruit (*mil.*); الجندى المجهول the Unknown Soldier

جندية *jundīya* military affairs; the army, the military; military service

تجنيد *tajnīd* draft, enlistment (*mil.*); recruitment; mobilization (of the army, also of workers, of energies) | التجنيد الاجبارى (*ijbārī*) military conscription

تجند *tajannud* military service

مجند *mujannad* enlisted; (pl. *-ūn*) conscript, draftee (*mil.*) | عسكرى مجند (*'askarī*) recruit (*Eg.*, *Syr.*; *mil.*)

جندارى *gindārī* standard-bearer, cornet (*Eg.*)

جندب *jundub* pl. جنادب *janādib*[2] grasshopper

[1]جندر *gandara* (*eg.*) to mangle (ه laundry)

جندرة *gandara* mangling (of laundry); press; ○ rotary press (*typ.*)

[2]جنداري look up alphabetically

جندرمة *žandarma* gendarmery

جندرمى *žandarmī* gendarme

جندفلى *ganduflī* (*eg.*) oysters

[1]جندل *jandala* to throw to the ground, bring down, fell (ه s.o.)

جندل *jandal* pl. جنادل *janādil*[2] stone; pl. جنادل cataract, waterfall (*eg.*)

[2]جندول *gundūl* (*eg.*) pl. جناديل *ganādīl*[2] gondola

جنرال *jenərāl, ginrāl* (*eg.*) pl. *-āt* general (military rank)

جنز II to say the burial prayers, conduct the funeral service (ه for the deceased; *Chr.*)

جنازة *jināza, janāza* pl. *-āt* جنائز *janā'iz*[2] bier; funeral procession

جناز *junnāz* pl. جنانيز *janānīz*[2] requiem, funeral rites, obsequies; funeral procession

جنزبيل *janzabīl* (= زنجبيل) ginger

[1]جنزر *janzara* (= زنجر) to be or become covered with verdigris

جنزار *jinzār* (= زنجار) verdigris

[2]جنزير *jinzīr* (= زنجير) pl. جنازير *janāzīr*[2] chain; track (of a caterpillar, of a tank, etc.); a linear measure (= 5 *qaṣaba* = 17.75 m; also = 20 m; *Eg.*) | طارة جنزير *ṭārat j.* track sprocket, sprocket wheel

مجنزر *mujanzar* track-laying (vehicle)

جنس II to make alike, make similar (ه s.th.); to assimilate, naturalize (ه s.o.); to class, classify, sort, categorize (ه s.th.) III to be akin, be related, similar (ه, ه to), be of the same kind or nature (ه as s.o., ه as s.th.), be like s.o. or s.th. (ه, ه), resemble (ه s.o., ه s.th.) V to have o.s. naturalized, acquire the citizenship (ب); to be naturalized VI to be akin, related, of the same kind or nature, homogeneous

جنس *jins* pl. اجناس *ajnās* kind, sort, variety, species, class, genus; category; sex (male, female); gender (*gram.*); race; nation | اسم الجنس *ism al-j.* (*gram.*) noun designating a kind, genus or species, generic term, see also اسم (under سم); الجنس البشرى (*bašarī*) the human race; ابناء جنسنا *abnā' jinsinā* our fellow tribesmen; هو مصرى الجنس he is Egyptian by nationality; الجنس اللطيف the fair sex; الجنس الخشن the strong sex; ○ جنس شكلى (*šaklī*) form class (*gram.*)

جنسى *jinsī* generic; sexual; racial | مشاكل جنسية sexual problems; فيلم جنسى sex film, porno

لاجنسى *lā-jinsī* asexual, sexless

جنسية *jinsīya* sexuality; (pl. *-āt*) nationality, citizenship | الجنسية المثلية (*miṯlīya*) homosexuality

تجنيس *tajnīs* naturalization; paronomasia (*rhet.*)

جناس *jinās* (*rhet.*) assonance, pun, paronomasia

مجانسة *mujānasa* relatedness, kinship, affinity; similarity, likeness, resemblance

تجنس *tajannus* acquisition of citizenship, naturalization

تجانس *tajānus* homogeneity, homogeneousness; likeness, similarity, resemblance

○ استجناس *istijnās* homosexuality

مجنس *mujannas* mongrel, bastard

مجانس *mujānis* similar, like, related; homogeneous

متجنس *mutajannis* naturalized

متجانس *mutajānis* akin, related, of the same kind or nature, homogeneous

جنطيانا (Lat. *Gentiana*) gentian (*eg.*)

[1]جنف VI to deviate (عن from); to incline, be inclined (الى or ل to s.th.)

[2]جنيف look up alphabetically

جنفاص *junfāṣ*, جنفيص *junfaiṣ* sackcloth, sacking

جنك *junk* pl. جنوك *junūk* harp

جنوا *janowā, jiniwā* Genoa (seaport in NW Italy)

جنى *janā i* (*jany*) to pick, gather, harvest, reap (ه s.th., also the fruits of one's work); to pocket, rake in, collect (ه s.th.); to derive (ه profit, من from); to secure, realize (ه profits, an advantage); to incur (ه evil, harm, punishment); to cause, provoke, bring about (ه s.th.); — (جناية *jināya*) to commit a crime, an outrage (على on); to offend, sin (على against); to commit, perpetrate (جناية, ذنبا *danban* a crime, an offense; على, less frequently الى, on or against); to inflict (ه some evil, على on s.o.); to harm (على s.o., s.th.) | ما جنت يداه (*yadāhu*) the crime that he has committed **V** to incriminate, accuse, charge with a crime (على s.o.), lay the blame (على on s.o.), blame (على s.o.); to act meanly **VIII** to gather, harvest (ه s.th.)

جنى *jany* harvest: reaping (fig.); — *janan* (coll.) fruits

جناية *jināya* pl. *-āt* perpetration of a crime; felony (*jur.*; in the strictly legal sense, more than a misdemeanor, جنحة, and an infraction, مخالفة), capital offense | محكمة الجنايات *maḥkamat al-j.* criminal court

جنائى *jinā'ī* criminal | محكمة جنائية (*maḥkama*) criminal court; القانون الجنائى criminal law, penal law

مجنى *majnan* pl. مجان *majānin* that which is picked or harvested, a crop; source of profit or advantage

تجن *tajannin* incrimination, accusation (على of s.o.); mean way of acting, low, underhand dealings

جان *jānin* pl. جناة *junāh* perpetrator (of a delict); delinquent, criminal

جانية *jāniya* criminal (fem.)

مجنى عليه *majnīy 'alaihi* harmed, injured; aggrieved party; victim of a crime

جنيف (Fr. *Genève*) *žənēf, jinēv* Geneva

جنيه (Engl. *guinea*) *ginēh*, also *gunaih* pl. *-āt* pound (*eg.*) | جنيه استرلينى (*istarlīnī*) pound sterling, English pound; جنيه مصرى Egyptian pound (abbreviation: ج م)

جهة see وجه

جهبذ *jahbad, jihbid*, جهبيذ *jihbīd* pl. جهابذة *jahābida* man endowed with a critical mind; great scholar; coryphaeus of science; bright, brilliant, intelligent

جهد *jahada a* (*jahd*) to endeavor, strive, labor, take pains, put o.s. out; to overwork, overtax, fatigue, exhaust (ه s.o.) **III** to endeavor, strive; to fight (فى سبيل الشىء for s.th.); to wage holy war against the infidels **IV** to strain, exert (ه s.th.); to tire, wear out, fatigue (ه s.o.), give trouble (ه to) | اجهد نفسه (*nafsahū*) to exert oneself, take great pains; to go to great lengths, go out of one's way (فى for or in s.th.); اجهد فكره فى (*fikrahū*) to concentrate on, put one's mind to, apply o.s. to **VIII** to put o.s. out (فى for s.th.), work hard; (*Isl. Law*) to formulate an independent judgment in a legal or theological question (based on the application of the 4 *uṣūl*; as opposed to *taqlīd*, q.v.)

جهد *jahd* pl. جهود *juhūd* strain; exertion; endeavor, attempt, effort; trouble, pains (فى on behalf or for the sake of s.th.); ○ voltage, tension (*el.*) | جهد جهده *jahada jahdahū*, also عمل (حاول) جهده to do (try) one's utmost, do (try) all in one's power, make every conceivable effort; بجهد جهيد *bi-jahdin jahīdin* with great difficulty, by dint of strenuous efforts;

جهد بعد جهد جهيد after a lot of trouble ○ جهد عال (*ʿālin*) high tension (*el.*)

جهد *juhd* strain, exertion; *juhda* (used prepositionally) to the limit of ... | جهد الطاقة *juhda ṭ-ṭāqa* as far as possible, as much as possible; جهد طاقته *j. ṭāqatihī* as much as he can, to the limit of his abilities; جهد امكانه *juhda imkānihī* do.; جهد ما *juhda mā* as much as, to the limits of what ...; جهدى *juhdī* as far as I can

جهيد *jahīd* see جهد *jahd*

جهاد *jihād* fight, battle; jihad, holy war (against the infidels, as a religious duty)

جهادى *jihādī* fighting, military

مجاهدة *mujāhada* fight, battle

اجهاد *ijhād* pl. *-āt* strain, stress, effort, exertion; overexertion, overstrain(ing)

اجتهاد *ijtihād* effort, exertion, endeavor, pains, trouble; application, industry, diligence; (*Isl. Law*) independent judgment in a legal or theological question, based on the interpretation and application of the 4 *uṣūl*, as opposed to *taqlīd*, q.v.; individual judgment

مجهود *majhūd* pl. *-āt* endeavor, effort, exertion, pains, trouble, work; ○ voltage, tension (*el.*) | بذل مجهوداته to make every effort, go to greatest lengths

مجاهد *mujāhid* pl. *-ūn* fighter, freedom fighter; warrior; sergeant (formerly, *Eg.*; *mil.*) | قدماء المجاهدين *qudamā' al-m.* (*Alg.*) veterans

مجهد *mujhid* strenuous, exacting, trying, grueling; — *mujhad* overworked, exhausted

مجتهد *mujtahid* diligent, industrious; (pl. *-ūn*) mujtahid, a legist formulating independent decisions in legal or theological matters, based on the interpretation and application of the four *uṣūl*, as opposed to *muqallid*, q.v.

جهر *jahara a* (*jahr*, جهار *jihār*) to be brought to light, come out, show, appear; — to declare publicly, announce (ه or ب s.th.); to avow in public, proclaim (ب s.th.); to raise (ه the voice); — *jahura u* (جهارة *jahāra*) to be loud, be clearly audible (voice) **III** to declare or say openly, voice, utter, express frankly (ب s.th.)

جهر *jahr* and جهار *jihār* publicness, publicity, notoriety; جهرا *jahran* and جهارا *jihāran* publicly, in public

جهرة *jahratan* openly, overtly, frankly, publicly

جهرى *jahrī* notorious, well-known, public

جهير *jahīr* loud (voice, shout)

اجهر *ajhar*² day-blind

اجهر *ajhar*² (elative) louder, more audible

جهورى *jahwarī* loud (voice)

مجهر *mijhar* loud-voiced

مجهر *mijhar* pl. مجاهر *majāhir*² microscope

مجهرى *mijharī* microscopic(al)

مجهار *mijhār* loud-voiced; ○ loudspeaker

مجاهرة *mujāhara* frankness, candor (of one's words)

مجهور *majhūr* loud and perceptible; voiced (*phon.*)

جهز *jahaza a* to finish off (على a wounded man), deliver the coup de grâce to (على) **II** to make ready (ه s.th.); to prepare (ه s.th., also a meal); to do up, refurbish (ه a room, a dwelling); to arrange (ه s.th.); to provide, supply (ه s.th.); to equip, fit out, furnish, supply, provide (ب ه or ه s.th. or s.o. with) **IV** to finish off (على a wounded man), deliver the coup de grâce to (على); to finish, ruin (على s.o.) **V** to be equipped, furnished, supplied, provided; to equip o.s.; to prepare o.s., get ready; to be ready, be prepared

جهاز *jihāz* (also pronounced *jahāz*) pl. *-āt*, اجهزة *ajhiza* equipment, appliances, outfit, gear, rig; trousseau; contrivance, gadget; implement, appliance, utensil; installation, apparatus (*techn.*); (pl. اجهزة) system, apparatus (*anat.*, also fig., = administrative apparatus, etc.); corporation, committee (*Tun.*) | جهاز لاسلكى (*lā-silkī*) wireless set, radio; جهاز راديو radio (receiving set); جهاز مستقبل (*mustaqbil*), جهاز الالتقاط, جهاز الاستقبال receiver, receiving set (radio); جهاز مذيع (*muḏī'*), جهاز الارسال *j. al-irsāl* transmitter (radio); جهاز تليفزيونى television set; جهاز الحفر *j. al-ḥafr* drilling rig; oil derrick; جهاز حكومى (*ḥukūmī*) government machine; جهاز دورى (*daurī*) circulatory system (*anat.*); جهاز ادارى (*idārī*) administrative apparatus; جهاز الدولة *j. ad-daula* state machinery; جهاز رادار radar installation; جهاز لتسجيل الاهتزازات الارضية or جهاز قياس الهزات الارضية (*hazzāt, arḍīya*) seismograph; جهاز سرى (*sirrī*) secret organization, underground organization; جهاز الاستماع sound locator; جهاز تشريعى legislative body; الجهاز العصبى (*'aṣabī*) the nervous system; جهاز التعليم educational system; جهاز كشف الكذب *j. kašf al-kiḏb* lie detector; جهاز المسح الرادارى (*j. al-masḥ*) radar measuring equipment; جهاز الهضم *j. al-haḍm* digestive apparatus; اجهزة الامن *a. al-amn* security apparatuses

تجهيز *tajhīz* equipment, furnishment; preparation; pl. تجهيزات equipment, gear

تجهيزى *tajhīzī* preparatory; (of a school) preparing for college

جاهز *jāhiz* ready, prepared; ready-made; equipped | البسة (ملابس, ملبوسات) جاهزة (*albisa*) ready-made clothes

مجهز *mujahhiz* pl. *-ūn* (*alg.*) supplier of equipment, technical installations

مجهز *mujahhaz* equipped, provided, furnished, supplied (ب with); armed (ب with guns; of a ship, tank, etc.); prepared (meal); refurbished (dwelling)

جهش IV to sob, break into sobs | اجهش بالبكاء (*bukā'*) to be on the verge of tears, struggle with tears; to break into tears

جهشة *jahša* (n. vic.) pl. *-āt* sob; outburst of tears

اجهاش *ijhāš* outburst of tears

جهض IV to give birth prematurely; to have a miscarriage (woman); to induce abortion | اجهضت نفسها (*nafsahā*) she induced an abortion

جهض *jihḍ* miscarried fetus

جهيض *jahīḍ* miscarried fetus

اجهاض *ijhāḍ* miscarriage, abortion; induced abortion

مجهض *mujhiḍ* abortifacient (drug)

جهل *jahila a* (*jahl*, جهالة *jahāla*) to be ignorant; not to know (ب or ه s.th., how to do s.th.); to be irrational, foolish; to behave foolishly (على toward) II to call (ه s.o.) stupid; to stupefy, make stupid (ه s.o.) VI to ignore (ه s.th.); to refuse to have anything to do (ه with), shut one's eyes (ه to), disregard (ه a fact); to affect ignorance, pretend to know nothing X to consider ignorant or stupid (ه s.o.)

جهل *jahl* and جهالة *jahāla* ignorance; folly, foolishness, stupidity; impetuosity, licentiousness, dissoluteness | عن جهل out of ignorance

جهول *jahūl* ignorant; foolish, stupid

مجهل *majhal* pl. مجاهل *majāhil*² unknown region, unexplored territory | مجاهل افريقيا unknown Africa

تجهيل *tajhīl* stultification

تجاهل *tajāhul* ignoring, disregard(ing)

جاهل *jāhil* pl. جهلة *jahala*, جهل *juhhal*, جهال *juhhāl*, جهلاء *juhalā'*² not knowing (ب s.th., how to do s.th.); ignorant, uneducated, illiterate; foolish; reckless, impetuous, uninhibited, unrestrained, without consideration

جاهلى *jāhilī* pagan, of or pertaining to pre-Islamic times | العصر الجاهلى (*ʿaṣr*) the pre-Islamic period

جاهلية *jāhilīya* state of ignorance; pre-Islamic paganism, pre-Islamic times; barbarism, licentiousness

مجهول *majhūl* unknown; anonymous (also مجهول الاسم *m. al-ism*); (pl. *-ūn*) an unknown (person); pl. مجاهيل *majāhīl*² unknown things | صيغة المجهول *ṣīğat al-m.* passive voice (*gram.*); شركة مجهولة الاسم *širka m. al-ism* (*Mor.*) joint-stock company (= Fr. *société anonyme*)

مجهولية *majhūlīya* being unknown, unknown nature

جهم *jahuma u* (جهامة *jahāma*, جهومة *juhūma*) to frown, glower **V** to frown, scowl, glower; to regard with displeasure (ه, ه or ل s.o. or s.th.), frown (ه or ل on); to eye gloomily, coolly, grimly (ه, ه or ل s.o., s.th.); to become sullen, gloomy (face)

جهم *jahm* sullen, glum, morose, gloomy (face)

جهام *jahām* clouds

جهامة *jahāma* and جهومة *juhūma* grim look, sullen expression; gloominess; brooding silence

جهنم *jahannam*² f. hell

جهنمى *jahannamī* hellish, infernal

جهوى see وجه

جو *jaww* pl. اجواء *ajwāʾ*, جواء *jiwāʾ* (pl. frequently with singular meaning) air; atmosphere (also fig.); sky; weather; sphere, milieu, environment; جوا *jawwan* by air; by telegraph, telegraphically | بريد الجو air mail; طبقات الجو *ṭabaqāt al-j.* air layers; فى جو ممطر (*mumṭir*) in rainy weather; صور مأخوذة جوا (*ṣuwar, jawwan*) aerial photographs

جوى *jawwī* air, aerial, aero- (in compounds); airy, atmospheric(al); weather (used attributively), meteorologic(al) | الضغط الجوى (*ḍağṭ*) atmospheric pressure; طبقات جوية (*ṭabaqāt*) air layers; اسطول جوى (*usṭūl*) air fleet; غارة جوية air raid; القوات الجوية (*qūwāt*) air force; الملاحة الجوية aviation; ميناء جوى and ميناء جوية (*mīnāʾ*) airport; ارصاد جوية meteorological observations; حجر جوى (*ḥajar*) meteorite; صورة جوية aerial photograph; التصوير الجوى aerial photography; منظر جوى (*manẓar*) aerial view

جوا (*colloq.*) *juwwā* in it, within, inside

جوانى *juwwānī* inner, inside, interior

جواتيمالا (Eg. spelling) *gwatimālā* Guatemala

جوافة *guwāfa* (*eg.*) guava (fruit); guava shrub

جوال (*eg.*) *guwāl* pl. *-āt* sack

جوان (Fr. *juin*) *žwān* (*Alg., Tun.*) June

جوانتى (It. *guanti; eg.*) gloves

¹جوب (Fr. *jupe*) and (*eg.*) جوبه *žūba* pl. *-āt* skirt

²(جوب) جاب *jāba u* (*jaub*, تجواب *tajwāb*) to travel, wander (ه through), traverse, roam, tour (ه s.th., e.g., foreign lands); to pierce, penetrate (ه s.th.), cut through (ه); to wander, cruise (ه about a place), cruise back and forth (ه through the streets) **III** to answer (ه s.o., على s.th.), reply, respond (ه to s.o., على to s.th.); to comply (ه with), accede (ه to) **IV** to answer (ه or الى s.o., عن or على a question), reply, respond (ه or الى to s.o., على to s.th.); to react positively (to a stimulus, invitation, challenge); to comply (ه with a request), accede, defer (ه to); to hear (ه s.o.), accede to the request or wishes of (ه); to fulfill, grant (ه a wish); to consent, assent, agree (الى to); to concur (الى in) | اجاب الى طلبه (*ṭalabihī*) to comply with s.o.'s request **VI** to reply to one

another; to echo (ه, ب from); to ring out (voices); to resound (noise); to be (mutually) corresponding, harmonize; to be favorable, propitious (مع to s.o.; situation); to adjust or attune oneself (مع to s.th.) **VII** to scatter, break up, pass over (clouds); to be dispelled, disappear, vanish (worries); to fade (darkness) **X** استجاب to hear, answer (ه a prayer), grant (ه a request); to comply with the request of (ل), accede or defer to the wishes of (ل); to react (ل to); to react positively (to a stimulus); to respond (ل to, ب with), listen, pay attention (ل to), show interest (ل in); to meet, answer (ل ب s.o. with), reply (ل ب to s.o. with or by doing s.th.); to resound, reverberate, re-echo; to resonate (ل or الى to s.th.), be in resonance with (*phys.*); — استجوب *istajwaba* to interrogate, examine, question (ه s.o.); to hear (ه the defendant or witness); to interpellate (ه s.o.; in parliament)

جوب *jaub* traversing, touring (of foreign countries); piercing, penetration

جوبة *jauba* pl. *-āt*, جوب *juwab* opening, gap; hole, pit

جواب *jawāb* pl. اجوبة *ajwiba* answer, reply; octave (to a given tone; *mus.*); (*eg.*; pronounced *gawāb* pl. *-āt*) letter, message | جواب الشرط *j. aš-šarṭ* main clause (conclusion) of a conditional sentence, apodosis

جوابى *jawābī* answering (used attributively) | الفعل الجوابى (*fiʿl*) the verb in the apodosis of a conditional sentence

جواب *jawwāb* traverser (of foreign countries); s.o. constantly under way, travelling through the world, globe-trotter; traveler, explorer

تجواب *tajwāb* traversing; wandering (through unknown country)

اجابة *ijāba* response, respondence; compliance; fulfillment, granting (of a request); accession; consent, assent; (pl. *-āt*) answer, reply | اجابة لطلبكم *ijābatan li-ṭalabikum* in compliance with your request; in answer to your request

تجاوب *tajāwub* agreement, conformity; harmony

استجابة *istijāba* hearing, answering (of a prayer); granting, fulfillment (of a request); response, reaction (to a stimulus); resonance, consonance (*phys.*) | استجابة ل *istijābatan li* in compliance with, in answer to, in deference to

استجواب *istijwāb* pl. *-āt* interrogation, questioning; hearing; interview; interpellation (in parliament)

متجاوب *mutajāwib* harmonious

مستجيب *mustajīb* hearing, answering, granting; reverberant, resonant, resonating; responsive, susceptible, impressible

جوت *jūt* and جوتا *jūtā* f. jute (*bot.*); jute fiber

(جوح) جاح *jāḥa u* (*jauḥ*), **IV** and **VIII** to annihilate, destroy, ruin; to devastate (ه a region) **VIII** to sweep away (ه, ه s.o., s.th.; storm, also fig.), put down, quell (ه, e.g., a riot); to strike, afflict, smite (ه a country or region; natural catastrophe, disaster)

اجاحة *ijāḥa* destruction, annihilation; crop damage, crop failure, bad harvest

اجتياح *ijtiyāḥ* destruction, annihilation; subdual, suppression

جائح *jā'iḥ* crushing, devastating; disastrous

جائحة *jā'iḥa* pl. جوائح *jawā'iḥ*² calamity, disaster, catastrophe; storm, tempest; epidemic; plague; crop damage

جوخ *jūḵ* pl. اجواخ *ajwāḵ* broadcloth

(جود) جاد *jāda u* (جودة *jūda*) to be or become good, become better, improve; — (*jūd*) to grant generously (ب s.th.), be so generous as to do s.th. (ب with verbal noun); to be liberal, openhanded (ب with s.th., على toward s.o.), bestow liberally (ب s.th., على upon s.o.), grant, give lavishly (ب of s.th., على to s.o.), shower (ب على s.o. with); to donate (ب a sum of money, etc.) | جاد بنفسه to sacrifice o.s.; to give up the ghost; جادت عيناه بالدمع (*'aināhu bi-d-dam'*) tears welled from his eyes; جادت السماء (heavens granted rain) it rained **II** to do well (ه s.th.); to make better, improve, better, ameliorate (ه s.th.); to recite (the Koran; cf. تجويد) **IV** to do well, do excellently (ه s.th.); to master (ه s.th.), be skilled, proficient (ه in), be an expert (ه at), be conversant (ه with an art); to ameliorate (ه s.th.); to accomplish or say good, excellent things; to achieve excellent results; to be excellent, outstanding, distinguish o.s. (e.g., as a poet) | اجاد لغة (*luğatan*) to master a language; اجاد العزف على البيانو (*'azfa*) to play the piano well **X** to think (ه s.th.) good or excellent, approve of (ه); to consider (ه s.th.) suitable for or appropriate to (ل)

جود *jūd* openhandedness, liberality, generosity

جود *jaud* heavy rains

جادة see under ²جد

جودة *jūda* goodness, excellence; good quality (of commodities, products)

جيد *jayyid* pl. جياد *jiyād* good, perfect, faultless; outstanding, excellent, first-rate; good (as an examination grade); جيدا *jayyidan* well, excellently; thoroughly | جيد جدا (*jiddan*) very good (also as an examination grade)

اجود *ajwad*² better

جواد *jawād* pl. اجواد *ajwād*, اجاود *ajāwid*², اجاويد *ajāwīd*², جود *jūd* openhanded, liberal, generous, magnanimous; *jawād* pl. جياد *jiyād*, اجياد *ajyād*, اجاويد *ajāwīd*² horse; race horse, racer; charger, steed | ابن الاجواد noble man

تجويد *tajwīd* art of reciting the Koran, Koran reading (in accordance with established rules of pronunciation and intonation)

اجادة *ijāda* good, excellent performance or accomplishment, etc.; improvement, amelioration

مجود *mujawwid* pl. *-ūn* Koran reciter

مجيد *mujīd* adept, efficient, proficient

جوذار *jaudār* see جاودار (alphabetically)

جودو *jūdō* judo

جار (جور) *jāra u* (*jaur*) to deviate, stray (عن from); to commit an outrage (على on), bear down (على upon), wrong, persecute, oppress, tyrannize (على s.o.); to encroach, make inroads (على on another's territory) | جارت به الطريق the way led him astray; he got off on the wrong path **III** to be the neighbor of s.o. (ه), live next door to (ه); to be adjacent, be next (ه to s.th.), adjoin (ه s.th.); to be in the immediate vicinity of (ه, ه), be close to (ه, ه); to border (ه on) **IV** to grant asylum or a sanctuary (ه to s.o.); to protect (ه s.o., من from), take (ه s.o.) under one's wing; to stand by s.o. (ه), aid (ه s.o.) **VI** to be neighbors; to be adjacent; to have a common border **X** to seek protection, seek refuge (ب with s.o., من from s.th.), appeal for aid (ه to s.o., من against s.th.)

جور *jaur* injustice; oppression, tyranny; outrage; wanton deviation (عن from)

جار *jār* pl. جيران *jīrān* neighbor; refugee; protégé, charge

جارة *jāra* pl. *-āt* neighboress

جيرة *jīra* neighborhood

جورة *jūra* pl. جور *juwar* pit, hole

جورى see alphabetically

جوار *jiwār* neighborhood, proximity; بجوار in the neighborhood of, in the vicinity of, near, close to | الى جواره beside him, at his side

مجاورة *mujāwara* neighborhood, proximity

اجارة *ijāra* protection, granting of asylum

تجاور *tajāwur* neighborhood (reciprocal); contiguity, relationship (of several things)

جائر *jā'ir* pl. جورة *jawara*, جارة *jāra* unjust, unfair; tyrannical, despotic; tyrant, oppressor, despot

مجاور *mujāwir* neighboring, adjacent; near, close by; (pl. *-ūn*) student (esp. of Al Azhar University; living in the vicinity of the Mosque)

مجير *mujīr* protector

متجاور *mutajāwir* having a common border; adjoining, adjacent, contiguous

جورب *jaurab* pl. جوارب *jawārib*[2] stocking; sock

جورجيا *jorjiyā* Georgia (republic of the U.S.S.R.)

جوری[1] *jūrī* damask rose (Rosa damascena, *bot.*); crimson

جوری[2] (Engl.) *jūrī* jury

جاز (جوز)[1] *jāza u* (جواز *jawāz*) to pass, come, travel (ه through); to walk through (ب or ه a place); to pass (ه an examination, a test); to be allowed, permitted, permissible; to be possible, conceivable; to work, succeed (عليه with s.o.; deceit, artifice) | جازت عليه الحيلة (*ḥīla*) the trick worked with him, he fell for the trick **II** to permit, allow (ه s.th.); to approve (ه of), sanction, warrant, authorize (ه s.th.) **III** to pass (ه s.th. or by s.th.), go or walk past s.th. (ه); to go beyond s.th. (ه), overstep, cross, leave behind (ه s.th.), also, e.g., جاوز الثلاثين من العمر (*'umr*) he is past thirty; to exceed, surpass (ه s.th.); to pass over s.th. (عن), disregard (عن s.th.), pay no attention (عن to); to let (عن s.th.) go unpunished; to give up, forgo, relinquish (عن s.th.) | جاوزت الساعة الواحدة (*as-sā'atu l-wāḥidata*) it is after one o'clock, past one o'clock **IV** to traverse, cross (ه s.th., الى on the way to); to permit, allow (ه ل to s.o. s.th.); to authorize (ه ل s.o. to do s.th., also ه ه); to license (ه s.th.); to approve, confirm, endorse (ه a decision, a judgment); to approve (ه of s.th.), sanction (ه s.th.) **V** to tolerate, suffer, bear; to speak metaphorically or in a figurative sense **VI** to pass (ه s.th. or by s.th.), go or walk past s.th. (ه); to go beyond s.th. (ه), overstep, cross, leave behind (ه s.th., also an age of life, as in III); to exceed, surpass (ه s.th., also على); to go too far, overstep all bounds, encroach, make inroads; to pass over s.th. (عن), disregard (عن s.th.), pay no attention (عن to); to skip over (عن s.th.); to give up, forgo, relinquish (ه s.th.); to refrain (عن from) **VIII** to pass, run, go (ه through), cut across (ه); to cross (ه a border, a street, a mountain range); to traverse (ه a country or sea); to cover (ه a distance); to pass (ه through the mind; said of ideas, thoughts); to go (ه through hard times or a crisis); to surmount, overcome (ه a crisis) | اجتاز العقبات (*'aqabāt*) to overcome obstacles **X** to deem permissible (ه s.th.); to ask permission

جوز *jauz* pl. اجواز *ajwāz* heart, center (of a desert, of a large area, etc.) | فى اجواز amid, in the middle of, in; فى اجواز الفضاء (*faḍā'*) in space

جواز *jawāz* permissibility, admissibility; lawfulness, legality; permission, (official) permit, license, authorization; possibility, conceivability; passing (of an examination); (pl. *-āt*) passport, also جواز السفر *j. as-safar*

مجاز *majāz* crossing; passage; corridor (*pol.-geogr.*); metaphor, figurative expression (*rhet.*); meaning extension of an Arabic word, use in a wider, figurative sense (as a means of rendering western terminology; *lex.*) | مجازا *majāzan*, على سبيل المجاز figuratively, metaphorically

مجازى *majāzī* figurative, metaphorical

اجازة *ijāza* pl. *-āt* permission, authorization; approval; license; = Fr. *licence* as an academic degree; permit; vacation, leave (of absence) | اجازة الحصر *i. al-ḥaṣr* grant of patent, issue of letters patent; patent; اجازة سوق *i. sauq* (*Ir.*), اجازة قيادة *i. qiyāda* (*Kuwait*) driver's license; اجازة قنصلية (*qunṣulīya*) exequatur of a consul (*dipl.*); اجازة مرضية (*maraḍīya*) sick leave; الاجازات المدرسية (*madrasīya*) school vacation; غائب بالاجازة on leave, on vacation

مجاوزة *mujāwaza* and تجاوز *tajāwuz* crossing; exceeding; overdraft, overdrawing (of an account); disregard (عن for); relinquishment (عن of s.th.)

تجوزا *tajawwuzan* in a figurative sense, metaphorically

اجتياز *ijtiyāz* traversing, crossing; passage; transit; covering (of a distance); passing (of an examination); surmounting (of difficulties)

جائز *jā'iz* permitted, lawful, legal; conceivable, thinkable

جائزة *jā'iza* pl. جوائز *jawā'iz*[2] prize, reward, premium | جائزة دراسية (*dirāsīya*) stipend, scholarship

مجاز *mujāz* licensed; (pl. *-ūn*) licentiate (as an academic title, = Fr. *licencié*; e.g., مجاز فى العلوم *licencié ès sciences*)

[2] □ جوز = زوج II to give in marriage

□ جوز *jauz* pl. اجواز *ajwāz* = زوج couple

□ مجوز (*syr.*; pronounced *məžwez*, < مزوج *muzwaj*) wind instrument with a double pipe, corresponding to the Egyptian *zummāra*)

[3] الجوزاء *al-jauzā'* Gemini (sign of the zodiac; *astron.*); the third month of the solar year (*Saudi Ar.*, cf. حمل *ḥamal*)

[4] جوز *jauz* (coll.; n. un. ة, pl. *-āt*) walnut | جوز الطيب *j. aṭ-ṭīb* nutmeg; جوز القىء *j. al-qai'* nux vomica; جوز الهند *j. al-hind*, جوز هندى (*hindī*) coconut; جوز القز *j. alqazz* cocoon, chrysalis of the silkworm

جوزة *gōza* (*eg.*) narghile

جوزى *jauzī* nut (used attributively and in compounds); nut-brown, hazel

[5] جاز look up alphabetically

جوزل *jauzal* pl. جوازل *jawāzil*[2] young pigeon

جاس (جوس) *jāsa u* to peer around, pry around, look around (خلال *kilāla* in); to search, investigate, explore (ه s.th.) VIII to search, investigate, explore (ه s.th.)

جوسق *jausaq* pl. جواسق *jawāsiq*[2] palace; manor, villa

جويطة *gawīṭa* pl. جوائط *gawā'iṭ*[2] (*eg.*) dowel, peg

جاع (جوع) *jā'a u* (*jau'*) to be hungry; to starve II to cause (ه s.o.) to starve, starve out, famish (ه s.o.) IV do.

جوع *jū'* hunger, starvation | مات جوعا to starve to death

جوعة *jau'a* (n. vic.) hunger

جوعان *jau'ān*[2], f. جوعى *jau'ā*, pl. جياع *jiyā'* hungry, starved, famished

مجاعة *majā'a* pl. *-āt* famine

جائع *jā'i'* pl. جياع *jiyā'*, جوع *juwwa'* hungry, starved, famished

تجويع *tajwī'* starving out

اجاعة *ijā'a* starving out

[1] جوف II to make hollow, hollow out (ه s.th.)

جوف *jauf* pl. اجواف *ajwāf* hollow, cavity; depression; interior, inside, center, heart; belly, abdomen; north (*mağr.*) | فى جوف inside, in the interior of, in the middle of; فى جوف الليل (*j. il-lail*) or جوف الليل (*jaufa*) in the middle of the night

جوفى *jaufī* inner, interior, inside; subterranean, underground, subsurface (of geological strata); northern (*maḡr.*) | مياه جوفية ground water

اجوف *ajwaf*[2], f. جوفاء *jaufā'*[2], pl. جوف *jūf* hollow; empty; vain, futile, inane, pointless, senseless

تجويف *tajwīf* pl. تجاويف *tajāwīf*[2] hollow, hollow space; cavity (also *anat.*) | تجويف البطن *t. al-baṭn* abdominal cavity (*anat.*); تجويف القلب *t. al-qalb* heart ventricle (*anat.*)

مجوف *mujawwaf* hollowed out, hollow

جوافة[2] look up alphabetically

جوق *jauq* pl. اجواق *ajwāq* and جوقة *jauqa* pl. *-āt* troop, group; theatrical troupe, operatic company; choir (*mus.*); orchestra, band (also جوقة موسيقية) | مدير الجوق *mudīr al-j.* conductor, bandleader, choir leader; جوقة الشرف *j. aš-šaraf* Legion of Honor

(جول)[1] جال *jāla u* (*jaul*, جولة *jaula*, تجوال *tajwāl*, جولان *jawalān*) to roam, rove, wander about; to move freely, be at home (فى in a field of learning), occupy o.s. (فى with); to be circulated, go the rounds; to pass (فى, ب through the mind) | جال برأسه and جال بباله to run through or go on in s.o.'s mind; to preoccupy s.o.; ما يجول فى خاطره (بخاطره) what he is preoccupied with, what is on his mind; جال الدمع فى عينيه (*dam'*, *'ainaihi*) his eyes swam in tears; جالت يده فى (*yaduhū*) he laid his hands on, he committed defalcations of **IV** to circulate, pass around (ه s.th.) | اجال الرأى فى (*ra'ya*) to weigh s.th. thoroughly, ponder s.th.; اجال النظر (*naẓara*) to let one's eyes wander about; to look around **V** to roam, rove, wander about, move around; to patrol, go the rounds; to cruise; to tour, travel from place to place, travel about

جولة *jaula* pl. *-āt* circuit, round; patrol; excursion, outing; tour; (round) trip; voyage, run (of a steamer); (round-trip) flight (of an airplane); round (in sports, also of discussions, negotiations)

جوال *jawwāl* wandering, migrant, itinerant, roving; cruising; traveling; ambulant; — (pl. ة) traveler, tourist; hiker; wanderer; see also alphabetically | بائع جوال peddler, hawker, wandering street merchant; جوال تجارى (*tijārī*) commercial traveler, traveling salesman; رام جوال *rāmin jawwāl* pl. رماة جوالة *rumāh jawwāla* rifleman (*mil.*; *Syr.*)

جوالة *jawwāla* one given to roaming or traveling; hiker; wanderer, wayfarer; ○ motorcycle; cruiser

تجوال *tajwāl* migration, wandering, roving, traveling; tour, circuit; walking tour, hike; nomadic life, nomadism | تجوال الشعوب migration of peoples

الجولان *al-jaulān* the Golan region | مرتفعات الجولان *murtafa'āt al-j.* the Golan Heights

جولان *jawalān* migration, wandering, roving, traveling; nomadic life, nomadism | جولان اليد *j. al-yad* embezzlement, defalcation

مجال *majāl* pl. *-āt* room, space (ل for s.th.); field, domain, sphere; scope, extent; reach; range; elbowroom, free scope; play, clearance; field (*magn.*) | ما ترك مجالا للشك (*šakk*) to admit of no doubt; لا مجال ل (*majāla*) there is no possibility of or for ..., it can't even be considered; لا مجال للطعن فيه (*majāla, ṭa'n*) (it is) incontestable; فى هذا المجال in this connection; فى المجال السياسى in the political sphere; فى مختلف المجالات in various fields; ودع المجال امامه فسيحا (*amāmahū*) to give s.o. a free hand, wide scope of action; مجال جوى (*jawwī*) air space; مجال حيوى (*ḥayawī*) lebensraum; مجال العمل *m. al-'amal* field of activity; مجال كهربائى (*kahrabā'ī*) electric field; مجال مغنطيسى (*maḡna-

ṭīsī) magnetic field; شدة المجال *šiddat al-m.* field intensity (*magn.*)

تجول *tajawwul* roaming, roving, wandering, migration; going out, moving about; patrol, round; (round) trip, tour; traveling | منع التجول *man' at-t.* and حظر التجول *ḥaẓr at-t.* barring of traffic, traffic ban; curfew

بائع جائل *bā'i' jā'il* pl. باعة جائلون peddler, hawker, street vendor

متجول *mutajawwil* wandering, migrant, roaming, roving, itinerant; ambulant; traveling; traveler | وكيل متجول traveling salesman; بياع متجول (*bayyā'*) peddler, hawker; قسيس متجول (*qissīs*) itinerant preacher

²جوال look up alphabetically

جولف (Eg. spelling) *golf* golf

جام look up alphabetically

¹جون *jūn* pl. اجوان *ajwān* gulf, inlet, bay

²جوان look up alphabetically

جونلة, جونلا, جونيلة (It. *gonnella*) *gonella* pl. *-āt* (woman's) skirt (*eg.*)

جاه look up alphabetically

جوهر II *tajauhara* to become substance

جوهر *jauhar* pl. جواهر *jawāhir*² intrinsic, essential nature, essence; content, substance (as opposed to form; *philos.*); matter, substance; atom; jewel, gem; pl. jewelry | الزيف والجوهر (*zaif*) the spurious and the genuine

جوهرة *jauhara* jewel, gem

جوهرى *jauharī* substantial; intrinsic, essential, inherent; fundamental, main, chief, principal; material; jeweler | غير جوهرى unessential

جوهرجى *jauharjī* and (*eg.*) جواهرجى *gawāhirgī* jeweler

مجوهر *mujauhar* decorated with jewels; pl. مجوهرات jewelry, trinkets; jewels, gems

¹جوى *jawiya a* (*jawan*) to be passionately stirred by love or grief

جوى *jawan* ardent love, passion

²جاوى look up alphabetically

جاودار = جويدار look up alphabetically

جويلية (Fr. *juillet*) *žwīlya* (*Alg.*, *Tun.*) July

جاء (جيء) *jā'a* يجيء *yajī'u* (مجيء *majī'*) to come (ه, ه to); to get (ه to), reach (ه a place); to arrive; to happen; to bring (ب s.th.; ب ه to s.o. s.th.); to bring forth, produce (ب s.th.); to set forth (ب s.th.); to do, perform; to commit, perpetrate (ه s.th.); to occur, be mentioned, be said (فى in an article, document or book); (with foll. imperf.) to be about or set out to do s.th. | جاء ذكره (*ḏikruhū*) the discussion turned to him, people started to talk about him; جاء فى جريدة الاهرام ان the newspaper "Al Ahram" reports that ...; جاء من باريس ان a report from Paris says that...; جاءت نتائجه مطابقة ل (*muṭābiqatan*) its results coincided with ...

جيئة *jī'a*, *jai'a* coming, arrival | جيئة وذهاب (*ḏahāb*) coming and going, ذهب جيئة وذهابا to pace the floor, walk up and down

مجيء *majī'* coming, arrival, advent

الجائيات *al-jā'iyāt* the things to come

¹جيب *jaib* pl. جيوب *juyūb* breast, bosom, heart; sine (*math.*); hole, hollow, cavity, excavation; pocket; purse | الجيب الخاص (*ḵāṣṣ*) the privy purse; تمام الجيب *tamām al-j.*, جيب التمام cosine (*math.*); ساعة الجيب pocket watch; مصروف الجيب pocket money; الجيوب الانفية (*anfīya*) the nasal sinuses (*anat.*); جيوب المقاومة *j. al-muqāwama* pockets of resistance (*mil.*); مسرح الجيب *masraḥ al j.* little theater; سيارة الجيب *sayyārat al-j.* small car, compact, minicar

جيبى *jaibī* pocket (adj.)

[2]جيپ *jīp*, جيب *jīb* and سيارة جيب *sayyārat j.* jeep

چيت (*ir.*) *čīt* a colorful cotton fabric, chintz

[1]جيد *jīd* pl. اجياد *ajyād*, جيود *juyūd* neck

[2]جيد *jayyid* see جود

[3]جياد, اجياد see جواد *jawād*

[1]جير *jairi* surely, truly, verily

[2]جير *jīr* lime

جيرى *jīrī* calcareous, lime (adj.)

جيار *jayyār* unslaked lime

جيارة *jayyāra* limekiln

[3]جير II to endorse (*fin.*)

جيرو (It. *giro*) endorsement (*fin.*)

[4]جيرة, جيران see جور

الجيزة *al-gīza* Giza (city in N Egypt); جيزة a brand of Egyptian cotton

(جيش) جاش *jāša i* (جيشان *jayašān*) to be excited, be agitated; to rage, storm; to boil, simmer II to levy troops, mobilize an army X to raise, mobilize (ه an army, also, e.g., انصارا *anṣāran* followers)

جيش *jaiš* pl. جيوش *juyūš* army; troops, armed forces | جيش الاحتلال occupation forces; جيش احتياطى army reserve; جيش مرابط (*murābiṭ*) territorial army; جيش الانقاذ *j. al-inqād* Salvation Army; جيش المساء *al-masā'* dusk, evening twilight

جياش *jayyāš* agitated, impassioned; excited, boiling up; ebullient; pleasurably excited, happily stimulated

جيشان *jayašān* excitement, agitation; raging

(جيف) جاف *jāfa i*, II and V to be putrid, stink (decaying cadaver)

جيفة *jīfa* pl. جيف *jiyaf*, اجياف *ajyāf* corpse, cadaver

چيكى *čīkī* Czech

جيل *jīl* pl. اجيال *ajyāl* race of men; coevals; generation; century; epoch, era | جيلا بعد جيل (*jīlan*) generation after generation

جيلاتى (It. *gelati*) *jēlātī* ice cream

جيم *jīm* name of the letter ج

جين (Fr. *gaine*) corselet, sheath corset (*eg.*)

جيوغرافيا *jiyoğrāfiyā* geography | الجيوغرافيا البشرية (*bašarīya*) anthropogeography

جيوغرافى *jiyoğrāfī* geographical

جيوفيزيا *jiyofīziyā* geophysics

جيوفيزيائى *jiyofīziyā'ī* geophysical; (pl. *-ūn*) geophysicist | السنة الجيوفيزيائية (*sana*) the geophysical year

جيوفيزيقى *jiyofīzīqī* geophysical

جيولوجيا *jiyolōjiyā* geology

جيولوجى *jiyolōjī* geologic(al); (pl. *-ūn*) geologist

ح

حاء *ḥā'* name of the letter ح

حاتى *ḥātī* (*eg.*) grillroom keeper

حاخام *ḥākām* rabbi | الحاخام الاكبر the chief rabbi

حاف *ḥāf* see [2]حفى

حوول see حول

حام *ḥām* Ham (son of Noah)

حامى *ḥāmī* Hamitic; (pl. *-ūn*) Hamite

حان and حانة see حين

حانبة (pronounced *ḥamba*) pl. حوانب *ḥawānib*[2] (formerly *Tun.*) hamba, palace gendarme of the Bey of Tunis

حانوت *ḥānūt* pl. حوانيت *ḥawānīt*[2] wineshop, tavern; bar, pub; shop

حانوتى *ḥānūtī* pl. *-īya* (*eg.*) shop keeper; undertaker, corpse washer

حب[1] *ḥabba i* (*ḥubb*) to love, like **II** to evoke (الى in s.o.) love or a liking (ه, ه for s.th. or s.o.), make (الى s.o.) love or like (ه, ه s.th. or s.o.); to endear (الى ه s.th. to s.o.), make (ه s.th.) dear, lovable, attractive (الى for s.o.), make (ه s.th.) palatable, acceptable (الى to s.o.); to urge (الى ه s.th. on s.o.), suggest (الى ه s.th. to s.o.) **IV** (حب *ḥubb*, محبة *maḥabba*) to love, like (ه, ه s.o., s.th.); to wish, want, or like, to do s.th. (ان) | احب ان *uḥibbu an* I should like to . . .; احب له ان to like about s.o. that he . . .; لا يحب الخير له (*kaira*) he doesn't want him to be happy, he grudges him everything **V** to show love, reveal one's affections (الى to s.o.); to endear o.s. (الى to s.o.), make o.s. popular, ingratiate o.s. (الى with s.o.); to court, woo (الى a woman) **VI** to love one another **X** to like (ه s.th.); to deem (ه s.th.) desirable, recommendable; to prefer (على ه s.th. to s.th. else)

حب *ḥubb* love; affection, attachment | حب الذات *ḥ. aḏ-ḏāt* self-love, amour-propre; حب الاستطلاع curiosity, inquisitiveness; حب الوطن *ḥ. al-waṭan* patriotism; حبا ل (*ḥubban*) out of love or affection for, out of friendship for; حبا فى in the desire to . . .

حبى *ḥubbī* friendly, amicable, loving; حبيا *ḥubbīyan* in an amicable manner, amicably; by fair means (*jur.*)

حب *ḥibb* pl. احباب *aḥbāb* darling, dear, dearest (one)

حباب *ḥabāb* aim, goal, end

حبيب *ḥabīb* pl. احباء *aḥibbā'*[2], احبة *aḥibba*, احباب *aḥbāb* beloved, sweetheart, lover; darling; dear one, friend; dear (الى to s.o.); popular; الاحباب the beloved ones, the dear ones

حبيبة *ḥabība* pl. *-āt*, حبائب *ḥabā'ib*[2] sweetheart, darling, beloved woman

احب *aḥabb*[2] dearer, more desirable, preferable (الى to s.o.)

حبذا *ḥabbaḏā* (with foll. nominative) how nice, how lovely is . . .! how good, excellent, perfect is . . .! | حبذا لو how nice it would be if . . .; حبذا الحال لو فعل *ḥ. l-ḥālu lau fa'ala* it would be nice, or he would do well, if he did it; يا حبذا الحال (*ḥālu*) that's just wonderful!

محبة *maḥabba* love; affection, attachment | محبة الوطن *m. al-waṭan* patriotism

تحبب *taḥabbub* courtship, wooing

تحابب *taḥābub* mutual love, concord, harmony

محبوب *maḥbūb* beloved; dear; lovable, desirable; popular; favorite; beloved one, lover; (pl. محابيب *maḥābīb*[2]) gold piece, sequin (in Ottoman times; *eg.*)

محبوبة *maḥbūba* sweetheart, darling, beloved woman

محبب *muḥabbab* agreeable, pleasant, desirable, lovable, dear (الى to s.o.); nice, likable

محب *muḥibb* pl. *-ūn* loving; lover; fancier, amateur, fan; friend | محب للناس philanthropic(al), affable; محبنا العزيز our dear friend; محبو الآثار friends of archeology; محب لذاته (*li-ḏātihi*) egoist

متحاب *mutaḥābb* loving one another, concordant

مستحب *mustaḥabb* (re)commendable, desirable (said of acts whose neglect is not punished by God, but whose performance is rewarded; *Isl. Law*); well-liked, popular

²حب II to produce seed, go to seed (plant); to bear seed (grain); to granulate, become granulated; to granulate (ه s.th.) IV to produce seed

حب *ḥabb* (coll.; n. un. ة) grains; seed; — pl. حبوب *ḥubūb* grain, cereals, corn; seed(s); grains, kernels; granules; pellets; pills, pastilles; berries; acne, pustules, pimples | حب العزيز chufa (Cyperus esculentus L.; *bot.*); حب الفقد *ḥ. al-faqad* chaste tree (Vitex agnus castus L.; *bot.*); حب الملوك croton seeds (seeds of Croton tiglium; *bot.*); (*maġr.*) cherries; حب الهال *ḥ. al-hāl* and حب الهان (حبهان) *ḥ. al-hān* cardamom (Amomum cardamomum L.; *bot.*); حب الغمام *ḥ. al-ġamām* hail, hailstones

حبة *ḥabba* (n. un.; see also حب *ḥabb*) pl. *-āt*, حبوب *ḥubūb* grain, granule; seed; (coffee) bean; kernel; pill, pastille; tablet, troche, lozenge (*med.*, *pharm.*); berry; pustule, pimple; triviality, trifle; a square measure (*Eg.*; = 58.345 m²); pl. حبات beads (of the rosary) | حبة شعير *ḥ. šaʿīr* a linear measure (*Eg.*; = 0.205 cm); حبة حلوة (*ḥulwa*) aniseed; حبة سوداء (*saudāʾ*) black caraway (Nigella sativa L.; *bot.*); حبات الرمال grains of sand; حبة رش *ḥ. rašš* grain of shot, pellet; حبة العين *ḥ. al-ʿain* eyeball; pupil (of the eye); حبة القلب *ḥ. al-qalb* dearest one, beloved, darling; حبة منع الحمل *ḥ. manʿ al-ḥaml* contraceptive pill, the pill; حبوب مخدرة (*mukaddira*) drugs, pills

حبب *ḥabab* blister

حبيبة *ḥubaiba* pl. *-āt* little grain, small kernel; small pimple or postule | دقيق الحبيبات fine-grained; خشن الحبيبات *kašin al-ḥ.* coarse-grained

حبيبي *ḥubaibī* granular, granulated | الرمد الحبيبي (*ramad*) trachoma (*med.*)

حبحب *ḥabḥab* (coll.) watermelon (*ḥij.*)

حباحب *ḥubāḥib* firefly, glowworm

حبذ II to approve, think well (ه of s.th.), commend (ه s.th.); to applaud, acclaim, cheer (ه s.o., ه s.th.)

حبذا see ¹حب

تحبيذ *taḥbīḏ* approval; acclamation, acclaim, applause, cheering

حبر *ḥabara u* (*ḥabr*) to gladden, make happy, delight (ه s.o.); — *ḥabira a* (حبور *ḥubūr*) to be glad, happy II to embellish, refine, make workmanlike (ه s.th.); to compose (ه s.th.) in elegant style; to write, compose (ه s.th.)

حبر *ḥibr* ink | ام الحبر *umm al-ḥ.* squid, cuttlefish; حبر على ورق (*waraq*) mere ink on paper, of no effect (e.g., an agreement, a treaty)

حبر *ḥabr*, *ḥibr* pl. احبار *aḥbār* a non-Muslim religious authority, learned man, scribe; bishop; rabbi | الحبر الاعظم the Pope; سفر الاحبار *sifr al-a.* Leviticus (Old Test.)

حبرى *ḥabrī* pontifical | قداس حبرى (*quddās*) pontifical mass (*Chr.*)

حبرية *ḥabrīya* office or dignity of a bishop, bishopric, pontificate

حبرة *ḥabara*, *ḥibara* pl. *-āt* silken shawl or wrap (worn in public by ladies)

حبار *ḥabār*, *ḥibār* pl. *-āt* mark, trace, (esp. of blows), welt, wale

حبور *ḥubūr* joy

حبار *ḥabbār* cuttlefish, squid (*zool.*)

حبارى *ḥubārā* pl. حباريات *ḥubārayāt* bustard (*zool.*)

يحبور *yaḥbūr* bustard chick (*zool.*)

محبرة *miḥbara*, *maḥbara* pl. محابر *maḥābir*² inkwell

حبس *ḥabasa i* (*ḥabs*) to obstruct, shut off, confine (ه, ه s.o., s.th.), block, bar, hold back, check (ه s.th. عن from; also tears, laughter, etc.); to withhold (ه عن from s.o. s.th.); to hold in custody, detain (ه s.o.); to apprehend, arrest, jail, imprison (ه s.o.); to keep, keep back, put aside, put away (ه على s.th. for); to tie up, invest inalienably (ه capital) | حبس نفسه على (nafsahū) to devote o.s. entirely to . . .; حبس يده عن (yadahū) to take (s.th.) out from under s.o.'s power; حبس عليه انفاسه (anfāsahū) to make s.o. catch his breath, take s.o.'s breath away; حبس مع الشغل ḥubisa maʿa š-šuḡl he was committed to prison under hard labor **II** to tie up inalienably (ه funds, على for, esp. for a pious purpose), make a religious bequest (ه, for the benefit of على) **VII** to be held back, be held up, stop, be interrupted, intermit; to restrain o.s., hold back **VIII** to block, obstruct, bar, confine (ه, ه s.o., s.th.); to detain, hold in custody (ه, ه s.o., s.th.); to hold back, retain, suppress (ه, ه s.o., s.th.); to be detained, held up; to be impeded, held back; to falter, break, fail (voice), stop (breath)

حبس *ḥabs* (act of) holding or keeping back, obstruction, check, repression; blocking off, barring, confinement; damming up, staving off; safekeeping, custody, retention; imprisonment, arrest, detention, jailing; (pl. حبوس *ḥubūs*) prison, jail | حبس احتياطى (*iḥtiyāṭī*) preventive custody, preventive detention (*jur.*); حبس انفرادى (*infirādī*) solitary confinement; حبس شديد penal servitude

حبس *ḥibs* pl. احباس *aḥbās* dam, weir, barrage

حبس *ḥubs, ḥubus* pl. احباس *aḥbās* (*Tun., Alg., Mor.* = *waqf*) inalienable property the yield of which is devoted to pious purposes, religious bequest, (*Fr. jur.*) "habous" | حبس عام (*ʿāmm*) public habous, حبس خاص (*ḵāṣṣ*) private habous; كان حبسا على (= كان وقفا على) to be entirely dependent on . . .

حبسة *ḥubsa* speech defect, impediment of speech; ○ aphasia (*psych.*)

حبيس *ḥabīs* blocked-off, shut-off, barred, confined, locked-up; secluded; bated (breath); choking (voice); restrained, barely audible (words); (pl. حبساء *ḥubasā'*[2]) hermit

حبوس *ḥabūs* (*Mor., Alg.*) habous = حبس *ḥubs, ḥubus*

محبس *maḥbas, maḥbis* pl. محابس *maḥābis*[2] place where s.th. is confined or locked up; jail, prison; (prison) cell

محبس *miḥbas* pl. محابس *maḥābis*[2] device for shutting off or blocking off; shutoff valve, tap (of a water pipe)

محبسة *maḥbasa* hermitage

انحباس *inḥibās* seclusion, confinement; stoppage, interruption; cessation

احتباس *iḥtibās* retention, restraint; inhibition, impediment, obstruction, stoppage | احتباس البول *iḥtibās al-baul* suppression of urine, ischuria

محبوس *maḥbūs* shut-off (from the outside world), isolated, secluded, confined, locked-up; imprisoned, captive; tied-up (funds); (pl. محابيس *maḥābīs*[2]) prisoner, prison inmate, convict

محبس *muḥabbis* donor of a habous (see حبس *ḥubs*)

المحبس عليه *al-muḥabbas ʿalaihi* beneficiary of a habous (see حبس *ḥubs*)

منحبس *munḥabis* secluded, shut-off

الحبش *al-ḥabaš* Abyssinia, Ethiopia; (pl. الاحباش *al-aḥbāš*) the Abyssinians, Ethiopians

الحبشة *al-ḥabaša* (and بلاد الحبشة) Abyssinia, Ethiopia

حبشى *ḥabašī* pl. احباش *aḥbāš* Abyssinian, Ethiopian; الحبشية the Ethiopian language

حبط *ḥabaṭa* i (حبوط *ḥubūṭ*) and *ḥabiṭa* a to come to nothing, fail, miscarry, go wrong; to be futile, be of no avail, be lost **IV** to frustrate, thwart, foil, defeat (ه s.th., ه على in s.th. s.o.; negotiations, efforts, an attempt, etc.)

حبط *ḥabaṭ* scar of a wound, wale, welt

حبوط *ḥubūṭ* futility, failure

احباط *iḥbāṭ* frustration, thwarting, foiling

حبق *ḥabaq* basil (*bot.*); (*eg.*) a variety of speedwell (Veronica anagallis aquatica L.)

حبك *ḥabaka i u* (*ḥabk*) to weave well and tight (ه s.th.); to braid, plait (ه hair), twist (ه a rope); to knit (ه stockings); to tighten, draw tight, make firm and solid (ه s.th.); to bind (ه a book); to contrive, devise (ه a plan or plot) **II** to plait, twist (ه s.th.); to tighten, make firm (ه s.th.); to interlace (ه s.th.) **VIII** to weave well and tight (ه s.th.); to be or become interlaced, interwoven, be arranged crosswise (like threads of a fabric)

حبك *ḥabk*: جيد الحبك *jayyid al-ḥ.* well and tightly woven; tight-fitting, well-made

حبكة *ḥabka* texture, structure; web of the plot, plot (of a drama, novel)

حبكة *ḥubka* pl. حبك *ḥubak* belt, girdle

حبك *ḥubuk*: حبك النجوم *ḥ. an-nujūm* the orbits of the celestial bodies

حباكة *ḥibāka* weaver's trade, weaving

محبوك *maḥbūk* tightly woven; tight, tightly drawn; well-knit, sturdy, firm, solid; solidly worked, well-made

¹حبل **VIII** to ensnare, catch in a snare (ه, ه s.o., s.th.)

حبل *ḥabl* pl. حبال *ḥibāl*, احبل *aḥbul*, حبول *ḥubūl*, احبال *aḥbāl* rope, cable, hawser; cord, string, thread; (pl. حبال *ḥibāl*) beam, ray (e.g., of the sun, of light), jet (e.g., of water); vein; sinew, tendon | حبل الوريد jugular vein; الحبل السرى (*surrī*) umbilical cord; الحبل الشوكى (*šaukī*) spine; حبال صوتية (*ṣautīya*) vocal cords; حبل المساكين ivy (*bot.*); حبال الماء jets of water; القى (اطلق) الحبل على الغارب *alqā* (*aṭlaqa*) *l-ḥabla ʿalā l-ġārib* to let things go, slacken the reins, give a free hand, impose no restraint; ارتخاء الحبل slackening of the reins, yielding; relenting; اضطرب حبله *iḍṭaraba ḥabluhū* to get into a state of disorder, of disorganization, of disintegration, get out of control; لعب على الحبلين (*laʿiba, ḥablain*) to play a double game, work both sides of the street

احبولة *uḥbūla* pl. احابيل *aḥābīl*² snare, net; rope with a noose; pl. احابيل tricks, wiles, artifices, stratagems (in order to get s.th.)

حبالة *ḥibāla* pl. حبائل *ḥabāʾil*² snare, net

حابل *ḥābil*: اختلط الحابل بالنابل (*iḵtalaṭa*) everything became confused, got into a state of utter confusion; حابلهم ونابلهم all together, all in a medley

²حبل *ḥabila a* (*ḥabal*) to be or become pregnant, conceive **II** and **IV** to make pregnant (ها a woman)

حبل *ḥabal* conception; pregnancy

حبلى *ḥublā* pl. حبالى *ḥabālā* and حبلانة *ḥablāna* pregnant

حبن *ḥaban* dropsy

حبهان (حب الهان *ḥabb al-hān*) cardamom (Amomum cardamomum L.; *bot.*)

حبا (حبو) *ḥabā u* (*ḥabw*) to crawl, creep; to present (ه ه s.o. with s.th.), give, award (ه ه to s.o. s.th.) **III** to be obliging (ه to s.o.), show one's good will (ه toward s.o.); to favor (ه s.o.); to side (ه with s.o.), be partial (ه to s.o.); to show respect, deference (ه to s.o.) **VIII** to sit with one's legs drawn up and wrapped in one's garment

حبوة *ḥibwa, ḥubwa, ḥabwa* gift, present

حباء *ḥibāʾ* gift, present

محاباة *muḥābāh* obligingness, complaisance, courtesy; favor(ing), favoritism, partiality; protection

حت *ḥatta u* (*ḥatt*) to rub off, scrape off, scratch off (ه s.th.)

حتة *ḥitta* pl. حتت *ḥitat* (*eg.*) piece, bit, morsel

حتات *ḥutāt* scraps; morsels, crumbs

تحات *taḥātt* corrosion; erosion (*geol.*)

حتد *ḥatida a* (*ḥatad*) to be of pure origin

محتد *maḥtid* descent, origin, lineage

حترة *ḥutra* small piece, bit, trifle

حتار *ḥitār* pl. حتر *ḥutur* border, edge, fringe, surroundings, vicinity

حتف *ḥatf* pl. حتوف *ḥutūf* death | يبحث عن (يسعى الى) حتفه بظلفه *yabḥaṯu ʿan* (*yasʿā ilā*) *ḥatfihī bi-ẓilfihī* he brings about his own destruction, digs his own grave; مات حتف انفه *māta ḥatfa anfihī* he died a natural death; لقى حتفه (*laqiya*) to find death, die

1حتم *ḥatama i* (*ḥatm*) to decree, make necessary, prescribe (على ه s.th. for s.o.), make (ه s.th.) a duty, a necessity (على for s.o.); to impose, enjoin (على ه s.th. upon s.o.); to decide, determine definitely (ب s.th.) **II** to decree, make necessary, prescribe (على ه s.th. for s.o.), make (ه s.th.) a duty, a necessity (على for s.o.) **V** to be necessary; to be s.o.'s (على) duty, be incumbent (على upon s.o.)

حتم *ḥatm* pl. حتوم *ḥutūm* imposition, injunction; final decision, resolution, determination; حتما *ḥatman* decidedly, definitely, necessarily, inevitably

حتمى *ḥatmī* decided, definite, final, conclusive, definitive, unalterable, irrevocable, inevitable

حتمية *ḥatmīya* decidedness, definiteness, definitiveness, determinateness, unalterableness; necessity; determinism (*philos.*)

لاحتمية *lā-ḥatmīya* indeterminism (*philos.*)

محتوم *maḥtūm* imposed, enjoined, obligatory; determined, definitive, determinate, unalterable, inevitable; destined, predestined, ordained (fate)

محتم *muḥattam* imposed, enjoined, obligatory; determined, definitive, determinate, unalterable, inevitable; destined, predestined, ordained (fate)

متحتم *mutaḥattim* absolutely necessary; imperative (duty)

2حتام *ḥattā-ma* see حتى

حتى *ḥattā* (prep.) until, till, up to, as far as; (conj.; with perf.) until, till; (with subj.) until, that, so that, in order that; — (particle) even, eventually even; and even; (with preceding negation) not even, and be it only ... | حتى لو even if; حتام *ḥattā-ma* until when?

1حث *ḥaṯṯa u* (*ḥaṯṯ*) to urge, incite, prompt, goad, spur on, egg on, prod, provoke, impel (ه s.o., على to do s.th.) | حث خطاه (*ḵuṭāhu*) to quicken one's pace, hurry (الى to a place); حث الطريق (*ṭarīqa*) to hurry, hasten; حث قدميه (*qadamaihi*) to quicken one's pace, break into a run **VIII** and **X** = **I**

حثيث *ḥaṯīṯ* fast, rapid, quick

O حاثة *ḥāṯṯa* hormone

2حثى *ḥiṯṯī* Hittite (n. and adj.)

حثالة *ḥuṯāla* dregs, lees, sediment; scum (fig.); offal, discard, scraps | حثالة الحرير silk combings

(حثو) حثا *ḥaṯā u* (*ḥaṯw*) to strew, scatter, spread, disperse (ه s.th.)

حج *ḥajja u* to overcome, defeat (ه s.o., with arguments, with evidence), confute (ه s.o.); to convince (ه s.o.); — (*ḥajj*) to make the pilgrimage (to Mecca), perform the hadj **III** to dispute, debate, argue, reason (ه with s.o.) **VI** to argue against each other, carry on a dispute, to debate; to take counsel **VIII** to advance (ب s.th.)

as an argument, plea, excuse, or pretext; to allege in support or vindication, plead (ب s.th.); to vindicate, justify (ل s.th.); to protest, remonstrate (على against), object, raise objections (على to)

حج *ḥajj* and حجة *ḥijja* pl. *-āt*, حجج *ḥijaj* pilgrimage; hadj, the official Muslim pilgrimage to Mecca | ذو الحجة *ḏū l-ḥijja* Zu'lhijjah, the last month of the Islamic calendar

حجة *ḥujja* pl. حجج *ḥujaj* argument; pretense, pretext, plea; proof, evidence; document, writ, deed, record; authoritative source, competent authority | بحجة ان under the pretense that ..., on the plea ..., on the pretext of ...; حجة استحكام document covering right of possession, confirmation of ownership (by a religious court, على for s.th.)

حجية *ḥujjīya* demonstrative power, conclusiveness, authoritative nature, authority (of a source, tradition, etc.)

حجاج *ḥajāj* pl. احجة *aḥijja* circumorbital ring (*anat.*)

محج *maḥajj* destination (of a journey)

محجة *maḥajja* pl. محاج *maḥājj*[2] destination of a pilgrimage, object of pilgrimage, shrine; destination (of a journey); goal; road; way; procedure, method | محجة الصواب *m. aṣ-ṣawāb* the Right Way, the Straight Path; محجة الحديد railroad

حجاج *ḥijāj* argument, dispute, debate

تحجج *taḥajjuj* argumentation, pleading, offering of a pretext, pretense, excuse

احتجاج *iḥtijāj* pl. *-āt* argumentation; pretext, excuse, plea, pretense; protest, remonstrance (على against), objection, exception (على to) | احتجاجا على (*iḥtijājan*) in protest against

حاج *ḥājj* pl. حجاج *ḥujjāj*, حجيج *ḥajīj* pilgrim; hadji, Mecca pilgrim, honorific title of one who has performed the pilgrimage to Mecca

محتج *muḥtajj* pl. *-ūn* protester

حجب *ḥajaba u* (*ḥajb*) to veil, cover, screen, shelter, seclude (ه على s.th. from); to hide, obscure (ه عن s.th. from s.th. else, e.g., from sight); to prevent (ه the viewing of s.th.); to hide from sight, keep in seclusion (ها a woman); to eclipse, outshine, overshadow (ه s.o.); to make imperceptible, invisible (ه عن s.th. to); to conceal (ه عن s.th. from s.o.); to make or form a separation (بين — وبين between — and) **II** to veil, hide, conceal; to hide from sight, keep in seclusion (ها a woman); to disguise, mask (ه ب s.th. with) **V** to conceal o.s., hide (عن from), flee from sight, veil o.s. **VII** to veil o.s., conceal o.s.; to be covered up, become hidden, be obscured **VIII** to vanish, become invisible, disappear from sight; to veil o.s., conceal o.s., hide; to become hidden, be concealed (عن from); to withdraw; to elude perception; to cease or interrupt publication (newspaper, periodical)

حجب *ḥajb* seclusion; screening off; keeping away, keeping off

حجاب *ḥijāb* pl. حجب *ḥujub*, احجبة *aḥjiba* cover, wrap, drape; curtain; woman's veil; screen, partition, folding screen; barrier, bar; diaphragm (also الحجاب الحاجز; *anat.*); amulet

حجابة *ḥijāba* office of gatekeeper

احتجاب *iḥtijāb* concealment, hiddenness, seclusion; veiledness, veiling, purdah

حاجب *ḥājib* concealing, screening, protecting; (pl. حجاب *ḥujjāb*, حجبة *ḥajaba*) doorman, gatekeeper; chamberlain; orderly (*Syr.*, *mil.*); (pl. حواجب *ḥawājib*[2]) eyebrow | حاجب المحكمة *ḥ. al-maḥkama* court usher; حاجب الهواء *ḥ. al-hawā'* airtight, hermetic

محجوب *maḥjūb* concealed, hidden, veiled

محجب *muḥajjab* veiled (woman)

حجر[1] *ḥajara u* (*ḥajr*, *ḥijr*, *ḥujr*, حجران *ḥijrān*, *ḥujrān*) to deny access (على to s.o.); to stop, detain, hinder (على or ه s.o.); to forbid, interdict (على ه s.th. to s.o.), prohibit (على s.o.) from doing s.th. (ه); to place (على s.o.) under guardianship, declare (على s.o.) legally incompetent

حجر *ḥajr* restriction, curb(ing), check(ing), obstruction, impeding, limitation, curtailing (على of s.th.); barring, closing, debarment, preclusion; detention; blocking, confinement, containment, suppression (as a protective measure); interdiction, prohibition, ban; revocation, or limitation, of s.o.'s (على) legal competence | حجر صحى (*ṣiḥḥī*) quarantine; الحجر على الافكار thought-ban, mind control

حجر *ḥijr* forbidden, interdicted, prohibited; lap; (pl. احجار *aḥjār*, حجور *ḥujūr*, حجورة *ḥujūra*) mare

حجرة *ḥujra* pl. *ḥujarāt*, حجر *ḥujar* room; cell; (railroad) compartment; chamber | حجرة الانتظار waiting room; حجرة النوم *ḥ. an-naum* bedroom; الحجرة الفلاحية (*fallāḥīya*) chamber of agriculture

محجر *maḥjar* pl. محاجر *maḥājir*[2] military hospital, infirmary; prison, jail, dungeon | محجر صحى (*ṣiḥḥī*) quarantine, quarantine station

محجر *maḥjir*, *miḥjar*, *maḥjar* pl. محاجر *maḥājir*[2] (= محجر العين *m. al-ʿain*) eye socket; see also below

تحجير *taḥjīr* interdiction, prohibition, ban; see also below

محجور *maḥjūr* pl. محاجير *maḥājīr*[2] (and محجور عليه) one placed under guardianship; minor; ward, charge

حجر[2] **II** to petrify, turn into stone (ه s.th.); to make hard as stone (ه s.th.) **V** to turn to stone, petrify, become petrified; to fossilize, become fossilized **X** = **V**

حجر *ḥajar* pl. احجار *aḥjār*, حجارة *ḥijāra*, حجار *ḥijār* stone; weight (placed as an equipoise on the scale of a balance) | حجر اساسى (*asāsī*) and حجر الاساس foundation stone, cornerstone; وضع الحجر الاساسى (*waḍʿ*) laying of the cornerstone; حجر البلاط *ḥ. al-balāṭ* flagstone, paving stone; حجر جهنم *ḥ. jahannam* lunar caustic, silver nitrate; حجر الجير *ḥ. al-jīr* limestone; حجر الزاوية *ḥ. az-zāwiya* cornerstone; foundation, main thing; الحجر السماق or حجر السماق (*summāqī*) porphyry; الحجر الاسود (*aswad*) the Black Stone (of the Kaaba); حجر الشادنة hematite (*min.*); حجر العثرة *ḥ. al-ʿaṯra* stumbling block; حجر الفلاسفة philosopher's stone; ○ حجر القمر *ḥ. al-qamar* selenite; حجر كريم and حجر ثمين precious stone, gem; طبع على الحجر (*ṭabʿ*) lithograph; طباعة الحجر lithography

حجرى *ḥajarī* stony, stone (adj.) | العصر الحجرى (*ʿaṣr*) the Stone Age; العصر الحجرى الحديث the Neolithic period; العصر الحجرى القديم the Paleolithic period

حجر *ḥajir* stony, petrified

حجار *ḥajjār* stone mason, stone cutter

محجر *maḥjir* pl. محاجر *maḥājir*[2] (stone) quarry

تحجير *taḥjīr* petrification; stone quarrying

تحجر *taḥajjur* petrification; fossilization

متحجر *mutaḥajjir* petrified; fossil

مستحجر *mustaḥjir* petrified; fossil

حجز *ḥajaza u i* (*ḥajz*) to hold back, restrain, hinder, prevent (عن ه s.th. from); to keep away (عن ه s.th. from); to block (off), close, bar; to lock (ه the door, دون on s.o., against s.o.); to postpone (ه a case, للحكم *li-l-ḥukm* until sentencing; *jur.*); to isolate, insulate, confine, seclude; to make inaccessible; to set apart; to separate (بين two things); to arrest, detain; to seize, sequester, impound (على or ه s.th., e.g., s.o.'s property, salary); to confiscate, safeguard (ه s.th.); to reserve (ه s.th.); to make a reservation (ه for a theater seat, a steamer cabin, a ticket, etc.); to book (ه a seat, e.g., on a plane) **VIII** to retain for o.s., reserve to o.s. (ه s.th.); to seize, arrest (ه s.o.); to hold captive (ه e.g., hostages); to confiscate (ه s.th.)

حجز *ḥajz* curbing, prevention, restraint; seclusion, confinement, containment, isolation, insulation, separation; arrest, detention, seizure, confiscation, sequestration (على of s.th.); reservation (of seats), advance booking; advance order (*com.*) | حجز الحرية *ḥ. al-ḥurrīya* deprivation of liberty, unlawful detention, duress (*jur.*); القى الحجز على (*alqā*) to confiscate s.th.; شباك الحجز *šubbāk al-ḥ.* ticket office

الحجاز *al-ḥijāz* Hejaz, region in W Arabia, on the Red Sea coast

حجازى *ḥijāzī* of or pertaining to Hejaz; (pl. *-ūn*) an inhabitant of Hejaz

احتجاز *iḥtijāz* arrest, detention, seizure; confiscation | احتجاز رهائن seizure of hostages

حاجز *ḥājiz* and حاجزة pl. حواجز *ḥawājiz*[2] obstacle, hindrance, impediment, obstruction; partition, screen, dividing wall; block, blockade, road block; fence, gate, railing, balustrade; hurdle; bar, barrier; barricade | الحجاب الحاجز diaphragm (*anat.*); ○ حاجز الامواج breakwater; الحواجز القمرقية (الجمركية) (*qumruqīya, gumrukīya*) customs barriers; حاجز الامن *ḥ. al-amn* security barrier; حاجز الريح *ḥ. ar-rīḥ* windshield; حاجز الاصطدام *ḥ. al-iṣṭidām* shock absorber, bumper; ○ حاجزة الصواعق lightning rod; حاجز الصوت *ḥ. aṣ-ṣaut* sound barrier; حاجز ملغم (*mulaǧǧam*) mine barrier; سباق حواجز *sibāq ḥ.* steeplechase; hurdle race (sport); ○ موظف حاجز *muwaẓẓaf ḥājiz* approx.: bailiff

محتجز *muḥtajaz* pl. *-ūn* s.o. held under arrest; hostage, detainee

محاجفة[1] *muḥājafa* singlestick fencing

احجاف[2] *iḥjāf* = اجحاف

حجل *ḥajala u i* (*ḥajl*, حجلان *ḥajalān*) to hop, leap; to skip, gambol

حجل *ḥajl, ḥijl* pl. حجول *ḥujūl*, احجال *aḥjāl* anklet

حجل *ḥajal* (coll.; n. un. ة) pl. حجلان *ḥijlān*, حجلى *ḥijlā* partridge; mountain partridge, mountain quail

حجلة *ḥajala* pl. حجال *ḥijāl* curtained canopy, or alcove, for the bride | ربات الحجال *rabbāt al-ḥ.* the ladies

لعبة الحجلة *laʿbat al-ḥajla* hopscotch

محجل *muḥajjal* wearing anklets (woman); white-footed (horse); bright, brilliant, radiant; unique, singular, esp. in the phrase اغر محجل (*aǧarr*[2])

حجم *ḥajama u* (*ḥajm*) to cup (ه s.o.; *med.*) **IV** to recoil, shrink, flinch (عن from); to desist, abstain, refrain (عن from), forbear (عن s.th.); to withdraw, retreat

حجم *ḥajm* pl. حجوم *ḥujūm*, احجام *aḥjām* bulk, size, volume; caliber (of a cannon) | كبير الحجم bulky, sizable, massive; حجم نقدى (*naqdī*) money volume (*fin.*)

حجام *ḥajjām* cupper

حجامة *ḥijāma* cupping, scarification, art of cupping

محجم *miḥjam*, محجمة *miḥjama* pl. محاجم *maḥājim*[2] cupping glass

احجام *iḥjām* desistance, abstention; restraint, aloofness, reserve

حجن *ḥajana i* (*ḥajn*) to bend, curve, crook (ه s.th.) **VIII** to snatch up, grab (ه s.th.), take hold (ه of s.th.)

احجن *aḥjan*[2] curved, crooked, bent

محجن *miḥjan* pl. محاجن *maḥājin*² staff or stick with a crooked end, crosier; hook

(حجو) حجا به خيرا *ḥajā bihī kairan* to think well of s.o., have a good opinion of s.o. III to propose a riddle (ه to s.o.); to speak in riddles, be enigmatic

حجا, حجى *ḥijan* pl. احجاء *aḥjā'* intellect, brains, understanding, discernment, acumen, sagacity, wit, intelligence

حجى *ḥajīy* appropriate, suitable, proper (ب for)

حجاية *ḥujjāya* pl. *-āt* (*mor.*) puzzle

احجى *aḥjā* more appropriate, more suitable, more proper; more correct, better

احجية *uḥjīya* pl. احاجى *aḥājīy*, احاج *aḥājin* riddle, puzzle, enigma

حخام *ḥakām* = حاخام (look up alphabetically)

حد *ḥadda u* (*ḥadd*) to sharpen, hone (ه a knife); to delimit, delineate, demarcate, mark off, stake off (ه land, من from); to set bounds (من or ه to s.th.), limit, restrict, confine (من or ه s.th.); to impede, hinder, curb, check (من or ه s.th.); to put a halt (من to s.th.); — *i* (حدة *ḥidda*) to become furious, angry (على at); — *i u* (حداد *ḥidād*) to wear mourning, mourn (على the deceased) II to sharpen, hone (ه a knife); to forge (ه s.th.; *syr.*); to delimit, demarcate (ه s.th.); to set bounds (ه to s.th.), circumscribe, mark off, delineate sharply; to limit, restrict, confine (من or ه s.th.); to determine, appoint, assign, schedule, lay down, set down, establish (ه s.th.); to fix (ه e.g., prices); to define (ه s.th.) | حدد بصره (*baṣarahū*) to dart sharp glances; to scrutinize (ف s.th.), look sharply (ف at s.th.) III to oppose (ه, ه s.o., s.th.), act contrary (ه, ه to s.o., to s.th.), contravene, counteract, violate (ه s.th.) IV to sharpen, make sharp (ه s.th.) | احد النظر الى (*naẓar*) to look sharply at, stare at; احد بصره (*baṣarahū*) to dart sharp glances; to scrutinize (ف s.th.), look sharply (ف at s.th.); احد من بصره (*baṣarihī*) to glance sharply; — to put on garments of mourning V to be delimited, be delineated, be bounded, be circumscribed; to be determined, be established, be set down, be scheduled, be fixed; to be defined, be definable VIII to be or become angry; to become infuriated, be furious (على at), be exasperated (على with); to be agitated, be upset, be in a state of commotion

حد *ḥadd*: الحد من prevention, limitation (of s.th.); restriction (of the number or quantity of s.th.)

حد *ḥadd* pl. حدود *ḥudūd* (cutting) edge (of a knife, of a sword); edge, border, brink, brim, verge; border (of a country), boundary, borderline; limit (fig.), the utmost, extremity, termination, end, terminal point, terminus; a (certain) measure, extent, or degree (attained); (*math.*) member (of an equation), term (of a fraction, of a proportion); divine ordinance, divine statute; legal punishment (*Isl. Law*) | لحد *li-ḥaddi* or الى حد until, till, up to, to the extent of, الى حد لحد الآن, *li-ḥ. l-āna* up to now, so far; الى حد ما (*ḥaddin*) to a certain degree, to a certain extent; الى حد بعيد, الى حد كبير to a considerable extent or degree, considerably, extensively; الى اى حد (*ayyi ḥaddin*) how far, to what degree or extent; لا حد له (*ḥadda*) boundless, infinite, unbounded, unlimited; بلا حد *bi-lā ḥaddin*, الى غير حد *ilā ġairi ḥaddin* boundless, unlimited, without limits; على حد سواء *'alā ḥaddin sawā'in*, على حد سوى *'alā ḥ. siwan* in the same manner; equally, likewise; على حد ضيق (*ḥaddin ḍayyiqin*) within narrow confines, on a limited scope; على حد (*ḥaddi*) according to, commensurate with;

على حد قوله (qaulihī) according to his statement, as he asserts, in his own words; فى حد ذاته fī ḥaddi ḏātihī and بحد ذاته in itself, as such; هم فى حد ذاتهم they . . . in themselves, by themselves, they alone; الحد الاعلى (aʿlā), الحد الاقصى (aqṣā) the maximum; الحد الادنى (adnā) the minimum; حد عمرى (ʿumrī) age limit; ذو حدين ḏū ḥaddain two-edged; فى حدود (ḥudūdi) within, within the framework of; بلغ حدا ان it reached such a pass, it went so far that . . .; بلغ اقصى حدوده (aqṣā ḥudūdihī) to attain its highest degree; حدود الله the bounds or restrictions that God has placed on man's freedom of action

حدودى ḥudūdī located on the border | بلدة حدودية (balda) border town; مناطق حدودية border regions (of a country)

حدة ḥidda sharpness, keenness; shrillness (of a high-pitched sound), stridency; sharp lineament (of features); vehemence, violence, impetuosity; fury, rage, wrath, ire, anger; excitability, irascibility, passionateness | فى حدة sharply; keenly; vehemently, violently

حدة ḥida see وحد

حدد ḥadad forbidden

حداد ḥidād (act of) mourning (على over) | ثوب الحداد ṯaub al-ḥ. garments of mourning; حداد البلاط ḥ. al-balāṭ court mourning

حديد ḥadīd iron; pl. حدائد ḥadāʾid[2] iron parts (of a structure); forgings, hardware, ironware | حديد خام crude iron, pig iron, iron ore; ○ حديد مطاوع (muṭāwiʿ) wrought iron; حديد غفل (ḡufl) unprocessed iron, pig iron; ظهر الحديد ẓahr al-ḥ., حديد الظهر cast iron; سكة الحديد sikkat al-ḥ. railroad; ضرب فى حديد بارد see ضرب

حديد ḥadīd pl. حداد ḥidād, احداء aḥiddāʾ[2], احدة aḥidda sharp (knife, eye, tongue, etc.), keen (mind)

احد aḥadd[2] sharper, keener; more vehement, more violent

حديدة ḥadīda pl. حدائد ḥadāʾid[2] piece of iron; object or tool made of iron | حديدة الحرث ḥ. al-ḥarṯ plowshare; على الحديدة (eg.) in financial straits, pinched for money

حديدى ḥadīdī iron (adj.) | سكة حديدية (sikka) railroad; العصر الحديدى (ʿaṣr) the Iron Age

الحديدة al-ḥudaida Hodeida (seaport in the Yemen Arab Republic)

حداد ḥaddād ironsmith, blacksmith

حدادة ḥidāda smithcraft, art of smithing

تحديد taḥdīd pl. -āt limitation, delimitation; delineation, demarcation; restriction, curb, confinement; determination, fixation, appointment; definition | على وجه التحديد (wajhi t-t.) and على التحديد to be exact . . ., strictly speaking . . .; precisely, exactly; تحديد النسل t. an-nasl birth control

حاد ḥādd sharp (also, fig., of a glance), keen (mind); high-pitched (tone); shrill (whistle); stormy (applause); vehement, fiery, impetuous; fierce; vivid; acute (illness) | حاد المزاج ḥ. al-mizāj, حاد الطبع ḥ. aṭ-ṭabʿ hot-blooded, hot-headed, hot-tempered, irascible; زاوية حادة (zāwiya) acute angle; تحت الحاد subacute

محدود maḥdūd bounded, bordered (ب by); circumscribed, confined; limited (= small, e.g., number, knowledge, etc.); delimited, determinate, fixed, definite, definitive | محدود الافق m. al-ufuq of limited horizon; محدود المعنى m. al-maʿnā unambiguous; محدود الضمان m. aḍ-ḍamān of limited liability; شركة محدودة (المسئولية) (širka) limited company, corporation

محدد muḥaddid: محدد قياس m. qiyās gauge, measuring instrument

محدد muḥaddad sharpened, sharp; determined, fixed, appointed, destined (ل for); set, determined, given (time); strictly delimited, clearly defined; sharply delineated

محتد *muḥtadd* angry, furious, exasperated

حدأة *ḥid'a*, pl. حدأ *ḥida'*, حداء *ḥidā'*, حدآن *ḥid'ān* kite (*zool.*)

حدأة *ḥada'a* pl. حداء *ḥidā'* double-bladed axe

حدب *ḥadiba a* (*ḥadab*) to be convex, dome-shaped, cambered, bent outward; to be hunchbacked; to be nice, kind, friendly (على or ب to s.o.), be solicitous (على or ب about s.o.), care (على or ب for s.o.), take care (على or ب of s.o.) **II** to make convex; to arch, bow upward, bend outward (ه a surface) **V** and **XII** احدودب *iḥdaudaba* to be convex; to be bowed upward, be bent outward; to have a hump, be humpbacked; to be humped (back)

حدب *ḥadab* affection, fondness, love; kindliness; solicitude, care; (pl. حداب *ḥidāb*, احداب *aḥdāb*) elevation of the ground | من كل حدب وصوب (*wa-ṣaubin*) or من كل صوب وحدب from all sides, from all directions, from everywhere; فى كل صوب وحدب everywhere, in every quarter, on all sides

حدب *ḥadib* arched, bowed upwardly or outwardly; hunchbacked; kindly, friendly

حدبة *ḥadaba* hunchback, hump; vaulting

احدب *aḥdab*², f. حدباء *ḥadbā'*², pl. حدب *ḥudb* hunchbacked, humped; — (elative) kindlier, friendlier

احديداب *iḥdīdāb*: احديداب الظهر *i. aẓ-ẓahr* spinal deformation, kyphosis

محدب *muḥaddab* convex; arched, bowed upwardly or outwardly; having a hump-back, hunchbacked | ○ طية محدبة (*ṭayya*) saddle of a geological fault, anticline (*geol.*)

محدودب *muḥdaudib* mounded (sand, the ground), bowed upward; hunchbacked, deformed (spine)

حدث *ḥadaṯa u* (حدوث *ḥudūṯ*) to happen, occur, take place, come to pass; — *ḥaduṯa u* (حداثة *ḥadāṯa*) to be new, recent; to be young **II** to tell, relate, report (ه to s.o., ب or ه s.th., فى, عن about); to speak, talk (ه to s.o., عن or فى about, of) | حدثه قلبه *ḥaddaṯahū qalbuhū* and حدثته نفسه *ḥaddaṯathu nafsuhū* his heart, his innermost feeling told him (ب s.th.); he had a presentiment or premonition (ب of), he had a suspicion (بأن that); حدث نفسه ب (*nafsahū*) to talk o.s. into (s.th.), try to believe s.th. or see s.th. (as factual); to resolve, make up one's mind to do s.th.; حدث نفسه ان he said to himself, told himself that ... **III** to speak, talk (عن or فى ه to s.o. about s.th.); to discuss (عن or فى ه with s.o. s.th.), converse (عن or فى ه with s.o. about); to negotiate, confer (ه with s.o.); to address, accost (ه s.o.); to call up (ه s.o., by telephone) **IV** to bring forth, produce, create, originate (ه s.th.); to found, establish (ه s.th.); to bring about, cause, occasion, provoke, effect (ه s.th.); to drop excrement | احدث حدثا (*ḥadaṯan*) to bring about s.th.; to cause or do s.th., esp., s.th. evil, do mischief **V** to speak, talk (الى to s.o., عن, ب or فى about or of s.th.), converse, chat (الى or مع with s.o., عن, ب or فى about s.th.) **VI** to talk with one another, converse, have a conversation; to chat, talk (مع with s.o.) **X** to renew (ه s.th.); to buy new (ه s.th.); to introduce, start, invent, originate, create (ه s.th.); to find or deem (ه s.o.) to be young

حدث *ḥadaṯ* pl. احداث *aḥdāṯ* a new, unprecedented thing, a novelty, innovation; event, incident, occurrence, happening; phenomenon; evil symptom; misdeed; misfortune; ritual impurity (*Isl. Law*); excrement, feces; (pl. احداث, حدثان *ḥudṯān*) young man, youth; احداث juveniles

حديث *ḥadīṯ* pl. حداث *ḥidāṯ*, حدثاء *ḥu-daṯā'*² new, novel, recent, late; modern;

حديثا *ḥadīṯan* recently, lately | حديث البناء *ḥ. al-binā'* new-built, recently built; حديث السن *ḥ. as-sinn* young; حديث العهد *ḥ. al-'ahd* of recent date, recent, new, young; حديث عهد ب, حديث العهد ب (*ḥ. 'ahdin*) having adopted or acquired (s.th.) recently; not long accustomed to (s.th.), inexperienced at (s.th.), new at (s.th.), newly, e.g., حديث العهد بالولادة (*bi-l-wilāda*) newborn, حديث العهد بالزواج (*bi-z-zawāj*) newly wed; كان حديث العهد بأوربا he had not known Europe until recently

حديث *ḥadīṯ* pl. احاديث *aḥādīṯ*[2], حدثان *ḥidṯān* speech; chat, chitchat, small talk; conversation, talk, discussion; interview; prattle, gossip; report, account, tale, narrative; Prophetic tradition, Hadith, narrative relating deeds and utterances of the Prophet and his Companions | حديث خرافة *ḥ. ḫurāfa* fabulous story, silly talk; حديث صحفي (*ṣuḥufī*) press interview; حديث قدسي (*qudsī*) Muslim tradition in which God Himself speaks, as opposed to حديث نبوى (*nabawī*) an ordinary Prophetic tradition; حديث النفس *ḥ. an-nafs* pl. احاديث النفس s.th. one talks o.s. into; premonition; misgiving; pleasurable imaginings, bright expectation; احاديث اذاعية (*idā'īya*) broadcast talks (radio), talk shows (TV)

حدوث *ḥudūṯ* setting in (of a state or condition), occurrence, incidence (of a phenomenon); occurrence, incident, happening

حداثة *ḥadāṯa* newness, recency, novelty; youth, youthfulness

حواديت *ḥawādīt* (*eg.*) folk tales, fairy stories

احدث *aḥdaṯ*[2] newer, more recent

حدثان الدهر *ḥidṯān* (or *ḥadaṯān*) *ad-dahr* misfortune, adversities, reverses

احدوثة *uḥdūṯa* pl. احاديث *aḥādīṯ*[2] speech; discussion, talk, conversation; chatter; fabling, fibbing; topic, subject of a conversation; gossip, rumor (about a person) | حسن الاحدوثة *ḥusn al-u.* praise (of s.o.); سوء الاحدوثة *sū' al-u.* slander, defamation

محادثة *muḥādaṯa* pl. *-āt* discourse, conversation, discussion, talk, parley

احداث *iḥdāṯ* production, creation, invention, origination; causation, effectuation

احداثيات *iḥdāṯīyāt* (pl.) co-ordinates (*math.*) | احداثيات عمودية (*'amūdīya*) ordinates; احداثيات افقية (*ufqīya*) abscissas (*math.*)

استحداث *istiḥdāṯ* invention, creation, production, origination

حادث *ḥādiṯ* occurring, happening, taking place; new, recent; fresh; — (pl. حوادث *ḥawādiṯ*[2], also *-āt*) occurrence, incident, event, happening; episode; case (*jur.*); accident, mishap | حادث تزوير a case of forgery; مكان الحادث *makān al-ḥ.* site of action, scene of the crime, locus delicti

حادثة *ḥādiṯa* pl. حوادث *ḥawādiṯ*[2] occurrence, event, happening; plot (of a play); incident, episode; accident, mishap | حادثة المرور *ḥ. al-murūr* traffic accident

محدث *muḥaddiṯ* pl. *-ūn* speaker, talker; spokesman; conversation partner, interlocutor; relator, narrator; a transmitter of Prophetic traditions, traditionary, representative of the science or study of Hadith (see above); ○ phonograph, gramophone

محدث *muḥdaṯ* new, novel, recent, late; modern; upstart, nouveau riche; المحدثون the Moderns

متحدث *mutaḥaddiṯ* spokesman, speaker | المتحدث الرسمي (*rasmī*) the government spokesman; المتحدث بلسان وزارة الخارجية (*bi-lisāni w.*) the spokesman of the foreign ministry

مستحدث *mustaḥdaṯ* newly made, new-fangled, of late date; — (pl. *-āt*) novelty, innovation; recent invention, modern product; neologism

خدج *ḥadaja i* and II to stare, look sharply (ه, ، at s.o., at s.th., often with ببصره *bi-baṣarihī* or بنظره *bi-naẓarihī*)

حدج *ḥidj* pl. حدوج *ḥudūj*, احداج *aḥdāj* load, burden, encumbrance

ابو حديج *abū ḥudaij* stork

حداجة *ḥidāja* pl. حدائج *ḥadā'ij*[2] camel saddle

حدر *ḥadara, ḥadura u* (*ḥadr*, حدارة *ḥadāra*) to be thick; — *ḥadara u i* (*ḥadr*, حدور *ḥudūr*) to bring down, lower (ه s.th.); to cause (ه s.th.) to descend; to drop (ه s.th.); to shed (ه tears); حدر حدرا (*ḥadran*) to rattle off, express quickly (an utterance, a thought); — (*ḥadr*) to come down, step down, descend; to glide down, swoop **II** to drop (ه s.th.); to lower, incline, dip (ه s.th.) **V** to descend gradually; to glide down; to come down, descend; to flow down (tears); to derive, stem, originate (من from) **VII** to come or go down, descend; to go downhill (of a person); to alight (from), get out (of a car); to glide down, sink down; to be in decline, be on the downgrade; to decline, wane; to flow down (tears); to slope down, slant down, be inclined (terrain); to reach back into the past, extend back to former times and be transmitted from them; to derive, stem, originate (من from); to come (الى to a place), arrive (الى at)

حدر *ḥadr* rapid recitation of the Koran (a terminus technicus of *tajwīd*)

حدور *ḥadūr* slope, downgrade, declivity, declivitous terrain

تحدر *taḥaddur* descent, slant, slope, inclination, incline, declivity

انحدار *inḥidār* slant, dip, pitch, inclination, descent, slope; declivity; fall (of a river), gradient (of a street, of a slope); decline, waning; ruin, decay, decadence; descent, lineage (من from) | سباق انحدار *sibāq i.* downhill race (skiing)

حادر *ḥādir* thick

متحدر *mutaḥaddir* descending, slanting, sloping downward

منحدر *munḥadir* descending; lowered, dipped; slanting, sloping, declivitous (terrain); declining, waning, being on the downgrade, in a state of decadence or decline; run-down, seedy, down-at-the-heels, down-and-out

منحدر *munḥadar* pl. *-āt* sloping ground; talus, incline, descent, declivity; fall (of a river)

حدس *ḥadasa i u* (*ḥads*) to surmise, guess, conjecture (ه s.th.)

حدس *ḥads* surmise, guess, conjecture; ○ intuition

□ حداف *ḥaddāf* (> حذاف), حداف الماكوك (*syr.*) shuttle (weaving)

□ طارة حدافة *ṭāra ḥaddāfa* (*syr.*) flywheel

حدق[1] *ḥadaqa i* (*ḥadq*) to surround, encircle, encompass (ب s.o., s.th.); (with بعينه *bi-'ainihī*) to look, glance (، at s.o.) **II** to look, glance, gaze, stare (الى or فى at, also ب) | حدق النظر فى (*naẓara*) to fix one's glance on . . . **IV** to surround, encircle, encompass, enclose (ب s.o., s.th.); to look, glance (فى, الى or ب at) | احدق النظر فى (*naẓara*) to fix one's glance on . . .

حدقة *ḥadaqa* pl. *-āt*, حدق *ḥadaq*, حداق *ḥidāq*, احداق *aḥdāq* pupil (of the eye); pl. احداق glances

حديقة *ḥadīqa* pl. حدائق *ḥadā'iq*[2] garden | حديقة الحيوانات *ḥ. al-ḥayawānāt* zoological garden, zoo

احداق *iḥdāq* encirclement, encompassment (ب of)

خطر محدق *kaṭar muḥdiq* imminent danger

²□ حدق II (= حذق) to make acid, sour, tart, or sharp (ه s.th.)

□ حادق *hādiq* (= حاذق) sour, tart, acid, sharp (taste)

حدل *ḥadala* i to flatten, level, even, roll (ه s.th.); (*ḥadl*, حدول *ḥudūl*) to treat unjustly (على s.o.)

محدلة *miḥdala* pl. محادل *maḥādil*² roller, steamroller

حدم VIII to burn, glow, blaze; to burn up, be consumed by fire; to flare up, break out (fight); to be furious, burn with wrath (على at, over), also احتدم غيظا (*ḡaiẓan*)

احتدام *iḥtidām* paroxysm

محتدم *muḥtadim* heated (e.g., debate); furious, infuriated, enraged

حدة *ḥida* see وحد

¹□ حدوة *ḥidwa* horseshoe

²(حدو) حدا *ḥadā* u (*ḥadw*, حداء *ḥudā'*, *ḥidā'*) to urge forward by singing (ه camels); to urge, spur on, egg on, prompt, instigate, induce, move (ب or ه s.o., الى to s.th., to do s.th.); حدا ب to instigate s.th. | يحدوهم الامل فى (*amal*) the hope of ... spurs them on; حدا بهم الحديث الى their conversation led them to ...; غرض تحدى اليه الركائب (*ḡaraḍun tuḥdā*) a goal much sought after or worth striving for V to compete, vie (ه with s.o.); to urge (ه ب s.o. to, بأن to do s.th.); to challenge, provoke (ه, ه s.o., s.th.; ه ب s.o. to, بأن to do s.th.); to defy (ه, ه s.o., s.th.); to incite, stimulate, arouse, animate, sharpen (ه s.th.; ذكاءه *ḏakā'ahū* s.o.'s intellect); to intend (ه s.th., to do s.th.), be bent (ه on doing s.th.) | تحدى الموت (*mauta*) to provoke, invite death, defy death; تحدى عاديات الزمان (*'ādiyāti z-zamān*) to brave the buffetings of fate

حداء *ḥudā'* animating singsong, chanting of the caravan leader

حداء *ḥaddā'* camel driver, cameleer

احدوة *uḥdūwa*, احدية *uḥdīya* song of the camel drivers

تحد *taḥaddin* pl. تحديات *taḥaddiyāt* challenge; urging (ب to s.th.); provocation

حاد *ḥādin* pl. حداة *ḥudāh* caravan leader (who urges the camels forward by singing); camel driver, cameleer; leader

متحد *mutaḥaddin* challenger, provoker

¹حدى *ḥadiya* a to remain, stay (ب at a place), stick (ب to a place)

²حادى عشر see احد

³□ حداية *ḥidāya*, *ḥiddāya* = حدأة *ḥid'a*

حذر *ḥaḏira* a (*ḥiḏr*, *ḥaḏar*) to be cautious, wary, to beware (من or ه, ه of s.o., of s.th.), be on one's guard (من or ه, ه against) II to warn, caution (ه من s.o. of or about), put (ه s.o.) on his guard (من against) III to watch out, be careful; to be on one's guard (ه against), be wary (ه of s.o.) V to beware, be wary (من of) VIII = I

حذر *ḥiḏr* and *ḥaḏar* caution, watchfulness, alertness, wariness, circumspection; precaution | اخذ حذره to be on one's guard; على حذر cautiously, warily; on one's guard (من against)

حذر *ḥaḏir* cautious, wary

حذار *ḥaḏāri* beware (ان of doing ..., من of s.th.)! watch out (من for)! be careful (من of)!

تحذير *taḥḏīr* warning, cautioning (من of, against)

محاذرة *muḥāḏara* caution, precaution, precautionary measure

محذور *maḥḏūr* that of which one should beware, against which one should guard; object of caution; — (pl. *-āt*) danger, peril; trouble, difficulty, misfortune

حذف *ḥaḏafa i* (*ḥaḏf*) to shorten, clip, curtail (ه or من s.th.); to take s.th. away, cut s.th. off, clip s.th. off (من from s.th.), reduce (من s.th.), strike or cross s.th. (من off s.th.); to cancel, strike out, delete, drop, leave out, omit, suppress (ه s.th.); (*gram.*) to elide, apocopate, drop by aphaeresis; to deduct, subtract (ه s.th.); to throw (ه ب at s.o. s.th.), pelt (ه ب s.o. with s.th.); to cast away, throw away, discard (ب s.th.) **II** to clip, trim (ه s.th.); to give (ه s.th.) shape, to trim, clip, or cut (ه s.th.) into proper shape

حذف *ḥaḏf* shortening, curtailing, cutting off, trimming, etc.; canceling, cancellation, striking off, crossing off, deletion; omission, dropping, suppression; (*gram.*) elision, ellipsis, apocopation

حذافير *ḥaḏāfīr*²: بحذافيره , بحذافيرها all of it, entirely, without exception; اخذه بحذافيره he took all of it, he took it lock, stock and barrel

حذق *ḥaḏiqa a, ḥaḏaqa i* (*ḥiḏq*, حذاقة *ḥaḏāqa*) to be skilled, skillful, well-versed, proficient (ه or في in s.th.), master (ه s.th.); —*ḥaḏaqa u* (حذوق *ḥuḏūq*) to turn sour (milk) **V** to feign skillfulness, proficiency, cleverness or smartness

حذق *ḥiḏq* and حذاقة *ḥaḏāqa* skill, dexterity, proficiency; smartness, cleverness, intelligence; perspicacity, sagacity, acumen

حاذق *ḥāḏiq* pl. حذاق *ḥuddāq* skillful, skilled, proficient; well-versed, clever, smart, intelligent; sour

حذلق **II** *taḥaḏlaqa* to show or display affected, exaggerated erudition; to be pedantic

حذلقة *ḥaḏlaqa* exaggerated, pedantic erudition; affected, forced style; pedantry

متحذلق *mutaḥaḏliq* pl. *-ūn* pedant

(حذو) حذا *ḥaḏā u*: حذا حذوه (*ḥaḏwahū*) to imitate s.o., take after s.o., follow s.o.'s example **III** to be opposite s.th. (ه), face, parallel (ه s.th.), run parallel (ه to); to stand opposite (ه s.o.), stand in front (ه ,ه of s.o. or s.th.) **VI** to be opposite each other, be parallel **VIII** to imitate, copy (ب or على s.o., s.th., also ه s.th.), take or follow (ب or على s.o., s.th., also ه s.th.) as an example or model; to be shod; to wear (ه s.th.) as footgear

حذو *ḥaḏwa* (prep.) opposite, face to face with | حذوك النعل بالنعل *ḥaḏwaka n-na'la bi-n-na'l* in a completely identical manner, to a T, like two peas in a pod

حذاء *ḥiḏā'* pl. احذية *aḥḏiya* (pair of) leather boots or shoes | حذاء الفروسية *ḥ. al-furūsīya* (pair of) riding boots, high boots; صانع الاحذية shoemaker

حذاء *ḥiḏā'a* (prep.) and بحذاء *bi-ḥiḏā'i* opposite, face to face with

حذاء *ḥaddā'* shoemaker, cobbler

على (في) محاذاة *'alā* (*fī*) *muḥāḏāti* along, alongside of, parallel to

احتذاء *iḥtiḏā'* imitation, copying

محاذ *muḥāḏin* opposite, facing

حر *ḥarra u i* (*ḥarr*, حرارة *ḥarāra*) to be hot **II** to liberate (ه s.o.): to free, set free, release (ه s.o.); to emancipate (ه s.o.); to consecrate (ه s.o.) to the service of God; to draw up, make out accurately (ه an account, a calculation); to adjust, render accurate (ه a weight, measure); to point or direct (ه a gun at s.th.); to revise (ه a book); to edit, redact (ه a book, a periodical); to write, pen, indite, compose (ه s.th.); (from حرير *ḥarīr*) to mercerize (ه cotton yarn or fabrics to achieve a silky lustre) **V** to become free; to be freed, be liberated (من from); to be emancipated; to be written, be composed **X** to become hot, be heated, flare up (quarrel, fight); to be kindled, be ardent or burning (feeling, desire)

حر *ḥarr* heat, warmth | وا حر قلباه see وا

حر *ḥurr* pl. m. احرار *aḥrār*, pl. f. حرائر *ḥarā'ir*[2] noble, free-born; genuine (jewels, etc.), pure, unadulterated; free; living in freedom; freeman; independent; free, unrestrained; liberal (*pol.*; الاحرار the Liberals); frank, candid, open (على toward s.o.); free, available, uninvested (money) | الاحتياطى الحر (*iḥtiyāṭī*) free reserves, unencumbered reserves; سباحة حرة (*sibāḥa*) freestyle swimming; مصارعة حرة (*muṣāra'a*) freestyle wrestling; من حر ماله *min ḥurri mālihī* with his own cash, with funds at his disposal

حرة *ḥarra* pl. *-āt* stony area; volcanic country, lava field

حرية *ḥurrīya* pl. *-āt* freedom, liberty; independence, unrestraint, license (e.g., poetic) | حرية العبادة *ḥ. al-'ibāda* freedom of worship; حرية الفكر *ḥ. al-fikr* freedom of thought; حرية الكلام *ḥ. al-kalām* freedom of speech; حرية النشر (or الصحافة) *ḥ. an-našr* (*aṣ-ṣiḥāfa*) liberty of the press; حرية التصرف *ḥ. at-taṣarruf* free disposal, right of disposition; authority, free hand

حرير *ḥarīr* silk; pl. حرائر *ḥarā'ir*[2] (حراير) silken wares, silks | حرير صخرى (*ṣakrī*) asbestos; حرير صناعى rayon

حريرى *ḥarīrī* silken, silky, of silk

حرائرى *ḥarā'irī* silken, silk- (in compounds), of silk; silk weaver

حرار *ḥarrār* silk weaver

حرارة *ḥarāra* heat; warmth; fever heat, fever; temperature; ardor, fervor (of emotion), passion; eagerness, enthusiasm, zeal; vehemence, violence, intensity; burning (of the skin)

حريرة *ḥuraira* pl. *-āt* calorie

حرارى *ḥarārī* thermal, thermic, thermo-, heat (used attributively); caloric | وحدة حرارية (*waḥda*) calorie

○ حرارية *ḥarārīya* pl. *-āt* calorie

حرور *ḥarūr* f., pl. حرائر *ḥarā'ir*[2] hot wind

حران *ḥarrān*[2], f. حرى *ḥarrā*, pl. حرار *ḥirār*, حرارى *ḥarārā* thirsty; passionate, fervent, hot (fig.) | زفرة حرى (*zafra*) a fervent sigh; دموع حرى hot tears

احر *aḥarr*[2] hotter, warmer | احر التهانئ warmest congratulations; على احر من الجمر (*jamr*) on pins and needles, on tenterhooks, in greatest suspense or excitement

○ محر *miḥarr* heating system, heating installation

تحرير *taḥrīr* liberation; release; emancipation; record(ing), writing; editing, redaction; editorship (of a newspaper, a periodical); (pl. *-āt*, تحارير *taḥārīr*[2]) piece of writing, record, brief, document | رئيس التحرير editor-in-chief; ادارة التحرير board of editors, editorial staff; تحريرا فى (*taḥrīran*) issued, made out on (with the date; on documents and certifications)

تحريرى *taḥrīrī* liberational; emancipational; liberal; recorded in writing, written, in writing

تحرر *taḥarrur* liberation, emancipation (intr.)

حار *ḥārr* hot; warm; ardent, glowing, fervent, passionate

محرور *maḥrūr* hot-tempered, hot-headed, fiery, passionate, furious

محرر *muḥarrir* pl. *-ūn* liberator, emancipator; writer, clerk; issuer (of a document); editor (of a newspaper, of a periodical)

محرر *muḥarrar* consecrated to God; set down in writing, recorded in writing, written; booked; pl. محررات bookings, entries

متحرر *mutaḥarrir* emancipated; an advocate of emancipation

حرب *ḥariba a* (*ḥarab*) to be furious, enraged, angry III to fight, combat (ه s.o.), battle, wage war (ه against s.o.) **VI** to fight (one another), be engaged in war **VIII** = **VI**

حرب *ḥarb* f., pl. حروب *ḥurūb* war, warfare; fight, combat, battle; enemy, enemies (على or ل of s.o.) | حرب اهلية (*ahlīya*) civil war; حرب دفاعية (*difāʿīya*) defensive war; حرب هجومية (*hujūmīya*) offensive war; حرب صحافية (*ṣiḥāfīya*) press feud; الحروب الصليبية (*ṣalībīya*) the Crusades; الحرب العظمى (*ʿuẓmā*), الحرب العالمية (*ʿālamīya*), الحرب العامة (*ʿāmma*) World War I; كشفت الحرب عن ساقها *kašafat il-ḥarbu ʿan sāqihā* and قامت الحرب على ساق *qāmat il-ḥ. ʿalā sāqin* war flared up, fierce fighting broke out

حربى *ḥarbī* warlike, bellicose, belligerent, martial, war (adj.), military; (pl. *-ūn*) warrior, soldier, military man | البوليس الحربى (*būlīs*) military police

حربية *ḥarbīya* military affairs | وزير الحربية minister of war

حربة *ḥarba* pl. حراب *ḥirāb* lance, spear; spearhead; bayonet, sidearm

حرباء *ḥirbāʾ* pl. حرابى *ḥarābīy* chameleon (*zool.*)

وا حرباه *wā ḥarabāh!* (exclamation of lament) alas! goodness no! oh my!

محراب *miḥrāb* pl. محاريب *maḥārīb*[2] a recess in a mosque indicating the direction of prayer, prayer niche, mihrab; (fig.) sanctum, holy of holies

محاربة *muḥāraba* struggle, combat, fight, battle; warfare

احتراب *iḥtirāb* mutual struggle

محارب *muḥārib* warring, belligerent; pl. *-ūn*) warrior, combatant, fighter; corporal (formerly, *Eg.*; *mil.*) | محارب قديم old combatant or campaigner, war horse

المتحاربون *al-mutaḥāribūn* the belligerents, the warring parties

حربوشة *ḥarbūša* pl. حرابش *ḥarābiš*[2] (*tun.*) pastille, pill

حرث **ḥaraṯa** *i u* (*ḥarṯ*) to plow (ه the soil); to cultivate, till (ه the ground)

حرث *ḥarṯ* plowing, tilling, tillage, cultivation of the soil; arable land, tilth; plantation, culture

حرثة *ḥarṯa* (n. un.) arable land, tilth

حراثة *ḥirāṯa* cultivation of the soil, farming, agriculture

حراث *ḥarrāṯ* plowman

محراث *miḥrāṯ* pl. محاريث *maḥārīṯ*[2] plow

حارث *ḥāriṯ* pl. حراث *ḥurrāṯ* plowman | ابو الحارث *abū l-ḥ.* lion

حرج **ḥarija** *a* (*ḥaraj*) to be close, tight, narrow; to be straitened, be confined, get into a strait, be cornered, be hard pressed; to be oppressed, be anguished (heart); to be forbidden (على to s.o.) **II** to narrow, tighten, straiten (ه s.th.); to complicate (ه s.th.), make (ه s.th.) difficult; to forbid (على ه s.th. to s.o.); to persist (فى in s.th.) **IV** to narrow, straiten, confine, cramp, hamper, impede, restrict (ه s.th.); to complicate, make difficult, aggravate, jeopardize (ه a situation, s.o.'s position); to embarrass (ه s.o.); to coerce, constrain, press (ه الى s.o. to); to forbid (على ه s.th. to (s.o.) | احرج موقفه (*mauqifahū*) to put s.o. under pressure, threaten s.o.'s position **V** to refrain from sin or evildoing; to abstain, refrain (من from), avoid (من s.th.); to be cornered, be forced to the wall; to become or be oppressed, anguished, distressed; to become critical, become complicated or difficult, be aggravated (situation), be jeopardized (s.o.'s position) | تحرج صدره من (ب) (*ṣadruhū*) to feel depressed by, feel annoyed at; تحرج به الناس this made things difficult for people

حرج *ḥaraj* closeness, tightness, narrowness; confinement, straitness, constriction, crampedness; restriction, impediment; oppression, distress, anguish; difficulty; critical situation; prohibition, interdiction; s.th. forbidden, s.th. interdicted, sin | لا حرج (*ḥaraja*) there is no objection; لا حرج عليك nothing stands in your way, you are at liberty; بلا حرج (*bi-lā*) unhesitatingly, without restraint or fear; اى حرج فى (*ayyu ḥarajin*) why should one feel restrained in . . .? لا يرى حرجا من he feels no hesitation about, will not hesitate to . . .

حرج *ḥaraj* (coll.; n. un. ة) pl. *-āt*, حراج *ḥirāj*, احراج *aḥrāj* thicket; dense forest; woodland, timberland

حرج *ḥarij* narrow, close, tight, confined, straitened; oppressed, hard pressed, harassed; critical (situation, position)

احرج *aḥraj*[2] narrower, closer, tighter, more straitened; more critical

حراج *ḥarāg* (*eg.*) auction

حراجة *ḥarāja* seriousness, gravity, difficulty, complicatedness (of a situation)

تحريج *taḥrīj* forestation, afforestation

تحرج *taḥarruj* restraint, reserve, aloofness; timidity, diffidence, faint-heartedness; critical complication, gravity, difficulty (of a situation)

محرجات *muḥarrijāt*: محرجات الايمان *m. al-aimān* binding, committing, or solemn, oaths

محرج *muḥrij* disconcerting, embarrassing

محرج *muḥraj* hard pressed, in a critical situation; embarrassed

متحرج *mutaḥarrij*: متحرج الصدر *m. aṣ-ṣadr* annoyed, vexed, anguished, oppressed

حرد *ḥarida a* (*ḥarad*) to be annoyed, disgruntled, angry, furious (على at, with)

حرد *ḥarad* anger, annoyance

حارد *ḥārid*, حرد *ḥarid* and حردان *ḥardān* annoyed, disgruntled, angry, furious

حرذون *ḥirḏaun* pl. حراذين *ḥarāḏīn*[2] lizard

حرز *ḥaraza u* (*ḥarz*) to keep, guard, protect, preserve (ه s.th.), take care (ه of); — *ḥaruza u* (حرازة *ḥarāza*) to be strong be strongly fortified, be impregnable **IV** to keep, preserve, guard (ه s.th.); to obtain, attain, achieve, win (ه, على s.th.) | احرز نصرا (انتصارا) (*naṣran*) to win a victory; احرز قصب السبق (*qaṣaba s-sabq*) to come through with flying colors, carry the day, score a great success **V** to be wary (من of), be on one's guard (من against) **VIII** to be wary (من of), guard, be on one's guard (من against), be careful, take heed, take precautions

حرز *ḥirz* pl. احراز *aḥrāz* fortified place; refuge, sanctuary, retreat; a safe place (for objects, valuables, money; e.g., a cupboard, chest, purse); (pl. احراز, حروز *ḥurūz*) amulet

حريز *ḥarīz* strongly fortified, guarded; inaccessible, impregnable

احراز *iḥrāz* acquisition, acquirement, obtainment, attainment, achievement, winning, gaining

احتراز *iḥtirāz* pl. *-āt* caution, wariness, prudence, circumspection; reservation, reserve | بكامل الاحتراز with all reservation

○ حارزة *ḥāriza* fuse (*el.*)

محرز *muḥriz* pl. *-ūn* obtainer, acquirer, winner, gainer; possessor, holder (على of s.th.) | محرز على البكالوريا (*bakālōriyā*) holder of a secondary school diploma (*Tun.*); holder of a B. A. degree

حرس *ḥarasa u* (*ḥars*, حراسة *ḥirāsa*) to guard, watch, control (ه, ه s.th., s.o.); to

مجروس *maḥrūs* guarded, safeguarded, secured; protected by God, preserved; المحروس (lit. the one protected, i.e.) the son; your son, your child; المحروسون your children, your family; المحروسة an epithet of Cairo and other cities

محترس *muḥtaris* cautious, wary, careful

حرش *haraša i* (*harš*) to scratch (ه, ه s.o., s.th.) **II** to instigate, prod, incite, provoke, incense (ه s.o.); to set (بين people against each other), sow discord, dissension (بين among) **V** to pick a quarrel, start a brawl (ب with s.o.), provoke (ب s.o.)

حرش *ḥirš, ḥurš* pl. احراش *aḥrāš*, حروش *ḥurūš* forest, wood(s)

حرش *ḥariš* and احرش *aḥraš*[2] rough, coarse, scabrous

حرش *ḥaraš*, حرشة *ḥurša*, حراشة *ḥarāša* roughness, coarseness, scabrousness

تحريش *taḥrīš* instigation, prodding, incitement, provocation, agitation, incensement

تحرش *taḥarruš* provocation, importunity, obtrusion, meddling, uncalled-for interference; pl. تحرشات trespasses, encroachments

حرشف *haršaf* pl. حراشف *ḥarāšif*[2] scales (of fish)

حرص *ḥaraṣa i* and *ḥariṣa a* (*ḥirṣ*) to desire, want, covet (على s.th.); to be intent, be bent (على on); to strive (على for), aspire (على to)

حرص *ḥirṣ* greed, avidity, cupidity, covetousness; desire; aspiration, endeavor, wish (على for); avarice | حرصا على in the desire for . . ., in the endeavor to . . .; out of concern or consideration for . . .; حرصا على الارواح danger! (on warning signs)

oversee, supervise, superintend (ه, ه s.th., s.o.); to secure, protect, safeguard, preserve, keep (ه, ه s.th., s.o.); to watch (على over) **V** and **VIII** to beware, be wary (من of), guard, be on one's guard (من against); احترس *iḥtaris* caution!

حرس *ḥaras* watch; guard, escort; bodyguard | الحرس السيار (*sayyār*) militia, "garde mobile" (*Syr.*); حرس الشرف *ḥ. aš-šaraf* honor guard; الحرس الملكى (*malakī*) the royal guard (formerly *Ir., Eg.*); الحرس الملوكى (*mulūkī*) (formerly) bodyguard of the Bey (*Tun.*); الحرس الوطنى (*waṭanī*) the National Guard; حرس الحدود border guard; حرس السواحل coast guard

حراسة *ḥirāsa* guarding, watching, control; watch, guard, guard duty; supervision, superintendence; guardianship, tutelage, custody, care, protection; safe conduct, escort; compulsory administration, sequestration; state control; administration of an estate (*jur.*); sequester | حراسة السواحل coastal protection or guarding; اصبح فى حراسة الدولة to be operated under state control (of expropriated businesses)

احتراس *iḥtirās* caution, wariness, prudence; (pl. *-āt*) precaution, precautionary measure | احتراسا من for protection from or against

حارس *ḥāris* pl. حرسة *ḥarasa*, حراس *ḥurrās* vigilant, watchful; watchman; attendant, keeper (e.g., in a zoo); sentry, sentinel, guard; overseer, supervisor, superintendent; administrator; guardian, custodian, keeper, protector; tutelary (in compounds); (= حارس المرمى *ḥ. al-marmā*) goal keeper (sport) | حارس التركة *ḥ. at-tirka* administrator of an estate; حارس الخواتم keeper of the seal; حارس قضائى (*qaḍā'ī*) sequestrator, receiver (in bankruptcy, in equity); ملاك حارس (*mal'ak*) guardian angel (*Chr.*); حارس الليل *ḥ. al-lail* night watchman

حريص *ḥarīṣ* pl. حراص *ḥirāṣ*, حرصاء *ḥuraṣā'*[2] covetous, greedy, avid, eager (على for); bent (على on), desirous (على of)

احرص *aḥraṣ*[2] more covetous, greedier

حرض II to goad, prod, spur on, egg on, incite, rouse, provoke (على ه s.o. to s.th. or to do s.th.); to instigate, abet, stir up, agitate (على ه s.o. to or against); ○ to induce (*el.*)

تحريض *taḥrīḍ* incitement, provocation; instigation, abetment, agitation (على to); inflammatory propaganda (على against s.o.); ○ induction (*el.*) | ○ تحريض ذاتى self-induction (*el.*)

تحريضى *taḥrīḍī* inciting, instigative, agitative, inflammatory; provocative

حارض *hāriḍ* bad, wicked, evil

محرض *muḥarriḍ* pl. *-ūn* inciter, baiter; instigator, abettor; demagogue, rabble rouser; agitator, provocator; ○ inductor (*el.*)

متحرض *mutaḥarriḍ* ○ induced (*el.*)

حرف II to slant, incline, make oblique (ه s.th.); to bend off, up, down or back, turn up, down or back, deflect (ه s.th.); to distort, corrupt, twist, pervert, misconstrue, falsify (ه s.th.) | حرفه عن موضعه (*'an mauḍi'ihī*) to distort the sense of s.th., rob s.th. of its true meaning **V** to turn off, branch off, take a turning; to deviate, depart, digress (عن from); to avoid (عن s.th.); to be or become bent off, distorted, corrupted, perverted **VII** to turn off, branch off, take a turning; to deviate, depart, digress, turn away (عن from); to slope down, slant, be inclined (terrain); to turn (الى to, toward); to be twisted, be distorted; to be oblique, slanting; to be cocked, rakish (headgear); with ب: to make s.th. appear oblique, slanted, or distorted; to be corrupted, perverted | انحرف به عن to turn s.o. away from; to dissuade s.o. from; انحرف مزاجه (*mizājuhū*) to be indisposed, be ill **VIII** to do (ه s.th.) professionally, practice (ه s.th.) as a profession; to strive for success

حرف *ḥarf* pl. حرف *ḥiraf* (cutting) edge (of a knife, of a sword); sharp edge; border, edge, rim, brink, verge; — (pl. حروف *ḥurūf*, احرف *aḥruf*) letter; consonant; particle (*gram.*); type (*typ.*) | على حرف irresolute, wavering, on the fence; الفاظه بحروفها *alfāẓuhū bi-ḥurūfihā* his words literally; بالحرف or بالحرف الواحد literally, verbatim, to the letter; حرفا بحرف *ḥarfan bi-ḥarfin* literally, word for word; وقع بالاحرف الاولى (*waqqa'a, ūlā*) to initial (e.g., معاهدة *mu'āhadatan* a treaty); الحروف الابجدية (*abjadīya*) the alphabetic letters, the alphabet; حروف مجموعة matter (*typ.*); الحروف الشمسية (*šamsīya*) the sun letters (i.e., sibilants, dentals, *r*, *l*, *n* to which the *l* of the article assimilates), الحروف القمرية (*qamarīya*) the moon letters (to which the *l* of the article does not assimilate); حرف الجر *ḥ. al-jarr* preposition (*gram.*); حرف الخفض *ḥ. al-kafḍ* do.; حرف التعريف article (*gram.*); حرف العطف *ḥ. al-'aṭf* coordinating conjunction (*gram.*); حرف الاستفهام interrogative particle (*gram.*); حرف القسم *ḥ. al-qasam* particle introducing oaths (*gram.*); الحرف العربى Arabic type (*typ.*); for other compounds look up the second word

حرفى *ḥarfī* literal

حرفية *ḥarfīya* wording, literal meaning (of a text) | اخذ بحرفية القانون to hold to the letter of the law

حرف *ḥurf* common garden pepper cress (Lepidium sativum L.; *bot.*)

حرفة *ḥirfa* pl. حرف *ḥiraf* occupation (esp. carried on independently); trade; handicraft (also حرفة يدوية *ḥirfa yadawīya*)

حرفى *ḥirafī* (and *ḥirfī*) industrial, trade (in compounds), professional; (pl. *-ūn*) independent tradesman; craftsman

حريف *ḥarīf* pl. حرفاء *ḥurafā'*[2] customer, patron, client (*tun.*, *mor.*)

حريف *ḥirrīf* pungent, acrid (taste); حريفات spicy food, delicacies

حرافة *ḥarāfa* pungency, acridity (taste)

تحريف *taḥrīf* pl. *-āt* alteration, change; distortion; perversion, corruption, esp. phonetic corruption of a word

تحريفية *taḥrīfīya* revisionism (in socialist countries)

انحراف *inḥirāf* pl. *-āt* deviation, digression; obliqueness, obliquity, inclination, slant; declination (*astron.*); ailment, indisposition, also انحراف المزاج; perversion (sexual); aberration (*opt.*)

انحرافى *inḥirāfī* pl. *-ūn* deviationist

احتراف *iḥtirāf* professional pursuit (of a trade, etc.); professionalism (in sports)

محرف *muḥarraf* corrupted (word)

منحرف *munḥarif* oblique; slanted, slanting, sloping, inclined; distorted, perverted, corrupted, twisted; deviating, divergent; (pl. *-āt*) trapezium (*geom.*) | شبه منحرف *šibh m.* trapezoid (*geom.*)

محترف *muḥtarif* one gainfully employed (ب in), person doing s.th. (ب) professionally; professional, a pro (sports); professional (adj.), e.g., صحافى محترف (*ṣiḥāfī*) professional journalist; climber, careerist

○ محترف *muḥtaraf* pl. *-āt* studio, atelier

حرق **ḥaraqa** *i* (*ḥarq*) to burn (ه s.th.); to burn, hurt, sting, smart | حرق قلبه (*qalbahū*), pl. حرق قلوبهم (*qulūbahum*) to vex, exasperate s.o.; — *u* (*ḥarq*) to rub together (ه s.th.) | حرق اسنانه (*asnānahū*), حرق الارم (*urram*) to gnash one's teeth **II** to burn (ه s.th.); **IV** to burn (ه s.th.); to destroy by fire (ه s.th.); to singe, scorch, parch (ه s.th.); to scald (ه s.th.); to kindle, ignite, set on fire (ه s.th.) | احرق فحمة ليله فى (*faḥmata lailihī*) to spend the night doing (s.th.), burn the midnight oil over ... **V** to burn, be aflame, burn up, take fire, be consumed by fire, be burned; to be consumed (by an emotion), pine away (ه with), be pained (ه by), eat one's heart out | تحرق شوقا (*šauqan*) to be overcome with longing or nostalgia **VIII** to burn, be aflame, burn up, take fire, be consumed by fire, be burned

حرق *ḥarq* burning, incineration, combustion; kindling, igniting, setting afire; arson, incendiarism; (pl. حروق *ḥurūq*) a burning, painful effect; pl. حروق burns (*med.*)

حرق *ḥaraq* fire, conflagration

حرقة *ḥurqa*, *ḥarqa* burning, incineration, combustion; stinging, smarting, burning (as a physical sensation); torture, torment, agony, pain, ordeal

حراق *ḥurāq*, *ḥurrāq* tinder

حراق *ḥarrāq* burning, aflame, afire; hot

حريق *ḥarīq* and حريقة pl. حرائق *ḥarā'iq*[2] fire; conflagration

○ حراقة *ḥarrāqa* torpedo

حرقان *ḥaraqān* burning, stinging, smarting (as a painful sensation; e.g., of the feet)

○ محرق *maḥraq* pl. محارق *maḥāriq*[2] focus (*phys.*)

تحاريق *taḥārīq*[2] (*Eg.*) season of the Nile's lowest water level, hottest season of the year

احراق *iḥrāq* burning, incineration, combustion

تحرق *taḥarruq* burning, combustion; burning desire (الى for)

احتراق *iḥtirāq* burning, combustion; fire, conflagration | ○ غرفة الاحتراق *ġurfat al-i.* combustion chamber (*techn.*); قابل الاحتراق *qābil al-i.* combustible

حارق *ḥāriq* pl. *-ūn*, حراق *ḥurrāq* arsonist, incendiary; igniter, burner (person)

محروق *maḥrūq* burned, charred, scorched, parched; reddish, bronze-colored; combustible, serving as fuel; pl. محروقات combustible materials or substances; fuel | فخار محروق (*fakkār*) fired clay

محرق *muḥriq*: قنبلة محرقة (*qunbula*) incendiary bomb

○ محرق *muḥraq* crematory

محرقة *muḥraqa* burnt sacrifice

حرقدة *ḥarqada* pl. حراقد *ḥarāqid*[2] Adam's apple

حرقفة *ḥarqafa* pl. حراقف *ḥarāqif*[2] protruding part of the hipbone

حرك **II** to move, set in motion, drive, propel, operate (ه s.th.); to march, move (ه troops); to stir (ه s.th.); to start, get started, get underway (ه s.th.); to agitate, excite, stimulate (ه s.th.); to incite, instigate, goad, prod, provoke, actuate, urge (على ه s.o. to do s.th.); to awaken, arouse, foment, stir up (ه s.th.); to vowel, vowelize (*gram.*, ه a consonant) | حرك مشاعره (*mašā'irahū*) to grip, excite, thrill s.o.; حرك العواطف to affect the feelings, be touching, moving, pathetic; لا يحرك ساكنا (*sākinan*) he doesn't budge, he doesn't bend his little finger, he remains immobile, apathetic; حرك ساكنه (*sākinahū*) to rouse s.o., put s.o. in a state of excitement, commotion or agitation **V** to move, be in motion, stir, budge; to start moving, get moving; to seize the initiative; to undertake independent measures; to start out, get underway (traveler); to depart, leave (train); to put out, to sail (fleet); to be set in motion, be driven, be operated; to be agitated, be excited, be stimulated; to be awakened, be roused, be fomented, be provoked, be caused

حرك *ḥarik* lively, active, brisk, agile, nimble

حركة *ḥaraka* pl. *-āt* movement, motion; commotion; physical exercise; stirring, impulse; proceeding, procedure, policy; action, undertaking, enterprise; military operation; continuation, progress; traffic (rail, shipping, street); movement (as a social phenomenon); vowel (*gram.*) | فى حركاته وسكناته (*sakanātihī*) in all his doings; in every situation; حركة المرور (through) traffic; حركة المراكب shipping traffic; حركة البضائع exchange of goods; merchandise traffic, freight traffic; حركة سياحية (*siyāḥīya*) tourist traffic, tourism; حركة الاموال turnover (*com.*); الحركة النسوية (*niswīya*) feminist movement; خفيف الحركة nimble, lithe, light, quick, agile, adroit; ثقيل الحركة slow in motion, heavy-handed, clumsy, sluggish, lumbering, inert, indolent; حركات تعبيرية expressive gestures; mimic art

حركى *ḥarakī* kinetic (*phys.*)

○ حركية *ḥarakīya* strategy

حراك *ḥarāk* movement, motion

محرك *maḥrak* path, trajectory (of a projectile)

محراك *miḥrāk* poker, fire iron

تحريكى *taḥrīkī* dynamic

تحرك *taḥarruk* pl. *-āt* movement, motion; forward motion; initiative; start; departure; sailing (of a fleet) | تحرك دبلوماسى (*diblōmāsī*) diplomatic initiative, demarche

حارك *ḥārik* withers

محرك *muḥarrik* mover, stirrer; rouser, inciter, fomenter, awakener, agent; instigator; — (pl. *-āt*) motive, springs, incentive, spur, motivating circumstance, causative factor; motor, engine (*techn.*) | محرك كهربائى (*kahrabā'ī*) electric motor; محرك نفاث (*naffāṯ*) jet engine; القوة المحركة (*quwwa*) motive power (*phys.*, *techn.*)

متحرك *mutaḥarrik* moving, movable, mobile; pronounced with following vowel, voweled, vowelized (consonant; *gram.*) | صور متحركة (*ṣuwar*) movies, motion pictures

حركث *ḥarkaṯa* (and حركش *ḥarkaša*) to stir up, agitate, excite, thrill

حرم *ḥaruma u*, *ḥarima a* to be forbidden, prohibited, interdicted, unlawful, unpermitted (على to s.o.); — *ḥarama i* (*ḥirm*, حرمان *ḥirmān*) to deprive, bereave, dispossess, divest (ه ه or من ه s.o. of s.th.), take away, withdraw, withhold (ه ه or ه من or من ه from s.o. s.th.), deny, refuse (ه ه or ه من or من ه to s.o. s.th.); to exclude, debar, preclude, cut off (ه ه or من ه s.o. from s.th.); to excommunicate (ه s.o.; *Chr.*) **II** to declare (ه s.th.) sacred, sacrosanct, inviolable, or taboo, to taboo (ه s.th.); to declare (ه s.th.) unlawful, not permissible, forbid, interdict, proscribe (ه s.th., على to s.o.); to render (ه s.o.) immune or proof (من against), immunize (من ه s.o. against) | حرمه على نفسه to deny o.s. s.th., abstain, refrain from s.th. **IV** to excommunicate (ه s.o.; *Chr.*); to enter into the state of ritual consecration (esp., of a Mecca pilgrim; see احرام *iḥrām*) **V** to be forbidden, interdicted, prohibited; to be holy, sacred, sacrosanct, inviolable **VIII** to honor, revere, venerate, esteem, respect (ه, ه s.o., s.th.) | احترم نفسه to be self-respecting **X** to deem (ه s.th.) sacrosanct, sacred, holy, inviolable; to deem (ه s.th.) unlawful or unpermissible

حرم *ḥirm* excommunication (*Chr.*)

حرم *ḥaram* pl. احرام *aḥrām* forbidden, prohibited, interdicted; taboo; holy, sacred, sacrosanct; s.th. sacred, sacred object; sacred possession; wife; sanctum, sanctuary, sacred precinct; (= حرم جامعى) campus, university grounds; الحرمان the two Holy Places, Mecca and Medina | ثالث الحرمين *ṯāliṯ al-ḥaramain* the third Holy Place, i.e., Jerusalem

حرمة *ḥurma* pl. حرم *ḥuram*, *ḥurumāt*, *ḥuramāt* that which is holy, sacred, sacrosanct, inviolable, or taboo; woman, lady, wife; — holiness, sacredness, sanctity, sacrosanctity, inviolability; reverence, veneration, esteem, deference, respect

حرام *ḥarām* pl. حرم *ḥurum* forbidden, interdicted, prohibited, unlawful; s.th. forbidden, offense, sin; inviolable, taboo; sacred, sacrosanct; cursed, accursed | ابن حرام *ibn ḥ.* illegitimate son, bastard; الاراضى الحرام no man's land; neutral territory; البيت الحرام (*bait*) the Kaaba; الشهر الحرام (*šahr*) the Holy Month Muharram; المسجد الحرام (*masjid*) the Holy Mosque in Mecca; منطقة حرام (*minṭaqa*) no man's land; حرام عليك you mustn't do (say) that! بالحرام illicitly, illegally, unlawfully

حرام *ḥirām* pl. -*āt*, احرمة *aḥrima* a woolen blanket (worn as a garment around head and body)

حريم *ḥarīm* pl. حرم *ḥurum* a sacred, inviolable place, sanctum, sanctuary, sacred precinct; harem; female members of the family, women; wife

حريمى *ḥarīmī* women's (in compounds), for women

حروم *ḥurūm* pl. -*āt* excommunication (*Chr.*)

حرامى *ḥarāmī* pl. -*īya* thief, robber, bandit

حرمان *ḥirmān* deprivation, bereavement, dispossession (of s.o., من of s.th.); prohibition (with genit.: to s.o., من from doing s.th.), revocation (من of a permission); banning, disqualification (of s.o., من from); debarment, exclusion, preclusion (من from); excommunication (*Chr.*); suspension (of a player, etc.; sport); privation; destitution, poverty | حرمان الارث *ḥ. al-irṯ* exclusion from inheritance, disinheritance (*Isl. Law*) | حرمانه من قيادة السيارة (*qiyādat as-sayyāra*) revocation of s.o.'s driver's license

محرم *maḥram* pl. محارم *maḥārim*[2] s.th. forbidden, inviolable, taboo, sacrosanct, holy, or sacred; unmarriageable, being in a degree of consanguinity precluding marriage (*Isl. Law*); pl. محارم close female relatives (of a man)

محرمة *maḥrama* pl. محارم *maḥārim*[2] handkerchief

تحريم *taḥrīm* forbiddance, interdiction, prohibition, ban

احرام *iḥrām* state of ritual consecration of the Mecca pilgrim (during which the pilgrim, wearing two seamless woolen or linen sheets, usually white, neither combs nor shaves, and observes sexual continence); garments of the Mecca pilgrim

احترام *iḥtirām* pl. *-āt* deference, respect, regard, esteem, reverence; honoring (e.g., of a privilege); pl. honors, respects, tributes | احترام الذات self-respect, self-esteem

محروم *maḥrūm* deprived, bereaved, bereft (من of); excluded, precluded, debarred (من from); suffering privation (as opposed to مرزوق); poor; excommunicated (*Chr.*)

محرم *muḥarram* forbidden, interdicted; Muharram, name of the first Islamic month; محرم الحرام *m. al-ḥarām* honorific name of this month

محرم *muḥrim* Mecca pilgrim who has entered the state of ritual consecration (see احرام *iḥrām*)

محترم *muḥtaram* honored, revered, venerated, esteemed, respected; (in the salutation of letters:) my dear . . .; venerable, reverend; notable, remarkable, considerable

حرمل *ḥarmal* African rue (Peganum harmala L.; *bot.*)

حرملة *ḥarmala* pl. حرامل *ḥarāmil*[2] a loose wrap worn over the shoulders (garment of the dervishes); cape, short wrap for women

حرن *ḥarana*, *ḥaruna u* (حران *ḥirān*, *ḥurān*) to be obstinate, stubborn, headstrong

حرون *ḥarūn* pl. حرن *ḥurun* obstinate, stubborn, refractory, reluctant, resistant

حارون *ḥārūn* brazier

حروة *ḥarwa* burning; wrath, rage; acridity, pungency (of taste); pungent, disagreeable odor

حرى V to seek, pursue (ه s.th.), strive (ه for), aspire (ه to); to examine, investigate (ه s.th.); to inquire (عن or ه into), make inquiries (عن or ه about); to be intent (ه on s.th.), take care (ه of s.th.), attend (ه to s.th., also في), look (ه after s.th., also في); to see to it (ان that)

بالحرى *bi-l-ḥarā* hardly, barely

حرى *ḥarīy* pl. احرياء *aḥriyā'*[2] adequate, appropriate, suitable (ب for), worthy (ب of s.th.) | حرى بالذكر (*ḏikr*) worth mentioning, considerable; حرى بالتصديق credible, believable; او بالحرى or to be exact, or rather

حراء *ḥirā'*(2) Hira (mountain northeast of Mecca)

احرى *aḥrā* more adequate, more proper, more appropriate | او بالاحرى or to tell the truth, or more explicitly, or put more exactly, or rather

تحر *taḥarrin* pl. تحريات *taḥarriyāt* inquiry; investigation | شرطة التحرى *šurṭat at-t.* or مصلحة التحرى *maṣlaḥat at-t.* secret police

حز *ḥazza u* (*ḥazz*) to notch, nick, incise, indent (فى s.th.), make an incision, cut (فى into s.th.) II and VIII = I

حز *ḥazz* pl. حزوز *ḥuzūz* incision, notch, nick; the right time, the nick of time

حزة *ḥazza* incision, notch, nick; time; the right time, the nick of time; predicament, plight

حزاز *ḥazāz* head scurf, ringworm; tetter, eruption (*med.*)

حزازة *ḥazāza* rancor, hatred, hate

محز *maḥazz* notch, nick | اصاب المحز to find the right solution, hit the nail on the head, hit the mark, strike home

حزب *ḥazaba u* (*ḥazb*) to befall (ه s.o.), happen, occur (ه to s.o.) | حزب الامر the matter became serious II to rally (ه s.o.); to form or found a party III to side, take sides (ه with), be an adherent (ه of s.o.) V to take sides; to form a party, make common cause, join forces

حزب *ḥizb* pl. احزاب *aḥzāb* group, troop, band, gang; party (*pol.*); the 60th part of the Koran | هو من احزابه he belongs to his clique, he is of the same breed

حزبى *ḥizbī* party (adj.), factional; (pl. -*ūn*) party man, party-liner

حزبية *ḥizbīya* party activities; partisanship, partiality; factionalism

حيزبون *ḥaizabūn* old hag

تحزب *taḥazzub* factiousness; factionalism

حازب *ḥāzib*: حزبه حازب *ḥazabahū ḥ.* he met with a mishap

متحزب *mutaḥazzib* partial, biased; partisan

¹حزر *ḥazara i u* (*ḥazr*, محزرة *maḥzara*) to estimate, assess, appraise (ه s.th.); to make a rough estimate (ه of s.th.), guess (ه s.th.)

حزر *ḥazr* estimation, assessment, appraisal; conjecture, guess, surmise

حزورة *ḥazzūra* riddle, puzzle

محزرة *maḥzara* estimation, assessment, appraisal; conjecture, guess, surmise

²حزيران *ḥazīrān*² June (*Syr.*, *Leb.*, *Ir.*, *Jord.*)

حزقانى *ḥuzuqqānī* choleric

حزوقة *ḥazūqa*, حازوقة *ḥāzūqa* hiccups

محازق *maḥāziq*² (*alg.*) pl. nuts (of bolts)

حزم *ḥazama i* (*ḥazm*) to tie up, bundle, wrap up, pack, do up in a package or bundle (ه s.th.); to girth (ه an animal); to buckle, fasten (ه a belt, a seatbelt); to make fast, fasten, tie (ه s.th.) | حزم امره (*amrahū*) to take matters firmly in hand; — *ḥazuma u* (*ḥazm*, حزامة *ḥazāma*, حزومة *ḥuzūma*) to be resolute, firm, stouthearted, intrepid II to tie together, pack (ه s.th.); to gird (ه s.o.) | حزم متاعه (*matāʿahū*) to pack one's things, tie up one's effects V and VIII to be girded; to gird o.s., put on a belt

حزم *ḥazm* packing, packaging, wrapping; determination, resoluteness, firmness, energy; judiciousness, discretion, prudence

حزمة *ḥuzma* pl. حزم *ḥuzam* s.th. wrapped up or tied up; bundle, fagot, fascine; beam of rays, radiation beam (*phys.*); bunch (of herbs, etc.); sheaf; package, parcel

حزام *ḥizām* pl. -*āt*, احزمة *aḥzima*, حزم *ḥuzum* belt, girth; girdle; cummerbund, waistband (worn over the caftan to fasten it); sword belt | حزام الامن *ḥ. al-amn* and حزام الامان *ḥ. al-amān* safety belt; حزام شعاعى (*šuʿāʿī*) radiation belt (*phys.*); حزام متحرك (*mutaḥarrik*) conveyor, conveyor belt (*techn.*)

احزم *aḥzam*[2] more resolute; more judicious

تحزيم *taḥzīm* packing up, wrapping up

حازم *ḥāzim* pl. حزمة *ḥazama* and حزيم *ḥazīm* pl. حزماء *ḥuzamā'*[2] resolute, energetic; judicious, discreet, prudent

حزن **ḥazana** *u* to make sad, sadden, grieve (ه s.o.); — *ḥazina a* (*ḥuzn, ḥazan*) to be sad, grieved (ل or على at or because of); to grieve, mourn (على over) **II** and **IV** to make sad, sadden, grieve (ه s. o.)

حزن *ḥuzn* pl. احزان *aḥzān* sadness, grief, sorrow, affliction

حزن *ḥazn* pl. حزون *ḥuzūn* rough, rugged, hard ground

حزن *ḥazin* sad, mournful, grieved

حزين *ḥazīn* pl. حزناء *ḥuzanā'*[2], حزان *ḥizān*, حزانى *ḥazānā* sad; mourning (for a deceased person); sorrowing, mournful, grieved | الجمعة الحزينة (*jum'a*) Good Friday (*Chr.*)

حزنان *ḥaznān*[2] very sad, very grieved, worried; in mourning

□ حزايني *ḥazāyinī* (حزائني *ḥazā'inī*) sad, mournful, melancholic; mourning- (in compounds), mortuary, funereal | قماش حزايني (*qumāš*) cloth for mourning garments

تحزن *taḥazzun* sadness; behavior of a mourner

محزون *maḥzūn* grieved, grief-stricken, pained, sad, saddened

محزن *muḥzin* grievous, saddening; sad; melancholic; tragic; محزنات *muḥzināt* grievous things | قصة تمثيلية محزنة (*qiṣṣa tamṯīlīya*) and رواية محزنة (*riwāya*) tragedy (*theat.*)

حس **ḥassa** (1st pers. perf. *ḥasastu*) *u* (*ḥass*) to curry, currycomb (ه an animal); to feel, sense (ه s.th.); — *ḥassa* (1st pers. perf. *ḥasastu*) *i*, (1st pers. perf. *ḥasistu*) *a* to feel sorry, feel sympathy or compassion (ل for), sympathize (ل with) **II** to grope, feel **IV** to perceive, sense, experience (ه or ب s.th.); to feel (ه or ب s.th.); to notice (ه or ب s.th.); to hear (ه a sound, a noise, etc.); to take notice (ه of s.o.) **V** to grope, probe (ه for s.th.), finger, handle, touch (ه s.th.), run the hand (ه over s.th.); to grope about, feel around; to grope, feel (ه one's way, الى to); to try to locate or detect (ه s.th.); to seek information, make inquiries (من about); to sense, experience, perceive (ه, ب s.th.); to feel (ب s.th.); to be affected, be deeply touched (ب by s.th.)

حس *ḥass* sensation, perception, feeling, sentiment

حس *ḥiss* sensory perception, sensation; feeling, sentiment; sense; voice; sound; noise | حس متبلد (*mutaballid*) apathy, emotional dullness; حس مشترك (*muštarak*) community feeling or spirit

حسى *ḥissī* sensory; sensuous; perceptible; palpable | ○ المذهب الحسى (*madhab*) sensationalism, sensualism; ○ الفلسفة الحسية (*falsafa*) do.

حسيات *ḥissīyāt* sensations

حسيس *ḥasīs* faint noise; soft sound of voices, whispering

حساس *ḥassās* sensitive; sensible; readily affected, susceptible; sensual (pleasure) | ورق حساس (*waraq*) photo-sensitive paper, photographic paper; حساس للضوء (*ḍau'*) light-sensitive

حساسة *ḥassāsa* sensory organ

حساسى *ḥassāsī* allergic | امراض حساسية allergic diseases, allergies (*med.*)

حساسية *ḥassāsīya* sensitivity (also *techn.*); sensibility; faculty of sensory perception; susceptibility; sensuality | مرض الحساسية *maraḍ al-ḥ.* allergy (*med.*)

محسة *miḥassa* currycomb

احساس *iḥsās* pl. *-āt,* احاسيس *aḥāsīs*² feel› feeling; sensation, sense (ب of s.th.); perception (ب of s.th.); sensitivity; pl. احساسات feelings, sentiments | ○ احساس بالنور sensitivity to light; ○ شديد الاحساس highly sensitive; احساس مشترك (*muštarak*) feeling of harmony, concord, unanimity; قلة الاحساس *qillat al-i.* insensitivity, dullness, obtuseness

○ الطائفة الاحساسية *aṭ-ṭā'ifa al-iḥsāsīya* the impressionists

تحسس *taḥassus*: التحسس البعيد remote sensing (oil production)

حاسة *ḥāssa* pl. حواس *ḥawāss*² sensation; sense | الحواس الخمس the five senses

محسوس *maḥsūs* felt; sensed; perceptible, noticeable, palpable, tangible; appreciable, considerable (e.g., loss); المحسوس that which is perceptible through the senses; appearance, evidence; المحسوسات things perceptible through the senses

حسب *ḥasaba u* (*ḥasb,* حساب *ḥisāb,* حسبان *hisbān, ḥusbān*) to compute, reckon, calculate; to count; to charge, debit (ه على s.th. to s.o., to s.o.'s account); to credit (ه ل s.th. to s.o., to s.o.'s account) | حسب حسابه (*ḥisābahū*) to take s.th. or s.o. into account or into consideration, reckon with s.th. or s.o., count on s.th. or s.o.; حسب حسابا ل (*ḥisāban*) do.; to attach importance to s.o. or s.th.; حسب الف حساب ل (*alfa*) to have a thousand apprehensions about...; — *ḥasiba a i* (حسبان *ḥisbān,* محسبة *maḥsaba, maḥsiba*) to regard (ه ه s.o. as), consider, deem (ه ه s.o. to be ...); to think, believe, suppose, assume; to consider, regard (ه من, ه s.o., s.th. as belonging to), count (ه من s.o. among); to see (ه في in s.o. s.th.); — *ḥasuba u* (*ḥasab,* حسابة *ḥasāba*) to be of noble origin, be highborn; to be highly esteemed, be valued III to settle an account, get even (ه with s.o.); to call (ه s.o.) to account, ask (ه s.o.) for an accounting; to hold (ه s. o.) responsible, make (ه s.o.) answerable | حاسب على نفسه to be careful, be on one's guard V to reckon (ل with an event); to be careful, be on one's guard; to take precautions; to seek to know, try to find out (ه s.th.) VI to settle a mutual account VIII to debit or credit; to take into account, take into consideration (ب or ه s.th.); to reckon (ب or ه with); (to anticipate a reward in the hereafter by adding a pious deed to one's account with God — such as resigning in God's will at the death of a relative; hence:) احتسب ولدا (*waladan*) to give a son, be bereaved of a son; احتسب عند الله الشيء to sacrifice s.th. in anticipation of God's reward in the hereafter; to charge (ه على s.th. for); to think, believe, suppose; to take (ه ه s.o. for or to be ...); to be content, content o.s. (ب with); to disapprove (ه على of s.th. in s.o.), take exception (ه على to s.th. in s.o.), reject (ه على s.th. in s.o.); to call (على s.o.) to account, ask (على s.o.) for an accounting

حسب *ḥasb* reckoning, computing, calculation; thinking, opinion, view; sufficiency | حسبك (or بحسبك) درهم *ḥasbuka* (*bi-ḥasbika*) *dirhamun* one dirham is enough for you; حسبك ان it suffices to say that...; you know enough when you hear that...; you need only...; بحسبك مقنعا ان (*muqni'an*) it will be enough to convince you if...; وحسبك بهذا كله شرا (*bi-hāḏā kullihī šarran*) but enough of all these negative aspects! فحسب *fa-ḥasb* and that's all, and no more, only (interchangeable with فقط)

حسبي *ḥasbī*: مجلس حسبي (*majlis*) pl. مجالس حسبية guardianship court, probate court (*Eg.*)

حسب *ḥasab* pl. احساب *aḥsāb* measure, extent, degree, quantity, amount; value; esteem, high regard enjoyed by s.o.; noble descent; *ḥasaba* (prep.), بحسب *bi-*

ḥasabi and على حسب *'alā ḥasabi* according to, in accordance with, commensurate with, depending on | ذو حسب ونسب (*na=sab*) of noble descent

حسبما *ḥasabamā* (conj.) according to what ..., as, depending on how ... | حسبما اتفق (*ttafaqa*) as chance will have it

حسبة *ḥisba* arithmetical problem, sum; calculation, reckoning

حسيب *ḥasīb* pl. حسباء *ḥusabā'*[2] respected, esteemed; noble, of noble birth, highborn

حسبان *ḥusbān* calculation, reckoning, accounting; computation | كان فى الحسبان to be taken into account, be taken into consideration; to be expected, be anticipated; كان فى الحسبان ان it was expected that ...; حسبانى ان I expect that ...

حساب *ḥisāb* arithmetic, reckoning, calculus; computation; calculation, estimation, appraisal; accounting, settlement; — (pl. *-āt*) reflection, consideration; weighing; bill, invoice; statement of costs; (bank) account; pl. حسابات bookkeeping | حساب الجمل *ḥ. al-jummal* (*al-jumal*) use of the alphabetic letters according to their numerical value; علم الحساب *'ilm al-ḥ.* arithmetic; حساب الاحتمال calculus of probability; حساب التفاضل *ḥ. at-tafāḍul* differential calculus; حساب التكامل *ḥ. at-takāmul* integral calculus; كان فى حسابه he reckoned with it, he expected it, he was prepared for it; عمل حسابا له to take s.o. or s.th. into consideration; to reckon with s.o. or s.th.; رتب حساباته على (*rat=taba*) to take s.th. into account or into consideration, be prepared for s.th. or to do s.th.; الحساب الختامى (*ḵitāmī*) and حساب نهائى (*nihā'ī*) final statement of account, final accounting; دعاه الى الحساب (*da'āhu*) he called him to account; يوم الحساب *yaum al-ḥ.* the Day of Reckoning, Judgment Day; اقام حسابا ل to render account to s.o.; بلا حساب without limit or bounds, to excess, to an unlimited extent; من غير حساب blindly, without forethought, at random; لحساب فلان to s.o.'s credit, to s.o.'s advantage; على حساب فلان to s.o.'s debit, at s.o.'s expense, to s.o.'s disadvantage; لقى سوء الحساب *laqiya sū'a l-ḥ.* he got a raw deal, he was in for it; حساب مثلثات *ḥ. muṯallaṯāt* trigonometry; حساب جار (*jārin*) current account; حسابات صندوق التوفير *ḥ. ṣundūq at-t.* savings-bank accounts; حساب موقوف blocked account; حسابات دوبيه (*dobya*) double-entry bookkeeping; الحساب الشرقى (*šarqī*) the Julian calendar; الحساب الغربى (*ğarbī*) the Gregorian calendar; انا على حسابك (*leb.*) I am at your service

حسابى *ḥisābī* arithmetical, mathematical, computational

حسابيات *ḥisābīyāt* arithmetic

محاسبة *muḥāsaba* pl. *-āt* accounting; clearing (*com.*); bookkeeping; request for accounting; examination of conscience (*theol.*) | قسم المحاسبة *qism al-m.* accounting department, comptroller's office; clearing house; ديوان المحاسبة audit office

احتساب *iḥtisāb* computation; calculation, consideration, reflection; debiting; crediting; valuation; contentedness, satisfaction

حاسب *ḥāsib* pl. *-ūn* counter, reckoner, arithmetician, calculator, computer; — (pl. *-āt*) calculating machine | حاسب الكترونى (*iliktrōnī*) electronic calculator, computer

محسوب *maḥsūb* pl. *-ūn*, محاسيب *maḥāsīb*[2] protégé, pet, favorite; محسوبك your obedient servant; — enjoying s.o.'s protection or shelter; calculated; measured, sedate (movements of a person, gestures, etc.)

محسوبية *maḥsūbīya* esteem enjoyed by s.o., position of distinction; patronage, favored position, favoritism

محاسب *muḥāsib* pl. *-ūn* accountant, bookkeeper; comptroller, auditor

محتسب *muḥtasib* (*Tun.*) bursar, treasurer (of a university, etc.)

محتسب *muḥtasab* that for which one can expect reward in the hereafter (e.g., suffering, loss, etc.)

حسد *ḥasada u* (*ḥasad*) to envy, grudge (ه s.o., على or ه s.th.), be envious (ه of s.o., على or ه because of s.th.) **VI** to envy each other

حسد *ḥasad* envy

حسود *ḥasūd* pl. حسد *ḥusud* envious

تحاسد *taḥāsud* mutual envy

حاسد *ḥāsid* pl. *-ūn*, حساد *ḥussād*, حسدة *ḥasada* envious; envier, grudger

محسود *maḥsūd* envied; smitten by the evil eye

حسر *ḥasara u i* (*ḥasr*) to pull away or off, remove (ه عن s.th., a cover, a veil, from); to uncover, lay bare, unveil (عن s.th.); — *u i* (حسور *ḥusūr*) to be uncovered, bared; to become dim (sight); — *ḥasira a* (*ḥasar*, حسرة *ḥasra*) to regret (على s.th.), be grieved, be pained (على by s.th.); to sigh (على over s.th.); — *ḥasara i*, *ḥasira a* (*ḥasar*) to become tired, fatigued **II** to fatigue, tire, weaken, sap (ه s.o.); to grieve, sadden (ه s.o.), cause pain or grief (ه to s.o.); to remove (ه a cover, عن from), lay bare, unveil (عن s.th.) **V** to be distressed, be pained, be grieved (على by); to sigh (على over) **VII** to be pulled away or off, be removed (عن from); to be rolled up, be turned back (sleeve, عن from the arm); to fall, drop (e.g., veil, water level); to recede, subside, abate (flood, etc.); to disappear suddenly (عن from); to drop one's veil; to become apparent, be unveiled, be revealed; to unveil, cause to become visible (عن s.th.)

حسر *ḥasar* fatigue, debility, weakness | حسر البصر *ḥ. al-baṣar* nearsightedness, myopia

حسر *ḥasir* grieved, sad; fatigued, languid, weary, tired

حسرة *ḥasra* pl. *ḥasarāt* grief, sorrow, pain, distress, affliction; sigh | يا للحسرة *yā la-l-ḥasrati* alas! unfortunately! يا حسرتى *yā ḥasratī* and وا حسرتاه *wā ḥasratāh* what a pity! too bad!

حسير *ḥasīr* pl. حسرى *ḥasrā* tired, weary, fatigued, exhausted; dim, dull (eye), nearsighted | حسير البصر *ḥ. al-baṣar* nearsighted, myopic

حسور *ḥusūr* nearsightedness, myopia

حسران *ḥasrān* regretful, sorry, sad, distressed, grieved

تحسر *taḥassur* sighing; regret

حاسر *ḥāsir* pl. حواسر *ḥawāsir*[2] bared, denuded; uncovered, bare; unveiled (woman, her hair and face; invar. for gender) | حاسر البصر *ḥ. al-baṣar* nearsighted, myopic; حاسر الرأس *ḥ. ar-ra's* bareheaded, hatless

حسك *ḥasak* (coll.; n. un. ة) thorns, spines; spikes, pricks; fishbones; awns, beard (*bot.*); name of several prickly herbs, esp. of the genus Tribulus

حسكى *ḥasakī* thorny, prickly, spiny

حسم *ḥasama i* (*ḥasm*) to cut, sever, cut off (ه s.th.); to finish (ه s.th.), put a stop or end (ه to s.th.); to terminate (ه e.g., a poor state of affairs, a nuisance); to decide (ه a question); to settle (ه an argument); to deduct, discount (ه an amount from a sum of money) **VII** to be severed, be cut off; to be finished, be completed, be terminated; to be settled (argument)

حسم *ḥasm* finishing, stop, end, termination; decision; settling, settlement (of an argument); discontinuance, shutdown, closing down; deduction, discounting (of an amount)

حسام *ḥusām* sword, sword edge

حسوم *ḥusūm* fatal, trying, grueling (pl.; days, nights, also years)

حاسم *ḥāsim* decisive; final, peremptory, conclusive, definite, definitive

حسن *ḥasuna u* (*ḥusn*) to be handsome, beautiful, lovely, nice, fine, good; to be expedient, advisable, suitable, proper, fitting; to be in a proper state, be in a desirable condition | ان حسن لديك *in ḥ. ladaika* if you like it, if it seems all right to you; يحسن بك ان it is to your advantage that you ...; you ought to ...; حسن استعداده ل he was all willing to ... **II** to beautify, embellish (ه s.th.); to adorn, decorate (ه s.th.); to improve, put into better form, ameliorate, better (ه s.th.); to make a better presentation (ه of s.th.); to present in a favorable light, depict as nice or desirable (ه ل s.th. to s.o.); to sugar-coat, make more palatable (ه s.th. unpleasant, s.th. disadvantageous) **III** to treat (ه s.o.) with kindliness **IV** to do right, act well; to do (ه s.th.) well, expertly, nicely; to know (ه how to do s.th.), be able (ه to do s.th.); to master (ه s.th.), have command (ه of s.th.), be proficient (ه in s.th.; a language, an art, a handicraft, etc.), be conversant (ه with s.th.); to do good, be charitable; to do favors, do good (الى or ب to s.o.), do (الى or ب s.o.) a good turn, be nice, friendly (الى or ب to s.o.); to give alms, give charity (الى to s.o.) | ما احسنه *mā aḥsanahū* how good he is! how handsome he is! احسنت *aḥsanta* well done! bravo! احسن الالمانية (*almānīya*) to master the German language, know German well; احسن الاختيار to make a good choice or selection; احسن التسديد to aim well or accurately; احسن مشورته (*mašūratahū*) to give good advice; احسن تطبيقه to make a good practical application of s.th.; احسن الظن ب (*ẓanna*) to have a good opinion of ..., judge s.th. favorably; احسن معاملته (*mu'āmalatahū*) to treat s.o. well; احسن فهمه (*fahmahū*) to grasp or understand s.th. well; لا يحسن ان (*yuḥsinu*) he is not capable of ..., he is not able to ... **V** to become nicer, more handsome, more beautiful; to improve, ameliorate, get better **X** to deem (ه s.th.) nice, etc., or good; to regard (ه s.th.) as right, advisable or appropriate; to approve (ه of s.th.), sanction, condone (ه s.th.); to come to like, to appreciate (ه s.th.), find pleasure (ه in s.th.); also = **IV**: استحسن الانجليزية (*ingilīzīya*) to know English well; pass. *ustuḥsina* to be good, commendable, advisable

حسن *ḥusn* beauty, handsomeness, prettiness, loveliness; excellence, superiority, perfection | لحسن الحظ *li-ḥ. il-ḥaẓẓ* fortunately; حسن السلوك good manners, good behavior; good conduct; حسن السير والسلوك (*ḥ. as-sair*) an irreproachable life; حسن التصرف *ḥ. at-taṣarruf* discretion, individual judgment; حسن الظن *ḥ. aẓ-ẓann* good opinion, favorable judgment; حسن التعبير euphemism; حسن القصد (النية) *ḥ. al-qaṣd* (*an-nīya*) good intention, good will, good faith; حسن يوسف *ḥ. yūsuf* beauty spot, patch; ست الحسن *sitt al-ḥusn* a kind of bindweed (Convolvulus cairicus L.; *bot.*); deadly nightshade, belladonna

حسن *ḥasan* pl. حسان *ḥisān* beautiful, handsome, lovely; pretty, nice; good, agreeable; excellent, superior, exquisite; حسنا *ḥasanan* well, splendidly, excellently, beautifully; الحسان the ladies; — high sandhill | وحسنا فعلت اذ (*fa'altu*) how well I did that I ...!

الحسنيون *al-ḥasanīyūn* the Hasanides, the descendants of Ḥasan, son of 'Alī and Fāṭima

احسن *aḥsan*[2] pl. احاسن *aḥāsin*[2] better;

nicer, lovelier, more beautiful; more excellent, more splendid, more admirable | هو احسن حالا منهم he is better off than they are; بالتى هى احسن (*bi-llatī*) in a friendly manner, amicably, with kindness

حسناء *ḥasnā'*[2] pl. حسان *ḥisān* (of a woman) beautiful, a beauty, a belle

الحسنى *al-ḥusnā* pl. *-āt* (f. of الاحسن *al-aḥsan*) the best outcome, the happy ending; fair means, amicable manner | بالحسنى amicably, by fair means, in a friendly manner; الاسماء الحسنى (*asmā'*) the 99 attributes of God

حسنة *ḥasana* pl. *-āt* good deed, benefaction; charity, alms; pl. حسنات advantages, merits

حسون *ḥassūn* pl. حساسين *ḥasāsīn*[2] goldfinch

محسنة *maḥsana* s.th. nice, s.th. good; advantage; pl. محاسن *maḥāsin*[2] beauties, charms, attractions, merits, advantages, good qualities | محاسن اجتماعية (*Alg.*) social privileges, services, social benefits

تحسين *taḥsīn* pl. *-āt* beautification, embellishment; improvement, amelioration, betterment; processing, refining, finishing; (pl. تحاسين *taḥāsīn*[2]) ornament, decoration | تحسين النسل *t. an-nasl* eugenics

محاسنة *muḥāsana* friendly treatment, kindliness, amicability

احسان *iḥsān* beneficence, charity, almsgiving, performance of good deeds

تحسن *taḥassun* improvement, amelioration | فى التحسن on the way to recovery

استحسان *istiḥsān* approval, consent; acclaim; discretion; application of discretion in a legal decision (*Isl. Law*) | شهادة استحسان *š. istiḥsān* certificate of achievement, citation of excellence

محسن *muḥassin* embellisher, beautifier, improver; pl. محسنات *muḥassināt* cosmetics

محسن *muḥsin* beneficent, charitable

مستحسن *mustaḥsan* approved, commendable; pleasant, agreeable

حسا (حسو) *ḥasā u* (*ḥasw*), V and VIII to drink noisily, sip, slurp (ه s.th.)

حسو *ḥasw* soup, broth

حسوة *ḥaswa* pl. *ḥasawāt* a sip

حسوة *ḥuswa* pl. *ḥusuwāt*, *ḥusawāt*, احسية *aḥsiya* a sip, small quantity of liquid; soup, broth: bouillon

حساء *ḥasā'* soup; broth | حساء البصل *ḥ. al-baṣal* onion soup; حساء الطماطم *ḥ. aṭ-ṭamāṭim* tomato soup; حساء العدس *ḥ. al-'adas* lentil soup; حساء لحم *ḥ. laḥm* and حساء من اللحوم consommé, bouillon

الاحساء (حسى) *al-aḥsā'* Al Hasa (province and administrative district in E Arabia)

حش *ḥašša u* (*ḥašš*) to mow, cut (ه s.th.) II to smoke hashish

حشيش *ḥašīš* (coll.) pl. حشائش *ḥašā'iš*[2] herbs, grasses; weeds; hay; hemp (Cannabis sativa L.; *bot.*), hashish, cannabis; stillborn child | حشيش الدينار *ḥ. ad-dīnār* hops

حشيشة *ḥašīša* (n. un.) herb | حشيشة الدينار hop (*bot.*)

حشاش *ḥaššāš* pl. *-ūn* smoker or chewer of hashish, hashish addict

حشاش *ḥušāš*, حشاشة *ḥušāša* last breath, last spark of life

حشيشى *ḥašīšī* (*eg.*) sap-green, reseda-colored

محش *miḥašš*, محشة *miḥašša* pl. محاش *maḥāšš*[2] sickle, scythe; fire iron, poker

محشة *miḥašša* pl. *-āt* (*eg.*) tool for weeding, weeder

محشش *maḥšaš*, محشش خانة *m.-ḵāna* hashish den

محششة *maḥšaša* pl. محاشش *maḥāšiš*² hashish den

حشد *ḥašada i u* (*ḥašd*) to gather, concentrate, mass (ه esp. troops), call up, mobilize (ه an army); to pile up, store up, accumulate (ه s.th., الى at a place) **II** to amass, accumulate (ه s.th.), mass, concentrate (ه esp. troops) **V** and **VIII** to rally, come together, assemble, gather, crowd together, throng together; to be concentrated, be massed (troops); to fall into line (troops)

حشد *ḥašd* pl. حشود *ḥušūd* assembling, rallying; gathering, assembly, crowd, throng; concentration, massing (esp. of troops; *mil.*); summoning up, mobilization (e.g., of all powers, means, possibilities)

تحشد *taḥaššud* pl. *-āt* concentration (of troops)

احتشاد *iḥtišād* pl. *-āt* gathering, crowd; concentration (of troops)

حاشد *ḥāšid* numerous (of an assembly), crowded (of a public demonstration)

○ حاشدة *ḥāšida* battery (*el.*)

حشر *ḥašara i u* (*ḥašr*) to gather, assemble, rally (ه people); to cram, crowd, pack, jam (together); to squeeze, press, force, stuff, tuck (بين or في ه s.th. into) | حشر نفسه بين الناس (*nafsahū*) to push one's way through the crowd

يوم الحشر *yaum al-ḥašr* the day of congregation (of the dead), the Day of Resurrection

حشرة *ḥašara* pl. *-āt* insect; pl. vermin, insect pests | علم الحشرات *ʿilm al-ḥ.* entomology

حشرى *ḥašarī* insectile, insectival, insect- (in compounds); entomologic(al)

حشرج *ḥašraja* and **II** *taḥašraja* to rattle in the throat

حشرجة *ḥašraja* rattling, rattle in the throat

حشف **V** to be dressed shabbily, dress slovenly

حشف *ḥašaf* dates of inferior quality

حشفة *ḥašafa* glans (penis; *anat.*)

حشك *ḥašaka i* (*ḥašk*) to cram, jam, squeeze, stuff (في ه s.th. into)

حشم *ḥašama i* (*ḥašm*) to shame, put to shame (ه s.o.) **II** and **IV** do. **V** and **VIII** to be ashamed to face s.o. (من or عن); to be reticent, modest, shy, bashful, diffident

حشم *ḥašam* servants, retinue, entourage, suite

حشمة *ḥišma* shame, bashfulness, timidity, diffidence; modesty; decency, decorum

حشيم *ḥašīm* pl. حشماء *ḥušamā'*² modest, timid, bashful, shy, diffident

محاشم *maḥāšim*² pubes, genitals

تحشم *taḥaššum* and احتشام *iḥtišām* shame, shyness, modesty, reticence, decency, decorum

محتشم *muḥtašim* shy, bashful; modest, reticent, decent, decorous

حشا (حشو) *ḥašā u* (*ḥašw*) to stuff, fill, dress (ب ه s.th. with; esp. fowl, etc.); to fill in (ه s.th.); to load (ه a firearm; ه ه s.th. with, e.g., a camera); to fill (ه a tooth); to insert (ه s.th.) **II** to interpolate (ه s.th.); to insert (ه s.th.); to provide (ه s.th.) with a margin; to hem (ه a dress); to supply (ه a book) with marginal notes or glosses **III** to except, exclude (من ه s.o. from) **V** to keep away, stand aloof, abstain (من from), avoid, shun (من s.th.), beware (من of), be on one's guard (من against) **VI** to keep away, abstain (عن or من from), beware (ه or عن or من of), avoid, shun (ه or عن or من s.th.)

حشو *ḥašw* that with which s.th. is stuffed or filled; dressing, stuffing (of fowl, etc.); filling (of teeth); insertion; ○ infix (*gram.*); parenthesis; interpolation

حشوة *ḥašwa* pl. *-āt* filling, stuffing (cushion, cookery, etc.); load (of a cartridge), charge (of a mine); panel, inlay, inserted piece (in paneling, in a door)

حشا *ḥašan* pl. احشاء *aḥšā'* bowels, intestines; interior, inside; pl. احشاء interior of the body; womb | فى احشاء in the interior of, within, in

حشى *ḥašan* = حشا *ḥašan*

حشية *ḥašīya* pl. *-āt*, حشايا *ḥašāyā* cushion, pillow; mattress

حاشا, حاشى *ḥāšā* (with genit., acc. or ل) except, save | حاشا لله, حاشى لله God forbid! حاشا لك ان far be it from you that you...; حاشا لك, حاشا لله = (*ḥāša*) حاش لك, حاش لله; حاشى ان تفعل far be it that you do it, (but with pers. suffix in connection with 1st pers. of the verb) حاشاى ان افعل (*ḥāšāya*) far be it that I do it

تحشية *taḥšiya* insertion; interpolation

تحاش *taḥāšin* avoidance

حاشية *ḥāšiya* pl. حواش *ḥawāšin* border; seam, hem; edge; margin (of a book); marginal gloss; marginal notes; commentary on certain words and passages of a book, supercommentary; footnote; postscript; retinue, entourage, suite, servants; dependents; pl. حواش critical apparatus | رقيق الحاشية and رقيق الحواشى nice, polite, courteous, gracious, amiable, kindly, friendly; رقة الحاشية *riqqat al-ḥ.* niceness, amiability, graciousness

محشو *maḥšūw* filled, dressed; stuffed; loaded (firearm); pl. محشوات *maḥšūwāt* filled, or stuffed, dishes

□ محشى *maḥšīy* (*colloq. máḥši*) filled, stuffed (food); stuffed meal, a dish filled with rice, chopped meat, etc.; محشية *maḥšīya* pl. *-āt* (*eg.*) candy with a filling

حص *ḥaṣṣa* *u* to fall as a share (ه to s.o.) III to share (ه ه s.th. with s.o.) IV to allot s.o. (ه) his share

حص *ḥuṣṣ* saffron

حصة *ḥiṣṣa* pl. حصص *ḥiṣaṣ* share, portion, allotment; share (*fin.*); contingent, quota; span of time; lesson, class period | حصة فى الربح *ḥ. fī r-rabḥ* dividend (*fin.*); ○ حصة التأسيس founders' share; ○ نظام الحصص quota system, apportionment; فى حصة وجيزة in a short time

تحصيص *taḥṣīṣ* quota system, apportionment

محاصة *muḥāṣṣa* allotment; sharing (with s.o.), partaking, participation

حصالبان see حصى

حصب *ḥaṣaba* *i u* to cover or strew with pebbles or gravel (ه ground); to macadamize (ه ground), metal (ه a road); — *ḥaṣiba* *a* and pass. *ḥuṣiba* to have the measles II to cover or strew with pebbles or gravel (ه ground); to macadamize (ه ground), metal (ه a road)

حصب *ḥaṣab* road metal, crushed rock, ballast

حصباء *ḥaṣbā'*[2] (coll.) pebbles; gravel

حصبة *ḥaṣba* measles (*med.*)

حاصبة *ḥāṣiba* storm, hurricane

حصحص *ḥaṣḥaṣa* to be or become clear, plain, manifest; to come to light (truth)

حصد *ḥaṣada* *i u* (*ḥaṣd*, حصاد *ḥaṣād*, *ḥiṣād*) to harvest, reap (ه s.th.); to mow (ه s.th.) IV, VIII and X to be ripe

حصد *ḥaṣd* and حصاد *ḥiṣād* harvesting, reaping, harvest; حصاد harvest time

حصيد *ḥaṣīd*, حصيدة *ḥaṣīda* pl. حصائد *ḥaṣā'id*² crop, harvest yield | قائم وحصيد everything without exception

حصاد *ḥaṣṣād* reaper; harvester

محصد *miḥṣad* pl. محاصد *maḥāṣid*² sickle

○ حصادة *ḥaṣṣāda* and ○ محصدة *miḥṣada* mowing machine, mower | ○ حصادة دراسة (*darrāsa*) combine

حاصد *ḥāṣid* reaper

○ حاصدة *ḥāṣida* mowing machine, mower

محصود *maḥṣūd* harvested, reaped, mown

محصد *muḥṣid* and مستحصد *mustaḥṣid* ripe

حصر *ḥaṣara i u* (*ḥaṣr*) to surround, encircle, encompass, ring (ه s.th.); to enclose (ه s.th.); to parenthesize (ه a word); to blockade (ه, ه s.o., s.th.); to besiege, beleaguer (ه, ه s.o., s.th.); to detain, deter, restrain, contain, hold back (ه s.o.); to limit, restrict (ه في or ب s.th. to); to condense, reduce in scope (ه s.th.); to narrow down, confine (ه في s.th. to, also a suspicion to s.o.); to bring together, compile, arrange (ه في s.th. under a rubric); to enter (ه في s.th. in a list); to put together, set up, list, enumerate (ه s.th.); to comprise, contain, include, involve (ه s.th.); — *ḥaṣira a* (*ḥaṣar*) to be in a fix, be in a dilemma **III** to encircle, envelop, enclose (ه s.o., esp. enemies); to beleaguer, besiege (ه a place); to blockade, cut off from supplies (ه, ه s.o., s.th.); to press hard, corner (ه s.o.), put the screws (ه on s.o.) **VII** to be straitened, confined, narrowed in; to be or become restricted, limited (على or في to); to limit o.s. (على or في to); to be condensed (في to), be concentrated (في in); to be or become united (e.g., تحت حكمه under s.o.'s rule); to be reducible (في to), be expressible (في in terms of), consist (في in)

حصر *ḥaṣr* encirclement, encompassment, enclosure, corralling; parenthesizing; blocking, blockading, beleaguering, siege; detention, determent; restraint, retention, containment, check; limitation, restriction, confinement; narrowing; gathering, collecting (of s.th. scattered), compilation; enumeration, listing, counting, computing; inventory, stock-taking (e.g., of goods, money, libraries); centralization, concentration; (tobacco) monopoly | بالحصر strictly speaking; على سبيل الحصر exhaustively; حصر التموين *ḥ. at-tamwīn* rationing; علامة الحصر *ʿalāmat al-ḥ.* parentheses, brackets (*typ.*); لا يدخل تحت الحصر (*yadkulu*) or لا حصر له (*ḥaṣra*) boundless, infinite, immeasurable, innumerable; يفوق الحصر *yafūqu l-ḥaṣra* do.; ○ اجازة الحصر *ijāzat al-ḥ.* patent on an invention; ادارة حصر التبغ والتنباك *idārat ḥ. at-tibğ wa-t-tumbāk* Government Tobacco Monopoly (*Syr.*)

حصر *ḥuṣr* retention (of urine); constipation

حصر *ḥaṣar* dyslogia, inability to express o.s. effectively

حصير *ḥaṣīr* pl. حصر *ḥuṣur* mat

حصيرة *ḥaṣīra* pl. حصائر *ḥaṣā'ir*² mat

حصار *ḥaṣṣār* pl. *-ūn* mat weaver

حصار *ḥiṣār* encirclement; blockade; siege | حصار اقتصادى economic blockade

محاصرة *muḥāṣara* encirclement; blockade; siege

انحصار *inḥiṣār* restrictedness, limitation, confinement; (tobacco) monopoly; ○ obsession (by an idea; *psych.*)

محصور *maḥṣūr* blocked, blockaded; beleaguered, besieged; limited, restricted, confined (في to); narrow; narrowly circumscribed

حصرم *ḥiṣrim* (coll.; n. un. ة) unripe and sour grapes (*syr.*)

حصف *ḥaṣufa u* (حصافة *ḥaṣāfa*) to have sound judgment, be judicious, discriminating

حصف *ḥaṣif* endowed with sound judgment, judicious, discriminating

حصيف *ḥaṣīf* endowed with sound judgment, judicious, discriminating; down-to-earth; (pl. حصفاء *ḥuṣafā'*²) realist

حصافة *ḥaṣāfa* sound judgment, judiciousness

حصل *ḥaṣala u* (حصول *ḥuṣūl*) to set in; to be there, be existent, extant; to arise, come about; to result, come out; to happen, occur, transpire, come to pass, take place; to happen, occur (ل to s.o.), come (ل upon s.o.), befall, overtake (ل s.o.); to originate, emanate, derive, stem (من from), be caused, be produced (من by); to attain, obtain, get, receive, achieve (على s.th.), win (على s.th., e.g., a prize); to come into possession (على of s.th.); to collect, recover (على a debt), call in (على funds); to receive, take in (على s.th.) **II** to cause s.th. (ه) to happen or set in; to attain, obtain (ه, على s.th.); to acquire (ه, على s.th., also knowledge); to infer, deduce (ه s.th.); to collect (ه a fee, fare, etc.), levy (ه taxes, fees, etc.), call in (ه money); to summarize, sum up (ه s.th.) **V** to result (من from), come out (sum); to be obtained, be attained; to be raised, be levied, be required, be demanded; to be taken in, come in (fees, taxes, funds); to be collected (taxes); to procure for o.s., get (على s.th.); to attain, receive, obtain (على s.th.); to acquire (على s.th.); to collect (على fees) **X** to procure for o.s., get (على s.th.); to attain, receive, obtain (على s.th.); to acquire (على s.th.); to levy, collect (ه money, fees)

حصول *ḥuṣūl* setting in, occurrence, incidence, happening (of an event or process); obtainment, attainment (على of s.th.); achievement (على of s.th.); acquisition (على of s.th.)

حصيلة *ḥaṣīla* pl. حصائل *ḥaṣā'il*² result; yield; winnings; amount collected, proceeds, returns; revenue, receipts

حوصل, حوصلة and حويصلة look up alphabetically

حصالة *ḥaṣṣāla* pl. *-āt* collection box, alms box; money box; cashbox

محصل *maḥṣal* result, outcome, upshot, issue

تحصيل *taḥṣīl* pl. *-āt* attainment, obtainment, gain; acquisition (also of knowledge); learning, studying, scientific studies; collection, raising, levy(ing), calling in (of funds, taxes); income, revenue, receipts, returns, proceeds; résumé, summary, gist (of a speech or opinion) | تحصيل الحاصل tautology

تحصيلجي *taḥṣīlgī* (*eg.*) = محصل *muḥaṣṣil*

حاصل *ḥāṣil* pl. حواصل *ḥawāṣil*² setting in, occurring, taking place, happening; result, outcome, sum, total, product (also *math.*); revenues, receipts, proceeds, gain; income, returns; crop, harvest; warehouse, storehouse, granary, depot, magazine; main content, purport, gist, essence, substance (of a speech); — (pl. *-ūn*) holder (على of, e.g., a certificate); الحاصل briefly, in short; pl. حاصلات product(s), yield, produce, production (*econ.*)

محصول *maḥṣūl* pl. *-āt*, محاصيل *maḥāṣīl*² result, outcome, issue; yield, gain; product, produce; crop, harvest; production

محصل *muḥaṣṣil* collector; tax collector; cashier; (bus, streetcar) conductor

محصل عليه *muḥaṣṣal ʿalaihi* received, attained, acquired

متحصل *mutaḥaṣṣil* yield, revenue, proceeds, receipts, returns (من from)

حصن **ḥaṣuna** *u* (حصانة *ḥaṣāna*) to be inaccessible, be well fortified; to be chaste (woman) II to make inaccessible (ه s.th.); to strengthen (ه s.th.); to fortify, entrench (ه s.th.); to immunize, make proof (ضد *ḍidda* against) IV to make inaccessible (ه s.th.); to fortify, entrench (ه s.th.); to be chaste, pure (woman); to remain chaste, be of unblemished reputation (woman) V to strengthen one's position, protect o.s.; to be fortified; to be secure, be protected

حصن *ḥiṣn* pl. حصون *ḥuṣūn* fortress, fort, castle, citadel, stronghold; fortification, entrenchment; protection | حصن طائر Flying Fortress

حصان *ḥiṣān* pl. حصن *ḥuṣun*, احصنة *aḥṣina* horse; stallion | حصان البحر *ḥ. al-baḥr* hippopotamus; حصان بخارى (*bukārī*) iron horse; قوة حصان *quwwat ḥ.*, or حصان alone, horse power

حصين *ḥaṣīn* inaccessible, strong, fortified, firm, secure(d), protected; immune, proof, invulnerable (ضد *ḍidda* against) | الحصن الحصين (*ḥiṣn*) stronghold (fig.; e.g., of radicalism)

ابو الحصين *abū l-ḥuṣain* fox

حصانة *ḥaṣāna* strength, ruggedness, forbiddingness, impregnability, inaccessibility; shelteredness, chastity (of a woman); invulnerability, inviolability; immunity (of deputies, diplomats; against illness)

تحصين *taḥṣīn* pl. *-āt* fortification, entrenchment; strengthening, cementing, solidification; immunization

احصان *iḥṣān* blamelessness, unblemished reputation, integrity (*Isl. Law*); chastity

تحصن *taḥaṣṣun* securing, safeguarding, protection, protectedness

محصن *muḥaṣṣan* fortified; entrenched; immune, proof (ضد *ḍidda* against)

محصنة *muḥṣina*, *muḥṣana* sheltered, well-protected, chaste; of unblemished reputation (woman; *Isl. Law*)

حصوى , حصوة see under حصى

حصى IV to count, enumerate (ه s.th.); to calculate, compute (ه s.th. من from); to debit, charge (ه على s.th. to s.o.'s account), hold (ه s.th. على against s.o.) | لا يحصى (*yuḥṣā*) innumerable

حصى *ḥaṣan* (coll.) pebbles, little stones

حصاة *ḥaṣāh*, حصوة *ḥaṣwa* pl. *ḥaṣawāt*, حصيات *ḥaṣayāt* little stone, pebble; calculus, stone (*med.*) | حصاة بولية (*baulīya*) cystic calculus; حصاة صفراوية (*ṣafrāwīya*) gallstone, biliary calculus

حصى لبان *ḥaṣā lubān*, حصالبان rosemary (*bot.*)

حصوى *ḥaṣawī* stony, pebbly, gravelly

احصاء *iḥṣā'* pl. *-āt* count, counting; enumeration; calculation, computation; statistics | احصاء السكان *i. as-sukkān* census

احصائى *iḥṣā'ī* statistic(al); (pl. *-ūn*) statistician

احصائية *iḥṣā'īya* pl. *-āt* statistics

حض **ḥaḍḍa** *u* (*ḥaḍḍ*) and II to spur on, incite (ه s.o., على to), goad, prod (ه s.o., على to do s.th.)

حض *ḥaḍḍ* incitement, inducement, prodding, prompting, instigation

حضيض *ḥaḍīḍ* pl. حضض *ḥuḍuḍ*, احضة *aḥiḍḍa* foot of a mountain; lowland; ground; bottom; lowest point; perigee (*astron.*); depth; state of decay | نزل الى الحضيض to sink low (fig.); دكه الى الحضيض (*dakkahū*) to ruin s.th. completely, run s.th. into the ground

حضر **ḥaḍara** *u* (حضور *ḥuḍūr*) to be present (ه at), be in the presence (ه of s.o.); to attend (ه s.th.); to be present (ه in s.o.'s mind), be readily recalled (ه by s.o.); to take part, participate (مجلسا majlisan in a meeting); to come, get (الى or ه, ه to s.o., to a place), arrive (الى or ه at a place); to visit (ه a place), attend (ه a public event), go (ه to a performance, etc.); to appear (امام before a judge, etc., الى in, at), show up (الى in, at); to betake o.s., go (الى من from ... to); — (حضارة ḥaḍāra) to be settled, sedentary (in a civilized region, as opposed to nomadic existence) **II** to ready, make ready, prepare (ه s.th., also, e.g., a medicine = to compound), make, produce, manufacture (ه s.th.); to study, prepare (ه a lesson); to fetch, get, bring (ه s.o., ه s.th.), procure, supply (ه s.th.); to settle (ه s.o.), make s.o. (ه) sedentary; to civilize (ه s.o., ه s.th.) **III** to give a lecture, present s.th. in a lecture (ه to s.o.); to lecture, give a course of lectures **IV** to fetch, get, bring (ه, ه s.o., s.th.), procure, supply (ه s.th.); to take (ه s.o., ه s.th., الى to a place) | احضره معه to have s.th. with one, bring s.th. along **V** to prepare o.s., ready o.s., get ready (ل for); to be ready, prepared; to become settled, be sedentary in a civilized region; to be civilized, be in a state of civilization; to become urbanized, become a town dweller **VIII** to come (ه to s.o.), be in the presence (ه of s.o.); to live in a civilized region; pass. *uḥtuḍira* to die **X** to have s.th. (ه) brought, to call, send (ه, ه for s.o., for s.th.), have s.o. (ه) come; to summon (ه s.o.); to fetch, procure, supply, get, bring (ه s.th.); to conjure, call up, evoke (ه a spirit); to visualize, envision, call to mind (ه s.th.); to carry with o.s., bring along (ه s.th.); to prepare (ه, e.g., a medicinal preparation)

حضر *ḥaḍar* a civilized region with towns and villages and a settled population (as opposed to desert, steppe); settled population, town dwellers (as opposed to nomads)

حضرى *ḥaḍarī* settled, sedentary, resident, not nomadic, non-Bedouin, like urbanites; civilized; urban; town dweller

حضرة *ḥaḍra* presence | فى حضرة in the presence of...; الحضرة العلية (*ʿalīya*) His Highness (formerly, title of the Bey of Tunis); حضرتكم a respectful form of address, esp. in letters; حضرة الدكتور cf. Fr. *Monsieur le docteur*

حضور *ḥuḍūr* presence; visit, participation, attendance; (as one pl. of حاضر) those present | بحضوره in his presence; حضور الحفلة *ḥ. al-ḥafla* attendance of the celebration; حضور الذهن *ḥ. aḏ-ḏihn* presence of mind; ورقة حضور *waraqat ḥ.* summons (*jur.*); حضور الصالون those present in the salon; حضور المقهى *ḥ. al-maqhā* the customers present in the café

حضورى *ḥuḍūrī*: احكام حضورية (*aḥkām*) judgments delivered in the presence of the litigant parties after oral proceedings (*jur.*); حضوريا *ḥuḍūrīyan* contradictorily (*jur.*)

حضارة *ḥaḍāra* pl. *-āt* civilization; culture; — settledness, sedentariness

حضارى *ḥaḍārī* civilizational; cultural

حضيرة *ḥaḍīra* pl. حضائر *ḥaḍāʾir*² a small group of 6 to 12 people (specif., the smallest unit of boy scouts = patrol); section (*mil.*)

محضر *maḥḍar* presence; attendance, coming, appearance (of s.o.); assembly, meeting, gathering, convention; (pl. محاضر *maḥāḍir*²) minutes, official report, procès-verbal, record of the factual findings | محضر الجرد *m. al-jard* inventory list; بمحضر منه *bi-maḥḍarin minhu* in s.o.'s presence

تحضير *taḥḍīr* preparing, readying, making ready; (pl. *-āt*) preparation (ل for; also e.g., for an examination); making, preparation, cooking (of food, etc.), production, manufacture; (*Maġr.*) dressing, finish, sizing (of textiles)

تحضيرى *taḥḍīrī* preparatory, preparative | المدارس التحضيرية للمعلمين (*muʿallimīn*) preparatory institutes for teachers, teachers' colleges (*Eg.*)

محاضرة *muḥāḍara* pl. *-āt* lecture

احضار *iḥḍār* procurement, supply, fetching, bringing

تحضر *taḥaḍḍur* civilized way of life

احتضار *iḥtiḍār* demise, death

استحضار *istiḥḍār* making, production, manufacture; preparation; summoning | استحضار الارواح *istiḥḍār al-arwāḥ* evocation of spirits, spiritism

حاضر *ḥāḍir* pl. حضر *ḥuḍḍar*, حضور *ḥuḍūr* present; attending; الحاضر the present (time); prepared (ل for); ready; (pl. حضار *ḥuḍḍār*, حضرة *ḥaḍara*) settled, sedentary, resident, village or town dweller, not nomadic | فى الحاضر or فى الوقت الحاضر at present, now; حاضر الفكر *ḥ. al-fikr* quick-witted, quick at repartee; نقد حاضر (*naqd*) cash, ready money; بالحاضر in cash, for cash; ادى فريضة الصلاة حاضرة *addā f. aṣ-ṣalāti ḥāḍiratan* to perform the prescribed prayer promptly and on time (within the stipulated interval)

حاضرة *ḥāḍira* pl. حواضر *ḥawāḍir*[2] capital city, metropolis; city (as a center of civilization)

محضور *maḥḍūr* possessed, haunted or inhabited by a jinni; demoniac

محضر *muḥaḍḍir* maker, producer, manufacturer; dissector (*med.*)

محضر *muḥaḍḍar* ready, at hand

محاضر *muḥāḍir* lecturer, speaker; (*Ir.*) university lecturer; (*Eg.*) reader (at a university)

محضر *muḥḍir* court usher

متحضر *mutaḥaḍḍir* civilized

محتضر *muḥtaḍar* dying, in the throes of death, on the brink of death; a dying person; haunted or inhabited by a jinni; demoniac

مستحضر *mustaḥḍar* pl. *-āt* preparation (*chem.*, *pharm.*) | مستحضر دوائى (*dawāʾī*) medicinal preparation

حضرموت *ḥaḍramaut*[2] Hadhramaut

حضرمى *ḥaḍramī* pl. حضارم *ḥaḍārim*[2] man from Hadhramaut; Hadhramautian (adj.)

حضن *ḥaḍana u* (*ḥaḍn*, حضانة *ḥiḍāna*) to clasp in one's arms, embrace, hug (ه s.o.); to nurse, bring up, raise (ه a child); (*ḥaḍn*, حضان *ḥiḍān*, حضانة *ḥiḍāna*, حضون *ḥuḍūn*) to hatch, brood, incubate (ه an egg; of a bird) VI to embrace one another, cling to one another, nestle against each other VIII to clasp in one's arms, embrace, hug (ه, ه s.o., s.th.); to hold or carry in one's arms (ه an object); to harbor in one's bosom (ه feeling); to hatch, concoct, contrive (ه s.th.); to bring up, raise (ه a child); to include, enclose, encompass (ه s.th.; loan translation of Engl. *to embrace*, Fr. *embrasser*)

حضن *ḥiḍn* pl. احضان *aḥḍān* breast, bosom (between the outstretched arms); armful, that which can be carried in one's arms | قبله بالحضن (*qabilahū*) he received him with open arms; بين احضان and فى احضان amid, among; with, in the presence of (s.o.); فى احضان الصحراء (*ṣaḥrāʾ*) in the heart (or folds) of the desert; اخذتنى بين احضانها she took me in her arms

حضانة *ḥiḍāna*, *ḥaḍāna* raising, bringing up, nursing (of a child); hatching (of an egg), incubation | دار الحضانة children's home, day nursery, crèche

حضين *ḥaḍīn* embraced, hugged, resting in s.o.'s arms

محضن *maḥḍan* pl. محاضن *maḥāḍin*² children's home, day nursery, crèche

احتضان *iḥtiḍān* embrace, hug(ging), accolade

حاضنة *ḥāḍina* pl. حواضن *ḥawāḍin*² nursemaid, dry nurse

محتضن *muḥtaḍin* embracing, hugging; tender, affectionate

حط *ḥaṭṭa u* (*ḥaṭṭ*) to put, place, put down, set down (ه s.th.); to take down (ه a load, burden); to lower, decrease, diminish, reduce (ه or من s.th.); to depreciate (من قدره *min qadrihī* or من قيمته *min qīmatihī* the value of s.th.) | حط الرحال (*riḥāla*) to halt, make a stop, dismount, encamp (while traveling on horseback, camelback, etc.); — *u* (*ḥaṭṭ*, حطوط *ḥuṭūṭ*) to sink, descend, go down; to alight (bird); to land (airplane); to drop (price) **II** to put down, set down, take off, unload (ه a load) **VII** to sink, descend, go down; to decrease, diminish; to decline, decay, wane **VIII** to put down, set down, take down (ه s.th.)

حط *ḥaṭṭ* (act of) putting or setting down; depreciation, belittling, derogation, disparagement (من of s.th.); reduction, diminution, decrease (من of s.th.)

حطة *ḥiṭṭa* alleviation, relief, mitigation; abasement, debasement, demotion, degradation (in rank, dignity, prestige); humiliation, insult, indignity

احط *aḥaṭṭ*² lower; meaner, viler, more vulgar

حطيطة *ḥaṭīṭa* price reduction

محط *maḥaṭṭ* place at which s.th. is put down or deposited; stopping place, stop; pause, fermata, hold, concluding strain, cadence (*mus.*) | محط الآمال object of hope, that on which one's hopes are pinned; كان محط الانظار to attract the glances, draw attention to o.s.; محط الكلام *m. al-kalām* sense, or meaning, of one's words

محطة *maḥaṭṭa* pl. *-āt* stopping place, stop (also of public conveyances); station, post; railroad station; broadcasting station, radio station | محطة تحويل التيار *m. taḥwīl at-tayyār* transformer station; محطة الاذاعة (اللاسلكية) *m. al-iḏāʿa* (*al-lā-silkīya*) broadcasting station, radio station; transmitter (station); محطة رئيسية (*ra'īsīya*) (railroad) main station; محطة الاشارات *m. al-išārāt* signal post; محطة ارسال *m. irsāl* broadcasting station (radio, TV); محطة للارصاد الجوية (*li-l-arṣād al-jawwīya*) meteorological station, weather station; محطة الصرف *m. aṣ-ṣarf* (*Eg.*) pump station (for drainage); power plant; محطة الاستقبال receiving station (radio); محطة لاسلكية قصيرة الامواج (*lā-silkīya qaṣīrat al-amwāj*) short-wave transmitter station; محطة توليد الكهرباء *m. taulīd al-kahrabā'* and محطة كهربائية power plant; محطة ارضية (*arḍīya*) ground station; محطة بحوث research station; محطة تجارب *m. tajārib* experimental station; محطة ضخ *m. ḍaḵḵ* pump station (oil industry); محطة فضاء *m. faḍā'* space station; محطة وقود *m. waqūd* and محطة بنزين *m. banzīn* gas(oline) station

انحطاط *inḥiṭāṭ* decline, fall, decay, decadence; inferiority | احساس الانحطاط *iḥsās al-inḥ.* sense of inferiority

انحطاطى *inḥiṭāṭī* postclassical writer

منحط *munḥaṭṭ* low, base, low-level, low-grade; fallen, degraded (woman); mean, vile, vulgar; inferior

حطب *ḥaṭaba i* to gather firewood | حطب فى حبله (*fī ḥablihī*) to support s.o., stand by s.o., back s.o. up **VIII** to gather firewood

حطب *ḥaṭab* pl. احطاب *aḥṭāb* firewood

حطاب *ḥaṭṭāb* wood gatherer; woodcutter, lumberjack; vendor of firewood

تحطيب *taḥṭīb* singlestick fencing (a popular game, esp. in rural areas; *eg.*)

حاطب *ḥāṭib* wood gatherer; woodcutter, lumberjack; vendor of firewood | كحاطب ليل *ka-ḥāṭibi lailin* lit.: like one who gathers wood at night, i.e., blindly, at random, heedlessly (said of s.o. who does not realize, or think about, what he is doing)

حطم **ḥaṭama** *i* (*ḥaṭm*) and **II** to shatter, smash, wreck, demolish (ه s.th.) **II** to split (ه atoms); to break (ه a record, s.o.'s pride); to dispel (ه discord), break down (ه enmity) **V** to break, go to pieces; to be broken (also of a record; sports), be smashed, be shattered; to crash (e.g., airplane, structure, etc.); to be wrecked (ship) **VII** = **V**

حطمة *ḥiṭma* pl. حطم *ḥiṭam* particle, small piece, shred, bit, morsel; s.th. broken

حطام *ḥuṭām* debris, rubble; fragments, shards, broken pieces; wreckage, wreck (of a ship or plane), crashed airplane; ruins, demolished site, shambles; razed house (by explosives, etc.) | حطام الدنيا *ḥ. ad-dunyā* the ephemeral things of this world, the vanities of the world

حطيم *ḥaṭīm* smashed, shattered, wrecked

تحطيم *taḥṭīm* smashing, shattering, wrecking, breaking, demolition, destruction, disruption | ○ سفينة تحطيم الجليد icebreaker (*naut.*); تحطيم الذرة *t. aḏ-ḏarra* nuclear fission (*phys.*)

تحطم *taḥaṭṭum* crumbling, disintegration; crash (of an airplane); collapse, breakdown

حاطمة *ḥāṭima*: ○ حاطمة الجليد icebreaker (*naut.*)

محطم *muḥaṭṭim* crashing, thundering, roaring (of an explosion, etc.); — *muḥaṭṭam* broken (language)

محطمة *muḥaṭṭima*: محطمة ثلجية (*ṯaljīya*) icebreaker (*naut.*)

حظ **ḥaẓẓa** *a* (*ḥaẓẓ*) to be lucky, fortunate **IV** = **I**

حظ *ḥaẓẓ* pl. حظوظ *ḥuẓūẓ* part, portion, share, allotment; lot, fate, destiny; good luck, good fortune; affluence, wealth, fortune; prosperity; pleasure | ذو حظ من endowed with; لحسن الحظ *li-ḥusni l-ḥ.* and من حسن الحظ fortunately, luckily; سوء الحظ *sū' al-ḥ.* bad luck, misfortune; سيء الحظ *sayyi' al-ḥ.* unlucky, unfortunate; لسوء الحظ unfortunately; من حسن حظي luckily for me, fortunately; كان من حسن حظه ان he was lucky in that he...; ليس احسن منها حظا he is no better off than she is; لا حظ له من علم (*ḥaẓẓa, ʿilm*) he has absolutely no knowledge; ليس لها حظ من عقل (*ʿaql*) she has no brains at all

حظيظ *ḥaẓīẓ* lucky, fortunate

محظوظ *maḥẓūẓ* lucky, fortunate; content(ed), happy, glad

حظر **ḥaẓara** *u* (*ḥaẓr*) to fence in, hedge in (ه s.th.); to forbid (ه على to s.o. s.th.), prohibit (ه على s.o. from doing s.th.)

حظر *ḥaẓr* forbiddance, interdiction, prohibition, ban; embargo | حظر التجول *ḥ. at-tajawwul* barring of traffic, traffic ban

حظار *ḥiẓār, ḥaẓār* wall, partition, screen; fence, palisade, railing

حظيرة *ḥaẓīra* pl. حظائر *ḥaẓā'ir*[2] enclosure, railing, fence, palisade, hedge; compound, yard, pound, pinfold; corral, pen, paddock, coop; hangar, shed; field, domain, realm (fig.) | فى حظيرة (with foll. genit.) inside of, within; جذبه الى حظيرته (*jaḏabahū*) to bring s.o. under one's influence; حظيرة زجاجية (*zujājīya*) show case; حظيرة سيارات *ḥ. sayyārāt* (*saud.-ar.*) car garage; حظائر الطائرات aircraft hangars; حظيرة القدس *ḥ. al-quds* Paradise

تحظير *taḥẓīr* ban, prohibition, interdiction

محظور *maḥẓūr* interdicted, prohibited, forbidden (على to s.o.); embargoed; pl. محظورات forbidden things, restrictions

(حظو and حظى) حظى *ḥaẓiya a* (حظوة *ḥuẓwa, ḥiẓwa*) to enjoy the favor or good graces of s.o. (عند), be in s.o.'s (عند) favor or good graces; to acquire, obtain, attain, gain, win (ب s.th.)

حظوة *ḥuẓwa, ḥiẓwa* favored position, role of favorite; precedence; favor, grace; good will, benevolence; prestige, credit, standing, respect, esteem | نال حظوة عند (لدى) to find favor with s.o.

حظى *ḥaẓīy* enjoying (ب s.o.'s attention or interest), favored (ب by s.th.)

حظية *ḥaẓīya* pl. حظايا *ḥaẓāyā* paramour, mistress, concubine

محظى *maḥẓīy* pl. *-ūn* favorite, darling; favored (by s.o.) | محظى بثقته (*bi-ṯiqatihī*) enjoying s.o.'s confidence

محظية *maḥẓīya* pl. *-āt* paramour, mistress, concubine

حف *ḥaffa u* (*ḥaff*) to surround (ب ,ه ,ه s.o., s.th. with, also ب and حول s.o., s.th.), enclose, encompass, border (ب, ه s.th.); to line on both sides (ه e.g., a street); to depilate (ه a part of the body), unhair (ه the skin); to trim, clip (ه the beard); to chafe, rub off, abrade (ه s.th.); to wipe (يديه *yadaihi* one's hands, ب on s.th.) | تحف به العيون he is the object of admiring glances, he is the center of attention, all eyes are upon him; تحف به شمائل الطيبة (*ṭība*) he is obviously a good person; — *i* (حفيف *ḥafīf*) to rustle II and VIII to surround (ب,حول ,ه ,ه s.o., s.th.), enclose, encompass, border (ب,حول ,ه s.th.)

حفاف *ḥifāf* pl. احفة *aḥiffa* border, side; ○ sidewalk

حفيف *ḥafīf* rustle, rustling

محفة *miḥaffa* (also *maḥaffa*) pl. *-āt* litter, stretcher; roller stretcher; sedan

حاف *ḥāff*: خبز حاف (*ḵubz*) plain bread (without anything to go with it); see also حفى[2]

حافة *ḥāffa* pl. *-āt*, حواف *ḥawāff*[2] border, fringe, hem, edge; rim (of a plate, etc.); brim (of a hat); bank (of a river), shore; see also *ḥāfa* (under حوف)

محفوف *maḥfūf*: محفوف بالمخاطر (*maḵāṭir*) surrounded by dangers

حفيد *ḥafīd* pl. احفاد *aḥfād*, حفدة *ḥafada* grandson; descendant, offspring, scion

حفيدة *ḥafīda* granddaughter

حفر *ḥafara i* (*ḥafr*) to dig (ه s.th.); to drill (for oil); to excavate (*archeol.*); to carve (ه s.th.); to engrave, etch (ه metal) | حفر خنادق to dig trenches; حفر حفرة (*ḥufratan*) to prepare a pitfall, prepare an ambush VII pass. of I; VIII to dig

حفر *ḥafr* digging, earthwork, excavation (also *archeol.*); unearthing; drilling (for oil); carving, inscribing (e.g., of letters); engraving, etching; graphic arts (etching, wood engraving); scurvy (*syr.*) | جهاز الحفر *jahāz al-ḥ.* oil rig; oil derrick

حفرة *ḥufra* pl. حفر *ḥufar* pit; hollow, cavity, excavation; hole

حفرى *ḥafrī* excavation (in compounds); drilling (in compounds); graphic (art) | اعمال حفرية graphics; عمليات حفرية (*ʿamalīyāt*) excavations; drilling operations

حفرية *ḥafrīya* digging, excavation; ○ gravure; pl. حفريات excavations (*archeol.*); archaeological finds | علم

علم الحفريات *ʻilm al-ḥ.* archaeology; paleontology; علماء الحفريات excavators

حفار **ḥaffār** pl. *-ūn* digger; excavation laborer (*archeol.*); engraver; graphic artist; driller; drill crew member (oil industry); stone mason | حفار القبور gravedigger

حفارة **ḥaffāra** pl. *-āt* drilling rig, drill tower (for oil production); drilling machine; ditching machine; tractor

حفير **ḥafīr** dug, dug out, excavated, unearthed

حفيرة **ḥafīra** pl. حفائر *ḥafā'ir*² s.th. excavated or unearthed; pl. excavations (*archeol.*)

احفور **uḥfūr** pl. احافير *aḥāfīr*² s.th. excavated; fossil; pl. excavations (*archeol.*) | علم الاحافير *ʻilm al-a.* paleontology

محفر **miḥfar** pl. محافر *maḥāfir*² spade

حافر **ḥāfir** pl. حوافر *ḥawāfir*² hoof | وقع الحافر على الحافر to coincide, happen to correspond exactly; على الحافر on the spot, right away, at once

حافرى **ḥāfirī** ungular, ungulate

حافرة **ḥāfira** original condition, beginning | عند الحافرة on the spot, right away, at once; رجع الى حافرته to revert to its original state or origin

محفور **maḥfūr** dug; inscribed, engraved; carved; pl. محفورات graphics (woodcuts, etchings)

حفز **ḥafaza** *i* (*ḥafz*) to pierce, stab (ه s.o., ب with the spear); to incite, instigate, urge, prompt, induce (على or الى ه s.o. to s.th.) **V** to prepare o.s., get ready, be ready, be about to do s.th. (ل or الى), set out to do s.th. (ل or الى); to get ready to jump, make a running start; to listen, pay attention **VIII** to be about to do s.th., be ready (ل for)

تحفز **taḥaffuz** preparedness, readiness; vim, dash, verve, sweep, élan

حافز **ḥāfiz** pl. حوافز *ḥawāfiz*² spur, drive (على to do s.th.), incentive (على to); initiative; stimulus, motive

متحفز **mutaḥaffiz** ready, prepared (ل for)

حفظ **ḥafiẓa** *a* (*ḥifẓ*) to preserve (ه s.th.); to protect, guard, defend (ه s.o.); to observe, bear in mind (ه s.th.), comply (ه with s.th.), be mindful, be heedful (ه of s.th.); to keep up, maintain, sustain, retain, uphold (ه s.th.); to hold, have in safekeeping (ه s.th.), take care (ه of s.th.); to keep, put away, save, store (ه s.th); to conserve, preserve (ه s.th.); to retain in one's memory, remember, know by heart (ه s.th.); to memorize, learn by heart, commit to memory (ه s.th., esp. the Koran); to reserve (ه لنفسه for o.s. s.th.); to stay, discontinue, suspend (التحقيق a judicial investigation; *jur.*) | حفظه الله may God protect him! حفظ بالبريد to hold in care of general delivery (ه s.th.); يحفظ فى البوسطة (*yuḥfaẓu*) in care of general delivery, poste restante; حفظ كلمته (*kalimatahū*) to keep one's word; حفظ الوفاء ل (*wafā'a*) to be loyal to s.o., keep faith with s.o. **II** to have s.o. (ه) memorize (ه s.th.) **III** to preserve, keep up, maintain, uphold, sustain (على s.th.); to supervise, control (على s.th.), watch (على over s.th.); to watch out (على for), take care, be heedful, be mindful (على of), look (على after), attend, pay attention (على to); to keep, follow, observe, bear in mind (على s.th.), comply (على with), conform (على to); to protect, guard, defend (ه and على, also عن s.th.) **IV** to vex, annoy, gall, irritate, hurt, offend (ه s.o.) **V** to keep up, maintain, preserve (ب s.th.); to observe, keep in mind (ب s.th.), be mindful, be heedful, take care (ب of s.th.), be concerned (ب with); to be cautious, be wary, be on one's

حفيظة *ḥafīẓa* pl. حفائظ *ḥafā'iẓ*² grudge, resentment, rancor; — حفيظة النفوس (*Saudi Ar.*) identity card

محفظة *maḥfaẓa, miḥfaẓa* pl. *-āt*, محافظ *maḥāfiẓ*² folder, bag, satchel, briefcase, dispatch case, portfolio; etui; wallet, billfold

محفظة *miḥfaẓa* capsule

تحفيظ *taḥfīẓ* memorization drill, inculcation (esp. of the Koran)

حفاظ *ḥifāẓ* defense, protection, guarding (esp. of cherished, sacred things); preservation, maintenance (على of interests); keeping, upholding (of loyalty), adherence (to a commitment); (pl. *-āt*) dressing, ligature, bandage | حفاظ الحيض *ḥ. al-ḥaiḍ* sanitary napkin

محافظة *muḥāfaẓa* guarding; safeguarding; preservation; protection, defense; conservation, sustaining, upholding; retention, maintenance (على of s.th.) conservativism (*pol.*), conservative attitude; following, observance (على of s.th.), compliance (على with s.th.), adherence (على to); guarding (من against misfortune), saving (من from misadventure); garrison (*mil.*); (pl. *-āt*) governorate, administrative district; province (in *Eg.* one of the 25 administrative districts, each with its own governmental agencies); office of the *muḥāfiẓ* (see below) | المحافظة على النفس self-preservation; مذهب المحافظة *maḏhab al-m.* conservative movement, conservativism, Toryism; المحافظة على البيئة (*bī'a*) preservation of the environment; المحافظة على نقاوة الهواء (*naqāwat al-hawā'*) prevention of air pollution

تحفظ *taḥaffuẓ* caution, wariness, restraint, reticence, reserve, aloofness; preventive custody (على of s.o.); — (pl. *-āt*) precaution, precautionary measure; reservation, limiting condition, condi-

guard; to be reserved, aloof; to have reservations; to impound, take into custody, seize (على s.th.; of the police); to arrest, take into custody (على s.o., e.g., a murder suspect) **VIII** to maintain, uphold (ب or ه s.th., e.g., بحقوقه one's rights); to keep up, maintain, retain (ب or ه s.th., e.g., a posture, a characteristic); to take care, take over custody (ب of s.o.), protect, guard (ب s.o.); to defend (against encroachment), hold, maintain (ب a possession); to preserve, sustain, continue, keep up (ب s.th.); to hold, possess (ب s.th.); to put away, hold, have in safekeeping (ب s.th.), take care (ب of s.th.); to keep, retain (ب s.th.); احتفظ لنفسه to keep for o.s., appropriate, reserve for o.s. (ب or ه s.th.), take complete possession (ه of) **X** to ask s.o. (ه) to guard or protect (ه or على s.th.); to entrust (على or ه ه to s.o. s.th.), commit s.th. (على or ه) to the charge of s.o. (ه)

حفظ *ḥifẓ* preservation; maintenance, sustentation, conservation, upholding; protection, defense, guarding; custody, safekeeping, keeping, storage; retention; observance, compliance (with); memorizing, memorization; memory; (*jur.*) discontinuance, stay, suspension (of legal action, of a judicial investigation) | حفظ الآثار preservation of ancient monuments (*Eg.*); حفظ الامانات *ḥ. al-amānāt* deposition for safe-keeping; checking of baggage; حفظ الصحة *ḥ. aṣ-ṣiḥḥa* hygiene, sanitation; رجال الحفظ police; غرفة حفظ *ġurfat ḥ.* archive of a governmental agency (*Eg.*)

حفظة *ḥifẓa* anger, indignation, resentment, rancor

حفيظ *ḥafīẓ* attentive, heedful, mindful; preserving, keeping, guarding (على s.th.)

tional stipulation, proviso | مع التحفظ with full reservation

تحفظى *taḥaffuẓī* precautionary, preventive; cautious, reserved, with reservation | اجراءات تحفظية (*ijrā'āt*) precautionary measures; صلح تحفظى (*ṣulḥ*) settlement before action, preventive settlement (*jur.*)

احتفاظ *iḥtifāẓ* guarding, safeguarding; preservation; retention, maintenance, continuation, conservation, defense, protection, vindication, sustaining, upholding; keeping, holding, safekeeping, custody (ب of s.th.)

حافظ *ḥāfiẓ* keeper, guarder, guardian, custodian, caretaker; (pl. حفاظ *ḥuffāẓ*, حفظة *ḥafaẓa*) one who knows the Koran by heart (formerly an honorific epithet)

حافظة *ḥāfiẓa* memory; — (pl. -*āt*, حوافظ *ḥawāfiẓ*[2]) wallet, billfold; coupon of a money order, etc., receipt-slip (*Eg.*)

محفوظ *maḥfūẓ* kept, held in safekeeping, deposited, guarded, preserved; memorized, committed to memory, etc.; conserved, preserved (food); reserved; ensured, secured, safeguarded; — pl. محفوظات canned goods, conserves; records (of an agency); archives; memorized material, what s.o. knows by heart | دار المحفوظات المصرية the Egyptian Public Record Office; كاتب المحفوظات records clerk, filing clerk; مأكولات محفوظة conserves, canned goods; جميع الحقوق محفوظة all rights reserved

محافظ *muḥāfiẓ* supervisory, controlling; observing (على s.th.), complying (على with), etc.; conservative (*pol.*), المحافظون the Conservatives, the Tories; (pl. -*ūn*) keeper, guarder, guardian, custodian; governor, president of a province (*muḥāfaẓa*; *Eg.*); mayor (Cairo); (as Brit. *governor*) director general, president

متحفظ *mutaḥaffiẓ* vigilant, alert, wary, cautious; reticent, reserved, aloof; staid, sedate

مستحفظ *mustaḥfaẓ* pl. -*āt* reserve (*mil.*)

حفل *ḥafala* i (*ḥafl*) to gather, assemble, congregate; to flow copiously; to be replete, teem, superabound (ب with); to pay attention, attend, give one's mind (ب or ل to s.th.), concern o.s. (ب with), make much (ب of), set great store (ب by) | لا حفل به (*ḥafla*) indifferent, of no consequence **II** to adorn, decorate, ornament (ب ه s.th. with) **VIII** to gather, rally, throng together; to celebrate (ب s.th., s.o.); to concern o.s. (ب or ل with), attend, pay attention, give one's mind (ب or ل to s.th.); to honor, welcome, receive kindly (ب s.o.)

حفل *ḥafl* gathering, meeting, assembling; assembly, congregation, throng, crowd; performance, show, public event; celebration; feast, festival | حفل ختامى (*kitāmī*) and حفل ختام closing ceremony; حفل رياضى (*riyāḍī*) sports festival; حفل ساهر soirée; evening celebration; حفل افتتاح opening ceremony

حفلة *ḥafla* pl. -*āt* assembly, gathering, meeting, congregation; party; (social or public) event; show, performance (theater, cinema); concert; festivity, ceremony, festival, festive event, celebration | حفلة التأبين commemoration, commemorative ceremony for a deceased person; الحفلة الاولى (*ūlā*) premiere; حفلة حافلة numerous assembly; حفلة خيرية (*kairīya*) charity performance, charity event; حفلة الدفن *ḥ. ad-dafn* funeral ceremony, obsequies; حفلة دينية (*dīnīya*) religious ceremony, Divine Service; حفلة ساهرة evening party, evening gathering, evening show or performance, soirée; حفلة سمر *ḥ. samar* evening party, soirée; حفلة سينمائية motion-picture show; حفلة

الشاى tea party; حفلة العرس *ḥ. al-ʿurs* wedding; حفلة الاستقبال (public) reception; حفلة موسيقية concert

حفيل *ḥafīl* eager, assiduous, diligent

محفل *maḥfil* pl. محافل *maḥāfil*[2] assembly, congregation, meeting, gathering; party; body, collective whole; circle, quarter | محفل ماسونى Masonic lodge; المحافل الرسمية (السياسية) (*rasmīya, siyāsīya*) the official (political) circles or quarters

احتفال *iḥtifāl* pl. *-āt* celebration, ceremony, festival, festivities

احتفالى *iḥtifālī* ceremonial, festive

حافل *ḥāfil* pl. حفل *ḥuffal*, حوافل *ḥawāfil*[2] full (ب of), filled, replete (ب with); abundant, copious, lavish; eventful, rich in content (history); much frequented, well attended (by visitors, participants, etc.), numerous (of attendance); solemn, ceremonial, festive

حافلة *ḥāfila* pl. *-āt*, حوافل *ḥawāfil*[2] autobus; streetcar | حافلة نقل *ḥ. naql* bus, city bus

محتفل *muḥtafil*: المحتفلون the participants in a festive event, the celebrators

محتفل *muḥtafal* assembly place, gathering place; party; محتفل به celebrated

حفن *ḥafana u* to scoop up with both hands (ه s.th.); to give a little (ل to s.o.)

حفنة *ḥafna* pl. *ḥafanāt* handful

حفو[1] and حفى) حفى *ḥafiya a* (حفاوة *ḥafāwa*) to receive kindly and hospitably, to welcome, receive with honors, honor (ب s.o.) **V** to behave with affection, be affectionate (ب toward) **VIII** do.; to celebrate (ب an occasion, a festival)

حفى *ḥafīy* welcoming, receiving kindly, greeting (ب s.o., s.th.)

حفاوة *ḥafāwa* friendly reception, welcoming, welcome, salutation (ب of s.o.)

احتفاء *iḥtifā'* reception, welcome, salutation (ب of s.o.); celebration, festivity

حفى[2] *ḥafiya a* (حفاء *ḥafā'*) to go barefoot; to have sore feet

حاف *ḥāfin* pl. حفاة *ḥufāh* barefoot(ed); — (*eg., leb.*) *ḥāf* dry (bread); plain and simple, without anything else

حق *ḥaqqa i u* to be true, turn out to be true, be confirmed; to be right, correct; (also pass. *ḥuqqa*) to be necessary, obligatory, requisite, imperative (على for s.o.), be incumbent (على upon s.o.); to be adequate, suitable, fitting, appropriate (على for s.o.); to be due (ل s.o.); يحق له he is entitled to it, he has a right to it; يحق له ان he has every reason to . . .; حق عليه he deserved it (punishment); — *u* to ascertain (ه s.th.), make sure, be sure (ه of s.th.); to recognize, identify (ه s.o.) **II** to make s.th. (ه) come true; to realize (ه s.th., e.g., a hope), carry out (ه e.g., a wish), carry into effect, fulfill, put into action, consummate, effect, actualize (ه s.th.); to set, establish (ه a record; sport); to implement (ه e.g., an agreement); to produce, bring on, yield (ه results); to determine, ascertain, find out, pinpoint, identify (ه s.th.); to prove s.th. (ه) to be true, verify, establish, substantiate (ه s.th.); to establish, recognize the true nature (ه of s.th.); to confirm, assert, aver, avouch, affirm (ه s.th.); to be exact, painstaking, meticulous, careful (ه in doing s.th.), e.g., حقق النظر (*naẓara*) to look closely; to study, examine, investigate, explore (ه s.th.), look, inquire (ه into s.th.); to verify, check (ه or فى s.th.); to edit critically (ه a text; *phil.*); to investigate (فى s.th.; police); to make an official inquiry (ه into s.th.), institute an investigation (ه of or into; court; *jur.*); to interrogate (مع s.o.), conduct a hearing (مع of s.o.; *jur.*) **III** to contend for a right (ه with s.o.), contest or litigate a right (ه against s.o.) **IV** to tell the truth; to be right (فى in s.th.); to enforce (ه s.th., e.g., a legal claim); to make into a duty (ه s.th., of God) | احق الحق (*ḥaqqa*) to help truth come into its own **V** to prove true, turn out to be true, be confirmed, prove to be correct; to materialize, become a fact; to be realized, be effected, come into effect; to be examined, be explored; to ascertain (ه s.th., also من), make sure, reassure o.s., gain proof, convince o.s., be convinced, be sure, be certain (ه of s.th.); to check, verify (ه or من s.th.); to be serious (ب about s.th.) **X** to be entitled, have a claim (ه to s.th.); to claim (ه s.th.), lay claim (ه to); to deserve, merit (ه s.th.), be worthy (ه of); to require, demand, necessitate, make requisite (ه s.th.); to fall due, become payable (sum of money), mature, become due (note); to be due (ل s.o.) | يستحق الذكر (*dikra*) worth mentioning, noteworthy; لا يستحق عليه الرسم (*rasmu*) not subject to a fee, free of charge

حق *ḥaqq* truth; correctness, rightness; rightful possession, property; one's due; duty; proper manner; true, authentic, real; right, fair and reasonable; correct, sound, valid; الحق an attribute of God; (pl. حقوق *ḥuqūq*) right, title, claim, legal claim (فى to); pl. حقوق (*Mag̃r.*) fees, dues, duties, taxes (loan translation from Fr. *droits*); الحقوق law, jurisprudence, legal science; حقا *ḥaqqan* really, in reality, in effect, actually, in fact, indeed, truly, in truth; justly, rightly, by rights | احقا ذلك؟ is that (really) so? really? بحق justly, rightly, by rights; بالحق truly, in reality, actually; properly, appropriately, in a suitable manner; بحق *bi-haqqi* and فى حق as to ..., as for ..., with respect to, concerning, regarding; وحق *wa-ḥaqqi* by the truth of ..., وحق جميع القديسين (*qiddīsīn*) by all the saints, by all that's holy! بحق السماء by the truth of heaven! هو على حق he is in the right; الحق معك you are right; الحق عليك you are wrong; هو حق عليك it is your duty; هذا حق عليكم you owe this to me; عرفانا لحقها عليه (*ʿirfānan*) in recognition of what he owed her; حقه what he can claim, what is his due; من حقه he is entitled to it, it is his due; كان من حقه ان he should have ..., he ought to have ...; له الحق فى he is entitled to ...; والحق يقال (*yuqāl*) one may say, it must be admitted, it's only fair to say, say what you will ..., ... though (as a parenthetical phrase); عرف حق المعرفة (*ḥaqqa l-maʿrifa*) to know exactly, know for certain, know very well, also علم حق العلم (*ḥaqqa l-ʿilm*); فهم حق الفهم *fahima ḥaqqa l-fahm* to understand precisely, comprehend thoroughly, be fully aware; حق التأليف author's rights; حق الشعوب international law; حقوق الطبع *ḥ. aṭ-ṭabʿ* printing rights, copyrights; حق تقرير المصير (*t. al-maṣīr*) right to self-determination; الحقوق المدنية (*madanīya*) civil rights; صاحب الحق claimant, one entitled to a claim; كلية الحقوق *kullīyat al-ḥ.* law school, faculty of law; — (as attrib. of a fem. n. also variable for gender) السعادة الحقة (*saʿāda*) true happiness, الوطنية الحقة (*waṭanīya*) real or true patriotism

حق *ḥuqq* hollow, cavity; socket of a joint (*anat.*); also = حقة *ḥuqqa*

حقة *ḥuqqa* pl. حقق *ḥuqaq*, حقاق *ḥiqāq*, احقاق *aḥqāq* small box, case, pot or jar; receptacle, container; — (pl. *-āt*, حقق *ḥuqaq*) a weight (*Syr., Pal.*) = اقة *uqqa*; حقة استانبولية = 1.280 kg (*Ir.*)

حقيق *ḥaqīq* pl. احقاء *aḥiqqāʾ*[2] worthy, deserving (ب of s.th.), fit, competent, qualified; entitled (ب to)

حقيقة *ḥaqīqa* pl. حقائق *ḥaqāʾiq*[2] truth, reality (also *philos.*); fact; the true state of affairs, the facts; true nature, essence; real meaning, true sense; *ḥaqīqatan* really, in reality, in effect, actually, in fact, indeed, truly, in truth | رأيته على حقيقته I saw its true nature, as it really is; في حقيقة الامر in reality, really, actually; ليس له حقيقة it does not really exist, it is not real

حقيقى *ḥaqīqī* real, true; actual; proper, intrinsic, essential; genuine; authentic; positive

حقوقى *ḥuqūqī* juristic(al); (pl. *-ūn*) jurist, jurisprudent, lawyer

احق *aḥaqq*² worthier, more deserving (ب of s.th.); more entitled (ب to s.th.); الاحق s.o. having the better (or best) legal claim, the preferential claimant

احقية *aḥaqqīya* better legal claim, preference, priority

حقانى *ḥaqqānī* correct, right, proper, sound, valid, legitimate, legal

حقانية *ḥaqqānīya* justice, law | وزارة الحقانية Ministry of Justice (formerly *Eg.*)

تحقيق *taḥqīq* realization, actualization, effectuation, implementation; fulfillment (of a claim, of a wish, etc.); achievement, accomplishment, execution; conduct (of a press interview); setting (of a record; sport); ascertainment, determination, identification, verification; substantiation; assertion, affirmation, confirmation; pinpointing, precise determination; exactness, accurateness, precision; (= تحقيق النطق *t. an-nuṭq*) precise pronunciation; critical edition (of a text; *phil.*); — (pl. *-āt*) verification, check, checkup, investigation; official or judicial inquiry, inquest | التحقيق ان it is a matter of fact that ..., it is certain that ...; على التحقيق properly speaking, strictly speaking, actually; exactly, precisely; positively, definitely; عند التحقيق properly speaking, strictly speaking, actually; تحقيق الشخصية *t. aš-šaḵṣīya* identification (of a person), proof of identity; شهادة تحقيق الشخصية *šahādat t. aš-šaḵṣīya* identity card; قلم تحقيق الشخصية *qalam t. aš-š.* bureau of identification; تحقيق الذاتية *t. aḏ-ḏātīya* identification; قاضى التحقيق examining magistrate; تحقيقات النيابة *t. an-niyāba* investigations of the public prosecutor's office; لجنة تحقيق *lajnat t.* committee of inquiry; تحقيق الارباح realization of profits (stock market); اعتقال رهن التحقيق (*rahna*) detention pending investigation (*jur.*); كتب التحقيق *kutub at-t.* critical editions of texts (*phil.*)

احقاق *iḥqāq*: احقاقا للحق *iḥqāqan li-l-ḥaqq* (so) that truth may prevail

تحقق *taḥaqquq* ascertainment, making sure; conviction, certainty, certitude; verification, check, checkup

استحقاق *istiḥqāq* pl. *-āt* worthiness, deservingness, merit; one's due or desert; maturity, payability, falling due (of a sum of money); re-claiming or calling in of s.th. due, demand of a right; claim (of s.o., في for a payment, a possession, etc.); vindication (*Isl. Law*), replevin, detinue | عن استحقاق deservedly, justly, by rights; بدون استحقاق undeservedly; تاريخ الاستحقاق date of maturity (e.g., of a bond); الاستحقاق اللبنانى (*lubnānī*) name of a Lebanese order of merit

محقوق *maḥqūq* worthy, deserving (ب, ل of), fit, competent, qualifying (ب, ل for); wrong, at fault, on the wrong track

محقق *muḥaqqiq* pl. *-ūn* investigator; inquirer; examining magistrate; editor (of a text), editor of a critical edition (*phil.*)

محقق *muḥaqqaq* sure, certain, beyond doubt, unquestionable, indubitable; assured, established, accepted, recognized | من المحقق ان it is certain that ..., it is a fact that ...

محق *muḥiqq* telling the truth, in the right, being right

متحقق *mutaḥaqqiq* convinced, sure, certain, positive

مستحق *mustaḥiqq* entitled (في to a payment, etc.); claiming; beneficiary (of a wakf); deserving, worthy; due (a sum, payment, على to s.o.'s debit) | مستحق الدفع *m. ad-daf'* due, payable (sum), mature (bill); مستحق الرسم *m. ar-rasm* subject or liable to charges; الضرائب المستحقة عليه the taxes which he owes, which are due

حقب VIII to put into one's bag, to bag (ه s.th.)

حقب *ḥuqb* pl. احقاب *aḥqāb*, حقاب *ḥiqāb* long stretch of time, long period

حقبة *ḥiqba* pl. حقب *ḥiqab*, *ḥiqabāt*, احقاب *aḥqāb* long time, stretch of time; period, age, historical epoch | حقبة من الزمان *ḥiqbatan min az-zamān* for quite a time, for some time

حقب *ḥaqab* pl. احقاب *aḥqāb* a kind of ornamental belt

حقاب *ḥiqāb* pl. حقب *ḥuqub* a kind of ornamental belt

حقيبة *ḥaqība* pl. حقائب *ḥaqā'ib*² valise, suitcase, traveling bag; leather bag; briefcase, portfolio; handbag | حقيبة دبلوماسية diplomatic pouch; حقيبة النقود portemonnaie, change purse; حقيبة اليد *ḥ. al-yad* ladies' purse, handbag

حقد *ḥaqida a*, *ḥaqada i* (*ḥaqd*, *ḥiqd*) to harbor feelings of hatred (على against) IV to incite to hatred or resentment, embitter, envenom (ه s.o.) V = I; VI to hate one another

حقد *ḥiqd* pl. احقاد *aḥqād*, حقود *ḥuqūd* hatred, malice, spite, resentment, rancor

حقيدة *ḥaqīda* pl. حقائد *ḥaqā'id*² hatred, malice, spite, resentment, rancor

حقود *ḥaqūd* full of hatred, spiteful, resentful, malicious, malevolent, rancorous

حاقد *ḥāqid* full of hatred, spiteful, resentful, malicious, malevolent, rancorous; pl. *-ūn*, حقدة *ḥaqada* haters, malevolent people

حقر *ḥaqara i* (*ḥaqr*) to despise, scorn, disdain (ه s.o., ه s.th.); to look down (ه, ه on), have a low opinion (ه, ه of); — *ḥaqura u* to be low, base, contemptible, despicable; to be despised, degraded, humiliated II to disparage, decry, depreciate (ه s.o.), detract, derogate (ه from s.o.); to degrade, debase, humble, humiliate; to regard with contempt, despise, scorn, disdain (ه s.o., ه s.th.) VIII to despise, scorn, disdain (ه s.o., ه s.th.), look down (ه, ه on) X to regard as contemptible or despicable, disdain, despise (ه s.o., ه s.th.), look down (ه, ه on)

حقير *ḥaqīr* pl. حقراء *ḥuqarā'*² low, base, mean, vulgar, vile; little, small, paltry, inconsiderable, poor, wretched, miserable; despised; despicable, contemptible

احقر *aḥqar*² lower, baser, more contemptible

حقارة *ḥaqāra* lowness, vulgarity, baseness, vileness, meanness; smallness, paltriness, insignificance, poorness, wretchedness, miserableness; despicability, contemptibleness; ignominy, infamy

تحقير *taḥqīr* contempt, disdain, scorn; degradation, humiliation, abasement

احتقار *iḥtiqār* contempt, disdain, scorn | نظر اليه بعين الاحتقار (*bi-'aini l-iḥt.*) to regard s.o. with contempt, look down one's nose at s.o.

محتقر *muḥtaqar* despised; contemptible, despicable

حقل *ḥaql* pl. حقول *ḥuqūl* field (also fig. = domain); arable land, acreage; oil field;

rubric | حقل البترول *ḥ. al-bitrōl*, حقل الزيت *ḥ. az-zait*, حقل النفط *ḥ. an-nafṭ* oil field; oil area; حقول التجارب experimental fields; حقل كهربائى (*kahrabā'ī*) electric field; حقل الغام minefield (*mil.*)

حقلى *ḥaqlī* field- (in compounds)

محاقلة *muḥāqala* sale of grain while still in growth, dealing in grain futures (*Isl. Law*)

حقن **ḥaqana** *i u* (*ḥaqn*) to hold back, withhold, keep back, detain, retain (ه s.th.); to suppress, repress, restrain (ه s.th.); to keep to o.s. (السر *as-sirra* the secret); to spare (دمه *damahū* s.o.'s blood or life); to inject (ه in s.th., العروق in the veins, ب s.th.); to squirt, inject (ه s.th., فى in); to give (ه s.o.) an injection (*med.*) | حقنه بمخدر (*bi-mukaddir*) to give s.o. an anesthetic injection **VIII** to become congested (esp. blood); to suffer from strangury; to take an enema, a clyster; to be injected | احتقن وجهه (*wajhuhū*) his face was flushed, his face turned red

حقن *ḥaqn* retention, withholding; sparing; injecting, injection (*med.*) | حقنا لدمائهم *ḥaqnan li-dimā'ihim* in order to spare their blood; حقن فى الوريد intravenous injection (*med.*); حقن الماء water injection, حقن الغاز gas injection (فى into the field, oil industry)

حقنة *ḥuqna* pl. حقن *ḥuqan* injection (*med.*); hypodermic | حقنة شرجية (*šarajīya*) clyster, enema

محقنة *miḥqana* pl. محاقن *maḥāqin*[2] syringe (*med.*)

احتقان *iḥtiqān* congestion | احتقان الدم *iḥt. ad-dam* vascular congestion

محتقن *muḥtaqan* reddened by blood congestion, flushed, red (face)

حقو *ḥaqw* pl. حقاء *ḥiqā'*, احقاء *aḥqā'* loin, groin | شدد حقويه *šaddada ḥaqwaihi* to gird one's loins

[1]حك **ḥakka** *u* (*ḥakk*) to rub, chafe; to scrape; to scratch; to rub off, scrape off, scratch off, abrade (ه s.th.) | حك فى صدره (*ṣadrihī*) it impressed him, affected him, touched s.th. inside him **IV** to itch **V** to rub o.s., scrape, chafe (ب against); to pick a quarrel (ب with s.o.) **VI** to rub or scrape against each other **VIII** to rub o.s., scrape, chafe (ب against); to be in contact, in touch (ب with) | احتك فى صدره (*ṣadrihī*) it impressed him, affected him, touched s.th. inside him

حك *ḥakk* rubbing, chafing; friction; scratching

حكة *ḥikka* itching; scabies, itch (*med.*)

حكاك *ḥakkāk* lapidary

محك *miḥakk* touchstone; test | ثبت على محك النظر *ṯabata 'alā m. an-naẓar* to stand a critical test

محكة *miḥakka* currycomb

تحاك *taḥākk* (reciprocal) friction

احتكاك *iḥtikāk* pl. *-āt* (reciprocal) friction; close touch or contact; friction (fig., = dissension, controversy) | من غير احتكاك *min ğairi ḥt.* frictionless

احتكاكى *iḥtikākī* friction (in compounds), frictional | صوت احتكاكى fricative (*phon.*)

محكك *muḥakkak* chafed, worn away

[2]حكة **ḥukka** (*tun.*, = *ḥuqqa*) pl. حكك *ḥukak* small box, case, pot or jar

حكر **VIII** to buy up, hoard and withhold, corner (ه a commodity); to monopolize (ه a commercial article); to have exclusive possession (ه of s.th.), hold a monopoly (ه over s.th.)

حكر *ḥukr* monopoly (على for s.o.)

حكر *ḥikr*, *ḥukr* and اجرة الحكر *ujrat al-ḥ.* ground rent, quitrent

حكر *ḥakar*, *ḥukar* hoarded

حكرة *ḥukra* hoarding (of goods); monopoly

حاكورة *ḥākūra* small vegetable garden

احتكار *iḥtikār* pl. *-āt* cornering, buying up; monopoly; preferential position; supremacy, hegemony | احتكار تجارة البن *iḥt. t. al-bunn* coffee-trade monopoly; احتكار السكر *iḥt. as-sukkar* sugar monopoly; احتكار تجارى (*tijārī*) commercial monopoly; الاحتكار الرأسمالى monopoly capitalism

احتكارى *iḥtikārī* rapacious, grasping, greedy; monopoly (in compounds)

احتكارية *iḥtikārīya* monopolism

محتكر *muḥtakir* pl. *-ūn* monopolist, owner of a monopoly

حكم *ḥakama u* (*ḥukm*) to pass judgment, express an opinion (على ,فى on s.th.), judge (على s.th., ب by, from); to decide, give a decision, pass a verdict, pass sentence (على on); to sentence (على s.o., ب to a penalty; said of the judge), impose, inflict (ب a penalty) on s.o. (على); to pronounce a verdict or judgment, deliver judgment, rule (ل in s.o.'s favor); to adjudicate, adjudge, award (ب ل to s.o. s.th.); to take (ب s.th.) as a standard or norm; to have judicial power, have jurisdiction, have authority (على and ه over); to govern, rule, dominate, control (ه s.o.); to order, command (ب s.th.); to bridle, check, curb (ه, ه s.th., s.o.); to determine, judge, decide (ب with *maṣdar*, that s.th. is the case, exists, or must happen) | حكم عليه بالاعدام (*ḥukima, i'dām*) he was sentenced to death; حكم بادانته (*bi-idānatihī*) to convict s.o., find s.o. guilty (*jur.*); حكم ببراءته (*bi-barā'atihī*) to acquit s.o. (*jur.*); حكم بصحته (*bi-ṣiḥḥatihī*) to determine that s.th. is right, correct, appropriate; حكم فيه بتحريم he decreed it to be forbidden, ruled that it should be considered unlawful (*Isl. Law*); حكم بتجهيل الرجل he decided that the man should be declared *jāhil*, i.e., non responsible for his actions; حكم على ان he judged or decided that . . . **II** to appoint (ه s.o.) as ruler; to choose (ه s.o.) as arbitrator, make (ه s.o.) the judge (فى over or in s.th., بين between) **III** to prosecute (ه s.o.); to arraign, bring to trial, hale into court (ه s.o.); to interrogate, hear (ه s.o.); to put on trial, take severely to task (ه s.o., ه s.th.) **IV** to make (ه s.th.) firm, strong, sturdy, solid; to fortify (ه s.th.); to strengthen, consolidate (ه s.th.); to do well, do expertly, master (ه field, work), be proficient (ه in) | احكم امره (*amrahū*) to do s.th. thoroughly, carefully, properly; احكم تدابيره (*tadābīrahū*) to plan one's actions precisely, organize well; احكم ربطه (*rabṭahū*) to tie, bind up s.th. tightly; احكم السدود to erect solid barriers, take strong safety measures (against an enemy); احكم قفل الباب (*qafla l-bāb*) to lock the door firmly; احكم لغة (*luğatan*) to master a language **V** to have one's own way (فى in), proceed (فى with) at random, at will, handle (فى s.th.) arbitrarily; to pass arbitrary judgment (فى on); to make o.s. the judge (على of), pass judgment (على on); to decide (ب on); to rule, reign, hold sway (فى over); to dominate, control (فى s.th.), be in control, be in command (فى of) **VI** to bring one another before the judge (الى الحاكم); to appeal (الى to) for a legal decision; to be interrogated, be heard (in court) **VIII** to have one's own way (فى in), proceed (فى with, in s.th.) at will, at random, handle (فى s.th.) arbitrarily, judge arbitrarily; to rule, reign, hold sway (على ,فى over); to be in control, be in possession (على of); to appeal (الى to) for a legal decision, seek a decision (الى from), have s.o. (الى) decide **X** to be strong, sturdy, solid, firm; to become stronger, be strengthened, be consolidated; to take root, be or become deep-rooted, deep-seated, ingrained, inveterate, marked, pronounced (feeling, trait)

حكم *ḥukm* pl. احكام *aḥkām* judgment, valuation, opinion; decision; (legal) judgment, verdict, sentence; condemnation, conviction; administration of justice; jurisdiction; legal consequence of the facts of a case (*Isl. Law*); regulation, rule, provision, order, ordinance, decree; legal provision (also *Isl. Law*); judiciousness, wisdom; judgeship; command, authority, control, dominion, power; government, regime; pl. احكام statutes, by-laws, regulations, rules, provisions, stipulations, principles, precepts; حكما *ḥukman* virtually; legally | بحكم *bi-ḥukmi* by virtue of, on the strength of, pursuant to; by force of; بحكم وظيفته *bi-ḥ. waẓīfatihī* ex officio; فى حكم as good as, all but, e.g., هو فى حكم العدم (*fī ḥukmi l-ʿadam*) it is as good as nothing, it is practically nonexistent; اصبح فى حكم المقرر *aṣbaḥa fī ḥukmi l-muqarrar* it is all but decided; كان فى حكم الشىء also: to be subject to s.th.; نزل على حكمه to give in, yield to s.o.; حكم البراءة *ḥ. al-barāʾa* acquittal; حكم حضورى (*ḥuḍūrī*) judgment delivered in the presence of the litigant parties, after oral proceedings (*jur.*); حكم محلى (*maḥallī*) local administration; حكم شرعى (*šarʿī*) sentence, verdict, judgment based on the Sharia; الحكم بالاعدام (*iʿdām*) death sentence; حكم غيابى (*ġiyābī*) judgment by default (*jur.*); حكم قضائى (*qaḍāʾī*) legal verdict; حكم اقلية *ḥ. aqallīya* minority rule; الحكم الذاتى (*ḏātī*) self-determination, autonomy (*pol.*); الحكم الجمهورى (*jumhūrī*) the republican form of government, the republican regime; الحكم المطلق (*muṭlaq*) the absolute, i.e., authoritarian, regime; الحكم النيابى (*niyābī*) the parliamentary regime, parliamentarianism; لجنة الحكم *lajnat al-ḥ.* board of examiners, review board; احكام الله God's commands; الاحكام العرفية (*ʿurfīya*) martial law; احكام انتقالية (*intiqālīya*) provisional regulations (*jur.*); احكام ختامية (*ḵitāmīya*) final regulations (*jur.*); احكام خاصة (*ḵāṣṣa*) special regulations; لكل سن حكمه (*sinn*) every age has its own set of rules, must be judged by its own standards; للضرورة احكام (*li-ḍ-ḍarūra*) necessity has its (own) rules, (approx.: necessity knows no law); علم الاحكام *ʿilm al-a.* judicial astrology

حكمى *ḥukmī* legal

حكمدار (*eg.*; pronounced *ḥikimdār*) commandant; chief of police

حكمدارية (*eg.*; pronounced *ḥikimdārīya*) commandant's office

حكم *ḥakam* pl. حكام *ḥukkām* arbitrator, arbiter; umpire, referee

حكمة *ḥikma* pl. حكم *ḥikam* wisdom; sagacity; wise saying, aphorism; maxim; underlying reason | لحكمة (with foll. genit.) on account of, because of

حكمى *ḥikmī* gnomic, aphoristic, expressing maxims | الشعر الحكمى (*šiʿr*) gnomic poetry

حكمة *ḥakama* pl. *-āt* bit (of a horse's bridle)

حكيم *ḥakīm* pl. حكماء *ḥukamāʾ*[2] wise, judicious; wise man, sage; philosopher; physician, doctor

حكيمباشى *ḥakīmbāšī* senior physician, chief surgeon

حكومة *ḥukūma* pl. *-āt* government

حكومى *ḥukūmī* of government, governmental; official; state-owned, state-controlled, of the state, state- (in compounds)

احكم *aḥkam*[2] wiser

محكمة *maḥkama* pl. محاكم *maḥākim*[2] court, tribunal | محكمة الاستئناف *m. al-*

isti'nāf and محكمة استئنافية court of appeal, appellate court; محكمة اهلية (*ahlīya*) indigenous court (formerly, *Eg.*; jurisdiction limited to Egyptian nationals); محكمة ابتدائية (*ibtidā'īya*) court of first instance; محكمة الثورة *m. at-taura* revolutionary tribunal; محكمة جزئية (*juz'īya*) district court; summary court; محكمة الجنايات *m. al-jināyāt* criminal court; محاكم الاحوال الشخصية (*šakṣīya*) courts dealing with vital statistics; محكمة مختلطة (*muktaliṭa*) mixed court (formerly, *Eg.*; with jurisdiction over residents of foreign nationality); محكمة شرعية (*šar'īya*) canonical court (administering justice on the basis of the Sharia), court dealing with family matters of Muslims; محكمة الشعب *m. aš-ša'b* people's court; محكمة عسكرية (*'askarīya*) and محكمة عرفية (*'urfīya*) court-martial; محكمة مدنية (*madanīya*) civil court; محكمة مركزية (*markazīya*) county court; محكمة القضاء الادارى *m. al-qaḍā' al-idārī* administrative court; محكمة النقض والابرام *m. an-naqḍ wa-l-ibrām* Court of Cassation, the highest court of appeal in Egypt; محكمة التمييز Court of Cassation (*Syr., Leb.* = محكمة النقض والابرام in Eg.); ساحات المحاكم tribunals

تحكيم *taḥkīm* appointment of an arbitrator; arbitration; arbitral decision, award; carrying out the duties of a referee or umpire (sport); pl. تحكيمات fortifications | تحكيم الحال starting from the present state of a court's findings (*Isl. Law*); هيئة التحكيم *hai'at at-t.* board of arbitration; jury (in competitions; sport, art), committee of judges, committee of umpires; committee of referees (in mil. maneuvers); لجنة تحكيمية (*lajna*) do.

محاكمة *muḥākama* judicial proceeding; trial, hearing (in court); legal prosecution

احكام *iḥkām* perfection; accuracy, exactness, exactitude, precision; exact performance, precise execution | بالاحكام accurately, exactly, precisely; بالغ فى الاحكام of highest perfection

تحكم *taḥakkum* arbitrariness, arbitrary powers or action; despotism; domination, dominion, rule; power of disposal (على over s.th.); authoritative attitude; imperious tone; regulation, control (فى of s.th., also *techn.*)

تحكمى *taḥakkumī* arbitrary; despotic

استحكام *istiḥkām* intensification, increase, strengthening; consolidation, stabilization; fortification; pl. استحكامات fortifications; see also حجة *ḥujja*

حاكم *ḥākim* judicious; ruling; decisive; —(pl. -*ūn*, حكام *ḥukkām*) ruler, sovereign; governor; judge | حاكم بامره (*bi-amrihī*) autocratic; autocrat, dictator; حاكم عام (*'āmm*) governor general; حاكم المباراة *ḥ. al-mubārāh* umpire, referee (*athlet.*); حاكم الصلح *ḥ. aṣ-ṣulḥ* (*Syr.*) justice of the peace; حاكم الناحية *ḥ. an-nāḥiya* judge of a local court; الحكام والمحكومون the rulers and the ruled, the governors and the governed

حاكمية *ḥākimīya* domination, dominion, rule, sovereignty; judgeship, judicature, jurisdiction (*ir.*)

محكوم *maḥkūm* governed, ruled, etc.; محكوم عليه sentenced (ب to) | المحكوم عليهم بالاعدام (*i'dām*) those sentenced to death; محكوم عليه بالفشل (*fašal*) doomed to fail

محكم *muḥakkam* pl. -*ūn* arbitrator, arbiter; umpire, referee (فى in, over)

محكم *muḥkam* strengthened, reinforced; firm, solid, sturdy; tight, taut; perfect, masterly, masterful; well-aimed (blow, hit); accurate, precise, exact | محكم التدبير well-planned, well-contrived; خطة محكمة (*kuṭṭa*) fixed plan; فريضة محكمة prescribed, obligatory religious duty

متحكم *mutaḥakkim* controller, control system (*techn.*); — *mutaḥakkam*: متحكم فيه controllable, under control

مستحكم *mustaḥkam* reinforced, fortified; strengthened, consolidated, strong; inveterate, deep-seated, deep-rooted, ingrained (custom, trait, etc.); pl. مستحكمات defenses, fortifications

حكدار, حكدارية see حكم

حكواتى see حكى

حكى *ḥakā i* (حكاية *ḥikāya*) to tell, relate (ه s.th.), report, give an account (ه of); to speak, talk (*syr.*, *leb.*); to imitate, copy (ه s.th.); to resemble (ه, ه s.o., s.th.) III to imitate, copy (ه s.th.), assimilate o.s. (ه to); to be similar (ه to), be like s.th. (ه), resemble (ه s.th.), be attuned, adjusted, adapted (ه to), be in harmony (ه with)

حكى *ḥaky* (*syr.*, *leb.*) speaking, talking; speech

حكاية *ḥikāya* pl. *-āt* story, tale, narrative; report (of occurrences), account; (*gram.*) literal quotation (of the words of others) | حكاية شعبية (*šaʿbīya*) folk tale, fairy story

حكواتى *ḥakawātī* (*syr.*) popular storyteller

حكاء *ḥakkā'* narrator

محاكاة *muḥākāh* imitation; similarity, resemblance; harmony | O محاكاة الاصوات echolalia (*psych.*)

حاك *ḥākin* narrator, storyteller; phonograph

محكى *maḥkīy* imitated, imitation (adj.); (*syr.*, *leb.*) spoken

حكيمباشى see حكم

¹حل *ḥalla u* (*ḥall*) to untie (ه a knot), unbind, unfasten, unravel, undo (ه s.th.); to solve (ه a problem, a puzzle); to decipher, decode (ه s.th.); to dissolve in water (ه s.th.; *chem.*); to resolve (ه s.th. into its components), analyze (ه s.th.); to melt (ه s.th.); to decompose, disintegrate (ه s.th.); to disband, break up, dissolve (ه an organization or party, parliament); to open, unpack (ه a package, and the like); to loosen, relax (ه s.th.); to release, set free, let go (ه s.th., ه s.o.); to clear, exonerate, exculpate (ه من s.o. from), absolve (ه s.o., من from his sins; *Chr.*); pass. *ḥulla* to be free; to be relaxed; — *i u* (حلول *ḥulūl*) to dismount, alight, stop, halt; to settle down, stay (ب at a place, also فى and ه; على with s.o., at s.o.'s house), come (for a visit, على to); to take up residence (ه in a place or country); to descend, come down; to descend (على upon s.o.; wrath); to overcome, overwhelm (على s.o.; sleep); to befall (ب and على s.o.; punishment, suffering), occur, happen (ب to s.o.); to become incarnate (فى in s.o.; God); to set in, arrive, begin (time, season); — *i* to pass into solution, dissolve; to fade (color); — *i* (*ḥill*) to be allowed, permitted, permissible, lawful; to be due, payable (debt) | حل فى منصب (*manṣib*) to take over or hold an office; حل ثالثا he came in third place (sport); حل محله (*maḥallahū*) to be in the right place; حل محل الشىء, حل محل فلان (*maḥalla*) to take the place of s.o. or s.th., replace, supersede s.o. or s.th., substitute for s.o. or s.th.; حلت فى قلبه محلا (*qalbihī*) she held a place in his heart; حل محل التقدير لديه (*maḥalla t-taqdīri ladaihi*) to enjoy s.o.'s high esteem; حل من نفوس القراء محل الاستحسان (*min nufūsi l-qurrā'i maḥalla l-istiḥsān*) to appeal to the readers, meet with the readers' approval II to dissolve, resolve (into its component parts), break up, decompose; to analyze (ه s.th.); to make a chemical analysis (ه of s.th.); to be dissolvent, act as a solvent (ه on;

med.); to discharge, absolve, clear, exonerate, exculpate (ه s.o.); (تحلة *taḥilla*) to expiate an oath; to make permissible or lawful, legitimate, sanction, justify, warrant (ه s.th.); to declare permissible or lawful, allow, permit (ه s.th.) **IV** to discharge, release, absolve, disengage (ه من s.o. from); to declare (ه s.th.) lawful, legally permissible, permit, allow (ه s.th.); to cause to set in or occur, bring about, produce, cause to take root, establish, stabilize (ه s.th.); to cause (ه s.th.) to take or occupy the place (ه of), shift, move, translocate (ه ه s.th., e.g., a tribe, to a place); to settle (ه بين s.th. among) | احله محله (*maḥallahū*) to cause s.o. or s.th. to take the place of s.o. or s.th. else, replace s.o. or s.th. by, substitute s.o. or s.th. for, take s.o. or s.th. as substitute for; احل الشيء محل العناية (*maḥalla l-ʿināya*) to pay attention to s.th., make s.th. one's concern **V** to dissolve, melt, disintegrate; to disengage o.s., disassociate o.s., extricate o.s., free o.s. (من from) **VII** to be untied (knot); to be solved, be unraveled (problem); to be dissolved, be broken up, be disbanded (also, of an organization, a party, etc.); to dissolve, melt; to become slack, limp, weak, loose, relaxed; to disintegrate; to melt away **VIII** to settle down (ه at a place); to occupy (*mil.*, ه a territory); to assume, take over, occupy, hold, have (ه a place, a rank, an office) | احتل المكان الاول (*al-makāna l-awwala*) to occupy the foremost place; احتل اعماله (*aʿmālahū*) to take over s.o.'s functions **X** to regard (ه s.th.) as permissible or lawful, think that one may do s.th. (ه); to regard as fair game, as easy prey, seize unlawfully, misappropriate, usurp (ه s.th.)

حل *ḥall* pl. حلول *ḥulūl* untying, unfastening, undoing (of a knot); solution (of a problem, of a puzzle, etc.); unriddling, unraveling, explanation; solution (*chem.*); dissolution, disbandment, breaking up (of an organization, etc.), abolition, cancellation, annulment; release, freeing, liberation; decontrol, release, unblocking (e.g., of a blocked sum); discharge, clearing, exoneration, exculpation; absolution (*Chr.*) | قابل للحل soluble, solvable; ○ الحل الطيفى (*ṭaifī*) spectral analysis; اهل الحل والعقد *ahl al-ḥ. wa-l-ʿaqd* or اهل الحل والربط (*rabṭ*) influential people, those in power; فى حله وترحاله (*tarḥālihī*) in all his doings, in everything he did; حل الشفرة *ḥ. aš-šifra* decoding, deciphering

حل *ḥill*: كان فى حل من (عن) (*ḥillin*) he was free to ..., he was at liberty to ...; he had free disposal of ...; انت فى حل من you're free to ..., you may readily ...

حلة *ḥalla* pl. حلل *ḥilal* low copper vessel; cooking pot (*eg.*)

حلة *ḥilla* way station, stopping place, stop, stopover; encampment; absolution (*Chr.*); dispensation (*Chr.*)

حلة *ḥulla* pl. حلل *ḥulal* clothing, dress, garb; vestments (ecclesiastic; *Chr.*); (complete) suit of clothes; (Western) suit | حلة رسمية (*rasmīya*) uniform; حلة السهرة *ḥ. as-sahra* formal dress

حلال *ḥalāl* that which is allowed, permitted or permissible; allowed, permitted, permissible, allowable, admissible, lawful, legal, licit, legitimate; lawful possession | ابن حلال *ibn ḥ.* legitimate son; respectable man, decent fellow

حلول *ḥulūl* stopping, putting up, staying; descending, coming on, befalling, overtaking; incarnation; setting in, advent, arrival (of a time, of a deadline), beginning, dawn; substitution (for s.o.)

حليل *ḥalīl* pl. احلاء *aḥillāʾ*[2] husband

حليلة *halīla* pl. حلائل *halā'il*² wife

احليل *iḥlīl* outer opening of the urethra; urethra (*anat.*)

محل *maḥall* pl. *-āt*, محال *maḥāll*² place, location, spot, site, locale, locality, center; (place of) residence; business; business house, firm, commercial house; store, shop; object, cause (e.g., of dispute, admiration, etc.); gear (automobile) | حل محله and احله محله see حل I and IV; محله (*maḥallahū*) in his (its) place; فى محله in his (its) place, in his (its) stead, instead of him; كان فى محله to be in the right place; to be appropriate, expedient, advisable; to be justified, warranted; فى غير محله improper, misplaced, unsuitable, ill-suited; out of place; inappropriate, inexpedient, inopportune; صادف محله *ṣādafa maḥallahū* to be convenient, be most opportune; لا محل ل (*maḥalla*) there is no room for ...; it is out of place, quite déplacé; محل العمل *m. al-ʿamal* place of employment; محل الاقامة *m. al-iqāma* (place of) residence, address; محل تجارى (*tijārī*) business house, commercial house; المحلات العمومية والتجارية (*ʿumūmīya, tijārīya*) public utilities and commercial houses; اسم المحل *ism al-m.* firm; محل رهونات *m. ruhūnāt* pawnshop; محلات السياحة *m. as-siyāḥa* travel agencies; محل مرطبات *m. muraṭṭibāt* refreshment parlor; محل اللهو *m. al-lahw* and محل الملاهى *m. al-malāhī* (pl. محال) amusement center; محل نزاع *m. nizāʿ* object of controversy, controversial matter; لا ارى محلا لعجب *lā arā m. li-ʿajabin* I don't see any reason for amazement, there is nothing to be astonished about; محل نظر *m. naẓar* s.th. deserving attention, a striking, remarkable thing; محلك سر *maḥallak sir* (*eg.*) in place, march! (command; *mil.*); محل هندسى (*handasī*) geometric locus (*math.*)

محلى *maḥallī* local; native, indigenous; parochial; pl. محليات local news, local page (of a newspaper)

محل *maḥill* due date; date of delivery

محلة *maḥalla* pl. *-āt* way station, stopping place, stop, stopover, encampment; camp; section, part, quarter (of a city) | المحلة الكبرى (*kubrā*) Mahalla el Kubra (city in N Egypt)

تحليل *taḥlīl* dissolution, resolution, breaking up, decomposition, specification, detailing, analyzation; (pl. *-āt*, تحاليل *taḥālīl*²) analysis (*chem.* and general); — absolution (*Chr.*) | بالتحليل in detail; معمل تحليل *maʿmal t.* laboratory for chemical analyses; تحليل العوامل factor analysis; تحليل كهربائى (*kahrabā'ī*) electrolysis; التحليل النفسى (النفسانى) (*nafsī*) psychoanalysis; تحليل وظيفى (*waẓīfī*) function analysis

تحليلى *taḥlīlī* analytic(al)

احلال *iḥlāl* substitution (e.g., *phon.*)

تحلل *taḥallul* dissolution, breakup; separation, disengagement, disassociation

انحلال *inḥilāl* dissolution, breakup, decomposition; disintegration; decay, putrefaction; slackening, exhaustion, prostration, weakness, impotence

احتلال *iḥtilāl* occupation (*mil.*) | جيوش الاحتلال occupation forces

احتلالى *iḥtilālī* occupying, occupation (used attributively); advocate of foreign occupation

محلول *maḥlūl* solved; dissolved, resolved, broken up; loose; untied, unfastened, unfettered, free, at large; weakened, prostrate, exhausted, languid; (pl. محاليل *maḥālīl*²) solution (liquid; *chem.*) | محلول الشعر *m. aš-šaʿr* with loose, disheveled hair

محلل *muḥallil* pl. *-ūn* analyzer, analyst | محلل نفسى (*nafsī*) psychoanalyst

منحل *munḥall* solved; dissolved, resolved, broken up; disbanded; languid, prostrate, weak; permitted, allowed

محتل *muḥtall* occupying (*mil.*); occupied (zone; *mil.*) | جيوش محتلة occupation forces; منطقة محتلة (*minṭaqa*) occupied territory

حيلولة[2] see حول

[1]حلب *ḥalaba i u* (*ḥalb*) to milk (ه an animal) | حلب الدهر اشطره *ḥalaba d-dahra ašṭurahū* he has seen good and bad days **V** to run, drip, trickle, ooze, seep, leak; to water, drool (mouth, with appetite) | تتحلب له الافواه (*afwāh*) making the mouth water, appetizing; تحلب اللعاب فى فمى (*al-luʿābu fī famī*) and تحلب ريقى (*rīqī*) my mouth was watering **VIII** to milk (ه an animal) **X** do.; to squeeze juice (ه from)

حلب *ḥalb* milking

حلب *ḥalab* milk

حلبة *ḥalba* pl. *ḥalabāt* race track; arena; dance floor; race horses; round (in boxing) | حلبة الرقص *ḥ. ar-raqṣ* dance floor; انه ليس من تلك الحلبة he is not made for that, he doesn't belong there, it is not in his line; فارس حلبة ب a master of, excelling or outstanding in

حلبة *ḥulba* fenugreek (Trigonella foenum-graecum; *bot.*); tonic, prepared of yellowish grains, for women in childbed (*eg., syr.*)

حليب *ḥalīb* milk | لبن حليب *laban ḥ.* cow's milk (*eg.*)

حليبى *ḥalībī* made of milk

حلوب *ḥalūb* lactiferous | بقرة حلوب (*baqara*) milk cow; الماشية الحلوب (*māšiya*) dairy cattle

حلابة *ḥilāba* dairy farming

حلاب *ḥallāb* milker

حلابة *ḥallāba* milkmaid, dairymaid; dairywoman; milk cow

محلب *maḥlab* mahaleb (Prunus mahaleb; *bot.*)

حالب *ḥālib* ureter

مستحلب *mustaḥlab* emulsion | مستحلب اللوز *m. al-lauz* almond milk

[2]حلب *ḥalab*[2] Aleppo

حلبى *ḥalabī* coming from or originating in Aleppo; an inhabitant of Aleppo | فستق حلبى (*fustuq*) pistachio, pistacia vera (*bot.*)

حلتيت *ḥiltīt, ḥaltīt* asafetida (Ferula assafoetida; *bot.*)

حلج *ḥalaja i u* (*ḥalj*, حليج *ḥalīj*) to gin (ه cotton)

حلج *ḥalj* ginning (of cotton)

حليج *ḥalīj* ginning (of cotton); ginned (cotton)

حلاجة *ḥilāja* cotton ginner's work or trade

حلاج *ḥallāj* cotton ginner

محلج *miḥlaj*, محلجة *miḥlaja* pl. محالج *maḥālij*[2] cotton gin

محلج *maḥlaj* pl. محالج *maḥālij*[2] cotton ginnery

حلحل *ḥalḥala* to remove, drive away, shove away **II** *taḥalḥala* to stir from one's place; to move, stir, budge

حلزون *ḥalazūn* snail; spiral

حلزونة *ḥalazūna* (n. un.) snail; spiral

حلزونى *ḥalazūnī* spiral, helical, volute, winding

حلس *ḥalisa a* to remain, stay permanently (ب at a place), stick (ب to a place)

حلس *ḥils* pl. احلاس *aḥlās* (with foll. genit.) one addicted or given to s.th., one adhering to s.th. | احلاس اللهو *a. al-lahw* people given to pleasure and amusement, bons vivants, playboys

حلس *ḥils* pl. احلاس *aḥlās*, حلوس *ḥulūs* saddle blanket

احلس *aḥlas*[2], f. حلساء *ḥalsā'*[2] bay, chestnut (horse)

حلف *ḥalafa i* (*ḥalf, ḥilf*) to swear (بالله by God) | حلف يمينا (*yamīnan*) to take an oath **II** to make (ه s.o.) swear; to put to oath, swear in (ه s.o.); to adjure, entreat earnestly (ه s.o.) **III** to enter into a confederation, into an alliance (ه with s.o.), become an ally (ه of s.o.) **VI** to commit one another by oath (على to do s.th.), join in alliance; to ally, make an alliance (مع with) **X** to make (ه s.o.) swear, exact an oath (ه from s.o.); to adjure, entreat earnestly (ه s.o.)

حلف *ḥalf, ḥilf* swearing, oath | حلف اليمين taking the oath

حلف *ḥilf* sworn alliance; pact (*pol.*), treaty; (pl. احلاف *aḥlāf*) ally | حلف عسكرى (*'askarī*) military alliance; الحلف الاطلنطى (*aṭlanṭī*) and حلف الاطلسى (*aṭlasī*) the Atlantic Pact; حلف وارسو *ḥ. warsō* the Warsaw Pact

حليف *ḥalīf* pl. حلفاء *ḥulafā'*[2] confederate; ally; allied | الحلفاء the Allies (*pol.*)

حليفة *ḥalīfa* pl. *-āt* f. of حليف

حلوف *ḥallūf* pl. حلاليف *ḥalālīf*[2] (*maġr., eg.*) wild boar; pig, swine

حلفاء *ḥalfā'* und حلفة *ḥalfa* (*bot.*) alfa, esparto

تحليف *taḥlīf* swearing in | لجنة التحليف *lajnat at-t.* (obs.) the jury (in court)

محالفة *muḥālafa* alliance

تحالف *taḥāluf* state of alliance; alliance

محلف *muḥallaf* sworn, bound by oath; (pl. *-ūn*) juror (in court) | المحلفون and هيئة المحلفين *hai'at al-m.* the jury (in court)

متحالف *mutaḥālif* interallied, allied

حلق *ḥalaqa i* (*ḥalq*) to shave (ه the head, the face); to shave off (ه the beard) **II** to circle in the air, hover; to fly, soar (bird, airplane, also of pilots; على and فوق over or above s.th.); to round, make round, circular or ring-shaped (ه s.th.); to ring, surround, encircle (على s.o., s.th.); to clothe **V** to form a circle, sit in a circle; to gather in a circle (على around s.o.)

حلق *ḥalq* shaving, shave; (pl. حلوق *ḥulūq*, احلاق *aḥlāq*) throat; back of the throat; pharynx; (fig.) chasm

حلقى *ḥalqī* guttural; laryngal (*phon.*); laryngeal, pharyngeal; see also *ḥalaqī*

حلق *ḥalaq* rings (coll.); (pl. حلقان *ḥulqān*, *eg.*) a pair of earrings

حلقة *ḥalqa* pl. *ḥalaqāt* ring (e.g., a metal ring of a door, also fig., of spies, criminals, etc.); link (of a chain); circle (also of people); group of students studying under a professor, hence: lecture, course (e.g., at Al Azhar University); seminar; part of a sequence or series; installment of a TV series; ringlet; disk; decade; market | حلقة النجاة *ḥ. an-najāh* life buoy, life preserver; حلقة الاتصال *ḥ. al-ittiṣāl* and حلقة الوصل *ḥ. al-waṣl* connecting link (بين between; fig.); الحلقة المفقودة the missing link, the intermediate form; فى الحلقة السادسة من عمره (*'umrihī*) in the sixth decade of his life, in his fifties; حلقة الاسماك fish market; حلقة القطن *ḥ. al-quṭn* cotton market; حلقة دراسية (*dirāsīya*) seminar, tutorial class; حلقة الذكر *ḥ. ad-ḏikr* (pl. حلقات الاذكار *ḥ. al-aḏkār*) collective liturgical exercise by a group of members of an order (Sufism), see ذكر *ḏikr*; حلقة مفرغة (*mufraḡa*) vicious circle; سلسلة حلقات *silsilat ḥ.* broadcast series, TV series; حلقات بصل *ḥ. baṣal* onion rings

حلقى *ḥalaqī*, *ḥalqī* annular, ring-shaped, circular; cyclical

حلاق *ḥallāq* pl. *-ūn* barber | حلاق صحى (*ṣiḥḥī*), حلاق الصحة *ḥ. aṣ-ṣiḥḥa* barber-surgeon

حليق *ḥalīq* shaved, shaven, shorn

حلاقة *ḥilāqa* shaving, shave; barber's trade | صابون الحلاقة *ṣābūn al-ḥ.* shaving soap; صالون الحلاقة barbershop; قاعة الحلاقة *qāʿat al-ḥ.* do.; ○ ماكينة الحلاقة and ○ آلة الحلاقة safety razor

محلق *miḥlaq* pl. محالق *maḥāliq*[2] straight razor

تحليق *taḥlīq* flying, flight (of an aircraft; على and فوق over a country); take-off (of an airplane); ○ laryngalization (*phon.*)

من حالق *min ḥāliq* from above

حلقوم *ḥulqūm* pl. حلاقيم *ḥalāqīm*[2] throat, gullet | راحة الحلقوم *rāḥat al-ḥ.* a kind of sweet made of cornstarch, sugar, mastic and pistachios (*eg.*)

حلك *ḥalika a* (*ḥalak*) to be pitch-black, deep-black XII احلولك *iḥlaulaka* do.

حلك *ḥalak* intense blackness

حلكة *ḥulka* intense blackness

حلك *ḥalik* pitch-black, deep-black; gloomy, murky

حلوكة *ḥulūka* gloominess, darkness; blackness

حالك *ḥālik* pitch-black, deep-black; gloomy, murky

حلم *ḥalama u* to dream (ب or عن of; فى ان of being, becoming, doing, etc., in the future); to muse, reflect, meditate (ب on s.th.); to attain puberty; — *ḥaluma u* to be gentle, mild-tempered VIII to attain puberty

حلم *ḥulm* pl. احلام *aḥlām* dream; pl. irreality, utopia | حلم اليقظة *ḥ. al-yaqẓa* daydream

حلمى *ḥulmī* dream- (in compounds), of or pertaining to dreams

حلم *ḥulum* sexual maturity, puberty | بلغ الحلم to attain puberty

حلم *ḥilm* pl. حلوم *ḥulūm*, احلام *aḥlām* gentleness, clemency, mildness; forbearance, indulgence; patience; insight, discernment, understanding, intelligence, reason | صغار الاحلام simple-minded people, simple souls

حلم *ḥalam* (coll.; n. un. ة) tick; mite; nipple, teat, mammilla (of the female breast)

حلمى *ḥalamī* parasitic; mammillary, nipple-shaped

حليم *ḥalīm* pl. حلماء *ḥulamā'*[2] mild, mild-tempered, gentle; patient

حلوم *ḥalūm*, حالوم *ḥālūm* a kind of Egyptian cheese

حالم *ḥālim* dreamy, dreamlike; (pl. *-ūn*) dreamer

محتلم *muḥtalim* sexually mature, pubescent, marriageable

حلنجى *ḥalangī* (*eg.*) swindler, cheat

(حلو and حلى) *ḥaluwa u*, *ḥaliya a*, حلا *ḥalā u* (حلاوة *ḥalāwa*, حلوان *ḥulwān*) to be sweet; to be pleasant, agreeable (ل to s.o.) | حلا له الشىء he enjoyed the thing; حلا له ان it pleased him that ..., he was delighted that ...; حسبما يحلو له (*ḥasabamā*) at his discretion, as he pleases; — حلى *ḥalā i* to adorn, grace;

— حلي *ḥaliya a* to be adorned (ب with) II to sweeten (ه s.th., e.g., a beverage with sugar); to adorn, bedeck, embellish, attire, furnish, provide (ه, ه s.o., s.th., ب with) | حلى ضرسه (*ḍirsahū*) to eat a sweet or sweet food, eat one's dessert V to adorn o.s., be adorned, decked out, embellished, graced, endowed, furnished, provided (ب with) X to find sweet or pleasant, like (ه s.th.), be delighted (ه by)

حلا *ḥalan* sweetness, pleasantness

حلو *ḥulw* sweet; pleasant, nice, charming, delightful, pretty | حلو الحديث a gifted raconteur, amusing, entertaining; الغدة الحلوة (*ğudda*) pancreas (*anat.*)

حلى *ḥaly* pl. حلى *ḥulīy* piece of jewelry, trinket

حلية *ḥilya* pl. حلى *ḥilan, ḥulan* decoration, embellishment, finery; trinket; ornament

حلوى *ḥalwā* pl. حلاوى *ḥalāwā* candy, confection, confectionery, sweetmeats; sweet pastry; dessert

حلواء *ḥalwā'*[2] candy, confection, confectionery, sweetmeats

حلوائى *ḥalwā'ī* confectioner, candy dealer; pastry cook, fancy baker

حلويات *ḥalwayāt* (*eg.*), *ḥulwīyāt* (*syr.-leb.*) sweets (in general); sweet pastry; candies, confectionery, sweetmeats; — *ḥalawīyāt* (*eg.*) delicacies, titbits of slaughtered animals, esp. kidneys and liver

حلاوة *ḥalāwa* sweetness; candies, confectionery, sweetmeats; grace, gracefulness, charm, refinement, wittiness, wit; present of money; ransom | حلاوة حمصية (*ḥummuṣīya*) a sweet made of roasted chick-peas; حلاوة طحينية (*ṭaḥīnīya*) a sweet made of sesame-seed meal; حلاوة لوزية (*lauzīya*) a sweet made of almonds; حلاوة الروح euphoria

حلوان *ḥulwān* present of money, gratuity, tip

حلوان *ḥulwān*[2] Helwan (town south of Cairo)

حلوانى *ḥulwānī* (*syr.-leb.*), *ḥilawānī* (*eg.*) confectioner, candy dealer; pastry cook, fancy baker

ما احيلى *mā uḥailā* oh, how sweet is ..., ما احيلاه oh, how sweet he is!

تحلية *taḥliya* decoration, embellishment, ornamentation; sweetening | تحلية المياه *t. al-miyāh* desalinization of water, production of fresh-water

محلى *muḥallan* sweetened; decorated, embellished, adorned, ornamented (ب with)

[1]حم *ḥam* pl. احماء *aḥmā'* father-in-law; pl. relatives of the wife by marriage, in-laws of the wife

حماة *ḥamāh* pl. حموات *ḥamawāt* mother-in-law; see also [1]حمى and [2]حمى

[2]حمة *ḥuma* see [2]حمو

[3]حم *ḥamma u* (*ḥamm*) to heat, make hot (ه s.th.); pass. *ḥumma* to be feverish, have a fever; — *u* (حموم *ḥumūm*) to decree (ه s.th., said of God) | حم القدر *ḥumma l-qadr* the fate was predetermined, the decision was already made; حم له ذلك (*ḥumma*) that was decreed to him, that is his lot, his destiny II to heat, make hot (ه s.th.); to bathe, wash (ه or ه s.o. or s.th.) IV to heat, make hot (ه s.th.) X to bathe, take a bath

حمة *ḥamma* hot spring

حمة *ḥumma* blackness, swarthiness, dark coloration; fever

حمم *ḥumam* magma; lava; embers, cinder

حمى *ḥummā* f., pl. حميات *ḥummayāt* fever, fever heat | الحمى التيفودية and الحمى التيفية (*tīfīya*) typhoid fever, typhus fever; حمى الدق *ḥ. d-diqq* hectic fever; حمى الربع *ḥ. r-ribʿ* quartan fever; الحمى الراجعة relapsing fever; الحمى الصفراء or الحمى الصفراوية (*ṣafrā'*, *ṣafrāwīya*) yellow fever; حمى الغب *ḥ. l-ġibb* tertian fever; الحمى الفحمية (*faḥmīya*) anthrax; الحمى القرمزية (*qirmizīya*) scarlet fever; حمى القش *ḥ. l-qašš* hayfever; الحمى القلاعية (*qulāʿīya*) foot-and-mouth disease; الحمى المخية الشوكية (*mukkīya, šaukīya*) cerebrospinal meningitis; الحمى المتموجة (*mutamawwija*) undulant fever, Malta fever, brucellosis; الحمى النفاسية (*nifāsīya*) puerperal fever, childbed fever; الحمى النمشية (*namašīya*) spotted fever ○

حمى *ḥummī* feverish, febrile, fever- (in compounds)

حمام *ḥamām* (coll.; n. un. ة) pl. *-āt*, حمائم *ḥamā'im*² dove, pigeon | حمام الزاجل carrier pigeon; ساق الحمام bugloss, oxtongue (Anchusa officinalis; *bot.*)

حمام *ḥimām* (fate of) death

حمام *ḥammām* pl. *-āt* bath; swimming pool; bathroom; Oriental bathhouse; spa; watering place | حمام شمس *ḥ. šams* sunbath; حمامات بحرية (*baḥrīya*) seaside resorts

حميم *ḥamīm* pl. احماء *aḥimmā'*² close friend; close, intimate; — hot water; the water reserved for sinners in hell

احم *aḥamm*², f. حماء *ḥammā'*², pl. حم *ḥumm* black

محم *miḥamm* hot-water kettle, caldron, boiler

استحمام *istiḥmām* bathing, bath

استحمامة (n. vic.) bath (which one takes)

محموم *maḥmūm* feverish, having a fever; frantic, hectic

حمأ[1] *ḥama'a a* to clean out, dredge (ه a well)

حمأ *ḥama'*, حمأة *ḥam'a* mud, mire, sludge; pl. حمآت *ḥama'āt* masses of mud

حمئ[2] *ḥami'a* to be or become angry, furious, mad (على at s.o.)

حمحم *ḥamḥama* (حمحمة *ḥamḥama*) to neigh, whinny (horse)

حمحمة *ḥamḥama* neigh(ing), whinnying, whinnies

حمحم *ḥimḥim* oxtongue, bugloss (Anchusa officinalis; *bot.*)

حمد *ḥamida a* (*ḥamd*) to praise, commend, laud, extol (على ه s.o. for, ه s.th.) II to praise highly (ه s.o.)

حمد *ḥamd* commendation, praise, laudation | الحمد لله *al-ḥamdu lillāh* thank God! praise be to God! praised be the Lord!

حميد *ḥamīd* praiseworthy, laudable, commendable; benign, harmless (disease)

حمود *ḥamūd* praiseworthy, laudable, commendable, praised

احمد *aḥmad*² more laudable, more commendable

الشريعة الاحمدية *aš-šarīʿa al-aḥmadīya* Mohammedan Law

محمدة *maḥmada* pl. محامد *maḥāmid*² commendable act; pl. محامد praises, encomiums

محمود *maḥmūd* praised; commendable, laudable, praiseworthy | محمود العواقب having favorable results, having a good outcome

محمد *muḥammad* praised; commendable, laudable

محمدى *muḥammadī* pertaining or attributable to Mohammed

حمدل *ḥamdala* to pronounce the formula الحمد لله "Praise be to God!"

حمدلة *ḥamdala* the formula الحمد لله (see above)

حمر II to redden, color or dye red (ه s.th.); to roast (ه s.th.); to fry (ه s.th.); to brown (ه flour in preparing a roux) **IX** to turn red, take on a reddish color, redden, blush

حمر *ḥumar* asphalt

حمرى *ḥumarī* asphaltic, asphalt, tar, tarry

حمرة *ḥumra* redness, red color(ation), red; rouge (*cosm.*); brick dust, brick rubble; erysipelas, St. Anthony's fire (*med.*) | اصبع حمرة *iṣba' ḥ.* lipstick

حمار *ḥimār* pl. حمير *ḥamīr*, حمر *ḥumur*, احمرة *aḥmira* donkey, ass | حمار الوحش *ḥ. al-waḥš* and حمار وحشى (*waḥšī*) wild ass, onager; سم الحمار *samm al-ḥ.* oleander (Nerium oleander; *bot.*)

حمارة *ḥimāra* pl. حمائر *ḥamā'ir*² she-ass, female donkey

حمور *ḥumūr* red, red color(ation), redness

حميرة *ḥumaira* redstart (*zool.*)

حمار *ḥammār* pl. ة donkey driver

احمر *aḥmar*², f. حمراء *ḥamrā'*², pl. حمر *ḥumr* red, red-colored, ruddy; rosy, pink; bloody, violent; excited, heated up (crowd) | تحت الاحمر, دون الاحمر infrared; البحر الاحمر the Red Sea; الصليب الاحمر the Red Cross; الموت الاحمر (*maut*) violent death; الهوى الاحمر (*hawā*) sexual intercourse; الاحمران ("the two red ones", i.e.) wine and meat; الاسود والاحمر ("the black and the red", i.e.) all mankind; احمر الشفاه and (*eg.*) احمر الشفايف lipstick

حمراء *ḥamrā'*² smut, rust (disease affecting cereals); الحمراء Alhambra, the Citadel of Granada

يحمور *yaḥmūr* red; deer, roe, roebuck; wild ass; hemoglobin (*physiol.*)

احمرار *iḥmirār* reddening, blush(ing), redness, red coloration; erythema (*med.*)

محمر *muḥammar* roasted, panfried | بطاطس محمرة (*baṭāṭis*) fried potatoes

حمز *ḥamaza i* (*ḥamz*) to bite, or burn, the tongue (taste)

حمس *ḥamisa a* (حماسة *ḥamāsa*) to be zealous, ardent, be enthusiastic; to be valiant, courageous **II** to fill with enthusiasm (ه s.o.) **V** to get heated, worked up; to be excited; to be enthusiastic (ل about), have a passion (ل for); to advocate fervently (ل s.th.); to be overzealous (فى in s.th.)

حمس *ḥamis* unflinching, ardent, eager, zealous, lively; enthusiastic, full of enthusiasm

حماس *ḥamās* enthusiasm, rapture; zeal; elan, fighting spirit

حماسة *ḥamāsa* enthusiasm, fire, ardor, fervor, zeal; valor, bravery, heroism; الحماسة the Hamasa (a famous collection of Arabic poems)

حماسى *ḥamāsī* enthusiastic, ardent, fiery, zealous, enraptured; enrapturing, stirring, rousing

احمس *aḥmas*², f. حمساء *ḥamsā'*², pl. حمس *ḥums* unflinching, tenacious, valiant; strenuous, zealous; enthusiastic

تحمس *taḥammus* unflinching zeal, enthusiasm (ل for), fanaticism

متحمس *mutaḥammis* enthusiastic, ardent, fiery, zealous; — (pl. *-ūn*) ardent follower, fanatic adherent, fanatic; fan (ل e.g., of a sport, of a trend in art)

حمش *ḥamaša u* to excite, irritate, infuriate, enrage (ه s.o.)

حمشة *ḥamša* catgut (*med.*)

¹حمص II to roast (ه s.th., esp. coffee); to toast (ه bread)

حمص *ḥimmiṣ, ḥimmaṣ*; (colloq.) *ḥummuṣ* (coll.; n. un. ة) chick-pea; — *ḥummuṣ* a dish made of ground chick-peas with sesame oil, etc.

محمصة *miḥmaṣa* coffee roaster

²حمص *ḥimṣ*² Homs (the ancient Emesa, city in central Syria)

حمض *ḥamuḍa u* (حموضة *ḥumūḍa*) to be or become sour II to make sour, sour, acidify, acidulate (ه s.th.); to develop (ه a photographic plate, a film; *phot.*); to cause (ه s.th.) to oxidize

حمض *ḥamḍ* pl. احماض *aḥmāḍ* acid (*chem.*) | حمض بولى (*baulī*) uric acid

شجر حمضى *šajar ḥamḍī* citrus trees

حمضية *ḥamḍīya* pl. -*āt* citrus fruit

حموضة *ḥumūḍa* sourness, acidity | مولد الحموضة *muwallid al-ḥ.* oxygen (*chem.*)

حماض *ḥummāḍ*, حميض *ḥummaiḍ* sorrel (*bot.*)

تحميض *taḥmīḍ* souring, acidification; development (*phot.*)

احماض *iḥmāḍ* jocular language, joking remark

حامض *ḥāmiḍ* sour, acid; acidulous; (pl. حوامض *ḥawāmiḍ*²) acid (*chem.*); pl. حوامض citrus fruits | حامض الفحم *ḥ. al-faḥm* carbonic acid; حامض كبريتى (*kibrītī*) sulphuric acid; حامض الليمون *ḥ. al-laimūn* citric acid

حماط *ḥamāṭ* (*saud.-ar.*) figs

حمق *ḥamiqa a* and *ḥamuqa u* (*ḥumq*, حماقة *ḥamāqa*) to be stupid, silly, foolish, fatuous; to become angry or furious II and IV to regard (ه s.o.) as a fool, consider (ه s.o.) dumb, stupid, idiotic VI pretend to be stupid VII to become angry or furious X to consider (ه s.o.) dumb, stupid, idiotic

حمق *ḥumq* stupidity, silliness, foolishness, folly

حماقة *ḥamāqa* stupidity, silliness, foolishness, folly; anger, wrath; pl. حماقات stupidities

حماق *ḥumāq, ḥamāq* smallpox, variola (*med.*)

احمق *aḥmaq*², f. حمقاء *ḥamqā'*², pl. حمق *ḥum(u)q*, حمقى *ḥamqā*, حماقى *ḥamāqā* dumb, stupid, silly, foolish, fatuous; fool, simpleton, imbecile

حمقان *ḥamqān* dumb, stupid, silly, foolish; angry, furious

حمل *ḥamala i* (*ḥaml*) to carry, bear (ه s.th.); to lift, pick up (ه s.th. in order to carry it), load up and take along (ه s.th.); to hold (ه s.th., in one's hand); to carry on or with one, take or bring along (ه s.th.); to transport, carry, convey (ه s.th.); to bring, take (الى or ل ه s.th. to s.o.); to take upon o.s. (عن instead of or for s.o., ه a burden), carry, assume (ه the burden, عن of s.o. else), relieve (ه عن s.o. from s.th.), take (ه a burden, a grievance, etc.) from s.o. (عن); to extend, show, evince, cherish, harbor (ه a feeling, ل toward s.o.); to become or be pregnant (من by s.o.); to bear fruit (tree); to induce, cause, prompt, get (على ه s.o. to do s.th.), make s.o. (ه) do s.th. (على); to convert, bring around, win over (على رأيه ه s.o. to one's opinion), convince (على رأيه ه s.o. of one's opinion); to attack (على s.o.), also حمل حملة على (*ḥamlatan*) to launch or make an attack on; to know by heart (ه a book); to relate, refer (على ه s.th. to), bring (ه s.th.) to bear (على upon s.th.), link, correlate, bring into relation (ه s.th., على with); to trace, trace back (على ه s.th.

to); to ascribe, attribute, impute (ه على s.th. to s.o.); to make (ه a word) agree grammatically (على with another) | حمل في نفسه to feel annoyed, be in a melancholy mood, feel blue; حمل على نفسه to pull o.s. together, brace o.s.; حمله على محمل (*maḥmali*) to take s.th. to mean ..., interpret or construe s.th. in the sense of ..., as if it were ...; حمله على غير محمله to misinterpret, misconstrue s.th.; حمله محمل الجد (*maḥmala l-jidd*) to take s.th. seriously, take s.th. at face value; حمل الاسلام to be a carrier of Islam (of a people or nation); حمل الدكتوراه (*doktōrāh*) to have a doctor's degree; حمل شهادة (*šahādatan*) to carry a certificate with one or on one's person; حمل فكرة (*fikratan*) to be a carrier, upholder of an idea; حمل القرآن to know the Koran by heart; حمل لقبا (*laqaban*) to hold a title; حمل مدنية (*madanīyatan*) to be a carrier of a civilization **II** to have or make (ه s.o.) carry or bear (ه s.th.), load, burden, charge, task (ه, ه s.o. or s.th. ه with), impose (ه ه on s.o. s.th.) **V** to bear, assume, take upon o.s. (ه s.th., e.g., النفقات *an-nafaqāt* the expenses, المسؤولية *al-mas'ūlīya* the responsibility); to bear up (ه under), bear, stand, sustain, endure, tolerate, stomach (ه s.th.); to undergo, suffer (ه s.th.); to be able to stand (ه s.o.) or put up (ه with s.o.); to hold up (ه against abuse), sustain (ه s.th., e.g., heavy usage or wear); to set out, get on one's way; to depart **VI** to maltreat, treat unjustly (على s.o.), be prejudiced, be biased, take sides (على against s.o.); to struggle to one's feet, rise with great effort | تحامل على نفسه (*nafsihī*) to brace o.s.; to pull o.s. together, take heart, pluck up courage **VIII** to carry, bring (ه s.th.); to carry away, take away, haul off, lug off (ه s.th.); to suffer, undergo, bear, stand, endure, sustain (ه s.th.); to allow, permit, suffer, tolerate, brook, stomach (ه s.th.), acquiesce (ه in), put up, bear (ه with s.th.); to hold (ه s.th.), have capacity (ه for); to imply that s.th. (ه) is possible, permissible, or conceivable; pass. يحتمل *yuḥtamalu* (it is) bearable, tolerable; (it is) conceivable, possible, probable, likely

حمل *ḥaml* carrying, bearing; inducement, prompting, encouragement (of s.o., على to); delivery; transport, transportation, conveyance; portage, carrying charges; — (pl. احمال *aḥmāl*, حمال *ḥimāl*) foetus; pregnancy | عدم الحمل *'adam al-ḥ.* sterility (of a woman)

حمل *ḥiml*, (*colloq.*) *ḥaml* pl. احمال *aḥmāl* cargo, load, burden | حمل حى (*ḥayy*) pay load, commercial load, live load; حمل ميت (*mayyit*) and حمل ساكن dead load, dead weight; حمل موازن (*muwāzin*) counterpoise, counterweight

حمل *ḥamal* pl. حملان *ḥumlān*, احمال *aḥmāl* lamb; (unconsecrated) Host (*Chr.-Copt.*); الحمل Aries, Ram (sign of the zodiac; *astron.*); the first month of the solar year (*Saudi Ar.*), counted from the Hegira and beginning on the 21st of March

حملة *ḥamla* pl. *ḥamalāt* attack (على on); offensive; campaign; military expedition; expeditionary force | حملة تأديبية (*ta'dībīya*) punitive expedition; حملة صحافية (*ṣiḥāfīya*) press campaign; حملة استكشافية (*istikšāfīya*) reconnaissance raid (*mil.*); حملة ميكانيكية motorized detachment (*mil.*); حملة انتخابية (*intikābīya*) election campaign; حملة تطهير clean-up campaign (*pol.*); حملة عالمية (*'ālamīya*) worldwide campaign; حملة توعية *ḥ. tau'iya* campaign of enlightenment

حملى *ḥamalī* pl. *-īya* ambulant water vendor

حميل *ḥamīl* foundling; child in the womb, fetus; guarantor, warrantor

حميلة على *ḥamīla 'alā* a burden to, completely dependent upon

حمول *ḥamūl* (m. and f.) long-suffering; patient, tolerant in suffering (of hardship, burdens); gentle, mild-tempered

حمال *ḥammāl* pl. *-ūn*, ة porter, carrier

حمالة *ḥimāla* work and trade of a porter or carrier

حمالة *ḥammāla* (carrier) beam, girder, support, base, post, pier, pillar; suspenders | حمالة الصدر (*ṣadr*) brassière

حمولة *ḥumūla* pl. *-āt* load capacity, load limit, capacity; tonnage (of a vessel); portage, freightage, transport charges; (pl. حمائل *ḥamā'il*[2]) family (*Ir.*)

احمل *aḥmal*[2] more tolerant or patient in suffering

محمل *maḥmal* see حمل *ḥamala*; also اخذ شيئا على محمل الجد (*m. il-jidd*) to take s.th. seriously

محمل *maḥmil*, (*colloq.*) *maḥmal* pl. محامل *maḥāmil*[2] camel-borne litter; mahmal, a richly decorated litter sent by Islamic rulers to Mecca as an emblem of their independence, at the time of the hadj; ○ bearing (*techn.*) | ○ محمل كريات *m. kuraiyāt* ball bearing (*techn.*)

تحميل *taḥmīl* burdening; encumbrance; imposition; loading (of ships; of goods); shipping, shipment

تحميلة *taḥmīla* pl. تحاميل *taḥāmīl*[2] suppository (*med.*)

تحمل *taḥammul* taking over, assumption (of burdens); bearing, standing, sufferance, endurance; durability; strength, hardiness, sturdiness, solidity (of a material); pl. تحملات assumed duties or tasks, obligations

تحامل *taḥāmul* prejudice, bias, partiality; intolerance

احتمال *iḥtimāl* bearing, standing, suffering, sufferance, toleration; durability, endurance (of a material or of goods); probability, likelihood, potentiality; pl. احتمالات probabilities; possibilities | صعب الاحتمال (*ṣa'b*) hard to bear, oppressive

حامل *ḥāmil* pl. حملة *ḥamala* porter, carrier; bearer (of a note, of a check, etc.; of an order or decoration); holder (of an identification paper, of a diploma, of a certificate, an academic title, a qualification, an idea); holding device, holder, clamp, fastener, hold, support (*techn.*); fighter (على against); (pl. حوامل *ḥawāmil*[2]) pregnant | حامل البريد courier; حملة الاسهم *ḥ. al-ashum* shareholders; حامل البكالوريا *ḥ. al-bakālōriyā* holder of a secondary school diploma (*Maḡr.*); s.o. having the degree of Baccalaureus; حامل العلم *ḥ. al-'alam* standard bearer, flagman; حامل اللقب *ḥ. al-laqab* titleholder (sport); حملة الاقلام the publicists, the writers; حامل كلام الله *ḥ. kalām allāh* one who knows the Koran by heart; تيار حامل (*tayyār*) carrier current (*el.*); موجات حاملة (*maujāt*) carrier waves (*el.*)

حاملة *ḥāmila* pl. *-āt* device for carrying, carrier; rack | حاملة خريطة map case; حاملة طائرات *ḥ. ṭā'irāt* aircraft carrier; حاملة قنابل bomber plane, bomber

محمول *maḥmūl* carried, borne; bearable, tolerable; load weight, service weight, cargo; tonnage (of a vessel); predicate, attribute (logic), محمول عليه subject (logic) | مشاة محمولة (*mušāh*) motorized infantry (*mil.*); جنود محمولون جوا (*jawwan*) airborne troops (*mil.*)

محمل *muḥammal* loaded, laden, heavily charged, burdened (ب with), encumbered (ب by)

محتمل *muḥtamal* bearable, tolerable; probable, likely | من المحتمل ان probably

حملق *ḥamlaqa* (حملقة *ḥamlaqa*) to stare, gaze (ب or ف at)

حملايا *ḥimalāyā* Himalaya

1حمو *ḥamū* (construct state of حم *ḥam*) and حماة *ḥamāh* see 1حم

2(حمو and حمى) حمى *ḥamiya* a to be or become hot; to glow (metal); to flare up; to fly into a rage, become furious (على at) | حمى الوطيس fierce fighting broke out II to make hot, heat (ه s.th.); to heat to glowing (ه metal); to fire up (ه a stove); to kindle, inflame, stir up, excite (ه s.th.); to bathe (= 3حم II) IV to make hot, heat (ه s.th.)

حمو *ḥamw* heat | حمو النيل *ḥ. an-nīl* prickly heat, heat rash, lichen tropicus (*eg.*)

حمو *ḥumūw* heat

حمة *ḥuma* pl. *-āt*, حمى *ḥuman* sting, stinger (of insects); prick, spine (of plants)

حمى *ḥamīy* hot, glowing; heated, excited

حمى *ḥummā* see 3حم

حمية *ḥamīya* zeal, ardor, fervor; enthusiasm, ardent zeal, fanaticism; violence, vehemence; passion, rage, fury; heat of excitement; temper, temperament | الحمية القومية (*qaumīya*) chauvinism

حميا *ḥumayyā* heat; excitement, agitation; enthusiasm; fire, passion, impetuosity, vehemence; fury, rage; wine

حماوة *ḥamāwa* heat

محمى *maḥman* fire chamber, furnace (of a stove, oven, etc.)

حام *ḥāmin* hot; heated, violent, fierce (e.g., a battle); glowing, passionate, fiery; burning

1حمى *ḥamā* i (*ḥamy*, حماية *ḥimāya*) to defend, guard (ه, ه s.o., s.th., من against), protect, shelter, shield (ه or ه من, ه s.o., s.th. from); to deny (المريض the patient) harmful food (ه; = to put him on diet); to forbid (ه ان s.o. to do s.th.) III to defend (من s.o. or s.th., also, of a lawyer in court); to shield, protect, support (عن s.o. or s.th.), take up the cause of (عن), stand up for (عن) VI to keep away (ه from), shun, avoid (ه s.th.) VIII to protect o.s. (ه, ه from s.th., from s.o.), defend o.s., cover o.s. (ب with s.th.), seek protection, seek shelter or refuge (ب with s.o., also عند; من from); to entrench oneself (ب in or at a place)

حمى *ḥiman* protection; defense; sanctuary

حمية *ḥimya* that which is defended; diet

حماية *ḥimāya* pl. *-āt* protection; patronage, sponsorship, auspices; protectorate (*pol.*) | حماية البيئة *ḥ. al-bī'a* environmental protection

محاماة *muḥāmāh* defense (*jur.*); legal profession, practicing of law | هيأة المحاماة *hai'at al-m.* the bar

احتماء *iḥtimā'* seeking cover, seeking protection; cover, shelter, protection

حام *ḥāmin* pl. حماة *ḥumāh* protector, defender, guardian; patron | الدولة الحامية (*daula*) protecting power (of a protectorate)

حامية *ḥāmiya* pl. *-āt* patroness, protectress; garrison (*mil.*)

محمى *maḥmīy* protected (ب by); being under a protectorate, having the status of a protectorate | منطقة محمية (*minṭaqa*) protectorate (country)

محمية *maḥmīya* pl. *-āt* protectorate (country; *pol.*)

محام *muḥāmin* pl. محامون *muḥāmūn* defense counsel, counselor-at-law, lawyer, barrister, attorney (at law), advocate

محامية *muḥāmiya* woman lawyer

محتم *muḥtamin* one who seeks protection; protégé; being under a protectorate, having the status of a protectorate

²حماة, حماه *ḥamāh* Hama (city in W Syria)

حموى *ḥamawī* pertaining to, or stemming from, Hama

حمير *ḥimyar*² the Himyarites

حميرى *ḥimyarī* Himyaritic

حن *ḥanna* *i* (حنين *ḥanīn*) to long, yearn, hanker (الى for), crave (الى s.th.); — (حنة *ḥanna*, حنان *ḥanān*) to feel tenderness, affection, sympathy (على for s.o.); to sympathize, commiserate (على with), feel compassion (على for); to pity (على s.o.), have mercy (على on) **II** to move, touch, fill with tenderness, soften, fill with compassion (قلبه *qalbahū* s.o.'s heart); to blossom, flower, be in bloom (tree) **V** to feel sympathy, feel pity, feel compassion (على for s.o.), commiserate (على with s.o.); to be tender, affectionate

حنة *ḥanna* sympathy; commiseration, compassion, pity; favorable aspect, advantage

حنان *ḥanān* sympathy, love, affection, tenderness; commiseration, compassion, pity; حنانيك *ḥanānaika* have pity! have mercy!

حنانة *ḥanāna* compassion, pity, commiseration

حنين *ḥanīn* longing, yearning, hankering, nostalgia, craving, desire (الى for)

حنون *ḥanūn* (m. and f.) affectionate, loving, softhearted, tenderhearted, compassionate, merciful; tender, soft, gentle, kind, moving, touching (voice)

حنان *ḥannān* affectionate, loving, tender; compassionate, sympathetic

تحنان *taḥnān* pity, compassion; sympathy, affection

تحنن *taḥannun* tenderness, affection, sympathy

حنأ **II** to dye red (ه s.th., with henna)

حناء *ḥinnā'* henna (a reddish-orange cosmetic gained from leaves and stalks of the henna plant) | ابو الحناء *abū l-ḥ.* robin (redbreast); تمر الحناء (colloq. *tamr el-ḥinna*) henna plant (Lawsonia inermis; *bot.*)

حانبة look up alphabetically

حنبلى *ḥanbalī* Hanbalitic, of or pertaining to the *maḏhab* of Aḥmad ibn Ḥanbal; puritanical, strict in religious matters; (pl. حنابلة *ḥanābila*) Hanbalite

الحنبلية *al-ḥanbalīya* the Hanbalitic school of Islamic Law

حانوت, حانوتى look up alphabetically

حنث *ḥaniṯa* *a* (*ḥinṯ*) with فى يمينه or بيمينه: to break one's oath **V** to practice piety, perform works of devotion; to seek religious purification; to scorn sin, not yield to sin

حنث *ḥinṯ* pl. احناث *aḥnāṯ* perjury; sin

حنجرة *ḥanjara* pl. حناجر *ḥanājir*² larynx, throat

حنجور *ḥunjūr* pl. حناجير *ḥanājīr*² larynx, throat

حنجل *ḥanjala* to prance (horse); to caper, gambol **II** *taḥanjala* to dance, caper, gambol, frisk

حندس *ḥindis* pl. حنادس *ḥanādis*² dark night

حندقوق *ḥandaqūq* (*bot.*) melilot, (yellow) sweet clover (Melilotus)

حنش *ḥanaš* pl. احناش *aḥnāš* snake

حنط II to embalm (ه a corpse); to stuff (ه a carcass)

حنطة *ḥinṭa* wheat

حنطى *ḥinṭī* wheat-colored, golden brown; tanned

حناطة *ḥināṭa* embalming

تحنط *taḥannuṭ* mummification

محنط *muḥannaṭ* mummified

حنطور *ḥanṭūr* (*eg.*) horse carriage with folding top

حنظل *ḥanẓal* (coll.; n. un. ة) colocynth (Citrullus colocynthis; *bot.*)

حنف *ḥanafa* *i* to turn or bend sideways

حنيف *ḥanīf* pl. حنفاء *ḥunafā'*[2] true believer, orthodox; one who scorns the false creeds surrounding him and professes the true religion; true (religion) | الدين الحنيف (*dīn*) the True (i.e., Islamic) Religion, also الحنيفة السمحاء (*samḥā'*)

حنفى *ḥanafī* pagan, heathen, idolater (*Chr.*); Hanafitic (see حنفية); (pl. *-ūn*) Hanafi

حنفية *ḥanafīya* paganism, heathendom (*Chr.*); الحنفية the Hanafitic school of Islamic Law; — (pl. *-āt*) faucet, tap; hydrant

الحنيفية *al-ḥanīfīya* the True (i.e., Islamic) Religion

احنف *aḥnaf*[2] afflicted with a distortion of the foot

حنق *ḥaniqa* *a* (*ḥanaq*) to be furious, mad, angry; to be annoyed, exasperated, peeved, irritated (على or من at, by), be resentful (على or من of) IV to infuriate, enrage, embitter, exasperate, irritate (ه s.o.)

حنق *ḥanaq* fury, rage, ire, wrath, anger, exasperation, resentment, rancor

حنق *ḥaniq* furious, mad, angry; resentful, bitter, embittered, annoyed, exasperated, peeved

حانق *ḥāniq* furious, mad, angry; resentful, bitter, embittered, annoyed, exasperated, peeved | حانق على الحياة (*ḥayāh*) weary of life, dispirited, dejected; حانق على النساء (*nisā'*) misogynist

محنق *muḥnaq* infuriated, enraged; embittered, bitter, angry, exasperated, resentful

حنك *ḥanaka* *i* *u*, II and IV to sophisticate, make experienced or worldly-wise through severe trials (said of fate, time, age)

حنك *ḥanak* pl. احناك *aḥnāk* palate

حنكى *ḥanakī* palatal

حنك *ḥunk*, *ḥink* and حنكة *ḥunka* worldly experience, practical ability won through experience; prudence, smartness, cleverness

محنك *muḥannak* experienced, worldly-wise, prudent, clever | محنك مبنك (*mubannak*) shrewd, smart, sharp

حنا (حنى and حنو) *ḥanā* *u* to bend, curve, twist, turn; to lean, incline (على or الى toward s.o.); to be attached (على to s.o.), have affection (على for s.o.); to feel for s.o. (على), sympathize (على with s.o.), commiserate, pity (على s.o.), feel compassion, feel pity (على for s.o.); — حنا and حنى *ḥanā* *i* to bend, bow, flex, curve, crook (ه s.th.) | حنى رأسه (*ra'sahū*) to bow one's head down IV to sympathize (على with s.o.), feel compassion, feel pity (على for s.o.), commiserate, pity (على s.o.) VII to bend, curve, twist, turn; to be winding, be tortuous, wind, meander (e.g., a road); to turn, deviate, digress (عن from); to bow (ل to s.o.); to lean, incline (على or فوق over s.th., الى toward s.o., toward s.th.); to devote o.s. eagerly (على to s.th.); to contain, harbor (على s.th.) | ان ضلوعى

لا تنحنى على ضغن (*ḍulūʿī, ḍiḡn*) I harbor no grudge, I feel no resentment

حنو *ḥanw* bending, deflection, flexing, flexure, curving, curvature, twisting, turning

حنو *ḥinw* pl. احناء *aḥnā'* bend, bow, turn, twist, curved line, curve, contour; pl. ribs | بين احنائها in her bosom

حنو *ḥunūw* sympathy, compassion, tenderness; loving affection (على for s.o.)

حنى *ḥany* bending, deflection, flexing, flexure, curving, curvature, twisting, turning

حنية *ḥanya* bend, turn, curve

حنية *ḥanīya* pl. حنايا *ḥanāyā* arc; camber, curvature | فى حنايا صدره in his bosom; فى حنايا نفسه in his heart, deep inside him

حناية *ḥināya* curving, curvature, twisting, turning, bending

محنى *maḥnan* pl. محان *maḥānin* curvature, bend, flexure, bow, turn, curve

انحناء *inḥinā'* pl. *-āt* bend, deflection, curvature; curve; arc; inclination, tilt; bow, curtsy

انحناءة *inḥinā'a* (n. vic.) bow, curtsy

الحوانى *al-ḥawānī* the longest ribs; (fig.) breast, bosom | بملء حوانيهم *bi-mil'i ḥ.* (they shouted) at the top of their lungs, with all their might

محنى *maḥnīy* bowed, inclined (head); bent forward, stooped (person); bent, curved, crooked

منحن *munḥanin* bent, curved, crooked, twisted; inclined, bowed

منحنى *munḥanan* pl. منحنيات *munḥanayāt* bend, flexure, deflection, curvature; turn, twist, break, angle; curve (of a road, and *math.*); slope

حواء *ḥawwā'*[2] Eve

حوب V to abstain from sin; to lead a pious life; to refrain, abstain (من from s.th.)

حوبة *ḥauba* sin, offense, misdeed, outrage

حوباء *ḥaubā'*[2] soul

حوت *ḥūt* pl. حيتان *ḥītān*, احوات *aḥwāt* fish; whale; — الحوت Pisces (sign of the zodiac; *astron.*); the twelfth month of the solar year (*Saudi Ar.*; cf. حمل *ḥamal*) | حوت سليمان *ḥ. sulaimān* salmon (*zool.*)

(حوث) X to dig out of the ground (ه s.th.)

مستحاث *mustaḥāṯ* pl. *-āt* fossil

حوج IV *aḥwaja* to have need, stand in need, be in want (الى of s.th.), need, require, want (الى s.th.); to put (ه s.o.) in need of (الى), make necessary (الى ه for s.o. s.th.), require (الى ه of s.o. s.th.), compel, oblige (الى ه s.o. to); to impoverish, reduce to poverty (ه s.o.) | ما احوجه الى (*aḥwajahū*) how much he stands in need of ...! how urgently he needs ...! VIII to have need, stand in need, be in want (الى of; also ل or ه), need, want, require (الى, also ل or ه, ه s.th., s.o.)

حوج *ḥauj* need, want, lack, deficiency, destitution

حاجة *ḥāja* pl. *-āt* need (الى or ب of); necessity, requirement, prerequisite; natural, bodily need; pressing need, neediness, poverty, indigence, destitution; object of need or desire; desire, wish, request; necessary article, requisite; matter, concern, business, job, work; thing, object; — pl. حوائج *ḥawā'ij*[2] needs, necessities, necessaries; everyday objects, effects, belongings, possessions, stuff; clothes, clothing | كان فى حاجة الى (ل) to stand in need, be in want of (s.th.), need, require (s.th.); (ل) لا حاجة الى (ḥājata) ... is not necessary, not required, there is no need of ...; لا حاجة لى به I don't need it; عند الحاجة if (or when) necessary, if need be, in case of need; فى غير حاجة (ġairi ḥājatin) unnecessarily; ما به الحاجة the essentials; محل الحاجة mahall al-ḥ. the essential passage, the gist, the substance, the crux, the interesting part (of an exposition); سد حاجته sadda ḥājatahū to meet s.o.'s needs, provide for s.o.'s needs; قضى حاجته qaḍā ḥājatahū to fulfill s.o.'s wish; قضى الحاجة to relieve nature

حاجيات ḥājīyāt everyday commodities, utensils, utilities, necessaries, necessities; needs

احوج aḥwaj² in greater need (الى of s.th.); more necessary

احتياج iḥtiyāj want, need, requirement, (pre)requisite, necessity; pl. -āt needs, necessities, necessaries

محاويج maḥāwīj² (pl. of محوج muḥwij) needy, poor, destitute people

محتاج muḥtāj in need, in want (الى of s.th.), requiring (الى s.th.); poor, destitute, indigent

حوجلة ḥaujala pl. حواجل ḥawājil² phial (chem.)

(حود) حاد ḥāda u (ḥaud) to turn aside, turn away (عن from), turn (عن off) II to turn off, take a turning

حودة ḥauda turn, turning

(حوذ) حاذ ḥāḏa u (ḥauḏ) to urge on, spur on (ه animals) IV احوذ aḥwaḏa do. X استحوذ istaḥwaḏa to overwhelm, overcome, overpower (على s.o.; esp. emotions), get the better of (على), gain mastery (على over); to capture (على the market); to seize (ه, على on), take possession (ه, على of), usurp (ه, على s.th.); to hold (ه s.o.'s attention)

حوذى ḥūḏī pl. -īya coachman, cabman, driver

حوذية ḥūḏīya coachman's work or trade

(حور) حار ḥāra u to return (الى to); to recede, decrease, diminish, be reduced (الى to) II to change, alter, amend, transform, reorganize, remodel, modify (ه or من s.th.); to roll out (ه dough); to make white, whiten (ه s.th.); to bleach (ه a fabric) III to talk, converse, have a conversation (ه with s.o.); to discuss, debate, argue IV (with جوابا jawāban) to answer, reply (with negations only) V to be altered, changed, amended, transformed, reorganized, remodeled, modified VI to carry on a discussion

حور ḥawar white poplar (also pronounced ḥaur); bark-tanned sheepskin, basil; marked contrast between the white of the cornea and the black of the iris

حارة ḥāra pl. -āt quarter, part, section (of a city); (Tun.) ghetto; lane, alley, side street (with occasional pl. حوارى ḥawārī) | حارة السد ḥ. as-sadd blind alley, dead-end street

احور aḥwar², f. حوراء ḥaurā'², pl. حور ḥūr having eyes with a marked contrast of white and black, (also, said of the eye:) intensely white and deep-black

حوارة ḥauwāra (ḥawāra?) cretaceous rock; chalk

حوارى ḥawārī pl. -ūn disciple, apostle (of Jesus Christ); disciple, follower

حوارى ḥuwwārā cretaceous rock; chalk

حورية ḥūrīya pl. -āt, حور ḥūr houri, virgin of paradise; nymph; (pl. -āt) young locust | حورية الماء water nymph, nixie

حوران *ḥaurān*² the Hauran, a mountainous plateau in SW Syria and N Jordan

محور *miḥwar* pl. محاور *maḥāwir*² axis (*math.*); axle, axletree; pivot, crucial point, that upon which s.th. hinges or depends; rolling pin | دول المحور *duwal al-m.* (formerly) the Axis Powers (*pol.*); O غلاف المحور المتعامد (*muta'āmid*) crankcase (*techn.*)

محورى *miḥwarī* axial (*math., techn.*)

محار *maḥār* (coll.; n. un. ة) oysters; shellfish, mussels; mother-of-pearl, nacre

محارة *maḥāra* (n. un.) oyster; oyster shell, mussel; trowel

تحوير *taḥwīr* alteration, change, transformation, reorganization, reshuffle, remodeling, modification

حوار *ḥiwār* talk, conversation, dialogue; argument, dispute; text (of a play); script, scenario (of a motion picture); libretto (of an opera)

محاورة *muḥāwara* talk, conversation, dialogue; argument, dispute

تحاور *taḥāwur* discussion

محاور *muḥāwir* pl. *-ūn* interlocutor, participant in a dialogue or conversation

(حوز and حيز) حاز *ḥāza u* (*ḥauz*, حيازة *ḥiyāza*) to possess, own, have (ه s.th.); to gain, win, get, receive, obtain, achieve, attain (على or ه s.th., e.g., success, victory, etc.); to gain possession, gain control (ه of s.th.), seize (ه s.th.); — *ḥāza i* (حيز *ḥaiz*) to drive on, urge on (ه camels) **V** *taḥawwaza* and *taḥayyaza* to writhe, twist, coil; — *taḥayyaza* to stay away, keep away, seclude o.s., isolate o.s. (عن from); to be disposed, incline, tend, lean (الى toward); to join (الى s.o. or s.th.); to side (ل, الى with), take sides (ل, الى in favor of) **VII** to isolate o.s., seclude o.s., separate, segregate, disengage o.s., dissociate o.s., stay away, keep away, retire, withdraw (عن or من from); to join (الى s.o. or s.th.); to unite (الى with); to side (الى or ل with), take sides (الى or ل in favor of) **VIII** to possess, own, have (ه s.th.); to take possession (ه of s.th.); to keep, prevent, hinder (ه عن s.o. from)

حوز *ḥauz* possession, holding, tenure; obtainment, attainment, acquisition; taking possession, occupation, occupancy; (*jur.*) tenancy; — (pl. احواز *aḥwāz*) enclosed area, enclosure; precinct(s), boundary, city limits

حوزى *ḥauzī* possessory, tenurial

حوزة *ḥauza* possession, holding, tenure; property; area, territory | فى حوزته or فى حوزة يده *fī ḥ. yadihī* in his possession; الدفاع عن حوزة مصر the defense of Egyptian territory

حيز *ḥayyiz*, *ḥaiz* pl. احياز *aḥyāz* scope, range, reach, extent, compass, confines, field, domain, realm; sphere | لا يدخل فى حيز المعقول (*yadkulu*) it is not within the bounds of reason; برز الى حيز المفعول (to advance to the realm of fact, i.e.) to become a reality; فى حيز الامكان *fī ḥ. il-imkān* within the realm of possibility, quite possible; دخل حيز التنفيذ to enter the stage of implementation; وضع فى حيز التنفيذ to put into force (ه s.th.)

حيازة *ḥiyāza* possession, holding, tenure; taking possession, occupation, occupancy; acquisition of title, acquisition of the right of possession; obtainment, attainment, acquisition

تحيز *taḥayyuz* partiality; prejudice, bias

انحياز *inḥiyāz* isolation, seclusion, retirement; partiality; prejudice, bias | عدم الانحياز *'adam al-i.* non-alignment (*pol.*);

دول عدم الانحياز *duwal ʿadam al-i.* the non-aligned states

حائز *ḥā'iz* pl. *-ūn* possessor, holder (على of, e.g., of a certificate)

متحيز *mutaḥayyiz* partial, prejudiced, biased

منحاز *munḥāz* secluded, retired, withdrawn, removed (عن from); an outsider, a stranger (عن to) | الدول (البلدان) غير المنحازة (*duwal, buldān*) the non-aligned states (countries)

حوس VIII (*eg.*) to be in a quandary, waver, hesitate

¹حاش (حوش) *ḥāša u* (*ḥauš*) to round up, drive into a trap (ه game); to stop, check, prevent, hinder (ه s.th.), stand in the way (ه of); to hold back, stem, stave off (ه s.th.) II to gather, collect, amass, accumulate, pile up, hoard (ه s.th.); to save, put by (ه money); to find (ه s.th.)

حوش *ḥauš* pl. احواش *aḥwāš*, حيشان *ḥīšān* enclosure, enclosed area; courtyard

حوش *ḥawaš* mob, rabble, riffraff

حوشى *ḥūšī* wild; unusual, odd, queer, strange

اسبوع الحاش *usbūʿ al-ḥāš* Passion Week (*Chr.*)

²حاشا, حاشى see حشو, حاش لله *ḥāša lillāh* = حاشى لله

حوص *ḥawaṣ* squinting of the eyes (caused by constant exposure to glaring light)

احوص *aḥwaṣ*,² f. حوصاء *ḥauṣā'*², pl. حوص *ḥūṣ* having narrow, squinting eyes

حياصة *ḥiyāṣa* girth

¹حوصل *ḥauṣal* craw (of a bird); pelican (*zool.*)

حوصلة *ḥauṣala* craw (of a bird); bladder (*anat.*) | الحوصلة الصفراوية (*ṣafrāwīya*) and الحوصلة المرارية (*marārīya*) gall bladder (*anat.*)

حويصل *ḥuwaiṣil* blister, bleb, vesicle; water blister

حويصلة *ḥuwaiṣila* pl. *-āt* blister, bleb, vesicle

²حوصلة *ḥauṣala* (*Tun.*) summary, resumé

حوض *ḥauḍ* pl. احواض *aḥwāḍ*, حياض *ḥiyāḍ*, حيضان *ḥīḍān* basin; water basin; trough, tank, cistern, reservoir, container; basin of a river or sea; pool; (in the Egyptian irrigation system) a patch of land surrounded by dikes, flooded by high water of the Nile; pond; pelvis (*anat.*); (garden) bed; dock; pl. حياض *ḥiyāḍ* (sacred) ground, area, domain (to be protected), sanctum | حوض جاف (*jāff*) dry dock; حوض حمام *ḥ. ḥammām* bathtub; حوض عوام (*ʿawwām*) floating dock; ذاد عن حياضه to assume the defense of s.o., make o.s. the champion of s.o.; to defend o.s.; ذب عن حياض الدين (*ḏabba*) to defend the faith; احواض الفحم والحديد coal and iron deposits; حوض الغسل *ḥ. al-ġasl* washbasin; حوض النيل the Nile basin, Egypt

O حويضة *ḥuwaiḍa* renal pelvis (*anat.*)

حاط (حوط) *ḥāṭa u* (*ḥauṭ*, حيطة *ḥīṭa*, حياطة *ḥiyāṭa*) to guard, protect (ه, ه s.o., s.th.), watch (ه, ه over s.o., over s.th.), have the custody (ه, ه of); to attend (ه to), take care (ه of), look after s.th. (ه); to surround, encircle, enclose, encompass (ب s.o., s.th.) II to build a wall (ه around s.th.), wall in (ه s.th.); to encircle, surround (ه s.th.), close in from all sides (ه on s.th.) III to try to outwit, dupe, or outsmart (ه s.o.); to mislead, lead astray, seduce (ه s.o.) **IV** to surround (ب s.o., s.th., also ه, ه s.o., s.th., ب with); to encompass, enclose, embrace, comprise, contain (ب s.th., also ه); to ring, encircle (ب s.o., s.th., also ه, ه s.o., s.th., ب with s.th.), close in from all sides (ب on); to know thoroughly, comprehend, grasp completely, understand fully (ب s.th.), be familiar, be thoroughly acquainted (ب with) | احاط به علما (*'ilman*) to know s.th. thoroughly, have comprehensive knowledge of s.th.; to take cognizance, take note of s.th.; احاطه علما ب he informed him of ..., he let him know about ...; he brought ... to his notice **V** to guard, protect (ه, ه s.o., s.th.); to take precautions (ه with regard to), attend (ه to); to be careful, be cautious, be on one's guard **VIII** to be careful, be cautious, watch out, be on one's guard; to take precautions, make provision (ل for, so as to ensure ...); to surround (ب s.o., s.th.); to guard, protect, preserve (ب s.th. from على), take care (ب of), attend (ب to), look after (ب), see to it (بأن that)

حيطة *ḥīṭa*, *ḥaiṭa*, حوطة *ḥauṭa* cautiousness, caution, provident care, prudence, circumspection | اخذ حيطته (*ḥīṭatahū*) to be on one's guard, take precautions; بلا حيطة thoughtlessly, unthinkingly, inadvertently

حياطة *ḥiyāṭa* guarding, custody, protection, care

تحويط *taḥwīṭ* encirclement

احاطة *iḥāṭa* encirclement, encompassment; comprehension, grasp, understanding, knowledge, cognizance (ب of s.th.), acquaintance, familiarity (ب with); information, communication | طلب احاطة *ṭalab i.* interpellation (*parl.*)

تحوط *taḥawwuṭ* provision, care, attention, precaution, prudence; pl. *-āt* precautionary measures, precautions

احتياط *iḥtiyāṭ* caution, cautiousness, prudence, circumspection, carefulness; provision, care, attention, precaution, prevention; reserve (also *mil.*); pl. *-āt* precautionary measures, precautions | على سبيل الاحتياط as a precaution, out of precaution, to be on the safe side

احتياطى *iḥtiyāṭī* precautionary; prophylactic; preventive; replacement; spare- (in compounds); reserve- (in compounds); stand-by; reserves, supplies; reserve funds, capital reserves (*fin.*); reserve (*mil.*) | اطار احتياطى (*iṭār*) spare tire; حبس احتياطى (*ḥabs*) preventive custody, preventive detention (*jur.*); الخدمة الاحتياطية (*ḵidma*) service in the reserves (*mil.*); تدابير احتياطية precautionary measures, precautions; قوات احتياطية (*quwwāt*) reserves (*mil.*); مال احتياطى capital reserve, reserve fund; احتياطى الزيت الخام (crude-)oil reserves; احتياطى الذهب *i. aḏ-ḏahab* gold reserve (*econ.*)

حائط *ḥā'iṭ* pl. حيطان *ḥīṭān*, حياط *ḥiyāṭ*, حوائط *ḥawā'iṭ*[2] wall | حائط المبكى *ḥ. al-mabkā* Wailing Wall (in Jerusalem); القى (ضرب) به عرض الحائط *alqā* (*ḍaraba*) *bihī 'urḍa l-ḥā'iṭ* not to give a hoot for s.th.; to disdain, despise, reject s.th.; to throw s.th. overboard, jettison s.th.

حائطى *ḥā'iṭī*: مجلة حائطية (*majalla*) and صحف حائطية (*ṣuḥuf*) wall newspaper (in socialist countries)

حويط *ḥawīṭ* (*eg.*) clever, smart, shrewd

محيط *muḥīṭ* surrounding (ب s.th.); comprehensive; familiar, acquainted (ب with); — (pl. *-āt*) circumference, periphery; extent, range, scope, compass, reach, domain, area; milieu, environment, surroundings; ocean; pl. محيطات surroundings, environment | المحيط الاطلنطى (*aṭlanṭī*) the Atlantic Ocean; المحيط الهادئ (*hādi'*) the Pacific Ocean

محاط *muḥāṭ* surrounded (ب by)

متحوط *mutaḥawwiṭ* cautious, prudent, provident, circumspect, careful, watchful

حوف *ḥauf* edge; brink; border, hem, fringe

حاف *ḥāf* see حفّ[2]

حافة *ḥāfa* pl. *-āt,* حواف *ḥawāfin* edge; border; fringe, hem; brink, verge; see also *ḥāffa* (under حف) | بين حوافيه within it, in it, therein; على حافة الخراب (*ḥ. al-ḵarāb*) on the brink of ruin; على حافة الهاوية on the verge of an abyss, on the rim of a precipice

حاق (حوق) *ḥāqa u* (*ḥauq*) to surround, enclose, infold, embrace (ب s.o., s.th.) II = I (على s.o., s.th.)

حوقل[1] *ḥauqala* (حوقلة *ḥauqala*) to pronounce the formula: لاحول ولا قوة الا بالله (see حول *ḥaul*)

حوقلة[2] *ḥauqala* pl. حواقل *ḥawāqil*[2] phial (*chem.*), Florence flask

حاك (حوك) *ḥāka u* (*ḥauk,* حياك *ḥiyāk,* حياكة *ḥiyāka*) to weave (ه s.th.); to interweave (ه s.th.); to knit (ه s.th.); to braid, plait (ه s.th.); to sew (ه a dress; *eg.*); to contrive, devise, hatch, concoct (ه s.th.; e.g., ruses, intrigues, pretexts), think up, fabricate, create (ه s.th. in one's imagination)

حياكة *ḥiyāka* weaving; knitting; braiding, plaiting; (*eg.*) sewing, needlework

حائك *ḥā'ik* pl. حاكة *ḥāka* weaver; — (*mor.*) an outer garment made of a long piece of white woolen material, covering body and head

حال (حول and حيل) *ḥāla u* to change, undergo a change, be transformed; to shift, turn, pass, grow (الى into s.th., also ه), become (الى s.th.); to deviate, depart (عن from, e.g., a commitment), dodge, evade, fail to meet (عن s.th.); to elapse, pass, go by (time); — (حيلولة *ḥailūla*) to prevent (دون s.th.); to intervene, interfere, interpose, come (بين between) | حال عن عهد (*'ahd*) to withdraw from a contract; حال بين فلان وبين الامر to make s.th. inaccessible to s.o., impossible for s.o.; to bar or obstruct s.o.'s way to s.th.; to prevent s.o. from s.th., deny s.o. s.th.; حال بين نفسه وبين الاشفاق (*išfāq*) to resist compassion, deny o.s. any sympathy **II** *ḥawwala* to change (الى ه or ه ه s.th. to s.th. else), transform, transmute, convert, turn, make (الى ه or ه ه s.th. into s.th. else); to transplant (ه s.th.); to transfer (ه s.th.); to convert (ه s.th., mathematically); to switch, commutate (ه current; *el.*); to convert, transform (ه current; *el.*); to shunt (ه a railroad car); to switch (ه a railroad track); to remit, send, transmit (ه s.th., e.g., money by mail, الى to s.o.); to pass on, hand on (الى ه s.th. to s.o.); to forward (الى ه s.th. to s.o. or to an address); to endorse (ه a bill of exchange, a promissory note); to direct, turn (ه s.th., also نظرة *naẓratan* a glance, الى to or toward); to divert, distract, keep (عن ه or ه s.o. or s.th. from); to turn away, avert (بصره عن *baṣarahū* one's eyes from); to turn off, switch off, disconnect (ه current; *el.*) | حول الدفة (*daffa*) to turn the helm, change the course **III** *ḥāwala* to try, attempt, endeavor (ه s.th., ان to do s.th.), make an attempt, make an effort (ان to do s.th.); to seek to gain (ه s.th.) by artful means; to deceive by pretenses, make excuses, hedge, dodge **IV** to change (ه ه or الى ه s.th. to), transform, transmute, turn, make (ه ه or الى ه s.th. into); to convert, translate (ه ه or الى ه s.th. into); to transfer (ه s.th.); to remit, send (ه s.th. الى or على to s.o.); to assign (ه, ه s.o., s.th., الى or على to s.o.); to turn over, hand over, pass on (على ه or ه s.o. or s.th. to); to forward (على ه s.th. to); to refer (ه الى s.o. to); to cede, transfer (ه a debt, على to s.o.; *jur.*) | احيل على (الى) المعاش (*uḥīla, maʿāš*) and احيل الى التقاعد (*taqāʿud*) he was pensioned off; احيلت الكمبيالة الى البروتستو the bill was protested (*fin.*) **V** *taḥawwala* to change, undergo a change; to be changed (الى to), be transformed, be transmuted, be converted (الى into), become (الى s.th.), turn, grow (الى into), transform (الى — من or عن from — into), change, develop, evolve (الى — من from — to); to withdraw, go away, leave; to move (الى to a residence); to turn away (من from), turn one's back (عن on); to deviate (عن from); to depart, digress, stray (عن الطريق from the way); to renounce, forgo, relinquish, disclaim (عن s.th.); to be transferred, brought over (الى to another place); to be transplanted, be moved (الى to); to be transmitted, be remitted (money); to proceed slyly or cunningly | تحول كل حيلة to use every conceivable trick; — *taḥayyala* to employ artful means; to ponder ways and means (ل to an end, in order to attain s.th.) **VI** *taḥāwala* to try, endeavor, take pains (على to do s.th.), strive (على for); — *taḥāyala* and **VIII** to employ artful means, resort to tricks, use stratagems (على against s.o.); to deceive, beguile, dupe, cheat, outwit, outsmart (على s.o.); to be out (على for s.th.) or achieve (على s.th.) by artful means, by tricks **VIII** to work or strive (on one's own resources), make efforts (on one's own) **IX** احول *iḥwalla* to be cross-eyed, to squint **X** to change (الى to, into), turn, be transformed, be converted (الى into); to be transubstantiated (bread and wine, الى into the body and blood of Christ; *Chr.*); to proceed, pass on, shift, switch (الى to s.th. new or s.th. different); to be impossible (على for s.o.); to be inconceivable, absurd, preposterous

حال *ḥāl* m. and f., pl. احوال *aḥwāl* condition, state; situation; position, status; attitude, bearing, posture (of a person); circumstance; case; present, actuality (as opposed to future); circumstantial expression or phrase (*gram.*); pl.: conditions, circumstances; matters, affairs, concerns; cases; *ḥāla* (prep.) during; immediately upon, right after; just at; in case of ..., in the event of ...; حالا *ḥālan* presently, immediately, at once, right away, without delay; now, actually, at present | فى الحال and للحال on the spot, at once, immediately; على كل حال (*kulli ḥālin*) and على اى حال (*ayyi ḥ.*) in any case, at any rate, anyhow; يبقى على حاله (*yabqā*) it remains unchanged, just as it is; فى حال من الاحوال in some case or other, anyway, if occasion should arise, possibly; (with neg.) by no means, under no circumstances, not at all, in no way; على حال, بحال, بأى حال *bi-ayyi ḥ.* with neg.: by no means, not at all, in no way; كذلك الحال فى the same goes for ..., it is the same with ..., it is also the case with ...; كما هو الحال فى as is the case with; كيف حالك how are you? شىء بحاله a thing in itself, a separate, independent thing; الاحوال الجوية (*jawwīya*) atmospheric conditions; الاحوال المناخية (*manākiya*) the climatic conditions; محاكم الاحوال الشخصية (*šakṣīya*) courts dealing with vital statistics; قانون (or نظام) الاحوال الشخصية personal statute; صاحب الحال noun referent of a circumstantial phrase (*gram.*); عرض حال *ʿarḍ ḥ.* application, memorial, petition; مضى الى حال سبيله (*ḥāli sabīlihī*) he went his own way, he went off on his own; لسان حاله , لسان الحال see لسان

حالما *ḥālamā* (conj.) as soon as

حالة *ḥāla* pl. *-āt* condition, state; situation; (possible, actual) case; (*gram.*) case; status, position of affairs; *ḥālata* (prep.) during | حالة ان *ḥālata an* (conj.) whereas; والحالة هذه under these circumstances, such being the case, things being as they are; فى حالة (*ḥālati*) in (the) case of ..., in the event of ..., e.g., فى حالة غيابه (*ġiyābihī*) in case of his absence, فى حالة الوفاة (*wafāh*) in case of death; فى هذه الحالة in this (that) case; لحالة ان *li-ḥālati an* in case that ..., in the event that ...; فى حالة ما اذا if; كما هى الحالة فى as is the case with ...; حالة اجتماعية (*ijtimāʿīya*) marital status; الحالات الجوية (*jawwīya*) atmospheric conditions; حالة الخطر *ḥ. al-ḵaṭar* stand-by, alert, state of alarm; الحالة الراهنة the status quo; حالة الطوارئ *ḥ. aṭ-ṭawāriʾ* state of emergency; حالة استعداد state of alert (*mil.*); فى حالة التلبس (*talabbus*) flagrante delicto (*jur.*); الحالة المدنية (*madanīya*) civil status, legal status; سوء الحالة *sūʾ al-ḥ.* predicament, plight; فى افضل الحالات in the best case, at best; فى حالة حرب (*ḥ. ḥarb*) in a state of war; دراسة الحالة *dirāsat al-ḥ.* case study (*psych.*); حالة الرفع *ḥ. ar-rafʿ* and حالة الفاعل nominative, حالة النصب *ḥ. an-naṣb* accusative, حالة المفعول به do., objective case, حالة الاضافة *ḥ. al-iḍāfa* and حالة المضاف اليه (*muḍāf*) genitive, ○ حالة المعطى له (*muʿṭā*) dative (*gram.*)

حالى *ḥālī* present, current, actual, existing; momentary, instantaneous; حاليا *ḥālīyan* at present, actually | صورة حالية (*ṣūra*) snapshot (*phot.*); فى الرابع من الحالى on the fourth of the current month

حالية *ḥālīya* actuality, topicality, timeliness

حول *ḥaul* pl. احوال *aḥwāl* year; might, power | لا حول ولا قوة الا بالله *lā ḥaula wa-lā qūwata illā bi-llāh* there is no power and no strength save in God; لا حول له ولا حيلة (*wa-lā ḥīlata*) he is completely powerless, he can do nothing, he is at the end of his resources

حول *ḥiwal* change of place, change | لا يبتغون عنه حولا (*yabtaġūna*) they don't want it otherwise, they ask for it

حول *ḥaula* (prep.) around, about; circa, about, some, approximately, roughly (with following number); about (esp. in news headings, approx. = re, concerning) | من حوله (*ḥaulihī*) (= حوله) around him (or it), about him (or it); من حوليهما (*ḥaulaihimā*) around the two of them, about them; from their vicinity, from their surroundings (dual)

حولى *ḥaulī* periodic, temporary, interim; one year old (animal), yearling; young animal; lamb, wether

حولية *ḥaulīya* pl. *-āt* yearbook (scientific publication); pl. حوليات annals (of a society, university, etc.)

حيل *ḥail* strength, force, power, vigor | على حيله (standing) upright, erect; لا قوة له ولا حيل (*qūwata*) completely helpless and paralyzed

حيلة *ḥīla* pl. حيل *ḥiyal*, احاييل *aḥāyīl*[2] artifice, ruse, stratagem, maneuver, subterfuge, wile, trick; device, shift; a means to accomplish an end; expedient, makeshift, dodge, way-out; legal stratagem (for the purpose of *in fraudem legis agere*) | ما الحيلة what's to be done? لا حيلة لى فى (*ḥīlata*) I have no possibility to ..., I am in no position to ...; ما بيدى حيلة (*bi-yadī*) I can do nothing, I can get nowhere; لم يجد حيلة الا *lam yajid ḥīlatan illā* he couldn't do anything except ..., he had no other choice than ...; اعيته الحيلة (*aʿyathu*) he was at a loss, he was at the end of his wits; حيل سينمائية (*sinamāʾīya*) film tricks, trick shots

حيلى *ḥiyalī* cunning, crafty, wily, sly, tricky, foxy

احيل *aḥyal*[2] craftier, wilier

حول *ḥawal* squinting, strabismus

احول *aḥwal*², f. حولاء *ḥaulā'*², pl. حول *ḥūl* squinting, squint-eyed, cross-eyed, walleyed

حؤول *ḥu'ūl* change, transformation, transmutation; prevention (دون of s.th.)

حوال *ḥiwāl* obstacle; partition, screen

حيال *ḥiyāla* (prep.) in view of ..., with regard to ..., in the face of, opposite, in front of, before

حوالة *ḥawāla* pl. *-āt* assignment, cession (*jur.*); bill of exchange, (promissory) note, check, draft | حوالة بريدية, حوالة البريد money order; حوالة سفر *ḥ. safar* traveler's check

حوالى *ḥawālā*, also pronounced *ḥawālay*, always thus before a suffix (prep.) around, about; circa, approximately, roughly, about, some (with following number)

حيلولة *ḥailūla* separation, interruption, disruption; prevention (دون of s.th.)

محولجى *miḥwalgī* pl. *-īya* (*eg.*) switchman (railroad)

لا محال *lā maḥāla* = لا محالة (see below)

محالة *maḥāla* roller, wheel (of a draw well)

لا محالة منه *lā maḥālata minhu* it is inevitable; there is no doubt about it; (also لا محالة alone) most certainly, positively, absolutely, by all means

تحويل *taḥwīl* transformation, transmutation, conversion (الى into s.th.); change, alteration, modification; transplantation; transposition, translocation, dislocation, displacement; transportation, transfer(ence); piping, routing (of s.th. to another place); conversion (e.g., of currency); conversion, transformation (of electric current); manufacture, processing (of raw material into finished goods, etc.); transfer (*fin.*; also تحويل الدين *t. ad-dain*); remittance (of money), transmittal, sending, forwarding; bill of exchange, promissory note, draft (*com.*); check; endorsement (*fin.*) | خط تحويل *ḵaṭṭ t.* transfer line (oil); قابل للتحويل convertible; transferable; قابلية العملة للتحويل (*qābilīyat al-ʿumla*) convertibility of currency

تحويلى *taḥwīlī*: صناعات تحويلية (*ṣināʿāt*) manufacturing or processing industries

تحويلة *taḥwīla* pl. *-āt*, تحاويل *taḥāwīl*² branch, offshoot; siding, sidetrack (railroad); side canal (irrigation; *Eg.*); switch (railroad)

محاولة *muḥāwala* pl. *-āt* attempt, try; effort, endeavor; recourse to expedients, shifts, or dodges, dodging, hedging | محاولة على حياته (*ḥayātihī*) attempt on s.o.'s life, murderous assault

احالة *iḥāla* transformation, conversion (الى into s.th.); transfer, conveyance, assignment; remittance; forwarding, referring (الى or على to a competent authority); transmission, transmittal; ○ transfer (*fin.*); cession, assignment (*Isl. Law*); absurdity | بالاحالة على with reference to; قاضى الاحالة magistrate sitting at defendant's arraignment, trial judge; احالة الى (على) المعاش (*maʿāš*) and احالة الى التقاعد (*taqāʿud*) pensioning off

تحول *taḥawwul* change, transformation, transmutation; abrupt change, sudden turn, reversal; shift, transition; departure, deviation, digression (عن from); renunciation (عن of) | نقطة التحول *nuqṭat at-t.* turning point

تحيل *taḥayyul* use of tricks, trickery

تحايل *taḥāyul* and احتيال *iḥtiyāl* use of tricks, trickery; cunning, craft, subtlety, artfulness; malice, treachery, perfidy; deception, fraud

تحايلى *taḥāyulī* and احتيالى *iḥtiyālī* fraudulent, e.g., افلاس احتيالى (*iflās*) fraudulent bankruptcy

استحالة *istiḥāla* change, transformation, transmutation, turn, shift, transition; transubstantiation (*Chr.*); impossibility, inconceivability, absurdity, preposterousness

حائل *ḥā'il* pl. حوائل *ḥawā'il*[2] obstacle, obstruction, impediment (دون on the way to s.th., بين — و see حال *ḥāla* I); barrier; partition, screen, folding screen; — (pl. حول *ḥuwwal*) changeable, variable, frequently changing; feeble, languid, wan, pallid

حائل *ḥā'il*[2] and حايل *ḥāyil* Hail (town and oasis in N Nejd)

محول *muḥawwil* pl. -*āt* converter, transformer (*el.*); switch lever (*el.*); reversing key (*el.*); buzzer, signal button (*tel.*); shift lever, shift key (typewriter); — (pl. -*ūn*) endorser (*fin.*); switchman (railroad)

محولة *muḥawwila* pl. -*āt* switch (railroad)

محول عليه *muḥawwal 'alaihi* c.o.d., cash on delivery; محول به collected on delivery

محيل *muḥīl* transferor, assignor (*Isl. Law*)

محال *muḥāl* inconceivable, unthinkable, impossible, absurd, preposterous, unattainable

متحول *mutaḥawwil* changeable, variable, changing; form-changing, metamorphic (e.g., *geol.*) | الاعياد المتحولة (*a'yād*) the movable feasts (*Chr.*)

محتال *muḥtāl* artful, cunning, deceitful, treacherous, perfidious, fraudulent; swindler, cheat, impostor, fraud; crook, scoundrel; assignee (*Isl. Law*) | محتال عليه debtor of a ceded claim, transferee (*Isl. Law*)

مستحيل *mustaḥīl* impossible, absurd, preposterous; مستحيلات impossible things, impossibilities, absurdities

حام (حوم) *ḥāma u* (*ḥaum*, حومان *ḥawamān*) to circle, hover, glide (in the air; of a bird, also of an aircraft); to hover, swarm, buzz (حول and على around) | حامت الشبهة ضده (*šubha, ḍiddahū*) suspicion concentrated on him, he was suspected **II** to circle in the air; to hover in circles, to circle; to go around, revolve (thoughts and images, in one's head or mind); to browse (في in a book)

حومة *ḥauma* pl. -*āt* turmoil of battle, thick of the fray; main part, bulk, main body; (*tun.*) quarter, section (of a city)

حوام *ḥawwām* gliding on an air cushion (vehicle) | مركب حوام (*markab*) pl. مراكب حوامة hovercraft

حوامة *ḥawwāma* pl. -*āt* hovercraft

حان and حانة see حين

حانوت look up alphabetically

حوين *ḥuwayyin* see حى

حوى *ḥawā i* to gather, collect, unite (ه s.th.); to encompass, embrace, contain, hold, enclose, comprise, include (ه s.th.); to possess, own, have (ه s.th.); to clasp (ه s.th., the hand) **V** to curl (up), coil (up) **VIII** to encompass, embrace, contain, hold, enclose, comprise, include (ه or على s.th.); to possess, own, have (ه or على s.th.); to take possession (ه of s.th.); to master by oneself (ه a problem)

حوية *ḥawīya* convolution, coil, curl, roll; pl. حوايا *ḥawāyā* intestines, bowels, entrails

حواية *ḥawāya* pl. *-āt* (*eg.*) wase, round pad to support a burden on the head or on the back

حاو *ḥāwin* pl. حواة *ḥuwāh* snake charmer; juggler, conjurer, magician

محتوى *muḥtawan* pl. *muḥtawayāt* content(s) (of a book, of a receptacle) | محتويات النفوس the innermost thoughts, the secrets of the heart

حي (حيو ,حى) حيي *ḥayiya*, حى *ḥayya* يحيا *yaḥyā* (حياة *ḥayāh*) to live; حى *ḥayya* to live to see, experience, witness (ه s.th.), live (ه through a time) | ليحى الملك *li-yaḥya l-malik* long live the king! — حيي *ḥayiya* يحيا *yaḥyā* (حياء *ḥayā'*) to be ashamed (من of, because of) **II** حيا *ḥayyā* to keep (ه s.o.) alive, grant (ه s.o.) a long life; to say to s.o. (ه): حياك الله may God preserve your life!; to greet, salute (ه s.o.) **IV** احيا *aḥyā* to lend life (ه, ه to s.o., to s.th.), enliven, animate, vitalize, endow with life, call into being (ه s.th.), give birth (ه to); to revive, reanimate, revivify (ه s.th.), give new life (ه to); to put on, produce, stage, arrange (ه e.g., a theatrical performance, a celebration, and the like); to celebrate (ه s.th., also a festival) | احيا الذكرى (*ḏikrā*) to commemorate (a deceased person), observe the anniversary (of s.o.'s death); احيا الليل (*lail*) to burn the midnight oil, احيا الليل صلاة (*ṣalātan*) to spend the night in prayer; احيا السهرة (*sahrata*) to perform in the evening (of an artist); احيا حفلة (*ḥaflatan*) to give a performance; to perform at a celebration (artist); قد احيت الفرقة ثلاث ايال *qad aḥyat il-firqatu ṯalāṯa layālin* the theatrical troupe gave three evening performances **X** استحيا *istaḥyā* to spare s.o.'s (ه) life, let live, keep alive (ه s.o.); استحيا *istaḥyā*, استحى *istaḥā* to be ashamed (ه to face s.o.; من of s.th., because of s.th.); to become or feel embarrassed (من in front of s.o.), be embarrassed (من by); to be bashful, shy, diffident

حى *ḥayy* pl. احياء *aḥyā'* living, live, alive; lively, lusty, animated, active, energetic, unbroken, undaunted, undismayed; living being, organism; tribe, tribal community; block of apartment houses; section, quarter (of a city); ward, district (of a city) | علم الاحياء *'ilm al-aḥyā'* biology; حى تجارى (*tijārī*) business district; حى جامعى university quarter; حى العالم *ḥ. al-'ālam* houseleek tree (Sempervivum arboreum L.; *bot.*); ذخيرة حية (*eg.*) live ammunition

حى *ḥayya*: حى على الصلاه *ḥayya 'alā ṣ-ṣalāh* come to prayer!

حية *ḥayya* pl. *-āt* snake, serpent, viper

احيائى ○ *aḥyā'ī* biologic(al); (pl. *-ūn*) biologist | كيمياء احيائية (*kīmiyā'*) biochemistry

حيي *ḥayīy* bashful, shy, diffident, modest

حياء *ḥayā'* shame, diffidence, bashfulness, timidity; shyness | قليل الحياء shameless, impudent; قلة الحياء *qillat al-ḥ.* shamelessness, impudence

حياة *ḥayāh* pl. حيوات *ḥayawāt* life; lifeblood; liveliness, animation | حياة الريف *ḥ. ar-rīf* country life, rural life; الحياة العامة (*'āmma*) public life; الحياة العائلية family life; مستوى الحياة *mustawā l-ḥ.* living standard; ○ علم الحياة *'ilm al-ḥ.* biology

حيوى *ḥayawī* lively, full of life, vital, vigorous; vital, essential to life; biotic (*biol.*, *med.*); biological | مضادات حيوية (*muḍāddāt*) antibiotics (*med.*)

حيوية *ḥayawīya* vitality, vigor, vim

حيويات *ḥayawīyāt*: مضادات الحيويات *muḍāddāt al-ḥ.* and مواد مضادة للحيويات (*mawādd muḍādda*) antibiotics (*med.*)

حياتى *ḥayātī* life (in compounds); biological | اوضاع حياتية living conditions; مشاكل حياتية problems of life

حيوان *ḥayawān* pl. *-āt* animal, beast; living being, living creature | حيوانات ثديية (*ṯadyīya*) mammals; حيوانات مجترة (*mujtarra*) ruminants; حيوان طفيلى (*ṭufailī*) parasite; علم الحيوان *'ilm al-ḥ.* zoology

حيوانى *ḥayawānī* animal (adj.); zoologic(al)

حيوانية *ḥayawānīya* bestiality; animality, animal nature

حوين *ḥuwayyin* pl. *-āt* minute animal, animalcule

احيى *aḥyā* livelier; more vigorous, more vital

تحية *taḥīya* pl. *-āt*, تحايا *taḥāyā* greeting, salutation; salute; cheer (= wish that God may give s.o. long life) | تحية لذكراه *taḥīyatan li-ḏikrāhu* in order to keep his memory alive, in remembrance of him; التحية العسكرية (*'askarīya*) military salute

احياء *iḥyā'* animation, enlivening; revival, revitalization, revivification; arranging, staging, conducting, putting on, holding (of a celebration) | احياء الذكرى *i. aḏ-ḏikrā* commemoration (of a deceased person); احياء لذكرى (*iḥyā'an*) (with foll. gen.) in commemoration of ..., in memoriam ...; احياء الموات *i. al-mawāt* cultivation of virgin land

استحياء *istiḥyā'* shame; diffidence, bashfulness, timidity; shyness

محيا *muḥayyan* face, countenance

الست المستحية *as-sitt al-mustaḥiya* sensitive plant (Mimosa pudica; *bot.*)

حيث[1] *ḥaiṯu* (conj.) where (place and direction); wherever; since, as, due to the fact that; whereas; inasmuch as | حيث ان (*inna* or *anna*) since, as, due to the fact that ...; in that ...; حيث كان wherever it be; in any case, at any rate; الى حيث *ilā ḥaiṯu* where (direction); to where ..., to the place where ...; من حيث *min ḥaiṯu* from where, whence, wherefrom; where (place); whereas; (with foll. nominative) as to, as for, concerning, regarding, with respect to, in view of, because of; من حيث الثقافة *min ḥ. ṯ-ṯaqāfatu* with regard to education, as far as education is concerned; من حيث يدرى ولا يدرى (*yadrī wa-lā yadrī*) whether he knows it or not, knowingly or without his knowledge; من حيث لا (with foll. imperf.) without (being, doing, etc.); من حيث هو as such, in itself, العالم من حيث هو (*'ālam*) the world in itself, the world as such; من حيث ان (*anna*) inasmuch as; in view of the fact that; since, as, due to the fact that; من حيث المبدأ (*mabda'u*) in principle, basically; بحيث *bi-ḥaiṯu* inasmuch as; in such a manner that ..., so as to ...; so that ...; such as ...; (he found himself) at a point or degree where, e.g., كانت من البراءة بحيث لا ترى (*barā'a, tarā*) = she was so naive that she couldn't see ...; بحيث لا insofar as ... not, provided that ... not; بحيث ان (*anna*) in such a manner that ..., so as to ..., so that ...

حيثما *ḥaiṯumā* wherever, wheresoever (place); wherever, no matter where ... (direction), in whichever direction | حيثما اتفق (*ittafaqa*) anywhere, wherever it be, haphazardly, at random

حيثية *ḥaiṯīya* pl. *-āt* standpoint; viewpoint, point of view, approach; aspect, respect, regard, consideration; high social standing, social distinction, dignity; pl. (= حيثيات الحكم *ḥ. al-ḥukm*) opinion of the court, reasons on which the judgment is based; declaratory part of a judgment (*jur.*) | ذوو الحيثيات (البارزة) (*ḏawū*) or اصحاب الحيثيات, اصحاب الحيثية people of (high) social standing, prominent people, people of distinction; من الحيثية الحيوانية (*ḥayawānīya*) from a zoological viewpoint

حيثى *ḥiṯī* Hittitic; (pl. *-ūn*) Hittite

حاد (حيد) *ḥāda* *i* (*ḥaid*, حيود *ḥuyūd*, حيدان *ḥayadān*, محيد *maḥīd*) to deviate, swerve, depart, desist (عن from); to leave, quit, give up, abandon, relinquish (عن s.th.); to turn (عن off the road), swerve off; حاد به عن to dissuade or get s.o. away from ...; to incline, tend (الى, نحو to, toward), shade, blend (الى, نحو into) **II** to keep aside, put aside (ه s.th.); to neutralize (ه a country) **III** to stay away, keep apart (ه, ه from s.o., from s.th.); to avoid, shun (ه, ه s.o., s.th.) **VII** to depart, deviate, digress, swerve (عن from)

حيد *ḥaid*, حيدان *ḥayadān* deviation, digression, departure, swerving, turning aside, turning away

حيدة *ḥaida* deviation, digression, swerving, departure (from a course); neutrality; impartiality | على حيدة aside, apart, to one side

حيود *ḥuyūd* deviation, deflection; (= حيود الضوء *ḥ. aḍ-ḍau'*) diffraction of light (*phys.*)

محيد *maḥīd* avoidance (عن of s.th.) | لا محيد عنه (*maḥīda*) it is unavoidable

تحييد *taḥyīd* neutralization (of a country)

حياد *ḥiyād* neutrality (*pol.*) | على الحياد neutral; حياد عن الخط (*ḵaṭṭ*) derailment (railroad)

حيادى *ḥiyādī* neutral (*pol.*)

حيادية *ḥiyādīya* neutralism (*pol.*)

محايدة *muḥāyada* neutrality (*pol.*)

حائد *ḥā'id* neutral (*pol.*)

محايد *muḥāyid* neutral (also *pol.*); neuter (*gram.*); المحايدون the neutrals (*pol.*)

متحايد *mutaḥāyid* neutral (*pol.*)

حيدراباد *ḥaidarābād*[2] Hydarabad

حار (حير) *ḥāra* (1st pers. perf. *ḥirtu*) *a* (حيرة *ḥaira*, حيران *ḥayarān*) to become confused; to become or be helpless, be at a loss, know nothing (فى of, about); to waver, hesitate, be unable to choose (بين — وبين between — and) | حار فى امره (*amrihī*) to be confused, baffled, bewildered, dismayed; to be at a loss, be at one's wit's end **II** to confuse, baffle, bewilder, nonplus, embarrass (ه s.o.); to puzzle, make uncertain (ه s.o.) **V** to become confused; to be or become dismayed, startled, baffled, perplexed (فى by), be at a loss (فى as to); to waver (uncertainly) (بين between); to gather without being able to flow away (water, tears in the eyes) | تحير فى امره (*amrihī*) to be confused, baffled, bewildered, disconcerted, be at a loss, be at one's wit's end; تحيرت فى مآقيه الدموع his eyes were brimming with tears **VIII** = *ḥāra*

حير *ḥair* fenced-in garden, enclosure | حير الحيوان *ḥ. al-ḥayawān* zoological garden, zoo

حيرة *ḥaira* confusion, perplexity, bewilderment, embarrassment, helplessness; uncertainty, lack of self-confidence; wavering (between two things) | فى حيرة embarrassed, at a loss, helpless

حيران *ḥairān*[2], f. حيرى *ḥairā*, pl. حيارى *ḥayārā*, *ḥuyārā* confused, perplexed, startled, dismayed, disconcerted, baffled, nonplused, bewildered, appalled, taken aback, stunned; embarrassed, at a loss, at one's wit's end; uncertain, helpless, sheepish (smile, etc.), confused, incoherent (words, and the like)

محارة *maḥāra* maze, puzzle box (for animal experiments; *psych.*)

تحير *taḥayyur* confusion, perplexity, bewilderment, dismay; embarrassment, helplessness

حائر *ḥā'ir* disconcerted, perplexed, startled, dismayed; embarrassed, helpless, at a loss, at one's wit's end; baffled, bewildered, confused, uncertain (فى about); straying, astray | حائر فى امره (*amrihī*) confused, baffled, bewildered, embarrassed, at a loss, helpless

محير *muḥayyar* embarrassed, at a loss, helpless

متحير *mutaḥayyir* and محتار *muḥtār* = حائر

حوز see حيز

حزب see حيزبون

(حيص) حاص *ḥāṣa* *i* (*ḥaiṣ*, حيصة *ḥaiṣa*, محيص *maḥīṣ*) to flee, escape (عن s.th. or from s.th.), run away (عن from), turn one's back (عن on) VII do.

حيص *ḥaiṣ*, حيصة *ḥaiṣa* flight, escape

وقع فى حيص بيص *waqa'a fī ḥaiṣa baiṣa* to get into a bad fix, meet with difficulties

حوص see حياصة

محيص *maḥīṣ* flight, escape; place of refuge, retreat, sanctuary | ما عنه محيص it is unavoidable; لم يكن لهم محيص من ان they couldn't but ..., they had no other alternative but to ...

(حيض) حاضت *ḥāḍat* *i* (*ḥaiḍ*, محيض *maḥīḍ*, محاض *maḥāḍ*) and V to menstruate, have a monthly period

حيض *ḥaiḍ* (n. un. حيضة) and حياض *ḥiyāḍ* menstruation, monthly period

حائض *ḥā'iḍ* (f.) and حائضة menstruating

حوط see حياط, حيطان, حياطة, حيطة

1(حيف) حاف *ḥāfa* *i* (*ḥaif*) to deal unjustly (على with s.o.), wrong, injure, harm (على s.o.); to restrict, limit, curtail, impair (على s.th.), encroach (على upon) V to impair, injure, prejudice, violate (ه or من s.th.), encroach, infringe (ه or من upon)

حيف *ḥaif* wrong, injustice; harm, damage, prejudice | حيف عليه what a pity! too bad! لا حيف به (*ḥaifa*) it is not out of place, it is quite appropriate

2حيفا *ḥaifā* Haifa (seaport in NW Israel)

(حيق) حاق *ḥāqa* *i* to surround, beset from all sides (ب s.o.); to fall, descend, come (ب upon s.o., punishment), befall, overtake, grip, seize, overcome (ب s.o.), happen, occur (ب to); to penetrate, pierce (فى the body; of a sword); to affect, influence (فى s.o., s.th.) IV to surround, beset from all sides (ب s.o.); to bring down (ه ب upon s.o. s.th.), cause s.th. (ه) to descend (ب upon s.o.)

حيق *ḥaiq* consequence, effect (of a misdeed redounding upon the evildoer)

حيك II to weave

حوك see حياكة

حيك *ḥaik* = حائك; see حوك

حيل V, حيلة, احيل, حيال, حيلولة, حائل, حايل, etc., see حول; احيل see حلو

(حين) حان *ḥāna* *i* to draw near, approach, come, arrive (time); to happen accidentally | حان الوقت the (right) time has come; now is the time; حان له ان the time has come for him to ...; اما حان لهم ان يفهموا (*a-mā, an yafhamū*) haven't they understood yet ...?; حانت منى التفاتة (*minnī ltifāta*) I happened to turn around (الى to), it just happened that my eyes fell on (الى) II to set a time (ه for s.o.) IV to destroy, wipe out (ه s.o.) V to watch, wait (ه for a time or an opportunity) | تحين الفرصة (*furṣata*) to wait for an opportunity, bide one's time X استحين *istaḥyana* to wait for the right time

حان *ḥān* bar, wineshop, wine tavern; pub; cabaret

حانة *ḥāna* pl. *-āt* bar, wineshop, wine tavern; pub, tavern

حانوت and حانوتى look up alphabetically

حين *ḥain* death, destruction

حين *ḥīn* pl. احيان *aḥyān*, احايين *aḥāyīn*[2] time; propitious time, good time, opportunity; *ḥīna* (prep.) at the time of ..., at, upon; (conj.) at the time when, when; as soon as; حينا *ḥīnan* for some time; once, one day; احيانا *aḥyānan* occasionally, from time to time, sometimes | حينا — حينا sometimes — sometimes, at times — at times; فى الاحايين at times, sometimes, once in a while; فى بعض الاحيان (الاحايين) *fī ba'ḍi l-a.* and بعض الاحيان *ba'ḍa l-a.* sometimes, occasionally, now and then, once in a while, from time to time, at times; فى اغلب الاحيان *fī aḡlabi l-a.* mostly, most of the time, in most cases; الى حين for some time; meanwhile, for the time being; فى حينه then, at the time, in his (its) time; in due time, at the appointed time; ذا الحين *ḏā l-ḥīna* just now, right now; من ذلك الحين from that time on, from then on; الى ذلك الحين until that time, till then; فى حين (with foll. verb) whereas; فى حين ان and على حين ان (*ḥīni*) at the same time when ..., while; whereas, also without ان, e.g., على حين هم يزعمون *'alā ḥīni hum yaz'umūna* whereas they, on the other hand, claim; حينا بعد حين, بين حين وحين, من حين الى حين, بين حين وآخر (*li-āḵara*) and من حين لآخر (*wa-āḵara*) from time to time, now and then, once in a while

حينئذ *ḥīna'iḏin* at that time, then, that day

حينذاك *ḥīnaḏāka* at that time, then, that day

حينما *ḥīnamā* (conj.) while; when, as

محيا, استحياء, احياء, حياء, استحيا, احيا, حيا, يحيا, حياة, حياتى, حيوى, حيوية, حيوان etc., see under حى

خ

خاء *ḵā'* name of the letter خ

خاتون *ḵātūn* pl. خواتين *ḵawātīn*[2] lady, socially prominent woman | زهرة الخاتون *zahrat al-ḵ.* little blue flower of the steppe (*syr.*)

خاخام *ḵāḵām* (= حاخام) rabbi

خارصين *ḵāraṣīn* and خارصينى *ḵāraṣīnī* (*eg.*) zinc

خازوق *ḵāzūq* pl. خوازيق *ḵawāzīq*[2] post, stake, pole; dirty trick | هذا خازوق that's tough luck!

خاقان *ḵāqān* pl. خواقين *ḵawāqīn*[2] overlord, ruler, sovereign, monarch, emperor

خاكى *ḵākī* earth-colored, khaki

خؤولة, خؤول see خول

خام *kām* (invar.) raw, unworked, unprocessed; untanned; linen; calico; (pl. *-āt*) raw material; inexperienced, green, untrained, unskilled, artless, uncouth, boorish; pl. خامات raw materials | جلود خام raw leather; خيوط خام raw fibers; زيت خام (*zait*) crude oil; سكر خام (*sukkar*) raw sugar; مادة خام (*mādda*) pl. مواد خام (*mawādd*) raw material

خان *kān* pl. *-āt* hostel, caravansary; inn | الخان الخليلي (*kalīlī*) district of Cairo (center of art trade and market activity); خان يونس Khan Yunis (town in Gaza sector)

خانة *kāna* pl. *-āt* column (e.g., of a newspaper); square (e.g., on a chessboard); compartment, partition, section (of a wardrobe, a refrigerator, etc.); place (of units, tens, etc.; *arith.*); place or rank (on a list or table; esp. sports) | خانة التصقيع deepfreeze compartment (of a refrigerator)

خب *kabba u* (*kabb*, خبب *kabab*, خبيب *kabīb*) to amble (animal); to trot (horse); to jog, saunter (person); to sink (في in sand); — *u* (*kabb*) to surge, heave, be rough (sea) **V** and **VIII** to amble (animal); to trot (horse)

خبب *kabab* amble; trot

خب *kabb*, *kibb* heaving, surging (of the sea), rough sea

خب *kabb* impostor, swindler

خبأ *kaba'a a* and **II** to hide, conceal (ه s.th.) **V** to hide, conceal o.s.; to be hidden, be concealed **VIII** to hide, conceal o.s.; to disappear; to be hidden, be concealed

خبء *kab'*, *kib'* that which is hidden, a hidden thing

خبيئة *kabī'a* pl. خبايا *kabāyā* that which is hidden; a hidden, secret thing; a cache | خبايا الارض *k. l-arḍ* that which is hidden in the earth; natural resources

مخبأ *makba'* pl. مخابئ *makābi'*[2] hiding place; hide-out, refuge, haunt, retreat; cellar, shelter, air-raid shelter

خباء *kibā'* pl. اخبئة *akbi'a*, اخبية *akbiya* tent; husk, hull (of grain)

خابئة *kābi'a*, خابية *kābiya* pl. خوابئ *kawābi'*[2], خواب *kawābin* large vessel, cask, jar

مخبآت *mukabba'āt* hidden, secret things; secrets

مختبئ *muktabi'* hidden, concealed

خبت **IV** to be humble (الى before God)

خبث *kabuṯa u* (*kubṯ*, خباثة *kabāṯa*) to be bad; to be wicked, evil, malicious, vicious, malignant **VI** to behave viciously, display malice; to feel awkward, feel embarrassed

خبث *kubṯ* badness, wickedness; malignancy (e.g., of a disease); malice, malevolence, viciousness

خبث *kabaṯ* refuse, scum, dross, slag

خبيث *kabīṯ* pl. خبث *kubuṯ*, خبثاء *kubaṯā'*[2], اخباث *akbāṯ*, خبثة *kabaṯa* bad, evil, wicked; malicious, vicious, spiteful; noxious, injurious, harmful; malignant (disease); offensive, repulsive, nauseating, disgusting (odor)

اخبث *akbaṯ*[2] worse; more wicked

خباثة *kabāṯa* badness, wickedness; malice, malevolence, viciousness, malignancy

خبر *kabara u* (*kubr*, خبرة *kibra*) to try, test (ه s.th.); to experience (ه s.th.); to have tried, have experienced, know by experience (ه s.th.); to get to know thoroughly, know well (ه s.th., ه s.o.); — *kabura u* to know thoroughly (ب or ه s.th.), be fully acquainted (ب or ه with s.th.) **II** to notify, advise, apprise, inform, tell (ه s.o., ب of or about) **III** to write (ه to s.o.), address (ه s.o.), turn, appeal (ه to s.o.), contact (ه s.o.) in writing; to communicate by telephone (ه with s.o.); to negotiate, treat, parley (ه with s.o.) IV to notify, inform, apprise, advise (ه ب s.o. of), let know, tell (ه ب s.o. about); to communicate, report, relate (ه ب to s.o. s.th.), tell (ه ب s.o. s.th.) V to inquire (ه of s.o.), ask (ه s.o.) VI to inform one another, notify one another, keep one another informed; to correspond, write each other; to negotiate, treat, parley (مع with s.o., فى about) VIII to explore (ه s.th.), search (ه into), seek information (ه about); to test, examine (ه s.o., ه s.th.); to try, put to the test (ه s.o., ه s.th.); to have tried, have experienced, know by experience (ه s.th.); to know well (ه s.th.) X to inquire (عن ه of s.o. about), ask (عن ه s.o. about)

خبر *ḵubr* knowledge; experience

خبر *ḵabar* pl. اخبار *aḵbār* news; information, intelligence; report, communication, message; notification; rumor; story; matter, affair; (*gram.*) predicate of a nominal clause; pl. annals | سأله عن اخباره to inquire of s.o. about s.o. else; دخل فى خبر كان or كان فى خبر كان (*ḵabari kāna*) to belong to the past, be passé, be no longer existent; see also ابيض and اسود

خبرة *ḵibra* pl. *ḵibarāt* experience (which s.o. has had); knowledge, skill resulting from experience | تبادل الخبرات *tabādul al-ḵ.* exchange of experience

خبير *ḵabīr* experienced, expert (ب in); familiar, conversant, well-acquainted (ب with), cognizant (ب of); الخبير the Knowing (one of the attributes of God); (pl. خبراء *ḵubarā'*[2]) expert, specialist | خبير الضرائب tax expert, tax adviser

خابور *ḵābūr* pl. خوابير *ḵawābīr*[2] peg; pin; wedge

مخبر *maḵbar* intrinsic significance; real message, sense, content (e.g., of a work of art; in contrast to its form); inner nature or being, spirit and soul (of a person; in contrast to مظهر *maẓhar* external appearance); (pl. مخابر *maḵābir*[2]) laboratory

مخبار *miḵbār* pl. مخابير *maḵābīr*[2] test tube (*chem.*)

مخابرة *muḵābara* pl. *-āt* correspondence, (esp. written) information (in classified ads: المخابرة ب please write to ..., please contact ...), notice, notification, communication; (= مخابرة تليفونية) telephone call, telephone conversation; pl. مخابرات intelligence service, secret service (*pol.*) | مخابرة خارجية (*ḵārijīya*) long-distance call; مخابرة سرية (*sirrīya*) secret communiqué; دائرة المخابرات and قلم المخابرات *qalam al-m.* intelligence bureau; وكالة المخابرات المركزية *wakālat al-m. al-markazīya* Central Intelligence Agency, CIA; المخابرات العامة (*'āmma*) General Intelligence (*Jord.*); المخابرة حضوريا (*ḥuḍūrīyan*) apply in person (in classified ads)

اخبار *iḵbār* notification, information, communication, note, message; report; indirect discourse, oratio obliqua (*gram.*)

اخبارى *iḵbārī* news-, information- (in compounds)

اخبارية *iḵbārīya* denouncing, informing (against s.o.)

تخابر *taḵābur* negotiation; correspondence; communication; intelligence contact (مع with a foreign power)

اختبار *iḵtibār* pl. *-āt* exploration, examination (of s.th., by one's own experience, experimentally); test; test item (of an examination); trial, probation, testing; experience, empirical knowledge; practical experience | اختبارات تحريرية (*taḥrīrīya*) written tests; اختبار ذاتى (*ḏātī*) self-probing, self-knowledge (through testing or experience); على سبيل الاختبار experimentally; تحت الاختبار on probation, on trial; حقول الاختبار experimental fields; اختبار بقع الحبر *i. buqaʿ al-ḥibr* Rorschach test (*psych.*); اختبارات على الحيوانات animal experiments

اختبارى *iḵtibārī* experimental; experiential; empirical | مسرح اختبارى (*masraḥ*) experimental theater

اختبارية *iḵtibārīya* empiricism

استخبار *istiḵbār* pl. *-āt* inquiry; pl. استخبارات secret service, intelligence service | دائرة الاستخبارات information bureau

استخبارى *istiḵbārī*: اعمال استخبارية undercover activities, intelligence operations

مخبر *muḵbir* pl. *-ūn* reporter; detective; informer, stool pigeon; denouncer

مختبر *muḵtabar* pl. *-āt* laboratory | مختبر لغة *m. luḡa* language laboratory; مختبر فضاء *m. faḍā'* space laboratory

مختبرى *muḵtabarī*: ابحاث مختبرية laboratory research; تجارب مختبرية laboratory experiments

خبز **ḵabaza** *i* (*ḵabz*) to bake (ه bread) **VIII** do.

خبز *ḵubz* pl. اخباز *aḵbāz* bread | خبز العباس *ḵ. al-ʿabbās* (*ir.*) baked dough filled with ground meat, saffron and greens

خبزة *ḵubza* loaf of bread

خباز *ḵabbāz* pl. *-ūn*, خبازة baker

خباز *ḵubbāz*, خبيز *ḵubbaiz*, خبازى *ḵubbāzā* mallow (*bot.*)

خبازة *ḵibāza* baker's trade, art of baking

مخبز *maḵbaz*, مخبزة *maḵbaza* pl. مخابز *maḵābiz*[2] bakery

مخبوزات *maḵbūzāt* bakery goods

خبص **ḵabaṣa** *i* (*ḵabṣ*) to mix, mingle, intermix (ه ب s.th. with) **II** to mix, mingle, intermix (ه s.th.); to muddle, jumble, confuse (ه s.th.), make a mess (ه of)

خبيص *ḵabīṣ*, خبيصة *ḵabīṣa* medley, mess, mishmash, hodgepodge; خبيصة a jellylike sweet

خباص *ḵabbāṣ* one who causes confusion, who messes things up; an irresponsible, light-minded person

خبط **ḵabaṭa** *i* (*ḵabṭ*) to beat, strike (ه s.th., against s.th.); to knock, rap (ه on, الباب on the door); to stamp (الارض the ground; of animals); to go stamping, trampling along (person; فى on a path) | يخبط خبط عشواء (*ḵabṭa ʿašwāʾa*) he acts haphazardly, he proceeds rashly or at random; خبط فيهم خبط عشواء he struck out blindly at them (with a cane) **V** to beat, strike, hit (ه s.o.); to bring down, fell, knock out, throw to the ground (ه s.o.); to bump, hit (ه against), collide (ه with), stumble (ه over); to be lost, wander about, stray; to wander about blindly, erratically (فى سيره *fī sairihī* in going); to wander aimlessly; to grope about, fumble about; to struggle, resist; to clatter over the ground, gallop (horse) **VIII** to bump (against); to struggle, resist; to grope about, fumble about; to be lost, wander around, stray; to stir, bustle

خبطة *ḵabṭa* blow, stroke; rap, knock; noise, din, uproar

خباط *ḵubāṭ* insanity, madness, mental disorder

مخبط *miḵbaṭ* pl. مخابط *maḵābiṭ*[2] drumstick

خبل **ḵabala** *u* (*ḵabl*) to confound, confuse, mess up, complicate (ه s.th.); to hinder, impede, handicap, stop, hold back (ه s.o.); to befuddle (ه s.o.), confuse s.o.'s (ه) mind, rob (ه s.o.) of his senses, make

(ه s.o.) crazy; — *kabila a* (*kabal,* خبال *kabāl*) to get confused; to be or become mentally disturbed, crazy, insane **II** to confound, confuse (ه s.th., ه s.o.); to complicate, entangle, mess up, muddle, throw into disorder (ه s.th.); to rob of his senses, drive insane (ه s.o.) **VIII** to become muddled, disordered (mind)

خبل *kabl, kabal* confusion; mental disorder, insanity

خبل *kabil* mad, crazy, insane; feeble-minded, dim-witted

اخبل *akbal*[2] mad, crazy, insane; feeble-minded, dim-witted

اختبال *iktibāl* mental disorder

مخبول *makbūl* mad, crazy, idiotic, imbecilic, mentally deranged, insane; muddlehead, dolt, fool

مخبل *mukabbal* confused, baffled, perplexed, dismayed; muddled, confused, mixed up

خبا (خبو) *kabā u* (*kabw, kubūw*) to go out, die (fire)

خبايا and خباء pl. اخبية see خبأ

خابية pl. خواب see خبأ

خبيارى *kibyārī* caviar

ختر *katara i* (*katr*) to betray (ه s.o.), act perfidiously, disloyally (ه toward s.o.); to deceive, cheat, dupe (ه s.o.)

ختر *katr* disloyalty, breach of confidence, perfidy, treachery, betrayal, deception

ختار *kattār* traitor, disloyal person, cheat, swindler

خاتر *kātir* treacherous, perfidious, disloyal

ختل *katala i u* (*katl,* ختلان *katalān*) to dupe, gull, cheat, double-cross, deceive (ه s.o.) **III** to deceive, cheat, dupe (ه s.o.); to behave hypocritically **VIII** = **I**

ختل *katl* and مخاتلة *mukātala* deception, trickery, double-dealing, duplicity, duping, gulling

مخاتل *mukātil* deceitful, crafty, wily, foxy

ختم *katama i* (*katm,* ختام *kitām*) to seal, provide with a seal or signet (ه s.th.); to stamp, impress with a stamp (ه s.th.); to seal off, close, make impervious or inaccessible (ه s.th.; also على the hearts, said of God); to put one's seal (ه on), conclude, terminate (ه s.th.); to wind up, finish, complete (ه s.th.); to close, heal, cicatrize (wound) **V** to put on or wear a ring (ب) | تختم بالذهب (*dahab*) to wear a golden ring **VIII** to conclude, finish, terminate, wind up (ه s.th.)

ختم *katm* sealing; — (pl. اختام *aktām,* ختوم *kutūm*) seal, signet, seal imprint; stamp, stamp imprint; also = ختمة (see below) | ختم البريد postmark, (postal) cancellation stamp; شمع الختم *šamʿ al-k.* sealing wax

ختمة *katma* pl. *katamāt* recital of the entire Koran, esp. on festive occasions

خاتم *kātam, kātim* pl. خواتم *kawātim*[2] seal ring, signet ring; ring, finger ring; seal, signet; stamp | خاتم الزواج *k. az-zawāj* wedding ring; خاتم النبيين *k. an-nabīyīn* the Seal (i.e., the last) of the Prophets = Mohammed; خاتم الدولة *k. ad-daula* official seal (of a government agency)

خاتام *kātām* pl. خواتيم *kawātīm*[2] seal ring, signet ring; ring

ختام *kitām* sealing wax; end, close, conclusion, termination | فى الختام at the end, at last, finally, eventually

ختامى *kitāmī* final, concluding | كلمة ختامية (*kalima*) concluding speech

اختتام *iḵtitām* end, close, conclusion, termination

خاتمة *ḵātima* pl. خواتم *ḵawātim*[2], خواتيم *ḵawātīm*[2] end, close, conclusion, termination; epilogue (of a book); خواتيم final stage

مختم *muḵattam* ringed, adorned with a ring or rings (hand)

مختتم *muḵtatam* end, close, conclusion, termination

ختن[1] *ḵatana* *i* (*ḵatn*) to circumcise (ه a boy) **VIII** pass.

ختن *ḵatn* circumcision

ختن *ḵatan* pl. اختان *aḵtān* son-in-law; bridegroom

ختان *ḵitān*, ختانة *ḵitāna* circumcision

خاتون[2] look up alphabetically

اختيار see ختيار □

خثر *ḵaṯara* *u* and *ḵaṯira* *a* to become solid, become thick, solidify, thicken; to be or become viscous, sirupy; to clot, coagulate (liquid); to curdle (milk) **II** and **IV** to thicken, inspissate, condense, coagulate (ه liquid); to curdle (ه milk) **V** = **I**

○ خثرة *ḵaṯra* thrombosis (*med.*)

خثار *ḵuṯār* dregs (of a liquid); scum of the earth, riffraff, mob

خثارة *ḵuṯāra* dregs (of a liquid); sediment, lees

تخثر *taḵaṯṯur* coagulation | ○ تخثر فى المخ (*muḵḵ*) cerebral thrombosis

خاثر *ḵāṯir* thickened, inspissated, condensed; viscous, ropy, sirupy; curdled, coagulated, clotted; yoghurt, curd

مخثرات *muḵaṯṯirāt* coagulants (esp. *med.*)

مخثر *muḵaṯṯar* thickened, inspissated, condensed; viscous, ropy, sirupy; curdled, coagulated, clotted

خجل *ḵajila* *a* (*ḵajal*) to become embarrassed; to be ashamed (من of s.th. or to face s.o.), be abashed (من by s.th.), feel embarrassed (من about s.th. or in front of s.o.) **II** and **IV** to shame (ه s.o.); to embarrass, abash, put to shame (ه s.o.)

خجل *ḵajal* shame (من at); bashfulness, diffidence, timidity, shyness; abashment; disgrace, shame, ignominy | يا للخجل (*la-l-ḵ.*) O disgrace! the shame of it!

خجل *ḵajil* abashed, embarrassed; bashful, diffident, shy, timid; overgrown with luxuriant, profuse vegetation; long and flowing (garment)

خجول *ḵajūl* abashed, ashamed, shamefaced; shy, bashful, diffident, timid

خجلان *ḵajlān*[2] abashed, ashamed, shamefaced; shy, bashful, diffident, timid; bewildered with shame, embarrassed

مخجول *maḵjūl* ashamed, shamefaced

مخجل *muḵjil* arousing shame, shameful; shocking, disgraceful, ignominious | الاعضاء المخجلة (*a'ḍā'*) the pudenda

خد *ḵadda* *u* to furrow, plow (ه the ground) **V** to be furrowed; to become wrinkled (skin)

خد *ḵadd* pl. خدود *ḵudūd* cheek; lateral portion, side | صعر خده *ṣa''ara ḵaddahū* to put on a contemptuous mien

خد *ḵadd* and خدة *ḵudda* pl. خدد *ḵudad* furrow, ridge, groove, rut

اخدود *uḵdūd* pl. اخاديد *aḵādīd*[2] furrow, ridge, groove, rut; trench, excavation; pl. اخاديد furrows, wrinkles, engraved lines (in a face)

مخدة *miḵadda* pl. مخاد *maḵādd*[2] cushion, pillow; seat cushion

خديج *ḵadīj* premature child

خداج *ḵidāj* abortion, miscarriage

خدر *kadira a* (*kadar*) to be numb, prickle, tingle (leg, arm); to be or become limp, benumbed, paralyzed; — *kadara u* to confine to women's quarters, keep in seclusion (ها a girl) **II** to numb, benumb, stupefy (ه s.o., ه s.th.); to anesthetize, narcotize, put to sleep (ه s.o., ه s.th.; *med.*); to confine to women's quarters, keep in seclusion (ها a girl) **IV** to make torpid, stupefy, benumb, deprive of sensation, narcotize (ه s.o., ه s.th.) **V** to be numbed, be stunned, be stupefied, be deprived of sensation; to come to rest, calm down

خدر *kidr* pl. خدور *kudūr*, اخدار *akdār*, اخادير *akādīr*² curtain, drape; women's quarters of a tent; boudoir, private room (of a lady)

خدر *kadar* and خدرة *kudra* numbness, insensibility (esp. of a limb gone to sleep); daze, torpor, stupor

خدر *kadir* numb (limb); benumbed, torpid, dazed

خدران *kadrān* numb (limb); dazed

تخدير *takdīr* anesthetization, narcotization; anesthesia (*med.*) | تخدير موضعى (*mauḍiʿī*) local anesthesia (*med.*)

○ اخدار *ikdār* analgesia (*med.*)

خادر *kādir* limp, languid; benumbed, torpid, dazed; hidden in his den, lurking (lion)

خادرة *kādira* chrysalis (of a caterpillar; *zool.*)

مخدر *mukaddir* anesthetic, painkilling, tranquilizing; (pl. *-āt*) an anesthetic; a narcotic, drug, dope

مخدر *mukaddar* numb, torpid, insensible; (*eg.*) tipsy, fuddled, drunk

مخدرة *mukaddara* girl kept in seclusion from the outside world

خدش *kadaša i* (*kadš*) to scratch (with one's nails, ه s.th.); to make scratch marks (ه on s.th.); to violate (ه s.o.'s honor), offend (ه the ear, the sense of shame, rules of decency); to disturb (ه the peace or silence); to harm, damage (سمعته *sumʿatahū* s.o.'s reputation) **II** to scratch severely (ه s.th.); to hurt, injure (ه s.o.'s hands, etc.); to offend (ه the ears) **V** pass. of **II**

خدش *kadš* pl. خدوش *kudūš*, اخداش *akdāš* scratch, scratch mark; graze, abrasion

خدع *kadaʿa a* to cheat (ه s.o., عن out of s.th.); to deceive, mislead, dupe, gull (ه s.o.); pass. *kudiʿa* to be mistaken, be wrong (عن about); to fail to see clearly (عن with regard to), get the wrong impression (عن of s.th.) | خدعه عن نفسه to mislead, dupe s.o. **III** to cheat, dupe, deceive, take in (ه s.o.); to try to deceive or double-cross (ه s.o.) **VII** to let o.s. be deceived, be deceived, deluded, misled (ب by); to be mistaken, be wrong

خدع *kadʿ* cheating; deceit, deception

خدعة *kudʿa* pl. خدع *kudaʿ*, *-āt* deception, cheating, swindle

خدعة *kudaʿa* impostor, swindler, cheat, sharper

سوى اخدعه *sawwā akdaʿahū* to crush s.o.'s pride, humble s.o.

خديعة *kadīʿa* pl. خدائع *kadāʾiʿ*² deception, deceit, betrayal, treachery, perfidy, trickery, imposture

خداع *kaddāʿ* impostor, swindler, sharper, cheat, crook; deceptive, delusive

خيدع *kaidaʿ* fata morgana, mirage

اخاديع *akādīʿ*² swindles, underhand dealings, crooked practices; phantoms, phantasms, delusions

مخدع *mikdaʿ*, *mukdaʿ*, *makdaʿ* pl. مخادع *makādiʿ*² small room, chamber, cabinet; bedchamber

خداع *kidā'* deception, deceit, swindle, imposture, betrayal, treachery, perfidy, trickery, duplicity

خداعى *kidā'ī* deceitful, fraudulent; deceptive, delusive, fallacious

خادع *kādi'* deceiving, deceitful; deceptive

مخادع *mukādi'* swindler, impostor, cheat, sharper, crook

خدل **kadila** *a* to stiffen, become rigid; to become numb, torpid, limp

خدم **kadama** *i u* (خدمة *kidma*) to serve, be at service, do service; to have a job; to work; to wait (ه on s.o.); to serve (ه s.o., ه s.th.); to render a service (ه to s.o., ه to s.th.), stand up (ه for s.o.) | خدم الارض to till or cultivate the soil; خدمه خدمات كثيرة (*kidamātin katīratan*) he rendered him many services; خدم ركاب فلان (*rikāba*) to be at s.o.'s beck and call; خدم مصالح فلان (*maṣāliha*) to serve s.o.'s interests; خدم القداس (*quddāsa*) to celebrate Mass (*Chr.*); طريقة اخدم نفسك بنفسك (*ikdim nafsaka bi-n.*) self-service **II** to employ, hire (ه s.o.), engage the services (ه of s.o.); to give work (ه to s.o.), provide work (ه for) **X** to employ, hire, take on (ه s.o., ل for s.th.), engage the services (ه ل of s.o. for s.th.); to put in operation, operate (ه e.g., a public utility); to employ, use (ه s.th., ل for), make use, avail o.s. (ه of s.th., ل for a purpose)

خدم *kadam* servants, attendants

خدمة *kidma* pl. خدم *kidam*, *-āt* a service (rendered); attendance, service; operation; office, employment, occupation, job; work | فى خدمة شىء in the service of s.th.; فى خدمتكم at your service; خدمة للحقيقة (*kidmatan*) in the interest of truth, for the sake of truth; الخدمة العسكرية (*'askarīya*) military service; الخدمة الاجبارية (*ijbārīya*) conscription, compulsory service; الخدمة السرية (*sirrīya*) secret service (*pol.*); خدمة القداس *k. al-quddās* celebration of Mass (*Chr.*); خدمة الارض *k. al-arḍ* cultivation of the soil; خدمة احتياطية reserve duty (*mil.*); خدمة العلم *k. al-'alam* (*Syr.*) military service; الخدمات العامة public services; خدمات صحية (*ṣiḥḥīya*) health services; خدمة سائرة pl. خدم سائرة (*eg.*) non-tenured workers, workers paid by the day; seasonal laborers; labor force not on regular appointment

خدام *kaddām* pl. ة manservant, servant, attendant; woman servant, female domestic servant, maid

خدامة *kadāma* attendance, service; employment, occupation, office, job

خدامة *kaddāma* pl. *-āt* woman servant, female domestic servant, maid

تخديم *takdīm* work, occupation or duty of an employment agent (مخدم *mukaddim* see below) | مكتب التخديم *maktab at-t.* labor office, employment bureau

استخدام *istikdām* (putting into) operation; use, utilization; employment, hiring (of an employee); (pl. *-āt*) service, occupation, position, job; pl. استخدامات modes of utilization or application

خادم *kādim* pl. خدام *kuddām*, خدمة *kadama* domestic servant, help; manservant; woman servant; employee; attendant; waiter; deacon (*Chr.*)

خادمة *kādima* woman servant; female domestic servant, maid; woman attendant

خادمية *kādimīya* status of a servant

مخدوم *makdūm* pl. *-ūn*, مخاديم *makādīm*[2] master, employer

مخدومة *makdūma* mistress, lady (of the house), woman employer

مخدومية *makdūmīya* status of the master or employer

مخدم *mukaddim* pl. *-ūn* employment agent

مستخدم *mustakdim* pl. *-ūn* employer; — *mustakdam* (colloq. *mustakdim*) pl. *-ūn* employee, official

خدن III to befriend (ه s.o.), make friends (ه with s.o.); to associate socially (ه with)

خدن *kidn* pl. اخدان *akdān* (intimate) friend, companion, confidant

خدين *kadīn* (intimate) friend, companion, confidant

خديو *kidīw*, خديوى *kudaiwī* khedive

خديوى *kidīwī* khedivial

خذأ X to submit, subject o.s.

مستخذئ *mustakdi'* submissive, servile, subservient, obedient

خذروف *kudrūf* pl. خذاريف *kadārīf*[2] (spinning) top

خذروفى *kudrūfī* turbinate, toplike

خذف *kadafa i* (*kadf*) to hurl away (ه, ب s.th.)

مخذفة *mikdafa* sling, slingshot, catapult

خذل *kadala u* (*kadl*, خذلان *kidlān*) to leave, abandon, forsake, desert, leave in the lurch (ه or عن s.o.); to stay behind; to disappoint; pass. *kudila* to fail, suffer a setback, meet with disappointment **III** to leave, abandon, forsake, desert, leave in the lurch (ه s.o.) **VI** to let up, flag, grow slack, languish, wane, decrease, fade, grow feeble **VII** to be left in the lurch; to be helpless; to be defeated; to meet with disappointment

خذلان *kidlān* disappointment; defeat, setback, failure

تخاذل *takādul* fatigue, languor, weakness, feebleness; relaxation, lessening of tension; disagreement, dissent, disunion

انخذال *inkidāl* forsakenness, desertedness, abandonment; defeat

متخاذل *mutakādil* languid, weak, exhausted, spent, effete

(خذو) **X** to submit, subject o.s.; to be or feel humiliated

استخذاء *istikdā'* subservience, submissiveness, servility

مستخذ *mustakdin* submissive, servile, subservient, obedient

خر *karra i u* (خرير *karīr*) to murmur, bubble, gurgle, purl (of running water); to ripple, trickle; to snore; — (*karr*, خرور *kurūr*) to fall, fall down, drop; to sink to the ground, prostrate o.s. | خر على الارض to fall to the ground; خر بين يديه (*baina yadaihi*) he prostrated himself before him; خر تحت قدميه (*taḥta qadamaihi*) he fell at his feet

خرير *karīr* purl, murmur, ripple (of water)

خرئ *kari'a a* (خرء *kar'*) to evacuate the bowels, defecate

خرء *kur'* and خراء *karā'* excrement, feces

خراسان *kurāsān*[2] Khurasan (province in NE Iran)

[1]خرب *karaba i* (*karb*) to destroy, wreck, demolish, shatter, devastate, lay waste (ه s.th.); — *kariba a* (خراب *karāb*) to be or become destroyed, ruined, waste, go to ruin, fall apart, disintegrate; to be out of order, be in need of repair **II** to devastate, lay waste, destroy, wreck, demolish, ruin, lay in ruins (ه s.th.) **IV** = **II**; **V** to be or become destroyed, ruined, waste, go to ruin, fall apart, disintegrate

خرب *karb* destruction, devastation

خرب ḵurb hole; eye of a needle; anus

خرب ḵarib destroyed, demolished, wrecked, devastated, waste; dilapidated, tumble-down, ramshackle; broken, ruined; kaput, out of order, in need of repair

خربة ḵirba pl. خرب ḵirab (site of) ruins; ruin, disintegrating structure

خربة ḵarba, ḵurba irreligion, lawlessness

خربة ḵurba pl. خرب ḵurab hole; eye of a needle; anus

خربة ḵariba (site of) ruins

خراب ḵarāb ruin, ruination; state of destruction or dilapidation; desolation; (pl. اخربة aḵriba) (site of) ruins

خرابة ḵarāba pl. *-āt*, خرائب ḵarā'ib[2] disintegrating structure, ruin, ruins

خربان ḵarbān, ḵirbān destroyed, wrecked, demolished, devastated, waste; ruined, broken, out of order

تخريب *taḵrīb* pl. *-āt* devastation, destruction, wrecking, demolition; sabotage

عمل تخريبي *'amal taḵrībī* act of sabotage

خارب ḵārib annihilator, destroyer

مخرب *muḵarrib* pl. *-ūn* annihilator, destroyer; saboteur

مخرب *muḵrib* annihilator, destroyer

[2]خروب ḵarrūb (coll.; n. un. ة) carob, locust; carob bean, locust pod, St.-John's-bread

خروبة ḵarrūba pl. *-āt* kharouba, a dry measure (*Eg.*; = $^1/_{16}$ قدح = .129 l)

خربش ḵarbaša to scratch (intr. and ه s.o.); to scrawl, scribble

خربوش ḵarbūš pl. خرابيش ḵarābīš[2] (*syr.*) tent

○ مخربشات *muḵarbašāt* graffiti

خربط ḵarbaṭa to throw into disorder, disarrange, confuse (ه s.th.)

خربطة ḵarbaṭa disorder, confusion

خربق ḵarbaqa to perforate, riddle (ه s.th.); to spoil, mar (ه s.th.)

خربق ḵarbaq hellebore (*bot.*)

خرت ḵarata *u* (ḵart) to pierce, bore, perforate (ه s.th.), make a hole (ه in)

خرت ḵurt, ḵart pl. اخرات aḵrāt, خروت ḵurūt hole; bore, drill hole; ring, eye, eyelet

خريت ḵirrīt experienced, practiced, skilled; guide

خرتيت ḵartīt rhinoceros

خرج ḵaraja *u* (خروج ḵurūj) to go out, walk out; to come out (من of), emerge (من from); to drive or ride out, go out (in a vehicle); to flow out, exude, effuse; to go away, depart, leave, retire; to protrude, project, stick out; to leave (من s.th.); to drop out (من from a competition; sport); to dismount, alight, disembark (من from), get out, step out (من of); to emanate, issue, arise, originate, result (من from); to draw away, segregate, separate, secede, dissent (عن from), disagree (عن with); to deviate, depart (عن from an arrangement, from a principle); to be an exception (عن to); to be outside a given subject (عن), go beyond a topic (عن), exceed (عن a topic); to be alien (عن to), be extraneous (عن from), not to belong (عن to), be not included (عن in), have nothing to do with (عن); لا يخرج عن it is limited to ..., it is nothing but ...; to go forth (into battle); to attack (على s.o., s.th.), rise, fight (على against); to rebel, revolt (على against); to violate, break, infringe (على a rule, a regulation); خرج عليه ب to come up to s.o. with ..., confront s.o. with ...; to get out, bring out, take out (ب s.o.); to turn out, oust, dislodge (ب s.o.); to lead away, dissuade (ب عن s.o. from); to find out, discover (ب s.th.) | خرج عن الخط (*katt*) to be derailed, run off the track (train); خرج منه فى عافية (*'āfiya*) to recover nicely from s.th.; خرج منه ظافرا غانما (*zāfiran ğāniman*) to overcome s.th. successfully, surmount s.th. triumphantly **II** to move out, take out, dislodge (ه s.o., ه s.th.); to turn out, oust, expel, evict, drive out (ه s.o., ه s.th.); to remove, eliminate (ه s.o., ه s.th.); to exclude, except (ه s.th.); to train (ه s.o., فى in a skill, and the like); to educate, bring up (ه s.o.); to distill (ه s.th.); to pull out, extract (ه s.th.); to gather, deduce, infer (ه s.th.) **IV** to move out, take out, get out, bring out, dislodge (ه s.o., ه s.th.); to pull out (ه من s.th. of); to unpack (ه things); to unload (ه s.th.), disembark, detrain, etc. (ه s.o., e.g., troops); to turn out, oust (ه s.o.); to emit, send out (ه s.th., e.g., electric waves); to stick out (ه e.g., the tongue); to fish out (ه s.th. from the pocket); to bring out into the open, make public (ه s.th.); to bring out, publish (ه a new work); to remove, extract (ه s.th.); to eliminate (ه s.th.); to evict (ه s.o.), remove (ه s.o., من from a dwelling); to expel, exile, expatriate (ه s.o., من from a country); to dismiss, fire, remove (ه s.o., من from an office); اخرجه من ثروته (*tarwatihī*) to rob s.o. of his property, dispossess, expropriate s.o.; to give off, sound, emit (ه s.th., e.g., a tone; said of a musical instrument); to set forth, state, express, utter, voice (ه an opinion); to break (ريحا *rīhan* wind); to educate, bring up (ه s.o.); to train (ه s.o.); to stage, produce (ه a play; *theat.*); to bring out, make, shoot (رواية *riwāyatan* a film, said of a director); to except, exclude (ه s.th., عن from); to pull out, extract (ه s.th.); to select (ه s.th.) **V** to be educated; to be trained (فى in a school, college, also من; فى in a field); to graduate (فى from a school, from a college, also من) **VI** to part company, separate; to disengage, disassociate, withdraw from one another; to cede, assign, transfer, make over (عن ل s.th. to s.o.) **X** to get out, move out, remove (ه s.th., من from); to take out, draw (ه s.th., من from); to pull out, extract (ه s.th., من from); to mine, extract, recover (ه mineral resources); to win, gain, make (ه a product, من from); to copy, excerpt (ه s.th., من from a book or document); to derive, draw, deduce, figure out, compute (ه من s.th. from); to elicit (ه s.th., e.g., astonishment, من from s.o.); to evoke (ه e.g., laughter, من from s.o.); to find out, discover (ه s.th.)

خرج *karj* expenditure, outlay, expense(s), costs; land tax; s.th. appropriate or suitable, that which is s.o.'s due, which s.o. deserves, which s.o. needs; (*eg.*) ration (food); (pl. خروجات *kurūjāt*) trimming; edge, edging, piping; pl. lace; trimmings | هذا خرجك that's what you need, what you deserve; خرج المشنقة *k. al-mašnaqa* one who deserves to be hanged

خرج *kurj* pl. خرجة *kiraja* saddlebag, portmanteau

خرجة *karja* pl. *karajāt* exit, departure; protrusion, protuberance, projection, salient part; (*eg.*) funeral

خراج *karāj* tax; kharaj, land tax (*Isl. Law*)

خراجى *karājī* of or pertaining to land tax; of or pertaining to the taxed and cultivable area

خراج *kurāj* pl. *-āt* abscess (*med.*)

خروج *kurūj* exit; egression, emergence; departure; exodus; emigration; raid, foray, sortie (على against), attack, assault (على on); offense (على against), violation (على of) | خروج عن الخط (katt) derailment (of a train); سفر الخروج sifr al-k. the Book of Exodus; خروج على القاعدة violation of a rule; خروج عن القياس (qiyās) abnormality, irregularity

خريج kirrīj pl. -ūn graduate (of a school, college, or university) | مؤتمر الخريجين العرب mu'tamar al-k. al-ʿarab Congress of Arab Graduates (a supra-national organization of university graduates advocating a unified Arab world)

مخرج makraj pl. مخارج makārij[2] (place of) exit; way out (of a difficult situation), outlet, escape, loophole, shift, dodge, excuse; articulation (of a sound); ○ cathode (el.); denominator (arith.) | مخرج مشترك (muštarak) common denominator (arith.); علم مخارج الحروف phonetics; لا مخرج منه (makraja) hopeless (situation)

تخريج takrīj education, training (in schools, colleges); raising, upbringing, rearing (of children); extraction; derivation, deduction

اخراج ikrāj taking out, moving out, removal; unloading, disembarkment, detrainment; emission; moving, carting away, hauling off; evacuation; publication, publicizing, bringing before the public; extraction, removal; elimination; dismissal, removal (from an office); ousting, expulsion, eviction, expatriation, banishment (from a country); excretion (biol.); finding out, discovery, figuring out; training, formation, education; direction, production, staging (motion pictures, theater) | تولى الاخراج (tawallā) to have the direction (motion pictures, theater); من اخراج ... directed by ... (motion picture)

تخرج takarruj graduation (from a school or college)

تخارج takāruj separation, disassociation, disengagement, (mutual) withdrawal

استخراج istikrāj taking out, moving out, pulling out, removal; withdrawing; extraction, derivation, gaining (of industrial products, etc.), mining, recovery (of mineral resources); preparation of an extract; excerpting, copying; deduction, inference; solution (of a problem)

خارج kārij outer, outside, outward, exterior; external, foreign; outside, exterior (n.); foreign country or countries; quotient (arith.); kārija (prep.) outside, out of; خارجا kārijan outside | خارجا عن outside of, apart from; في الخارج abroad, in foreign countries; outside; الى الخارج abroad, to foreign countries; to the outside, outward, out

الخارجة El Khârga (town in central Egypt, in Khârga oasis)

خارجى kārijī outer, out- (in compounds), outside, outward, exterior, external; foreign; nonresident; objective, based on external aspects (opposite of subjective) | عيادة خارجية (ʿiyāda) policlinic; تلميذ خارجى (tilmīd) a student not living at a boarding school, a day student; اثبات خارجى (iṯbāt) objective proof

خوارج kawārij[2] the Khawarij, Kharijites (the oldest religious sect of Islam); dissenters, dissidents, backsliders, rebels

الخارجية al-kārijīya the sect of the Kharijites, see خوارج; foreign affairs | وزارة الخارجية ministry of foreign (external) affairs, foreign ministry

مخرج mukrij pl. -ūn (screen or stage) director

مخرج mukraj excerpt, extract (from a book); مخرجات excretions (biol.)

متخرج *mutakarrij* pl. *-ūn* graduate (ف or من of a school or college)

مستخرج *mustakraj* pl. *-āt* extract; excerpt (من from), partial copy (من of)

خرخر *karkara* to snore

[1]خرد *karida a* to be a virgin, be untouched, innocent, chaste

خريدة *karīda* pl. خرائد *karā'id*[2], خرد *kurud* virgin; unbored pearl

[2]خردة *kurda* scrap metal, scrap iron; pl. خردوات *kurdawāt* notions, smallwares; small goods, smalls, miscellaneous small articles; (*eg.* also) novelties, fancy goods for ladies

خردجى *kurdajī* dealer in miscellaneous smallwares

خردق *kurdaq, kurduq* small shot, buckshot

خردل *kardal* (coll.; n. un. ة) mustard seeds; mustard

خرز *karaza i u* to pierce, bore (ه s.th.)

خرز *karaz* (coll.; n.un. ة) pl. *-āt* beads, specif., strung beads

خراز *karrāz* pl. *-ūn* cobbler

مخرز *mikraz* pl. مخارز *makāriz*[2] awl; punch

مخراز *mikrāz* pl. مخارز *makārīz*[2] awl; punch

خرزانة *karzāna* (*eg.*) switch, rod

[1]خرس *karisa a* (*karas*) to be dumb, mute; to become silent, keep silent, hold one's tongue **IV** to silence, reduce to silence, gag (ه s.o.)

خرس *karas* dumbness, muteness

اخرس *akras*[2], f. خرساء *karsā'*[2], pl. خرس *kurs*, خرسان *kursān* dumb, mute

خرسان *karsān*[2] dumb, mute

[2]خرسان *karasān*, خرسانة *karasāna* concrete (béton) | ○ خرسانة مسلحة (*musallaḥa*) armored (or reinforced) concrete

خرشوف *kuršūf* (coll.; n. un. ة) pl. خراشيف *karāšīf*[2] artichoke

خرص *karaṣa u* (*karṣ*) to guess, estimate (ه s.th.); to conjecture, surmise (ه s.th.), form conjectures (ه about); to tell an untruth, a falsehood, to lie **V** to fabricate lies (على against s.o.); to raise false accusations (على against s.o.)

خرص *kirṣ, kurṣ* pl. خرصان *kirṣān, kurṣān* earring

خراص *karrāṣ* pl. *-ūn* liar, slanderer, calumniator

خرط *karaṭa u i* (*karṭ*) to pull off, strip (ه leaves from a tree); to turn, lathe, shape with a lathe (ه wood, metal); to exaggerate, boast, brag, lie; — *u* (*eg.*) to cut into small pieces; to mince, chop, dice (ه meat, carrots, etc.) **II** (*eg.*) to cut into small pieces, mince, chop (ه s.th.) **VII** to be turned, be lathed, be shaped with a lathe; to join, enter (ف, ف سلك *fī silk* an organization, a community), affiliate (ف, ف سلك with an organization, a community); to penetrate (ف s.th. or into); to plunge headlong (ف into), embark rashly (ف upon); to labor, slave, toil | انخرط ف البكاء (*bukā'*) to break into tears

خرط *karṭ* pulling-off (of leaves); دون خرط القتاد see دون ذلك; turning, turnery

خراط *karrāṭ* pl. *-ūn* turner, lather; braggart, bluffer, storyteller

خراطة *kirāṭa* turner's trade, turnery, art of turning

خراطة *kurāṭa* turnings, filings, millings, shavings

خراطة *karrāṭa* skirt (*syr.*)

خريطة *karīṭa* pl. خرائط *karā'iṭ*[2], خرط *kuruṭ* map, chart

خرائطى *karā'iṭī* cartographic(al)

مخرطة *mikraṭa, makraṭa* pl. مخارط *ma-kāriṭ*[2] lathe

انخراط *inkirāṭ* joining (فى of), entry (فى into)

خارطة *kāriṭa* pl. *-āt* map, chart

مخروط *makrūṭ* cone (*math.*); conic

مخروطى *makrūṭī* conic

خرطوش *karṭūš* bullets, cartridges; — خرطوشة (n. un.) pl. خراطيش *karāṭīš*[2] cartridge; lead (of a pencil); cartouche (*arch.*); daybook | خرطوشة سجائر (*eg.*) a carton of cigarettes

خرطال *karṭāl* oats

خرطوم *kurṭūm* pl. خراطيم *karāṭīm*[2] proboscis, trunk (of the elephant); hose

الخرطوم *al-kurṭūm*, (also pronounced *al-karṭūm*) Khartoum (capital of the Sudanese Republic)

خراطين *karāṭīn*[2] a kind of earthworm

خراطينى *karāṭīnī* wormlike, vermiform

خرطيط *karṭīṭ* rhinoceros

خرع *karu'a u* (*kur'*, خراعة *karā'a*) and *kari'a a* (*kara'*) to droop, be or become slack, limp, flabby; to be or become languid, soft, spineless, yielding **VII** do. **VIII** to invent, devise, contrive (ه s.th.); to create, originate (ه s.th.)

خرع *kari'* and خريع *karī'* soft, languid, yielding, spineless, devoid of energy, nerveless

خروع *kirwa'* castor-oil plant, palma Christi (Ricinus communis; *bot.*)

اختراع *iktirā'* pl. *-āt* invention

مخترع *muktari'* pl. *-ūn* inventor

مخترع *muktara'* pl. *-āt* invention

خرف *karifa a* (*karaf*) and **II** to dote, be senile and feeble-minded; to drivel, talk foolishly

خرف *karaf* feeble-mindedness, dotage, senility; childishness (of an old man)

خرف *karif* and خرفان *karfān* feeble-minded, doting; childish; dotard

خريف *karīf* autumn, fall

خريفى *karīfī* autumnal

خروف *karūf* pl. خراف *kirāf*, اخرفة *akrifa*, خرفان *kirfān* young sheep, lamb, yearling; wether

خرافة *kurāfa* pl. *-āt* superstition; fable, fairy tale

خرافى *kurāfī* fabulous, fictitious, legendary

مخرفة *makrafa* prattle, drivel, twaddle, bosh

تخريف *takrīf* folly, delusion; foolish talk, drivel, twaddle, bosh, buncombe

مخرف *mukarrif* senile and feeble-minded; foolish; (pl. *-ūn*) prattler, chatterbox, windbag; charlatan

خرفش *karfaša* to shuffle, mix (ه s.th.)

خرفوشة *karfūša* pl. خرافيش *karāfīš*[2] card of low value, discard (in card playing)

خرق *karaqa i u* (*karq*) to tear, rend, tear apart (ه s.th.); to make a hole (ه in); to perforate, pierce, bore (ه s.th.); to penetrate (ه s.th.), break, pass (ه through s.th.); to traverse, cross, transit (ه s.th., a country); to violate, impair, infringe

(ه s.th.), encroach (ه upon); to break (ه a vow, and the like), commit a breach of (ه); to exceed the ordinary, be unusual, extraordinary, unprecedented, unheard-of | خرق العادة to go beyond what is ordinary or customary **IV** to lurk, lie in wait **V** and **VII** to be torn, be rent, be pierced, be broken **VIII** to pierce (ه s.th.); to cut, break, pass (ه through s.th.), penetrate (ه s.th.); to traverse, cross, transit (ه s.th.), travel through s.th. (ه); to pass through (ه a street, an alley); to exceed (ه e.g., a limit), go beyond s.th. (ه) | اخترق مسامعه (*masāmi'ahū*) to shrill in s.o.'s ears

خرق *k̲arq* tearing, rending, laceration; piercing, boring, perforation; penetration; disruption; breakthrough; traversion, crossing, transit; violation, breach; (pl. خروق *k̲urūq*) hole, aperture, opening | خرق الامن العام *k̲. al-amn al-'āmm* violation of public security; خرق العادات offense against common usage, violation of mores; اتسع الخرق على الراقع (*ittasa'a*) the rent is beyond repair

خرق *k̲urq* and خرقة *k̲urqa* awkwardness, clumsiness; stupidity | خرق فى الرأى (*ra'y*) stupidity; folly, madness; من الخرق فى الرأى ان ... it would be very unwise to ...

خرقة *k̲irqa* pl. خرق *k̲iraq* tatter, shred; rag; scrap (of paper); polishing cloth; eraser (cloth)

اخرق *ak̲raq*², f. خرقاء *k̲arqā'*², pl. خرق *k̲urq* clumsy, awkward; stupid; crazy, foolish; irregular; illegal, illicit, unlawful

مخرقة *mak̲raqa* trickery, sleight of hand, legerdemain, hocus-pocus, swindle

مخارق *mak̲āriq*² a kind of pastry (*tun.*)

اختراق *ik̲tirāq* penetration; piercing, disruption; traversion, crossing, transit; اختراق الضاحية see سباق سباق

خارق *k̲āriq* and (للعادة or) خارق العادة exceeding the customary, unusual, extraordinary, unprecedented, unheard-of; pl. خوارق *k̲awāriq*² preternatural phenomena, miracles; that which transcends the conceivable or the rational | خارق الطبيعة supernatural; خوارق المصادفات *k̲. al-muṣādafāt* miraculous coincidences

خارقة *k̲āriqa* pl. خوارق *k̲awāriq*² miracle

مخترق *muk̲taraq* passage, passageway

خرم *k̲arama i* (*k̲arm*) and **II** to pierce (ه s.th.), make a hole or holes (ه in); to perforate (ه s.th.) **VII** to be pierced, be riddled, be torn; to be deranged, unsettled, disorganized; to come to an end, run out, peter out, get lost **VIII** to destroy, annihilate (ه s.o.); to carry off, carry away (ه s.o., of death); to break (الصفوف the ranks), pass through s.th. (ه)

خرم *k̲arm* pl. خروم *k̲urūm* gap, blank (e.g., in a manuscript, or the like)

خرم *k̲urm* hole | خرم الابرة *k̲. al-ibra* eye of the needle

خرامة *k̲arrāma* drill, bit, auger, gimlet; punch, perforator

اخرم *ak̲ram*² having a perforated nasal septum

تخريم *tak̲rīm* piercing, boring, drilling; perforation; punching; lacemaking, lacework

تخريمة *tak̲rīma* lace, lacework, openwork, filigree

انخرام *ink̲irām* state of unsettlement, disturbance, disorganization, derangement | انخرام فى التوازن (*tawāzun*) disturbance of equilibrium

مخروم *mak̲rūm* defective, incomplete (e.g., a manuscript)

مخرم *mukarram* perforated; done in openwork, in filigree

خرماشة *kurmāša* pl. *-āt* (*ir.*) harrow

خرمنجي (Turk.) *karmangī* pl. *-īya* (*eg.*) tobacco tester, tobacco blender

خرنوب *kurnūb* carob, locust; carob bean, locust pod, St.-John's-bread

خرنق *kirniq* pl. خرانق *karāniq*² young hare, leveret

خروع *kirwaʿ* castor-oil plant, palma Christi (Ricinus communis; *bot.*)

¹خز *kazza* *u* to pierce, transfix (ه s.o.); to stab (ه s.o., ب with) **VIII** to pierce, transfix (ه s.o., ب with)

²خز *kazz* pl. خزوز *kuzūz* silk, silk fabric

¹خزر *kazara* *u* to look askance (ه at s.o.), give s.o. (ه) a sidelong glance

²الخزر بحر *baḥr al-kazar* the Caspian Sea

خيزران *kaizurān* pl. خيازر *kayāzir*² cane, reed; rattan; bamboo

خيزرانة *kaizurāna* cane, stick

خزع *kazaʿa* *a* (*kazʿ*) to cut, sever (ه s.th.)

خزعبل *kuzaʿbal* idle talk, bosh

خزعبلة *kuzaʿbala* pl. *-āt* idle talk, bosh; joke, jest, hoax; fib, yarn; cock and bull story

خزف *kazaf* potter's earth, clay; pottery, earthenware; ceramics | خزف صينى (*ṣīnī*) porcelain

خزفى *kazafī* earthen, made of clay; made of porcelain; porcelaneous, porcelain, china (adj.); ceramic; pl. خزفيات ceramics | طين خزفى (*ṭīn*) argillaceous earth; porcelain clay, kaolin

خزاف *kazzāf* pottery and ceramics merchant; dealer in chinaware; potter

خزافة *kizāfa* potter's trade, pottery

¹خزق *kazaqa* *i* to pierce, stab, transfix (ه, ه s.o., s.th.); to drive, ram (ه فى الارض s.th. into the ground); to tear, rend, rip apart (ه s.th.) **II** to tear, rend, rip apart (ه s.th.) **V** and **VII** pass of **I** and **II**

خزق *kazq* rip, rent, tear, hole (in a garment)

خازوق *kāzūq* pl. خوازيق *kawāzīq*² post, stake, pole; dirty trick | هذا خازوق that's tough luck!

²خوزق look up alphabetically

خزل *kazala* *i* (*kazl*) to cut off, sever (ه s.th.); to hinder, prevent, hold back, restrain, keep (ه s.o., عن from) **VIII** to cut off, cut short, end abruptly (ه s.th.); to shorten, abridge, abbreviate (ه s.th.); to stand alone (ب with an opinion)

اختزال *iktizāl* abridgment, abbreviation; shorthand, stenography

مختزل *muktazil* stenographer

خزم *kazama* *i* (*kazm*) to string, thread (ه pearls) | خزم انفه (*anfahū*) to pierce the nasal septum (of a camel) and insert the nose ring for the bridle; to make s.o. subservient to one's will

خزام *kizām*, خزامة *kizāma* pl. خزائم *kazāʾim*² nose ring

خزامى *kuzāmā* lavender (*bot.*)

خزن *kazana* *u* (*kazn*) to store, stock, lay up, hoard, amass, accumulate; to contain, conceal (ه s.th., e.g., oil, minerals; of discovery sites); to keep secret, keep (ه a secret) **II** to store, stock, lay up, warehouse (ه s.th.); to hoard, accumulate (ه provisions); to keep, put in safekeeping (ه s.th., esp. valuables); to dam, dam up

(ه water in a basin or reservoir); to store up (ه energy, etc.; *phys., techn.*) VIII to store, stock, hoard, accumulate (ه s.th.); to keep, put in safekeeping (ه s.th.)

خزن *ḵazn* storing; accumulation, hoarding, amassing; storage, warehousing

خزنة *ḵazna* treasure house; safe, coffer, vault; wardrobe, locker; cupboard

خزانة *ḵizāna* pl. *-āt*, خزائن *ḵazā'in*² treasure house; money-box; vault, safe; treasury, treasury department (of an official agency), any office for the deposit and disbursement of funds; locker, wardrobe, closet; cupboard; library | خزانة الدولة *ḵ. ad-daula* and خزانة عامة (*'āmma*) public treasury, exchequer; خزانة الثلج *ḵ. aṯ-ṯalj* icebox, refrigerator; خزانة الكتب *ḵ. al-kutub* bookcase; library; خزانة خصوصية (*ḵuṣūṣīya*) private library; خزانة الملابس wardrobe, closet, locker

خزينة *ḵazīna* pl. خزائن *ḵazā'in*² treasure house; public treasury, exchequer; treasury, treasury department (of an official agency), any office for the deposit and disbursement of funds; cashier's office; vault, coffer, safe; cashbox, till (of a merchant) | الخزينة الخاصة (*ḵāṣṣa*) (formerly) the Royal Privy Purse (*Ir.*); خزينة الدولة *ḵ. ad-daula* public treasury, exchequer; خزينة نقود راصدة, خزينة راصدة cash register

خزان *ḵazzān* pl. *-āt*, خزازين *ḵazāzīn*² dam; reservoir; basin, sump, pool; storage tank (also for oil); — (pl. *-ūn*) storehouseman, warehouseman | خزان الوقود *ḵ. al-waqūd* gasoline tank (of an auto)

مخزن *maḵzan* pl. مخازن *maḵāzin*² storeroom, storehouse; depository; stockroom, storage room; depot, magazine, warehouse; store, shop, department store; المخزن *al-maḵzan* the Makhzan, the Moroccan government (formerly: governmental finance department; *Mor.*) | مخزن ادوية *m. adwiya* drugstore; مخزن الاصدار *m. al-iṣdār* shipping room (*com.*)

مخزني *maḵzanī* being under government control or administration, belonging to the government, administrative (*Mor.*) | املاك مخزنية (*amlāk*) government land (*Mor.*)

مخازني *maḵāzinī* pl. *-īya* native gendarme (*Mor.*)

مخازن *maḵāzin*²: مخازن الطريق *m. aṭ-ṭarīq* the nearest, shortest way, a short cut

مخزنجي *maḵzanjī* storehouseman, warehouseman

خزندار *ḵazandār*, *ḵaznadār* treasurer

تخزين *taḵzīn* storage (also *phys., techn.*); accumulation; damming; safekeeping | تخزين الطاقة energy storage (*phys., techn.*)

خازن *ḵāzin* pl. خزنة *ḵazana*, خزان *ḵuzzān* treasurer

مخزون *maḵzūn* stored, stored up, deposited, warehoused; in stock, in inventory (goods, materials); (pl. *-āt*) stock, store, supplies; reserves, deposits (of oil, in the ground, at a discovery site)

خزى *ḵaziya a* (*ḵizy*, *ḵazan*) to be or become base, vile, despicable, contemptible; (خزاية *ḵazāya*) to be ashamed (من of); — *ḵazā i* to disgrace, dishonor, discredit, put to shame (ه s.o.); to shame, abash, embarrass (ه s.o.) IV to humiliate, degrade, dishonor (ه s.o.); to shame, put to shame (ه s.o.) X to be ashamed

خزى *ḵizy*, *ḵazan* shame, disgrace, ignominy | يا للخزى! *yā la-l-ḵazā* what a shame!

خزيان *ḵazyān*², f. خزيا *ḵazyā*, pl. خزايا *ḵazāyā* ashamed, shamefaced, abashed; shameful, disgraceful, scandalous, infamous, base, mean, vile

مخزاة *makzāh* pl. مخاز *makāzin* a shameful thing, a disgrace; reason for shame; pl. shameful things, disgraceful acts, infamies

مخزى *makzīy* ashamed, shamefaced, abashed; embarrassed, confused; المخزى the Devil

مخز *mukzin* disgraceful, shameful, scandalous, infamous

مخزية *mukziya* pl. *-āt* disgraceful act, infamy

خس *kassa* (1st pers. perf. *kasistu*) *a* (خسة *kissa*, خساسة *kasāsa*) to be mean, base, vile; to become less, decrease, diminish, depreciate, fall in value; — *kassa u* to lessen, reduce, diminish (ه s.th.) **II** to lessen, reduce, diminish (ه s.th.)

خس *kass* lettuce (Lactuca sativa; *bot.*)

خسة *kassa* (n. un.) head of lettuce

خسة *kissa* and خساسة *kasāsa* meanness, baseness, vileness

خسيس *kasīs* pl. اخساء *akissā'*[2] mean, base, low, vile, despicable, contemptible, miserable

خسيسة *kasīsa* pl. خسائس *kasā'is*[2] mean trick, infamy

خسأ *kasa'a a* (*kas'*) to chase away (ه s.o.); — خسئ *kasi'a a* to be driven away, make off | خسئت *kasi'ta* beat it! scram! اخسأ اليك *iksa' ilaika* do.

اخسأ *aksa'*[2] baser, meaner, more despicable; weaker

خاسئ *kāsi'* spurned, rejected, outcast; low, base, vulgar, despicable, contemptible; disgraceful, shameful, scandalous, infamous; futile, vain (attempt); weak, feeble, languid

خستكة *kastaka* indisposition

مخستك *mukastak* indisposed, unwell, sickly

خسر *kasira a* (*kusr*, خسار *kasār*, خسارة *kasāra*, خسران *kusrān*) to incur a loss, suffer damage; to lose, forfeit (ه s.th.); to lose a match, lose (امام to a team); to go astray, lose one's way, get lost; to perish **II** to cause loss or damage (ه to s.o.); to do harm (ه to s.o.); to destroy, ruin (ه s.o.); to corrupt, deprave (ه s.o.) **IV** to cause a loss (ه to s.o.); to shorten, cut, reduce (ه s.th.) **X** to grudge (على or في s.o. ه s.th.), envy s.o. (على or في) the possession of (ه)

خسر *kusr* loss, damage

خسران *kusrān* loss, damage, forfeiture; decline, deterioration; depravity, profligacy

خسارة *kasāra* pl. خسائر *kasā'ir*[2] loss, damage; pl. losses, casualties (في in; *mil.*) | يا خسارة what a pity! too bad!

خسران *kasrān* (*eg.*) loser; affected by damage or loss

خاسر *kāsir* losing, loser (also in sports); lost, hopeless; involving substantial losses; depraved, corrupted; profligate, disreputable person, scoundrel

مخسر *mukassir* causing damage, harmful, noxious, injurious, detrimental

خسف *kasafa i* (*kasf*, خسوف *kusūf*) to sink, sink down, give way, cave in, disappear, go down; to be eclipsed (moon); — *i* (*kasf*) to cause to sink, cause to give way | خسف الله به الارض *k. llāhu bihī l-arḍa* God made him sink into the ground, God made the ground swallow him up **VII** to sink, sink down, go down

خسف *kasf* baseness, ignominy, disgrace, shame; inferiority | سام خسفا *sāma kasfan* to humiliate, abase, degrade (ه s.o.)

خسوف *ḵusūf* occultation (*astron.*); lunar eclipse

خش *ḵašša i u* (*ḵašš*) to enter (في s.th.)

خشاش *ḵišāš* vermin, insects

خشب II to lignify, become woody or woodlike; to line, face or case with wood, to panel, wainscot (ه s.th.) V to lignify, become woody or woodlike; to become hard, stiff, firm, rigid; to stiffen, freeze (e.g., with panic)

خشب *ḵašab* pl. اخشاب *aḵšāb* wood, lumber, timber | خشب الانبياء *ḵ. al-anbiyā'* guaiacum wood, lignum vitae

خشبة *ḵašaba* pl. *-āt*, اخشاب *aḵšāb* piece of wood; a timber; pale, post; plank, board | خشبة الميت *ḵ. al-mayyit* coffin; خشبة المسرح *ḵ. al-masraḥ* stage (of a theater), على خشبة المسرح on the "boards"

خشبي *ḵašabī* wooden, woody, ligneous, made of wood; timber-, lumber- (in compounds)

خشاب *ḵaššāb* pl. ة lumber merchant

تخشيب *taḵšīb* paneling, wainscoting

تخشيبة *taḵšība* pl. *-āt*, تخاشيب *taḵāšīb*² barrack, wooden shed

تخشب *taḵaššub* stiffness, rigor, rigidity; stiffening

متخشب *mutaḵaššib* frozen, rigid; stiff, hard, firm

خشت *ḵušt* pl. خشوت *ḵušūt* javelin

¹خشخاش *ḵašḵāš* (coll.; n. un. ة) pl. خشاخيش *ḵašāḵīš*² poppy

²خشخش *ḵašḵaša* to rattle, crackle; to clatter; to clink, chink; to rustle

خشخشة *ḵašḵaša* pl. *-āt* rattle; clatter; crackling noise; clink, chink; rustle

خشخيشة *ḵušḵēša* pl. خشاخيش *ḵašāḵīš*² (*eg.*) baby's rattle

خشارة *ḵušāra* leftover (of a meal); offal, refuse; a discard, a worthless thing

خشع *ḵaša'a a* (خشوع *ḵušū'*) to be submissive, be humble; to humble o.s.; to fade (voice) | خشع ببصره (*baṣarihī*) to lower one's eyes II to humble, reduce to submission (ه s.o.) V to display humility; to be humble; to be moved, be touched

خشوع *ḵušū'* submissiveness, submission, humility

خاشع *ḵāši'* pl. خشعة *ḵaša'a* submissive, humble

خشاف *ḵušāf* various fruits, stewed and soaked in sirup or rose water, compote

خشكار *ḵuškār* coarsely ground grain, grits

خشكريشة *ḵaškarīša* scab, slough, scurf

خشم II to intoxicate, make drunk (ه s.o.)

خشم *ḵašm* nose; mouth; vent, outlet

خيشوم *ḵaišūm* pl. خياشيم *ḵayāšīm*² nostril; gill; also pl. خياشيم nose

خشن *ḵašuna u* (خشونة *ḵušūna*) to be rough, coarse, crude; to be raw, uncut, unpolished II to roughen, coarsen, make crude (ه s.th.) III to be rude, uncivil, boorish (ه to s.o.) V to display rough, rude, or coarse, manners; to be rough, uneven; to lead a rough life XII اخشوشن *iḵšaušana* to be rough, coarse, crude; to lead a rough life; to harden or toughen oneself

خشن *ḵašin* pl. خشان *ḵišān* rough, crude; coarse (as opposed to ناعم *nā'im*); rude, unpolished, uncouth; tough, harsh (life); hoarse, raucous (voice) | خشن اللمس *ḵ. al-lams* coarse to the touch, rough, uneven, wrinkled; خشن الخلق *ḵ. al-ḵulq* uncouth, boorish; خشن القشرة *ḵ. al-qišra* thick-shelled; الجنس الخشن (*jins*) the strong sex

خشانة *ḵašāna* roughness; crudity; rudeness

اخشن *aḵšan*², f. خشناء *ḵašnā'*², pl. خشن *ḵušn* rough, tough, harsh, rude, uncouth

الخشناء *al-ḵašnā'* the vulgar, uneducated people

خشونة *ḵušūna* roughness, coarseness; crudeness; rudeness; tough way of life, life of hardship

خشى **ḵašiya** *a* (*ḵašy*, خشية *ḵašya*) to fear, dread (ه s.o., ه s.th., على for s.o. or s.th.), be afraid (ه of) **II** to frighten, scare, terrify, alarm (ه s.o.) **V** = **I**; **VIII** to be embarrassed; to be ashamed

خشية *ḵašya* fear, anxiety, apprehension | خشية من *ḵašyatan min* for fear of; خشية ان (*ḵašyata*) out of fear that . . .

اخشى *aḵšā* more timorous, more fearful; more to be feared, more frightening

مخشاة *maḵšāh* fear, anxiety, apprehension

خشيان *ḵašyān*², f. خشيا *ḵašyā*, pl. خشايا *ḵašāyā* timorous, timid, anxious, apprehensive

خاش *ḵāšin* timorous, timid, anxious, apprehensive

خص **ḵaṣṣa** *u* to distinguish, favor (especially, before others), single out (ه s.o.), bestow special honors (ه upon s.o., in preference to others); to endow (ب ه s.o. with), confer, bestow (ب ه upon s.o. s.th.); to apportion, allot, assign, accord, give, dedicate, devote (ب ه to s.o. s.th., in preference to others); with لنفسه: to take possession (ه of), demand (ه s.th.; also خص به نفسه *nafsahū*); to be specifically associated (ه with s.o.), be characteristic (ه of s.o.), be peculiar (ه to); to apply in particular (ه to), be especially valid (ه for); to concern, regard (ه s.o., ه s.th.), have special relevance (ه to), bear (ه on) | خصه بعنايته (*bi-'ināyatihī*) to devote one's attention to s.o., favor s.o. with one's attention; خصه بالذكر (*bi-ḏ-ḏikr*) to make special mention of s.o. or s.th.; واخص منهم (*aḵuṣṣu*) I mention, among them, especially (with foll. acc.); هذا لا يخصنى this does not concern me, this is none of my business **II** to specify, particularize, itemize (ه s.th.); to specialize (ه s.th.), narrow, restrict (ه ل s.th. to); to designate, destine, set aside, earmark, single out (ه ل or ه s.o. or s.th. for a purpose); to devote in particular, dedicate, assign (ه ل s.th. to); to allocate, allot, apportion (ه ل s.th. to); to appropriate (ه ل funds for); to reserve, hold, withhold (ه ل s.th. for); to tie down (ب ه s.o. to a special field) **V** to specialize (ل in, also ب or فى, in a scientific field); to devote all one's attention (ل to s.th.); to apply o.s. (ل to), go in for s.th. (ل); to be peculiar (ب to); to be chosen, destined, earmarked (ل for) **VIII** to distinguish, favor (ب ه s.o. with), confer distinction (ب ه upon s.o. by); to devote, give, accord, afford (ب ه to s.o. s.th., in preference to others); to dedicate (ب ه to s.o. s.th., e.g., one's services); (with لنفسه) to take exclusive possession (ه of), claim, demand (ه s.th.), lay special claim (ه to; also اختص به نفسه *nafsahū*); to be distinguished, be marked (ب by); to possess alone, in distinction from all others, have above others (ب s.th.), have the advantage over others (ب that); to be peculiar (ب to); to concern, regard (ب s.th.), bear (ب on); to be pertinent, have relevance (ب to), have to do (ب with); to be duly qualified, be competent, have jurisdiction (ب in; e.g., an authority); to have as a special function or task (ب s.th.)

خس *ḵass* lettuce (*bot.*)

خص *ḵuṣṣ* pl. خصاص *ḵiṣāṣ*, اخصاص *aḵṣāṣ*, خصوص *ḵuṣūṣ* hut, shack, shanty, hovel

خصة *ḵaṣṣa* jet of water

خصاص *ḵaṣāṣ* interstice, interval, crevice, crack, gap

خصاصة *ḵaṣāṣa* crevice, crack, interval, gap

خصيصة *ḵaṣīṣa* pl. خصائص *ḵaṣā'iṣ*[2] special characteristic or quality, specialty, particularity, peculiarity

خصيصا *ḵiṣṣīṣan* particularly, especially, specifically

خصوص *ḵuṣūṣ* specialness; خصوصا *ḵuṣūṣan* especially, in particular, specifically | من خصوص في خصوص, بخصوص and (with foll. genit.) as to, concerning, regarding, with respect to, as regards; من هذا الخصوص and بهذا الخصوص in this connection, in this matter, in this respect, about this, concerning this; على الخصوص and على وجه الخصوص (*wajhi l-ḵ.*) especially, particularly, in particular, specifically; خصوصا وأن *ḵuṣūṣan wa-anna* especially for the reason that

خصوصى *ḵuṣūṣī* special; private, personal; pl. خصوصيات private affairs

خصاصة *ḵaṣāṣa* poverty, penury, privation, destitution, want

اخص *aḵaṣṣ*[2] more special, more specific | على الاخص especially; فى الاخص do.; اخص الخاصة *a. al-ḵāṣṣa* the most select elite, the crème de la crème

اخصاء *aḵiṣṣā'*[2] intimate friends, confidants

اخصائى *aḵiṣṣā'ī* (widespread wrong pronun. instead of *iḵṣā'ī*, see [2]خصى) pl. *-ūn* specialist; expert (of a specialized field); اخصائية pl. *-āt* do. (fem.)

تخصيص *taḵṣīṣ* specialization; specification, particularization, itemization; designation, destination (for a purpose); allotment, apportionment, allocation; reservation; — (pl. *-āt*) appropriation, ration; financial allocation; credit | على تخصيص and على وجه التخصيص specifically

تخصص *taḵaṣṣuṣ* specialization (esp., in a scientific field)

تخصصى *taḵaṣṣuṣī* special, specialized, specialist (in compounds) | تدريب تخصصى special training

اختصاص *iḵtiṣāṣ* pl. *-āt* jurisdiction, competence; special province or domain, bailiwick (fig.); pl. اختصاصات special traits, characteristics, particularities or features; prerogatives, privileges, monopolies; concessions (*Intern. Law*) | ذو (ذات) الاختصاص duly qualified, authorized, responsible, competent; دائرة الاختصاص scope of competence, sphere of authority, jurisdiction, province, domain, field

اختصاصى *iḵtiṣāṣī* pl. *-ūn* specialist

خاص *ḵāṣṣ* special, particular; specific, peculiar; relative, relevant, pertinent (ب to), concerning (ب s.th.); earmarked, designated, destined, set aside (ب for); especially valid or true (ب for), especially applicable (ب to), characteristic (ب of); distinguished; private; exclusive, not public | جريدة خاصة ب professional journal for ...; الخاص والعام (*'āmm*) the special and the general; high and low, all people; راس مال خاص private capital; الطبيب الخاص physician in ordinary; علاقات خاصة (*'alāqāt*) private connections; تعليم خاص special instruction (for handicapped children); مدرسة خاصة (*madrasa*) special school (for the handicapped); private school

خاصة *ḵāṣṣa* pl. خواص *ḵawāṣṣ*[2] exclusive property; private possession; specialty, particularity, peculiarity, characteristic, property, attribute; essence, intrinsic nature; leading personalities, people of distinction, الخاصة the upper class, the educated, the elite; *ḵāṣṣatan* and بخاصة *bi-ḵāṣṣatin* especially, in particular | خاصة وأن *ḵāṣṣatan wa-anna* especially for the reason that; خاصة الخاصة the most select elite; فى خاصة انفسهم *fī ḵ. anfusihim* at the bottom of their hearts, deep inside

خاصية *ḵāṣṣīya* pl. *-āt*, خصائص *ḵaṣā'iṣ*² specialty, particularity, characteristic, peculiarity, property, special attribute, feature, trait, qualification; prerogative, privilege; jurisdiction, competence

خويصة *ḵuwaiṣṣa* (dimin. of خاصة *ḵāṣṣa*) one's own business, private affair | يدخل فى خويصة امرى he meddles in my private affairs

مخصوص *maḵṣūṣ* special | القسم المخصوص (*qism*) secret political police (*Eg.*)

مخصص *muḵaṣṣaṣ* chosen, set aside, earmarked, designated, destined (ل for); allotted, apportioned, allocated; — pl. مخصصات (financial) allocations; appropriations, credits; (daily) allowances; (food) rations | مخصصات اضافية (*iḍāfīya*) extra allowances; مخصصات الملك *m. al-malik* civil list

مختص *muḵtaṣṣ* pertaining, pertinent, relevant, relative (ب to); duly qualified, authorized, responsible, competent; special; pl. مختصات *muḵtaṣṣāt* competences | المقامات المختصة the competent authorities; الدوائر المختصة competent (or authoritative) quarters

خصب *ḵaṣaba i* and *ḵaṣiba a* (*ḵiṣb*) to be fertile (soil) **II** to make fertile (ه s.th.); to fructify, fertilize (ه s.th.) **IV** = **I**

خصب *ḵiṣb* fertility; abundance, plenty; superabundance, profusion

خصب *ḵaṣib* and خصيب *ḵaṣīb* fertile, productive, fat

خصوبة *ḵuṣūba* fertility

مخصاب *miḵṣāb* very fertile, productive

تخصيب *taḵṣīb* fructification, fertilization

اخصاب *iḵṣāb* fertility; fertilization

مخصب *muḵaṣṣib* pl. *-āt* fertilizer (*chem.*)

مخصب *muḵṣib* fertile, productive, fat

خصر *ḵaṣira a* (*ḵaṣar*) to become cold; to suffer from the cold **III** to clasp (ه s.o.) around the waist, put one's arm around s.o.'s (ه) waist **VI** to put the arms around each other's hips; to dance together (ه the dabka, see دبكة) **VIII** to shorten, condense, abridge, epitomize (ه s.th.); to summarize (ه s.th.)

خصر *ḵaṣr* pl. خصور *ḵuṣūr* hip, haunch, waist

مخصرة *miḵṣara* pl. مخاصر *maḵāṣir*² stick, baton, wand; mace, scepter

اختصار *iḵtiṣār* shortening, condensation, abridgment, summarization, epitomizing (of a statement); (pl. *-āt*) abbreviation; abridgment, shortened version or adaptation (of a book); brevity | بالاختصار and باختصار briefly, in short, in a few words

مختصر *muḵtaṣar* shortened, condensed, abridged; brief, short; concise, terse, succinct; — (pl. *-āt*) short excerpt, brief exposition, synopsis, outline, summary, abstract, epitome, compendium; abbreviation; abridgment, shortened version (of a book)

خاصرة *ḵāṣira* pl. خواصر *ḵawāṣir*² hip, haunch, waist | شوكة فى خاصرته (*šauka*) a thorn in his side

خصف *ḵaṣafa i* (*ḵaṣf*) to mend, repair, sew (ه a shoe)

خصفة *ḵaṣfa* pl. خصاف *ḵiṣāf* basket (made of palm leaves)

خصلة *ḵuṣla* pl. خصل *ḵuṣal*, *-āt* tuft; bunch, cluster; lock, wisp (of hair)

خصلة *kaṣla* pl. خصال *kiṣāl* quality, property, characteristic, peculiarity, trait; (natural) disposition

خصم *kaṣama* *i* to defeat (ه an opponent) in argument; to deduct, subtract (ه s.th., من from); to discount (ه a bill, a note) **III** to argue, quarrel, dispute (ه with s.o.); to bring legal action (ه against s.o.), sue (ه s.o.), litigate (ه with); **VI** to quarrel, argue, have a fight; to go to law, carry on a lawsuit, litigate (مع with s.o.) **VII** to be deducted, be subtracted **VIII** to quarrel, argue, have a fight; to be in conflict with one another (e.g., traits in a person)

خصم *kaṣm* pl. خصوم *kuṣūm*, اخصام *akṣām* adversary, antagonist, opponent; opposing party (in a lawsuit)

خصم *kaṣm* deduction; subtraction; rebate; discount; pl. خصوم *kuṣūm* liabilities (*fin.*) | سعر الخصم *si'r al-k.* discount rate, bank rate; خصم الكمبيالات *k. al-kambiyālāt* bill discount

خصيم *kaṣīm* pl. خصماء *kuṣamā'*[2], خصمان *kuṣmān* adversary, antagonist, opponent

خصومة *kuṣūma* quarrel, argument, dispute, controversy, feud; lawsuit

خصام *kiṣām* quarrel argument, dispute, controversy, feud; lawsuit

مخاصمة *mukāṣama* quarrel, argument, dispute, controversy, feud; lawsuit

اختصام *iktiṣām* contradiction, conflict

مخاصم *mukāṣim* adversary, opponent, opposing party (in a lawsuit); antagonist; litigant

[1]خصى *kaṣā* *i* (خصاء *kiṣā'*) to castrate, emasculate (ه s.o.)

خصي *kaṣīy* pl. خصيان *kiṣyān*, خصية *kiṣya* a castrate, eunuch; — castrated | ديك خصي (*dīk*) capon

خصية *kuṣya* pl. خصى *kuṣan* testicle

خصاء *kiṣā'* castration

مخصي *mukṣīy* castrated, emasculated | فرس مخصي (*faras*) gelding

[2]اخصائي *ikṣā'ī* pl. *-ūn* specialist; expert (of a specialized field); اخصائية pl. *-āt* do. (fem.)

خض *kaḍḍa* (*kaḍḍ*) to jolt, jog (ه s.th.); to shake (ه s.th.); to frighten, scare (ه s.o.)

لبن خض *laban kaḍḍ* buttermilk

خضة *kaḍḍa* concussion, shock, jolt; fright, scare; psychic shock

خضب *kaḍaba* *i* (*kaḍb*) to dye, color, tinge (ه s.th.); — *kaḍaba* *i* and *kaḍiba* *a* (خضوب *kuḍūb*) to be or become green (plant) **II** to color, tinge (ه s.th.); to dye (ه s.th) **XII** اخضوضب *ikḍauḍaba* to be or become green (plant)

○ خضب *kaḍb* chlorophyll (*biol.*)

خضاب *kiḍāb* dye, dyestuff | ○ خضاب الدم *k. ad-dam* hemoglobin (*biol.*)

خضوب *kuḍūb* green, greenness, green color

خضيب *kaḍīb* dyed

مخضب *mukaḍḍab*: مخضب بالدماء (*dimā'*) smeared with blood

خضخض *kaḍkaḍa* (خضخضة *kaḍkaḍa*) to set in motion, upset, rock, shake (ه s.th.) **II** to be jolted, be rocked, be shaken

خضخضة *kaḍkaḍa* concussion, shock, jolt

خضد *kaḍada* *i* (*kaḍd*) to cut off, break off (ه thorns) | خضد شوكته (*šaukatahū*) to tame s.o., hold s.o. in check, curb s.o.'s power

خضر *kaḍira* *a* (*kaḍar*) to be green **II** to make green, dye or color green (ه s.th.) | خضر الارض (*arḍ*) to sow the land, till the earth

IX to be or become green XII اخضوضر *ikḍauḍara* = IX

خضر *kaḍir* green, verdant; verdure, greenery; young green crop (of grain)

الخضر *al-kaḍir, al-kiḍr* a well-known legendary figure

خضرة *kuḍra* green, greenness, green color; — (pl. خضر *kuḍar*) vegetation, verdure, greenery, greens; meadow; خضر vegetables

خضرى *kuḍarī* greengrocer

خضار *kaḍār* green, greenness, green color; greens, herbs, potherbs

خضير *kaḍīr* green

خضارة *kuḍāra* greens, herbs, potherbs

خضار *kaḍḍār* greengrocer

اخضر *akḍar*[2], f. خضراء *kaḍrā'*[2], pl. خضر *kuḍr* green | اتى على الاخضر واليابس (*atā*) to destroy everything, wreak havoc

الخضراء *al-kaḍrā'* "the Verdant" (epithet of Tunis); the sky

خضراوات *kaḍrāwāt* vegetables; greens, herbs, potherbs

الخضيراء *al-kuḍairā'* Paradise

O يخضور *yakḍūr* chlorophyll (*biol.*)

مخضرة *makḍara* meadow, lawn, turf, sod, greens, verdant land

مخضرات *mukaḍḍarāt* vegetables

خضرم *kiḍrim* pl. خضارم *kaḍārim*[2] abundant, copious; well-watered, abounding in water; openhanded, generous, liberal, munificent

مخضرم *mukaḍram* designation of such contemporaries of Mohammed, esp. of poets, whose life span bridges the time of paganism and that of Islam; an old man who has lived through several generations or historical epochs

خضع *kaḍa'a a* (خضوع *kuḍū'*) to bow, defer, submit, yield, surrender (ل to s.o., to s.th.), humble o.s. (ل before), obey, follow (ل s.o. or s.th.); to be subject (ل e.g., to a law, to a power, to a test, a modification or improvement, etc.); to be under s.o.'s (ل or ال) control II and IV to humble, subjugate, subdue, make tractable (ه s.o.); to submit, subject, expose (ل ه or ه s.th. or s.o. to s.th.) VIII = *kaḍa'a*

خضوع *kuḍū'* submission, obedience, humility, subjection

خضوع *kaḍū'* pl. خضع *kuḍu'* submissive, humble

اخضاع *ikḍā'* subjugation, subdual; subjection

خاضع *kāḍi'* pl. خضع *kuḍḍa'*, خضعان *kuḍ'ān, kiḍ'ān* submissive, humble; obedient, pliant, tractable; subject, liable, prone (ل to s.th.)

خضل *kaḍila a* to be or become moist II and IV to moisten, wet (ه s.th.) IX = I

خضل *kaḍil* moist, wet; juicy, succulent; refreshing, gay, lighthearted

خضم *kaḍama i* (*kaḍm*) to munch (ه s.th., with a full mouth), bite (ه into s.th.)

خضم *kiḍamm* vast (said of the sea); sea, ocean

خط *kaṭṭa u* (*kaṭṭ*) to draw or trace a line (على on); to draw, trace, sketch, design (ه s.th.); to write, pen (ه s.th.); to carve, engrave, inscribe (ه s.th.); to outline, mark, trace out, prescribe (ه ل for s.o. s.th.) | خط خطا (سطرا) (*kaṭṭan, saṭran*) to draw a line; خطه الشيب (*šaibu*) his hair turned gray II to draw lines; to rule (ه s.th.); to furrow, ridge (ه s.th.); to mark with lines or stripes, stripe, streak (ه s.th.); to pencil (ه the eyebrows); to mark, designate, earmark, indicate (ه s.th.); to demarcate, delimit, delineate, stake out, survey (ه land, real estate); to lay out, map out (ه roads); to make or work out plans (ل for a project) **VIII** to trace out, mark, outline, prescribe (ه a way); to mark, demarcate, delimit, stake out, delineate (ه s.th.); to map out, plan, project (ه e.g., the construction of a city); to make, design, devise (ه a plan); to plan (ه s.th.), make plans (ه for)

خط *ḵaṭṭ* pl. خطوط *ḵuṭūṭ* line; stroke; stripe, streak; (railroad) line, line of communication; telephone line; frontline (*mil.*); furrow, ridge; handwriting; writing, script; calligraphy, penmanship | ○ خط ارضى (*arḍī*) ground wire (radio); الخط الاسفينى (*isfīnī*) cuneiform writing; الخطوط الامامية (*amāmīya*) the foremost lines, battle lines (*mil.*); خط بارز (*bāriz*) relievo script; خط تليفونى and خط هاتفى (*hātifī*) telephone line; خط (تليفونى) ساخن hot-line, direct telephonic connection; خط تجميع assembly line; خطوط جوية (*jawwīya*) airlines; خط حديدى (*ḥadīdī*) and خط سكة الحديد *ḵ. sikkat al-ḥadīd* railroad line, railroad track; خط تحويل transfer line (oil); خط الزوال *ḵ. az-zawāl* meridian (*astron.*; = خط نصف النهار *ḵ. niṣf an-nahār*); الخط المسمارى (*mismārī*) cuneiform writing; خط الاستواء *ḵ. al-istiwā'* equator; خط الطول *ḵ. aṭ-ṭūl* or خط طولى (*ṭūlī*) circle of longitude, meridian (*geogr.*); خط العرض *ḵ. al-ʿarḍ* or خط عرضى (*ʿarḍī*) parallel (of latitude) (*geogr.*); الخطوط العريضة broad outlines; وضع الخطوط العريضة ل (*waḍaʿa*) to outline (ه s.th.) in the broadest terms; خط تقسيم المياه *ḵ. taqsīm al-miyāh* divide, watershed; خط القوة الكهربائية *ḵ. al-quwwa al-kahrabāʾīya* power line; خط الموت *ḵ. al-maut* death strip, no man's land; خط مموج (*mumawwaj*) wavy line; خطوط الانابيب pipelines; خطوط النار lines of fire (war); خط الهاجرة meridian (*geogr.*); خط الهدنة *ḵ. al-hudna* armistice line; فن الخط *fann al-ḵ.* calligraphy; خرج عن الخط to derail, run off the rails (train); على خط مستقيم (*mustaqīm*) straightaway, in a straight line; outright, out and out; على طول الخط (*ṭūl al-ḵ.*) all along the line; بخط اليد (*ḵ. al-yad*) handwritten

خط *ḵuṭṭ* pl. اخطاط *aḵṭāṭ* section, district, quarter (of a city)

خطى *ḵaṭṭī* handwritten; linear; spear

خطة *ḵiṭṭa* pl. خطط *ḵiṭaṭ* a piece of land acquired for the purpose of building a house; a piece of real estate, lot; district; map or plan of a piece of real estate, layout; — *ḵuṭṭa* pl. *ḵuṭaṭ*, also pronounced *ḵiṭṭa*, plan, project; line of action, course, guiding principle; office, function, post, position | خطة العمل *ḵ. al-ʿamal* operation plan, work plan; خطة الانتاج *ḵ. al-intāj* production plan; خطة المسرح *ḵ. al-masraḥ* repertoire, program (*theat.*); طبقا لخطة مرسومة (*ṭibqan*) according to schedule, as scheduled or planned

خطاط *ḵaṭṭāṭ* pl. *-ūn* penman, calligrapher; — tracing lines, leaving a straight trace | فشك خطاط (*fašak*) or قذيفة خطاطة tracer bullet, tracer (*mil.*)

تخطيط *taḵṭīṭ* pl. *-āt* ruling, drawing of, or marking with, lines; lineation; designation, marking, earmarking; surveying, survey (of land); planning; projecting, mapping out, laying out (of cities, of roads); plan, design | تخطيط صحى (*ṣiḥḥī*) health planning; تخطيط المدن *t. al-mudun* city planning

تخطيطى *taḵṭīṭī* planning (in compounds); concerning the ground plan | رسم تخطيطى (*rasm*) ground plan, construction drawing, design

مخطوط *maḵṭūṭ* handwritten; manuscript

مخطوطة *maḵṭūṭa* pl. *-āt* manuscript

مخطط *muḵaṭṭaṭ* striped, streaked, ruled; furrowed; designated, marked, earmarked; planned, guided, controlled; (pl. *-āt*) sketch, design, plan, layout; map (of a city)

خطئ *kaṭi'a a* (خطأ *kaṭa'*) to be mistaken; to commit an error, make a mistake; to sin **II** to charge with an offense, incriminate, declare guilty (ه s.o.); to accuse (ه s.o.) of an error or mistake; to fine (ه s.o.; *tun.*) **IV** to be mistaken, to err, commit an error, be at fault (فى in); to be wrong (فى about, in); to make a mistake (فى in, with); to miss (ه s.o., e.g., a shot; ه the target); to escape (ه s.o. or s.o.'s notice; a fact) | اخطأ فأله (*fa'luhū*) (his omen was wrong, i.e.) his expectations do not come true, are not fulfilled; that's where he is wrong, that's where he made a mistake! اخطأه الشىء (*šai'u*) (lit.: the thing escaped him, missed him, i.e.) he lacked it; اخطأه التوفيق he failed, was unsuccessful; اخطأ فى استنتاجاته he drew the wrong conclusions; اخطأ بين الشيئين he confused the two things, he mistook one thing for the other

خطء *kiṭ'* slip, lapse, fault, offense, sin

خطأ *kaṭa'* and خطاء *kaṭā'* error; mistake, incorrectness; offense, fault; *kaṭa'an* erroneously, by mistake | من الخطأ ان ... it is (would be) wrong to ...; اصلاح الخطأ *iṣlāḥ al-k.* corrigenda, errata, list of corrections; قتل الخطأ *qatl al-k.* accidental homicide (*jur.*); خطأ مطبعى (*maṭba'ī*) misprint

خطيئة *kaṭī'a* pl. *-āt*, خطايا *kaṭāyā* mistake, blunder; slip, lapse; fault, offense; crime, sin; fine (*tun.*)

خاطئ *kāṭi'* wrong, incorrect, erroneous; mistaken, at fault; (pl. خطاة *kuṭāh*, actually, pl. of colloq. *kāṭī*), f. خاطئة *kāṭi'a* pl. خواطئ *kawāṭi'*[2] sinner

مخطئ *mukṭi'* mistaken, at fault, wrong; incorrect, wrong, erroneous

خطب *kaṭaba u* (خطبة *kuṭba*, خطابة *kaṭāba*) to deliver a public address, make a speech; to preach, deliver a sermon (فى الناس and الناس *an-nāsa* to the people); — (*kaṭb*, خطبة *kiṭba*) to propose (ها to a girl; said of the man), ask for a girl's hand (ها) in marriage (ل on behalf of s.o.; said of the matchmaker); to give in marriage, betroth, affiance, engage (بنته ل or على one's daughter to s.o.) | خطب ودها (*wuddahā*) and خطب مودتها (*mawaddatahā*) he courted her love **III** to address (ه s.o.), speak, talk, direct one's words (ه to s.o.), turn (ه to s.o., orally or in writing) | خاطبه بالتليفون to telephone s.o., call s.o. up; خاطبه بالكاف (*bi-l-kāf*) to address s.o. on an intimate first-name basis **VI** to talk to one another; to converse, confer, have a talk, carry on a conversation; to write each other, correspond, carry on a correspondence **VIII** to seek a girl's (ها) hand in marriage, ask for a girl's hand

خطب *kaṭb* pl. خطوب *kuṭūb* matter, affair, concern, business; situation, conditions, circumstances; misadventure, mishap; calamity | ما خطبك what's happened to you? what's the trouble? what's the matter with you? ما خطبه فى what concern of his is ...? what has he to do with ...? ما خطب ذلك what's it all about?

خطبة *kiṭba* courtship; betrothal, engagement

خطبة *kuṭba* pl. خطب *kuṭab* public address; speech; lecture, discourse; oration; sermon, specif., Muslim Friday sermon, khutbah | خطبة الافتتاح opening address

خطاب *kiṭāb* pl. *-āt*, اخطبة *akṭiba* public address, speech; oration; letter, note, message | خطاب ترحيب welcoming address; خطاب العرش *k. al-'arš* speech from the throne; خطاب مستعجل (*musta'jil*) express letter, special-delivery letter; خطاب تقدمة *k. taqdima* letter of introduction; ○ خطابات ذات القيمة المقررة (*ḏāt al-qīma al-muqarrara*)

(= lettres avec valeur déclarée) registered, insured letters (*eg.*); فصل الخطاب *faṣl al-ḵ.* (in letters:) conclusion of the formal greetings by the words اما بعد *ammā baʿdu*; conclusion, termination, end; decision; unmistakable judgment; بينى وبينك فصل الخطاب we're through with one another once and for all

خطابى *ḵiṭābī* oratorical, rhetorical; speech-, lecturing (in compounds)

خطيب *ḵaṭīb* pl. خطباء *ḵuṭabāʾ*[2] (public) speaker; orator; lecturer; preacher, khatib; suitor (for the hand of a girl); fiancé

خطيبة *ḵaṭība* fiancée

خطابة *ḵaṭāba* preaching, sermonizing, oratory

خطابة *ḵiṭāba* rhetoric, oratory; art of eloquence; speech, lecture, discourse

خطوبة *ḵuṭūba* courtship; betrothal, engagement

مخاطبة *muḵāṭaba* pl. *-āt* address; public address, speech; proclamation; conversation, talk; conference, parley | مخاطبة تليفونية telephone conversation, telephone call

تخاطب *taḵāṭub* conversation; talk, discussion; (inter)communication (also, e.g., telephonic, by radio, etc.) | لغة التخاطب *luḡat at-t.* colloquial language

خاطب *ḵāṭib* pl. خطباء *ḵuṭabāʾ*[2], خطاب *ḵuṭṭāb* suitor; matchmaker; engaged, betrothed; fiancé

خاطبة *ḵāṭiba* pl. خطاب *ḵuṭṭāb* woman matchmaker

مخطوبة *maḵṭūba* fiancée

مخاطب *muḵāṭib* interlocutor, conversation partner

مخاطب *muḵāṭab* addressed, spoken to; (*gram.*) second person

اخطبوط look up alphabetically

خطر *ḵaṭara i* (خطران *ḵaṭarān*) to swing, wave, brandish (ب s.th.); to shake, tremble, vibrate; to walk with a (proud) swinging gait; to stride with a graceful gait; — *i u* (خطور *ḵuṭūr*) to occur (ل to s.o.), come to s.o.'s (ل) mind | خطر الامر على باله (*bālihī*) the matter came to his mind, occurred to him, he recalled the matter (also فى باله and ببال or على قلبه); خطر له خاطر he had an idea; امر لم يخطر ببال (*lam yaḵṭir bi-bālin*) an unexpected matter, s.th. one wouldn't dream of; — *ḵaṭura u* (خطورة *ḵuṭūra*) to be weighty; to be important, significant; to be grave, serious, momentous, dangerous, perilous, risky, hazardous **III** to risk, hazard, stake (ب s.th., بنفسه one's life); to incur the danger, run the risk (ب of), risk (ب s.th.); to bet, wager (ه s.o., على a stake) **IV** to notify, inform (ه s.o.), let (ه s.o.) know (ب about s.th.); to warn, caution (ه s.o.) **V** to walk with a lofty, proud gait; to stride, strut (with a swinging gait); to pendulate, oscillate, vibrate **VI** to make a bet (على against a stake)

خطر *ḵaṭar* weightiness, momentousness; importance, consequence, significance; seriousness, gravity; — (pl. *-āt*, اخطار *aḵṭār*) danger, peril, menace (على to); riskiness, dangerousness; risk; hazard; (pl. خطار *ḵiṭār*) stake, bet, wager | جليل الخطر of very great importance, momentous; ذو خطر important, weighty, to be taken seriously; dangerous, perilous; معرض للخطر (*muʿarraḍ*) endangered, jeopardized; اشارة الخطر *išārat al-ḵ.* alarm signal; warning sign

خطر *ḵaṭir* dangerous, perilous, risky, hazardous; serious, grave, weighty, important, significant

خطرة *ḵaṭra* pl. *ḵaṭarāt* pompous walk, strut; swinging gait; idea, thought, notion

خطار *ḵaṭṭār* pendulum (*phys.*)

خطير *ḵaṭīr* pl. خطر *ḵuṭr* weighty, momentous; important, significant; grave, serious; dangerous | خطير الشأن of great importance

خطورة *ḵuṭūra* weight(iness), importance, moment(ousness); consequence, significance; gravity, seriousness; danger; dangerousness

خطران *ḵaṭarān* swinging, oscillation, vibration

اخطر *aḵṭar*[2] more dangerous, riskier; weightier, of greater consequence; more serious, graver

مخطرة look up alphabetically

مخاطر *maḵāṭir*[2] dangers, perils

مخاطرة *muḵāṭara* pl. *-āt* venture, risk, hazard

اخطار *iḵṭār* notification, information; warning

خاطر *ḵāṭir* pl. خواطر *ḵawāṭir*[2] idea, thought, notion; mind; desire; pl. ideas, aphorisms | لاجل خاطرك (*li-ajli*) for your sake; من كل خاطر *min kulli ḵāṭirin* with all one's heart, most gladly; عن طيبة خاطر *ʿan ṭībati ḵāṭirin* gladly, with pleasure; of one's own free will, voluntarily; على خاطرك as you like; من خاطره of one's own accord, voluntarily; اخذ بخاطره to afford satisfaction to s.o., to comfort, reassure s.o.; اخذ على خاطره من to feel offended by, take offense at; راعى خاطره (*rāʿā*) to have regard for s.o.'s feelings, respect s.o.'s wishes; صدع خاطره *ṣaddaʿa ḵāṭirahū* to trouble, bother s.o.; طمن الخواطر (*ṭammana*) to calm the excitement; مر بخاطره ان (*marra*) the thought crossed his mind that ...; اكراما لخاطرك (*ikrāman*) for your sake, to please you; سرعة الخاطر *surʿat al-ḵ.* presence of mind; سريع الخاطر quick-witted

مخاطر *muḵāṭir* one who risks s.th., who takes a chance; daring, bold, venturesome; (pl. *-ūn*) adventurer

مخطر *muḵṭir* dangerous, perilous, risky, hazardous

خطرف *ḵaṭrafa* (*eg.*) to be delirious, to rave, talk irrationally

خطرفة *ḵaṭrafa* delirium, raving

خطف *ḵaṭifa a*, *ḵaṭafa i* (*ḵaṭf*) to snatch, wrench or wrest away, seize, grab (ه s.th.); to make off (ه with s.th.); to abduct, kidnap (ه s.o.); to dazzle (البصر *al-baṣara* the eyes) **V** to grab, seize, snatch away (ه s.th.); to carry away, sweep away (ه s.o.) **VI** to snatch or seize (ه s.th.) from one another **VII** to be snatched away, be wrested away; to be carried away, be swept away **VIII** to grab, seize, take forcibly (ه s.th.); to snatch, wrest, wrench (ه من s.th. from s.o.); to abduct, kidnap (ه s.o.); to hijack (ه an airplane); to run away, elope (ها with a woman); to make off (ه with s.th.); to dazzle (البصر *al-baṣara* the eyes) | اختطف الكلام (*kalāma*) to talk rapidly and breathlessly, half swallowing one's words

خطف *ḵaṭf* grabbing, forcible seizure, rape; abduction, kidnaping; خطفا *ḵaṭfan* rapidly, quickly; by force

خطفة *ḵaṭfa* pl. *ḵaṭafāt* (n. vic.) a snatching away, a grab; sudden stirring, flash | فى خطفة البرق (*barq*) instantly, in a trice, like a streak of lightning; خطفة من خطفات الشعور an impulse, a sudden emotion

خطاف *ḵaṭṭāf* rapacious; robber

خطاف *ḵuṭṭāf* pl. خطاطيف *ḵaṭāṭīf*[2] (iron) hook; fishhook; (coll.; n. un. ة) swift, a variety of swallow

خطيف *ḵaṭṭīf* pl. خطاطيف *ḵaṭāṭīf*[2] iron hook

اختطاف iḵtiṭāf grabbing, forcible seizure, rape; abduction, kidnaping; hijacking (e.g., of an airplane)

خاطف ḵāṭif pl. خواطف ḵawāṭif[2] ravenous; rapacious; rapid, prompt; quick, sudden; lightninglike; fleeting; short, brief | ذئاب خاطفة ravenous wolves; صورة خاطفة (ṣūra) snapshot; حرب خاطفة (ḥarb) blitzkrieg; لحظة خاطفة (laḥẓa) a fleeting glance

مخطوف maḵṭūf: ○ حركة مخطوفة (ḥaraka) anaptyctic vowel (phon.)

مختطف muḵtaṭif pl. -ūn abductor, kidnapper

خطل ḵaṭila a (ḵaṭal) to talk nonsense **IV** do. **V** to strut, walk with a pompous gait; to walk with a proud, swinging gait

خطل ḵaṭal idle talk, prattle

خطل ḵaṭil garrulous, chattering, given to silly talk; stupid, foolish

خطم ḵaṭm nose, snout, muzzle (of an animal); front part (nose and mouth); foremost or first part; important matter | اطل بخطمه (aṭalla) approx.: to manifest its force, set in (e.g., of a disaster)

خطمى ḵiṭmī, ḵaṭmī (coll.; n. un. ة) marsh mallow (Althaea officinalis; bot.)

خطام ḵiṭām pl. خطم ḵuṭum noseband, halter (of a camel)

خطا (خطو) ḵaṭā u (ḵaṭw) to step, pace, walk; to proceed, advance, progress | خطا خطوات واسعة (ḵaṭawātin) to take large strides, also fig. = to make extraordinary progress **II** and **V** to overstep, transgress (ه s.th.); to cross (ه s.th.), go or walk through s.th. (ه); to ford (ه a river); to leave its banks, overflow (river); to cross, traverse (البحار the seas); to omit, disregard, ignore, pass by (ه s o.); to go beyond s.th. (ه); to extend (الى to); to exceed, transcend (ه s.th.); to excel, surpass, outstrip, outdo (ه s.o.); to proceed, pass (ه through s.th., الى to), leave s.th. (ه) behind and turn to s.th. else (الى); to disregard (ه, ه s.o., s.th.) in order to turn one's attention to (الى) | تخطى به الى الامام (ilā l-amāmi) to promote, advance s.th. **VIII** to step, pace, walk; to proceed, advance, progress

خطو ḵaṭw gait, manner of walking

خطوة ḵaṭwa pl. ḵaṭawāt and ḵuṭwa pl. ḵuṭwāt, ḵuṭuwāt, خطى ḵuṭan step, pace, stride | سار فى خطاه (ḵuṭāhu) to walk, or follow, in s.o.'s footsteps; تقدم خطوة فخطوة taqaddama ḵuṭwatan fa-ḵuṭwatan to proceed or advance step by step; اتخذ خطوة حاسمة (ittaḵada) to take a decisive step; خطوتان وقفزة ḵaṭwatān wa-qafza hop, skip and jump (athlet.); خطوة الاوزة ḵ. al-iwazza single or Indian file; خطوة تبديل change of step (while marching); سريع الخطى s. al-ḵuṭā walking rapidly, taking long strides

خطية ḵaṭīya (= خطيئة) slip, lapse, transgression, fault, offense, sin

خطاة ḵuṭāh pl. of خاطئ ḵāṭi' sinner

خف ḵaffa i to be light (of weight); to be slight, insignificant; to become lighter, decrease in weight, lose weight; to abate, reduce, become less (عن in its effect on s.o. or s.th., of a pressure or a force); to decrease in intensity, grow lighter (color); to become lower (noise); to be nimble, agile, quick; to hasten, hurry, rush (الى to) **II** to make lighter (ه s.th.), reduce the weight of (ه); to ease, lighten, relieve, soften (ه عن for s.o. s.th. difficult or oppressive, also ه على; من s.th., e.g., s.o.'s situation); to lessen, decrease, reduce, diminish (ه or من s.th.); to mitigate, alleviate, moderate, temper (ه or من s.th.); to thin, dilute (ه e.g., a liquid); (gram.) to pronounce (ه a consonant) without taš-

dīd | خفف عنك *kaffif ʿanka!* cheer up! take it easy! خفف من سرعتك *kaffif min surʿatika!* slow down! خفف الآلام عنه to soothe s.o.'s pains **V** to dress lightly; to disburden, relieve o.s. (of a burden); to rid o.s., free o.s. (من of s.th.); to hurry away (عن from), leave (عن s.th.) in a hurry **X** to deem (ه s.th.) light; to value lightly, disdain, scorn, despise (ب s.o. or s.th.), look down (ب upon), think nothing (ب of), make light (ب of), set little store (ب by); not to take seriously (ب s.th.), attach no importance (ب to); to carry away, transport (ه or ب s.o., e.g., joy) | استخفه الطرب (*ṭarab*) he was beside himself with joy; استخفت به الحماسة (*ḥamāsa*) he got carried away by enthusiasm

خف *kuff* pl. خفاف *kifāf*, اخفاف *akfāf* a pair of shoes, slippers (of light leather, without heels); — (pl. اخفاف *akfāf*) camel hoof; foot (of the ostrich); sole (of the foot) | رجع بخفى حنين *rajaʿa bi-kuffai ḥunain* to return with empty hands, without having achieved one's mission; to accomplish nothing, fail, be unsuccessful

خفة *kiffa* lightless (of weight); slightness, insignificance, triviality; sprightliness, buoyancy; agility, nimbleness; inconstancy, fickleness, flightiness, levity, frivolity; high spirits | خفة الحركة *k. al-ḥaraka*, خفة فى الحركة nimbleness, agility, quickness; خفة الدم *k. ad-dam* amiability, charm; خفة الروح *k. ar-rūḥ* do.; خفة الظل *k. az-zill* amiability, friendliness; خفة العقل *k. al-ʿaql* lightheadedness; خفة اليد *k. al-yad* manual skill, dexterity, deftness

اخف *akaff*[2] lighter; lesser, slighter; weaker | اخف الضررين *a. aḍ-ḍararain* the lesser of two evils

خفاف *kafāf*, حجر الخفاف *ḥajar al-k.* pumice, pumice stone

خفان *kuffān* pumice, pumice stone

خفيف *kafīf* pl. خفاف *kifāf*, اخفاف *akfāf*, اخفاء *akiffāʾ*[2] light (of weight); slight, little, trivial, insignificant; thin, scanty, sparse; nimble, agile, sprightly, lively; — الخفيف name of a poetic meter | رياح خفيفة (*riyāḥ*) light winds; خفيف الحركة *k. al-ḥaraka* easily movable, very mobile; nimble, agile; خفيف الدم *k. ad-dam* amiable, charming; خفيف الروح *k. ar-rūḥ* likable, charming, winning, amiable; vivacious, merry, cheerful; خفيف الظل *k. az-zill* likable, nice (person); خفيف العارضين *k. al-ʿāriḍain* having a thin beard; خفيف العقل *k. al-ʿaql* feeble-minded, dimwitted; خفيف اليد *k. al-yad* nimble-fingered, deft; شاى خفيف weak tea

تخفيف *takfīf* lightening, easing; lessening, decrease, diminution; reduction; allaying, mitigation, alleviation, palliation, moderation; commutation (*jur.*); relief; thinning, dilution (e.g., of a liquid) | ظروف التخفيف extenuating circumstances (*jur.*); تخفيف حدة التوتر *t. ḥiddat at-tawattur* détente, easing of tension (*pol.*)

استخفاف *istikfāf* disdain, scorn, contempt; levity, frivolity

ظروف مخففة *ẓurūf mukaffifa* extenuating circumstances (*jur.*)

مخفف *mukaffaf* thin, diluted; pronounced without doubling (*gram.*)

خفت *kafata u* (خفوت *kufūt*) to become inaudible, die down, die away (sound, voice); to become silent, become still; to become faint, dim, soft (light, color) **III** خافت بكلامه, بصوته (*bi-kalāmihī, bi-ṣautihī*) to lower one's voice **IV** to silence, reduce to silence (ه s.o.) **VIII** = **I**

خفوت *kufūt* fading (*radio*)

خافت *kāfit* dying away, dying down, becoming silent; inaudible; faint, dying, fading, trailing off (sound, voice); soft, subdued (light, color)

مختفت *muktafit* soft, low, subdued

خفر *kafara u* (*kafr*, خفارة *kifāra*) to watch (ه, ه s.o., s.th. or over s.o., over s.th.), guard, protect (ه s.o., ه s.th.); — *kafira a* (*kafar*, خفارة *kafāra*) to be timid, shy, bashful II = I *kafara* V = I *kafira*

خفر *kafr* watching, watch, guard(ing)

خفر *kafar* guard detachment, guard; escort | خفر السواحل coast guard (*Eg.*)

خفر *kafar* timidity, shyness, bashfulness, diffidence

خفر *kafir* bashful, diffident, timid, shy, embarrassed, coy

خفير *kafīr* pl. خفراء *kufarā'*[2] watchman; protector, guardian; guard, sentry, sentinel

خفارة *kifāra* watch(ing), guard(ing), protection; guard duty

مخفر *makfar* pl. مخافر *makāfir*[2] guardhouse, guardroom; guard, control post | مخفر الشرطة *m. aš-šurṭa* police station

خافرة *kāfira*: خافرة السواحل *k. as-sawāḥil* coastguard cruiser (*Eg.*)

مخفور *makfūr* under escort, escorted; covered, sheltered, protected

خفس *kafasa u* (*kafs*) to ridicule, scorn (ه s.o.), laugh, mock (ه at); to destroy, demolish, tear down (ه a house)

خفش *kafaš* day blindness, hemeralopia

اخفش *akfaš*[2], f. خفشاء *kafšā'*[2], pl. خفش *kufš* day blind, hemeralopic; weak-sighted, afflicted with defective vision

خفاش *kuffāš* pl. خفافيش *kafāfīš*[2] bat (*zool.*)

خفض *kafaḍa i* (*kafḍ*) to make lower (ه s.th.); to lower, decrease, reduce, lessen, diminish (ه s.th.); to lower, drop (ه, من s.th., also, e.g., the voice); (*gram.*) to pronounce the final consonant of a word with *i*; to put (ه a word) in the genitive | خفض جناحه ل (*janāḥahū*) to unbend toward s.o., show o.s. open-minded, responsive, accessible to; — *kafuḍa u* to be carefree, easy, comfortable (life); to sink, dip, drop, settle, subside; to become low, drop to an undertone (voice) II to lower, decrease, reduce (ه s.th., price); to diminish, lessen (ه s.th.); to dim (ه the light); to devaluate (ه, e.g., قيمة الدولار *qīmat ad-dōlār* the dollar) | خفض عليك *kaffiḍ ʿalaika* take it easy! خفض عليك جأشك (*ja'šaka*) cool off! calm down! relax! خفض السرعة (*surʿa*) to reduce one's speed, slow down; خفض صوته (*ṣautahū*) he lowered his voice V to be lowered, reduced (price) VII to be inclined, lowered (to the ground, e.g., heads); to sink, dip, drop, settle, subside; to be lowered, be reduced (price); to decrease, grow less; to be diminished

خفض *kafḍ* lowering, lessening, decrease, diminution, reduction; subduing, lowering, muffling (of the voice); curtailment, limitation, restriction; ease (of life); (*gram.*) pronunciation of the final consonant with *i* | خفض القيمة *k. al-qīma* devaluation (of a currency); خفض العيش *k. al-ʿaiš* carefree, easy life; هو فى خفض من العيش he lives in ease and comfort; خفض الصوت *k. aṣ-ṣaut* lowering of the voice; حرف الخفض *ḥarf al-k.* preposition (*gram.*)

خفيض *kafīḍ* low, soft, subdued (voice)

تخفيض *takfīḍ* lowering, cutback, reduction (esp. of prices); diminution, decrease, lessening, curtailment, restriction, limitation | تخفيض القيمة *t. al-qīma* devaluation

انخفاض *inkifāḍ* sinking, dropping, subsidence; lowering, reduction; lessening, decrease, diminution, decrement; dropping of the water level, low water | انخفاض جوى (*jawwī*) low (*meteor.*)

مخفض *mukaffad* lowered, reduced, low, moderate (price, rate); lower

منخفض *munkafid* low (altitude, frequency, price, etc.); soft, low, subdued, muffled (voice) | الاراضى المنخفضة the Netherlands; — *munkafad* pl. *-āt* low ground; depression (*geogr.*) | منخفض جوى (*jawwī*) low, low-pressure area (*meteor.*)

خفق *kafaqa i u* (*kafq*, خفقان *kafaqān*, خفوق *kufūq*) to vibrate; to tremble, shake; to beat, throb, palpitate (heart); to flutter, wave, stream (flag); to flap the wings, flutter (bird); to waver, flicker; — (*kafq*) to flash (lightning); to beat, whip (ه s.th.; eggs, cream, etc.); to make the sound of footsteps (shoe); — (خفوق *kufūq*) to drop one's head drowsily, nod off, doze off (خفق خفقة *k. kafqatan*); — *i* (خفوق *kufūq*) to set, go down (celestial body) **II** to roughcast, plaster, stucco (ه a wall) **IV** to flap the wings, flutter (bird); to set, go down (celestial body); to be unsuccessful, go wrong, fail, miscarry, come to nothing, be abortive; to fail, be unsuccessful (فى in s.th.)

خفق *kafq* throb(bing) palpitation; beating, beat; footfall, footstep, tread (of a boot, of the foot)

خفقة *kafqa* pl. *kafaqāt* (n. vic.) beat, throb; tap, rap, knock; ticking noise, tick | خفقات القلب *k. al-qalb* heartbeats

خفقان *kafaqān* palpitation of the heart, heartbeat; throb(bing), beat(ing); fluttering, flutter

خفاق *kaffāq* palpitant, throbbing (heart); fluttering, waving, streaming (flag)

○ مخفقة *mikfaqa* whisk, eggbeater

اخفاق *ikfāq* failure, fizzle, flop, fiasco

خافق *kāfiq* palpitant, throbbing (heart); fluttering, waving, streaming (flag); الخافقان *al-kāfiqān* East and West; الخوافق *al-kawāfiq* the cardinal points, the four quarters of the world; الخافقات flags, banners

خافقى *kāfiqī* mortar, plaster, roughcast; stucco

خفان see خف

خفى *kafiya a* to be hidden, be concealed; to be unknown (a fact; على to s.o.); to disappear, hide | لا يخفى ان it is well known that ...; as everybody knows ..., it is obvious that ...; لا يخفى عليك you know very well ..., you are well aware (of it); — *kafā i* to hide, conceal (ه s.th.); to keep secret (ه s.th.) **IV** to hide, conceal (ه s.th.); to afford (ه s.o.) a place to hide, shelter, hide (ه s.o.); to keep secret (ه s.th.); to disguise, conceal (ه s.th., على or عن from s.o.) | اخفى الصوت to lower the voice, speak in an undertone **V** to hide, keep o.s. out of view; to disguise o.s. **VIII** to hide, keep o.s. out of view; to disappear, vanish; to be hidden, be unknown; to be lacking, be missing, be absent | اختفى عن الانظار to be hidden or disappear from sight **X** to hide, keep o.s. out of view; to be hidden, be concealed; to be hidden from s.o.'s (عن) view, become invisible (عن to s.o.), disappear from sight

خفى *kafīy* hidden, concealed; secret, unknown; unseen, invisible; mysterious | خفى الاسم *k. al-ism* anonymous; ○ انوار خفية (*anwār*) indirect lighting; شركة خفية الاسم (*širka*) joint-stock company (*Tun.*; = Fr. *société anonyme*)

خفية *kufya*, *kifya* secrecy; — *kufyatan*, *kifyatan* secretly, clandestinely, covertly | خفية عنه without his knowledge; فى خفية secretly, without anyone's noticing

خفية *kafīya* pl. خفايا *kafāyā* a secret, a secret affair

خفاء *kafā'* secrecy, hiddenness | فى الخفاء secretly, clandestinely, covertly; لا خفاء

فى ان (*kafā'a*) it is quite evident, it is quite obvious that ...

اخفاء *ikfā'* hiding, secretion; concealment; lowering of the voice

تخف *takaffin* disguise

اختفاء *iktifā'* disappearance

خاف *kāfin* hidden, concealed; secret, unknown; unseen, invisible

خافية *kāfiya* pl. خواف *kawāfin* a secret; — pl. الخوافى *al-kawāfī* the coverts, the secondaries (of a bird's wing)

مخفى *makfīy* hidden, concealed

متخف *mutakaffin* disguised, in disguise

مختف *muktafin* hidden, concealed, clandestine, covert, secret; disappearing, vanishing

مختفى *muktafan* hiding place, hide-out

خاقان look up alphabetically

خل *kalla* u (*kall*) to pierce, transfix (ه s.th.) II to turn sour; to make sour, to sour, acidify (ه s.th.); to pickle, marinate (ه s.th.); to salt, cure with salt or in brine (ه s.th.); to pick (ه the teeth); to run the fingers (ه through s.th.), part, comb (ه the hair, the beard, also with the fingers) III to treat (ه s.o.) as a friend IV to offend (ب against), infringe, transgress (ب s.th.); to violate, break (ب s.th., e.g., a rule, a custom); to fail to fulfill, fail to meet (ب an agreement); to forsake, desert, abandon (ب s.o., s.th.); to disturb, upset, harm, prejudice (ب s.th.) V to pass through (ه s.th.); to be, lie or come between s.th. (ه; also in time), intervene (ه between); to be located or situated, be interposed, be placed (ه between); to permeate, pervade, interpenetrate (ه s.th.), mix, mingle, blend (ه with); to be in (e.g., of an opening, a hole, ه in a wall); to be part of (ه s.th.), happen, take place (of events, ه in an episode, a period of time) VIII to be or become defective; to be in disorder, be faulty, deficient, imperfect; to become disordered; to be upset, be unbalanced; to be disturbed (order, system) | اختلت الشروط the conditions are not fulfilled; اختل توازنه (*tawāzunuhū*) to lose one's balance, become unbalanced; اختل عقله (*'aqluhū*) to be mentally deranged

خل *kall* vinegar

خليك look up alphabetically

خل *kill*, *kull* pl. اخلال *aklāl* friend, bosom friend

خلل *kalal* pl. خلال *kilāl* gap, interval, interstice; cleft, crack, rupture, fissure; a defective, unbalanced state, imbalance; defectiveness, imperfection; fault, flaw, defect, shortcoming; disturbance, upset, disorder; damage, injury, harm (that s.th. suffers or suffered); خلال *kilāla* during; between; through | فى خلل *fī kalali* and فى خلال *fī kilāli* during; in the course of, within, in a given period of; فى خلال ذلك meanwhile, in the meantime; من خلال *min kilāli* across, through, right through the middle of; out of, from within; (to judge, reason, draw conclusions, etc.) by, on the basis of, on the strength of, (to recognize) from; by means of

خلة *kalla* need, want, lack; — (pl. خلال *kilāl*) property, attribute, peculiarity; characteristic; natural disposition

خلة *kulla* pl. خلل *kulal* friendship

خلال *kilāl* pl. اخلة *akilla* boring or drilling implement; peg, pin; spit, skewer; (also خلالة, pl. *-āt*) toothpick; see also خلل *kalal*

خليل *kalīl* pl. اخلاء *akillā'*[2], خلان *kullān* friend, bosom friend; lover; الخليل Hebron (town in Jordanian Palestine) | خليل الله epithet of Abraham

خليلة *ḵalīla* pl. *-āt* girl friend, woman friend; sweetheart, paramour

ام الخلول *umm al-ḵulūl* river mussel (*zool.*)

اخلال *iḵlāl* pl. *-āt* breach, infraction, violation (of a law, of a treaty, and the like); offense (against), transgression, infringement (of); disturbance (of an order, of a system); impairment, injury, harm (to); average, damage by sea | مع عدم الاخلال ب (*ʿadami l-i.*) without prejudice to, without detriment to

اختلال *iḵtilāl* deficiency, defectiveness, imperfection; (a falling into) disrepair, deterioration; faultiness; disturbance (of a system, of a function, of the equilibrium, etc.); disorder, confusion | ○ اختلال الانية *i. al-anīya* personality disturbance (*psych.*)

مخلل *muḵallal* pickled; salted; (pl. *-āt*) pickles, pickled vegetables

مخل *muḵill* disgraceful, shameful | مخل بالآداب immoral, indecent, improper

مختل *muḵtall* defective; deficient; imperfect; disturbed

خلب **ḵalaba** *i u* (*ḵalb*) to seize with the claws, clutch (ه s.th.), pounce (ه on); — *u* (خلابة *ḵilāba*) to cajole, coax, wheedle (ه s.o.); to inveigle, beguile, bewitch, enchant (ه s.o., عقله *ʿaqlahū* s.o.'s mind); to charm, fascinate, captivate (ه s.o.) **III** to cajole, wheedle, coax. inveigle, beguile, bewitch, enchant (ه s.o.) **VIII** to seize with the claws, clutch (ه s.th.), pounce (ه on); to cajole, inveigle, beguile, bewitch, enchant (ه s.o.); to captivate (ه glance)

خلب *ḵilb* pl. اخلاب *aḵlāb* fingernail, claw, talon

برق خلب *barqun ḵullabun* and *barqu ḵullabin* lightning without a downpour; a disappointing, disillusioning matter; an unkept promise; letdown; خلب and خلب من برق do.

خلبي *ḵullabī*: فشك خلبي (*fašak*) blank cartridges (*Syr.*; *mil.*)

خلاب *ḵallāb* gripping, captivating, fascinating; attractive, engaging, winning; tempting, enticing; fraudulent, deceitful; deceptive, delusive, fallacious

خلابة *ḵilāba* engaging manners, attractiveness, charm

مخلب *miḵlab* pl. مخالب *maḵālib*[2] claw, talon | ذراع مخلب soil-sampling arm; gripping device (*techn.*)

خالب *ḵālib* = خلاب *ḵallāb*

خلبص **II** *taḵalbaṣa* (*eg.*) to clown

خلبوص *ḵalbūṣ* pl. خلابيص *ḵalābīṣ*[2], خلابصة *ḵalābiṣa* (*eg.*) clown, buffoon, harlequin

خلج **ḵalaja** *i* and **III** to be on s.o.'s (ه) mind, trouble, preoccupy, prepossess (ه s.o., s.o.'s mind; said of worries, doubts, etc.); to pervade, fill (ه s.o.; said of a feeling) | خالج قلبه (*qalbahū*) to be uppermost in s.o.'s heart **V** to be shaken, be convulsed, be rocked **VIII** to quiver, tremble, quake, shake; to twitch (eye, limb, body); to animate, move, stir, inspire, fill, pervade, possess (ه, في the heart; said of a feeling) | اختلج غما (*ġamman*) to be filled with sorrow, with grief (heart)

خلجة *ḵalja* pl. *ḵalajāt* emotion, sentiment; scruple, qualm, misgiving

خليج *ḵalīj* pl. خلج *ḵuluj*, خلجان *ḵuljān* bay, gulf; canal; الخليج name of Cairo's ancient city canal which was abandoned and leveled at the end of the 19th century; also = الخليج العربى | الخليج العربى the Arabian Gulf, = الخليج الفارسى the Persian Gulf; خليج العقبة *ḵ. al-ʿaqaba* the Gulf of ʿAqaba; خليج السويس *ḵ. as-suwēs* the Gulf of Suez

خلاج *ḵilāj* misgiving, doubt, scruple, qualm

اختلاجة *iḵtilāja* (n. vic.) convulsion, jerk, twitch; tremor

خالجة *ḵālija* pl. خوالج *ḵawālij*[2] emotion, sentiment; scruple, qualm; idea

خلخل *ḵalḵala* to shake, convulse, rock (ه s.th.); to rarefy (ه s.th., e.g., air; *chem.-phys.*) II *taḵalḵala* to be shaken, be rocked; to come off, become disjointed, become detached; to become loose, work loose; to be or become rarefied (*chem.-phys.*)

خلخل *ḵalḵal* pl. خلاخل *ḵalāḵil*[2] anklet

خلخال *ḵalḵāl* pl. خلاخيل *ḵalāḵīl*[2] anklet

تخلخل *taḵalḵul* rarefication

مخلخل *muḵalḵal* and متخلخل *mutaḵalḵil* rarefied

خلد *ḵalada* u (خلود *ḵulūd*) to remain or last forever, be everlasting; to be immortal, deathless, undying; to abide forever (الى or ب in, with); to remain, stay (الى or ب or فى at a place) | خلد الى الراحة to rest, betake oneself to one's nightly rest; خلد الى النوم (*naum*) to lie down to sleep **II** to make eternal or everlasting, perpetuate, eternalize (ه s.th.), make immortal, immortalize (ه s.o.); to make ineffaceable, unforgettable (ه s.th.; a memory); to remain, stay, abide, linger (ب at, in a place); to grow very old, enjoy a long life, be long-lived **IV** to eternize, immortalize, make immortal (ه s.o., ه s.th.); to perpetuate (ه s.th.); to remain, stay, abide, linger (الى or ب at, in a place); to dwell (الى on an idea, an image); to be disposed, incline, lean, tend (الى to) | اخلد الى الراحة = خلد الى الراحة **V** to become eternal or immortal, perpetuate o.s.; to be or become long, lasting, perpetual

خلد *ḵuld* infinite duration, endless time, perpetuity, eternity | دار الخلد Paradise, the hereafter

خلد *ḵuld* mole (*zool.*)

خلد *ḵalad*, pl. اخلاد *aḵlād* mind, heart, spirit, temper

خلود *ḵulūd* infinite duration, endless time, perpetuity, eternity; eternal life, immortality; abiding, remaining, staying

تخليد *taḵlīd* perpetuation, eternization, immortalization | تخليدا لذكراه (*li-ḏikrāhu*) for preserving the memory of him, in memoriam ...

خالد *ḵālid* everlasting, perpetual, eternal; immortal, deathless, undying; unforgettable, glorious; pl. خوالد *ḵawālid*[2] mountains | الجزائر الخالدات the Canary Islands

مخلد *muḵlid* disposed, inclined, tending (الى to)

خلس *ḵalasa* i (*ḵals*) to steal (ه s.th.); to pilfer, filch, swipe, purloin (ه s.th.) **III** خالسه النظر (*naẓara*) to glance furtively at s.o. **VIII** to steal, pilfer, filch, swipe (ه s.th.); to get under false pretenses or by crooked means (ه s.th.); to embezzle, misappropriate (ه s.th.); to spend secretly (ه hours) | اختلس الخطى الى (*ḵuṭā*) to sneak up on s.o.; اختلس النظر الى (فى) to glance furtively at s.o.

خلسة *ḵulsatan* and فى خلسة by stealth, stealthily, surreptitiously, furtively; unobtrusively, unnoticeably

خلاسى *ḵilāsī* mulatto, bastard

اختلاس *iḵtilās* pl. *-āt* embezzlement, misappropriation, defalcation

مختلس *muḵtalis* embezzler, defalcator

مختلس *muḵtalas* fleeting, furtive (e.g., smile)

خلص *ḵalaṣa* u (خلوص *ḵulūṣ*) to be pure, unmixed, unadulterated; to be clear, unequivocal (goal, a chosen course, an idea); to belong (ل to s.o.); to finally arrive at, come to (الى s.th., e.g., a result, conclusions, etc.); — (خلاص *ḵalāṣ*) to be or become free, be freed, be liberated (من from), be cleared, get rid (من of); to be saved, be rescued, escape (من from); to be redeemed, be delivered, attain salvation (*Chr.*); — (*colloq.*) to be finished, be done, be through, be over; to be all gone **II** to clear, purify, refine, purge, rectify (ه s.th.); to clarify (ه a situation); to liberate, free, save, rescue (ه s.o., من from), rid (ه s.o., من of); to redeem, deliver (*Chr.*); to prepay the postage (على on); to pay duty (على البضائع on merchandise); to clear (على goods), make clear for dispatch (على luggage); to settle (ه a bill); (*colloq.*) to finish (ه s.th.) | خلص حقه (*ḥaqqahū*) to restore one's right, secure one's due **III** to act with integrity, with sincerity (ه toward s.o.), treat (ه s.o.) fair and square; to get even, become quits (ه with s.o.) **IV** to dedicate (ه ل to s.o. s.th.); to be loyal (ل to s.o.); to be devoted, be faithful (ل to) | اخلص له الحب (*ḥubba*) to love s.o. dearly; اخلص لله دينه (*li-llāhi dīnahū*) to worship God faithfully and sincerely **V** to rid o.s. (من of), free o.s. (من from), get rid (من of); to be freed, be delivered, be saved, be rescued, escape (من from) **VI** to act with reciprocal integrity and sincerity; to be quits, be even **X** to extract (ه s.th., من from); to copy, excerpt (ه s.th., من from); to abstract, take, gather, work out (ه s.th., as the quintessence, من of); to deduce, infer, derive (ه s.th., من from); to discover, make out, find out (ه s.th.); to select, choose (ه s.th.); to claim totally, demand, want wholly or entirely for oneself (ه s.th., ه s.o., also with لنفسه); to demand payment of a sum (ه) and get it (من from s.o.) | استخلص دروسا (*durūsan*) to learn a lesson, draw conclusions (من from s.th.); استخلص فائدة من to derive benefit from, profit, benefit from; استخلص منه وعدا (*wa'dan*) to exact a promise from s.o.

خلاص *ḵalāṣ* liberation, deliverance, riddance; rescue, salvation (من from); redemption (*Chr.*); payment, settlement, liquidation (of a bill); receipt; placenta, afterbirth

خلاصة *ḵulāṣa* pl. *-āt* excerpt; extract, essence; quintessence, substance, gist (of s.th.); abstract, résumé, summary, epitome; synopsis | خلاصة نهائية (*nihā'īya*) summation (*jur.*); الخلاصة اللاهوتية (*al-lāhūtīya*) the "summa theologica" (of Thomas Aquinas); خلاصة عطرية (*'iṭrīya*) perfume essence; والخلاصة in short, briefly, in a word (introducing a summary of the basic ideas)

خليص *ḵalīṣ* pl. خلصاء *ḵulaṣā'*[2] pure, clear, unmixed, unadulterated; sincere, faithful, loyal; loyal adherent

خلوص *ḵulūṣ* clearness, purity; sincerity, candor, frankness

خلاص *ḵallāṣ* (*maḡr.*) tax collector

مخلص *maḵlaṣ* safe place; refuge, escape, rescue, salvation, deliverance

تخليص *taḵlīṣ* clearing, purification, refining, rectification; clarification; liberation, extrication, deliverance, rescue, salvation; payment, settlement, liquidation; prepayment of postage (على on); customs clearance, payment of duty (على البضائع on merchandise; also تخليص البضائع)

مخالصة *muḵālaṣa* pl. *-āt* receipt

اخلاص *iḵlāṣ* sincere devotion, loyal attachment, sincere affection; sincerity, frankness, candor; loyalty, faithfulness, fidelity, allegiance (ل to); purity and innocence (of a love, of a kiss)

تخلص *taḵalluṣ* freedom, liberation, release, extrication, escape (من from)

استخلاص *istiḵlāṣ* extraction; excerption; short digest, summary, summing-up of the main contents; derivation, deduction; selection; collecting (of a sum of money)

خالص *ḵāliṣ* pl. خلص *ḵullaṣ* clear; pure, unmixed, unadulterated; sincere, frank, candid, true; free, exempt (من from) | خالص الاجرة *ḵ. al-ujra* post-free; خالص الرد *ḵ. ar-radd* prepaid, reply paid for (telegram); خالص من الكمرك (*gumrug*) dutyfree; خالص الضريبة tax-exempt

مخلص *muḵalliṣ* liberator; Savior, Redeemer (*Chr.*)

مخلص (عليه) *muḵallaṣ* (*ʿalaihi*) postage paid

مخلص *muḵliṣ* devoted; sincere, frank, candid; loyal; faithful (ل to s.o., to s.th.); purehearted, virtuous, righteous; المخلص (in letters) approx.: yours truly ..., sincerely yours ...; المخلصون sincere, upright people

مستخلص *mustaḵlaṣ* pl. *-āt* extract, excerpt

خلط *ḵalaṭa i* (*ḵalṭ*) to mix, mingle, commingle, blend (ه ب s.th. with); to confuse, confound, mix up (بين two things; بين — و s.th. with), mistake (بين — و s.th. for) | خلط فى كلامه (*kalāmihī*) to talk confusedly; خلط عليه تفكيره (*tafkīrahū*) to confuse s.o.'s thinking **II** to mix, mingle, commingle, blend (ه s.th.); to cause confusion **III** to mix, mingle, blend, merge, fuse (ه with s.th.); to meddle (ه in), interfere (ه with); to mingle (هم with or among a crowd, with a group of people); to associate (هم with people), have to do (هم with others) | خالط نفسه (*nafsahū*) to befall, attack s.o. (pain, etc.); خولط فى عقله *ḵūliṭa fī ʿaqlihī* to be or become disordered in mind **VIII** to be mixed, mix, mingle, form a mixture or blend; to consist of a heterogeneous mixture, be motley, promiscuous; to associate, be on intimate terms (ب with); to be or become confused, get all mixed up

خلط *ḵalṭ* mixing, blending; combination; mingling, commingling (ب with); confusing, confounding, mistaking, mix-up, confusion

خلط *ḵilṭ* pl. اخلاط *aḵlāṭ* component of a mixture; ingredient; pl. mixture, blend | اخلاط الانسان the four humors of the human body (blood, phlegm, yellow bile, and black bile); اخلاط من الناس common people, populace, rabble, riffraff, mob; خلط ملط *ḵilṭ milṭ*, *ḵalṭ malṭ* motley, pell-mell, promiscuously

خلطة *ḵalṭa* pl. *ḵalaṭāt* mixture, blend, medley

خلطة *ḵulṭa* company; mixture

خلاط *ḵallāṭ* and خلاطة *ḵallāṭa* pl. *-āt* mixer, mixing machine; mortar box

خليط *ḵalīṭ* mixed, blended; motley, heterogeneous, promiscuous; mixture, blend (من of); medley, hodgepodge; (pl. خلطاء *ḵulaṭāʾ*[2]) associate, companion, comrade

تخليط *taḵlīṭ* pl. *-āt* insanity; delirium

مخالطة *muḵālaṭa* company, intercourse, association

اختلاط *iḵtilāṭ* (process of) mixing, blending; mingling, commingling; mixture, confused muddle; confusion; mental disorder; (social) intercourse, association, dealings (ب with)

مخلوط *maḵlūṭ* pl. مخاليط *maḵālīṭ*[2] mixture, blend; alloy

مخلط *muḵallaṭ* confused, disordered

مخالط *muḵālaṭ* stricken, afflicted (ب e.g., by a disease)

مختلط *muḵtaliṭ* mixed | المحاكم المختلطة the mixed courts, see محكمة; تعليم مختلط coeducation

خلع *ḵalaʿa a* (*ḵalʿ*) to take off, put off, slip off (ه a garment); to doff, take off (طربوشه

one's tarboosh); to extract, pull (ه a tooth); to tear out, rip out; to pull away (ه s.th.); to wrench, dislocate, luxate (ه a joint); to depose, remove, dismiss, discharge (ه s.o., من from an office); to renounce, forgo, give up (ه s.th.), withdraw (ه from); to throw off, cast off (عذاره *ʿiḏārahū* one's restraint, one's inhibitions); to refuse (الطاعة obedience); to disown, repudiate (ابنه one's son); to divorce (ها one's wife) in return for a compensation to be paid by her; to get through, have done (ه with s.th.), be through, have gone through s.th. (ه, e.g., a hard day); to impart (ه على s.th. to); to confer, bestow (ه على s.th. upon s.o.), grant, award (ه على s.th. to s.o.) | خلع ثيابه (*ṯiyābahū*) to undress; خلعه من العرش (*ʿarš*) to dethrone s.o.; خلع عليه خلعة (*kilʿatan*) to bestow a robe of honor upon s.o.; خلع على نفسه حق (*ḥaqqa*) to arrogate to o.s. the right of ...; — *kaluʿa u* (خلاعة *kalāʿa*) to be dissolute, morally depraved **II** to take away, remove, displace, dislocate (ه s.th.); to knock out of joint, take or break apart (ه s.th.); pass. *kulliʿa* to fall to pieces, get out of joint **III** to divorce (ها one's wife, in return for a compensation to be paid by her) **V** to go to pieces, fall apart, break; to become or be luxated, dislocated (joint); to take a vacation in the country (*tun.*) | تخلع فى الشراب (*šarāb*) to be addicted to drinking, drink heavily **VII** to be torn out, be ripped out or pulled away; to become or be luxated (joint, limb); to be displaced, be dislocated, be removed; to be divested, be deprived, be stripped (من of s.th.), forfeit, lose (من s.th.) | انخلع قلبه (*qalbuhū*) he was completely taken aback, he was alarmed, startled

خلع *kalʿ* slipping off, taking off (of clothes); deposition (e.g., of a ruler); dislocation, luxation | خلع الاسنان extraction of teeth

خلع *kulʿ* khula, divorce at the instance of the wife, who must pay a compensation (*Isl. Law*)

خلعة *kilʿa* pl. خلع *kilaʿ* robe of honor

خليع *kalīʿ* pl. خلعاء *kulaʿāʾ*[2] deposed, dismissed, discharged (from an office); repudiated, disowned; wanton, dissolute, dissipated, profligate, morally depraved

خلاع *kallāʿ* wild, unruly, wanton, shameless, impudent

خلاعة *kalāʿa* dissoluteness, dissipation, profligacy, wantonness, licentiousness, moral depravity; (*tun.*) recreation in the country, summer vacation

خولع *kaulaʿ* fool, dolt, simpleton

خالع *kāliʿ*: خالع العذار *k. al-ʿiḏār* unrestrained, uninhibited, wanton; libertine, debauchee, roué, rake

مخلوع *maklūʿ* unrestrained, uninhibited, wanton; wild, unruly; reckless, heedless, irresponsible; crazy, mad

خلف *kalafa u* to be the successor (ه of s.o.), succeed (ه s.o.); to follow (ه s.o.), come after s.o. (ه); to take the place of s.o. (ه), substitute (ه for s.o.); to replace (ه s.o., ه s.th.); to lag behind s.o. (عن); to stay behind (عن after s.o.'s departure); to be detained, be held back, be kept away, stay away (عن from) **II** to appoint as successor (ه s.o.); to leave behind, leave (ه, ه s.o., s.th.); to have descendants, have offspring | خلفه وراءه to leave s.th. behind **III** to be contradictory, contrary, opposed (ه to); to conflict, clash, be at variance (ه with); to contradict (ه s.o., ه s.th.); to be different, differ, diverge (ه from), be inconsistent, incompatible, not in keeping, not harmonizing (ه with); to distinguish between, not confuse (بين two things); to offend (ه against a command, a rule), break, violate, disobey (ه a command, a rule) **IV** to leave

(ه offspring, children); to compensate, requite, recompense (على s.o.; said of God); to break, fail to keep (وعده *wa'dahū* one's promise), go back on one's word; to disappoint (الرجاء *ar-rajā'a* the hopes) **V** to stay behind; to lag or fall behind (عن); to stay, stay on, remain; to fail to appear or show up; to play truant; to be absent; to stay away (عن from), not go (عن to), not attend (عن s.th.) | تخلف عن المجىء (*majī'*) to fail to come or arrive; تخلف عن العودة (*'auda*) not to return **VI** to disagree, differ, be at variance; to differ in opinion, be of a different mind **VIII** to differ, be different, vary (عن from); to be varied, varying, variable, various, diverse, dissimilar; to vary (بين between); to be controversial, disputed, debated (عليهم among people; judgment, value, interpretation); to differ in opinion, be at variance, argue, quarrel, dispute (فى about), disagree (مع فى with s.o. or s.th. in certain matters); to come or go frequently (الى to), frequent, patronize (الى a place), visit frequently (الى s.o., s.th.), come and go (الى at); to pass over s.o. (عليه) successively or by turns (of the stages of one's life, events, etc.); to come, descend (على upon s.o.; said of afflictions), befall, overtake (على s.o.) | اختلف باختلاف (with genit.) to be different, differ according to the kind of . . . **X** to appoint as successor or vicar (ه s.o.)

خلف *ḵalf* back, rear, rear part or portion; successors; *ḵalfu* and من خلف *min ḵalfu* (adv.) at the back, in the rear; *ḵalfa* (prep.) behind, after, in the rear of | جرى خلفها he ran after her; من خلف *min ḵalfi* behind, in the rear of; من الخلف from behind, from the rear; الى الخلف to the rear, backward, back; الى خلف الشىء in the wake of s.th.; فى الخلف in the rear; at the back, in the background; للخلف در (*dur*) about face! (command; *mil.*)

خلفى *ḵalfī* rear, hind, hinder, back; pertaining to background; cryptic, enigmatic, recondite

خلفية *ḵalfīya* background (of a picture and fig.); cryptic or recondite nature or character (of s.th.)

خلف *ḵilf* pl. اخلاف *aḵlāf* teat, nipple, mammilla

خلف *ḵulf* dissimilarity, disparity, difference, contrast, variance, discrepancy

خلف *ḵalaf* pl. اخلاف *aḵlāf* substitute; successor; descendant, offspring, scion

خلفة *ḵilfa* dissimilarity, disparity, difference; that which follows s.th. and replaces it (e.g., second growth of plants, day and night, etc.)

خليفة *ḵalīfa* pl. خلفاء *ḵulafā'*[2], خلائف *ḵalā'if*[2] vicar, deputy; successor; caliph; (formerly) senior official of the native administration in Tunis, assigned to a قائد; (formerly) title of the ruler of Spanish Morocco

المنطقة الخليفية *al-minṭaqa al-ḵalīfīya* the Caliphate Zone (formerly, designation of Spanish Morocco)

خلافة *ḵilāfa* vicarship, deputyship; succession; caliphate, office or rule of a caliph; (formerly) administrative department of a خليفة (*Tun.*), see above

مخلاف *miḵlāf* pl. مخاليف *maḵālīf*[2] province (Yemen)

خلاف *ḵilāf* pl. *-āt* difference, disparity, dissimilarity; divergence, deviation; contrast, contrariety, incongruity, contradiction, conflict; disagreement, difference of opinion (على or فى about); dispute, controversy; *ḵilāfa* (prep.) beside, apart from, aside from | خلافه *ḵilāfuhū* (= غيره) other, the like, خلافهم others (than those mentioned), وخلافه and the like (after an enumeration); بخلاف *bi-ḵilāfi* beside, apart from, aside from; contrary to, as

مختلف *mutakallif* residual; left over; retarded, backward, underdeveloped (mentally, in growth, etc.); (pl. *-ūn*) one left behind; straggler; — pl. متخلفات heritage, legacy, estate; leftovers; scraps, refuse, offal | اتربة متخلفة (*atriba*) waste material, overburden, superstratum (in mining); المياه المتخلفة (*miyāh*) waste water, sewage

مختلف *muktalif* different, varying, divergent (من from); varied, various, diverse; having a different opinion, disagreeing (في or على about)

مختلف فيه (عليه) *muktalaf fīhi* (*ʿalaihi*) controversial, disputed

خلق *kalaqa u* (*kalq*) to create, make, originate (ه s.th.); to shape, form, mold (ه s.th.); — *kaliqa a* and *kaluqa u* to be old, worn, shabby (garment); — *kaluqa u* (خلاقة *kalāqa*) to be fit, suitable, suited **II** to perfume (ه s.th.) **IV** to wear out (ه s.th.), let (ه s.th.) become old and shabby **V** pass. of **II**; to be molded, be shaped (ب by a model or pattern), change (ب with a model); to become angry **VIII** to invent, contrive, devise (ه s.th.); to fabricate, concoct, think up (ه s.th.); to attribute falsely (ه على to s.o. s.th.)

خلق *kalq* creation; making; origination; s.th. which is created, a creation; creatures; people, man, mankind; physical constitution

خلق *kulq, kuluq* pl. اخلاق *aklāq* nature, temper, disposition, character (of a person); noble character; morality; — pl. اخلاق character (of persons); morals; morality | سوء الخلق *sūʾ al-k.* ill nature; سيئ الخلق *sayyiʾ al-k.* ill-natured; سهل الخلق *sahl al-k.* complaisant, obliging; ضيق الخلق *ḍayyiq al-k.* illiberal, ungenerous; impatient; annoyed; علم الاخلاق *ʿilm al-a.* ethics; moral science, morals; سمو الاخلاق *sumūw al-a.* nobility of character; مكارم

opposed to, unlike; خلافا ل *kilāfan li* contrary to, against, in contradiction to; على خلاف ذلك unlike that, contrary to that, on the contrary, on the other hand

خلافى *kilāfī* controversial, disputed

مخالفة *mukālafa* pl. *-āt* contrast, contrariety; contradiction, inconsistency; contravention, infringement, violation; wrong conduct; infraction (*jur.*; as distinguished from جنحة and جناية); foul (soccer, sport); fine (for an infraction) | مخالفة سلوكية (*sulūkīya*) misdemeanor, misbehavior, offense

تخلف *takalluf* staying away, nonappearance, nonattendance, nonpresence, absence, truancy (also تخلف عن الحضور); staying behind, staying on; stopover (railroad); backwardness; retardation (in development) | تخلف عقلى (*ʿaqlī*) mental retardation, mental disturbance

○ تخالف *takāluf* dissimilation (*phon.*) | ○ تخالف جزئى (تقدمى ,رجعى ,كلى) *t. juzʾī* (*taqaddumī, rajʿī, kullī*) partial (progressive, regressive, total) dissimilation

اختلاف *iktilāf* pl. *-āt* difference, dissimilarity, disparity; diversity, variety; variant, variation; difference of opinion, disagreement; controversy | الرعية على اختلاف المذاهب الدينية (*raʿīya, dīnīya*) the subjects of every (= irrespective of their) religious denomination; على اختلاف احزابهم whichever party they may belong to; الفواكه على اختلافها all the different fruits, fruits of every kind

مخلوفة *maklūfa* pl. *-āt* camel saddle

مخلف *mukallaf* left, left behind; left over; pl. مخلفات heritage, legacy, estate; scraps, leftovers | مخلفات البطون feces

مخالف *mukālif* divergent, varying, different; inconsistent, incompatible, contradictory, contrasting, conflicting; (pl. *-ūn*) transgressor (of a command)

الاخلاق noble manners, high moral standards; شرطة الاخلاق *šurṭat al-a.* vice squad

خلقى *kulqī* ethic(al), moral | جرائم خلقية offenses against public morals

خلق *kalaq* (m. and f.) pl. خلقان *kulqān*, اخلاق *aklāq* shabby, threadbare, worn (garment)

خلقة *kilqa* pl. خلق *kilaq* innate character, inborn disposition, personal nature (of s.o.); external appearance (of living beings), countenance, physiognomy; *kilqatan* by nature

خلقى *kilqī* natural, native, congenital, innate, inborn, inbred

خلقة *kalaqa* rag, tatter

خلاق *kalāq* share (of positive qualities, of religion) | لا خلاق له (*kalāqa*) disgraceful, ignominious, despicable; a worthless fellow, a good-for-nothing

خليق *kalīq* pl. خلقاء *kulaqā'*[2] fit, qualified, suitable, appropriate (ب, ل for s.th., ان to do s.th.); apt (ان to do s.th.); in keeping with (ب), adequate (ب to), worthy (ب of) | نحن خليقون ان it is (would be) only fair that we ..., we should ..., we ought to ...; هو خليق ان he is apt to ..., it is only natural for him that he ...; خليق بهذا ان يكون مؤلما (*mu'liman*) this is apt to be painful, it is only natural that this is painful; نظرة يسيرة خليقة ان تقنعنا بأن (*tuqni'anā*) no more than a quick glance is apt to convince us that ...

خلوق *kalūq* of firm character, steadfast, upright

اخلق *aklaq*[2] more adequate, more appropriate, more natural

خلاق *kallāq* creative; creator, artist (of a work of art); الخلاق the Creator, Maker (God)

خليقة *kalīqa* the creation, the universe created by God; nature; natural disposition, trait, characteristic; creatures, created beings; pl. خلائق *kalā'iq*[2] creatures, created beings

اخلاقى *aklāqī* moral; ethic(al); ethicist, moral philosopher | جرم اخلاقى (*jurm*) offense against public morals; الفلسفة الاخلاقية (*falsafa*) moral science, moral philosophy; ethics

اخلاقية *aklāqīya* pl. *-āt* morality, moral practice | اخلاقيات العمل *a. al-'amal* working morale

خلقانى *kulqānī* dealer in old clothes

خالق *kāliq* creative; Creator, Maker (God)

مخلوق *maklūq* created; (pl. *-āt*, مخاليق *makālīq*[2]) creature, created being

مختلق *muktaliq* inventor, fabricator (of untruths)

مختلق *muktalaq* fabricated, trumped up, invented, fictitious; apocryphal; pl. *-āt* lies, falsehoods, fabrications, fictions

خلقين *kalqīn* pl. خلاقين *kalāqīn*[2] caldron, boiler, kettle

[1]خلنج *kalanj* heath, erica (*bot.*)

[2]خلنجان *kulungān* (*eg.*) (rhizome of) galingale (Polypodium Calaguala Kz.; *bot.*)

(خلو) خلا *kalā u* (*kulūw*, خلاء *kalā'*) to be empty, vacant; — (*kulūw*) to be free (من or عن from); to be devoid (من of s.th.), lack, want (من s.th.), be in need (من of); to be vacant (office); — (خلوة *kalwa*) to be alone (ب, الى, مع with s.o., الى also: with or in s.th.); to isolate o.s., seclude o.s.; to withdraw, retire (للمداولة *li-l-mudāwala* for deliberation; court, jury); to withdraw for spiritual communion, in order to take counsel (الى with); to devote o.s., apply o.s., give one's attention (ل to s.th.); خلا به to forsake, desert s.o., leave s.o. in the lurch; — to pass (ه s.o.), go by s.o. (ه); to pass, elapse, go by, be bygone, past, over (time) | خلا له الجو (*jaww*) to have free scope, have freedom of action; لا يخلو من جمال (*jamāl*) it is not without a certain beauty; لا يخلو من مبالغة (*mubālaġa*) it is slightly exaggerated; لا يخلو من فائدة it is not quite useless; خلا الى نفسه to be alone with o.s.; to commune with o.s., take counsel with o.s., search one's heart; منذ عشر سنوات خلت *mundu ʿašri sanawātin kalat* for the past ten years **II** to vacate, evacuate (ه s.th.); to leave, leave alone (ه s.o.); to release, let go (ه s.o., ه s.th.); to desist, abstain, refrain (عن from), give up (عن s.th.) | خلى سبيله (*sabīlahū*) to let s.o. off, let s.o. go, release s.o.; خلى بين فلان وبين الشىء to give s.o. a free hand in, let s.o. have his own way with or in, let s.o. alone with; to open the way for s.o. to; خل عنك هذه الميول *kalli ʿanka h. l-muyūla* desist from such desires! خل عنك هذا الهراء (*hurāʾa*) stop this nonsense! **IV** to empty, void, drain, deplete (ه من s.th. of); to vacate, leave uninhabited or untenanted (ه a place); to evacuate (ه a city); to remove, transport (ه s.o., esp. an injured person) | اخلى سبيله (*sabīlahū*) to let s.o. off, let s.o. go, release s.o.; اخلى السبيل ل to open the way for ...; اخلى طرفه (*ṭarafahū*) to dismiss, discharge s.o., send s.o. away; to exonerate, exculpate, clear s.o.; اخلى سمعه ل (*samʿahū*) to be all ears for..., listen intently to ...; اخلى بينه وبين ما يقول to let s.o. say whatever he likes, let s.o. talk freely **V** to give up, relinquish, forgo, abandon (عن or من s.th.), withdraw, resign (عن or من from); to leave in the lurch (عن s.o.); to cede, leave, surrender (عن s.th. to s.o.); to lay down (عن an office) **VIII** to retire, withdraw, step aside, be alone (ب or مع with)

خلو *kilw* free (من from), devoid (من of)

خلو *kulūw* emptiness, vacuity; freedom (من from) | خلو الرجل *k. ar-rigl* (*eg.*) acceptance of an illegal bonus in renting an apartment, or payment of a bonus by the applicant for preference in renting

خلا *kalā* and ما خلا (with foll. acc. or genit.) except, save, with the exception of

خلاء *kalāʾ* emptiness, vacuity; empty space, void, vacancy, vacuum; open country; (as predicate, invar.) empty | فى الخلاء or تحت الخلاء under the open sky, outdoors, in the open air; بيت الخلاء *bait al-k.* toilet, water closet

خلوة *kalwa* pl. *kalawāt* privacy, solitude; seclusion, isolation, retirement; place of retirement or seclusion, retreat, recess; secluded room; hermitage; religious assembly hall of the Druses; booth, cabin | على خلوة alone; in retirement, in seclusion; خلوة الحمام *k. al-ḥammām* bathhouse

خلوى *kalawī* lonely, solitary, secluded, isolated, outlying; located in the open country, rural, rustic, country | بيت خلوى (*bait*) country house

خلى *kalīy* pl. اخلياء *akliyāʾ*[2] free (من from), void, devoid (من of) | خلى البال carefree, easygoing, happy-go-lucky

خلية *kalīya* pl. خلايا *kalāyā* beehive; cell (*biol.*) | ○ الخلية الحيوية الاولى (*al-ḥayawīya l-ūlā*) protoplasm; من خلايا from within..., from inside ..., out of ...

مخلاة *miklāh* nosebag; bag, sack

تخلية *takliya* vacating, evacuation

اخلاء *iklāʾ* emptying, voiding, draining; clearing; vacating, evacuation | اخلاء سبيله *i. sabīlihī* his release

تخل *takallin* relinquishment, abandonment, surrender, renunciation, resignation (عن of s.th.)

اختلاء *iktilāʾ* privacy, solitude

خال *kālin* empty, void; open, vacant (office, position); free, unrestrained, untrammeled, unencumbered; free (من from), devoid (من of) | in numerous compounds corresponding to Engl. -less or un-, e.g., خال من الفائدة useless, خال من السكان (*sukkān*) uninhabited, untenanted, unoccupied, خال من العمل (*'amal*) unemployed; خالى الدين *kālī d-dain* not bound by, without obligation to, free (من from); خالى البال carefree, easygoing, happy-go-lucky; — (pl. خوال *kawālin*) past, bygone (time) | القرون الخالية the past centuries; فى الايام الخوالى *fī l-ayyāmi l-kawālī* in the days past

خليك *kallīk* (from *kall* vinegar) acetic | حامض الخليك acetic acid

خم *kamma u* (*kamm*) to sweep (ه a room); — *i u* (*kamm*, خموم *kumūm*) to exude a rotten, foul smell; to rot, putrify, decay

خم *kumm* pl. اخمام *akmām* coop, chicken coop, brooder; poultry pen

خمة *kamma* putrid smell, stench

خام *kāmm* stinking, rotten, putrid, foul-smelling; *kām* look up alphabetically

مخم *mukimm* stinking, rotten, putrid, foul-smelling

خمج *kamija a* (*kamaj*) to spoil, rot, decay

خمد *kamada u* (خمود *kumūd*) to go out, die (fire); to abate, subside, let up, calm down, cease, die down **IV** to extinguish, put out (ه fire); to calm, appease, placate, soothe, lull, still, quiet (ه s.th.); to suppress, quell (ه s.th.); to subdue, soften, deaden, dull (ه s.th.); to stifle, smother, kill (ه s.th.; fig.)

خمود *kumūd* extinction; decline, degeneration, deterioration; quietness, stillness, tranquillity, calm; immobility, motionlessness

اخماد *ikmād* extinction, putting out; calming, soothing, placation, appeasement, lulling, stilling; subduing, softening, dulling; settlement; suppression, quelling (of a riot)

خامد *kāmid* dying; abating, subsiding; calm, tranquil, still, quiet

خمر *kamara u* (*kamr*) and **II** to cover, hide, conceal (ه s.th.); to leaven, raise (ه dough); to ferment (ه s.th.), cause fermentation (ه in) **III** to permeate, pervade (ه s.th.), mix, blend (ه with); to seize, permeate (ه s.o., feeling, thought, doubt) **IV** to leaven, raise (ه dough); to ferment (ه s.th.), cause fermentation (ه in); to harbor, entertain (ه s.th.); to bear a grudge, feel resentment (ل against s.o.) **V** to ferment, be in a state of fermentation; to rise (dough); to veil the head and face (woman) **VI** to conspire, plot, collude, scheme, intrigue (على against) **VIII** to ferment, be in a state of fermentation; to rise (dough); to become ripe, ripen (also fig.: an idea in s.o.'s mind)

خمر *kamr* m. and f., pl. خمور *kumūr* wine; pl. alcoholic beverages, liquor

خمرة *kamra* wine

خمرى *kamrī* golden brown, reddish brown, bronze-colored (actually, wine-colored)

خمرية *kamrīya* pl. *-āt* wine poem, bacchanalian verse

خمار *kimār* pl. اخمرة *akmira*, خمر *kumur* veil covering head and face of a woman

خمار *kumār* aftereffect of intoxication, hang-over

خمير *kamīr* leavened (dough); ripe, mature, mellow; leaven; leavened bread

خميرة *kamīra* pl. خمائر *kamā'ir*[2] leaven; ferment; barm, yeast; enzyme (*chem.*); (fig.) starter, nucleus, basis (from which s.th. greater develops)

خمار *ḵammār* wine merchant, keeper of a wineshop

خمارة *ḵammāra* wineshop, tavern; bar

خمير *ḵimmīr* winebibber, drunkard, tippler, sot

تخمير *taḵmīr* leavening, raising (of dough); fermenting, fermentation

اختمار *iḵtimār* (process of) fermentation

مخمور *maḵmūr* drunk, intoxicated, inebriated

مختمر *muḵtamir* fermenting, fermented; alcoholic

خمس **II** to quintuple, make fivefold, multiply by five (ه s.th.); to make pentagonal (ه s.th.); to divide into five parts (ه s.th.)

خمس *ḵums* pl. اخماس *aḵmās* one fifth | ضرب اخماسه فى اسداسه *ḍaraba aḵmāsahū fī asdāsihī* and ضرب اخماسا لاسداس (*li-asdāsin*) to brood, rack one's brain in search of a way out; to be at one's wit's end; to scheme, intrigue; to fantasize, build air castles; to daydream

خمسة *ḵamsa* (f. خمس *ḵams*) five

خمسة عشر *ḵamsata ʿašara* (f. خمس عشرة *ḵamsa ʿašrata*) fifteen

خمسى *ḵamsī*: خطة خمسية (*ḵiṭṭa*) five-year plan

خمسون *ḵamsūn* fifty | عيد الخمسين *ʿīd al-ḵ.* Whitsuntide, Pentecost; احد الخمسين *aḥad al-ḵ.* Whitsunday; ايام الخماسين *ayyām al-ḵamāsīn* the period of about 50 days between Easter and Whitsuntide; □ خمسين and خماسين khamsin, a hot southerly wind in Egypt

الخمسينات *al-ḵamsīnāt* the fifties (decade of a century)

عيد خمسينى *ʿīd ḵamsīnī* 50th anniversary; العقد الخمسينى (*ʿaqd*) the fifties (decade of a century)

خميس *ḵamīs* and يوم الخميس *yaum al-ḵ.* Thursday | خميس الجسد *ḵ. al-jasad* Corpus Christi Day (*Chr.*); خميس الفصح *ḵ. al-fiṣḥ*, خميس الاسرار *ḵ. al-asrār*, and خميس العهد *ḵ. al-ʿahd* Maundy Thursday (*Chr.*)

خماس *ḵammās* pl. خمامسة *ḵamāmisa* (*maḡr.*) sharecropper receiving one fifth of the crop as wages

خماسى *ḵumāsī* fivefold, quintuple; quintet (*mus.*); pentathlon (*athlet.*); consisting of five consonants (*gram.*) | خماسى الزوايا (*zawāyā*) pentagonal, five-cornered; خطة خماسية (*ḵiṭṭa*) and مخطط خماسى (*muḵaṭṭaṭ*) five-year plan

خميسة *ḵumaisa* (*mor.*, pronounced *ḵmīsa*) ornament in the shape of a hand (worn by women and children as a talisman against the evil eye)

الخامس *al-ḵāmis* the fifth

مخمس *muḵammas* pentagonal, five-cornered; pentagon; fivefold, quintuple; ○ pentameter

خمش *ḵamaša i u* (*ḵamš*) and **II** to scratch (ه e.g., the face, the skin, with the nails)

خمش *ḵamš* pl. خموش *ḵumūš* scratch, scratch mark, scar

خماشة *ḵumāša* pl. *-āt* scratch, scar

خمص *ḵamaṣa u* and *ḵamiṣa a* to be empty, hungry (stomach)

خميص *ḵamīṣ*, خميص البطن *ḵ. al-baṭn*, خميص الحشا *ḵ. al-ḥašā* with an empty stomach, hungry

اخمص القدم *aḵmaṣ al-qadam* pl. اخامص *aḵāmiṣ*[2] hollow of the sole (of the foot) | من الرأس الى اخمص القدم from head to toe

خمع *ḵamaʿa a* (*ḵamʿ*, خموع *ḵumūʿ*) to limp, walk with a limp

خمل *ḵamala u* (خمول *ḵumūl*) to be unknown, obscure, undistinguished; to be weak, languid | خمل ذكره (*ḏikruhū*) to have fallen into oblivion, be forgotten

خمل *ḵaml* and خملة *ḵamla* nap, the rough, hairy surface of a fabric; fibers

خمل *ḵamil* languid, sluggish, dull, listless

خمول *ḵumūl* obscurity; weakness, lassitude, languor, lethargy; indolence, sluggishness, inactivity; apathy, indifference; inertness (also *chem.*); drowsiness

خميلة *ḵamīla* pl. خمائل *ḵamā'il*² place with luxuriant tree growth; thicket, brush, scrub

خامل *ḵāmil* unknown, obscure, undistinguished, unimportant, minor; weak, languid, sluggish

مخمل *muḵmal* velvet-like fabric, velvet

مخملى *muḵmalī* velvety | جلد مخملى (*jild*) deerskin, buckskin

خمن II to guess, conjecture, surmise; to make conjectures (ه as to); to assess, appraise, estimate (ه s.th.)

تخمين *taḵmīn* appraisal, assessment, estimation; تخمينا *taḵmīnan* and على تخمين approximately, roughly

مخمن *muḵammin* appraiser, assessor

¹خن *ḵanna i* (خنين *ḵanīn*) to speak nasally, nasalize; to twang, speak through the nose

خنة *ḵunna* nasal twang

خنين *ḵanīn* twanging, nasal twang

اخن *aḵann*², f. خناء *ḵannā'*² twanging, speaking through the nose

²خن *ḵunn* (= خم *ḵumm*) pl. اخنان *aḵnān* coop, chicken coop, brooder

خنث *ḵaniṯa a* to be soft, effeminate V to display effeminate manners, become or be effeminate

خنث *ḵaniṯ* soft, effeminate

خنثى *ḵunṯā* pl. خناث *ḵināṯ*, خناثى *ḵanāṯā* hermaphrodite

خنوثة *ḵunūṯa* effeminacy

تخنث *taḵannuṯ* effeminacy

مخنث *muḵannaṯ* bisexual; effeminate; powerless, impotent, weak

خنجر *ḵanjar* pl. خناجر *ḵanājir*² dagger

خنخن *ḵanḵana* to nasalize, speak nasally; to twang, speak through the nose

خندق *ḵandaqa* to dig a ditch or trench (خندقا); to take up positions, prepare for battle

خندق *ḵandaq* pl. خنادق *ḵanādiq*² ditch; trench

خنزوانية *ḵunzuwānīya* megalomania

خنزب *ḵanzab* Satan, Devil

خنزير *ḵinzīr* pl. خنازير *ḵanāzīr*² swine, pig, hog; خنازير scrofula, scrofulosis (*med.*) | خنزير برى (*barrī*) wild boar; خنزير الهند *ḵ. al-hind* and خنزير هندى (*hindī*) guinea pig

خنزيرة *ḵinzīra* sow

خنازيرى *ḵanāzīrī* scrofulous

الخناس *al-ḵannās* epithet of the Devil (properly speaking, he who withdraws when the name of God is mentioned)

اخنس *aḵnas*², f. خنساء *ḵansā'*², pl. خنس *ḵuns* pugnosed

خنشار *ḵinšār* fern (*bot.*)

خنوص *ḵinnauṣ* pl. خنانيص *ḵanānīṣ*² piglet

خنصر *ḵinṣir* pl. خناصر *ḵanāṣir*² little finger | عقد الخنصر (الخناصر) على to give s.th. top-rating because of its excellence, put s.th. above everything else

خنع *ḵana'a a* (خنوع *ḵunū'*) to yield, surrender, bow, stoop (ل or الى to s.o.), humble o.s., cringe (ل or الى before s.o.)

خنوع *ḵanūʿ* submissive, servile, meek, humble; treacherous, perfidious, disloyal

خنوع *ḵunūʿ* submissiveness, meekness, servility

خانع *ḵāniʿ* submissive, servile, humble; treacherous, disloyal

خنف *ḵanaf* (*eg.*) twanging, nasal twang

خنفر *ḵanfara* to snuffle, snort

خنفس *ḵunfus* and خنفساء *ḵunfusāʾ* pl. خنافس *ḵanāfis*² dung beetle, scarab; pl. الخنافس and فرقة الخنافس *firqat al-ḵ.* the Beatles

خنق *ḵanaqa u* (*ḵanq*) to choke (ه s.o.); to suffocate, stifle, smother, strangle, throttle, choke to death (ه s.o.); to throttle down (*techn.*; ه s.th.); to slow down, cut, check, suppress (ه s.th.) **III** to quarrel, have a fight (ه with s.o.) **VI** to quarrel, dispute, have a fight (مع with s.o.) **VII** pass. of **I**; **VIII** to be throttled, be suppressed; to be tight, constricted (throat); to be strangled, be choked to death

خنق *ḵanq* strangling, strangulation; throttling, suppression | خنق الانوار *ḵ. al-anwār* dim-out

خنقة اليد *ḵanqat* (*ḵunqat*) *al-yad* wrist

خناق *ḵunāq* suffocation; angina (*med.*); *ḵunāq* and خانوق *ḵānūq* quinsy, diphtheria (*med.*); pl. خوانق *ḵawāniq*² and خوانيق *ḵawānīq*² do.

خناق *ḵannāq* choking, throttling, strangling

مخنق *maḵnaq* neck, throat | اخذه بمخنقه to grab s.o. by the throat, bear down on s.o.; to have power over s.o.

خناق *ḵināq* strangling cord; neck, throat | ضيق الخناق على (*ḍayyaqa*) to tighten the grip around s.o.'s throat, tread on s.o.'s neck, oppress s.o., beset s.o. grievously; اخذ بخناقه to grab s.o. by the throat

خناق *ḵināq* and خناقة *ḵināqa* quarrel, fight, row

اختناق *iḵtināq* pl. *-āt* suffocation, asphyxiation; constriction; asphyxia (*med.*); stoppage | اختناق المرور traffic jam; نقط اختناق *nuqaṭ i.* bottlenecks (in street traffic)

خانق *ḵāniq* choking, strangling; suffocating, asphyxiating, stifling, smothering; throttling, throttle- (in compounds; *techn.*); — (pl. خوانق *ḵawāniq*²) choke coil (*el.*); throttle, throttle valve (*techn.*); gorge, ravine, canyon | غاز خانق asphyxiating gas; خانق الذئب *ḵ. aḏ-ḏiʾb* wolfsbane, monkshood, aconite (*bot.*)

مخنوق *maḵnūq* strangled; suffocated, stifled, smothered; suppressed, choking (voice, laughter, etc.); constricted; strangulated; throttled

مختنق *muḵtaniq* crammed, jammed, crowded, chock-full (ب with)

(خنو and خنى) خنا *ḵanā u*, خنى *ḵaniya a* (خنى *ḵanan*) to use obscene language **IV** to hit hard, afflict grievously, wear down, ruin, destroy, crush (على s.o., s.th.; said of fate)

خنى *ḵanan* obscene language; s.th. indecent or obscene; prostitution; fornication

خواجة *ḵawāja* pl. *-āt* sir, Mr. (title and form of address, esp., for Christians and Westerners, used with or without the name of the person so addressed)

خوان *ḵuwān*, *ḵiwān* pl. اخونة *aḵwina*, اخاوين *aḵāwīn*² table | خوان الزينة *ḵ. az-zīna* dressing table

خوجة *ḵōga* (*eg.*) teacher, schoolmaster

خوخ **II** (*eg.*) to rot, decay, spoil

خوخ *ḵauḵ* (coll.; n. un. ة) peach (*eg.*, *ir.*); plum (*syr.*)

خوخة *ḵauḵa* pl. خوخ *ḵuwaḵ* skylight, windowlike opening; wicket (of a canal lock, of a gate); (*eg.*) alley connecting two streets

خوذة *kūḏa* pl. *-āt*, خوذ *kuwaḏ* helmet

[1](خور) خار *kāra u* (خوار *kuwār*) to low, moo (cattle); — خور *kawira a* (خور *kawar*) and خار *kāra u* to decline in force or vigor; to grow weak, spiritless, languid, to languish, flag; to dwindle, give out (strength)

خور *kaur* pl. اخوار *akwār*, خيران *kīrān* inlet, bay

خور *kawar* weakness, fatigue, enervation, languor, lassitude

خوار *kuwār* lowing, mooing

خوار *kawwār* weak, languid, strengthless

[2]خورى *kūrī* pl. خوارنة *kawārina* parson, curate, priest (*Chr.*) | الخورى الاسقفى (*usqufī*) representative of the bishop (*Chr.*); see also اخير *akyar*[2]

خورس *kūrus* choir (of a church)

خورفسقفوس *kūrfisqufūs* representative of the bishop (*Chr.*; *syr.*)

خوزق *kauzaqa* to impale (ه s.o.); to corner, drive into a corner, get into a bad fix (ه s.o.)

خازوق see خزق

ورق خوشق *waraq kaušaq* wrapping paper; blotting paper

[1]خوص *kūṣ* (coll.; n. un. ة) palm leaves

خوصة *kūṣa* (*eg.*) plaitwork of palm leaves (resembling that of Panama hats; used as a tarboosh lining)

خواصة *kiwāṣa* art of palm-leaf plaiting

[2]خوص *kawaṣ* and اخوص see حوص

[3]خويصة see خص

[1](خوض) خاض *kāḍa u* (خوض *kauḍ*, خياض *kiyāḍ*) to wade (ه into water); to plunge, dive, rush (ه into s.th.), tackle courageously (ه s.th.), embark boldly (ه on); to penetrate (ه or فى into), become absorbed, engrossed (ه or فى in); to go into a subject (فى), take up (فى a subject), deal (فى with) | خاض المعركة (*ma'raka*) to rush into battle; خاض غمار الحرب (*ġimāra l-ḥarb*) to enter the war II to wade (ه into)

خوض *kauḍ* plunge, rush (into); entering, entry (into, e.g., into war, into negotiations); penetration; search (فى into), examination, discussion, treatment (فى of a subject)

مخاضة *makāḍa* pl. *-āt*, مخاوض *makāwiḍ*[2] ford

[2]مخاض see مخض

(خوف) خاف *kāfa* (1st pers. perf. *kiftu*) *a* (*kauf*, مخافة *makāfa*, خيفة *kīfa*) to be frightened, scared; to be afraid (ه, ه or من of), dread (ه, ه or من s.o. or s.th.); to fear (ه, ه or من s.o., s.th.; على for s.o., for s.th.; ان that) II and IV to frighten, scare, alarm, fill with fear (ه s.o.) V = I

خوف *kauf* fear, dread (من of); خوفا *kaufan* for fear (من of), fearing (على for) | خوف مرضى (*maraḍī*) phobia (*psych.*)

خيفة *kīfa* fear, dread (من of)

خواف *kawwāf*, خويف *kawwīf* fainthearted, fearful, timid, timorous; coward, poltroon

اخوف *akwaf*[2] more timorous; more dreadful, more to be feared

مخافة *makāfa* fear, dread | مخافة ان (*makāfatan*) for fear that ..., afraid that ...

مخاوف *makāwif*[2] (pl. of مخافة) fears, apprehensions, anxieties; horrors, dangers, perils

تخويف *takwīf* and اخافة *ikāfa* intimidation, bullying, cowing, frightening, scaring

تخوف *taḵawwuf* fear, dread

خائف *ḵā'if* pl. خوف *ḵuwwaf* fearful, timid, timorous; scared, frightened, alarmed (من by); afraid (من of); anxious (على about), apprehensive (على for)

مخوف *maḵūf* feared, dreaded; dangerous, perilous

مخيف *muḵīf* fear-inspiring, frightful, dreadful, terrible, horrible

خوفو *ḵūfū* Cheops

خاكى look up alphabetically

خول II to grant, accord, give, concede (ه ‿ to s.o. s.th., also ه ل; esp., the right, the power to do s.th.), bestow, confer (ه ‿ upon s.o. s.th., also ه ل), vest, endow (ه ‿ s.o. with s.th., also ه ل)

خال *ḵāl* pl. اخوال *aḵwāl*, خؤول *ḵu'ūl*, خؤولة *ḵu'ūla* (maternal) uncle; — (pl. خيلان *ḵīlān*) mole, birthmark (on the face); ○ patch, beauty spot

خالة *ḵāla* pl. *-āt* (maternal) aunt

خول *ḵawal* chattels, property, esp., that consisting in livestock and slaves; servants; (*eg.*) dancer; effeminate person, sissy

خولى *ḵaulī* supervisor, overseer (of a plantation); gardener

خؤولة *ḵu'ūla* relationship of the maternal uncle

مخول *muḵawwal* authorized (ب to)

خام look up alphabetically

[1](خون) خان *ḵāna u* (*ḵaun*, خيانة *ḵiyāna*) to be disloyal, faithless, false, treacherous, perfidious, act disloyally, treacherously, perfidiously (ه toward s.o.); to betray (ه s.o.); to cheat, dupe, gull, hoodwink (ه s.o.), impose (ه upon), deceive (زوجته one's wife); to fool, deceive, mislead (ه s.o.; said, e.g., of the memory); to forsake, let down, desert (ه s.o.); to fail (ه s.o.; e.g., the voice, and the like); to fail to keep (ه e.g., a promise), break (عهدا *'ahdan* a contract) | خانه جيبه (*jaibuhū*) his purse let him down, he didn't have enough money; خانه التوفيق success eluded him, he failed II to regard as or call faithless, false, disloyal, treacherous, dishonest, unreliable (ه s.o.); to distrust, mistrust (ه s.o.) V to impair, harm, hurt, prejudice (ه s.th.) VIII to dupe, gull, cheat, deceive, double-cross, betray (ه s.o.) X استخون *istaḵwana* to distrust, mistrust (ه s.o.)

خيانة *ḵiyāna* faithlessness, falseness, disloyalty, treachery, perfidy; breach of faith, betrayal; treason; deception, fooling | خيانة الامانة *ḵ. al-amāna* breach of faith; خيانة عظمى (*'uẓmā*) high treason; خيانة الوعود breach of promise

خؤون *ḵa'ūn* faithless, false, disloyal, traitorous, treacherous, perfidious; unreliable, tricky, deceptive

خوان *ḵawwān* unreliable, faithless, disloyal, treacherous, perfidious; traitor

خائن *ḵā'in* pl. خوان *ḵuwwān*, خونة *ḵawana* disloyal, faithless, false, unreliable, traitorous, treacherous, perfidious; traitor

[2]خان and خانة look up alphabetically

[3]خوان look up alphabetically

[1]خوى *ḵawā i* (خواء *ḵawā'*, خوى *ḵawan*) to be empty (من of); to be hungry | خوى مما حوى *ḵawā mimmā ḥawā* to have become empty (e.g., purse); — *ḵawiya a* (خواء *ḵawā'*) to be empty, bare, dreary, desolate, waste

خواء *ḵawā'* and خوى *ḵawan* emptiness (of the stomach), hunger

خاو *ḵāwin* empty, vacant; dreary, waste, desolate | خاو على عروشه (*'urūšihī*) completely devastated; خاوى الوفاض *ḵ. l-wifāḍ* (= خالى الوفاض) with an empty pouch, empty-handed, without a catch

[2]خوى III to join (ه s.o.), join the company of (ه), accompany (ه s.o.)

خوى *ḵuwaiy* little brother

خوة *ḵūwa* brotherliness, fraternity (= اخوة *uḵūwa*)

مخاو *muḵāwin* brotherly, fraternal

خيار *ḵiyār* (coll.; n. un. ة) cucumber | خيار شنبر *ḵ. šanbar* (*eg.*) drumstick tree, purging cassia (Cassia fistula; *bot.*); خيار قشة *ḵ. qašša* (*eg.*) gherkins, pickles

(خيب) خاب *ḵāba* *i* (خيبة *ḵaiba*) to fail, miscarry, be without success, be unsuccessful; to be frustrated, be dashed, be disappointed (hopes); to go wrong **II** and **IV** to cause to fail; to thwart, frustrate, foil, defeat (ه s.th.); to disappoint, dash (آماله *āmālahū* s.o.'s hopes) **V** = **I**

خيبة *ḵaiba* failure, miscarriage, defeat, frustration; fizzle, flop; disappointment | ولد خيبة *walad ḵ.*, f. بنت خيبة *bint ḵ.* (*eg.*) a good-for-nothing, a ne'er-do-well

خائب *ḵā'ib* failing; abortive, unsuccessful; disappointed

(خير) خار *ḵāra* *i* to choose, make one's choice; to prefer (ه على s.th. to) **II** to make or let (ه s.o.) choose (بين between, فى from), give (ه s.o.) the alternative, option or choice (بين between, فى in); to prefer (ه على s.th. to) **III** to vie, compete (ه with s.o.); to make or let (ه s.o.) choose, give (ه s.o.) the choice, option or alternative **V** to choose, select, pick (ه, ه s.o., s.th.) **VIII** to choose, make one's choice; to choose, select, elect, pick (ه, ه s.o., s.th.), fix upon s.o. or s.th. (ه, ه); to prefer (ه على s.th. to) | اختار الله الى جواره ... (*jiwārihī*) approx.: the Lord has taken ... unto Himself **X** to seek or request what is good or best (ه) for o.s. (ه from s.o.); to consult an oracle, cast lots | استخار الله فى to ask God for proper guidance in

خير *ḵair* pl. خيار *ḵiyār*, اخيار *aḵyār* good; excellent, outstanding, superior, admirable; better; best; — (pl. خيور *ḵuyūr*) good thing, blessing; wealth, property; — good, benefit, interest, advantage; welfare; charity | خير الناس the best of all people; اخيار الناس, خيار الناس the best people, the pick of the human race; هو خير منك he is better than you; هو خير لك it is better for you; الخير كل الخير the very best; الخير العام (*'āmm*) the commonweal, general welfare; دولة الخير العام welfare state; لخير for the benefit of; لخير انفسهم *li-ḵ. anfusihim* for their own good; اعمال الخير charitable deeds; صباح الخير *ṣabāḥ al-ḵ.* and صباحك بالخير good morning! ذكره بالخير (*ḏakarahū*) to retain a good impression of s.o.; to speak well of s.o.; بخير *bi-ḵair* fine, in good health (as an answer to inquiries about one's health and in wishes); اخو الخير a good, benevolent person; اهل الخير *ahl al-ḵ.* charitable people

خيرى *ḵairī* charitable, beneficent, benevolent, philanthropic | جمعية خيرية (*jam'īya*) charitable organization

خيرية *ḵairīya* charity, charitableness, benevolence, beneficence

خير *ḵayyir* good; virtuous; generous, liberal, openhanded, munificent; charitable, beneficent, benevolent; benign, gracious, kind

خيرة *ḵaira* pl. *-āt* good deed, good thing; pl. خيرات resources, treasures (e.g., of the earth, of a country), boons, blessings

خيرة *ḵīra* and *ḵiyara* the best, choice, prime, flower, pick, elite

خيرى *ḵīrī* gillyflower (*bot.*)

اخير *aḵyar*[2], f. خيرى *ḵīrā*, خورى *ḵūrā*, pl. اخاير *aḵāyir*[2] better, superior

خيار *ḵiyār* choice; option, exercise of the power of choice (*Isl. Law*); refusal, right of withdrawal (*Isl. Law*); the best, choice, prime, flower, pick, elite; see also alphabetically

خيارى *ḵiyārī* optional, facultative; voluntary

اختيار *iḵtiyār* choice; election (also *pol.*; pl. *-āt*); selection; preference (على to); option; free will (*philos.*); اختيارا *iḵtiyāran* of one's own accord, spontaneously, voluntarily

اختيار (Turk.) *iḵtiyār* pl. *-īya* (*ir.*, *syr.*, *jord.*), also □ ختيار *ḵityār* pl. *-īya* old; an old man; elder, senior person in a community

اختيارى *iḵtiyārī* voluntary, facultative, elective (studies)

مخير *muḵayyar* having the choice or option

مختار *muḵtār* free to choose, having the choice or option (فى in), volunteering, مختارا *muḵtāran* (adv.) voluntarily, spontaneously, of one's own accord; choice, select, exquisite; chosen, preferred, favorite; a favorite; مختارات selection, selected writings, anthology; (pl. مخاتير *maḵātīr*[2]) village chief, mayor of a village; mayor of a city district (*Syr.*, *Leb.*, *Ir.*)

خيزران see خزر

(خيس) خاس *ḵāsa* *i* (خيس *ḵais*, خيسان *ḵayasān*) to break (ب an agreement, a promise)

خيش *ḵaiš* sackcloth, sacking, canvas

خيشة *ḵaiša* pl. *-āt*, خيش *ḵiyaš* piece of sackcloth; cleaning rag; floorcloth; sack; straw mattress, pallet; Bedouin tent

خيشوم see خشم

(خيط) خاط *ḵāṭa* *i* (*ḵaiṭ*) and **II** to sew, stitch (ه s.th.)

خيط *ḵaiṭ* pl. خيوط *ḵuyūṭ*, اخياط *aḵyāṭ*, خيطان *ḵīṭān* thread; twine, cord; packthread, string; fiber; filament (*bot.*); ray | خيوط الفجر الاولى *ḵ. al-fajr al-ūlā* the first rays of the sun, the crack of dawn; خيط امل *ḵ. amal* a spark of hope, a thread of hope

خيطى *ḵaiṭī* threadlike; fibrous

خياط *ḵiyāṭ* needle

خياطة *ḵiyāṭa* sewing; needlework, tailoring, dressmaking | آلة الخياطة sewing machine

خياط *ḵayyāṭ* pl. *-ūn* tailor

خياطة *ḵayyāṭa* pl. *-āt* dressmaker; seamstress

مخيط *miḵyaṭ* needle

خائط *ḵā'iṭ* tailor

[1](خيل) خال *ḵāla* *a* to imagine, fancy, think, believe, suppose (ان that); to consider, deem, think (ه ه s.o. to be ..., ه ه s.th. to be ...), regard (ه ه s.o. as, ه ه s.th. as) **II** to make (الى s.o.) believe (ان that), suggest (الى to s.o., ه s.th.), give s.o. (الى) the impression that (ه) | خيل اليه (له) ان (*ḵuyyila*) he imagined, fancied, thought that ..., it seemed, it appeared to him that ...; على ما خيلت (*ḵayyalat*; النفس being understood) as the heart dictates, i.e., as chance will have it, at random, unhesitatingly **IV** to be dubious, doubtful, uncertain, intricate **V** to imagine, fancy (ه s.th.); to present itself, reveal itself (ل to s.o.'s mind), become the object of imagination, appear (= **II** *ḵuyyila*; ل to s.o.) | تخيل فيه الخير (*ḵaira*) to suspect good qualities in s.o., have an inkling of s.o.'s good qualities, think well of s.o., have a good opinion of s.o. **VI** to pretend (ل ب to s.o. s.th., that ...), act (ل toward s.o., ب as if); to feel self-important, be conceited; to behave in a pompous manner, swagger, strut about; to conceive eccentric ideas, get all kinds of fantastic notions, have a bee in one's bonnet; to appear dimly, in shadowy outlines; to appear, show (على on), hover (على about; e.g., a smile about s.o.'s

lips), flit (على across, e.g., a shadow across s.o.'s face, etc.) VIII to feel self-important, be conceited; to behave in a pompous manner, swagger, strut about

خيال *ḵayāl* pl. اخيلة *aḵyila* disembodied spirit, ghost, specter; imagination; phantom, apparition; phantasm, fantasy, chimera, vision; shadow, trace, dim reflection | خيال شك *ḵ. šakk* slightest doubt; خيال الصحراء *ḵ. aṣ-ṣaḥrā'* scarecrow; خيال الظل *ḵ. aẓ-ẓill* shadow play; الخيال المبتكر (*mubtakir*) and الخيال الخلاق (*ḵallāq*) creative imagination; هذا خيال فى خيال that is sheer fantasy!

خيالة *ḵayāla* pl. *-āt* ghost, spirit, specter; phantom; phantasm, fantasy, chimera

خيالى *ḵayālī* imaginary, unreal; ideal, ideational, conceptual; utopian

اخيل *aḵyal*[2] more conceited, haughtier, prouder

اخيل *aḵyal* pl. خيل *ḵīl*, اخايل *aḵāyil*[2] green woodpecker

خيلاء *ḵuyalā'*[2] conceit, conceitedness, haughtiness, pride; الخيلاء *al-ḵuyalā'a* haughtily, proudly

خيلولة *ḵailūla* conceit, conceitedness, snobbery, arrogance, haughtiness

مخيلة *maḵīla* conceit, conceitedness, snobbery, arrogance, haughtiness; (pl. مخايل *maḵāyil*[2]) indication, sign, symptom, characteristic; pl. مخايل visions, mental images, imagery

تخييل *taḵyīl* fantastic deception, sham; play acting | فن التخييل *fann at-t.* dramatic art

تخيل *taḵayyul* pl. *-āt* imagination, phantasy; delusion, hallucination, fancy, whim, fantastic notion

تخيلى *taḵayyulī* fantastic, fanciful, imaginary

اختيال *iḵtiyāl* pride; arrogance, haughtiness

مخيلة *muḵayyila* imagination, phantasy

مخيل *muḵīl* dubious, doubtful, uncertain, intricate, tangled, confused; confusing, bewildering

مختال *muḵtāl* conceited, haughty, arrogant

[2]خيل II to gallop (on horseback)

خيل *ḵail* (coll.) pl. خيول *ḵuyūl* horses; horsepower, H.P. | سباق الخيل horse racing, horse race; ليس هناك لا خيل ولا خيالة (*ḵail, ḵayyāla*) approx.: all is desolate and empty, deathlike, without civilization

خيال *ḵayyāl* pl. ة, *-ūn* horseman, rider

خيالة *ḵayyāla* cavalry (*mil.*) | سرية خيالة *sarīya ḵayyāla* cavalry squadron (*mil.*)

[3]خال see خول

[1]خيم II to pitch one's tent, to camp; to settle down; to stay, linger, rest, lie down, lie (على on, فى or ب at a place); (fig.) to reign (e.g., calm, silence, peace, etc.; فى or ب at, in), settle (على over) V to pitch one's tent; to camp

خيمة *ḵaima* pl. *-āt*, خيام *ḵiyām*, خيم *ḵiyam* tent; tarpaulin; arbor, bower; pavilion

خيام *ḵayyām* tentmaker

مخيم *muḵayyam* pl. *-āt* camping ground, camp, encampment | مخيمات الشباب *m. aš-šabāb* youth camps

[2]خيم *ḵīm* natural disposition, nature, temper, character; inclination, bent, tendency | اخذ خيمه (*eg.*) to feel s.o.'s pulse, sound s.o. out

[3]خام look up alphabetically

□ خية *ḵayya* pl. *-āt* noose

د

د abbreviation of دقيقة minute, درهم dirham, دينار dinar (د ج = دينار جزائرى Algerian dinar, د ل = دينار ليبى Libyan dinar); د. for دكتور Doctor, Dr.

دأب *da'aba a* (*da'b, da'ab,* دؤوب *du'ūb*) to persist, persevere, be indefatigable, untiring, tireless (فى or على in s.th.); to go in for s.th. (على), apply o.s., devote o.s. (على to), practice eagerly (على s.th.)

دأب *da'b* pl. ادؤب *ad'ub* habit

دأب *da'b, da'ab* and دؤوب *du'ūb* persistence, perseverance, tirelessness, indefatigability, assiduity, eagerness

دئب *da'ib* and دائب *dā'ib* addicted, devoted, persistent, assiduous, eager, indefatigable, untiring, tireless (على in)

دءوب *da'ūb* untiring, tireless, indefatigable, persevering, persistent

ادأب *ad'ab*[2] more persistent, more assiduous

دادة *dāda* governess, dry nurse, nurse

دار صينى *dār ṣīnī* bark of Cinnamomum zeylanicum (*bot.*); cinnamon; a refreshing cinnamon drink

دار فلفل *dār fulful, dārafilfil* (*eg.*) a variety of peppers (Piper Chaba; *bot.*)

داغ *dāğ* pl. *-āt* brand (made on cattle, etc.)

داكا *dakkā* Dacca

دال *dāl* name of the letter د

داليا *dāliyā* dahlia(s) (*bot.*)

داما *dāmā* checkers | لوحة الداما *lauḥat ad-d.* checkerboard

داماجانة see دمجانة

دانتيل *dantīl* = دانتيلا

دانتيلا (Fr. *dentelle*) *dantillā, dantellā* lace

دانق *dānaq, dāniq* pl. دوانق *dawāniq*[2] an ancient coin, = $^1/_6$ dirham; small coin; a square measure (*Eg.*; = 4 *sahm* = 29.17 m²)

الدانمارك *ad-danmark* Denmark

دانماركى *danmarkī* Danish

الدانوب *ad-dānūb* the Danube

داهومى *dahōmī* Dahomey (former name of Benin, country in W Africa)

داود *dāwūd*[2] David | داود باشا (*syr.*) meal of rice and meat

داى[1] *dāy* pl. *āt* dey (former Turkish title for the ruler of Algiers and Tunis)

داية[2] *dāya* pl. *-āt* wet nurse; midwife

دب *dabba i* (*dabb,* دبيب *dabīb*) to creep, crawl (reptile, insect); to proceed, advance, or move slowly; to go on all fours; to enter (فى s.th.), come (فى into); to steal, creep (فى نفسه into s.o.'s heart; of a feeling, e.g., doubt); to spread (فى over, in, through), fill, pervade, invade (فى s.th.); to gain ground; to gain ascendancy (فى in s.o.; of a condition, an idea, a sensation); to stream in, rush in (of sensations, فى upon s.o.) | دب فيه دبيب الحياة (*d. al-ḥayāh*) to gain vitality **II** to sharpen, point, taper (ه s.th.)

دب *dubb* pl. ادباب *adbāb,* دببة *dibaba* bear | الدب الاصغر (*aṣğar*) Little Bear, Ursa Minor (*astron.*); الدب الاكبر (*akbar*) Great Bear, Ursa Major (*astron.*)

دبى *dubbī* ursine

دبة *dubba* she-bear

دبة *dabba* sand hill, mound

دبيب *dabīb* creeping, crawling; infiltration; influx, inflow, flow (e.g., of sensations, of life, of vigor); reptile

دباب *dabbāb* creeping, crawling, repent, reptant

دبابة *dabbāba* pl. *-āt* tank, armored car

مدب *madabb*: من مدب النيل الى مصبه (*maṣabbihī*) from the lower Nile to its mouth

دابة *dābba* pl. دواب *dawābb*² animal, beast; riding animal (horse, mule, donkey)

دويبة *duwaibba* tiny animal, animalcule; insect

مدبب *mudabbab* pointed, tapered

دبج II to embellish, decorate, adorn, ornament (ه s.th.); to put in good style, formulate, compose, write down, put down in writing (ه s.th.)

ديباج *dībāj* pl. دبابيج *dabābīj*² silk brocade

ديباجة *dībāja* (n. un. of ديباج) brocade; introductory verses or lines, proem, preamble; face, visage; style, elegance of style; renown, repute, standing, prestige

تدبيج *tadbīj* embellishment, adornment, ornamentation; composition, writing (of a book)

مدبجات *mudabbajāt* embellishments of speech, fine figures of speech

دبدب *dabdaba* to tread, tap; to step noisily, clatter; to clop; to patter

دبدبة *dabdaba* sound of footsteps, footfall, pitapat; pattering or clattering noise; snapping, flapping noise

دبدوبة *dabdūba* pl. دباديب *dabādīb*² point, tip, tapered end

¹دبر *dabara u* (دبور *dubūr*) to turn one's back; to elapse, pass, go by (time) **II** to make arrangements, make plans (ه for), prepare, plan, organize, design, frame, devise, concert, arrange, get up, bring about (ه s.th.); to hatch (ه a plot, etc.); to contrive, work up (ه a ruse); to direct, conduct, manage, run, engineer, steer, marshal, regulate (ه s.th.), be in charge (ه of); to manage well, economize (ه s.th.) | دبر خطة (*kiṭṭatan*) to devise a plan; دبر الشؤون to conduct the course of business, be in charge **IV** to turn one's back (عن or على on s.o.); to flee, run away; to escape, dodge; to slip away **V** to be prepared, planned, organized, managed; to reflect, ponder (فى or ه on); to consider, weigh, contemplate (فى or ه s.th.); to treat or handle with care, with circumspection (فى s.th.); to proceed or behave in a well-planned and prudent manner (ه in an affair) **VI** to face in opposite directions, stand back to back; to be contrary, opposite, opposed; to be inconsistent, incompatible **X** to turn the back (ه on s.o.)

دبر *dubr, dubur* pl. ادبار *adbār* rump backside, buttocks, posteriors; rear part, rear, hindpart; back; last part, end, tail | من دبر behind, at the back, in the rear; from behind, from the rear; ولى دبره *wallā duburahū* to turn one's back; to flee, run away

دبرى *dabarī* trailing behind, belated, late

دبرة *dabra* turn (of fate)

دبور *dabūr* f. west wind

دبور *dabbūr* pl. دبابير *dabābīr*² hornet; wasp

تدبير *tadbīr* pl. *-āt* planning, organization; direction, management, disposal, regulation; economy, economization; — (pl. تدابير *tadābīr*²) measure, move, step | تدبير المنزل *t. al-manzil* housekeeping, household management; تدبير منزلى (*manzilī*) do.; قام بالتدابير اللازمة and اتخذ التدابير اللازمة (*ittakada*) to take the necessary measures; احسن تدبيره (*aḥsana*) to take good care of s.th., be economical; to plan or organize s.th. well

ادبار *idbār* flight, retreat

تدبر *tadabbur* reflection, meditation (فى on), thinking (فى about); consideration, contemplation (فى of); deliberation

تدابر *tadābur* disparity, dissimilarity, contrast

دابر *dābir* past, bygone (time); the ultimate, utmost, extremity, end; root | قطع دابر الشىء (*dābira š-šai'*) to eradicate, root out s.th., suppress s.th. radically; بالامس الدابر (*amsi*) sometime in the past; ذهب كامس الدابر (*ka-amsi d-dābiri*) to vanish into thin air, disappear without leaving a trace (actually: like yesterday gone by)

مدبر *mudabbir* manager, director; ruler, disposer; leader; ringleader | مدبر المكائد schemer, intriguer, intrigant

مدبر *mudbir*: مدبرا ومقبلا *mudbiran wamuqbilan* from the rear and from in front

[2]دبارة *dubāra* (= دوبارة) packthread, string, twine, cord, rope; thread

دبرياج (Fr. *débrayage*) *dibriyāj* clutch (auto)

[1]دبس *dibs* sirup, molasses, treacle, esp. of grapes

[2]دبوس *dabbūs* pl. دبابيس *dabābīs*[2] pin; safety pin | دبوس انكليزى safety pin; دبوس الكرافتة *d. al-kravatta* tie pin

دبش *dabaš* pl. ادباش *adbāš* junk, rubbish, trash; household goods; furnishings, furniture; — *dabš* rubblestone, rubble; crushed rock (used as substratum in macadamizing)

دبغ *dabaġa a i u* (*dabġ*) to tan (ه a hide) **VII** to be tanned

دباغة *dibāġa* tanning, tanner's trade

دباغ *dabbāġ* tanner

مدبغة *madbaġa* pl. مدابغ *madābiġ*[2] tannery

دبق *dabiqa a* (*dabaq*) to stick, adhere (ب to); to cleave, cling (ب to) **II** to catch with birdlime (ه a bird)

دبق *dibq* birdlime

دبق *dabiq* sticky, gluey, limy

دبك *dabaka u* (*dabk*) to stamp the feet; to dance the *dabka* (see below)

دبكة *dabka* (*syr.*) a group dance in which the dancers, lined up with locked arms or holding hands, stamp out the rhythm and sing

دبلة *dibla* pl. دبل *dibal* ring

دبلوم *diblōm* and دبلومة *diblōma* pl. *-āt* diploma

دبلوماسى *diblōmāsī* diplomatic; (pl. *-ūn*) diplomat

دبلوماسية *diblōmāsīya* diplomacy

دبى *dubaiy*[2] Dubai, name of an emirate on the Persian Gulf

دثر *daṯara u* (دثور *duṯūr*) to fall into oblivion, be forgotten, become obsolete, antiquated, extinct; to be blotted out, wiped out, effaced, obliterated (track by the wind) **II** to cover, envelop (ه s.o.); to destroy, annihilate (ه s.th.) **V** to wrap o.s. (فى in), cover o.s. (فى with) **VII** to be or become wiped out, blotted out, effaced, obliterated; to be old; to be forgotten, have fallen into oblivion, be obsolete **VIII** *iddaṯara* to wrap o.s. (ب in), cover o.s. (ب with)

دثار *diṯār* pl. دثر *duṯur* blanket, cover

مدثور *madṯūr* past, bygone, ancient (time)

دج *dajja* i (*dajj*, دجيج *dajīj*) to walk slowly II دججه بالسلاح to arm s.o. to the teeth V تدجج بالسلاح to be armed to the teeth

دج *dujj* (*syr.*) thrush (*zool.*)

دجة *dujja* intense darkness, pitch-darkness

دجاج *dajāj* (coll.) chickens; fowl (as a generic designation)

دجاجة *dajāja* (n. un.) hen; chicken | دجاجة الحبش *d. al-ḥabaš* guinea fowl

مدجج بالسلاح *mudajjaj bi-s-silāḥ* heavily armed, bristling with arms

دجر *dajira* a (*dajar*) to be embarrassed, be at a loss

ديجور *daijūr* pl. دياجير *dayājīr*² gloom, darkness, dark

ديجورى *daijūrī* dark, gloomy

دجل¹ *dajala* u to deceive, dupe, cheat, take in (على s.o.); to be a swindler, a charlatan, a quack II to coat, smear (ه s.th.); to gild (ه s.th.); to deceive, dupe, cheat, take in (على s.o.), impose (على on)

دجل *dajl* deceit, trickery, humbug, swindle

دجال *dajjāl* pl. *-ūn*, دجاجلة *dajājila* swindler, cheat, imposter; quack, charlatan (fem. دجالة); (also المسيح الدجال) Antichrist

تدجيل *tadjīl* imposture, humbug; charlatanry, quackery

دجلة² *dijla*² the Tigris river

دجن *dajana* u (*dajn*, دجون *dujūn*) to be dusky, murky, gloomy (day); — (*dujūn*) to remain, stay; to get used, become accustomed, become habituated; to become tame, be domesticated II to tame; to domesticate (ه an animal) | دجنه لخدمة فلان (*li-ḵidmati f.*) to put s.th. or s.o. to use for s.o., make s.th. or s.o. of service to s.o. III to flatter, cajole, coax, wheedle, try to win or entice by gentle courtesy (ه s.o.) IV to be murky, gloomy, overcast (day); to be dark (night)

دجنة *dujna*, *dujunna* darkness, gloominess, gloom

ادجن *adjan*² dark

داجن *dājin* tame, tamed, domesticated (animal); dark, gloomy | حيوانات داجنة (*ḥayawānāt*) domestic animals

دواجن *dawājin*² poultry

مدجن *mudajjan* tamed; domesticated; pl. المدجنون the Mudejars, Muslims allowed to remain after the Christian reconquest of Spain

دجنبر *dužambir* (*Mor.*) December

دجا (دجو) *dajā* u to be dark, gloomy, dusky; to overshadow, cover, veil, shroud, blanket (ه s.th.), spread (ه over) III to play the hypocrite, pose as a friend (ه of s.o.); to cajole, flatter (ه s.o.)

دجى *dujan* gloom, darkness, duskiness

دياجى الليل *dayājī l-lail* dark of night

مداجاة *mudājāh* hypocrisy; flattery, adulation, sycophancy

داج *dājin* dark, gloomy

دحدح II *tadaḥdaḥa* to waddle

دحدح *daḥdaḥ* and دحداح *daḥdāḥ* dumpy, squat, stocky

دحر *daḥara* a (*daḥr*, دحور *duḥūr*) to drive away, chase away (ه s.o.); to dislodge, remove (ه s.o.); to defeat (ه an army) VIII to be driven away, be routed, be repelled, be thrown back; to be defeated (army); to go under, go to ruin, succumb, break down, collapse

اندحار *indiḥār* banishment, rejection; (pl. *-āt*) defeat (*mil.*); ruin, fall, breakdown, collapse; catastrophe | اندحار الكون *ind. al-kaun* end of the world

مدحور *madḥūr* routed, repelled; expelled, cast out; ostracized, banished

دحرج *daḥraja* to roll (ه s.th.) **II** *tadaḥraja* to roll, roll along; to roll down

داحس *dāḥis* pl. دواحس *dawāḥis* whitlow, felon (*med.*)

دحش *daḥaša a* (*daḥš*) to insert, thrust in, shove in, foist in, smuggle in **VII** to interfere, meddle; to mix

دحض *daḥaḍa a* to be invalid, void, untenable (argument); to disprove, refute, invalidate (ه an argument) **II** and **IV** to disprove, refute, invalidate (ه an argument) | لا يدحض (*yudḥaḍu*) irrefutable

دحض *daḥḍ* refutation, disproof

دحوض *duḥūḍ* invalidity, shakiness, weakness, refutability (of an argument or a claim)

مدحاض *midḥāḍ*: دعوى مدحاض (*da'wā*) an invalid, unjustified claim

دحل *daḥal* (*leb.*) marbles

(دحو) دحا *daḥā u* (*daḥw*) to spread out, flatten, level, unroll

ادحية *udḥīya* ostrich nest in the ground

O مدحى *midḥan* pl. مداح *madāḥin* roller, steamroller

ادخر *iddakara*, ادخار *iddikār*, مدخر *muddakir*, *muddakar*, مدخرة *muddakira* see ذخر

دخس *dukas* dolphin

دخل *dakala u* (دخول *dukūl*) to enter (ه, less frequently في, also الى, s.th.), go, step, walk, move, come, get (ه, في, الى into); to penetrate, pierce (ه, في, الى s.th.); to take possession of s.o. (ه), befall, seize (ه s.o.; e.g., doubt); to take up (خدمة a post), start at a job; to enter s.o.'s (على) room or house, drop in on s.o. (على), come to see s.o. (على); to call on s.o. (على); to consummate the marriage, cohabit, sleep (ب or على with a woman); to come (على over s.o.; e.g., joy); (*gram.*) to be added (على to); to supervene, enter as a new factor, aspect, element, etc. (على upon s.th.), be newly introduced (على into s.th.); to make one's own, acquire (على s.th.); to join, enter (ه or في e.g., a religious community); to participate, take part (ه in); to set in, begin (time, event); to be included (في in; also ضمن *ḍimna*), fall, come (في, ضمن, تحت under), belong, pertain (في, ضمن, تحت to), be within s.th. (في, ضمن, تحت); pass.: *dukila* to be sickly, diseased, abnormal | دخل على الامر تعديل (*ta'dīlun*) the matter has undergone modification; دخل الخدمة (*kidma*) to take up one's post, start at a job, report for work; دخل المدرسة (*madrasa*) to enter school; دخل الميناء (*mīnā'*) to enter the harbor, put in; دخل فى الموضوع to come to the point; دخل فى عقله (فى جسمه) *dukila fī 'aqlihī* (*fī jismihī*) to suffer from a mental (physical) disturbance **II** to make or let enter, bring in, let in (ه, ه s.o., s.th.); to enter, insert, include (ه s.th., في or ه in) **III** to come over s.o. (ه), befall, seize (ه s.o.; e.g., doubt, suspicion, despair) **IV** to make or let enter, bring in, let in, admit, lead in, show in (ه s.o., ه into a house or room), take (ه ه s.o. to); to move, take, haul (على or في ه s.th. into); to incorporate, include, embody, insert (في or ه ه s.th. in); to cause to set in, bring about, produce, set off, trigger (على ه s.th. in); to introduce (ه s.th., e.g., an innovation, an improvement, على in or on s.th.) | ادخله المدرسة (*madrasa*) to send s.o. to school; to take s.o. to school; ادخل المستشفى *udkila l-mustašfā* to be taken to the hospital; ادخل تغييرا على to bring about a change in ...; ادخلت عليه تعديلات (*udkilat*) the matter was subjected to modifications **V** to meddle (في in), interfere (ف in, with); to interpose, intervene (ف in); to invade (ف s.th.), intrude, obtrude (ف on), disturb (ف s.th.); to interlock, mesh, gear **VI** to meddle (ف in, e.g., ف شؤونه in s.o.'s affairs), butt in (ف الحديث on a conversation); to interfere (ف in, with), interpose, intervene (ف in); to interlock, mesh, gear; to be superimposed; to be intertwined (e.g., streets); to intergrade, shade, blend (ببعض or بعضه فى بعض one into the other); to come over s.o. (ه), befall, strike, seize (ه s.o.; e.g., doubt, grief)

دخل *dakl* income; revenues, receipts, returns, takings (as opposed to خرج *karj*); interference, intervention; doubt, misgiving | ضريبة الدخل income tax; الدخل القومى (*qaumī*) national income, gross national product, GNP; الدخل الصافى net income; ليس له اى دخل فيه (*ayyu daklin*) and (ب or) لا دخل له فى (*dakla*) he should not meddle in . . ., he has nothing to do with . . ., it is none of his business; ما دخلك ؟ what's that got to do with you?

دخل *dakal* disturbance, derangement, disorder, imbalance, or defect of the mind; defect, infirmity

دخلة *dikla* intrinsic nature, essence; inner self, innermost, heart, soul (of a person); secret intention | راجع دخلته *rāja'a diklatahū* to commune with o.s., search one's soul

دخلة *dukla*: ليلة الدخلة *lailat ad-d.* wedding night

دخلة *dukkala* a variety of warbler

دخيل *dakīl* inner, inward, internal; inner self, heart, core; adopted from outside; taken from a foreign language (into Arabic); — (pl. دخلاء *dukalā'*[2]) newly added (على to); extraneous, not indigenous, alien; foreigner, alien, stranger; newcomer, novice; (new) convert; guest; protégé, charge, ward | كلمة دخيلة (*kalima*), لفظ دخيل (*lafẓ*) foreign word or expression; (*syr.-pal.*) دخيلك (*dakīlak*) please, if you please

دخيلة *dakīla* pl. دخائل *dakā'il*[2] inner self, inmost being, intrinsic nature; innermost thought | فى دخيلة نفسه inwardly, inside, in his heart; دخائل نفوسنا our inmost being; دخائل الامور the underlying nature of things, the factors at the bottom of things; دخائل شؤونه *d. šu'ūnihī* his private affairs; its internal affairs

دخول *dukūl* entry, entrance, admission; entering, ingress; beginning, setting in; penetration; intrusion, invasion; first coition in marriage (*Isl. Law*) | دخول الحرب *d. al-ḥarb* entry into war

دخولية *dukūlīya* octroi, city toll; (*syr.-leb.*) entrance fee

مدخل *madkal* pl. مداخل *madākil*[2] entrance; hallway, vestibule, anteroom; entrance hall, lobby, foyer; mouth (of a port, of a canal); entry or access road, highway leading into a metropolis; ○ anode (*el.*); behavior, conduct; see also *mudkal* | مدخل للسيارات (*sayyārāt*) driveway; حسن المدخل *ḥusn al-m.* good manners, good conduct

مداخلة *mudākala* interference, intervention; participation, interest (ف in)

ادخال *idkāl* leading in, showing in, bringing in, taking in, hauling in; involvement, implication; insertion, interpolation, incorporation, inclusion; introduction (e.g., of a constitution; of an improvement, على on an apparatus, or the like)

تدخل *tadakkul* entry, entrance; invasion; interference (ف with, in), intervention; intrusion, obtrusion | عدم التدخل *'adam at-t.* noninterference, nonintervention (*pol.*)

تداخل *tadākul* interference, intervention; interlock, interlocking, nexus, meshing; superimposition; intergradation; permeation, pervasion; ○ interference (*phys.*)

داخل *dāḵil* belonging, pertaining (في to), falling (في under), included (في in); inner, inward, inside, interior, internal; inside, interior (of s.th.); *dāḵila* (prep.) within, inside, in; داخلا *dāḵilan* inside (adv.) | من الداخل from within; from the inside

داخلة *dāḵila* pl. دواخل *dawāḵil*² interior, inside, inmost, hidden part; الداخلة the Dakhla oasis (in central Egypt)

داخلى *dāḵilī* inner, inward; internal; interior, inside; concerning internal services, used internally; domestic, home, inland (as opposed to خارجى *ḵārijī* external, foreign; *pol.*); indigenous, native; private; belonging to the house; داخليا *dāḵilīyan* inside (adv.) | تلاميذ داخلية boarding students (as opposed to خارجية day students); حرب داخلية (*ḥarb*) civil war; مدرسة داخلية (*madrasa*) boarding school; ملابس داخلية underwear; ملاحة داخلية inland navigation

داخلية *dāḵilīya* interior | داخلية البلاد the interior of the country, the inland; وزارة الداخلية ministry of the interior; وزير الداخلية minister of the interior

مدخول *madḵūl* sickly, diseased, abnormal; (mentally) disordered; weak-minded, mad, insane; of weak character, spineless; (pl. مداخيل *madāḵīl*²) revenue, receipts, takings, returns; income

مدخل *mudḵal* (also pronounced *madḵal*) introduction (إلى or ل to a field of learning, e.g., لدراسة القانون to the study of law)

دخمس *dakmasa* (دخمسة *dakmasa*) to fool (على s.o.) about one's real intentions, pull the wool over s.o.'s (على) eyes; to cheat; to be sly, crafty, artful

دخمسة *dakmasa* deception, fooling, trickery; cunning, craft, slyness

دخن *dakina a* to be smoky; to taste or smell of smoke; — *dakana a u* to smoke, emit smoke (fire) **II** to fumigate, fume (ه s.th.); to smoke, cure with smoke (ه foodstuffs); to smoke (ه a cigarette, tobacco, a pipe) **IV** to smoke, emit smoke (fire) **V** to be smoked, be cured with smoke; to be fumigated

دخن *dukn* pearl millet, dukhn

دخن *dakan* smoke, fume, vapor

دخان *dukān* (*dukkān*) pl. ادخنة *adkina* smoke, fume, vapor; tobacco

دخنة *dukna* smoke color; a kind of incense (Calamus aromaticus)

○ دخينة *dakīna* pl. دخائن *dakā'in*² cigarette

دخاخنى *dakākinī* (*eg., tun.*) tobacconist

مدخنة *madkana* pl. مداخن *madākin*² chimney, smokestack, funnel

تدخين *tadkīn* fumigation; smoking (e.g., of fish); (tobacco) smoking

داخنة *dākina* pl. دواخن *dawākin*² chimney, smokestack, funnel

مدخن *mudakkin* pl. -*ūn* smoker; — *mudakkan* smoked (foodstuffs)

ديدبان look up alphabetically

ديدن *daidan* habit, practice

ددى **III** to pamper, spoil (ه a child)

در *darra i u* (*darr*) to flow copiously; to stream, flow, well; to accrue (على to s.o.; profit, wealth); to be abundant, plentiful **IV** to make flow, cause to flow abundantly (ه s.th., e.g., sweat, milk); to bestow lavishly, heap (ه على s.th. upon s.o.), shower, overwhelm (ه على with s.th. s.o.); to yield (ه a profit, على to s.o.) **X** to stream, flow; to be abundant; to cause or try to bring about the abundant flow of (ه); to cause s.th. (ه) to yield in abundance; to be out for s.th. (ه), seek to gain (ه a profit), try to make (ه a living); to evoke, awaken (ه an emotion, e.g., sympathy)

در darr milk; achievement, accomplishment | لله دره li-llāhi darruhū (literally: his achievement is due to God) how capable, how good, how excellent he is!

در durr (coll.) pearls

درة durra (n. un.) pl. -āt, درر durar pearl; — a variety of parrot (Psittacus Alexandri L.)

درى durrī glittering, twinkling, brilliant (star)

درة dirra, darra pl. درر dirar teat; udder

مدرار midrār showering abundant rain (sky, cloud); spouting, pouring forth, welling out

ادرار idrār: ادرار البول i. al-baul copious urination, diuresis

دار dārr flowing copiously; productive, rich, lucrative; profitable

مدر mudirr: مدر للبول (baul) diuretic(al), pl. مدرات البول diuretics; مدر للعرق (ʿaraq) sudorific

درأ daraʾa (darʾ) to reject (ه s.th.); to avert, ward off (ه s.th., e.g., خطرا kaṭaran a danger, عن from) VI iddāraʾa to contend (فى for)

درء darʾ repulsion, prevention, averting; warding off, parrying

دريئة darīʾa pl. -āt target

درابزين darābazīn railing, parapet, banisters, balustrade

دراج Durrës (It. Durazzo, seaport in W Albania)

دراق durrāq (n. un. ة; syr.) peaches, peach

دراما drāmā drama

درامى drāmī dramatic

درامية drāmīya dramatics, dramatic nature

دراماتيكى drāmatīkī dramatic

درب dariba a (darab, دربة durba) to be accustomed, be used (ب to), be practiced, trained, skilled (ب in) II to habituate, accustom (ه, ه s.o., s.th., فى or ب or على to); to practice, drill (ه s.o., فى, ب or على in); to school, train, coach, tutor (ه s.o., فى, ب or على in) V to be accustomed, be used (على or فى to); to be or become practiced, skilled, trained, drilled, schooled (على or فى in); to train (athlet.)

درب darb pl. دروب durūb narrow mountain pass; path, trail, track; road; alley, lane | درب التبانة d. at-tabbāna the Milky Way

دربة durba habituation, habitude, habit; familiarity (with s.th.), experience; skill, practice

دريبة darība court of first instance (Tun.)

تدريب tadrīb habituation, accustoming; (pl. -āt) practice; drill; schooling, training, coaching, tutoring; continuation training | تدريب اساسى (asāsī) basic training; تدريب تخصصى (takaṣṣuṣī) specialized training; التدريب العسكرى (ʿaskarī) military training; تدريب فنى (fannī) technical training; تدريب مهنى (mihanī) vocational training

تدريبى tadrībī: دورة تدريبية (daura) training course; continuation course

مدرب mudarrib pl. -ūn instructor, drill instructor; trainer, coach (athlet.); tamer (of wild animals)

مدرب mudarrab experienced; practiced, skilled; trained; schooled

متدرب mutadarrib pl. -ūn trainee, trained person

درابزين darābazīn and دربزين darbazīn railing, parapet, banisters, balustrade

دربس darbasa to bolt (ه a door)

درباس *dirbās* pl. درابيس *darābīs*² bolt, doorbolt

دربكة *darabukka* (*eg.*), *dirbakka* (*syr.*) pl. *-āt* darabukka, a conical, one-headed hand drum, open at the small end

دربكة *darbaka* banging or rattling noise, din, uproar, turmoil

درج *daraja u* (دروج *durūj*) to go, walk, move' proceed, advance (slowly); to approach gradually, step by step (الى s.th.); to follow a course (على), proceed along the lines of (على), proceed in such and such a manner (على); to be accustomed, be used (على to do s.th.); to go away, leave, depart; to outgrow (من a nest, a habitation); to be past, bygone, over (time); to have passed away, be extinct; to circulate, be in circulation, be current, have currency; to grow up (child); — (*darj*) to roll up, roll together (ه s.th.); to wrap, wind, twist (ه على s.th. around); — *darija a* to rise or advance step by step | درج العرف على *daraja l-ʿurfu ʿalā* it has become the general practice to ... **II** to make (ه s.o.) rise or advance by steps, promote (ه s.o.) by degrees; to move or bring (ه s.th.) gradually closer (الى to); to approximate (ه الى s.th. to); to roll up, fold up (ه s.th.); to circulate, put into circulation (ه s.th.), give currency (ه to s.th.), make (ه s.th.) the general practice; to divide into degrees, steps or grades, graduate, grade, gradate (ه s.th.) **III** to go, keep up (ه with, e.g., with the time, with a fashion) **IV** to insert, include, incorporate, embody (ه فى s.th. in); to enter, register (ه فى s.th., e.g., in a list), book (ه s.th.); to enfold, wrap (ه فى s.o. in, a corpse in a shroud) **V** to progress by steps, advance gradually; to proceed step by step (الى to); to make progress (فى in); to graduate (فى e.g., in the grades of a school, of pupils); to grade, be graded, graduated, gradated **VII** to be inserted, entered, incorporated, embodied, included (فى in); to be classified (فى in, تحت under) **X** to make (ه s.o.) advance or rise gradually, promote (ه s.o.) by degrees; to lead (ه s.o.) gradually (الى to), bring (ه s.o.) around to (الى, ل); to bait, allure (ه s.o.); to entice, tempt, lure into destruction (ه s.o.)

درج *darj* entry, entering, registering, registration, recording; a rolled or folded paper; roll, scroll | فى درج الكتاب in the book; فى درج الكلام *fī d. il-kalām* in the course of the talk

درج *durj* pl. ادراج *adrāj*, دروج *durūj* drawer (of a table, desk, etc.); (pl. ادراج) desk (e.g., for pupils in school)

درج *daraj* pl. ادراج *adrāj* way, route, course; flight of steps, stairs, staircase | رجع ادراجه *rajaʿa adrājahū* (also عاد ادراجه) to retrace one's steps, go back the way one came; to go back, turn back; ذهب ادراج الرياح (*adrāja r-riyāḥ*) to go the ways of the winds, i.e., to pass unnoticed, without leaving a trace; to end in smoke, come to nothing, be futile, be in vain

درجة *daraja* pl. *-āt* step, stair; flight of steps, stairs, staircase; degree, step, tone (of a scale; *mus.*); degree (*math.*, *geogr.*; of temperature); grade, rate; degree, order, rank; class (also, e.g., in trains, of a decoration); phase, state, stage (of a development); mark, grade (in school) | درجة الحرارة *d. al-ḥarāra* (degree of) temperature; الدرجات العليا (*ʿulyā*) the maximal temperatures; الدرجات السفلى (*suflā*) the minimal temperatures; درجة صوتية (*ṣautīya*) tone level, pitch (*mus.*); درجة الطول *d. aṭ-ṭūl* degree of longitude (*geogr.*); درجة علمية (جامعية) (*ʿilmīya, jāmiʿīya*) academic degree; درجة العقل *d. al-ʿaql* level of intelligence, IQ; دفتر الدرجات report card (in school); كشف الدرجات *kašf ad-d.* report card, class report, school record; من (فى) الدرجة الاولى (*ūlā*) first-rate, first-class; ذو درجة of superior quality, high-grade, high-class; لدرجة ان (*li-darajati*) to the extent that ...; to such an extent that ..., so much that ...; لآخر درجة in the highest degree

دراج *durrāj* pl. دراريج *darārīj*² francolin (*zool.*); see also alphabetically

تدرج *tadruj*², تدرجة *tadruja* pheasant

دراج *darrāj* pl. *-ūn* (*Tun.*) bicyclist

دراجة *darrāja* pl. *-āt* bicycle | دراجة نارية and دراجة بخارية (*bukārīya*) motorcycle

مدرج *madraj* pl. مدارج *madārij*² way that one follows or pursues; course, route; road, path; starting point, outset, rise, growth, birth, dawn, beginning(s); tarmac, runway (of an airport); (as also *mudarraj*) amphitheater; (amphitheatered) auditorium or lecture room; grandstand, bleachers | منذ مدرجه since its beginnings; مدرج نشأته *m. naš'atihī* the place where he grew up; سار فى مدارج الرقى (*m. ir-ruqīy*) to travel the road of progress

مدرجة *madraja* pl. مدارج *madārij*² tarmac, runway (of an airport)

تدريج *tadrīj* division into degrees; gradation, graduation; gradual advance or increase | تدريجا *tadrījan*, على التدريج, بالتدريج, مع التدريج gradually, by and by, by degrees, by steps, step by step, more and more

تدريجى *tadrījī* gradual, gradatory, progressive; تدريجيا *tadrījīyan* gradually, by and by, by steps, by degrees, in stages

ادراج *idrāj* insertion, interpolation, incorporation; entry, registration, recording (فى in a list)

تدرج *tadarruj* gradual advance or progress; gradation, graduation | بالتدرج gradually, by and by; تدرج ارتقائه *t. irtiqā'ihī* his gradual rise

استدراج *istidrāj* capability of gradually winning s.o. over, persuasiveness, art of persuasion

دارج *dārij* current, prevalent, widespread, popular, common, in vogue, circulating, in circulation | الكلام الدارج (*kalām*) and اللغة الدارجة (*luğa*) the popular language, colloquial language

مدرج *mudarraj* graded, graduated; rising stepwise; terraced; — (pl. *-āt*) open staircase, open-air stairs; grandstand, bleachers; amphitheater; (amphitheatered) auditorium or lecture room; terraced slope of a mountain

مدرج *mudraj* inserted, interpolated, incorporated; entered, registered; contained, included (فى, ب in), comprised (ب, فى by)

متدرج *mutadarrij* pl. *-ūn* apprentice

درد *darida a* (*darad*) to become toothless, lose one's teeth

ادرد *adrad*² toothless

دردى *durdī* sediment, dregs, lees

دردبيس *dardabīs* ugly old woman, hag

دردرة *dardara* roar, rush (of water); idle talk, prattle, chatter

دردار *dardār* elm (*bot.*)

دردور *durdūr* eddy, whirlpool, vortex

دردشة *dardaša* idle talk, prattle, chatter

¹درز *daraza u* to sew, stitch

درز *darz* pl. دروز *durūz* seam, hem; suture

²درزى *durzī* pl. دروز *durūz* Druse | جبل الدروز *jabal ad-d.* the Jebel ed Druz, the mountainous homeland of the Druses in S Syria

درس *darasa u* (*dars*) to wipe out, blot out, obliterate, efface, extinguish (ه s.th.); to thresh (ه grain); to learn, study (ه s.th., على under s.o.), درس العلم على (*ʻilm*) to study under (a teacher, a professor); to make a study or investigation (ه of a problem), study precisely (ه a question); — *u* (دروس *durūs*) to be effaced, obliterated, blotted out, extinguished **II** to teach; to instruct (ه s.o., ه in s.th.); **III** to study (ه together with s.o.) **VI** to study (ه s.th.) carefully together **VII** to become or be wiped out, blotted out, effaced, obliterated, extinguished

درس *dars* effacement, obliteration, extinction; — (pl. دروس *durūs*) study, studies; lesson, chapter (of a textbook); class, class hour, period; lecture; lesson (taught by experience, etc.) | القى دروسا عن (*alqā*) to lecture on ...; اعطى دروسا (*aʻṭā*) to give lessons; اخذ دروسا to take lessons; to learn lessons (عن from); درس خصوصى (*ḵuṣūṣī*) private lesson, pl. دروس خصوصية private tutoring; دروس منزلية (*manzilīya*) homework (of a pupil or student)

دراس *dirās* threshing (of grain)

دراسة *dirāsa* pl. *-āt* studies; study; written study or treatment (of a problem) | دراسة عالية (*ʻāliya*) collegiate studies; دراسة ثانوية (*ṯānawīya*) attendance of a secondary school, secondary education, high-school education; دراسة متوسطة (*mutawassiṭa*) secondary education, high-school education (*Syr.*)

دراسى *dirāsī* of or pertaining to study or studies; scholastic, school; instructional, educational, teaching, tuitional | رسوم دراسية tuition fees; سنة دراسية (*sana*) academic year; scholastic year, school year

دريس *darīs* dried clover

عمال الدريسة *ʻummāl ad-darīsa* (*eg.*) railroad section gang, gandy dancers

دراس *darrās* pl. *-ūn* (eager) student

○ دراسة *darrāsa* flail; threshing machine | ○ حصادة دراسة (*ḥaṣṣāda*) combine

درواس *dirwās* mastiff

مدرسة *madrasa* pl. مدارس *madāris*[2] madrasah (a religious boarding school associated with a mosque); school (also = school of thought or artistic trend) | مدرسة ابتدائية (*ibtidāʼīya*) primary school; مدرسة اولية (*awwalīya*) old style elementary school; مدرسة ثانوية (*ṯānawīya*) secondary school, high school; مدرسة اعدادية (*iʻdādīya*) lower grade secondary school, intermediate school; مدرسة متوسطة (*mutawassiṭa*) do. (*Alg., Saudi Ar.*); مدرسة تجارية (*tijārīya*) commercial school; مدرسة حربية (*ḥarbīya*) military academy; مدرسة خاصة (*ḵāṣṣa*) special school (for the handicapped); private school; مدرسة داخلية (*dāḵilīya*) boarding school; مدرسة ريفية (*rīfīya*) village school (*Eg.*); مدرسة زراعية (*zirāʻīya*) agricultural school, secondary school emphasizing agriculture; مدرسة عالية (عليا) (*ʻāliya, ʻulyā*) college; مدرسة الفنون والصنائع school of industrial arts, school of applied art and handicraft; مدرسة كبرى (*kubrā*) college; المدرسة القديمة the old "school" (= intellectual or artistic movement); مدرسة مهنية (*mihanīya*) vocational school

مدرسى *madrasī* scholastic, school | سنة مدرسية (*sana*) school year; الشبيبة المدرسية school-age youth

تدريس *tadrīs* teaching, instruction, tuition | هيئة التدريس *haiʼat at-t.* teaching staff; faculty, professoriate (of an academic institution)

دارس *dāris* pl. *-ūn* student, university student; research worker; — (pl. دوارس *dawāris*[2]) effaced, obliterated; old, dilapidated, crumbling | تجدد دارسه *tajaddada dārisuhū* to rise from one's ashes

مدروس *madrūs* studied, investigated (problem); based on exact studies (plan, project); carefully studied, well-considered

مدرس *mudarris* pl. *-ūn* teacher (general); instructor; teacher at a higher school; (*Eg.*) lecturer | مدرس مساعد (*musā'id*) teaching assistant (university); assistant instructor; مدرس اول (*awwal*) head teacher at a higher school; مدرس الفصل *m. al-faṣl* class teacher

مدرسة *mudarrisa* pl. *-āt* teacher (fem.); lecturer (fem.)

درع **II** to arm; to armor, equip with armor (ه s.th.) **V** and **VIII** *iddara'a* to arm o.s., take up arms, put on armor

درع *dir'* m. and f., pl. دروع *durū'*, ادرع *adru'*, ادراع *adrā'* coat of mail, hauberk; (suit of) plate armor; armor plate; armor; armature; (pl. ادراع *adrā'*) chemise

دراعة *darrā'a* pl. *-āt* armored cruiser

دراعة *durrā'a* pl. دراريع *darārī'*[2] loose outer garment with sleeves, slit in front

دارع *dāri'* armored, armor-clad, ironclad

دارعة *dāri'a* pl. دوارع *dawāri'*[2] armored cruiser

مدرع *mudarra'* armored; armadillo (*zool.*) | قوة مدرعة (*qūwa*) tank corps; سيارة مدرعة (*sayyāra*) armored car; مشاة مدرعون (*mušāh*) armored infantry (*mil.*)

مدرعة *mudarra'a* pl. *-āt* armored cruiser; armored car

درف *darf* side, flank, wing; protection

درفة *darfa* pl. درف *diraf* leaf (of a double door or window)

درفل *darfala* (درفلة *darfala*) to roll, mill (ه metal into sheets; *techn.*)

درفيل *darfīl* pl. درافيل *darāfīl*[2] dolphin (*zool.*); roller (for flattening metal, for moving heavy loads); chock, brake shoe

درقة[1] *daraqa* (leather) shield

O درق *daraq* thyroid gland

درقي *daraqī* shield-shaped; thyroid | الغدة الدرقية (*ğudda*) thyroid gland

دراق[2] look up alphabetically

درك[1] **II** to last, continue, keep up (rains) **III** to reach, get, catch, overtake, outdistance, outrun (ه, ه s.o., s.th.), catch up, come up (ه, ه with); to keep up, continue without interruption (ه s.th.) **IV** to attain, reach (ه s.th.), arrive (ه at); to get, catch, overtake (ه s.o., ه s.th.), catch up, come up (ه, ه with); to come suddenly, unexpectedly (ه upon s.o.), overtake (ه s.o.; death); to obtain (ه s.th.); to grasp, comprehend (ه s.th.); to perceive, discern, notice (ه s.th.); to realize, understand (ه s.th.), become aware, become conscious (ه of s.th.); to mature, ripen (e.g., a fruit); to attain puberty, reach sexual maturity (boy) **V** تدركت الشمس الى المغيب (*šams, mağīb*) the sun prepared to set **VI** to reach and seize one another; to continue without interruption, go on incessantly; to face, meet, obviate, take steps to prevent (ه s.th.); to watch out, be on one's guard (ه against); to handle carefully (ه s.th.), be careful (ه with s.th.); to put in order, set right, correct (ه s.th.), make amends (ه for), provide compensation or indemnity (ه for a loss, or the like) **X** to correct, rectify, emend (ه s.th.); to set right, put in order, straighten out (ه s.th.); to make good, repair, redress (ه a damage, a mistake, etc.), make up (ه for); to supplement, supply (ه that which is missing); to anticipate, forestall, obviate (ه an event)

درك *darak* attainment, achievement, accomplishment; overtaking, catching up; police; (pl. ادراك *adrāk*) bottom, lowest level

دركي *darakī* pl. *-ūn* policeman

دركة *daraka* lowest level; pl. *-āt* descending steps (as opposed to درجات; cf. درجات الحياة ودركات الموت *darajāt al-ḥayāh wa-d. al-maut*)

دراك *darrāk* much-accomplishing, efficient, successful

مدارك *madārik*[2] mental faculties, mental powers; perceptive faculty; sensory perception | المدارك الخمس the five senses

دراكا *dirākan* (adv.) constantly, incessantly, without interruption

ادراك *idrāk* reaching, attainment, achievement, accomplishment; realization, perception, discernment, awareness, consciousness (فقد الادراك *faqd al-i.* unconsciousness); comprehension, understanding, grasp; reason, intelligence; sexual maturity, puberty; age of maturity | سن الادراك *sinn al-i.* age of discretion (*Isl. Law*)

تدرك *tadarruk* gradual decline

استدراك *istidrāk* pl. *-āt* redress, reparation; correction, emendation, rectification

مدرك *mudrik* rational, reasonable, endowed with reason, intelligent; (sexually) mature, pubescent, at the age of puberty

مدركات *mudrakāt* realizations; cognitions; fixed notions, established concepts

المتدارك *al-mutadārik* name of a poetical meter

درك[2] (Engl.) derrick, derrick crane

درم *darima a* to fall out (teeth) II to clip, trim (ه nails)

درن *darina a* (*daran*) to be dirty, filthy IV do. V to suffer from tuberculosis

درن *daran* pl. ادران *adrān* dirt, filth; tubercles; tuberculosis | درن رئوى (*ri'awī*) pulmonary tuberculosis; جبل الدرن *jabal ad-d.* the Atlas Mountains (in NW Africa)

درنة *darana* (n. un.) pl. *-āt* tubercle; small tumor, outgrowth, excrescence, tubercule, nodule

درنى *daranī* tubercular, tuberculous

تدرن *tadarrun* tuberculosis | تدرن رئوى (*ri'awī*) and تدرن الرئة *t. ar-ri'a* pulmonary tuberculosis

تدرنى *tadarrunī* tuberculous

متدرن *mutadarrin* affected with tubercles, tuberculated

مدره *midrah* pl. مداره *madārih*[2] spokesman

درهم *dirham* pl. دراهم *darāhim*[2] dirhem, drachma (*Ir.* = coin of 50 فلس); a weight (*Eg.* = $^1/_{12}$ اوقية = ca. 3.12 g); دراهم money, cash

دريهمات *duraihimāt* (dimin. with a derogatory sense; approx.:) pennies

دروة *dirwa* pl. *-āt* (*eg.*) protecting screen or wall; parapet

درواس *dirwās* mastiff

درويش *darwīš* pl. دراويش *darāwīš*[2] dervish

درى[1] *darā i* (دراية *dirāya*) to know (ب or ه s.th. or of s.th.); to be aware, be cognizant (ب or ه of); to have knowledge (عن of), know (عن about) | وما يدرى الا و... (*illā wa-*) all of a sudden there was ...; suddenly he noticed that ..., before he was even aware, it happened that ... III to flatter, treat with flattery or gentle courtesy, cajole, coax (ه s.o.); to deceive by friendliness, take in (ه s.o.); (*syr.*) to nurse (ه s.o., ه s.th.), attend to (ه), care for (ه); (*eg.*) to screen, shelter, cover protectively (ه s.th.); to hide (ه ب s.th. with or behind) IV to let (ه s.o.) know (ب s.th. or about s.th.), inform, notify, advise (ه ب s.o. of) | وما ادراك ما ... (*adrāka*), وما ادراك ب how can (or could) you know what ... is? you have no idea of ...! وما ادرانى بأن ... how should I know that ..., how was I to know that ...!

VI to hide oneself (ب with or behind, also fig.)

دراية *dirāya* knowledge, cognizance, acquaintance

ادرى *adrā* more knowledgeable, better informed, knowing better (ب s.o., s.th.), better acquainted (ب with)

لاادرى *lā-adrī* pl. *-ūn* a skeptic; an agnostic

لاادرية *lā-adrīya* skepticism; agnosticism

مداراة *mudārāh* flattery; affability, amiable behavior

دار *dārin* knowing, aware, cognizant (ب of s.th.)

²مدرى *midran*, مدرة *midra* (= مردى *mirdan*), مدراة *midrāh* pl. مدار *madārin* pole (esp. one for punting boats)

درياق *diryāq* (= ترياق) theriaca; antidote

دزينة (It. *dozzina*) *dazzīna* pl. *-āt* dozen

دس *dassa u* (*dass*) to put, get, slip, shove, thrust, insert (ه s.th. into ف); to bury (ه ف s.th. in the ground); to slip (ه الى s.th. to s.o.); to instill, infuse (ه ب, ف s.th. in); to administer surreptitiously (السم *as-samma* poison, ل to s.o.); to foist (ه ف s.th. into); to smuggle (ه ف s.th. into, ه بين s.o. among); to interpolate (ه s.th.); to intrigue, scheme, plot (على, ل against s.o.) | دس الدسائس to engage in secret machinations, intrigue, scheme II to put in, get in, slip in, shove in, thrust in, insert (ه s.th.); to hide, conceal (ه s.th.) V to engage (secretly, الى in); to be hidden (ف in) VII to slip (بين between or among, ف into), creep, steal, sneak (بين among, ف into), infiltrate (ف s.th.); to ingratiate o.s., insinuate o.s. (ف or الى to s.o., into s.o.'s confidence); to be hidden

دسيسة *dasīsa* pl. دسائس *dasā'is*² intrigue, machination, scheme, plot | دس الدسائس *dass ad-d.* machinations, intrigues, scheming, plotting (ضد against); plot, conspiracy

دساس *dassās* pl. *-ūn* intrigant, intriguer, schemer, plotter, conspirator; sand snake (Eryx jaculus)

¹دست *dast* pl. دسوت *dusūt* place of honor, seat of honor; seat of office; council | دست الحكم *d. al-ḥukm* (a ruler's) throne

²دست *dist* pl. دسوت *dusūt* kettle, boiler, caldron made of copper (*eg.*, *syr.*)

³دستة *dasta* dozen; pack, packet, package

دستور *dustūr* pl. دساتير *dasātīr*² statute; regulations; by-laws; (basic) constitutional law; constitution (*pol.*); — (*colloq.*) *dastūr* permission

دستورى *dustūrī* constitutional; (*Tun.*) belonging to the Destour party | النظام الدستورى constitutional form of government

دستورية *dustūrīya* constitutionality | عدم الدستورية *'adam ad-d.* unconstitutionality

دسر *dasara u* (*dasr*) to push, shove, push off (ه s.th.)

دسار *disār* pl. دسر *dusur* dowel

داسر *dāsir* propeller, airscrew ○

دسكرة *daskara* pl. دساكر *dasākir*² village

دسم *dasam* fatness (of meat); fat, grease; fat content (of foodstuffs)

دسم *dasim* fat; fatty, greasy, grimy, grubby; rich, abundant, substantial; meaty, pithy, full of thoughts (e.g., reading material)

ادسم *adsam*², f. دسماء *dasmā'*², pl. دسم *dusm* very fat; fatty, greasy, grimy, grubby; — richer, more substantial, pithier

دسامة *dasāma* fattiness, greasiness, griminess, grubbiness

دسومة *dusūma* fatness; richness, substantiality

دسام *disām* plug, stopper

ديسم *daisam* amaranth (*bot.*)

دسمبر *disembir, disambir* December

دسو II to introduce, bring in (ه s.th.) V to be hidden, concealed; to penetrate (الى into)

[1]دش *dašša u* (*dašš*) to crush, grind, bruise (ه e.g., grain)

دشيش *dašīš* and دشيشة a kind of porridge made of crushed wheat and butter

[2]دش (Fr. *douche*) *duš* shower, douche

دشت *dašt* junk, trash, rubbish, refuse

دشرة *dašra* pl. دشور *dušūr*, مداشر *madāšir*[2] (*alg.*) small village

دشن II to hand over, present (ه s.th.); to consecrate, dedicate, inaugurate (ه s.th.)

تدشين *tadšīn* consecration, dedication, inauguration | تدشين الكنيسة consecration of the church

تدشيني *tadšīnī* dedication, opening (in compounds) | حفلة تدشينية (*ḥafla*) dedication ceremony

دشو V to belch, burp, eruct

دعة *da'a* see ودع

دع *da''a* to rebuff, turn down (contemptuously, ه the poor, an orphan)

دعب *da'aba a* (دعابة *du'āba*) to joke, jest, make fun (ه with s.o.) III to play, toy (ه, ه with s.th., with s.o.); to joke, jest, make fun (ه with s.o.); to give (ه s.o.) a good-natured slap or smack (ب); to flirt (ها with a woman); to dally, philander, play around (ها with a woman); to play (ه about s.o.; e.g., waves); to stroke gently, caress, fondle (ه s.th.); to beguile, tempt, delude (ه s.o.; said of hopes); to play (ه a musical instrument) | داعب البيانو to play on the piano VI to make fun, have fun together, have a good time

دعب *da'ib* joking, jocose, playful, jolly, gay, funny

دعابة *du'āba* pl. *-āt* joking, jesting, funmaking, fun; joke, jest

دعاب *da''āb* jocose, playful, jolly, gay

مداعبة *mudā'aba* pl. *-āt* play, funmaking, fun; joke, jest; pleasantry; dalliance, flirtation, philandery

داعب *dā'ib* joking, jocose, playful, jolly, gay, funny

مداعب *mudā'ib* joking, jesting

دعبل *di'bil* frog spawn, frog's eggs

مدعبل *muda'bal* indisposed, out of sorts; round, ball-shaped

ادعج *ad'aj*[2], f. دعجاء *da'jā'*[2], pl. دعج *du'j* black-eyed; deep-black and large (eye)

دعر *da'ira a* (*da'ar*) to be immoral

دعر *da'ar* immorality, indecency

دعر *da'ir* unchaste, lewd, licentious, dissolute, obscene, bawdy, immoral, indecent

دعارة *da'āra, di'āra* indecency, immorality, licentiousness, debauchery | بيت الدعارة *bait ad-d.* brothel

داعر *dā'ir* pl. دعار *du''ār* unchaste, lewd, licentious, dissolute, obscene, bawdy, indecent, immoral

دعس *da'asa a* (*da's*) to tread underfoot, trample down, crush (ه s.th.); to knock down, run over (ه s.o.; automobile) **VII** pass. of **I**

دعسة *daʻsa* footprint

دعك *daʻaka a* (*daʻk*) to rub (ه s.th.); to scrub, scour (ه s.th.); to scrub on a washboard (ه laundry); to crush, squash, mash (ه s.th.); to crumple (ه paper)

دعم *daʻama a* (*daʻm*) to support, hold up, prop up, back (ه s.th.); to strengthen, promote (ه e.g., economic growth) **II** to support, hold up (ه s.th.); to prop, shore up, stay, buttress, underpin (ه s.th.); to cement, consolidate, strengthen (ه s.th.) **VIII** ادعم *iddaʻama* to be supported; to rest, be based (على on)

دعم *daʻm* support, assistance

دعمة *diʻma* pl. دعم *diʻam* support, prop

دعامة *diʻāma* pl. *-āt*, دعائم *daʻā'im*² support, prop, stay, shore; pier; buttress; pillar (esp. fig., e.g., دعائم السيادة pillars of authority)

تدعيم *tadʻīm* support, strengthening, reinforcement, consolidation, underpinning

دعا (دعو and دعى) *daʻā u* (دعاء *duʻā'*) to call (ه s.o.); to summon (ب or ه s.o.), call or send for s.o. (ب or ه); to call up (ه s.o., الى, ل for); to call, assign (ه s.o. الى to; government); to call upon s.o. (ه), appeal to s.o. (ه) for s.th. or to do s.th. (ل, الى), invite, urge (ل, ه الى s.o. to do s.th.); to invite, ask to come (ه الى s.o. to; e.g., to a banquet); to challenge, move, induce, prompt (ل, ه الى s.o. to do s.th.), prevail (ل, ه الى on s.o. to do s.th.); to call (ب, ه ه s.o. by a name), name (ب, ه ه s.o. so and so), pass.: دعى *duʻiya* to be called, be named; to invoke (الله God = to pray to); to wish (ل s.o.) well, bless (ل s.o.; properly: to invoke God in favor of s.o.), invoke a blessing (ب) upon s.o. (ل), pray (ب for s.th., ل on behalf of s.o.), implore (ب ل for s.o. s.th.); to curse (على s.o.; properly: to invoke God against s.o.), call down evil, invoke evil (على upon s.o.); to propagate, propagandize (الى s.th.), make propaganda, make publicity (الى, also ل, for); to demand, require (الى s.th.), call for (الى); to call forth, bring about, cause, provoke, occasion (الى s.th.), give rise (الى to) | دعى للاجتماع (*duʻiya*) to be summoned, be called into session (parliament); دعى الى حمل السلاح *duʻiya ilā ḥamli s-silāḥ* to be called up for military service, be called to the colors; رجل يدعى ... (*yudʻā*) a man called ..., a man by the name of ...; دعا له بطول العمر (*ṭūli l-ʻumr*) he wished him a long life **III** to challenge (ه s.o.); to pick a quarrel (ه with); to proceed judicially (ه against), prosecute (ه s.o.) **VI** to challenge each other, call each other forth or out, summon each other; to evoke one another (thoughts, reminiscences, sentiments); to be associated with each other (ideas, thoughts); to be dilapidated, be tumble-down, threaten to fall (walls); to sink, subside, cave in; to fall down, sink to the ground (person); to collapse, break down, decline, degenerate (fig., of a cultural phenomenon); to flock together, rally **VIII** ادعى *iddaʻā* to allege, claim, maintain (ه s.th., ان that); to lay claim (ه to s.th.), demand, claim (ه s.th.); to make undue claims (ه to s.th.), arrogate (to o.s.), assume unduly or presumptuously (ه s.th.); to affect, feign, simulate, pretend, purport (ب s.th.); to testify, give evidence (in court); to bring an accusation (in court, ضد *ḍidda* against s.o.); to accuse (ه على or ب s.o. of), charge (ب or ه على s.o. with), blame (ب or ه على s.o. for), hold s.th. (ب or ه) against s.o. (على) **X** to call or send (ه for s.o.), summon (ه s.o.); to cite, summon for examination or trial (ه s.o.; court, police); to call up (ه s.o., الى, also ل, for military duty); to recall (ه s.o., e.g., a diplomatic envoy); to call, appoint (ه s.o., e.g., a professor to a chair); to invoke (ه s.o.); to invite, urge (ه الى s.o. to do s.th.), suggest (ه الى to s.o. s.th. or to do s.th.), call upon s.o. (ه) to do s.th. (الى), appeal (ه الى to s.o. for s.th. or to do s.th.); to call for (ه), require, demand, necessitate, make necessary or requisite (ه s.th.)

دعوة *daʿwa* call; appeal; bidding, demand, request; call, convocation, summons (الى to), calling up, summoning; (official) summons, citation; invitation; claim, demand, plea; missionary activity, missionary work (also نشر الدعوة *našr ad-d.*), propaganda; — (pl. دعوات *daʿawāt*) invocation, imploration, supplication, prayer; good wish | بدعوة من at the invitation of; دعوات صالحات good wishes; دعوة بالشر (*šarr*) imprecation, curse; صاحب الدعوة host; الدعوة للخدمة (*lil-kidma*) call-up for military duty

دعوى *daʿwā* pl. دعاوى *daʿāwā*, دعاو *daʿāwin* allegation, pretension; claim; lawsuit, case, action, legal proceedings (*Isl. Law*) | بدعوى ان on the pretext that ...

دعى *daʿīy* pl. ادعياء *adʿiyā'*[2] adopted son; bastard; braggart, bigmouth, show-off; pretender; swindler, impostor

دعاء *duʿā'* pl. ادعية *adʿiya* call; invocation of God, supplication, prayer; request, plea; good wish (ل for s.o.); imprecation, curse (على against s.o.)

ادعى *adʿā* more conducive, more stimulating, of greater incentive (الى, ل to), causing or provoking to a greater extent (الى, ل s.th.)

دعاوة *daʿāwa*, *diʿāwa* pl. *-āt* propaganda (*pol.*); publicity (الى for)

دعاوى *daʿāwī*, *diʿāwī* propagandistic

دعاية *diʿāya* pl. *-āt* propaganda (*pol.*); advertising (*com.*)

دعائى *diʿā'ī* propagandistic

مدعاة *madʿāh* determining factor, decisive motive or incentive; reason, motive, cause (الى for) | مدعاة الى الشك (*šakk*) cause for doubt

تداع *tadāʿin* imminent collapse, impending breakdown; mutual summoning; association | تداعى المعانى *tadāʿī l-maʿānī* and تداعى الأفكار association of ideas; التداعى اللفظى (*lafẓī*) word association (*psych.*)

ادعاء *iddiʿā'* pl. *-āt* claim; arrogation, undue assumption, presumption; allegation; pretension, pretense; accusation, charge; الادعاء the prosecution (in a court of justice)

استدعاء *istidʿā'* pl. *-āt* summons, summoning; recall (of a diplomat), calling back; official summons, citation; desire, wish, longing; petition, application

داع *dāʿin* pl. دعاة *duʿāh* one who invites, inviter; propagandist; host; motive, reason, cause | لا داعى (*dāʿiya*) it is not necessary, there is no need, there is no cause (ل for)

داعية *dāʿiya* one who calls for s.th. (الى), invites to s.th. (الى); propagandist (with foll. genit. or الى: of s.th.), herald; (pl. دواع *dawāʿin*) motive, reason, cause, occasion; pl. دواع requirements, exigencies | داعية حرب warmonger; دواعى الدهر *d. ad-dahr* vicissitudes of fate; لدواع صحية *li-dawāʿin ṣiḥḥīya* for reasons of health; من دواعى سرورى it gives me great pleasure ...

مدعو *madʿūw* one invited, guest; called, named, by the name of | مدعو للسوق (*sawq*) called up for military duty

متداع *mutadāʿin* evoking one another, one leading to the other (reminiscences, thoughts); frail, shaky (constitution); dilapidated, tumble-down; ready to fall, threatened with collapse; declining, in a stage of decline, on the downgrade

مدع *mudda'in* pl. مدعون one who makes an allegation or pretension, alleger, pretender; claimer, claimant; plaintiff; prosecutor (*jur.*); — arrogant, presumptuous, bumptious | المدعى العمومى (*'umūmī*) the public prosecutor; المدعى العام (*'āmm*) do.

مدعى *mudda'an* claimed; المدعى عليه the defendant (*jur.*); pl. مدعيات *mudda'ayāt* claims, pretensions

مستدع *mustad'in* applicant, petitioner

مستدعى *mustad'an* conscript, draftee (for military service)

دغدغ **daḡdaḡa** to tickle (ه s.o.); to titillate (ه e.g., the imagination); to stimulate (ه the taste); (*eg.*) to crush; (*eg.*) to chew, munch (ه s.th.)

[1]دغر **daḡara** *a* (*daḡr*, دغرى *daḡrā*) to attack (على s.o.), fall upon s.o. (على)

دغر *daḡr* attack, assault

دغرى *daḡrā* attack, assault

[2]دغرى **duḡrī** (*eg.*, *syr.*) direct, straight; straight ahead

دغش IV ادغشت الدنيا *adḡašat id-dunyā* it became dark, twilight fell

دغش *daḡaš* darkness, dusk, twilight

دغيشة *daḡīša* darkness, dusk

دغص **daḡiṣa** *a* (*daḡaṣ*) to be chock-full, on the point of bursting

داغصة *dāḡiṣa* pl. دواغص *dawāḡiṣ*[2] kneepan, kneecap, patella

دغل **daḡal** pl. ادغال *adḡāl*, دغال *diḡāl* place with luxuriant tree growth; thicket, bush, jungle; — defectiveness, faultiness, corruption

دغل *daḡil* covered with dense undergrowth (place); impenetrable; corrupted

مدغل *mudḡil* covered with dense undergrowth (place); false, perfidious, insidious (in character)

دغم IV and VIII ادغم *iddaḡama* to put (ه فى s.th. into), insert. incorporate, embody (ه فى s.th. in); (*gram.*) to contract (ه فى one letter into another), assimilate (ه فى s.th. to) VII to be incorporated, embodied, merged, amalgamated; to be assimilated, contracted

ادغام *idḡām*, *iddiḡām* incorporation; contraction, assimilation (*gram.*); coalescence

دف **daffa** *i* (دفيف *dafīf*) to flap the wings (bird) II to hurry, rush

دف *daff* pl. دفوف *dufūf* side; lateral surface

دف *duff*, *daff* pl. دفوف *dufūf* tambourine

دفة *daffa* side; leaf (of a double door or window); cover (of a book), الدفتان the two covers of a book; rudder, helm | مدير الدفة or قائد الدفة *mudīr ad-d.* steersman, helmsman; قبض على دفة التنفيذ to take the helm, make o.s. the leader; يد الدفة *yad ad-d.* tiller; من الدفة للشابورة (*eg.*) all together, one and all, all without exception

دفية *diffīya* (*eg.*) loose woolen cloak

دفؤ **dafi'a** *a* and دفؤ *dafu'a* *u* to be warm; to feel warm II and IV to warm, heat (ه s.th.) V, VIII ادفأ *iddafa'a* and X to warm o.s.

دفء *dif'* warmth, warmness, heat

دفئ *dafi'* and دفىء *dafī'* warm

دفآن *daf'ān*[2], f. دفأى *daf'ā* warm

دفاء *difā'* heating

دفاءة *dafā'a* warmth, warmness, heat

☐ دفاية *daffāya* pl. *-āt* stove; central heating, heating system

مدفأ *midfa'* and مدفأة *midfa'a* pl. مداف *madāfi'*[2] stove, heating stove

تدفئة *tadfi'a* heating, generation of heat

دافئ *dāfi'* warm

دفتر *daftar* pl. دفاتر *dafātir*[2] booklet; notebook, copybook; daybook, journal; ledger (*com.*); roster, register, official register | دفتر حسابى (*ḥisābī*) account book; bankbook, passbook; دفتر خدمة العلم *d. kidmat al-ʿalam* (*Syr.*) service record (*mil.*); دفتر الخطابات *d. al-kiṭābāt* letter file, letter book, folder, portfolio; دفتر الشروط publication setting forth the terms of a purchase, the conditions of a lease, the stipulations of a contract, or the like; دفتر الاشتراك subscription booklet; دفتر الصندوق *d. aṣ-ṣundūq* cashbook (*com.*); دفتر المساحة cadastre, land register; دفتر التوفير savings account book; دفتر المواليد birth register; دفتر اليومية *d. al-yaumīya* diary, journal; مسك الدفاتر *mask ad-d.* bookkeeping

دفترخانة *daftarkāna* archives, public records office (*Eg.*) | دفترخانة الاملاك العقارية *d. al-amlāk al-ʿaqārīya* land-registry office (*Tun.*)

دفتريا *difteriyā*, دفتيريا *diftēriyā* diphtheria (*med.*)

دفر *dafara* to push, push back (ه s.o.); — *dafira a* (*dafar*) to stink

دفر *dafar* stench

دفر *dafir* stinking, fetid

دفس *dafasa* to hide (ه s.th.); to push

دفع *dafaʿa a* (*dafʿ*) to push; to push away, shove away, push back, drive back, repel, remove, dislodge, drive away (ه, ه عن s.o., s.th. from); دفعه جانبا (*jāniban*) to push, shove, or elbow, s.o. aside; to rid (عن نفسه o.s., ه of s.th.), get rid of s.th.; to get the better of (ه, ه s.o., s.th.); to fight (ه ب s.th. with); to reject, repudiate (ه s.th.); to rebut, refute, disprove (ه s.th.); to propel, drive (ه s.th.); to move, cause, urge, impel, egg on, goad (ه or ب s.o., الى or ل to do s.th.), induce, incite, force, compel, oblige (ه or ب s.o., الى or ل to), make s.o. (ب or ه) do s.th. (الى or ل); to hand over, present, turn over (ل or الى ه s.th. to s.o.); to pay (ثمنا *ṯamanan* a price, الى or ل to s.o.) | دفع خطاه الى (*kuṭāhu*) to wend one's way to **III** to resist, withstand (ه s.o., ه s.th.), offer resistance (ه, ه to); to contradict, oppose (ه s.o., عن so as to make him abstain from s.th.), dissuade (ه s.o., عن from); to suppress (ه s.th.); to defend (عن s.o., s.th.), uphold (عن s.th.); to be entrusted with the defense (عن of s.th., of s.o., also *jur.*) **V** to dash forward; to dart off, rush off; to pour forth, flow, stream, gush forth (water); to spring up, make itself felt (an idea, a social tendency, and the like) **VI** to shove or push one another; to push or shove one another away or aside; to push off, shove off (عن from); to issue in intermittent bursts, gush forth intermittently; to burst forth, rush out, sally (من from); to be propelled, be driven forward; to storm forward; to hurry along, hasten, go quickly **VII** to dart off, rush off; to proceed rashly, blindly, without forethought; to be too impetuous, be too hotheaded; to plunge headlong (فى into s.th.); to hasten, hurry; to dash along (cars); to rush, dart, make (الى at s.th.), pounce (الى on s.th.); to rush off, hurry off, go quickly (الى, نحو to; with foll. imperf.: to do s.th.); to give o.s. (ل to s.o.); to burst forth, gush out, pour forth, spurt, spout, flow, run (من from; water); to be pushed, propelled or driven (الى الامام forward, وراء by a force), let o.s. be carried away or be overcome (وراء by s.th., e.g., وراء شهواته *šahawātihī* by one's bodily appetites, وراء شعوره by one's feelings, وراء العاجلة by worldly things); to proceed, set out, begin (with foll. imperf.:

to do s.th.) X to try to ward off or stave off (ه s.th., ب by)

دفع *daf'* pushing, propelling, driving forward; propulsion; kickoff (sport); pushing back, shoving aside; repulsion, driving away, driving off; dispelling; parrying, warding off, staving off; repulse, rejection, repudiation; rebuttal; handing over, turning in; payment | الدفع النفاث (*naffāṯ*) jet propulsion; قوة الدفع *quwwat ad-d.* impetus, kicking power

دفعة *daf'a* (n. vic.) pl. *dafa'āt* shove, push, thrust; impetus, impact, momentum, forceful impulse, drive; ejaculation; payment; deposit; disbursement; pl. issues (stock market)

دفعة *duf'a* pl. *dufu'āt, dufa'āt* that which issues at any one time, a burst, a gush, a spurt, and the like; time, instance | دفعة واحدة (*duf'atan*) all at one time, all at once, in one stroke, in one fell swoop; هذه الدفعة this time; ست دفعات six times; على دفعات متفاوتة (*mutafāwita*) at different times; دفعة جديدة من a new batch or onset of (people)

دفاع *daffā'* propelling, impelling, giving impetus; ○ piston (*techn.*)

مدفع *midfa'* pl. مدافع *madāfi'*[2] gun, cannon | ○ مدافع بعيدة المرمى (*ba'īdat al-marmā*) long-range guns; مدفع رشاش (*raššāš*) machine gun; ○ مدافع ضخمة (*ḍakma*) heavy artillery; المدافع المضادة للطائرات (*muḍādda*) or المدافع المقاومة للطائرات (*muqāwima*) anti-aircraft guns; مدفع ثلاثى مضاد للطائرات ○ (*ṯulāṯī, muḍādd*) three-barreled anti-aircraft gun (*mil.*); مدفع هاون *m. hāwun* mortar; ضرب مدفع الظهر *ḍarb m. aẓ-ẓuhr* marking of exact noon by cannon shot; مدفع سريع الطلقات (*s. aṭ-ṭalaqāt*) machine gun; submachine gun, tommy gun; مدفع مضاد للدبابات (*muḍādd, dabbābāt*) anti-tank gun

مدفعى *midfa'ī* gun-, cannon-, artillery- (in compounds); artilleryman, gunner, cannoneer

مدفعية *midfa'īya* artillery

مدفعجى *midfa'gī* (*eg.*) artilleryman

دفاع *difā'* protection; defense (عن of s.th., of s.o., also *jur.*) | خط الدفاع *kaṭṭ ad-d.* line of defense; halfbacks (soccer); مجلس الدفاع *majlis ad-d.* defense council; وزارة الدفاع *wizārat ad-d.* ministry of defense; الدفاع الوطنى (*waṭanī*) national defense; الدفاع المضاد للطائرات (*muḍādd*) anti-aircraft defense; دفاع شرعى legitimate self-defense

دفاعى *difā'ī* defensive, protective

مدافعة *mudāfa'a* defense (عن of s.th.)

اندفاع *indifā'* pl. *-āt* rush(ing), plunging, plunge (فى into); outburst, outbreak, eruption; élan, dash, impetuosity, hotheadedness, fire, exuberance, effusiveness; rashness, precipitance; self-abandon; اندفاعا *indifā'an* spontaneously

اندفاعة *indifā'a* (n. vic.) sudden outburst, outbreak (e.g., of wailing)

دافع *dāfi'* repellent, expellant; driving, pushing, giving impetus, incentive, impellent, propelling, propulsive, etc.; repeller; payer, e.g., دافعو الضرائب the taxpayers; (pl. دوافع *dawāfi'*[2]) incentive, impulse, impetus, spur, motive; drive, instinct (*psych.*) | بدافع (with foll. genit.) motivated by ..., by reason of ..., on the strength of ...; الدافع الجنسى (*jinsī*) sexual drive; دوافع فطرية (*fiṭrīya*) natural, innate drives

مدفوع *madfū'* completed payment(s), paid amounts of money; المدفوع اليه the receiver of payments | المدفوع من رأس المال capital investment

مدفوعة *madfū'a* pl. *-āt* payment, paid amount of money

مدافع *mudāfi'* pl. *-ūn* defender (عن of s.o., of s.th.); back (in soccer)

دفق *dafaqa u i* (*dafq*) to pour out, pour forth (ه s.th.); — *u* (*dafq*, دفوق *dufūq*) to be shed; to flow, well out, spout, gush forth; to overflow (ه with s.th.) **V** to pour forth, spout forth, gush forth; to rush in; to break forth, break out, burst out; to go off (shot); to plunge blindly (فى, الى into s.th.); to rush (على against); to crowd (على into) **VII** = **V**

دفق *dafq* pouring out, effusion

دفقة *dufqa* pl. *dufuqāt*, *dufaqāt*, *dufqāt* = دفعة *duf'a* | دفقة واحدة (*dufqatan*) = دفعة واحدة; دفقات الريح *d. ar-rīḥ* gusts; دفقة من الماء gush of water

دفاق *daffāq* bursting forth, darting out, rushing out

تدفق *tadaffuq* outpour, outflow, issue, effluence, efflux, effusion; influx, run, rush, inrush, inpour; outbreak, outburst; impulsiveness; exuberance, effusiveness

دافق *dāfiq* pl. دوافق *dawāfiq*[2] bursting forth, breaking out, erupting; gushing, torrential

متدفق *mutadaffiq* impulsive; exuberant, effusive

دفلى *diflā* oleander (Nerium oleander L.; *bot.*)

دفن *dafana i* (*dafn*) to bury, inter, inhume (ه s.o.); to hide, conceal, keep secret (ه s.th.) **VII** to be buried, be inhumed; to be hidden, be concealed, be kept secret

دفن *dafn* burial, interment, inhumation

دفين *dafīn* pl. دفناء *dufanā'*[2] buried, interred; hidden, secret

دفينة *dafīna* pl. دفائن *dafā'in*[2] hidden treasure, treasure-trove

مدفن *madfan*, مدفنة *madfana* pl. مدافن *madāfin*[2] burying place, burial ground, cemetery

مدفون *madfūn* buried, interred; hidden; secret, latent

دفاية see دفؤ

دق *daqqa i* (دقة *diqqa*) to be thin, fine, fragile, frail; to be little, small, tiny, minute; to be subtle, delicate; to be insignificant, unimportant, trifling, inconsiderable; to be too fine, too subtle (عن for perception); — *u* (*daqq*) to crush, bruise, bray (ه s.th.); to grind, pulverize, powder (ه s.th.); to pound (ه s.th., e.g., meat); to strike (clock); to beat, throb (heart); to hammer, throb (engine); to knock, rap, bang (الباب *al-bāba* on the door); to bump (رأسه بالحائط *ra'sahū bi-l-ḥā'iṭ* one's head against the wall); to drive (ه a nail); to ram in, drive in (*constr. eng.*); to beat, strum, play (على a musical instrument); to type (على on a typewriter); — to sound, resound, ring out (said of musical instruments) | دق الجرس (*jarasa*) to ring the bell; دق جرس الخطر (*j. al-kaṭar*) to sound the alarm; دق الجرس على to call s.o. up, give s.o. a ring; دق الجرس (*jarasu*) the bell rang; دقت الساعة the clock struck **II** to triturate, pulverize, reduce to powder (ه s.th.); to be precise, exact, strict, meticulous, painstaking, proceed with utmost accuracy or care (فى in s.th.); to scrutinize, examine closely, determine exactly (ه s.th.); to do (ه s.th.) carefully, with precision | دقق البحث (*baḥta*) to investigate carefully; دقق النظر (*naẓara*) to watch attentively or carefully, scrutinize, examine closely (فى s.th.); دقق الملاحظة (*mulāḥaẓata*) to observe closely **III** to deal scrupulously (ه with s.o.) **IV** to make fine, make thin (ه s.th.) **VII** to be crushed, brayed, pounded; to be broken | اندق عنقه (*'unquhū*) he broke his neck **X** to be or become thin or fine

دق *daqq* crushing, bruising, braying, pounding; pulverization, trituration; grinding (down); beat(ing), throb(bing); bang(ing), knock(ing), rap(ping); tattoo(ing) | دق الجرس *d. al-jaras* peal, ringing, sound of a bell; دق الحنك *d. al-ḥanak* chatter, prattle

دق *daqqī*: صانع دق (*eg.*) coppersmith; stonemason

دق *diqq* fine, thin; little, small, tiny, minute; delicate, fragile, frail | شجر دق (*šajar*) shrubbery, brush, scrub; حمى الدق *ḥummā d-d.* hectic fever

دقة *daqqa* (n. vic.) pl. *-āt* bang, knock, rap; beat, throb; stroke, striking (of a clock); hammer, hammering sound; thumping, thump | دقات القلب *d. al-qalb* heartbeats; دقة الجرس *d. al-jaras* peal, or ring, of a bell; telephone call, ring; من الدقة القديمة (*eg.*) old-fashioned, of the old guard

دقة *diqqa* thinness; fineness; smallness, tininess, minuteness; triviality, pettiness, paltriness; subtlety, subtleness, finesse; critical or precarious state, delicate situation; accuracy, exactness, exactitude, precision | بدقة exactly, accurately, precisely, minutely, painstakingly, meticulously, sharply; دقة الشعور acuteness of feeling, sensitivity, sensitiveness, sensibility

دقية *diqqīya* (*eg.*) small copper pot

دقة *duqqa* pl. دقق *duqaq* fine dust; powder

الدقى *ad-duqqī* El Dukki (city district in Cairo)

دقاق *duqāq* crushed, brayed, or pulverized, substance; powder; flour of lupine

دقيق *daqīq* pl. دقاق *diqāq*, ادقة *adiqqa* fine, thin; delicate, frail, fragile; little, small, tiny, puny, minute; subtle; paltry, petty, trifling, trivial; precise, accurate, exact; painstaking, scrupulous, meticulous; inexorable, relentless, strict, rigorous; delicate (situation), critical, trying, serious, precarious; — flour, meal | دقيق الحساب keeping strict account, strict, relentless, inexorable; دقيق الشعور sensitive; دقيق الصنع *d. aṣ-ṣanʿ* finely worked, of delicate workmanship; دقيق النظر *d. an-naẓar* clear-sighted, penetrating, discerning, sensitive; ابو دقيق *abū d.* butterfly; اداة دقيقة (*adāh*) and جهاز دقيق (*jahāz*) precision equipment, precision instrument; الاعضاء الدقيقة (*aʿḍāʾ*) the genitals; دقيق السمك *d. as-samak* fish meal

دقيقة *daqīqa* pl. دقائق *daqāʾiq*² particle; nicety; intricacy; detail, particular; minute (time unit) | دقائق الفا *d. alfā* alpha particles (*phys.*); دقائق الامور the niceties, intricacies, or secret implications of things; دقائق ذرية (*ḏarrīya*) atomic particles; دقائق ناعمة fine particles

دقيقى *daqīqī* particle-like, minute | تفاصيل دقيقية finest details

دقاق *daqqāq* grinder, crusher; flour merchant; frequently or constantly beating, striking, etc.; player of an instrument | ساعة دقاقة repeater (watch)

دقاقة *daqqāqa* knocker, rapper (of a door)

ادق *adaqq*² finer; more delicate; smaller, tinier; more accurate, preciser; stricter

مدق *midaqq* beetle; pounder, pestle; masher; (*eg.*) trail, footpath

مدقة *midaqqa* pl. مداق *madāqq*² pounder, pestle; beetle; clapper, tongue (of a bell)

تدقيق *tadqīq* accuracy, precision, exactness, exactitude | بتدقيق exactly, precisely, accurately, minutely

مدقوق *madqūq* crushed, ground; crumbled

مدقق *mudaqqiq* exact, accurate (scholar), thorough (investigator), painstaking, meticulous, strict, relentless

مدقق *mudaqqaq* precise, exact (data)

داقرة *dāqira* pl. دواقر *dawāqir*² clay vessel

(*tun.*); — stipend for underprivileged students (*tun.*)

دقشوم *daqšūm* (*eg.*) rubblestone, crushed rock; brickbats, gravel

دقع *daqiʿa a* (*daqaʿ*) to grovel, cringe; to be miserable, wretched, humble, abject; to live in poverty **IV** do.; to make miserable (ه s.o.; poverty)

ادقاع *idqāʿ* mass poverty

مدقع *mudqiʿ* miserable, wretched; degrading, abasing (poverty)

دقل *daqal* mast (of a ship); mainmast

دقلة *daqla* (*tun.*) designation of a kind of date

دقماق *duqmāq* pl. دقاميق *daqāmīq*[2] (*eg.*) mallet, beetle

[1]دك *dakka u* (*dakk*) to make flat, level or even, to smooth, level, ram, stamp, tamp (ه earth, the ground, a road); to press down, weigh down; to beat down; to devastate, demolish, destroy, ruin (ه s.th.) **II** to mix, mingle (ه s.th.) **VII** to be crushed; to be leveled

دك *dakk* pl. دكوك *dukūk* level ground; — devastation, demolition, destruction

دكة *dakka* pl. *-āt* rubblestone, crushed rock; ballast

دكة *dikka* pl. دكك *dikak* bench

دكان *dukkān* pl. دكاكين *dakākīn*[2] bench; store, shop

دكانة *dukkāna* small shop; small teashop (*eg.*); small coffeeshop (*syr.*)

دكانجى *dukkānjī* storekeeper, shopkeeper, retailer

مدك *midakk* pl. *-āt* ramrod; ○ tamper rammer

[2]دك **II** to provide (ه trousers) with a waistband (*dikka* or *tikka*)

دكة *dikka* (= تكة *tikka*) waistband (in the upper seam of trousers)

دكتاتور *diktātōr* dictator

دكتاتورى *diktātōrī* dictatorial; authoritarian

دكتاتورية *diktātōrīya* dictatorship

دكترة *daktara* conferment of a doctorate

دكتور *doktōr, duktōr* pl. دكاترة *dakātira* doctor | دكتور فى الحقوق doctor of laws, LL.D.; دكتور فى الطب (*ṭibb*) doctor of medicine, M.D.

دكتورة *doktōra, duktōra* pl. دكاترة *dakātira* doctor (fem.)

دكتوراة and دكتوراه *doktōrāh, duktōrāh* doctorate, doctor's degree, title of doctor | الدكتوراة الفخرية (*fakrīya*) honorary doctorate

ادكر *iddakara* see ذكر

دكريتو (It. *decreto*) *dikrītō* pl. دكريتات decree

[1]ادكن *adkan*[2], f. دكناء *daknā'*[2] pl. دكن *dukn* blackish, dark (color)

داكن *dākin* dark, dark-colored | اخضر داكن dark green; اصفر داكن yellowish, of a dingy yellow, mud-colored

[2]دكان, دكانة and دكانجى see [1]دك

دل *dalla u* (دلالة *dalāla*) to show, demonstrate, point out (ه على to s.o. s.th.); to lead, guide, direct, conduct (ه على or الى s.o. to), show s.o. (ه) the way (على or الى to); to show, indicate, mark (على s.th.); to point (على to s.th.), evince, indicate, denote, imply, bespeak, suggest (على s.th.), be indicative, be suggestive (على of); to furnish evidence (على for s.th.), prove (على s.th.); — (1st pers. perf. *dalaltu*) *i* (دلال *dalāl*) to be coquettish, flirt, dally (of a woman; على with s.o.) **II** to prove (على s.th.), furnish the proof (على for), confirm, corroborate (ب على s.th. with); to sell or put up at auction, auction off (على s.th.); to pamper, coddle, spoil (ه s.o.); to fondle, caress, pet (ه a child) **IV** to make free, take liberties (على with s.o.); to pride o.s. (ب on), be conceited (ب of) **V** to be coquettish, flirt, dally (of a woman; على with s.o.); to be coy, behave affectedly; to take liberties (على with s.o.); to pamper, coddle (على s.o.) **X** to ask to be shown (على s.th.); to inquire about the way, let oneself be shown the way (على toward, to); to seek information, inform o.s. (على about); to obtain information; to be informed (على about); to be guided (ب by), act or proceed in accordance with (ب); to conclude, gather, infer (على s.th., ب or من from), draw conclusions (ب or من from, على with regard to), judge (على s.th., ب or من by)

دل *dall* proper, dignified conduct; coquetry, flirtation

دلة *dalla* pl. دلال *dilāl* pot with long curved spout and handle used for making coffee (among Syrian nomads and in some parts of Saudi Arabia)

دلال *dalāl* coquetry, coquettishness; pampering, coddling, spoiling

دليل *dalīl* pl. ادلة *adilla*, دلائل *dalā'il*², ادلاء *adillā'*² (the latter of persons) indication (على of); sign, token; symptom; proof, evidence (على of); guide; tourist guide, cicerone; pilot (of a ship, of an airplane); guidebook, guide manual, handbook; directory, telephone directory; railroad guide, timetable; guide rail (*techn.*); roller path (in steel construction) | اقام الدليل على to furnish the proof for, demonstrate, prove s.th.; دليل سياحى (*siyāḥī*) tourist guide; دليل ظرفى (*ẓarfī*) circumstantial evidence; دليل قاطع cogent proof, conclusive evidence

دليلة *dalīla* guide (fem.) | دليلة سياحية (*siyāḥīya*) tourist guide (fem.)

دلال *dallāl* pl. *-ūn* auctioneer; broker, jobber, middleman, agent, commission merchant; real estate agent; hawker

دلالة *dalāla* pl. *-āt* pointing; guidance; leading, leadership; indication (على of); sign, token; sense, meaning | علم الدلالة *'ilm ad-d.* semantics

دلالى *dalālī* meaning (in compounds), semantic

دلالة *dilāla* auction, public sale; business of a broker or middleman; brokerage commission; trade of a dealer, jobber or agent

دلالة *dallāla* middlewoman, woman broker

ادل *adall*² proving more cogently (على s.th.), more indicative or suggestive (على of) | ادل دليل على (*dalīlin*) the surest evidence of, the best proof of

تدليل *tadlīl* reasoning, argumentation, demonstration; proving (على of), furnishing of proof or evidence (على for); corroboration, substantiation, confirmation; pampering, coddling, spoiling; fondling, petting, caressing; pet form (of a name) | اسم التدليل pet name; تدليلا من as a pet form of ...

ادلال *idlāl* arrogance; pride (ب in) | الادلال بنفسه self-elevation, conceit

تدلل *tadallul* coquetry, coquettishness; pampering, coddling, spoiling

استدلال *istidlāl* reasoning, argumentation, demonstration; conclusion, inference, deduction; proof, evidence (على of)

دال *dāll* meaningful; significant; ○ the word or form signifying (linguistics; Fr. *signifiant*, in contrast with ○ مدلول *madlūl* the thing signified, Fr. *signifié*)

دالة *dālla* familiarity, chumminess; liberty (that one takes with s.o.);

audacity, boldness; (pl. *-āt*) function (*math.*)

مدلول *madlūl* proven; (pl. *-āt*) meaning, sense; see also دال *dāll* | مدلولات الكلمات *m. al-kalimāt* lexical meanings

مدلل *mudallal* pampered, spoiled (child)

مدل *mudill* presumptuous, arrogant | مدل بنفسه (*bi-nafsihī*) conceited, self-important

[1]دلب *dulb* plane tree, sycamore (*bot.*)

[2]دولاب pl. دواليب look up alphabetically

دلتا delta; الدلتا the Nile Delta, Lower Egypt

دلج IV to set out at nightfall

دلوح *dalūḥ* pl. دلح *duluḥ* moisture-laden cloud

دلدل *daldala* to set into a swinging motion, dangle **II** *tadaldala* to hang loosely, dangle

دلدل *duldul* and دلدول *duldūl* porcupine (*zool.*)

دلس **II** to swindle, cheat; to counterfeit, forge, falsify (ه s.th.) **III** to deceive, defraud (ه s.o.), impose (ه on)

تدليس *tadlīs* deceit, fraud; swindle

تدليسى *tadlīsī* fraudulent

مدلس *mudallas* forged, counterfeit | نقود مدلسة counterfeit money; مفاتيح مدلسة forged keys

دلع *dalaʿa a* (*dalʿ*) with لسانه *lisānahū*: to stick out one's tongue; to loll, let the tongue hang out **II** to pamper, spoil (ه a child); to caress, fondle, pet (ه s.o.) **IV** شيء يدلع النفس (*eg.*) a nauseating, disgusting thing **VII** to stick out, be stuck out, hang out, loll (tongue); to dart out, lick out, leap out, flare up (flame); to break out (fire, war); to be pampered, spoiled (child)

دلع *dalʿ*: اسم الدلع *ism ad-d.* pet name

دلاع *dallāʿ* (coll.; n. un. ة) watermelon (*maḡr.*)

دلغان *dilḡān* clay

دلف *dalafa i* (*dalf*, دلوف *dulūf*, دلفان *dalafān*) to walk with short steps, toddle; to go or walk slowly, saunter, stroll (الى to); to advance (على toward); to approach step by step (الى s.o. or s.th.); to penetrate, reach (الى as far as); to grope (الى for, of the hand); to leak, drip, trickle (water)

○ دالف *dālif* pl. دوالف *dawālif*[2] ricochet (*mil.*)

دلفين *dulfīn* pl. دلافين *dalāfīn*[2] dolphin

دلق *dalaqa u* (*dalq*) to spill, pour out (ه a liquid) **VII** to be spilled (liquid); to pour, gush out; to stream (e.g., into the street; crowds); to dash forward (people); to be flabby and prominent or protruding (e.g., belly)

مندلق *mundaliq*: مندلق الكرش *m. al-kirš* with a hanging belly

دلك *dalaka u* (*dalk*) to rub (ه s.th.); to stroke (ه s.th.), pass the hand (ه over s.th.); to knead (العجين the dough); — *u* (دلوك *dulūk*) to set, go down (sun) **II** to rub (ه s.th., ه s.o.), embrocate (ه s.th.); to knead; to massage (ه s.o.)

دلك *dalk* rubbing; grazing, brushing, touching, touch

دلوك *dalūk* liniment

دلوك *dulūk*, دلوك الشمس *d. aš-šams* sunset

تدليك *tadlīk* embrocation; massage

مدلك *mudallik* pl. *-ūn* masseur

مدلكة *mudallika* pl. *-āt* masseuse

دله *daliha a* = **V**; **II** to rob s.o. (ه) of his senses, drive (ه s.o.) crazy (love) **V** to go out of one's mind, go crazy (with love) | تدلهت فى حبه (*ḥubbihī*) she has fallen madly in love with him

مدله *mudallah* madly in love

دلهم IV *idlahamma* to be dark, gloomy; to be deep-black

دلهم *dalham* dark, gloomy; deep-black

ادلهمام *idlihmām* a deep black

مدلهم *mudlahimm* dark, gloomy; deep-black

دلو II to let hang, dangle (ه s.th.); to hang, suspend (ه s.th.); to lower (ه s.th.); to drop, let down, let fall down (ه s.th.) IV = II; to cast down (ه glances, الى on s.o.); to let one's glance (بانظاره *bi-anẓārihī*) sweep down; to express, utter, voice (ب s.th., e.g., برأيه *bi-ra'yihī* one's opinion); to deliver, make (بتصريح a statement; *pol.*); to give (بصوته *bi-ṣautihī* one's vote, in an election); to adduce, present, advance, offer (بحجة *bi-ḥujjatin* an argument); to inform, notify, advise (ب الى s.o. of), let (الى s.o.) know (ب about); to offer, present (ب الى to s.o. s.th.); to grant, give (بحديث ل an interview to s.o.); to slander, defame, asperse (فى s.o.) | ادلى دلوه بين الدلاء (*dalwahū, dilā'*) or ادلى بدلوه فى الدلاء to make one's contribution (together with others), add one's touch, put in one's two bits' worth V to hang down, be suspended, dangle (من from); to be lowered, be let down; to be or become low; to sink, descend | تدلى للسقوط to threaten to fall down, be ready to fall

دلو *dalw* usually f., pl. ادل *adlin*, دلاء *dilā'*, ادلاء *adlā'* leather bucket; bucket, pail; الدلو Aquarius (sign of the zodiac; *astron.*); the eleventh month of the solar year (*Saudi Ar.*; cf. حمل *ḥamal*)

دلاية *dallāya* pendant

ادلاء *idlā'* delivery (of a statement); utterance, statement; presentation; granting

دالية *dāliya* pl. دوال *dawālin* water-wheel (for irrigation); trellis, espalier on which grapevines are trained; varix, varicose vein

متدل *mutadallin* pendent, suspended, hanging, dangling; projecting, overhanging, ready to fall down

داليا look up alphabetically

[1]دم *dam* pl. دماء *dimā'* blood; دماء homicide cases (*jur.*) | دم الاخوين *d. al-aḵawain* dragon's blood (a dark-red, resinous substance derived from the dragon tree, Dracaena draco)

دمى *damī* blood- (in compounds), sanguine

دموى *damawī* blood- (in compounds), sanguine; sanguinary, bloody

[2]دم *damma u* (*damm*) to coat, smear, besmear (ب ه s.th. with); to paint, daub, color, dye, tinge, tint (ب ه s.th. with) II to rub, embrocate, anoint (ب ه s.th. with)

دم *damm* ointment, unguent, salve, liniment, embrocation; paint; pigment, dye, dyestuff; rouge

دمام *dimām* ointment, unguent, salve, liniment, embrocation; paint; pigment, dye, dyestuff; rouge

دميم *damīm* pl. دمام *dimām* ugly; deformed, misshapen | دميم الخلقة *d. al-ḵilqa* ugly to look at, of repulsive appearance

دمامة *damāma* ugliness; ugly appearance; abominableness, monstrosity

الدمام *ad-dammām* Dammam (seaport in E Saudi Arabia, on the Persian Gulf)

دمث *damuṯa u* (دماثة *damāṯa*) to be gentle, mild (character) II to soften, mellow (ه s.th.)

دمث *damiṯ* pl. دماث *dimāṯ*: دمث الاخلاق gentle, mild-tempered

دماثة *damāṯa* mildness, gentleness (of character); good-naturedness; fine manner, politeness

دمج *damaja* u (دموج *dumūj*) to enter (في s.th.), go or come into (في), be inserted, incorporated (في in) **II** to write shorthand **IV** to twist tightly, twine firmly (ه s.th.); to enter, insert, include, incorporate, embody (في ه s.th. in); to introduce, interpolate, intercalate (في ه s.th. in); to annex (في ه s.th. to) **VII** to be inserted, be incorporated (في in); to be annexed (في to); to merge (في with), be swallowed up, be absorbed (في by); to be fused, fuse, amalgamate; to become identical, identify oneself

دمج *damj* insertion, incorporation, inclusion (في in)

تدميج *tadmīj* shorthand, stenography

ادماج *idmāj* insertion, incorporation, interpolation; inclusion (في in); assimilation

اندماج *indimāj* incorporation, insertion (في in); amalgamation, merger, merging (في with); absorption (في by); annexation (في to); fusion; assimilation

اندماجى *indimājī* coming into being as a result of consolidation or amalgamation

مدمج *mudmaj* firm, compact

مندمج *mundamij* firm, compact, tight

دمجانة *damajāna* (also داجانة) pl. *-āt* demijohn, carboy

دمدم *damdama* to mutter, grumble, growl, snarl

دمدمة *damdama* pl. *-āt* growl, snarl; rumbling noise, rumble

دمر[1] *damara* u to perish, be ruined, be destroyed **II** to annihilate, destroy, ruin, demolish, wreck (ه s.th.) **V** to be destroyed, demolished, ruined, wrecked **VII** to be destroyed, be annihilated

دمار *damār* ruin, destruction

تدمير *tadmīr* annihilation, destruction, demolition

اندمار *indimār* utter defeat, rout, destruction, annihilation

مدمرة *mudammira* pl. *-āt* destroyer (*naut.*)

دمور[2] *dammūr* (*eg.*) a coarse calico-like fabric

دمورى *dammūrī* (*eg.*) made of *dammūr* (see above)

دميرة[3] *damīra* (*eg.*) flood season of the Nile

[4]□ لا دومرى *lā dūmarī* (= لا تدمرى) nobody, no one, not a living soul

تدمر[5] *tadmur*[2], usually pronounced *tudmur*, Palmyra (ancient city in Syria, now a small village)

تدمرى *tadmurī*, usually pronounced *tudmurī*, someone, somebody; لا تدمرى nobody, no one, not a living soul

دمس *damasa* u to hide, conceal, disguise (ه s.th.); to bury (ه في الارض s.o. in the ground) **II** do.

دمس *dims* (*eg.*) cinders, ashes

دماسة *damāsa* darkness

ادماس *admās* (pl.) hovels, shanties, huts

دموس *dammūs* pl. دماميس *damāmīs*[2] cave, cavern

ديماس *dīmās* pl. دياميس *dayāmīs*[2], دماميس *damāmīs*[2] dungeon; underground vault; pl. catacombs

دامس *dāmis* pitch-dark; dark, gloomy, dusky

مدمس see فول فول

دمشق *dimašq*[2], *dimišq*[2] Damascus (capital of Syria)

دمشقى *dimašqī* Damascene (adj.); (pl. -*ūn*, دماشقة *damāšiqa*) a Damascene, resident of Damascus

مدمشق *mudamšaq* damascened, damasked; (*syr.*) having adopted a sophisticated style of living (imitating that of Damascus), urbanized

دمع *dama'a a* to water (eye) **IV** to cause to weep, evoke tears, make (the eyes) water

دمع *dam'* pl. دموع *dumū'* tears

دمعة *dam'a* (n.un.) tear, teardrop; (*eg.*) *dim'a* gravy

دمعى *dam'ī*: قنبلة دمعية (*qunbula*) tear-gas bomb

دمعة *dami'a* and دميع *damī'* pl. دمعى *dam'ā*, دمائع *damā'i'*[2] readily inclined to weep, frequently weeping, tearful, lachrymose (woman)

دموع *damū'* and دماع *dammā'* watering, watery, tearful (eyes)

مدمع *madma'* pl. مدامع *madāmi'*[2] lachrymal canal

[1]دمغ *damaġa a* to refute, invalidate (ه a falsehood, an error, a false accusation); to triumph (ه over falsehood; said of truth)

دماغ *dimāġ* pl. ادمغة *admiġa* brain

حجة دامغة *ḥujja dāmiġa* cogent argument; شهادة دامغة (*šahāda*) irrefutable testimony

[2]دمغ *damaġa u* (*damġ*) to stamp, provide or mark with a stamp (ه s.th.); to hallmark (ه gold and silver articles); to brand (ه an animal); to label, characterize (ه s.o., بأنه as)

دمغ *damġ* stamping | دمغ المصوغات *d. al-maṣūġāt* hallmarking of gold and silver articles

دمغة *damġa* stamp; hallmark (on gold and silver articles) | ورق دمغة *waraq d.* stamped paper

مدموغ *madmūġ* stamped, bearing a stamp

دمغجة *damġaja* (*tun.*) demagoguery

دمقراطى *dimuqrāṭī* democratic; democrat

دمقراطية *dimuqrāṭīya* democracy; democratic attitude or conviction

دمقس *dimaqs* raw silk

دمقسى *dimaqsī* silken, silky

مدماك *midmāk* row of stones or tiles (in the wall of a building)

مدموك *madmūk* and مدمك *mudmak* firm, tight, taut

دمل *damala u* (*daml*, دملان *damalān*) to fertilize, manure, dung (ه the soil); — *damila a* (*damal*) to heal, heal up, scar over, cicatrize (wound) **VII** to heal, heal up, scar over, cicatrize (wound); to fester, suppurate (sore)

دمل *dummal* (n. un. ة) pl. دمامل *damāmil*[2], دماميل *damāmīl*[2] abscess (*med.*), boil, sore, ulcer; furuncle; bubo, plague boil; inveterate evil | دمل الدماغ brain abscess (*med.*)

دملى (*dummalī*) furuncular | طاعون دملى bubonic plague

دملج *dumluj* pl. دمالج *damālij*[2] bracelet, bangle

[1]دمن *damana u* (*damn*) to fertilize, manure, dung (ه the soil) **IV** to give o.s. up, devote o.s., apply o.s. (على or ه to), go in for (على or ه); to be addicted (على e.g., to liquor)

دمن *dimn* (coll.; n. un. ة) pl. دمن *diman* fertilizer, manure, dung

دمنة *dimna* pl. دمن *diman* vestiges or remnants of a dwelling, ruins

دمان *damān* fertilizer, manure, dung

ادمان *idmān* addiction; excess; mania; dipsomania | ادمان المخدرات *i. al-mukaddirāt* drug addiction; ادمان المسكرات *i. al-muskirāt* alcoholism

مدمن *mudmin* addicted, given up (على e.g., to wine); an addict (على of) | مدمن المخدرات *m. al-mukaddirāt* drug addict; مدمن المسكرات *m. al-muskirāt* an alcoholic

دمان² *dumān* see دومان

دمنهور *damanhūr*² Damanhûr (city in N Egypt)

دموى see دم¹

دمى¹ *damiya a* to bleed **II** and **IV** to cause to bleed

دام *dāmin* bleeding, bloody, gory

مدمى *mudamman*, f. مدماة bloody; blood-red

دمية² *dumya* pl. دمى *duman* statue, statuette; image, effigy; dummy; doll; puppet | الدمى المتحركة (*mutaḥarrika*) puppet play, puppet show

دمياط *dimyāṭ*² (*eg.* *dumyāṭ*) Damietta (city in N Egypt)

دن *danna u* (*dann*, دنين *danīn*) to buzz, hum (insect); to drone

دن *dann* and دنين *danīn* buzz(ing), hum(ming), droning, drone

دن *dann* pl. دنان *dinān* earthen wine jug

دنأ *dana'a a* and دنؤ *danu'a u* (دنوءة *dunū'a*, دناءة *danā'a*) to be low, mean, base, vile, contemptible, despicable

دنىء *danī'* pl. ادنياء *adniyā'*², ادناء *adnā'* low, base, mean, vile, despicable, contemptible; inferior, second-rate, of poor quality

ادنأ *adna'*² lower, viler, meaner; more inferior, of poorer quality

دناءة *danā'a* lowness, baseness, meanness, vileness; inferiority

دنتلا, دنتلة (Fr. *dentelle*) *dantilla* lace, lacework

دنجل *dinjil* (*eg.*) pl. دناجل *danājil*² axle, axletree

دندرمه (Turk. *dondurma*) *dandurma* ice cream

دنادشة *danādiša* common people, people of no consequence

دندن *dandana* to buzz, hum; to drone; to hum softly, croon (a song); to murmur

دندى *dindī* (*eg.*) turkey

دينار pl. دنانير look up alphabetically

دنس *danisa a* (*danas*) to be soiled, sullied, defiled, polluted **II** to stain, soil, dirty, befoul, sully, pollute, contaminate (ه s.th.); to dishonor, disgrace (ه s.th.); to desecrate (ه s.th.) **V** pass. of **II**

دنس *danas* pl. ادناس *adnās* uncleanness, dirt, filth, squalor; stain, blemish, fault

دنس *danis* pl. ادناس *adnās*, دنساء *dunasā'*² unclean, soiled, sullied, foul, polluted, defiled, stained

تدنيس *tadnīs* pollution, defilement, soiling, sullying, contamination; dishonoring, disgracing; desecration, profanation

دنف *danifa a* (*danaf*) to be seriously ill **IV** do.

دنف *danif* pl. ادناف *adnāf* seriously ill

دنف *danaf* long illness; ○ cachexia, marasmus (*med.*)

مدنف *mudnif*, *mudnaf* emaciated, haggard, weak

دانق look up alphabetically

دنقلة *dunqula* Dongola (town in N Sudan, on the Nile)

دنجل = دنكل

الدنمرك, الدنمارك *ad-dinimark, ad-danmark* Denmark

دنمركى, دنماركى *dinimarkī, danmarkī* Danish; (pl. *-ūn*) Dane

دنا (دنى and دنو) *danā u* (دنو *dunūw*, دناوة *danāwa*) to be near, be close; to come or go near s.o. or s.th. (من or الى or ل), approach (من, الى, ل s.o., s.th.); to come close, get close (من, الى, ل to), approximate (من, الى, ل s.th.); to draw near, be imminent (time, event); دنا به من to bring s.o. close to ...; — دنى *daniya a* (دنا *danan*, دناية *danāya*) to be low, lowly; to be or become mean, base, vile, despicable, contemptible **II** to bring close (ه s.th., ه s.o., من to), bring, take or move (ه s.th., ه s.o.) near (من), approximate (ه s.th., من to); to apply o.s. (فى to s.th.), busy o.s. (فى with s.th.), delve (فى into); دنى نفسه (*nafsahū*) to lower o.s., abase o.s., humble o.s. **III** to approach (ه s.o., ه s.th.), come or get near s.o. or s.th. (ه, ه), come or get close (ه, ه to); to approximate (ه s.th.); to measure up (ه, ه to) | شىء لا يدانى (*yudānā*) an unequaled thing **IV** to be near, be close; to approach (من or الى or ل s.o. or s.th.), come, go or draw near s.o. or s.th. (من, الى, ل), come close, get close (من, الى, ل to); to bring close (ه s.o., ه s.th., من to), bring, take or move (ه s.o., ه s.th.) near (من), approximate (ه s.th., من to); to lower, drop (ه s.th., e.g., the veil) **V** to approach gradually (الى s.th. or s.o.); to be debased, sink low, sink, decline; to lower o.s., abase o.s., humble o.s. **VI** to come near each other, get close to each other, approach one another; to be close together; to approach, approximate (من s.th.) **VIII** ادنى *iddanā* to be near, be close, come or draw near, approach **X** to wish to be nearer or closer, try to come nearer or closer; to seek to fetch or bring closer (ه s.th., الى to, to o.s.), reach out (ه for s.th.), wish (ه اليه for s.th.)

دنو *dunūw* advent, approach; proximity, nearness, imminence (of an event)

دنى *danīy* pl. ادنياء *adniyā'*[2] near, close; low, lowly; mean, base, vile, despicable, contemptible, inferior, infamous, depraved

دنية *danīya* pl. *-āt*, دنايا *danāyā* a base quality or habit; s.th. disgraceful, infamy, vile action

ادنى *adnā*, f. دنيا *dunyā* pl. m. ادان *adānin*, ادنون *adnauna*, pl. f. دنى *dunan*, دنيوات *dunyawāt* nearer, closer; situated lower down, nether; lower, inferior; lowlier; smaller, of less significance; more appropriate, better suited, more suitable; pl. الاداني, f. الدنيوات the youngest age class (sport; *Tun.*) | الشرق الادنى (*šarq*) the Near East; المغرب الادنى (*magrib*) Algeria; ادنى من حبل الوريد (*ḥabli l-warīd*) very near or close, imminent; الاقارب الادنون the closest relatives; من ادناه الى اقصاه (*aqṣāhu*) from one end to the other; wholly, entirely, completely, altogether; الحد الادنى (*ḥadd*) the minimum; ادناه hereinafter, below (in writings, documents, etc.) e.g., الموقعون ادناه (*muwaqqi'ūn*) those signed below, the undersigned; لا ادنى (with foll. genit.) not the least, not a single, not one; ادنى الدرجات *a. d-darajāt* the lowest stage(s)

دنيا *dunyā* f., pl. دنييات *dunyayāt* world; earth; this world (as opposed to آخرة); life in this world, worldly existence; worldly, temporal things or possessions; earthly things or concerns | الحياة الدنيا life in this world; ام الدنيا *umm ad-d.* Cairo; اقام الدنيا واقعدها *aqāma d-d. wa-aq'adahā* approx.: to kick up a dust, make a stir, move heaven and earth

دنيوى *dunyawī*, دنياوى *dunyāwī* worldly, mundane, secular; earthly, temporal, transitory, transient; pl. الدنيويات worldly things

دناوة *danāwa* nearness, closeness, proximity, propinquity; lowness, lowliness; meanness, baseness, vileness

دناية *danāya* lowness, lowliness; meanness, baseness, vileness

تدن *tadannin* sinking, decline; low level, nadir (fig.) | التدنى الاخلاق (*aklāqī*) the low level of morality, the moral decline

دان *dānin* low; near, close

متدان *mutadānin* close together

دهر *dahr* pl. دهور *duhūr*, ادهر *adhur* course or passage of time; a transient period of time, long stretch of time; age; epoch; lifetime; eternal continuance, eternity; fickle fate | بنات الدهر *banāt ad-d.* blows of fate, trials, afflictions, misfortune; تصاريف الدهر and صروف الدهر vicissitudes of fate, changes of fortune; adversities, adverse circumstances; دهر الداهرين *dahra d-dāhirīn* for all eternity, forever and ever; الى آخر الدهر *ilā ākiri d-d.* do.; لا ... الدهر كله (*ad-dahra kullahū*) never in all one's life

دهرى *dahrī* temporal, worldly, secular; — (pl. *-ūn*) an adherent of the *dahrīya* (see below); materialist; atheist, freethinker

دهرى *duhrī* very old, far advanced in years

دهرية *dahrīya* doctrine of the eternity of the world, a materialistic, atheistic trend in medieval Islam; materialism

دهس *dahasa a* (*dahs*) to trample underfoot, trample down, crush (ه s.th.), tread (ه on s.th.); to run over (ه s.o.)

دهش *dahiša a* and pass. *duhiša* to be astonished, amazed, surprised (من or ل at); to wonder, marvel (من at); to be baffled, startled, puzzled, perplexed, taken aback (من or ل by) **II** and **IV** to astonish, amaze, surprise, baffle, puzzle, perplex, startle (ه s.o.) **VII** = *dahiša*

دهش *dahaš* perplexity, surprise, consternation, alarm, dismay

دهش *dahiš* astonished, amazed, surprised; baffled, puzzled, nonplused, perplexed, startled, disconcerted, alarmed, upset; dazed, stunned

دهشة *dahša* astonishment, amazement, surprise, wonder; perplexity, consternation, bafflement, bewilderment, dismay, alarm

اندهاش *indihāš* astonishment, amazement; perplexity, consternation, bafflement, bewilderment

مدهش *mudhiš* astonishing, amazing, surprising, marvelous; pl. *-āt* amazing things, marvels, wonders

مدهوش *madhūš* and مندهش *mundahiš* astonished, amazed, surprised; perplexed, baffled, puzzled, nonplused, startled; overwhelmed

دهق[1] *dahaq* stocks (to hold the feet of an offender by way of punishment)

دهاق *dihāq* full (cup), brimful

دهقان[2] *dihqān*, pl. دهاقنة *dahāqina*, دهاقين *dahāqīn*[2] man of importance, one who plays an important role, leading personality; grandee (in ancient Persia) | دهاقين السياسة *d. as-siyāsa* the political leaders

دهك *dahaka a* (*dahk*) to crush; to mash (ه s.th.)

دهلز **II** *tadahlaza* to stroll about, walk about (in a hall)

دهليز *dihlīz* pl. دهاليز *dahālīz*[2] anteroom, vestibule, lobby, foyer; corridor, hallway | ابن الدهليز *ibn ad-d.* pl. ابناء الدهاليز foundling

دهلى *dihlī* Delhi

دهم *dahama a* (*dahm*) and *dahima a* (*daham*) to come or descend (ه upon s.o.) suddenly; to surprise, take unawares, take by surprise (ه s.o.), come unexpectedly (ه to s.o.); to enter suddenly, raid, invade (ه s.th.) **II** to blacken (ه s.th.) **III** to befall, seize, grip, attack (ه s.o.), come over s.o. (ه; e.g., sickness, despair); to surprise, take unawares, catch red-handed (ه s.o.); to attack suddenly (ه s.o.), fall upon s.o. (ه), invade, raid (ه e.g., a house); to overtake (ه s.o.; fate), catch up with (ه) **IX** to be black

دهمة *duhma* blackness

ادهم *adham*², f. دهماء *dahmā'*², pl. دهم *duhm* black, deep-black | داهية دهماء (*dāhiya*) disaster, catastrophe

الدهماء *ad-dahmā'* the masses, the common people, the populace, also دهماء الناس

مداهمة *mudāhama* police raid; house search

مدهم *mudhamm* very dark, pitch-dark

دهن *dahana u* (*dahn*) to oil (ه, ه s.th., s.o., ب with); to anoint (ه, ه s.th., s.o., ب with); to grease, smear (ه, ه s.th., s.o., ب with); to rub, embrocate (ه, ه s.th., s.o., ب with); to paint, daub (ه s.th.); to varnish (ه s.th.) **II** do. **III** to treat with gentleness (ه s.o.); to cajole, flatter (ه s.o.), fawn (ه on s.o.); to cheat, dupe, gull, take in, outsmart (ه s.o.) **V** pass. of **I**

دهن *dahn* oiling, greasing; painting, daubing

دهن *duhn* pl. ادهان *adhān*, دهون *duhūn*, -*āt*, دهان *dihān* oil (edible, lubricating, for the skin); fat, grease

دهنى *duhnī* oily, oil, oleic, oleo- (in compounds); fatty, greasy

دهنيات *duhnīyāt* fats, oils; fatty substances

الدهناء *ad-dahnā'* Dahna, desert region in Arabia

دهان *dahhān* house painter, painter

دهينة *dahīna* pomade

دهان *dihān* pl. -*āt*, ادهنة *adhina* cosmetic cream, cold cream, salve, ointment, unguent; consecrated oil, anointing oil; paint, varnish; hypocrisy, dissimulation, deceit; — (without pl.) painting, daubing; whitewashing | ورشة للدهان (*warša*) paintshop

مداهنة *mudāhana* flattery, adulation, sycophancy, fawning; hypocrisy, dissimulation; deceit, trickery

مداهن *mudāhin* flatterer, adulator, sycophant; hypocrite

مدهن *mudhin* oily; fatty, greasy

دهور *dahwara* to hurl down (ه s.th.); to tear down, topple, overthrow (ه s.th.); to tip over, overturn (ه s.th.) **II** *tadahwara* pass. of **I**; to fall, tumble; to tip or turn over (intr.); to slump, sink; to be dragged down, sink to the lowest level

تدهور *tadahwur* fall, downfall; decline, slump; turnabout (of a situation), overturn

دهى *dahiya a* (دهاء *dahā'*) to be clever, smart, cunning, artful, wily; — *dahā a* to befall, overtake, hit, strike (ه s.o.), come over s.o. (ه; misfortune) **II** = *dahā* **VI** to pretend to be smart or cunning

دهاء *dahā'* smartness, slyness, shrewdness, subtlety, cunning, craft

ادهى *adhā* smarter, shrewder; craftier, wilier; more skillful, subtler, more resourceful; worse, more calamitous

داه *dāhin* pl. دهاة *duhāh* smart, sly, shrewd, subtle, cunning, wily, artful; resourceful person

داهية *dāhiya* smart fellow, old fox, sly dog

داهية *dāhiya* pl. دواه *dawāhin* calamity, disaster, catastrophe | داهية دهياء (*dahyā'*) and داهية دهماء (*dahmā'*) disaster, catastrophe; فليذهب فى داهية (*fal-yaḏhab*) let him go to hell! داهية فى امك *d. fī ummak* (*colloq.*) may misfortune overtake your mother! (curse on the one addressed = go to hell!)

(دوء) داء *dā'* pl. ادواء *adwā'* disease, malady | داء الثعلب *d. aṯ-ṯa'lab* alopecia, loss of the hair; ○ داء الرقص *d. ar-raqṣ* St. Vitus's dance; داء السكر *d. as-sukkar* diabetes; داء الفيل *d. al-fīl* elephantiasis; داء المنطقة *d. al-minṭaqa* shingles, herpes zoster (*med.*)

دوى see دواء

□ (دوب) داب *dāba u* (< ذاب, q.v.) to wear thin, be worn out (*eg.*) II to wear thin, wear out (ه s.th.; *eg.*)

دوبارة *dūbāra* packthread, string, twine, cord, rope; thread

دوبلاج (Fr.) *dublāž* dubbing, synchronization (of a film)

دوبلير (Fr.) *dublēr*, f. دوبليره *dublēra* a double (in films); stand-in, substitute actor, second cast

دوبيت *dūbait* a rhymed poem consisting of four hemistichs

دوبيه *dobya*, دوبيا *dobyā* (It.) double entry (*econ.*)

دوح VII to spread, spread out, extend

دوحة *dauḥa*, coll. دوح *dauḥ*, pl. ادواح *adwāḥ* large tree with widespread branches; family tree, genealogical table

(دوخ) داخ *dāḵa u* (*dauḵ*) to conquer, subjugate (ه a country); to resign o.s., humble o.s.; to be or become dizzy, have a feeling of dizziness; to feel ill, be sick, feel nausea II to conquer, subjugate (ه a people); to make submissive, subdue, humble, humiliate, degrade (ه s.o.); to make (ه s.o.) dizzy; to molest, bother, trouble (ه s.o.); to daze, stun (ه s.o.) | دوخ رأسه (*ra'sahū*) and دوخ دماغه (*dimāḡahū*) to make s.o.'s head go round, make s.o. dizzy

دوخة *dauḵa* vertigo, dizziness; coma; nausea

دائخ *dā'iḵ* dizzy

تدويخ *tadwīḵ* subjugation, conquest

دود[1] II to be or become worm-eaten

دود *dūd* (coll.; n. un. ة) pl. ديدان *dīdān* worm; maggot; larva; caterpillar | دودة الحرير and دودة القز *d. al-qazz* silkworm; دود القرع *d. al-qar'*, دود قرعى (*qar'ī*) ascarids; دود القرمز *d. al-qirmiz* cochineal; دود المش *d. al-mišš* cheese maggots; الدودة الوحيدة tapeworm

دودى *dūdī* wormlike, worm-shaped, vermiform

مدود *madūd*, *mudawwid* wormy, worm-eaten

□[2] مدود *midwad* = مذود

(دور) دار *dāra u* (*daur*, دوران *dawarān*) to turn, revolve, rotate, move in a circle (على, ب, حول around s.th. or s.o.), circle (على, ب, حول s.th. or s.o.); to begin to turn or rotate; to circulate; to go round, spread, be current, make the rounds (of rumors, etc.); to run, be in operation (of a machine or engine); to start running, start up (engine); to walk or go about, run around; to roam, rove, move about, wander about, gad about; to make the rounds (على among people), turn successively (على to several people); to turn, turn one's face, wheel around; to veer, shift, change its direction; to change, take a different turn, become different; to turn (على against s.o.); to have to do, deal (حول or على with), treat (حول or على of), refer (حول or على to), bear (حول or على on), concern (حول or على s.th.); to take place, be going on, be in progress, be under way; to be discussed, be talked about (بين among); to circulate, pass around (ب s.th.); to lead, guide or show around (ب s.o.); to let roam, let wander (بعينيه, بنظره, *bi-naẓarihī*, *bi-ʿainaihi* one's eyes, one's glance, فى over) | در *dur!* about face! (command; *mil.*); دار رأسه (*ra'suhū*) to be or become dizzy, giddy; دار مع الفرص (*furaṣ*) to trim sail, adapt o.s. to the situation; دارت رحى الحرب (*raḥā l-ḥarb*) war broke out; المعارك التى دارت رحاها امس the battles that raged yesterday; الساعة تدور فى الثانية it's almost 2 o'clock; دار فى فلكه (*falakihī*) to be s.o.'s satellite or faithful follower, side with s.o., follow s.o.'s path; دار فى خلده (*ḵaladihī*) it kept running through his head; دار فى باله do.; شىء لم يدر لاحد فى بال (*li-aḥadin*) a matter about which no one had thought; دار بنفسه (*bi-nafsihī*) it passed through his mind; دار على الالسن (*alsun*) to be much discussed, be on everyone's lips; يدور اسمه على السنتهم (*alsinatihim*) his name is on everybody's tongue; دار على الافواه واسلات الاقلام (*afwāh, asalāt al-aqlām*) to be current in both the spoken and written language, be in general use, be generally accepted (e.g., words); دار بلادا واكل اعيادا (*bilādan, aʿyādan*) he had been around in the world and had seen a lot; (*colloq.*) دار باله (*bālahū*) to pay attention (الى, على to), be careful (الى, على with); دارت عليهم الدائرة calamity overtook them **II** to turn in a circle, spin, whirl, rotate, revolve (ب, ه s.th.); to turn, turn around (ب, ه s.th.); to invert, reverse (ب, ه s.th.); to make round, to round (ه s.th.); to circulate, pass around (ه s.th.); to set going, set in motion, start (ه s.th.); to wind (ه a watch, a clock); to look, search (على for s.th.) | دور رأسه (*ra'sahū*) to turn s.o.'s head, persuade s.o., bring s.o. round **III** to go or walk around (ه with s.o.); to try to bring (ه s.o.) round; to ensnare, inveigle (ه s.o.); to try to ensnare (ه s.o.); to try to deceive (ه s.o.); to cheat, trick (ه s.o. عن or على out of s.th.); to get away, escape, dodge, duck out **IV** to turn, revolve, rotate, spin, whirl (ه s.th.); to turn around, turn (ه, ب s.th., رأسه الى one's head toward); to direct (ه الى or على s.th. to, toward), aim (ه الى or على s.th. at); to circulate, pass around (ه s.th.); to bind (ه على s.th. around, e.g., a bandage around the head or over the eyes); to set in operation, set going, set in motion (ه a machine, an apparatus); to start, start up (المحرك *al-muḥarrik* the motor); to play (ه a record); to play back (ه tapes); to act upon s.th. (ه), drive (ه s.th.); to get under way (ه a job, a project); to take up (ه s.th.); to initiate (ه s.th.); to divert, turn away (ه عن, ه s.o., s.th. from); to direct, conduct, steer, manage, head, run (ه s.th.), be in charge (ه of); to revolve in one's mind, think over, ponder (ه s.th., ان that) | ادار بوجهه الى (*bi-wajhihī*) to turn around to s.o., look back at s.o.; ادار رأسه (*ra'sahū*) to turn s.o.'s head, persuade s.o., bring s.o. round; to make s.o. giddy or drunk (with joy); ادار الحديث فى الموضوع to bring conversation around to a topic, broach or discuss a subject **V** to be or become round; to be circular **X** do.; to round out (of bodily forms); to go round s.th. (حول), surround (حول s.th.); to circle, rotate, revolve; to turn around (person), turn (on one's heel); to turn one's head, look back; to turn off (الى, نحو toward, in the direction of); to turn (الى to), face (الى s.o.)

دار *dār* f., pl. دور *dūr*, ديار *diyār*, ديارات *diyārāt*, ديرة *diyara* large, stately house; building, structure, edifice; habitation, dwelling, abode; residence, home; seat,

داری *dārī* domestic, native

دوری *dūrī* domestic (animal); عصفور دوری (*ʿuṣfūr*) and دوری house sparrow

دور *daur* pl. ادوار *adwār* round (of a patrol; in sports); role, part (played by s.o. or s.th.); film role, stage role; periodic change, rotation, alternation; crop rotation; period; (one's) turn; phase, stage, step, degree, station; epoch, age, era; fit, attack, paroxysm (of a disease); floor, story; musical composition; number, single performance (within a program) | دور وتسلسل (*wa-tasalsul*) vicious circle, circulus vitiosus; دور نهائى (*nihāʾī*) final round, finals (*athlet.*); دور نصف نهائى (*niṣfu nihāʾī*) semi-finals, دور ربع نهائى (*rubʿu n.*) quarter-finals (sport); دور الانعقاد *d. al-inʿiqād* session, term (*parl.*); الدور الاول (*awwal*) leading role, starring role; دور البطولة *d. al-buṭūla* do.; championship round (sport); قام بدور or لعب دورا (*laʿiba*) to play a part or role; دور ارضى (*arḍī*) ground floor, first floor; كان دوره it was his turn; جاء دوره his (or its) turn came up; الدور له it is his turn; (انا) بدورى I for one, (I) for my part, (هو) بدوره he in turn, (he) for his part; بالدور alternately, by turns

دورة *daura* pl. *-āt* turn, revolution, gyration, rotation; circulation; cycle; circuit; round, patrol; procession (*Chr.*); round trip; tour (in general, of an artist or performer); detour; period (○ also *el.*); work shift (industry); session (of parliament); study course, refresher course (several days or weeks); meeting, study session; sports events, games (lasting several days) | دورة اولمبية (*ōlimbīya*) Olympiad; الدورة الدموية (*damawīya*) blood circulation; الدورة الجوية (*jawwīya*) air circulation; دورة اجتياز (تجاوز) الرتبة *d. ijtiyāz* (*tajāwuz*) *ar-rutba* officers' training course (*mil.*, *Syr.*); دورة تدريبية training course; continuation course; دورة

site, locality; area, region; land, country (esp. pl. ديار, see below) | دار الآثار museum (of antiquities); دار البريد post office; دار البقاء *d. al-baqāʾ* the eternal abode, the hereafter; الدار الباقية (*bāqiya*) do.; انتقل للدار الباقية to pass away, die; دار البلدية *d. al-baladīya* town hall; الدار البيضاء (*baiḍāʾ*) Casablanca (seaport in W Morocco); the White House (in Washington); دار التجارة commercial house, business house; دار الحرب *d. al-ḥarb* war zone, enemy territory (*Isl. Law*: non-Muslim countries); دار الرياسة seat of the chief executive of a country; دار السعادة *d. as-saʿāda* Constantinople; دار السلطنة *d. as-salṭana* Constantinople (designation before World War I); دار السلام *d. as-salām* paradise, heaven; epithet of Baghdad; Dar es Salaam (seaport and capital of Tanganyika Territory); the region of peace, i.e., the territory of Islam (*Isl. Law*; opposite of دار الحرب see above); دور السينما cinemas, movie houses; دار الشرطة *d. aš-šurṭa* police headquarters; دار الصنعة or دار الصناعة arsenal; دار صينى see alphabetically; دار الضرب *d. aḍ-ḍarb* and دار السكة *d. as-sikka* mint (building); الديار العراقية (*ʿirāqīya*) Iraq; دار العلوم name of a college in Cairo; دار المعلمين *d. al-muʿallimīn* teachers' college; دار الافتاء *d. al-iftāʾ* building housing the office of the Grand Mufti; دار الفناء *d. al-fanāʾ* (as opposed to دار البقاء see above) the temporal world, this world; دار القضاء *d. al-qaḍāʾ* court of justice, tribunal; دار الكتب *d. al-kutub* public library; دور اللهو *d. al-lahw* amusement centers; night clubs; دار التمثيل theater, playhouse; دار الملك *d. al-mulk* (royal) residence; الديار المصرية (*miṣrīya*) Egypt; دار النشر *d. an-našr* pl. دور النشر publishing house; دار الهجرة *d. al-hijra* Medina; دار الايتام *d. al-aitām* orphanage, orphans' home

دارة *dāra* pl. *-āt* halo (of the moon); aureole (*astron.*, *el.*); small castle; villa

دراسية (*dirāsīya*) study course, study session; دورة زراعية (*zirā'īya*) crop rotation, system of farming by crop rotation; دورة تشريعية (*tašrī'īya*) legislative period; دورة صيفية (*ṣaifīya*) summer course; دورة الفلك *d. al-falak* revolution of celestial bodies; دورة التفافية (*iltifāfīya*) flanking maneuver (*mil.*); دورة ليلية (*lailīya*) night shift, دورة نهارية (*nahārīya*) day shift; دورة مالية (*mālīya*) financial period, fiscal year; دورة المياه *d. al-miyāh* lavatory (with running water), toilet, water closet

دورى *daurī* patrolling, patrol- (in compounds); periodic, occurring at regular stated times, recurring, intermittent; circulatory, cyclic, etc., see دور and دورة; (*eg.*) league (sport); دوريا *dauriyan* periodically | امر دورى (*amr*) daily order, order of the day; الجهاز الدورى (*jahāz*) the circulatory system; دورى عام (*eg.*) national league (sport), مباريات الدورى العام national league games, بطل الدورى *baṭal ad-d.* league champion

دورية *daurīya* pl. *-āt* work shift (industry); patrol, round; patrol, reconnaissance squad; periodical, magazine | دوريات الاستكشاف reconnaissance squads, patrols

□ داورية *dāwirīya* = دورية *daurīya*

دير *dair* pl. اديار *adyār*, اديرة *adyira*, ديورة *duyūra* monastery, convent, cloister

ديرى *dairī* monastic, monasterial, cloistral

ديرة *dīra* living place, abode, homeland (*bedouin*)

دوار *duwār* vertigo, dizziness, giddiness; nausea; seasickness | دوار الجو *d. al-jaww* airsickness

دوار *dawwār* rapidly or constantly turning, whirling, spinning, rotating, circling, circulating; revolving, rotary, rotatory; whirlpool, eddy, vortex; itinerant, ambulant, roving; — (pl. دواوير *dawāwīr*[2]) enclosure, corral; farmyard; (*eg.*) office of the village chief or mayor; *duwwār* (*alg.*, *mor.*) Bedouin camp or settlement, douar | باب دوار revolving door; بائع دوار peddler, hawker; جهاز حفر دوار (*jahāz ḥafr*) rotary drilling rig; دوار الشمس *d. aš-šams* sunflower; مسرح دوار (*masraḥ*) revolving stage; كرسى دوار (*kursī*) swivel chair

ديار *dayyār* monastic, friar, monk

ديرانى *dairānī* monastic, friar, monk

دوارة *dawwāra* whirlpool, eddy, vortex; ○ merry-go-round; top (toy); compass, pair of dividers (*syr.*) | ○ دوارة الهواء *d. al-hawā'* weather vane

ديارى *diyārī* domestic: native

دوران *dawarān* turn(ing), rotation, revolution, gyration; circulation, circling, circuiting; running (of a machine, of a tape, etc.); round; round trip, tour | الدوران البطىء (*baṭī'*) and الدوران على الفاضى slow running, idling, idle running (auto, *techn.*)

دورانى *dawarānī* rotational, pertaining to circular motion

ادور *adwar*[2] (elative): ادور على الالسن (*alsun*) more talked about, more frequently expressed or discussed

مدار *madār* pl. *-āt* orbit (of a planet or satellite, حول around); circling, circuiting, circuit, revolution; axis; pivot, (fig.) that upon which s.th. turns or depends, the central, cardinal, or crucial factor, the pivot; center; subject, topic, theme (of a conversation, of negotiations); scope, range, extent, sphere; tropic (*geogr.*); ○ steering wheel | مدار السرطان *m. as-saraṭān* Tropic of Cancer, مدار الجدى *m. al-jady* Tropic of Capricorn; كان مداره على it (i.e., the dispute, or the like) was about ..., it hinged on ...; على مدار السنة (*m. as-sana*) throughout the year, all year round; على مدار النهار (*m. an-nahār*) throughout the whole day; على مدار الساعة around the clock, day and night

مدارى *madārī* being in orbit, circling, orbiting

تدوير *tadwīr* recitation of the Koran at medium speed (between *tartīl* and *ḥadr*; a technical term of *tajwīd*)

مداورة *mudāwara* pl. *-āt* cheating, humbug, trickery; outwitting; attempted evasion or circumvention, shift, dodge; persuasion, inveigling, ensnaring

ادارة *idāra* turning; turning around or over, reverting, reversion, inversion; starting, setting in operation; operation; drive (*techn.*); direction, management; administration; (pl. *-āt*) administrative agency, department, office, bureau | ادارة الامن *i. al-amn* the police; ادارة التجنيد conscription office (*mil.*); ادارة الجوازات *i. al-jawāzāt* passport office; ادارة المخابرات *i. al-mukābarāt* secret service bureau, office of intelligence services; ادارة شؤون العاملين personnel office or administration (of an agency or company); ادارة عرفية (*'urfīya*) military administration; ادارة الامتحانات office of examinations (in a ministry of cultural affairs); سوء الادارة *sū' al-i.* mismanagement, maladministration; مجلس الادارة *majlis al-i.* board of directors, administrative board, committee of management; مركز الادارة *markaz al-i.* administration center, headquarters

ادارى *idārī* administrative, departmental; — (pl. *-ūn*) administrative officer; administrative expert; manager (*athlet.*); an official (sport); اداريا *idārīyan* through administrative channels, administratively, officially

استدارة *istidāra* roundness, rotundity, circularity

دائر *dā'ir* turning, revolving, spinning; circulating; current (e.g., expression), common; ambulant, itinerant; in progress, under way; working, in operation; running (machine, engine); round

دائرة *dā'ira* pl. دوائر *dawā'ir*[2] circle (also *math.*); ring; round slice; circuit, circumference; sphere, scope, range, compass, extent, circuit; field, domain (fig.); government office, agency, bureau (esp. *Syr.*, *Ir.*); division, chamber (of a court of justice; *jur.*); farm, country estate (*eg.*); (*Alg.*) administrative district (also with pl. *-āt*); misfortune, calamity, affliction | في دائرة . . . within the framework of . . .; على شكل نصف دائرة *'alā šakli niṣfi d.* semicircular; نقطة الدائرة *nuqṭat ad-d.* essential factor, pivot, crucial point, crux; دائرة كهربائية (*kahrabā'īya*) electric circuit; دائرة قصيرة short circuit (*el.*); دائرة المعارف encyclopedia; دائرة مشوية (*mašwīya*) grilled medallion, center cut; دائرة الاختصاص jurisdiction (of an official agency, esp. of a court of justice); دائرة البروج the zodiac (*astron.*); دائرة الامن العام *d. al-amn al-'āmm* department of public security; دائرة المحكمة *d. al-maḥkama* jurisdiction; chamber of a court of justice (*jur.*); الدائرة السنية (*sanīya*) administrative office of royal or government real estate (formerly, *Eg.*); دائرة استئنافية (*isti'nāfīya*) appellate court (*Eg.*; *jur.*); دائرة الاستخبارات (esp. *Tun.*) and دائرة المخابرات *d. al-mukābarāt* intelligence bureau (*pol.*); دائرة انتخابية (*intikābīya*) electoral district; دوائر الحكومة government agencies; دوائر رسمية (*rasmīya*) official circles; government agencies; دوائر سياسية (عسكرية) (*siyāsīya*, *'askarīya*) political (military) circles; دوائر الاعمال business circles; دارت عليه الدوائر to suffer adversities

دائرى *dā'irī* circular, ring-shaped, annular | نصف دائرى *niṣfu dā'irī* semicircular

□ داورية *dāwirīya* pl. *-āt* patrol, round

مدور *mudawwar* round, circular

مدير *mudīr* pl. *-ūn*, مدراء *mudarā'*[2] director; head, chief; manager; administrator; superintendent; rector (of a university); administrative officer at the head of a county or rural district, mudir; head of a department (of a ministry); (formerly, *Eg.*) president of a province (*mudīrīya*) | مدير الجوق *m. al-jauq* bandleader, conductor of an orchestra; مدير التحرير managing editor (of a newspaper); مدير المراسم and مدير التشريفات chief of protocol; مدير عام (*'āmm*) general manager; president of the board; مدير فنى (*fannī*) technical director

مديرة *mudīra* pl. *-āt* directress; manageress; woman administrator

مديرية *mudīrīya* direction; administration; management; — (pl. *-āt*) division, department (of a ministry); administrative district, county; (formerly, *Eg.*) province | مديرية الجمارك customs administration; مديرية النفوس (*Ir.*) residents' registration office

مستدير *mustadīr* round; circular | مؤتمر المائدة المستديرة (*mu'tamar al-m.*) round-table conference

دورق *dauraq* pl. دوارق *dawāriq*[2] (*eg.*) bulging vessel with a long, slender neck, carafe

دورو (Span.) *dūrō* coin of small value (*Alg.*)

دوزن *dauzana* to tune (a musical instrument); ○ to tune in (radio)

دوزان *dūzān* and دوزنة *dauzana* tuning (of a musical instrument); دوزنة ○ tuning (*radio*)

دوزينة (It. *dozzina*) *dōzīna* dozen

داس (دوس) *dāsa u* (*daus*, دياس *diyās*) to tread, step (ه on); to tread (ه s.th.); to tread down, trample down, trample underfoot, crush (ه s.th.); to thresh (grain); to treat with disdain, humiliate (ه s.o.); to run over (ه s.o.; automobile) VII pass. of I

دوس *daus* treading, trampling, tread, step

ديسة *dīsa* dense forest, jungle, thicket

دواسة *dawwāsa* pl. *-āt* pedal

مداس *madās* a pair of shoes or sandals

مدوس *madūs*, مداس *mudās* trodden, trampled down; crushed; run over

دوسنطاريا *dusinṭāriyā*, دوسنتاريا dysentery

دوسيه *dōsēh* and دوسييه *dosyēh* (Fr.) pl. *-āt* dossier, file

[1]دوش (*eg.*) *dawaš* to irritate (ه s.o.) or drive s.o. crazy by noise

دوشة *dauša* (*eg.*) din, noise, clamor, uproar, hubbub, hullabaloo

[2]دوش (Fr. *douche*) *dūš* pl. *-āt* shower, douche

دوطة (It. *dote*) *dōṭa* dowry

دوغ II to imprint a mark, to brand

داغ *dāġ* pl. *-āt* brand (on cattle)

داف (دوف) *dāfa u* (*dauf*) to mix, mingle (ه فى s.th. with); to add, admix (ه فى s.th. to)

دوق *dūq* duke

دوقة *dūqa* duchess

دوقى *dūqī* ducal

دوقية *dūqīya* dukedom, duchy; ducat

دوك II to chatter, prattle

دوكة *dauka* din, row, hubbub, tumult, confusion

[1]دال (دول) *dāla u* (دولة *daula*) to change periodically, take turns, alternate, rotate; to change, turn (time, fortune) | دالت دولة الاستبداد the time of absolutism is over,

belongs to the past; دالت له الدولة fortune has turned in his favor (عليه against him) **III** to alternate, rotate (ه, ه s.o., s.th.); to cause to succeed by turns or to follow one another (الايام *al-ayyāma* the days; God); to alternate (بين between); to confer, talk (ه with s.o., في about), discuss (ه في with s.o. s.th.) **IV** to give ascendancy, afford superiority, give the upper hand (ه من to s.o. over); to make victorious, let triumph (ه على s.o. over), grant victory (ه على to s.o. over); to replace (ه ب or من s.th. with), exchange, substitute (ه ب or من for s.th. s.th.) | اديل لبنى العباس من بنى امية *udīla li-banī l-ʿabbāsi min banī umayyata* the rule passed from the Ommaiads to the Abbasides **VI** to alternate, take turns (ه with or in s.th., e.g., in some work); to hand each other s.th. (ه), pass s.th. (ه) alternately between themselves; to handle alternately (ه different things), take now this, now that; to exchange (الرای *ar-ra'y* views); to make frequent use (ه of s.th.); to confer, have a discussion, take counsel, deliberate; to parley, negotiate; to circulate, be in circulation, be current, have currency | تداولته الايدى *tadāwalathu l-aidī* it passed from hand to hand, it made the rounds, it circulated; تداولته الالسن (*alsun*) it passed from mouth to mouth, it was the talk of the town, it was on everybody's lips; تداول الاحاديث to talk with one another, have conversations

دولة *daula* pl. دول *duwal* alternation, rotation, change; change of time, turn of fortune; dynasty; state, country; power, empire | صاحب الدولة title of the Prime Minister; دولة رئيس الحكومة *daulat r. al-ḥ.* His Excellency, the Prime Minister; فخامة الدولة *fakāmat ad-d.* title of the President of the Republic (*Syr.*, *Leb.*); الدولة العلية (*ʿalīya*) name of the ancient Ottoman Empire; الدول الكبرى (العظمى or) (*kubrā*, *ʿuẓmā*) the big powers; دولة منتدبة (*muntadaba*) mandatory power; الدول النامية (*nāmiya*) the developing countries; الدول الصناعية (*ṣināʿīya*) the industrialized countries; دولة اتحاد الامارات العربية and دولة الامارات see امارة

دولة (*dam.*, pronounced *dōle* = ركوة *rakwa*) metal vessel with long curved handle used for making coffee

دولى *daulī* state (adj.); *daulī* and *duwalī* international

دولية *duwalīya* internationality; internationalism; the International

دويلات *duwailāt* petty states, small countries

دواليك *dawālaika* alternately, by turns; successively, one by one, one after the other | وهكذا دواليك (*wa-hākaḏā*) and so forth, and so on

تدويل *tadwīl* internationalization

مداولة *mudāwala* pl. *-āt* parley, negotiation; deliberation, consultation; discussion; *mudāwalatan* alternately, one after the other, one at a time

تداول *tadāwul* alternation, rotation; circulation, currency; circulation of money | بالتداول alternately, by turns, in rotation

متداول *mutadāwal* current, circulating, in circulation; valid; common, in common use, prevailing | الكلام المتداول (*kalām*) the colloquial language

دوال[2] *dawālin* see دلو

دولاب *dūlāb* pl. دواليب *dawālīb*[2] wheel; tire; gearing, gears, wheels, mechanism, machine, machinery; closet, locker, cabinet, cupboard | دولاب للملابس wardrobe; دولاب الهدوم do.; دولاب الماء waterwheel, noria; دواليب المحفوظات filing cabinets

دولار *dōlār* pl. *-āt* dollar

[1](دوم) دام *dāma u* (*daum*, دوام *dawām*) to last. continue, go on; to persevere, persist | ما دام *mā dāma* as long as; (the more so) since, inasmuch as, as, because; while he is ..., when he is ...; ما دام حيا (*ḥayyan*) as long as he is alive; ما دمت معك (*dumtu*) so long as (or while) I am with you **II** to move in a circle, turn, spin, revolve, rotate, gyrate, circle; to turn, revolve, spin, twirl (ه s.th.) **III** to continue; to persevere, persist (على in); to apply o.s. diligently and steadily (على to), pursue with diligence and perseverance (على s.th.); to attend regularly (على a school class, instruction); to be on duty (official, employee) | داوم على العمل (*'amal*) to perform one's official duties, devote oneself to one's work **IV** to cause to last or continue, perpetuate, make lasting, make permanent (ه s.th.) **X** to make (ه s.th.) last or continue; to continue, go on (ه with s.th.)

دوم *daum* continuance, permanence, duration; دوما *dauman* constantly, at all times, ever, always; — doom palm (*bot.*)

ديمة *dīma* pl. ديم *diyam*, ديوم *duyūm* continuous rain

دوام *dawām* duration, continuance, permanence, perpetuity; uninterrupted succession; endurance, perseverance; abiding, stay (of s.o., في at a place); work during office hours; attendance during regular class hours (of pupils); دواما *dawāman* and على الدوام permanently, perpetually, at all times, ever, always | ساعات الدوام, اوقات الدوام, وقت الدوام working hours, office hours; انتظام الدوام regularity of attendance (esp. in school)

ديمومة *daimūma* duration | في ديمومة permanently, continuously

دوامة *duwwāma* top (child's toy); whirlpool, eddy, vortex

مداومة *mudāwama* perseverance, endurance, persistence; continuance, duration; continuation

دائم *dā'im* lasting, enduring; endless, eternal, perpetual, everlasting; perennial; continued, continuous, continual, incessant, unceasing, constant; permanent, standing, established; durable | دائم التقدم والنمو *d. at-taqaddum wa-n-numūw* in a state of constant progress and growth

دائما *dā'iman* always | دائما ابدا (*abadan*) always and ever

دائمى *dā'imī* = دائم | اوامر دائمية standing orders

مدام *mudām* wine

مستديم *mustadīm* constant, continuous, continual, incessant, uninterrupted | اوامر مستديمة standing orders

[2]دومان *dūmān* rudder, helm

دومانجى *dūmānjī* steersman, helmsman

[1]دون **II** to record, write down, set down, put down in writing (ه s.th.); to enter, list, register, book (ه s.th.); to collect (ه poems) | دون شرطا (*šarṭan*) to stipulate a condition **V** to be recorded, be written down, be put down in writing

ديوان *dīwān* pl. دواوين *dawāwīn*[2] account books of the treasury (in the older Islamic administration); divan, collection of poems written by one author; governmental office, administrative office; chancellery, office, bureau, secretariat; council of state, cabinet; council, consultative assembly, board of advisers, executive committee; government; court of justice, tribunal; hall; davenport, divan; (railway) compartment | لغة الدواوين *luğat ad-d.* official jargon, officialese; ديوان التفتيش inquisitional court; the Inquisition; ديوان المحاسبة *d. al-muḥāsaba* audit office, control bureau (of government funds); ديوان الموظفين *d. al-muwaẓẓafīn* (*Saudi Ar.*) agency for the appointment of officers in all ministries

ديوانى *dīwānī* administrative, administrational, official; an Ottoman style of cursive (used by the secretaries of the State Chancellery for treaties, diplomas, firmans, etc.)

تدوين *tadwīn* recording, writing down; entry, listing, booking; registering, registration

مدونة *mudawwana* pl. *-āt* record, note; entry; written document; body of laws; pl. مدونات writings, literature (on a given subject)

²دون *dūn* low, lowly; bad, poor, inferior; meager, inadequate | عامله بالدون (*ʿāmalahū*) he snubbed him

دون *dūna* (prep.) below, beneath, under (in rank, value, etc.); this side of, short of; before; without; more than; with the exclusion of, leaving ... aside, disregarding ...; and not by any means, but not | دون ذلك (with foll. nominative) on the way to that, there is ..., before accomplishing that one must ..., دون ذلك خرط القتاد (*karṭ al-qatād*) before one can do that, one must strip the tragacanth of its leaves, i.e., accomplish the impossible; من دون, بدون (*dūni*) without; with the exclusion of, excluding; بدون ان and من دون ان without (+ foll. gerund in Engl.); دونك *dūnaka* (with foll. acc.) here you are! take ...! watch out (ه for)! beware (ه of)! هو دونه he is below him, he doesn't measure up to him; كان دونه اهمية (*ahammīyatan*) to be of less importance than ...; اثم دونه كل اثم *iṯmun dūnahū kullu iṯmin* a sin to end all sins; الذين هم دون السن العسكرية (*sinn, ʿaskarīya*) those below the age for military service; دون ما نظر الى (*naẓarin*) regardless of, irrespective of; دون ما فائدة with no benefit at all; completely useless; تخشى ان يسعدن دونها (*takšā an yasʿadna*) she is afraid they will be happier than she is; تلك الكتب دون غيرها (*kutub, ġairihā*) those books and no others; انا متعجب من فضلك دون علمك (*mutaʿajjib, faḍlika, ʿilmika*) I admire your virtue, but not your knowledge, or, I admire your virtue more than your knowledge; كم الافواه دون التذمر والشكوى (*kamma, taḏammur, šakwā*) he stopped their mouths to keep them from muttering and complaining; اذا كان الغصن دون ما يحتمله (*ġuṣnu, yaḥtamiluhū*) if the branch is not strong enough to carry him; وصل دونهم الى الغاية it was he, not they, who reached the goal; اشاحت بوجهها دونه (*ašāḥat bi-wajhihā*) she averted her face so that he could not see her; الباب محجوز دون المراجعين (*murājiʿīn*) the door is barred to petitioners, solicitors; يوصد الباب دونهم (*yūṣidu*) he bars the door to them; تغلق من دونها الباب (*taġliqu*) she locks the door behind her; براءة دون براءة الاطفال (*barāʾa*) an innocence greater than the innocence of children; تحتاج الى ذلك دون غيرها she needs that to a far greater degree than others, more than anyone else; حال دون الشيء to prevent s.th.; الاشعة دون الحمراء (*ašiʿʿa, ḥamrāʾ*) infrared rays (*phys.*); الموجات دون القصيرة (*maujāt*) ultra-short waves (*phys.*)

دونم *dūnum* a square measure (*Ir.* = about 2500 m²; *Pal.* = roughly, 900 m²)

¹دوى *dawā i* and *dawiya a* to buzz, hum (of insects) **II** do.; to sound, resound, ring out; to drone; to echo, reverberate **III** to treat (ه a patient, ه a disease) **VI** to treat o.s. (with a medicine); to be cured

دوى *dawan* pl. ادواء *adwāʾ* sickness, illness, disease, malady

دوى *dawīy* sound, noise, ring, clang, roar, thunder, drone; echo, reverberation

دواة *dawāh* (□ دواية *dawāya*) pl. دوى *duwīy, diwīy*, دويات *dawayāt* inkwell | دواة المصباح *d. al-miṣbāḥ* socket of a light bulb

دواء *dawāʾ* pl. ادوية *adwiya* remedy, medicament, medication, medicine, drug

دوائى *dawāʾī* medicinal, medicative, curative

داء see دوء

دواء *diwāʾ* treatment, therapy (*med.*)

مداواة *mudāwāh* treatment, therapy (*med.*)

تداو *tadāwin* cure

مدو *mudawwin* loud, ringing, resounding

[2]دوى (Fr. *douille*) *dūy* socket (of a light bulb)

دويتو (It. *duetto*) *duwittō* duet (*mus.*)

ديالكتيك *diyalektīk* dialectics

ديالكتيكى *diyalektīkī* dialectical

ديالوج *diyalōg* (Eg. spelling) pl. *-āt* dialogue

ديباج and ديباجة see دبج

دبلوماسى = ديبلوماسى

ديوث *dayyūṯ* (□ ديوس) cuckold; procurer, pimp; a variety of warbler (*zool.*)

ديجور see دجر

الديجوليون *ad-dēgōlīyūn* (Eg. spelling) the Gaullists

دياجى see دجو

ديدان see دود

ديدبان *daidabān, daidubān* pl. *-āt,* ديادبة *dayādiba* guard, sentry; sentinel | ديدبان المراكب ship's pilot

ديدن see ددن

دير, ديرة, اديار, ادیرة, ديار, ديرانى see دور

ديزل *dīzil* diesel

ديس *dīs* diss (Ampelodesma tenax; *bot.*)

ديسم see دسم

ديسة see دوس

ديوس see ديوث

ديسمبر *disembir, disambir* December

ديفليه (Fr.) *dēfilē* a filing by, marching past, show (fashion)

ديك *dīk* pl. ديكة *diyaka,* ديوك *duyūk,* ادياك *adyāk* cock, rooster | ديك الحبش *d. al-ḥabaš* and ديك حبشى (*ḥabašī*) turkey, turkey cock; ديك رومى (*rūmī*) do.; وزن الديك *wazn ad-d.* bantamweight (sport)

السعال الديكي *as-suʿāl ad-dīkī* whooping cough

ديكاتلون *dīkatlūn* decathlon (sport)

ديكتاتور, ديكتاتورى, ديكتاتورية see دكتاتور

ديكور (Fr. *décor*) *dīkōr* pl. *-āt* décor, stage decoration, scenery; interior decoration

ديكولتيه (Fr.) *dēkoltēh* pl. *-āt* décolleté

ديماجوجية (Eg. spelling) *dīmāgōgīya* demagoguery

ديماس pl. دياميس see under دمس

ديمة, ديم, ديمومة see دوم

ديموطيق *dīmūṭīqī* demotic (writing)

ديمقراطى, ديموقراطى *dimuqrāṭī* democratic; democrat

ديمقراطية, ديموقراطية *dimuqrāṭīya* pl. *-āt* democracy; democratic attitude or conviction | ديموقراطية شعبية (*šaʿbīya*) people's democracy

[1](دين) دان *dāna i* to borrow, take up a loan; to be a debtor, be indebted; to owe (ل ب s.o. s.th., also, e.g., دان له بالشكر (*šukr*) *d. lahū bi-š-šukr* to owe s.o. one's thanks; ب s.th., e.g., بالحياة *bi-l-ḥayāh* one's life, ل to s.th. or s.o.); to be indebted (ل ب to s.o. for); to be subject, subject

o.s., bow, yield, (ل to s.o. or s.th.), be under s.o.'s (ل) power, owe allegiance (ل to s.o.), obey (ل s.o.); to grant a credit, give or sell on credit, grant a loan, lend money (ه to s.o.); to subject, subjugate (ه s.o.); to requite, repay (ه s.o.); to condemn (ه s.o.), pass judgment (ه on s.o.) **III** to have a debt (ه with s.o.), be indebted (ه to s.o.); to be the creditor (ه of s.o.), have a money claim (ه on s.o.) | داينه بمبلغ خمسة قروش (*bi-mablaḡ kamsat q.*) he had a claim of five piasters on him **IV** to lend money (ه to s.o.); to sell on credit (ه to s.o.); to convict, find guilty, pronounce guilty (ه s.o., ب of a crime); to condemn (morally, ه s.o., ه a country), censure (ه s.o.) **V** to be indebted, have debts; to subject o.s. (ل to) **VI** تداينوا بدين (*dain*) to contract a mutual loan, borrow money from each other **X** to make or incur debts, take up a loan

دين *dain* pl. ديون *duyūn* debt; pecuniary obligation, liability; obligation (*Isl. Law*); claim (*Isl. Law*), financial claim | بالدين on credit; رب الدين *rabb ad-d.* creditor; ديون الحرب *d. al-ḥarb* war debts; دين مضمون bonded, or funded, debt; دين ممتاز (*mumtāz*) preferred, or privileged, debt; دين موحد (*muwaḥḥad*) consolidated debt; دين مطلق (*muṭlaq*) debt not bound to the physical person of the debtor, but outliving him (*Isl. Law*); دين مستغرق (*mustaḡriq*) claims against an estate which exceed or equal the assets (*Isl. Law*)

دينونة *dainūna* judgment; Last Judgment

الديان *ad-dayyān* the Judge (attribute of God)

مدينة *madīna* and مدائن *madā'in*[2] see under مدن

ادانة *idāna* verdict of guilty; conviction; (moral) condemnation (e.g., of a country) | صدر الحكم بادانته *ṣadara l-ḥukmu bi-idānatihī* he was convicted

استدانة *istidāna* incurrence of debts

دائن *dā'in* creditor; lender; جانب الدائن see مدين *madīn*

مديون *madyūn* indebted, in debt; obligated, under obligation

مديونية *madyūnīya* indebtedness, obligation

مدين *madīn* owing; indebted, obligated, under obligation; (pl. *-ūn*) debtor | مدين بالشكر (*šukr*) owing gratitude, much obliged; كان مدينا ل to be indebted to s.o., stand in s.o.'s debt; جانب المدين وجانب الدائن the debit side and the credit side, debit and credit

مدين *mudīn* moneylender, creditor

مدان *mudān* convicted, found guilty; guilty; judged, condemned

[2](دين) دان *dāna i* to profess (ب a religion, a conviction, etc.) | دان بالاسلام to profess Islam; دان بعاداته (*bi-ʿādātihī*) to adhere to one's customs **V** to profess (ب a religion)

دين *dīn* pl. اديان *adyān* religion, creed, faith, belief | يوم الدين *yaum ad-d.* the Day of Judgment

دينى *dīnī* religious; spiritual | لادينى irreligious; ○ العلم الدينى (*ʿilm*) science of religion

دين *dayyin* religious, pious, godly, devout

ديانة *diyāna* pl. *-āt* religion; communion, confession, denomination, sect | صاحب الديانة founder of a religion

ديان *dayyān* pious, godly, devout, religious

تدين *tadayyun* piety, godliness, devoutness, religiousness, religiosity; bigotry

متدين *mutadayyin* pious, godly, devout, religious

متدينة *mutadayyina* religious community

دينار *dīnār* pl. دنانير *danānīr*[2] dinar, an ancient gold coin; a monetary unit = pound (*Ir., Jord.*), dinar (*Lib., Tun., Alg.*); pl. دنانير money

دينارى *dīnārī* diamonds (of a deck of cards)

دينامو *dīnāmō* dynamo, generator

ديناميت *dīnāmīt* dynamite

ديناميكية *dīnāmīkīya* dynamics; dynamism

O دينم *dainam* pl. ديانم *dayānim*[2] dynamo, generator

دية see ودى

ديوان pl. دواوين and ديوانى see دون[1]

ذ

ذا *ḏā* (demonstr. pron.) pl. اولاء *ulā'i* this one, this; بذا *bi-ḏā* by this, by this means, thereby; لذا *li-ḏā* therefore; كذا *ka-ḏā* so, thus, in this manner; so and so, so and so much; هكذا *hā-ka-ḏā* so, thus, in this manner; serves as intensifier after interrogative pronouns (roughly corresponding in English to such phrases as: ... on earth, ... then, or the like): ماذا what on earth? لماذا why then? why in heaven's name? — هو ذا *huwa ḏā*, f. هى ذى *hiya ḏī* that one; look at that one! why, that is ..., now if that isn't ...!; هاءنذا *hā'ana-ḏā* behold, it is I, here I am, pl. ها نحن اولاء (see also ها); — used as an accusative in the construct state: master, owner, or possessor of, with ذو nominative (q.v.), ذى as genitive; — ذاك *ḏāka*, f. تاك *tāka*, تيك *tīka*, pl. اولائك *ulā'ika* this, this one; اذ ذاك (*iḏ*) then, at that time; in those days; — ذلك *ḏālika*, f. تلك *tilka*, pl. اولائك *ulā'ika* that, that one; بذلك *bi-ḏālika* by that, by that means, in that manner; لذلك *li-ḏālika* therefore; بعد ذلك *ba'da ḏālika* after that, upon that, thereafter, thereupon; مع ذلك *ma'a ḏālika* yet, still, nevertheless, for all that; وذلك ان (*anna*) which means that ..., to be more precise, that is (to say), namely, to wit; وذلك لان (*li-anna*) and that is because ..., for the one reason that ...; ذلك بان (*bi-anna*) this is due to the fact that ...; كذلك *ka-ḏālika* so, thus, in that manner; equally, likewise, in the same manner; — ذلكم *ḏālikum*, f. تلكم *tilkum*, pl. اولائكم *ulā'ikum* that one; — هذا *hāḏā*, f. هذه *hāḏihī*, هذى *hāḏī*, pl. هؤلاء *hā'ulā'i*, dual m. هذان *hāḏāni*, f. هاتان *hātāni* this, this one, see هذا (alphabetically)

ذأب X to be wolflike, be fierce or cruel like a wolf

ذئب *ḏi'b* pl. ذئاب *ḏi'āb*, ذؤبان *ḏu'bān* dieb (Canis anthus), jackal; wolf | مرض الذئب الاحمر *maraḍ aḏ-ḏ. al-aḥmar* name of a noncontagious skin disease

ذؤابة *ḏu'āba* pl. ذوائب *ḏawā'ib*[2] lock, strand (of hair); tuft, wisp

ذات, ذاتى and ذاتية see ذو

ذاك see ذا

ذال *ḏāl* name of the letter ذ

ذب *ḏabba u* to drive away, chase away (ه, ه s.o., s.th.); to defend (عن s.o., s.th.)

ذباب *ḏubāb* (coll.; n.un. ة) pl. اذبة *aḏibba*, ذبان *ḏibbān* flies, fly | ذباب قارض gadfly, horsefly

ذبابة *ḏubāba* pl. *-āt* (n. un. of ذباب) fly; tip (of the sword, or the like)

ذبانة *ḏubbāna, ḏibbāna* fly; sight, bead (on a firearm)

مذبة *miḏabba* fly whisk, fly swatter

ذبح **ḏabaḥa** *a* (*ḏabḥ*) to kill (by slitting the throat); to slaughter, butcher; to massacre; to murder, slay; to sacrifice, offer up, immolate (ه an animal) **II** to kill, slaughter, butcher, massacre, murder

ذبح *ḏabḥ* slaughtering, slaughter

ذبح *ḏibḥ* sacrificial victim, blood sacrifice

ذبحة *ḏibḥa, ḏubḥa* angina (*med.*); diphtheria | الذبحة الصدرية (*ṣadrīya*) angina pectoris (*med.*); ○ الذبحة الفؤادية (*fu'ādīya*) do.

ذباح *ḏabbāḥ* slaughtering, killing, murdering; slaughterer, butcher

ذبيح *ḏabīḥ* slaughtered

ذبيحة *ḏabīḥa* pl. ذبائح *ḏabā'iḥ*[2] slaughter animal; sacrificial victim, blood sacrifice; sacrifice, immolation; offering, oblation

مذبح *maḏbaḥ* pl. مذابح *maḏābiḥ*[2] slaughterhouse; altar (*Chr.*)

مذبحة *maḏbaḥa* pl. مذابح *maḏābiḥ*[2] massacre, slaughter, carnage, butchery

ذبذب **ḏabḏaba** to set into a swinging motion, swing, dangle (ه s.th.) **II** *taḏabḏaba* to swing, pendulate; to oscillate (*el.*); to be deflected (magnetic needle); to vibrate; to fluctuate; to waver, vacillate, hesitate

ذبذبة *ḏabḏaba* pl. *-āt* pendulous motion, pendulation; oscillation (*el.*); vibration (*phys.*)

تذبذب *taḏabḏub* pendulous motion, pendulation, swinging; oscillation (*el.*); deflection (of a magnetic needle)

○ مذبذب *muḏabḏib* oscillator (*el.*)

مذبذب *muḏabḏab* fluctuating, variable; vacillating, wavering, hesitant, unsteady

متذبذب *mutaḏabḏib*: تيار متذبذب (*tayyār*) oscillating current (*el.*)

ذبل **ḏabala, ḏabula** *u* (*ḏabl*, ذبول *ḏubūl*) to be wilted, to wilt, wither; to fade; to become dry, dry up; to waste away; to become dull, lose its luster (eye)

ذبل *ḏabl* mother-of-pearl, nacre

ذبالة *ḏubāla* wick

ذابل *ḏābil* pl. ذبل *ḏubul* wilted, withered; dry, dried up; faded (color); languid, dull, lackluster, languishing (glance); feeble, weak, tired

ذحل **ḏaḥl** pl. اذحال *aḏḥāl*, ذحول *ḏuḥūl* resentment, rancor, hatred; revengefulness, vindictiveness; blood revenge

ذخر **ḏakara** *a* to keep, preserve, store away, put away (ه s.th.); to save, lay by (ه s.th.) **VIII** ادخر *iddakara* to keep, preserve, store away, put away (ه s.th.); to store, accumulate, gather, hoard, amass (ه s.th.); to lay by (ه s.th.); to save (ه s.th., also strength, trouble, etc.) | ادخر حبا ل (*ḥubban*) to harbor love for; لا يدخر جهدا (*juhdan*) he spares no effort

ذخر *ḏukr* pl. اذخار *aḏkār* s.th. stored away, put by, hoarded, or accumulated; stores, supplies; treasure

ذخيرة *ḏakīra* pl. ذخائر *ḏakā'ir*[2] treasure; stores, supplies; provisions, food; ammunition (*mil.*); (holy) relic

ادخار *iddikār* storage; hoarding, amassing, accumulation; storing, gathering; saving

ادخاري *iddikārī* savings (in compounds) | قدرة ادخارية (*qudra*) savings capacity (of a people)

مذخر *muḏakkir* pl. *-ūn* assistant gunner, ammunition passer (*mil., Syr.*)

مدخر *muddakir* pl. *-ūn* saver (*econ.*), s.o. with a savings account

مدخرة *muddakira* pl. *-āt* (*Syr.*) storage battery, battery

مدخر muddakar saved; hoarded; pl. مدخرات savings; hoarded monies, supplies

[1]ذرة dura see ذرو

[2]ذر darra u (darr) to strew, scatter, spread (ه s.th.); to sprinkle (ه ب on s.th. s.th.) | ذر الرماد فى عينيه (ar-ramāda fī ʿainaihi) to throw dust in s.o.'s eyes; — u (ذرور durūr) to rise, come up, rise resplendent over the horizon (sun) | ذر قرنه (qarnuhū) it began to show, it emerged

ذر darr strewing, scattering, sprinkling; (coll.) tiny particles, atoms, specks, motes

ذرة darra (n. un.) pl. -āt atom; tiny particle; speck, mote | مثقال ذرة mitqāl d. the weight of a dust particle, a tiny amount; a little bit; مقدار ذرة miqdār d. a tiny amount, a jot, an iota; ذرة من الشك (šakk) the least doubt

ذرى darrī atomic | قنبلة ذرية (qunbula) atomic bomb; النشاط الذرى (našāṭ) and طاقة ذرية (ṭāqa) atomic energy

ذرية darrīya: مذهب الذرية madhab ad-d. atomism (philos.)

ذرور darūr powder

ذرورى darūrī powdery, powdered, pulverized

ذريرة darīra pl. ذرائر durā'ir[2] fragrant powder, cosmetic scented powder

ذريرة duraira pl. -āt subatomic particle, smallest structural unit of the atomic nucleus (phys.)

ذرى durrī of or pertaining to the offspring or progeny | وقف ذرى waqf d. see وقف

ذرية durrīya pl. -āt, ذرارى darārīy progeny, descendants, children, offspring | وقف ذرية waqf d. see وقف

[3]يذر yadaru see (وذر)

[4]ذرة dura see (ذرو and ذرى)

ذرأ dara'a a to create; to sow (ه many or different things; fig.); to seed (ه the ground, a field)

ذرب dariba a (darab) to be sharp, cutting

ذرب darab diarrhea (med.)

ذرب darib pl. ذرب durb sharp, cutting | جرح ذرب (jurḥ) a malignant, incurable wound

ذراح durrāḥ pl. ذراريح darārīḥ[2] Spanish fly, blister beetle (zool.)

ذرع daraʿa a (darʿ) to measure (ه s.th.); to take the measure or measurements (ه of s.th.); to cover (ه a distance); to cross, traverse (ه a country), travel through (ه); to intercede, intervene, mediate, put in a word (ل for s.o., on behalf of s.o., عند with s.o. else) V to use, employ, apply (بذريعة bi-darīʿa or بوسيلة bi-wasīla a means, an expedient); to use as a pretext, as an excuse (ب s.th.); to use as a means (ب s.th., الى to an end) VII to proceed, advance; to intervene

ذرع darʿ power, ability, capability (ب to do s.th.) | ضاق ذرعا ب and ضاق عنه ذرعا (darʿan) not to be up to s.th., be unable to do or accomplish s.th.; to be unable to stand or bear s.th., be fed up with, be tired of, feel uneasy about, be oppressed by

ذراع dirāʿ f., pl. اذرع adruʿ, ذرعان durʿān arm; forearm; — (m.) lever, shift lever, lever arm (techn.); crank arm (techn.); jib, boom (of a crane); cubit, in Syria = .68 m | in Egypt: ذراع بلدى (baladī) = .58 m, ذراع استانبولى (istanbūlī) = .665 m, ذراع هندازة (hindāza) = .656 m, ذراع معمارى (miʿmārī) = ca. .75 m, ذراع مربع (murabbaʿ) = .5625 m²; in Iraq: ذراع حلبي (ḥalabī) = ca. .68 m, ذراع بغدادى (baġdādī) or ذراع بلدى (baladī) = ca.

.80 m, ذراع معمارى see above; ذراع التروس gear lever (*techn.*); ذراع مخلب (*miklab*) soil-sampling arm; gripping device (*techn.*)

ذريع *darīʿ* stepping lively, walking briskly; rapid, quick; torrential; rapidly spreading, sweeping (death); devastating; intercessor

ذريعة *darīʿa* pl. ذرائع *darāʾiʿ*[2] medium, means, expedient; pretext, excuse | مذهب الذرائع *madhab ad-d.* instrumentalism (*philos.*)

ذرف **darafa** *i* (*darf*, ذريف *darīf*, ذروف *durūf*, ذرفان *darafān*) to flow, well forth (tears); to shed (ه tears; said of the eye) **II** to exceed (على an age) **X** to let flow, shed (ه tears)

مذرف *madraf*: سالت مذارف عينيه (*m. ʿainaihi*) to shed tears

ذرق **daraqa** *i u* (*darq*) to drop excrement (bird) **IV** do.

ذرق *darq* droppings, excrement (of a bird)

(ذرو and ذرى) ذرا **darā** *u* (*darw*) to disperse, scatter (ه s.th.); to carry off, blow away (ه dust; said of the wind); to winnow, fan (ه grain); — ذرى *darā i* (*dary*) do. **II** do.; to atomize (ه s.th.) **IV** = **I**; to throw down, throw off (ه, ه s.o., s.th.) | اذرت العين الدمع (*damʿa*) the eye shed tears **V** to be winnowed, be fanned; to climb (ه on), scale (ه s.th.); to seek shade or shelter (ب in, at, under); to take refuge (ب with), flee (ب to) **X** to take refuge (ب with), place o.s. under s.o.'s (ب) protection, flee (ب to s.o.)

ذرة *dura* durra, a variety of sorghum | ذرة شامى (*eg.*) Indian corn, maize (Zea mays L.); ذرة صفراء (*ṣafrāʾ*) do. (*syr.*); ذرة عويجة (*eg.*) a variety of millet (Andropogon Sorghum Brot. var. Schweinfurthianus Kcke.); ذرة بيضاء (*baiḍāʾ*) millet (*syr.*)

ذرى *daran* protection, shelter

ذروة *durwa*, *dirwa* pl. ذرى *duran* summit; top; peak; culmination, climax, acme, apex | مؤتمر الذروة *muʾtamar ad-d.* summit conference

مذرى *midran* and مذراة *midrāh* pl. مذار *madārin* winnow, winnowing fork

تذرية *tadriya* atomization

ذعر **daʿara** *a* (*daʿr*) to frighten, scare, alarm, terrify (ه s.o.); pass. *duʿira* to be frightened (ل by), get alarmed (ل at); — *daʿira a* (*daʿar*) to be terrified, alarmed, dismayed **IV** to frighten, scare, alarm, terrify (ه s.o.) **V** and **VII** to be frightened, become alarmed

ذعر *duʿr*, fright, terror, alarm, panic

ذعر *daʿar* fright, alarm, dismay, consternation

ذعاف **duʿāf** lethal, deadly, immediately killing (poison) | موت ذعاف (*maut*) a sudden, immediate death

ذعق **daʿaqa** *a* (*daʿq*) to frighten (ه s.o.) by screaming

ذعن **daʿina** *a* (*daʿan*) and **IV** to submit, yield, give in (ل to s.o.), obey (ل s.o., an order, etc.); to concede voluntarily, grant willingly (ب ل to s.o. s.th.)

مذاعنة *mudāʿana* submissiveness, pliability, compliance, obedience

اذعان *idʿān* submissiveness, pliability, compliance, obedience

مذعن *mudʿin* submissive, pliable, tractable, obedient

مذعان *midʿān* pliable, tractable, docile, obedient, obliging, compliant

ذفر **dafar** pungent smell, stench

ذقن **daqan**, *diqan*, now most often pronounced *daqn* f., pl. اذقان *adqān*, ذقون *duqūn* chin; — *daqn* f., pl. ذقون *duqūn* beard | ذقن

الشيخ *d. aš-šaiḵ* wormwood, absinthe; خروا لاذقانهم *ḵarrū li-adqānihim* they prostrated themselves; غرق فى العمل حتى الذقن (*ğariqa fī l-ʿamal*) to be up to one's neck in work, be swamped by work (properly: to drown in work); ضحك على ذقنه (*ḍaḥika*) pl. على ذقونهم (*eg., syr.*) to fool s.o., make fun of s.o., lead s.o. around by the nose (ب with s.th.); to put on an act for s.o.; ضحك فى ذقنه to laugh in s.o.'s face

ذكر *dakara u* (*dikr*, تذكار *tadkār*) to remember, bear in mind (ه s.th.), think (ه of); to keep in mind (ه s.th.); to recall, recollect (ه s.th.); — (*dikr*) to speak, talk (ه of, about); to name, mention, cite, quote (ه s.th.); to state, designate, indicate (ه s.th.); to give (ه e.g., facts, data); to point, refer (ه to s.th.); to report, relate, tell (ه ل s.th. to s.o.) | تقدم يذكر *taqaddumun yudkaru* notable progress; لا يذكر (*yudkaru*) inconsiderable, not worth mentioning; ذكره بخير (بالخير) (*ḵair*) to have pleasant memories of s.o., hold s.o. in fond remembrance; to speak well of s.o.; ذكره بشر (*šarr*) to have unpleasant memories of s.o.; to speak ill of s.o. **II** to remind (ه ب s.o. of s.th.), point out (ه ب to s.o. s.th.), call s.o.'s (ه) attention (ب to); to make (ه a word) masculine (*gram.*) **III** to parley, negotiate, confer, have a talk, take counsel (ه with s.o.); to memorize, commit to memory, learn, study (ه one's assignment, one's lessons) | ذاكر دروسه (*durūsahū*) to study one's lessons, do one's homework **IV** to remind (ه ه s.o. of s.th.), call (ه s.th.) to s.o.'s (ه) mind **V** to remember, bear in mind (ه s.th.), think (ه of s.th.) **VI** to remind each other (ه of), revive each other's memory of (ه); to confer (together), have a talk, take counsel **VIII** ادكر *iddakara* = **V**; **X** to memorize, commit to memory, learn, study (ه one's assignment, one's lessons); to remember, recall, keep in mind, know by heart (ه s.th.)

ذكر *dikr* recollection, remembrance, reminiscence, memory, commemoration; reputation, repute, renown; naming, stating, mention(ing), quoting, citation; report, account, narration, narrative; invocation of God, mention of the Lord's name; (pl. اذكار *adkār*) collective liturgical exercises of Sufi orders, consisting in incessant repetition of certain words or formulas in praise of God, often accompanied by music and dancing | على ذكر (with foll. genit.) apropos of, speaking of ...; وعلى ذكر ذلك speaking of that, incidentally, in that connection; الذكر الحكيم the Koran; سالف الذكر above-mentioned, afore-mentioned; سعيد الذكر of blessed memory, deceased, late; اشاد بذكره (*ašāda*) to celebrate, praise, commend s.o. or s.th., speak in glowing terms of s.o. or s.th.; ما زال على ذكر من (*dikrin min*) he still remembered ..., he could still recall ...; جاء ذكره على لسانهم (*lisānihim*) they spoke in praise of him

ذكر *dakar* pl. ذكور *dukūr*, ذكورة *dukūra*, ذكران *dukrān* male; (pl. ذكور) penis

ذكرى *dakarī* male, masculine

ذكرة *dukra* reputation, repute, renown

ذكرى *dikrā* pl. ذكريات *dikrayāt* remembrance, recollection, memory; pl. reminiscences, memoirs | ذكرى سنوية (*sanawīya*) annual celebration or commemoration ceremony

ذكير *dakīr* steel

تذكار *tadkār*, *tidkār* remembrance; reminder, memento; memory, commemoration; souvenir, keepsake; memorial day | تذكار جميع القديسين *t. jamīʿ al-qiddīsīn* All Saints' Day (*Chr.*)

تذكارى *tadkārī*, *tidkārī* serving to remind, helping the memory; memorial, commemorative

تذكرة *tadkira* reminder; memento

تذكرة *tadkira*, mostly pronounced *tadkara*, pl. تذاكر *tadākir*[2] message, note; slip, paper, permit, pass; card; ticket; admission ticket | تذكرة بريد postcard; تذكرة اثبات الشخصية *t. itbāt aš-šakṣīya* identity card; تذكرة ذهاب واياب *t. dahāb wa-iyāb* round-trip ticket; تذكرة الرصيف (*eg.*) platform ticket; تذكرة اشتراك subscriptiou ticket; تذكرة طبية (*ṭibbīya*) medical prescription; تذكرة مرور permit, pass, laissez-passer; passport; تذكرة النفوس (*Syr.*) identity card (= بطاقة شخصية *Eg.*); تذكرة الهوية المدنية *t. al-huwīya al-madanīya* (*Syr.*, *Ir.*) civilian identity card; تذكرة الانتخاب *t. al-intikāb* ballot

تذكرجى *tadkarjī*, تذكرى *tadkarī* ticket seller, ticket clerk; (streetcar) conductor

تذكير *tadkīr* reminding (of s.o., ب of s.th.), reminder, memento; fecundation, pollination (of female blossoms; in pomiculture); masculine use of a word (*gram.*)

مذاكرة *mudākara* pl. *-āt* negotiation, consultation, conference; deliberation (of a court; *Syr.*); (*Mor.*) conversation; learning, memorizing, memorization; study

تذكر *tadakkur* memory, remembrance, recollection

استذكار *istidkār* memorizing, memorization, committing to memory

ذاكرة *dākira* memory

مذكور *madkūr* mentioned; said, above-mentioned; worthy of mention; celebrated | لم يكن شيئا مذكورا *lam yakun šai'an m.* it was of no importance, it was nothing

مذكر *mudakkar* masculine (*gram.*)

مذكرة *mudakkira* pl. *-āt* reminder; note; remark; notebook; memorandum, memorial, aide-mémoire, (diplomatic) note; ordinance, decree; treatise, paper, report (of a learned society, = Fr. *mémoires*); official report (concerning an incident); official notice; pl. reminiscences, memoirs | مذكرة الاتهام *m. al-ittihām* bill of indictment (*jur.*); مذكرة تبليغ السوق (*sauq*) official draft notice (for military duty; *Syr.*); مذكرة الجلب *m. al-jalb* writ of habeas corpus (*jur.*); مذكرة احتجاج protest note; مذكرة شفاهية (*šifāhīya*) verbal note (*dipl.*)

(ذكو and ذكى) ذكا *dakā u* (*dukūw*, ذكا *dakan*, ذكاء *dakā'*) to blaze, flare up (fire); to exude a strong odor; — ذكى *dakiya* (ذكاء *dakā'*) to be sharp-witted, intelligent II and IV to cause to blaze, fan (ه the fire); to kindle (ه s.th.) II to immolate an animal X = *dakā*

ذكاء *dakā'* acumen, mental acuteness, intelligence, brightness; — *dukā'*[2] the sun

ذكى *dakīy* pl. اذكياء *adkiyā'*[2] intelligent, sharp-witted, clever, bright; redolent, fragrant; tasty, savory, delicious

اذكى *adkā* brighter, smarter, more intelligent; more fragrant; more delicious

ذل *dalla i* (*dull*, *dull*, ذلالة *dalāla*, ذلة *dilla*, مذلة *madalla*) to be low, lowly, humble, despised, contemptible II to lower, debase, degrade, humiliate, humble (ه, ه s.o., s.th.); to subject, break, subdue, conquer (ه s.o.); to overcome, surmount (ه difficulties, obstacles) IV to lower, debase, degrade, humiliate, humble (ه, ه s.o., s.th.); to subject, break, subdue, conquer (ه, ه s.o., s.th.) V to lower o.s., humble o.s., cringe (الى or ل before s.o.); to be humble, obsequious X to think (ه s.o.) low or despicable; to think little (ه of), disesteem (ه s.o.); to deride, flout, disparage, run down (ه s.o.)

ذل *dull* lowness, lowliness, insignificance; ignominy, disgrace, shame, degradation, humiliation; humility, humbleness, meekness, submissiveness

ذلة *dilla* lowness, baseness, vileness,

depravity; submissiveness, obsequiousness

ذليل *ḏalīl* pl. اذلاء *aḏillā'*², اذلة *aḏilla* low, lowly; despised, despicable, contemptible; docile, tractable, pliable; humble, submissive, abject, servile; obsequious, cowering, cringing

ذلول *ḏalūl* pl. ذلل *ḏulul* docile, tractable, gentle (animal); female riding camel

مذلة *maḏalla* humbleness, meekness, submissiveness; humiliation

تذليل *taḏlīl* derogation, degradation, bemeaning; overcoming, conquering, surmounting (of difficulties, of an obstacle, and the like)

اذلال *iḏlāl* degradation, debasement, humiliation

تذلل *taḏallul* self-abasement

مذل *muḏill* humiliating, disgraceful

ذلذل *ḏulḏul* pl. ذلاذل *ḏalāḏil*² lowest, nethermost part of s.th.; train, hem (of a garment) | ذلاذل الناس the mob, the riffraff

اذلف *aḏlaf*², f. ذلفاء *ḏalfā'*², pl. ذلف *ḏulf* having a small and finely chiseled nose

ذلق *ḏalq* tip, point; tip of the tongue

ذلق *ḏalq*, *ḏaliq*, ذليق *ḏalīq* eloquent, glib (speaker); smooth, fluent (speech or style); pointed, sharp

اذلق *aḏlaq*² pl. ذلق *ḏulq* = ذلق *ḏalq*, *ḏaliq* | الحروف الذلق (*ḏulq*) = حروف الذلاقة

ذلاقة *ḏalāqa* eloquence, fluency, smoothness (of speech) | حروف الذلاقة the consonants *r*, *l*, *n*, *f*, *b*, *m* (*phon.*)

ذلك etc., see ذا

ذم *ḏamma* *u* (*ḏamm*, مذمة *maḏamma*) to blame, find blameworthy, dispraise, criticize (ه, ه s.o., s.th.), find fault (ه, ه with s.o. or s.th.) II to rebuke, censure sharply (ه, ه s.o., s.th.)

ذم *ḏamm* censure, dispraise, derogation, disparagement

ذمة *ḏimma* pl. ذمم *ḏimam* protection, care, custody; covenant of protection, compact; responsibility, answerableness; financial obligation, liability, debt; inviolability, security of life and property; safeguard, guarantee, security; conscience | بالذمة؟ honestly? really? seriously? فى ذمتى and على ذمتى upon my word, truly; فى ذمته ,بذمته in s.o.'s debt, indebted to s.o.; ما بذمته his debt; على ذمته under s.o.'s protection; at s.o.'s disposal; for the benefit of s.o. or s.th., for s.o. or some purpose (allocation of funds); هى على ذمته she is financially dependent on him, he has to support her; اهل الذمة *ahl aḏ-ḏ.* the free non-Muslim subjects living in Muslim countries who, in return for paying the capital tax, enjoyed protection and safety; طاهر الذمة of pure conscience, upright, honest; عديم الذمة and قليل الذمة dishonest; unscrupulous; برأ ذمته (*barra'a*) to relieve one's conscience, meet one's obligation; الدين المتبقى بذمته (*dain, mutabaqqī*) the balance of his unpaid debt; ترتب بذمته (*tarattaba*) to become the debtor of s.o.; to be to s.o.'s debit, be payable by s.o., fall due to s.o. (amount, debt); على ذمة وكالة الانباء as the news agency assures

ذمى *ḏimmī* a zimmi, a free non-Muslim subject living in a Muslim country (see ذمة *ḏimma*: اهل الذمة)

ذمام *ḏimām* pl. اذمة *aḏimma* right, claim, title; protection, custody; security of life and property | فى ذمام الليل *fī ḏ. al-lail* under cover of darkness

ذميم *ḏamīm* censured; blameworthy, objectionable, reprehensible; ugly, unfair, nasty

ذميمة *ḏamīma* pl. ذمائم *ḏamā'im*² blame, censure

مذمة *maḏamma* pl. *-āt* blame, censure

مذموم *madmūm* censured; blameworthy, objectionable, reprehensible

مذمم *mudammam* sharply censured; objectionable, reprehensible

ذمر V to grumble, complain (من or على about)

ذمار *dimār* sacred possession, cherished goods; honor

تذمر *tadammur* pl. *-āt* grumbling, complaint, grievance

ذمى *damiya a* (ذماء *damā'*) to be in the throes of death

ذماء *damā'* last remnant; last breath of life | ذماء من الحياة (*ḥayāh*) last breath of life

ذنب IV to do wrong, commit a sin, a crime, an offense; to be guilty, be culpable X to find or declare (ه s.o.) guilty of a sin, of a crime, of an offense

ذنب *danb* pl. ذنوب *dunūb* offense, sin, crime, misdeed

ذنب *danab* pl. اذناب *adnāb* tail; appendage; follower, henchman; pl. اذناب dependents, clique of followers, following (of s.o.) | ذوات الاذناب *dawāt al-a.* comets

ذنبى *danabī* caudal, tail-(in compounds); appendaged, appendant, dependent

ذنيب *dunaib* petiole, leafstalk (*bot.*)

مذنب *mudannab* pl. *-āt* comet

مذنب *mudnib* culpable, guilty; sinner; evildoer, delinquent, criminal

ذهب *dahaba a* (ذهاب *dahāb*, مذهب *madhab*) to go (الى to); to betake o.s., travel (الى to); to go away, leave, depart; to disappear, vanish, decline, dwindle; to perish, die, be destroyed; with ب: to carry s.th. off, take s.th. away, abduct, steal s.th., sweep s.th. or s.o. away, annihilate, destroy s.th. or s.o.; ذهب به الى to lead or conduct s.o. to, take s.o. along to; to think, believe (الى s.th.), hold the view, be of the opinion (الى that); to escape (عن s.o.; fig.), slip (عن s.o.'s mind), ذهب عنه ان to lose sight of the fact that ..., forget that ...; to ignore, skip, omit (عن s.th.); (with imperf.) to prepare to ..., be about to ... | ذهب وجاء to go back and forth, walk up and down; ذهب الى ابعد من (*ab'ada*) to go beyond ... (fig.); ما يذهب فى نزعته (*naz'atihī*) what follows along these lines; اين يذهب بك! (*yudhabu*) the idea of it! you can't mean it! ذهب سدى (*sudan*) to be futile, be in vain, be of no avail; ذهب ادراج الرياح (*adrāja r-riyāḥ*) to go the ways of the winds, i.e., to pass unnoticed, without leaving a trace; to end in smoke, come to nothing, be futile, be in vain; ذهب كامس الدابر (*ka-amsi d-dābir*) to vanish into thin air, disappear without leaving a trace (lit.: like yesterday gone by); ذهب ببهائه (*bi-bahā'ihī*) to take the glamor away from s.th.; ذهب بنفسه (*bi-nafsihī*) to kill s.o. (joy, terror, etc.); ذهب بخياله (*bi-kayālihī*) to let one's imagination wander (الى to); ذهب بصوابه (*bi-ṣawābihī*) to drive s.o. wild, drive s.o. out of his mind, make s.o. crazy; ذهب مذهبه (*madhabahū*) to embrace s.o.'s *madhab* (see below); to follow s.o.'s teaching, make s.o.'s belief one's own, embrace s.o.'s ideas; to adopt s.o.'s policy, proceed exactly like s.o.; ذهب كل مذهب (*kulla madhabin*) to do everything conceivable, leave no stone unturned, go to greatest lengths; ذهبوا مذاهب شتى (*šattā*) they followed different trends or orientations II to gild (ه s.th.) IV to cause to go away, make disappear, remove, eliminate (ه s.th.); to take away (ه s.th., عن from s.o.)

مذهب II *tamadhaba* (deriv. of مذهب *madhab*) to follow, adopt, embrace (ب a teaching, a religion, etc.); to be a disciple or adherent (ب of s.o.), follow s.o.'s (ب) teachings

ذهب *ḏahab* (m. and f.) gold; gold piece, gold coin | ○ ذهب ابيض (*abyaḍ*) platinum

ذهبى *ḏahabī* golden, of gold; gold-colored (hair); precious, excellent, apposite (e.g., advice, saying, etc.) | آية ذهبية golden word, maxim, epigram

ذهبية *ḏahabīya* pl. *-āt* dahabeah, a long light-draft houseboat, used on the Nile

ذهاب *ḏahāb* going; passing, passage, falling away, decrease, dwindling, loss, disappearance; leave, departure; trip, journey; outward-bound trip or journey (as opposed to اياب *iyāb* return trip; railroad); opinion, view (الى ان that) | ذهابا وايابا (*iyāban*) there and back; back and forth, up and down; تذكرة ذهاب واياب *taḏkarat ḏ. wa-iyāb* round-trip ticket; مقابلة الذهاب *muqābalat aḏ-ḏ.* first match (in soccer, in contrast to مقابلة الاياب *m. al-iyāb* return match; *Tun.*)

ذهوب *ḏuhūb* going | ذهوب ومآب coming and going; فى جيئة وذهوب coming and going, in a state of fluctuation, having its ups and downs

مذهب *maḏhab* pl. مذاهب *maḏāhib*² going, leave, departure; way out, escape (عن from); manner followed, adopted procedure or policy, road entered upon; opinion, view, belief; ideology; teaching, doctrine; movement, orientation, trend (also *pol.*); school; mazhab, orthodox rite of *fiqh* (*Isl. Law*); religious creed, faith, denomination | ○ مذهبه فى الحياة (*ḥayāh*) his philosophy of life, his weltanschauung; المذهب التاريخى historism; مذهب الروحية *m. ar-rūḥīya* spiritualism; المذهب الرواقى (*riwāqī*) stoicism; المذهب السلوكى (*sulūkī*) behaviorism; المذهب الاصلاحى (*iṣlāḥī*) reformism; المذهب الطبيعى (*ṭabīʿī*) naturalism; المذهب العقائدى (*ʿaqāʾidī*) dogmatism; ○ مذهب اللذة *m. al-laḏḏa* hedonism; مذهب المثالية *m. al-miṯālīya* idealism; المذهب المادى (*māddī*) the materialistic ideology, materialism; المذهب الواقعى and مذهب الواقعية realism; ذهب مذهبا بعيدا to go very far, be very extensive

مذهبى *maḏhabī* denominational, confessional; doctrinaire; following or representing a particular doctrine; sectarian

مذهبية *maḏhabīya* doctrinaire attitude, devotion to an ideology; sectarianism

ذاهب *ḏāhib*: ذاهب اللون *ḏ. al-laun* faded, colorless, discolored

مذهوب به *maḏhūb bihī* and مذهوب العقل *m. al-ʿaql* out of one's mind, demented

مذهب *muḏahhab, muḏhab* gilded

ذهل *ḏahala a* (*ḏahl*, ذهول *ḏuhūl*) and *ḏahila a* to be numbed, stunned, stupefied or dazed; to be absent-minded; to be indifferent (عن to or toward); to be perplexed, confused, speechless (by surprise or fright); to forget, ignore, neglect, overlook (عن s.th.); to be or become distracted (عن from) **IV** to baffle, startle, nonplus (ه s.o.); to distract (ه عن s.o. from), make (ه s.o.) forget (عن s.th.) **VI** to pretend forgetfulness, feign to have forgotten (عن s.th.) **VII** = *ḏahila*

ذهول *ḏuhūl* numbness, stupefaction, daze, stupor; absent-mindedness; drowsiness; indifference, disinterestedness; perplexion, confusion (by surprise or fright); distraction, distractedness (عن from)

ذاهل *ḏāhil* numbed, stupefied; in a stupor; absent-minded; drowsy; indifferent (عن to s.th.); perplexed; distracted (عن from)

مذهول *maḏhūl* seized by stupor or confusion, struck with surprise or fright; perplexed

مذهل *muḏhil* startling, baffling, amazing

منذهل *munḏahil* alarmed, dismayed,

perplexed, startled, baffled; distracted, absent-minded

ذهن *ḏihn* pl. اذهان *aḏhān* mind; intellect

ذهنى *ḏihnī* mental, intellectual

ذهنية *ḏihnīya* pl. *-āt* mentality

ذو *ḏū*, genit. ذى *ḏī*, acc. ذا *ḏā*, f. ذات *ḏāt*, pl. m. ذوو *ḏawū*, اولو *ulū*, pl. f. ذوات *ḏawāt* (with foll. genit.) possessor, owner, holder or master of, endowed or provided with, embodying or comprising s.th. | ذو عقل *ḏū ʿaql* endowed with brains, bright, intelligent; ذو مال rich, wealthy; ذو صحة *ḏū ṣiḥḥa* healthy; ذو بال see بال; ذو شأن *ḏū šaʾn* important, significant; a respected, influential man; ذو خطر وشأن (*ḏ. ḵaṭar*) a man of importance and reputation; ذو القربى *ḏū l-qurbā* relative, kin(sman); ذوو القرابة *ḏ. l-qarāba* relatives; غير ذى زرع (*zarʿin*) uncultivated (land); من ذى قبل *min ḏī qablu* than before; من ذى نفسه *min ḏī nafsihī* of one's own accord, spontaneously; ذووه *ḏawūhu* his relatives, his kin, his folks; ذوو المودة والمعرفة *ḏawū l-mawadda wa-l-maʿrifa* friends and acquaintances; ذوو الشبهات *ḏawū š-šubuhāt* dubious persons, people of ill repute; ذوو الشأن *ḏawū š-šaʾn* important, influential people; the competent people (or authorities), those concerned with the matter; اولو الامر *ulū l-amr* rulers, leaders; اولو الحل والعقد *ulū l-ḥall wa-l-ʿaqd* influential people, those in power

ذات *ḏāt* f., pl. ذوات *ḏawāt* being, essence, nature; self; person, personality; the same, the selfsame; -self; الذات the ego; one's own self; الذوات people of rank, people of distinction, notables; ذاتا *ḏātan* personally | الذات الانسانية (*insānīya*) the human personality; ذات بال f. of ذو بال see بال; ذات البين *ḏ. al-bain* disagreement, dissension, disunion, discord, enmity; friendship; ذات الجنب *ḏ. al-janb* pleurisy, (also = ذات الرئة) pneumonia (*med.*); ذوات الاذناب comets; ذات الرئة *ḏ. ar-riʾa* pneumonia (*med.*); ذوات الاربع *ḏ. al-arbaʿ* the quadrupeds; ذات الصدر *ḏ. aṣ-ṣadr* chest complaint; bottom of the heart, secret thoughts; ذات اليد *ḏ. al-yad* wealth, affluence; ذات ايدينا *ḏ. aidīnā* our possessions; ذات اليمين *ḏāta l-yamīni* to the right, ذات الشمال *ḏāta š-šimāli* to the left, ذات اليسار *ḏāta l-yasāri* do.; بلهجة ذات معنى (*lahja, maʿnan*) with a meaningful tone; ذات مرة *ḏāta marratin* once, one time, فى ذات مرة *fī ḏāti marratin* do.; ذات يوم *ḏāta yaumin* one day, فى ذات يوم *fī ḏāti yaumin* do.; فى ذات صباح (*ḏ. ṣabāḥin*) one morning, of a morning; ذات عام *ḏāta ʿāmin* in a certain year; فى ذات غد *fī ḏāti ġadin* sometime in the future, before long; ... فى ذات *fī ḏāti* ... (with foll. genit.) as to ..., concerning ..., with reference to ..., re; بالذات *bi-ḏ-ḏāt* none other than ..., ... of all things, ... of all people; personally, in person; انا بالذات I, of all people, ..., none other than I ...; فى لندن بالذات in London, of all places; السعادة بالذات (*saʿāda*) essential happiness, happiness proper; هذه العبارة بالذات (*ʿibāra*) exactly, precisely this expression; فى تلك الليلة بالذات in the very same night; ذواتهم their ego, their true selves; ذات نفسه *ḏ. nafsihī*, ذات انفسهم *ḏ. anfusihim* his self, their selves, his (their) very nature; هو بذاته, هو ذاته (he) himself; ذات الشىء the same thing; ذات الاشياء the same things; فى ذات السنة ذاتها (*sana*) the same year; فى ذات الوقت (*ḏ. al-waqt*) simultaneously, at the same time; يمثلون ذات ادوارهم (*yumaṯṯilūna*) they play their real-life roles (in a film); لذاته *li-ḏātihī* by himself (itself); in itself; as such; for his (its) own sake; فى ذاته in itself; فى حد ذاته *fī ḥaddi ḏ.* do.; قائم بذاته self-existent, independent, self-contained, isolated; الثقة بالذات (*ṯiqa*) self-confidence; حب الذات *ḥubb aḏ-ḏ.* and محبة الذات *maḥabbat aḏ-ḏ.* self-love, selfishness, egoism; احترام الذات self-respect; الاعتماد على الذات self-confidence, self-reliance; صريح بذاته

self-evident, self-explanatory; مناقض ذاته *munāqiḍ ḏātahū* self-contradictory; ابن ذوات *ibn ḏawāt* descended from a good family, highborn; اولاد الذوات children from good families

ذاتى *ḏātī* own, proper; self-produced, self-created, spontaneous; personal; self-acting, automatic; subjective (*philos.*); (pl. *-ūn*) subjectivist (*philos.*); ذاتيا *ḏātīyan* of o.s., by o.s.; personally, in person | ○ ذاتى المركز *ḏ. al-markaz* egocentric; الحكم الذاتى (*ḥukm*) autonomy; ملاحظة ذاتية self-observation, introspection; نقد ذاتى (*naqd*) self-criticism

ذاتية *ḏātīya* personality; subjectivism (*philos.*); identity (of a person) | تحقيق الذاتية identification (of a person)

لاذاتية *lā-ḏātīya* impersonality

ذواتى *ḏawātī* high-class, exclusive, luxurious

ذأب[1] see ذوابة

[2](ذوب) ذاب *ḏāba* u (*ḏaub*, ذوبان *ḏawabān*) to dissolve; to melt; to melt away; to liquefy, deliquesce; to dwindle away, vanish; to pine away, waste away (حسرة وأسى *ḥasratan wa-asan* with grief and sorrow) | ذاب حياء (*ḥayā'an*) to die of shame; ذابت اظفاره فى (*aẓfāruhū*) to strive in vain for, make futile efforts in order to **II** to dissolve, melt, liquefy (ه s.th.) **IV** to dissolve (also, e.g., tablets in water), liquefy (ه s.th.); to melt (ه s.th.); to smelt (ه metal); to consume, spend, exhaust, use up, sap (ه s.th.) | اذاب جهده (*juhdahū*) to exhaust s.o.'s energy; اذاب عصارة مخه فى (*'uṣārata mukkihī*) to rack one's brain with

ذوب *ḏaub* dissolution; solution (also, as a liquid)

ذوبان *ḏawabān* dissolution, melting, deliquescence, liquefaction | ذوبان الثلج (الثلوج) *ḏ. aṯ-ṯalj* (*aṯ-ṯulūj*) snowbreak, thaw; قابل للذوبان *qābil li-ḏ-ḏ.* meltable, soluble, dissoluble

تذويب *taḏwīb* dissolution, solution, melting, liquefaction

اذابة *iḏāba* dissolution, solution, melting, liquefaction

ذائب *ḏā'ib* dissolved; melted, molten; soluble, dissoluble

ذات and ذوات see ذو

(ذود) ذاد *ḏāda* u (*ḏaud*, ذياد *ḏiyād*) to scatter, drive away, chase away; to remove (ه ,ه عن s.o., s.th. from); to defend, protect (عن s.o., s.th.) | ذاد النوم عن عينيه (*an-nauma 'an 'ainaihi*) to drive or keep the sleep from his eyes

ذود *ḏaud* defense, protection (عن of s.th.)

ذياد *ḏiyād* defense, protection (عن of s.th.)

مذود *miḏwad* pl. مذاود *maḏāwid*[2] manger, crib, feeding trough

ذائد *ḏā'id* pl. ذادة *ḏāda* defender, protector

(ذوق) ذاق *ḏāqa* u (*ḏauq*, ذواق *ḏawāq*, مذاق *maḏāq*) to taste, sample (ه food, etc.); to try, try out, test (ه s.th.); to get a taste (ه of s.th.), experience, undergo, suffer (ه s.th.), go through s.th. (ه) | ذاق الموت (*maut*) to suffer death; لا يذوقون له طعما (*ṭa'man*) they have no sense of it, they have no feeling for it **IV** to have (ه s.o.) taste or sample (ه s.th.), give (ه ه s.o. s.th.) to taste **V** to taste (ه s.th.) slowly, repeatedly, thoroughly; to get a taste (ه of s.th.); to sense, perceive (ه s.th.); to enjoy thoroughly, savor, relish (ه s.th.); to derive pleasure (من from)

ذوق *ḏauq* pl. اذواق *aḏwāq* gustatory sense; taste (فى for; also, e.g., literary taste); perceptivity, responsiveness (ل for); sensitivity, sensitiveness; personal experience, firsthand knowledge of s.th.; savoir faire, suavity, urbanity, tact; liking, inclination; taste, flavor (of food, etc.) | الذوق السليم good taste

ذوقى *ḏauqī* of taste, gustative, gustatory

ذواق *ḏawāq* taste

ذواق *ḏawwāq* epicure, connoisseur, gourmet, bon vivant

ذواقة *ḏawwāqa* man of extraordinary good taste, connoisseur; gourmet

مذاق *maḏāq* taste

تذوق *taḏawwuq* enjoyment, relish, delight

ذائقة *ḏā'iqa* sense of taste

متذوق *mutaḏawwiq* a man of taste, connoisseur

ذولق **ḏaulaq** tip of the tongue

الحروف الذولقية (*ḏaulaqīya*) the consonants *r*, *l*, *n* (*phon.*)

ذوى **ḏawā** *i and* **ḏawiya** *a* to wither, wilt, fade; to be withered, be dry; to wear away, disappear, come to an end **IV** to cause to wilt, dry up

ذاو *ḏāwin* withered, faded, drooping

ذو see ذى

(ذيع) ذاع **ḏā'a** *i* (ذيوع *ḏuyū'*) to spread, get about, circulate, be spread, be disseminated, be or become widespread; to leak out, become public, become generally known **IV** to spread, spread out, disseminate, propagate (ه or ب s.th.); to make known, announce, make public, publicize, publish (ه or ب s.th.); to promulgate (ه or ب s.th.); to show, manifest, display (ه or ب s.th.), give evidence (ه or ب of); to reveal, disclose, divulge (ه or ب s.th.); to emit (ه electric waves); to broadcast, transmit (ه s.th., على to the public; radio); to radiate (ه s.th.) | اذاع بالتلفزة (*talfaza*) to telecast (ه s.th.); اذاع برنامجا (*barnāmajan*) to broadcast a program

ذيوع *ḏuyū'* widespreadness, commonness; spreading, spread, dispersion, diffusion; circulation (of news)

مذياع *miḏyā'* pl. مذاييع *maḏāyī'*[2] telltale, talebearer, tattler; communicative, indiscreet; radio set; microphone; ○ transmitter (radio)

اذاعة *iḏā'a* spreading, dissemination, propagation; announcement, proclamation; publication; revelation, disclosure; playback (of a tape; as opposed to recording); broadcasting, radio; (pl. *-āt*) (radio) broadcast, transmission | اذاعة الاخبار *i. al-akbār* newscast, news (radio); اذاعة تلفزية (*talfazīya*) television broadcast, telecast; اذاعة لاسلكية (*lā-silkīya*) and اذاعة راديوفونية radio broadcast; broadcasting, radio; اذاعة البوليس police radio; الاذاعة المرئية (*mar'īya*; *Lib.*) television; مجلة الاذاعة *majallat al-i.* radio magazine

اذاعى *iḏā'ī* radio, television, TV (in compounds) | حديث اذاعى radio talk; radio interview; محطة اذاعية radio station

ذائع *ḏā'i'* widespread, common, general; circulating, in circulation; widely known | ذائع الصيت *ḏ. aṣ-ṣīt* famous, noted, renowned, widely known

مذيع *muḏī'* pl. *-ūn* spreader, disseminator, propagator, proclaimer; broadcasting, transmitting (used attributively); (radio) transmitter; (radio and TV) announcer; speaker (at a microphone)

مذيعة *muḏī'a* pl. *-āt* (radio and TV) announcer (fem.)

ذيل II to furnish (ه s.th., esp. a book) with an appendix, add a supplement (ه to); to provide (ه s.th.) at the end (ب with); to extend (ه s.th.); pass.: to have a sequel or aftereffect; not to be at an end, be continued IV to trample underfoot, degrade, debase (ه s.th.)

ذيل *ḏail* pl. ذيول *ḏuyūl*, اذيال *aḏyāl* the lowest or rearmost part of s.th., lower end; tail; hem, border (of a garment); train (of a skirt); lappet, coat tail; bottom, foot, end (of a page); appendage, appendicle; addenda, supplement, appendix (of a book); retinue, attendants, suite; dependent; result, consequence | فى ذيله immediately thereafter; طاهر الذيل innocent, blameless, upright, honest; طهارة الذيل *ṭahārat aḏ-ḏ.* innocence, moral integrity, probity, uprightness, honesty; طويل الذيل long, lengthy, extensive; ذيل حصان *ḏ. ḥiṣān* ponytail; شوربة ذيل الثور *šorbat ḏ. aṯ-ṯaur* oxtail soup; تمسك باذياله *tamassaka bi-aḏyālihī* to cling to s.o.'s coat tails, hold on to s.o.; جر عليه ذيل العفاء (*jarra, ʿafāʾ*) to wipe out s.th., bring about the doom of s.th., let s.th. sink into oblivion; لاذ باذيال الشىء to resort to s.th.

تذييل *taḏyīl* addition of a supplement, of an extension

مذيل *muḏayyal* extended (by an addition, supplement, etc.)

ر

راء *rāʾ* name of the letter ر

رئة *riʾa* pl. رئون *riʾūn*, رئات *riʾāt* lung

رئوى *riʾawī* pulmonary, pulmonic, pneumonic, of or pertaining to the lung, lung (used attributively)

رأب *raʾaba a* (*raʾb*) to mend, repair, patch up (ه a rent, and the like); to rectify, put in order, set right (ه s.th.) | رأب الصدع (*ṣadʿa*) to mend a rift, bring about conciliation (بين between)

رؤبة *ruʾba* patch (for mending a rent)

مرأب *mirʾab* pl. مرائب *marāʾib*[2] repair shop, garage

رابور (Fr. *rapport*) report

راتينج *rātīnaj* resin

راتينة = رتينة (look up alphabetically)

راجا *rājā* pl. راجوات *rājawāt* Indian prince, rajah

رؤد *ruʾd* soft, tender; *ruʾd* and فتاة رؤد (*fatāh*) delicate young girl

رئد *riʾd* pl. ارآد *arʾād* person of approximately the same age, contemporary

رادار *rādār* radar

رادارى *rādārī* radar (in compounds) | امواج رادارية radar waves (*phys.*)

راديكالى *radikālī* radical

راديكالية *radikālīya* radicalism

راديو *rādiyō*, *rādyō* pl. راديوهات *rādiyōhāt*, *rādyōhāt* radio | راديو بيك اب *r. bik-ab* (Engl. *pickup*) radio-phonograph

راديوى *rādyawī* radio (in compounds) | اشارات راديوية (*išārāt*) radio signals; البث الراديوى (*baṯṯ*) broadcast of radio waves; امواج راديوية radio waves

راديولوجى *rādiyōlōjī* radiology

راديوم *rādiyūm* radium | ذو راديوم فاعل radioactive

bridgehead; رأس حامية (*ḥāmiya*) hothead, hotspur, firebrand; رأس الخيمة *r. al-kaima* Ras al Khaimah, name of an emirate on the Persian Gulf; رأس السنة *r. as-sana* New Year; رأس العمود *r. al-ʿamūd* capital (of a column or pilaster); رأس الكتاب letterhead; رأس مال pl. رؤوس اموال capital (*fin.*); مسقط الرأس *masqaṭ, masqiṭ ar-r.* birthplace, home town; سمت الرأس *samt ar-r.* zenith (*astron.*); البلد الرأس (*balad*) the capital city; رؤوس الاصابع tiptoes; fingertips; جزر الرأس الاخضر *juzur ar-r. al-akḍar* Cape Verde Islands

راسي *ra'sī* head (adj.), cephalic; main, chief, principal; perpendicular, vertical

رأسمال *ra's-māl* pl. رساميل *rasāmīl*[2] capital

رأسمالي *ra's-mālī* capitalistic; (pl. *-ūn*) capitalist

رأسمالية *ra's-mālīya* capitalism | الرأسمالية الاحتكارية monopoly capitalism

رئيس *ra'īs* pl. رؤساء *ru'asā'*[2] one at the head, or in charge, of; head; chieftain; leader; chief, boss; rais; director; headmaster, principal; chairman; governor; president; manager, superintendent; conductor (*mus.*); superior (as distinguished from مرؤوس subordinate); (*mil.*) captain (*Jord.*, formerly, *Ir.*, *Syr.*, etc.) | رئيس اول (*awwal*) major (formerly, *Syr.*, *Ir.*, *Jord.*; *mil.*); رئيس الاساقفة archbishop; رئيس البلدية *r. al-baladīya* chief of a municipality, mayor; رئيس التحرير editor-in-chief; رئيس الحكومة chief of government; رئيس اركان الحرب *r. arkān al-ḥarb* chief of general staff; رئيس التشريفات *r. at-tašrīfāt* chief of protocol, master of ceremonies; رئيس الشمامسة archdeacon; رئيس الاطباء *r. al-aṭibbā'* head doctor; رئيس عرفاء *r. ʿurafā'* sergeant major (*Ir.*; *mil.*); رئيس اعلى (*aʿlā*) supreme head; رئيس العمال *r. al-ʿummāl* supervisor of workers; foreman, chief workman; رئيس الفريق team captain (sports); رئيس قسم *r. qism* depart-

راديومي *rādiyūmī* radium (in compounds)

رأرأ *ra'ra'a*: رأرأ بعينيه (*bi-ʿainaihi*) to roll one's eyes

راس **ra'asa** *i a* (رئاسة *ri'āsa*) to be at the head, be the chairman, be in charge (ه of s.th.); to preside (ه over s.th.); to head, lead, direct, manage, run (ه s.th.); — رؤس *ra'usa u* to be the chief, the leader **II** to appoint as chief or head, make the director or leader, entrust with the direction, management or chairmanship (ه s.o.); to make (ه s.o.) president **V** = *ra'asa* **VIII** to become or be the chief, head, leader, or director

رأس *ra's* m. and f., pl. رؤوس *ru'ūs*, ارؤس *ar'us* head (also as a numerative of cattle); chief, chieftain, head, leader; upper part, upper end; tip; top, summit, peak; vertex, apex; extremity, end; promontory, headland, cape (*geogr.*); main part; beginning; رأسا *ra'san* directly, straightway; immediately | برأسه sui generis, in a class by itself, independent, self-contained, e.g., علم برأسه (*ʿilm*) a science in itself; رأس برأس (both) alike, one like the other, equally, without distinction; على رأس (with foll. genit.) at the head of; at the end of; at the beginning of, before, prior to; على الرأس والعين (*wa-l-ʿain*) very gladly; just as you wish! at your service! على رؤوس الاشهاد *ʿalā r. al-ašhād* in public, for all the world to see; رأسا على عقب *ra'san ʿalā ʿaqbin* upside down, topsy-turvy, e.g., قلبه رأسا على عقب (*qalabahū*) to turn s.th. completely upside down, upset s.th. from the bottom up; من الرأس الى القدم (*qadam*) or من الرأس الى اخمص القدم (*akmaṣi l-qadam*) from head to toe; رفع به رأسا to pay attention to s.th.; رأس الآفات the principal evil, the root of all evil; رأس تنورة Ras Tanura (cape, E Saudi Arabia, oil center); رأس ثوم *r. ṯūm* clove of garlic; رأس الجسر *r. al-jisr*

ment head (university); رئيس الاقسام *r. al-aqsām* technical director general (of the State Railways; *Eg.*); رئيس الكتبة *r. al-kataba* head secretary; رئيس النذل *r. an-nudul* headwaiter; رئيس النواب *r. an-nuwwāb* president of parliament, speaker of the (lower) house; رئيس هيئة اركان الحرب *r. hai'at arkān al-ḥarb* chief of general staff; رئيس الوزراء *r. al-wuzarā'* and رئيس الوزارة prime minister, premier

رئيسة *ra'īsa* manageress; directress; mother superior

رئيسى *ra'īsī* main, chief, principal, leading | دور رئيسى (*daur*) leading role, leading part; سبب رئيسى (*sabab*) principal cause, main reason; شارع رئيسى main street; طبق رئيسى (*ṭabaq*) main course (of a meal); الفضائل الرئيسية cardinal virtues (*Chr.*); مقالة رئيسية (*maqāla*) editorial, leading article, leader

رئاسة *ri'āsa*, رياسة *riyāsa* (also رآسة) leadership, leading position; management, direction; chairmanship; presidency, presidentship; supervision, superintendency | رئاسة عامة (*'āmma*) general management; general supervision; رئاسة الوزارة prime ministry, premiership; دار الرياسة presidential palace, seat of the chief executive of a country

رئاسى *ri'āsī*, رياسى *riyāsī* supervisory; presidential, president's; presidial; executive | اصدار عفو رئاسى (*iṣdār 'afw*) executive-clemency order

ترؤس *tara''us* direction, management; chairmanship

روائس *rawā'is*[2] cliffs lining river beds (wadis)

مرؤوس *mar'ūs* subordinate; (pl. *-ūn*) a subordinate, a subaltern

رأف *ra'afa a* and رؤف *ra'ufa u* (رأفة *ra'fa*, رآفة *ra'āfa*) to show mercy (ب on s.o.), have pity (ب with s.o.), be kind, gracious, merciful (ب to s.o.) V do.

رأفة *ra'fa* and رآفة *ra'āfa* mercy, compassion, pity; indulgence, decency; kindliness, graciousness

رؤوف *ra'ūf* merciful, compassionate; kind, benevolent; gracious

ارأف *ar'af*[2] kindlier, more gracious (ب toward)

رافيا *rāfiyā* raffia, raffia palm

[1]رأم *ra'ama a* (*ra'm*) to repair, mend (ه s.th.)

[2]رئم *ra'ima a* (رئمان *ri'mān*) to love tenderly (ه s.th.), be very fond (ه of); to treat tenderly, fondle, caress (ه s.th.)

رئم *ri'm* pl. آرام *ārām*, ارآم *ar'ām* white antelope, addax

رءوم *ra'ūm* loving, tender (mother to her children)

رام الله *rāmallah* Ramallah (town in W Jordan, N of Jerusalem)

رامية *rāmiya* ramie, a strong, lustrous bast fiber; China jute (*bot.*)

راوند *rāwand* rhubarb

[1]رأى *ra'ā* يرى *yarā* (*ra'y*, رؤية *ru'ya*) to see; to behold, descry, perceive, notice, observe, discern (ه s.th.); to look (ه ه at s.th. as), regard (ه ه s.th. as), consider, deem, think (ه ه s.th. to be ...); to judge; to be of the opinion (ان that), believe, think (ان that); to express one's opinion; to feel (ان that); to deem appropriate, think proper (ه s.th.), decide (ه on s.th., ان to do s.th.); to consider, contemplate | أرأيت *a-ra'aita* look at that! there you are! رأى العين (*ra'ya l-'ain*)

to see with one's own eyes; رأى رؤيا (*ru'yā*) to have a dream; رأى منه العجب (*'ajaba*) to be amazed at s.th.; رأى للشيء فائدة to expect some benefit from s.th.; رأى من واجبه (*min wājibihī*) to regard as one's duty, deem incumbent upon o.s.; رأى له ان to think that it would be in s.o.'s interest to ...; رأى رأيه (*ra'yahū*) to share s.o.'s opinion; pass.: رؤى ان (*ru'iya*) it was decided that ...; رؤى الشيء it was felt proper to do so, it was thought to be the right thing to do **III** to act ostentatiously, make a show before people, attitudinize; to do eyeservice; to behave hypocritically, act the hypocrite, (dis)simulate, dissemble (ه toward s.o.) **IV** ارى *arā* to show, demonstrate (ه ه to s.o. s.th.) | يا ترى *yā turā* (in interrogative sentences) what's your opinion? would you say ...? I wonder ..., متى يا ترى I wonder when ..., ترى هل *turā hal* I wonder if ..., would you say that... ? اتراها جاءت ? (*a-turāhā*) I wonder if she has come, would you say she has come? اترانى اعود ? would you say I should go back? هل تراك فى حاجة الى ذلك (*turāka*) do you think you really must have it? تراه لاحظ كيف (*turāhu lāḥaẓa*) I wonder if he noticed how ...? **V** to deem, think, believe; to show oneself (ل to s.o.) **VI** to present o.s. to or come into s.o.'s (ل) view, show o.s. (ل to s.o.); to appear, seem (ل to s.o.); to appear right, seem appropriate (ل to s.o.), be thought proper (ل by s.o.); to see one another; to look at o.s. (in a mirror); to act the hypocrite; to fake, feign, simulate (ب s.th.) **VIII** to consider, contemplate (ه s.th.); to be of the opinion (ان that), decide (ان that); to make up one's mind (ه about), decide (ه on s.th.) | ارتأى رأيا (*ra'yan*) to have an opinion; ارتأى رأيه (*ra'yahū*) to share s.o.'s opinion

رأى *ra'y* pl. آراء *ārā'* opinion, view; idea, notion, concept, conception; advice, suggestion, proposal; (*Isl. Law*) subjective opinion, decision based on one's individual judgment (not on Koran and Sunna) | فى رأيى and عند رأيى in my opinion; انا من هذا الرأى I am of this opinion; من رأيه ان he is of the opinion that ...; اخذ الرأى على (*ukiḏa*) it was put to the vote, (the matter) was voted upon; لم يكن عند رأيهم he was not what they had expected; لم يكن له فيه رأى he had no say in the matter; الرأى العام (*'āmm*) public opinion; ذو الرأى pl. ذوو الآراء sensible, judicious; man of good sense and judgment; well-informed, knowledgeable person, one in the know; تبادل الآراء *tabādul al-ā.* exchange of views; صلب الرأى *ṣulb ar-r.* obstinate, stubborn, opinionated; قسم الرأى *qism ar-r.* committee of experts, council on legal and economic matters (attached to the ministries; *Eg.*)

راية *rāya* pl. -*āt* banner, flag

رؤية *ru'ya* visual faculty; sight; view; seeing, viewing; vision; inspection, examination, reflection, consideration; opinion, view

رؤيا *ru'yā* pl. رؤى *ru'an* vision; dream | سفر الرؤيا *sifr ar-r.* the Apocalypse (*Chr.*)

مرأى *mar'an* pl. مراء *marā'in* sight, view; vision; apparition | على مرأى من before s.o.'s eyes; على مرأى ومسمع من (*wa-masma'in*) before the eyes and ears of; with full knowledge of

مرآة *mir'āh* pl. مراء *marā'in*, مرايا *marāyā* looking glass, mirror; reflection, reflected image

□ مراية *mirāya* pl. -*āt* looking glass, mirror

مرآوى *mir'āwī* mirror (in compounds), reflecting; ○ autoscopic (*psych.*)

رئاء *ri'ā'* and رياء *riyā'* eyeservice; hypocrisy, dissimulation; dissemblance; simulation (ب of s.th.)

مراآة, مراءاة *murā'āh* eyeservice; hypocrisy, dissimulation, dissemblance; simulation (ب of s.th.)

راء *rā'in* pl. راؤن, راؤون *rā'ūn* viewer, onlooker, spectator, observer

O رائية *rā'iya* pl. *-āt* view finder (of a camera)

مرئى *mar'īy* seen; visible; المرئيات the visible things, the visible world | صوتى مرئى *ṣautī-mar'īy* audio-visual

مراء *murā'in* pl. مراؤون *murā'ūn* hypocrite

رئة[2] and رئوى see رء

راى[3] *rāy* an Egyptian variety of salmon

راية[4] see رأى[1]

رايخ *rāyiḵ*: الرايخ الالمانى (*almānī*) the (former) German Empire

رب *rabba u* (*rabb*, ربابة *ribāba*) to be master, be lord, have possession (ه, ه of), control (ه, ه s.o., s.th.), have command or authority (ه, ه over); — *u* (*rabb*) and II to raise, bring up (ه a child) II to deify, idolize (ه, ه s.o., s.th.)

رب *rabb* pl. ارباب *arbāb* lord; master; owner, proprietor (*Isl. Law*); (with foll. genit.) one possessed of, endowed with, having to do with, etc.; الرب the Lord (= God); رب *rabbi* and رباه *rabbāh* oh my God! | رب العمل *r. al-'amal* employer; رب العائلة father of the family, paterfamilias; ارباب السلطان *a. as-sulṭān* the rulers; ارباب المصالح *a. al-maṣāliḥ* the people to whom it matters, the interested parties; ارباب المال the capitalists; صعود الرب the Ascension (*Chr.*); ارباب المعاشات *a. al-ma'āšāt* pensioners; ارباب السوابق those previously convicted, people with a criminal record; ارباب الفنون artists

ربة *rabba* pl. *-āt* mistress; lady | ربة المنزل *r. al-manzil* the lady of the house; ربة البيت *r. al-bait* landlady; ربة شعره *r. ši'rihī* his muse; ربات الحجال *r. al-ḥijāl* the ladies

رب *rubb* pl. رباب *ribāb*, ربوب *rubūb* rob, thickened juice (of fruit); mash, pulp | رب سوس *r. sūs* licorice rob

رب *rubba* (with foll. indet. genit.) many a, e.g., رب رجل (*rajulin*) many a man, رب مرة (*marratin*) many a time

ربما *rubbamā* sometimes; perhaps, maybe, possibly | (with perf. having conditional or future meaning) ربما غادرت القطر (*ḡādartu l-quṭra*) maybe I would leave the country; perhaps I shall leave the country; ربما لم يكف (*yakfi*) perhaps it won't be enough; ربما ضحكت منه (*ḍaḥikta*) perhaps you will laugh at him

ربة *rabba*, *ribba* a kind of skin eruption affecting the head and face

رباب *rabāb*, ربابة *rabāba* rebab or rebec, a stringed instrument of the Arabs resembling the fiddle, with one to three strings (in Eg. usually two-stringed)

ربيب *rabīb* pl. ارباء *aribbā'*[2] foster son, stepson; foster father; confederate, ally

ربيبة *rabība* pl. ربائب *rabā'ib*[2] foster daughter, stepdaughter; foster mother; (woman) ally

ربوبية *rubūbīya* divinity, deity, godship

ربان *rubbān* pl. *-īya*, ربابنة *rabābina* captain (formerly also as a naval rank, *Eg.*)

ربانى *rabbānī* divine; pertaining to God | الربانيات divine things; الصلاة الربانية (*ṣalāh*) the Lord's Prayer (*Chr.*)

مربة (*eg.*) *mirabba* (= مربى *murabban*) jam, preserved fruit

راب *rābb* stepfather

رابة *rābba* stepmother

ربأ *raba'a a* to hold in esteem, esteem highly (ب s.o.); ربأ به عن to consider s.o. above s.th., above doing s.th., have too high an opinion of s.o. as to suspect him of (doing) s.th. or as to expect him to do s.th.; ربأ بنفسه عن (*bi-nafsihī*) to deem o.s. above s.th., be too proud for, stand aloof from

ربيئة *rabī'a* pl. ربايا *rabāyā* guard

ربت *rabata i* (*rabt*) to pat, caress, stroke (ه s.o.) **II** do. | ربت على خده (*kaddihī*) to pat s.o.'s cheek; ربت على كتفه (*katifihī*) to pat s.o. on the shoulder; ربت نفسه to be self-satisfied, self-complacent, smug

ربح *rabiḥa a* (*ribḥ, rabaḥ*) to gain (ه من from s.th. s.th.), profit (من from); to win (sports, games) | ما ربحت تجارتهم (*tijāratuhum*) their business was unprofitable **II** and **IV** to make (ه s.o.) gain, allow s.o. (ه) a profit

ربح *ribḥ* pl. ارباح *arbāḥ* gain, profit; benefit; interest (on money); — pl. proceeds, returns, revenues; dividends (*fin.*) | ربح بسيط simple interest, ربح مركب (*murakkab*) compound interest; ارباح موزعة (*muwazza'a*) distributed dividends

رباح *rubbāḥ* pl. رباييح *rabābīḥ*[2] monkey

اربح *arbaḥ*[2] more profitable, more lucrative

مرابحة *murābaḥa* (*Isl. Law*) resale with specification of gain, resale with an advance

رابح *rābiḥ* profiteer, gainer, winner; beneficiary; lucrative, gainful, profitable (business)

مربح *murbiḥ* lucrative, gainful, profitable

ربد **V** to become clouded, become overcast (sky); to turn ashen, take on a glowering expression (face, with anger) **IX** to become ashen, assume a glowering expression (face)

مربد *murbadd* clouded; gloomy, morose (face)

ربسوس = رب سوس, see رب *rubb*

ربص *rabaṣa u* (*rabṣ*) to wait, look, watch, be on the lookout (ب for) **V** to lurk, lie in wait (ل for s.o.), waylay, ambush (ل s.o.); to lay an ambush, move into an ambush; to take up positions (*mil.*); to expect (ه, ب s.th.), wait (ه, ب for s.th.) | تربص الفرصة (*furṣata*) to wait (or look) for an opportunity; تربص به الامر (*amra*) to wait for s.th. to befall s.o. or to happen to s.o., e.g., تربص به الدوائر to wait for s.o. to meet with disaster; to wish s.o. every misfortune

تربص *tarabbuṣ* pl. *-āt* probationary term (*adm.*); (*Mağr.*) study session, training course, meeting or course for continuation training

تربصي *tarabbuṣī* (*Mağr.*) pertaining to continuation training, etc. | فترة تربصية (*fatra*) study session, training course

متربص *mutarabbiṣ* pl. *-ūn* candidate, aspirant; (*Mağr.*) participant in a study session or course

ربض *rabaḍa i* (*rabḍ*, ربوض *rubūḍ*) to lie down; to lie, rest (animals; with the chest to the ground); to lurk (ل for s.o.); to lie at anchor (ships); to be parked waiting (cars); to be in position (troops) | ربض على خطوط القتال to be stationed on the front lines

ربض *rabaḍ* pl. ارباض *arbāḍ* outskirts, suburb; place where animals lie down to rest

مربض *marbiḍ* pl. مرابض *marābiḍ*[2] place where animals lie down to rest; sheep pen, fold

ربط **rabaṭa** *u i* (*rabṭ*) to bind, tie up, make fast, moor (ه s.th.); to tie, fasten, attach, hitch (ه الى s.th. to); to connect (ه الى s.th. with); to fix, appoint, determine (ه s.th.); to value, rate, assess (ه s.th.); to add, append, affix (ه الى s.th. to); to insert (ه الى s.th. in); to combine, unite (ه s.th., بين — وبين s.th. with); to ligate (ه s.th.), apply a tourniquet (ه to); to bandage, dress (ه a wound); to bridle, check (ه, على s.th.); to brake (ه a train); to suspend (ه a cleric; *Chr.*) | ربط لسانه (*lisānahū*) to silence s.o.; ربط على قلبه (*qalbihī*) to fortify s.o., give s.o. patience (said of God); ربط جأشه (*ja'šahū*) to keep one's self-control, remain calm, be undismayed; ربط الطريق to practice highway robbery **III** to be lined up, posted, stationed (troops); to line up, take up positions; to camp; to be moored (ship); to move into fighting positions | رابط فى قضيته (*qaḍīyatihī*) to defend the cause of, fight for **VI** to be closely tied together, stand in close relation **VIII** to bind o.s., commit o.s., engage o.s.; to be bound (ب by, also, e.g., by an obligation), be tied (ب to); to be linked, be connected (ب with); to depend (ب on); to unite, join forces

ربط **rabṭ** binding, tying; fastening, joining, attaching, connecting; fixation, determination (of an amount, of a number); valuation, assessment | ربط الرزق *r. ar-rizq* setting of s.o.'s subsistence, allotment of food; ربط صلات *r. ṣilāt*, ربط علاقات *r. ʿalāqāt* connection of ties, relationships; establishment of relations; ربط الطريق highway robbery; ربط مالى financial allocation; اهل الحل والربط *ahl al-ḥall wa-r-r.* influential people, those in power; مكان الربط *makān ar-r.* (welded) seam, weld (*techn.*)

ربط **rabaṭ** (*tun.*) section, quarter (of a city), suburb

ربطة **rabṭa** pl. *rabaṭāt*, ربط *rubaṭ* ribbon, band, bandage; bundle; parcel, package; purse, wallet | ربطة الرقبة *r. ar-raqaba* and ربطة العنق *r. al-ʿunuq* necktie, cravat; ربطة الساق *r. as-sāq* garter; ربطة النقود money purse

رباط **ribāṭ** pl. *-āt*, ربط *rubuṭ*, اربطة *arbiṭa* ribbon, band; ligature, ligament; bandage; dressing (of a wound); bond, fetter, shackle; — suspension (of a cleric; *Chr.*); (pl. *-āt*, ربط *rubuṭ*) inn for travelers, caravansary; hospice (for Sufis or the poor) | رباط الاجربة *r. al-ajriba* garter; رباط الجزمة *r. al-jazma* and رباط الحذاء *r. al-ḥidā'* shoestring; رباط الرقبة *r. ar-raqaba* necktie

الرباط **ar-ribāṭ**, رباط الفتح *ribāṭ al-fatḥ* Rabat (capital of Morocco)

رباطة الجأش **ribāṭat al-ja'š** composure, self-control, calmness, intrepidity

مربط **marbiṭ**, *marbaṭ* pl. مرابط *marābiṭ*[2] place where animals are tied up; horse box

مربط **mirbaṭ** pl. مرابط *marābiṭ*[2] hawser, mooring cable; rope; ○ terminal (*el.*)

مرابطة **murābaṭa** the stationing (of troops)

ترابط **tarābuṭ** cohesion, close connection (بين between)

ارتباط **irtibāṭ** connectedness, connection, link; (pl. *-āt*) contact, liaison; tie (ب to); obligation, engagement, commitment; bearing (ب on), connection (ب with), relation (ب to); cohesion (of different things with one another); coherence; bond; correlation (*math.*) | بدون ارتباط *bidūn i.* not binding, without obligation (*com.*); ضابط ارتباط liaison officer; فك الارتباط *fakk al-i.* disengagement of forces (*mil.*)

رابط الجأش **rābiṭ al-ja'š** composed, calm, unruffled, undismayed, fearless

رابطة *rābiṭa* pl. روابط *rawābiṭ*[2] band; bond, tie; connection, link; confederation, union, league | روابط الصداقة *r. aṣ-ṣadāqa* bonds of friendship; الرابطة الاسلامية (*islāmīya*) the Moslem League; رابطة الشعوب League of Nations

مربوط *marbūṭ* bound; connected; fastened, tied, moored (الى to); fixed, appointed; fixed salary; estimate (of the budget)

مرابط *murābiṭ* posted, stationed; garrisoned (troops); Marabout; pl. المرابطون the Almoravids | الجيش المرابط (*jaiš*) the Territorial Army (*Eg.*)

مرابطى *murābiṭī* Almoravid (adj.)

مترابط *mutarābiṭ* closely tied together, standing in close relation

مرتبط *murtabiṭ* connected, linked (ب with); bound, committed (ب by); depending, conditional (ب on)

ربع *raba'a a* to gallop (horse); — to sit; to squat; to stay, live **II** to quadruple, multiply by four, increase fourfold (ه s.th.); to square (ه a number) **V** to sit or sit down cross-legged; to sit; to be situated, lie (على on, e.g., on the coast; place, town) | تربع على العرش (*'arš*) to mount the throne, sit on the throne

ربع *rab'* pl. ربوع *rubū'*, رباع *ribā'* living zone, region; residence, quarters; large tenement house; large group of people, clan; pl. ربوع inhabited area, territory | فى ربوع المدينة in the town area, in the city zone

ربع *rib'*: حمى الربع *ḥummā r-rib'* quartan (fever)

ربع *rub'* pl. ارباع *arba'* quarter, fourth part; roubouh, a dry measure (*Eg.* = 4 قدح = 8.25 l); (*syr.*) 25-piaster piece | ربع ساعة quarter of an hour; الساعة الثانية الا ربعا (*illā rub'an*) it is a quarter to two; الربع الخالى Rub' al Khali (desert region in S Arabia); آلة الربع quadrant (*naut.*); ربع سنوى *r. sanawī* quarterly, trimestral

ربعى *rub'ī* quarterly, trimestral

ربعة *rab'a* (m. and f.) pl. ربع *rab'* (also ربعة القوام *r. al-qawām* and ربعة القامة *r. al-qāma*) of medium height, medium-sized (of poeple), square-built, stocky

ربعة *rub'a* robhah, a dry measure (*Eg.*; = 1/4 قدح = 0.516 l)

رباع *rabbā'* athlete (boxer, wrestler, weight lifter, etc.)

ربيع *rabī'* spring, springtime, vernal season; name of the third and fourth months of the Muslim year (ربيع الاول *r. al-awwali* Rabia I, and ربيع الثانى *r. aṯ-ṯānī* Rabia II); quarter, fourth part

اربعة *arba'a* (f. اربع *arba'*) four | ذوات الاربع *ḏawāt al-a.* the quadrupeds

اربعة عشر *arba'ata 'ašara* (f. اربع عشرة *arba'a 'ašrata*) fourteen

اربعون *arba'ūn* forty; الاربعون a ceremony held on the 40th day after s.o.'s death | عيد الاربعين *'īd al-a.* Ascension Day (*Chr.*)

الاربعينات *al-arba'īnāt* the forties (decade of a century)

رباع *rubā'*[2] four at a time

رباعى *rubā'ī* consisting of four, quadripartite, fourfold, quadruple; quadrangular; tetragonal; (*gram.*) consisting of four radical letters, quadriliteral; quartet (*mus.*); relay team of four (sport); (pl. *-āt*) quatrain (*poet.*) | مؤتمر رباعى (*mu'tamar*) four-power conference; رباعى الاضلاع quadrilateral; رباعى الارجل *r. l-arjul* quadruped(al), four-footed; محرك رباعى المشوار *muḥarrik r. l-mišwār* four-cycle engine

الاربعاء *al-arbaʿāʾ*, *al-arbiʿāʾ*, يوم الاربعاء *yaum al-a.* Wednesday

يربوع *yarbūʿ* pl. يرابيع *yarābīʿ*² jerboa (Jaculus jaculus; *zool.*)

مربع *marbaʿ* pl. مرابع *marābiʿ*² meadow; pasture; place of entertainment

تربيع *tarbīʿ* lunar quarter; — (pl. ترابيع *tarābīʿ*²) quadrangle; square, plaza (surrounded by houses) | تربيع الدائرة quadrature of the circle

تربيعة *tarbīʿa* pl. ترابيع *tarābīʿ*² square, quadrangle; square, plaza; square panel; tile, floor tile

تربيعى *tarbīʿī* quadratic, square

الرابع *ar-rābiʿ* the fourth; رابعا *rābiʿan* fourthly, in the fourth place

مربوع *marbūʿ*, مربوع القامة of medium height, medium-sized (of people), square-built

مربع *murabbaʿ* fourfold, quadruple; quadrangular; tetragonal; square, quadratic; quadrangle; a square; (pl. *-āt*) quadrangular piece; quartet | متر مربع (*mitr*) square meter; مربع الاضلاع quadrilateral (*math.*)

مربعة *murabbaʿa* pl. *-āt* section, district, area

مرابع *murābiʿ* partner in an agricultural enterprise (sharing one quarter of the gains or losses)

جلس متربعا *jalasa mutarabbiʿan* to sit crosslegs

رابغ *rābiġ* pleasant, comfortable

ربق *ribq* lasso, lariat

ربقة *ribqa*, *rabqa* pl. ربق *ribaq*, رباق *ribāq*, ارباق *arbāq* noose

ربك *rabaka u* (*rabk*) to muddle, entangle, complicate (ه s.th.); to confuse, throw into confusion (ه, ه s.o., s.th.); — *rabika a* (*rabak*) to be in an involved, confused situation **IV** to confuse, embarrass, abash (ه s.o.) **VIII** to be confused; to become involved (فى in)

ربك *rabak* involved, confused situation; embarrassment

ربك *rabik* confused; embarrassed; in trouble, beset by difficulties

ارتباك *irtibāk* pl. *-āt* entanglement, involvement; snarl, tangle, muddle, mess; confusion; embarrassment; upset (of the stomach)

مربك *murbik* confusing, bewildering, disconcerting; embarrassing

مرتبك *murtabik* confused, complicated, involved; bewildered, disconcerted, embarrassed; involved (فى in)

ربل *rabil* plump, fleshy, fat (person)

ربلى *rablī*, *rabalī* fleshy

ربلة *rabla* pl. *rabalāt* (mass of) flesh (of the body)

ربيل *rabīl* fleshy, corpulent, fat

ربالة *rabāla* corpulence

ربما *rubbamā*, ربانى *rabbānī*, ربان *rubbān* and رباه *rabbāh* see under رب

ربا (ربو) *rabā u* (رباء *rabāʾ*, ربو *rubūw*) to increase; to grow; to grow up; to exceed, (على a number, also عن), be more than (على) | ما يربو على المئة more than a hundred **II** to make or let grow; to raise, rear, bring up (ه s.o.); to educate; to teach, instruct (ه a child); to breed, raise (ه e.g., poultry, cattle); to grow, cultivate (ه plants, flowers); to develop (ه e.g., a method) **III** to practice usury **IV** to make grow, augment, increase (ه s.th.); to exceed (على a number, an age, a measure) V to be brought up, be educated; to be bred, be raised

ربو *rabw* dyspnea, asthma (*med.*)

ربوة *rabwa* and *rubwa* pl. ربى *ruban* hill

ربوة *ribwa* pl. *-āt* ten thousand, myriad

ربا *riban* interest; usurious interest; usury

ربوى *ribawī* usurious

رباء *rabā'* surplus, excess; superiority (على over s.o.); favor

مربى *marban* place where s.o. grows up

تربية *tarbiya* education, upbringing; teaching, instruction; pedagogy; breeding, raising (of animals) | سيء التربية *sayyi' at-t.* ill-bred; قليل التربية ill-bred, uncivil, ill-mannered; علم التربية *'ilm at-t.* pedagogy, pedagogics; علم التربية الاجتماعية social pedagogy; تربية الاطفال baby care; التربية البدنية (*badanīya*) physical education, physical training; تربية الحرية المطلقة *t. al-ḥurrīya al-muṭlaqa* non-authoritative education; تربية الحيوان *t. al-ḥayawān* cattle farming, stockbreeding; تربية الدجاج *t. ad-dajāj* chicken farming, poultry husbandry; تربية السمك *t. as-samak* pisciculture; تربية النباتات *t. an-nabātāt* plant cultivation

تربوى *tarbawī*, تربيوى *tarbiyawī* pedagogic, pedagogical

رابية *rābiya* pl. رواب *rawābin* hill

مرب *murabbin* pl. مربون *murabbūn* educator; pedagogue; breeder (of livestock)

مربية *murabbiya* pl. *-āt* tutoress, governess; dry nurse, nursemaid

مربى *murabban* raised, brought up; educated; well-bred, well-mannered; jam, preserved fruit; pl. مربيات *murabbayāt* preserves

مراب *murābin* usurer

مترب *mutarabbin* well-bred, well-mannered

ريبورتاج (Fr. *reportage*) pl. *-āt* reportage, report

ربيان *rubyān* (*saud.-ar.*, *ir.*) shrimps (*zool.*)

ارت *aratt*², f. رتاء *rattā'*², pl. رت *rutt* afflicted with a speech defect

رتب II to array, arrange, dispose (ه s.th. in a regular sequence or order); to decorate, dress (ه a show window); to settle, determine, regulate (ه s.th.); to put into proper order, put together (ه words); to prepare, set aside, earmark (ه s.th.); to fix, appoint (ل ه a salary for s.o.); to make (ه s.th.) result or accrue (على from), derive (على ه s.th. from), make (ه s.th.) the result or consequence of (على) V to fall in line; to be arranged, organized or set up (along the lines of); to be set aside, be assigned; to be subordinate (على to s.th.), be the result or consequence (على of), result, follow, derive, spring (على from), be caused (على by) | ترتب بذمته (*bi-dimmatihī*) to become the debtor of s.o.

رتبة *rutba* pl. رتب *rutab* degree, grade, level; rank, standing, station; class, quality; (*mil.*) rank; clerical rank, order (of the Christian ministry); religious ceremony (*Chr.*) | رتبة شرف *r. šaraf* honorary rank (*mil.*); كتاب الرتب ritual (of the Roman Catholic Church)

رتابة *ratāba* monotony

رتيب *ratīb* monotonous; (pl. رتباء *rutabā'*²) noncommissioned officer (*Leb.*, *Syr.*; *mil.*)

مرتبة *martaba* pl. مراتب *marātib*² step;

a steplike elevation serving as a seat; mattress; grade, degree, rank, class | في المرتبة الاولى (*ūlā*) first (mortgage); احتل المرتبة الاولى (*iḥtalla*) to come in first or in first place (sport)

ترتيب *tartīb* pl. *-āt* order, arrangement, array; sequence, succession; ranking list, table (sport); make-up, setup; layout (of a complex, e.g., of houses); organization; preparation, arrangement, provision, measure, step; rite of administering a sacrament (*Chr.*) | بالترتيب one by one, in proper succession; من غير ترتيب disorderly, in confusion

ترتيبي *tartībī* ordinal | عدد ترتيبي (*'adad*) ordinal number

راتب *rātib* monotonous; (pl. رواتب *rawātib*[2]) salary, pay, emolument; pl. رواتب certain supererogatory exercises of devotion

مرتب *murattab* arranged; organized, set up, regulated, etc.; (pl. *-āt*) salary, pay, emolument

رتج *rataja* u (*ratj*) to lock, bar, bolt (ه the door); — *ratija* a (*rataj*) to be tongue-tied, be speechless, falter IV pass.: ارتج عليه (*urtija*) words failed him, he was speechless, he didn't know what to say, he was at a loss

رتاج *ritāj* pl. رتج *rutuj*, رتائج *ratā'ij*[2] gate, gateway | محكم الرتاج *muḥkam ar-r.* firmly bolted (gate)

رتوش look up alphabetically

رتع *rata'a* a (*rat'*, رتوع *rutū'*, رتاع *ritā'*) to pasture, graze; to gormandize, carouse, feast; to revel, indulge freely (في in) IV to pasture, put out to graze (ه cattle)

مرتع *marta'* pl. مراتع *marāti'*[2] rich grazing land, pasture; fertile ground (ل for; fig.); breeding ground, hotbed (of vice, of evil, etc.)

رتق *rataqa* u i (*ratq*) to mend, repair, patch up, sew up (ه s.th.)

رتق *ratq* pl. رتوق *rutūq* patching, mending, repair; darn (of a stocking)

[1]رتك *rataka* u i (*ratk*, *ratak*, رتكان *ratakān*) to run with short steps, trot

[2]مرتك *martak* litharge (*chem.*)

رتل *ratila* a (*ratal*) to be regular, well-ordered, neat, tidy II to articulate slowly, carefully and precisely (ه s.th.); to psalmodize, recite in a singsong; to present slowly and in a singing manner (القرآن the Koran); to sing, chant (ه spiritual songs, hymns; *Chr.*)

رتل *ratl* pl. ارتال *artāl* long line, file (of people), queue; column (e.g., of cars, tanks); railroad train | رتل آلي (*ālī*) motorized convoy (*mil.*)

رتيلاء *rutailā'*[2] harvestman (Phalangium), daddy longlegs; tarantula

ترتيل *tartīl* slow, chanting manner of Koran recitation (in contrast with *tajwīd*); psalmodizing, psalmody, singsong recitation; singing, chanting (of hymns, etc.; *Chr.*); — (pl. تراتيل *tarātīl*[2]) hymn; religious song (*Chr.*)

ترتيلة *tartīla* pl. تراتيل *tarātīl*[2] hymn

مرتل *murattil* church singer; choirboy, chorister (*Chr.*); singer, chanter

رتم *ratama* i (*ratm*) to utter, say (بكلمة *bi-kalima* a word; only with neg.)

رتم *ratam* (coll.; n. un. ة) retem (Retama raetam Webb., Genista raetam Forsk.; *bot.*)

رتمة *ratma* and رتيمة *ratīma* pl. رتائم *ratā'im*², رتام *ritām* thread wound around one's finger as a reminder

(رتو) رتا *ratā u* and II رتّى *rattā* to mend, darn (ه e.g., stockings)

رتوش (Fr. *retouche*) *ritūš*, (*eg.*) *rutūš* retouch; adornment, embellishment | بدون رتوش unvarnished, unadorned (fact, truth)

رتينج *ratīnaj* (= راتينج) resin

رتينة (It. *retina*) *ratīna* pl. رتائن *ratā'in*² incandescent mantle

رث *raṯṯa i* (رثاثة *raṯāṯa*, رثوثة *ruṯūṯa*) to be ragged, tattered, shabby, worn (garment)

رث *raṯṯ* pl. رثاث *riṯāṯ* old, shabby, worn, threadbare | رث الهيئة *r. al-hai'a* of shabby appearance

رثة *riṯṯa* old, outmoded things, worn clothes

رثيث *raṯīṯ* old, shabby, worn, threadbare

رثاثة *raṯāṯa* shabbiness, raggedness

رثوثة *ruṯūṯa* shabbiness, raggedness

(رثو and رثى) رثا *raṯā u* (*raṯw*) to bewail, lament, celebrate in an elegy, in a funeral oration (ه a deceased person); — رثى *raṯā i* (*raṯy*, رثاء *riṯā'*, مرثية *marṯiya*, مرثاة *marṯāh*) to bewail, lament, bemoan (ه a deceased person); to elegize, celebrate in an elegy, in a funeral oration (ه a deceased person); to mourn (ل for, over), deplore (ل s.o. or s.th.); to pity (ل s.o.), feel sorry (ل for) | رثاه بمرثاة to elegize s.o. (a deceased person), bewail and celebrate him in an elegy; شيء يرثى له (*yurṯā*) a deplorable, regrettable thing

رثى *raṯy* bewailing, bemoaning, lamentation

رثاء *riṯā'* bewailing, bemoaning, lamentation; regret; elegiac poetry

رثية *raṯya* pl. *raṯayāt* arthritis, gout

مرثية *marṯiya* and مرثاة *marṯāh* pl. مراث *marāṯin* elegy, dirge, epicedium; pl. مراث funeral orations

رج *rajja u* (*rajj*) to convulse, shake, rock (ه s.th.); pass. *rujja* to be shaken, tremble, shake, quake **VIII** to be convulsed, shake, tremble, quake

رج *rajj* shaking, rocking, convulsion

رجة *rajja* pl. *-āt* convulsion; shock, concussion

رجاج *rajjāj* trembling, quaking, shaking, rocking

ارتجاج *irtijāj* shock, concussion; trembling, tremor | ارتجاج المخ *irt. al-mukk* cerebral concussion (*med.*)

رجأ **IV** to postpone, adjourn, defer, put off (ه s.th.)

ارجاء *irjā'* postponement, deferment, adjournment

رجب *rajaba u* and *rajiba a* (*rajab*) to be afraid (من or عن of), be awed (من or عن by)

رجب *rajab* Rajab, the seventh month of the Muslim year

رجح *rajaḥa a i u* (رجوح *rujūḥ*, رجحان *rujḥān*) to incline (scale of a balance); to weigh more, be of greater weight; to preponderate, predominate; to surpass, excel (ه s.o.); to be very likely (ان that), رجح عنده ان it appeared to him most likely that ...; — to weigh (ه بيده s.th. in the hand) **II** to make (ه s.th.) outweigh (على s.th. else), give preponderance (ه to s.th., على over); to think (ه s.th.) weightier; to prefer (ه على s.th. to), give (ه s.th.) preference (على to), favor (على ه s.th. more than); to think likely or probable (ه s.th., ان that) V to carry greater weight, be weightier, preponderate; to swing back and forth, pendulate; to rock; to seesaw, teeter VIII to swing back and forth, pendulate; to rock; to seesaw, teeter

رجاحة *rajāḥa* forbearance, indulgence, leniency; composure, equanimity

رجحان *rujḥān* preponderance, predominance (على over), ascendancy, superiority

ارجح *arjaḥ*[2] superior in weight, preponderant; having more in its favor, more acceptable; preferable; more likely, more probable | الارجح ان it is most likely that ...; probably ...; على الارجح probably, in all probability

ارجحية *arjaḥīya* preponderance, predominance, prevalence

ارجوحة *urjūḥa* pl. اراجيح *arājīḥ*[2] seesaw; swing; cradle

راجح *rājiḥ* superior in weight, preponderant; having more in its favor, more acceptable; preferable; probable, likely

مرجوحة *marjūḥa* pl. مراجيح *marājīḥ*[2] seesaw; swing

مرجح *murajjiḥ* deciding (vote); — *murajjaḥ* favored, preferred; preponderant, predominant; probable, likely

رجرج *rajraja* to make shake, cause to jiggle or sway (ه s.th.); to quiver; to sway II *tarajraja* to tremble, quiver; to sway

رجراج *rajrāj* agitated; trembling, tremulous; swaying; quivering; الرجراج the sea

[1]رجز VIII to compose or declaim poems in the meter *rajaz*; to thunder, roar, surge (sea)

رجز *rujz, rijz* punishment (inflicted by God); dirt, filth

رجز *rajaz* name of a poetical meter

ارجاز *arjāz* verses in the meter *rajaz*; little (work) song

ارجوزة *urjūza* pl. اراجيز *arājīz*[2] poem in the meter *rajaz*

[2]ارجوز look up alphabetically

رجس *rajisa a* (*rajas*) and *rajusa u* (رجاسة *rajāsa*) to be dirty, filthy; to commit a shameful act, do s.th. disgraceful or dirty

رجس *rijs* pl. ارجاس *arjās* dirt, filth; dirty thing or act, atrocity

رجس *rajas* pl. ارجاس *arjās* dirt, filth

رجس *rajis* dirty, filthy

رجاسة *rajāsa* dirt, squalor

رجاس *rajjās* roaring, surging (sea); thundering

مرجاس *mirjās* plumb, lead line (for measuring the depth of water)

رجع *raja'a i* (رجوع *rujū'*) to come back, come again, return; to recur; to resort, turn (الى to); to recommence, begin again, resume (الى s.th.); to fall back (الى on), go back, revert (الى to); to look up (الى s.th. in a book), consult (الى a book); to go back, be traceable (الى to), be attributable (الى ان to the fact that ...), derive, stem, spring (الى from); رجع به الى to reduce s.th. to (its elements, or the like); to depend (الى on); to be due, belong by right (الى to); to fall under s.o.'s (ل) jurisdiction, be s.o.'s (ل) bailiwick; to desist, refrain (عن from); to withdraw (عن, also فى, e.g., what one has said), revoke, countermand, repeal, cancel (عن or فى, e.g., a decision); to turn against s.o.

(على); رجع به على فلان to claim restitution of s.th. from s.o.; to demand, claim (ب s.th., على from s.o.); to entail, involve (ب s.th., a consequence), to have a good effect (في on), be successful (في with) | رجع على عقبه (*ʿaqbihī*) pl. رجعوا على اعقابهم (*aʿqābihim*) to retrace one's steps, go back the way one came; رجع الى الصحة (*ṣiḥḥa*) to regain one's health; رجع الى صوابه (*ṣawābihī*) to come to one's senses; رجع الى نفسه to watch o.s., examine o.s.; يرجع ذلك الى ان this is due to the fact that ...; يرجع السبب الى (*sabab*) the reason is to be found in ...; رجعت به الذاكرة الى he recalled, remembered ...; رجع في كلامه (*kalāmihī*) to go back on one's word; رجع عن قصده (*qaṣdihī*) to give up one's intention; رجع البصر في (*baṣara*) and (ببصره) رجع بالبصر في to turn one's eyes toward; رجع البصر حوله (فيما حوله) to let one's eyes wander around; رجع البصر بين to let one's glance wander between (persons or things); رجعت يده من يده ب (*yaduhū*) to receive s.th. from s.o.'s hand, accept, take over **II** to cause to come back or return; to return, give back; to send back; to turn away (ه عن s.o. from); to sing or chant in a vibrant, quavering tone; to echo, reverberate (ه s.th.) | رجع صداه (*ṣadāhu*) to return the echo of s.th., echo s.th. **III** to return, come back (ه, ه to); to revert (ه to); to go over s.th. (ه) again, reiterate, repeat (ه s.th.); to go back, apply for information (ه to), consult (ه a book), look up (ه in a book); to turn (ه to s.o., في in s.th. for advice, etc.), consult, ask (ه s.o.); to present oneself (ه at an office); to refer (ه, ه to); to check, verify, examine critically (ه s.th.); to audit (ه accounts, etc.) | راجعه عقله (*ʿaqluhū*) to come to one's senses; راجع نفسه (*nafsahū*) to try to make up one's mind, reconsider the whole thing, think the matter over; يراجع *yurājaʿ* (in cross references) see ... **IV** to make or let return; to take back, turn back (ه الى s.o. to s.th.); to force (ه s.o.) to turn back; to ascribe, attribute, trace (ه الى s.th. to); to reduce (ه الى s.th. to) **V** to return, come again; to reverberate, echo **VI** to return to one another; to withdraw, retreat, fall back, back off; to retire, dissociate, distance oneself (من from); to retrograde, fall off, diminish, deteriorate; to depart gradually (عن from); to fall behind, lag behind; to change one's mind | تراجع خطوة (*ḵuṭwatan*) to take a step backwards **VIII** (*eg.*) to be stale, no longer be fresh **X** to demand the return of s.th. (ه), reclaim (ه s.th.); to get back, recover, retrieve, regain (ه s.th.); to take back, withdraw (e.g., وعدا *waʿdan* a promise), revoke, repeal, countermand, cancel (ه s.th., e.g., a decision); to say the words: انا لله وانا اليه راجعون *innā li-llāhi wa-innā ilaihi rājiʿūn* | استرجعه الى حافظته (*ḥāfiẓatihī*) to call s.th. to mind, recall s.th.

رجع *rajʿ* coming back, return; (also رجع الصوت *r. aṣ-ṣaut*, رجع الصدى *r. aṣ-ṣadā*) echo | رجع الحديث answer; كرجع البصر *ka-r. al-baṣar* in the twinkling of an eye, in a moment

رجعي *rajʿī* reactionary; retroactive; revocable (*Isl. Law*); ○ regressive (e.g., assimilation; *phon.*) | بأثر رجعي (*bi-aṯar*) with retroactive force (*jur.*)

رجعية *rajʿīya* reactionism; reaction (*pol.*)

رجعة *rajʿa* return; recurrence; revocation, cancellation; receipt, voucher; — *rajʿa*, *rijʿa* return to one's wife after divorce, remarriage with one's divorced wife (*Isl. Law*)

رجعى *rujʿā* reactionism, reaction

رجوع *rujūʿ* return; reverting, coming back (الى to); recourse (الى to); traceability (الى to); revocation, withdrawal, retraction (عن of s.th.); resignation, surrender (عن of s.th.); reclamation; recall; restitution, return | برجوع البريد by return mail

رجوعى *rujūʿī* directed backwards, toward the past; retrospective

رجيع *rajīʿ* excrement

مرجع *marjiʿ* pl. مراجع *marājiʿ*[2] return; authority to which one turns or appeals; place of refuge, retreat; recourse, resort; authority; competent authority, responsible agency; source (esp. scientific), authoritative reference work; resource; source to which s.th. goes back or to which s.th. can be attributed; starting point, origin; recourse (*jur.*) | المرجع السابق ibidem, loc. cit. (citations in books); مرجع النظر *m. an-naẓar* jurisdiction, competence; المرجع اليه he is the one to turn to; المرجع فى ذلك الى I am thereby referring to ...; كان مرجع هذا الشيء الى this was due to ..., was attributable to ...; اليهم مرجع الفضل (*m. al-faḍl*) the merit is due to them

مرجعية *marjiʿīya* authority

مراجعة *murājaʿa* reiteration, repetition; inspection, study, examination; consultation (of a reference work); request; application, petition (esp. to an authority); application for advice or instructions, etc., consultation (of s.o.); checking, verification, re-examination; auditing, audit (also مراجعة الحساب); revision, correction (of a manuscript) | مراجعة الدفاتر auditing; المراجعة لدى (in ads) please apply to ...! (for information, solicitation)

ارجاع *irjāʿ* return, restitution; refundment; attribution (الى to); reduction (الى to)

تراجع *tarājuʿ* withdrawal, retreat; change of mind; recession, retrogradation

ارتجاع *irtijāʿ* return to an older form or order, reactionism, reaction

ارتجاعى *irtijāʿī* reactionary

استرجاع *istirjāʿ* reclamation; recovery, retrieval; retraction, withdrawal, revocation

راجع *rājiʿ* returning, reverting, etc.; due, attributable (الى to); rightfully belonging (الى to s.o.); subject (ل to s.th.); depending (ل on) | الحمى الراجعة (*ḥummā*) relapsing fever

مراجع *murājiʿ* pl. *-ūn* checker, verifier, examiner; reviser; petitioner; patient (who consults a doctor) | مراجع الحسابات *m. al-ḥisābāt* auditor, comptroller

مرتجع *murtagiʿ* (*eg.*) old, stale, no longer fresh

رجف *rajafa u* (*rajf*, رجفان *rajafān*) to be convulsed, be shaken; to tremble, quake; to shiver, shudder; — to agitate, convulse, shake (ه s.o.) **IV** to make (ه s.o.) tremble or shudder; to convulse, shake, rock (ه s.th.); to spread lies, false rumors; also with ب, e.g., ارجف بافتراءات (*bi-ftirāʾāt*) to spread calumnies **VIII** to tremble, quake; to shudder

رجفة *rajfa* (n. vic.) trepidation, tremor; shudder, shiver, shivering fit

رجاف *rajjāf* trembling, quaking; shaken, convulsed

ارجاف *irjāf* pl. اراجيف *arājīf*[2] untrue, disquieting talk, false rumor

رجل *rajila a* to go on foot, walk **II** to comb (ه the hair); to let down (ه the hair), let it hang long **V** = **I**; to march; to dismount (من or عن from; rider); to get off (e.g., a streetcar); to assume masculine manners, behave like a man | ترجل فى طريقه to walk all the way **VIII** to improvise, extemporize, deliver offhand (ه a speech) **X** to become a man, reach the age of manhood, grow up; to act like a man, display masculine manners or qualities

رجل *rijl* f., pl. ارجل *arjul* foot; leg

رجل *rijl* pl. ارجال *arjāl* swarm (esp. of locusts); — common purslane (Portulaca oleracea L.; *bot.*)

رجل *rajil* going on foot, pedestrian, walking

رجل *rajul* pl. رجال *rijāl* man; pl. رجالات *rijālāt* great, important men, leading personalities, men of distinction | رجال الامن *r. al-amn* the police; رجال الابحاث researchers; رجال البحار *r. al-biḥār* navigators, seafarers; رجال الدولة *r. ad-daula* statesmen; رجال السند *r. as-sanad* informants, sources of information; رجال الاعمال business people

رجالى *rijālī* men's, gentlemen's, for men (e.g., apparel)

رجولة *rujūla* masculinity, virility, manhood

رجولية *rujūlīya* masculinity, virility, manhood

مرجل *mirjal* pl. مراجل *marājil*[2] cooking kettle, caldron; boiler

ارتجال *irtijāl* improvisation, extemporization, extemporary speech

ارتجالى *irtijālī* extemporary, improvised, impromptu, offhand, unprepared

ارتجالية *irtijālīya* unplanned, improvised procedure

راجل *rājil* pl. رجل *rajl*, رجالة *rajjāla*, رجال *rujjāl*, رجلان *rujlān* going on foot, walking; pedestrian

الراجلة *ar-rājila* pedestrians

مترجل *mutarajjil*: قوات مترجلة (*quwwāt*) foot soldiers, infantry

مرتجل *murtajal* improvised, extemporaneous, extemporary, impromptu, offhand

[1]رجم *rajama u* (*rajm*) to stone (ه s.o.); to curse, damn, abuse, revile (ه s.o.) | رجم بالغيب (*ġaib*) to talk about s.th. of which one knows nothing; to guess, surmise, make conjectures; to predict the future II رجم بالغيب do.

رجم *rajm* stoning; (pl. رجوم *rujūm*) missile | رجم بالغيب (*ġaib*) conjecture, guesswork; prophecy

رجم *rujum* shooting stars, meteorites

رجمة *rujma* pl. رجم *rujam*, رجام *rijām* tombstone

رجيم *rajīm* stoned; cursed, damned; see also alphabetically

[2]رجم, ترجمة look up alphabetically

مرجونة *marjūna* basket

رجا (رجو) *rajā u* (رجاء *rajā'*, رجاة *rajāh*, مرجاة *marjāh*) to hope; to hope for s.th. (ه); to expect, anticipate (ه s.th.), look forward (ه to); to wish (ه for s.th., ه ل s.o. s.th., e.g., success); to ask (ه for s.th., من or ه s.o., ان to do s.th.), request (ه s.th., من from s.o., ان that he ...) | رجاه فى الحاح (*ilḥāḥ*) to plead with s.o., implore s.o.; ارجو عدم المؤاخذة (*'adama l-mu'ākaḏa*) I must ask your indulgence V to hope (ه, ه for); to expect, anticipate (ه, ه s.th., s.o.), look forward (ه to); to request (ه s.o.); to ask (ه s.o.) VIII to hope (ه, ه for); to expect, anticipate (ه, ه s.th., s.o.), look forward (ه to); to dread (ه s.o.)

رجا *rajan* pl. ارجاء *arjā'* interior wall, inner surface (of a well); side wall; side, end; — pl. ارجاء periphery within which s.th. lies; total area, zones, quarters (of a city, etc.); فى ارجاء (prep.) inside, within, everywhere in . . . | تفسح فى ارجاء الحديقة (*tafassaḥa*) to stroll about in the garden; فى ارجاء الغرفة (*ġurfa*) all about the room; فى ارجاء البلاد all over the country, throughout the country; تجاوبت ارجاء الردهة بالتصفيق (a. ar-radha) the entire auditorium resounded with applause; واسع الارجاء and شاسع الارجاء vast in extent, vast-dimensioned

رجاء rajā' hope (ب, فى and genit.: of); expectation, anticipation; urgent request | على رجاء in the hope of, hoping for; برجاء imploringly, in a pleading voice; رجاء العلم rajā' al-'ilm for your information (on memos, records, etc.); رأس الرجاء الصالح Cape of Good Hope

رجاة rajāh hope, expectation, anticipation

رجية rajīya s.th. hoped for; hope

مرجاة marjāh hope

راج rājin hoping, full of hope

مرجو marjūw hoped for, expected; requested | المرجو من فضلك ان (min faḍlika) approx.: I hope you will be kind enough to ...; المرجو مراعاة ان (murā'ātu) please notice that ..., attention is called to the fact that ...

رجى rajiya a to become silent; to remain silent; pass. رجى عليه (rujiya) to be tongue-tied, be unable to utter a sound

رجيم (Fr. régime) rijīm diet

رحب raḥiba a (raḥab) and raḥuba u (ruḥb, رحابة raḥāba) to be wide, spacious, roomy II to welcome (ب s.o., also ب s.th., e.g., news), bid welcome (ب to s.o.); to receive graciously, make welcome (ب s.o.) V to welcome (ب s.o.), bid welcome (ب to)

رحب raḥb wide, spacious, roomy; unconfined | رحب الصدر r. aṣ-ṣadr generous, magnanimous; broad-minded, open-minded, liberal; frank, candid, open-hearted; carefree; صدر رحب (raḥb) generosity, magnanimity; open-mindedness, broad-mindedness, liberality; frankness, candor; رحب الباع generous, open-handed, liberal; رحب الذراع do.

رحب ruḥb vastness, wideness, spaciousness, unconfinedness | اتى على الرحب والسعة (atā, sa'a) to be welcome; وجد رحبا وسعة (sa'atan) to meet with a friendly reception

رحب raḥab vastness, wideness, spaciousness, unconfinedness | رحب الصدر r. aṣ-ṣadr magnanimity, generosity; lightheartedness

رحبة raḥba, raḥaba pl. raḥabāt, رحاب riḥāb wide area, wide space; large square; courtyard, inner court (e.g., of a mosque); pl. رحاب wideness, vastness; generosity, magnanimity, big-heartedness; sacred precinct, protected area | رحاب الكون riḥāb al-kaun and رحاب الفضاء r. al-faḍā' vastness of outer space; انا فى رحابك I am under your protection, in the realm of your generosity! (spoken at the grave of a saint); نزل فى رحابه ضيفا (ḍaifan) he came to him as a guest; رحاب الجامعة university grounds, campus

رحيب raḥīb = رحب raḥb

رحابة raḥāba wideness, vastness, spaciousness, unconfinedness | رحابة الصدر r. aṣ-ṣadr magnanimity, generosity

مرحبا بك marḥaban bika welcome!

ترحاب tarḥāb welcome, greeting | قابله بترحاب (qābalahū) to receive s.o. with open arms

ترحيب tarḥīb welcoming, welcome, greeting

ترحيبى tarḥībī: كلمة ترحيبية (kalima) welcoming speech, word of welcome

رحرح raḥraḥa: رحرح بالكلام (kalām) to equivocate, speak ambiguously, beat around the bush

The Rest of the Arabic-English Dictionary: The Hans Wehr Dictionary of Modern Written Arabic. Fourth Edition, continue in Volume 2 available at

www.snowballpublishing.com

CPSIA information can be obtained
at www.ICGtesting.com
Printed in the USA
LVHW021045010623
748480LV00004B/61